The Virginia Adventure

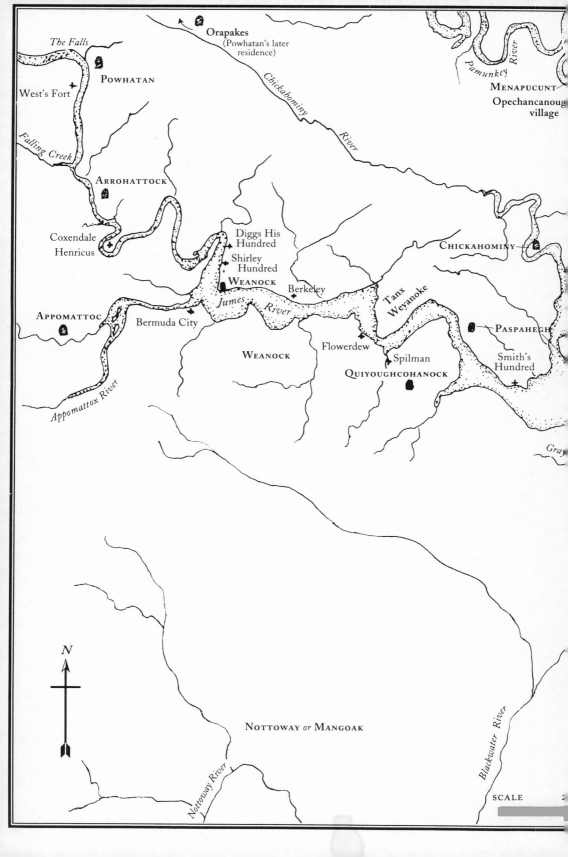

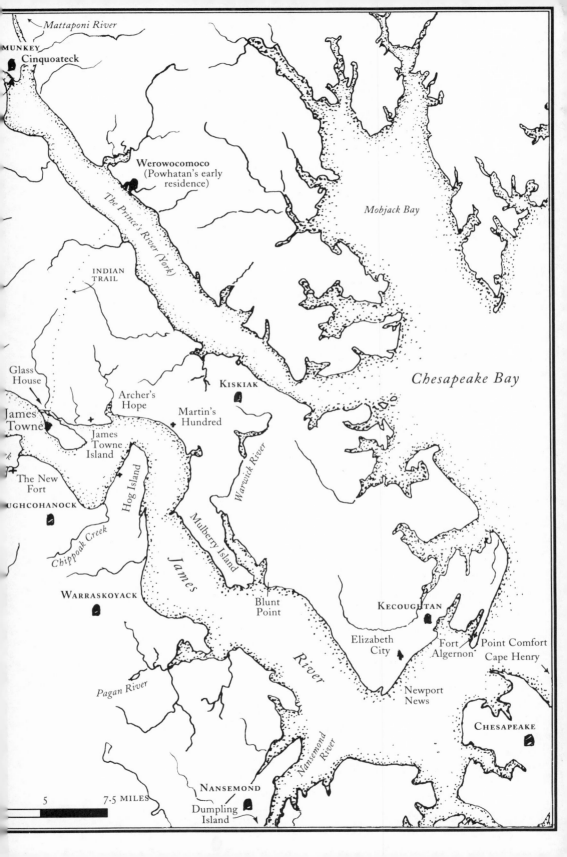

Mattaponi River

MUNKEY
Cinquoateck

Werowocomoco
(Powhatan's early
residence)

The Prince's River (York)

Mobjack Bay

INDIAN
TRAIL

Chesapeake Bay

Glass
House

KISKIAK

Archer's
Hope

Martin's
Hundred

James
Towne

James
Towne
Island

k

The New
Fort

Hog Island

Warwick River

UGHCOHANOCK

Chippoak Creek

Mulberry Island

James

WARRASKOYACK

Blunt
Point

KECOUGHTAN

River

Elizabeth
City

Fort
Algernon

Point Comfort
Cape Henry

Newport
News

Pagan River

CHESAPEAKE

Nansemond River

NANSEMOND

Dumpling
Island

5   7.5 MILES

The Virginia Bookshelf

The Virginia Bookshelf is a series of paperback reprints of classic works focusing on Virginia life, landscapes, and people.

The Virginia Adventure

ROANOKE TO JAMES TOWNE: AN ARCHAEOLOGICAL AND HISTORICAL ODYSSEY

❧ *by* ❧

IVOR NOËL HUME

University of Virginia Press
Charlottesville and London

UNIVERSITY OF VIRGINIA PRESS
Copyright © 1994 by Ivor Noël Hume
Reprinted by arrangement with Alfred A. Knopf, Inc.
Printed in the United States of America on acid-free paper

9   8   7   6   5   4   3

Library of Congress Cataloging-in-Publication Data

Noël Hume, Ivor.
    The Virginia adventure : Roanoke to James Towne : an
archaeological and historical odyssey / by Ivor Noël Hume.
        p.   cm.
    Includes bibliographical references (p.   ) and index.
    ISBN 0-8139-1758-1 (alk. paper)
        1. Roanoke Colony (Va.)—History.   2. Jamestown (Va.)—History.
I. Title.
F229.N84   1997
975.5′425—dc21

                                                            97-16651
                                                            CIP

In Memory of my Beloved
Audrey
who for 43 years did so much
of the work and received so little
of the credit
1927–1993

O, wonder!
How many goodly creatures are there here!
How beauteous mankind is! O brave new world,
That has such people in 't!
—William Shakespeare, *The Tempest*
Act V, Scene 1 (1611)

. . . In the midst of infinite business, as having,
amongst savages, the charge of wild men of mine
own nation, whose unruliness is such as not to
give leisure to the governor. . . .
—Governor Ralph Lane to Sir Philip Sidney
from Virginia, August 12, 1585

CONTENTS

❧

LIST OF ILLUSTRATIONS

ACKNOWLEDGMENTS

THESE are the pages that nobody reads save for one's friends, colleagues, and respondents, and then only to be sure that they have not been overlooked and that their names are correctly spelled. So concerned are we for the susceptibilities of the living that rarely do we feel the need to give credit to the dead. This book, however, owes almost everything to the people who lived its story and whose recollections and opinions color almost every page. They are the ghosts of Roanoke Island and James Towne whose words have kept me company for nigh on five years and who now can never be dismissed: Ralph Lane, John White, Sir Walter Ralegh, Christopher Newport, John Smith, George Percy, the Sir Thomases Gates and Dale, the Reverend Alexander Whitaker, the nervously soul-searching John Rolfe, and many others who I trust can find no means of complaining that their names are omitted.

As for the living, I hope that they will forgive me for not citing them in order of their contributions' magnitude, for in truth every idea offered or mistake identified has been help beyond price. The alternative of an alphabetical listing has the disadvantage of requiring the endless repetition of affiliations and of the assistance provided. Here, instead, is an assortment of thank-you's whose only correlation is that if I had a list, each would be at its head.

For help in chasing Sir Walter Ralegh's people around Roanoke Island, I am indebted to United States National Park Service ranger-historian Phillip W. Evans, to his superintendent, Thomas L. Hartman, and to the scholars who have contributed more to knowledge of the Roanoke voyages than anyone is ever likely to do, David and Alison Quinn. As for the Roanoke site's archaeology, my old and dear friend J. C. "Pinky" Harrington has made his mark there as lastingly as he has on Jamestown Island, and thanks to the wisdom of his wife, Virginia, who played a major research role at Jamestown in her own right, our occasional disagreements have always surrendered to the uncorking of good Scotch whisky. Among those still on staff at Jamestown and Yorktown, I am in debt to Assistant Superintendent James Haskett, who succeeded the late Charles E. Hatch as Jamestown's premier historian, also to past and present curators Susan Hanna and David Riggs; and to the Park Service's regional archaeologist, David Orr, who reviewed the drafts of the

Jamestown archaeological chapters, as did Phillip Evans for those relating to Roanoke.

From the Virginia Division of Historic Landmarks, state archaeologist Catherine Slusser and staff archaeologists David Hazzard and Anthony F. Oppermann have been unfailingly helpful both in offering the benefit of their own experience and in providing copies of reports by others. The ranks of American archaeologists experienced in excavating early-seventeenth-century sites are woefully thin, but two names are undisputed, the Thomas Jefferson Foundation's archaeological director William Kelso and contract archaeologist Nicholas Luccketti, both of whom have been generous with their information; so, too, has the staff of Flowerdew Hundred, from owner David Harrison and executive director Robert Wharton to their charismatic field director, James Deetz. Because much of the digging has taken place in libraries rather than in the ground, I am in debt to many, to me, nameless book fetchers, but specifically in the library of the Colonial Williamsburg Foundation, to Special Collections curator John Ingram and librarians Susan Berg and Liz Ackert. For help with the "Strachey" manuscript, I have to thank the Folger Shakespeare Library's associate director Philip A. Knachel, manuscripts curator Laetitia Yeandle and editor Barbara Mowat, and, in Bermuda, Edna and Teddy Tucker. Also in Bermuda, my special thanks to Peggy and Alan J. "Smokey" Wingood for their generosity in sharing the products of their *Sea Venture* research. Back in Virginia, I have appreciated the help of the Smithsonian Institution's anthropological curator emeritus T. Dale Stewart for providing information concerning 1938 excavations on Potomac Creek, and that of his department's archaeological technician Molly Coxson, who did her best to assist me in tracing Carl D. Manson and his silver wine taster.

My thanks, too, are due to the several who did their best to find me a source for hallucinogenic drugs—albeit in the seventeenth century: Dr. James Baker, medical director at Virginia's Eastern State Hospital, consulting psychiatrist Dr. Frank J. Ayd, Jr., and Virginia's ever-helpful deputy state medical examiner Dr. Marcella Fiero. For introducing me to the beauty and special properties of the fly agaric mushroom, I am indebted to Colonial Williamsburg's landscape supervisor Wesley Green and, in England, to fungologist Sir David Burnett.

Through more years than I care to recall, the staff at the Jamestown Festival Park (subsequently renamed the Jamestown Settlement) has provided unrestricted opportunities for me to study its fort reconstruction and has been unfailingly gracious in accepting criticism of its shortcomings. I am particularly grateful to the recent chairman of the Jamestown-Yorktown Foundation, the Honorable Hunter B. Andrews, and to his predecessor, the late Honorable Lewis A. McMurran, Jr., for inviting me to contribute to the many subsequent improvements, and to current park director Sara Patton and her colleagues for their advice and practical assistance. The Association for the Preservation of Virginia Antiquities' curator of Collections, Nancy M. Packer, has been unstintingly helpful in culling its archives and minute books for information about the John Smith and Pocahontas statues, as well as other tiresome questions concerning the APVA's early stewardship of its Jamestown acres. My inquiries concerning the origins of the Pocahontas portraits were received no less graciously by the National Portrait Gallery's senior curator, Robert G. Stewart, by Department of Paintings and Sculpture curator Ellen G. Miles, and by curator of prints Wendy Wick Reaves; likewise by Alan Jutzi, curator of rare books at the Huntington Library. Related, too, were inquiries at the British Museum's Department of Coins and Medals, where Michael Kent efficiently shot down a previously promising research balloon. I am indebted, too, to Mr. Wynn Dough, director of the North Carolina Outer Banks History Center, for his help in tracking down a photograph of the Elizabethan sixpence from Roanoke Island, and to Dr. David Phelps and East Carolina University for actually providing it.

As always, my gratitude goes out to that other sharpshooter, my late wife, Audrey, whose knowledge of the period was almost as valuable as her deflationary comments on my phraseological excesses—and the wisdom of using words like "phraseological." I am equally indebted to my editor and friend Barbara Bristol, who wisely, and frequently, advised me that history isn't supposed to be funny.

Finally, my thanks to all those who in their unremembered ways have contributed to what I hope is a memorable book.

James City County   I. N. H.
April 29, 1993

A WORD ABOUT WORDS

I N USING the testimony of contemporary eyewitnesses, rather than paraphrase their evidence I have chosen wherever possible to let them speak for themselves—or, more correctly, to write for themselves. Just as in court the character and veracity of a witness can be gauged by the words he or she uses to answer the questions, so we can get closer to the seventeenth-century deponents by retaining the eccentricities of their frequently phonetic spelling. Thus, as we read the words, we often come close to hearing them spoken. There are occasions, however, when the needs of the narrative transcend concern for historical purity, and on these occasions I have substituted modern spelling. In others where the absence of words or punctuation makes for difficult reading, I have inserted additions set within brackets. Then, too, some letter conventions have been modernized. Thus, for example, where *ff* means a capital *F* I have used the latter; the archaic long *s* has been replaced by the standard letter; and where *v* substitutes for *u*, and vice versa, I have used the appropriate modern letter. However, the common use of "then" to mean "than" has been retained, as have seventeenth-century abbreviations.

Although I have tried to keep as close to original texts as available sources permit, many have already been edited for publication, starting when they were first printed in the seventeenth century and continuing into our own. Modern scholars recognize the importance of publishing exact transcripts of such original manuscripts as survive, but some of the most important have been lost, and so in their extant versions they speak for the spelling of the copyists rather than for the educational standing or shortcomings of the original authors. Texts translated from the Spanish have in some instances suffered from the translator's unfamiliarity with the subtleties of archaic terminology, and certain passages consequently have an incongruously modern ring to them. Be that as it may, with the exception of the cited spelling deviations, I have refrained from tinkering. After all, words are to the historian as potsherds are to the archaeologist. Both are fragments of the past, and singly or collectively they need to be seen for what they are and for what they have to say.

Several proper names may appear oddly spelled—e.g., "Ralegh" for the more familiar "Raleigh" and "Hawkyns" for "Hawkins"—but as these seem to have been the spellings their Tudor and Stuart owners preferred,

I have stayed with them. Much more troublesome has been to decide how to present the most important name of all—Jamestown. At the outset in 1607 the settlers lived within James Fort, but they very quickly came to see themselves as inhabitants of a walled town, and so, as was common throughout the century, they called it James Towne. Before long, and as the Virginia Company established a series of key settlements distinct from the private communities, such as Wolstenholme Towne in Martin's Hundred, the principal towns were called cities. James City (usually spelled "Cittie" or "Citty") defined a community that extended beyond the palisaded area yet in reality never amounted to more than a village. It would become smaller still as its importance faded in the eighteenth century, at which time the previous century's "James Towne" was commonly written as "James-town." For my purposes, however, I have used "James Fort" in its original connotation, "James Towne" for the seventeenth-century palisaded township in all its phases, and the modern "Jamestown" for any references after 1699, when the Virginia legislature moved to Williamsburg.

Finally, a word about dates: In 1582 Pope Gregory XIII ordered a reformation of the calendar that dropped ten days following October 4 and began the new year on January 1. Although the new system was quickly accepted by most of Europe, England continued to use the "Old Style" Julian calendar, which began the new year at the Feast of the Annunciation on March 25. The Old Style calendar remained in use in Britain until 1752, when by an Act of Parliament (introduced the previous year by Lord Chesterfield) the country fell belatedly in line with the rest of Europe and officially adopted the Gregorian "New Style" calendar. The changeover by then necessitated the omission of eleven days between September 2 and 14. For the purposes of this book, however, all dates have been converted to New Style.

PROLOGUE

ॐ

UNTIL the summer of 1993, when it blew down, a lone cypress stood
in the river about three hundred feet from the Jamestown Island
shore. Though not a particularly large tree as cypresses go, it was there at
the turn of the century and before that for as long as anyone could then
remember. The tree has often been cited as marking the shoreline approximately as it was in the seventeenth century, and thus close to the site of
the first permanent English settlement in the New World, a revelation
that surprised tourists who assumed that the Jamestown they have come
to visit, and the remains they expect to see, are part of that first fragile
foothold. There is no denying that the James River has taken a sizable
bite out of the low-lying, clay-footed island since the first settlers
dropped anchor there on May 13, 1607; and because archaeologists have
found no trace of James Fort's wooden walls, it is convenient to conclude
that the site has been entirely lost to erosion—convenient, but not necessarily true.

A hundred and thirty-five miles away to the south, on another, equally
vulnerable island, the ravages of wind and water have done Anglo-American history a similar, if less drastic, disservice. Sheltered behind North
Carolina's ever-shifting Outer Banks, Roanoke Island was temporary
home to the four successive groups of Elizabethan adventurers whose
efforts scratched the name "Virginia" on land that Spain had hitherto
considered to lie within the perimeter of its own Terra Florida. On
Roanoke, over more than forty years visitors to the Fort Raleigh National
Historic Site have been shown a small, reconstructed earthwork barely
large enough to house twenty men, yet identified as the fort built to
defend more than a hundred. Called Fort Raleigh because the colonists
settled there under a patent issued to Sir Walter Ralegh in 1584, like
Jamestown, the site has been subjected to several archaeological excavations, digging which, until 1991, failed to define where those people lived
or worked, or why a grass-covered earthwork substituted for defenses
which the only surviving account described as being of wood.

What follows is indeed a tale of two cities: the interim "Cittie of
Ralegh" on North Carolina's Roanoke Island and the embryonic "James
Cittie" at its namesake island in modern Virginia. While lessons learned
from the failure of the first enterprise eventually helped the second suc-

ceed, and while some of the leadership contributed to both, the linkage reaches into the present century, for the pioneering American archaeologist Jean C. Harrington dug first at Jamestown and later at Fort Raleigh. More recently my own excavations on the early-seventeenth-century site of Wolstenholme Towne, about eight miles downriver from Jamestown, revealed the ground plan of a timber-built fort whose details threw fresh light on hitherto enigmatic traces found at Roanoke and described by Harrington as an "outwork." At the same time the Wolstenholme discoveries gave clearer meaning to the previously misinterpreted description of James Fort's palisades. Completing a circle of coincidence, a chance meeting with Harrington in London in 1950 brought me to America six years later and led eventually to my serving as a consultant at both Roanoke and Jamestown, and thence to the chapters now before you.

Although, to my shame, I have never been able to recall that first meeting with J. C. Harrington, my first encounter with James Fort, on a Sunday afternoon in September 1956, remains as vivid today as it was when I first caught sight of its pointed palisades thrusting menacingly upward amid the piney woods. As my wife and I returned from a visit to the site of the colonists' early-seventeenth-century glassmaking venture, the forest was eerily silent; nothing stirred but the occasional towhee scuffling for grubs in the underlying carpet of dead leaves. Even without a twig's warning crack, imagination had no difficulty conjuring breeze-stirred shadows into painted faces watching and waiting; I needed only the twang of a bowstring and the thud of an arrow to know that I was experiencing what parapsychologists define as retrocognition—stepping back in time. At any moment colonists nervously clutching their muskets and blowing on their fuses behind the palisade might begin firing from between its newly pointed posts.

The sinking yellow sun backlit the palisades, casting long, dramatic shadows into the trees closely ringed about it, indeed so closely that attackers would have enjoyed as much cover as the walls gave the defenders. That disturbing thought served to dilute my first awed impression, as did also the sunlight glinting on an outer barbed-wire fence of concentration camp stability.

On discovering that both fence and fort had open gates, we stepped cautiously inside, expecting any second to be challenged or set upon by dogs. But the fort was as silent as the woods around it. Thatch-roofed huts stood empty, some finished, others not. New boards leaned against walls; a pair of sawyers' trestles lay on their sides as though the place had been vacated in unseemly haste. Were it not for the presence of several rusty oil drums substituting for colonial wooden barrels, I could have been persuaded that we had indeed stepped through a time warp into the abandoned James Towne of June 7, 1610. Instead, we were trespassing in the partially completed reconstruction being readied for the 350th anniversary of the Jamestown Island landing, its exhibits scheduled to open on April 1, 1957.

Never again would the rebuilt fort recapture the sense of reality that emanated from its incomplete and chaotic state on that silent Sunday afternoon. Before long the magic of imagination would be replaced by the reality of ostrich-plumed halberdiers in sunglasses and fiberglass armor posing for tourists. Although the reconstruction had been intended to last a mere eighteen months or two years, the public's enthusiastic interest in the fort convinced the Virginia authorities to postpone its destruction— indefinitely, as it turned out. Thirty years later this onetime trespasser was asked to survey the by then crumbling reconstruction's shortcomings and to suggest, in the light of the Wolstenholme discoveries, how it might be made more authentic.

Lacking any shred of archaeological evidence from Jamestown Island, one naturally turned to the fort's only English-American predecessor, to the partially excavated Elizabethan site on Roanoke Island. What had begun for me with an unquestioning tourist's-eye visit in 1958 led in 1989 to a reevaluation of what little had been found in the ground there and to a sentence-by-sentence probing of the historical records to try to determine who did what at Roanoke between 1584, when the first English arrived, and 1590, when the last of them were deemed to be well and truly lost.

The notion that archaeologists might profitably employ historical sources as well as count potsherds has long raised skeptical eyebrows among professional historians who traditionally have scoffed at our insistence that artifacts can sometimes speak where the written record is silent. In truth, the discipline of historical archaeology, which grew out of prehistoric anthropology in the coaxing hands of Harrington at Jamestown in the 1930s, relies on the integration of artifactual and documentary evidence, bonded with the same kind of critical analysis and synthesis employed by conventional historians. Historical archaeology simply means hunting for physical evidence and reviewing it alongside the testimony of people who knew or saw what happened.

The building of the Jamestown fort, into whose replication two English visitors intruded on that September afternoon, is like a crime scene that sends us back through time, examining witnesses, checking leads, and analyzing clues. To twentieth-century eyes, much that occurred in Sir Walter Ralegh's "New found land" is hard to believe or even to understand, for having no experience of the Elizabethan world, we measure everything against the yardstick of what we consider acceptable or otherwise. Consequently, intelligently reaching out to the past—any past—is dependent on dichotomous notions. On the one hand, we must draw a cloak over our own life experience so that we learn to think as "they" did, and to do so within the limits of what they knew, but on the other, to render any of it of value to ourselves, we cannot help but draw modern comparisons.

For most of us, however, the romantic aspects of the past are the bits we remember, for these are the ones with which we feel comfortable. At Roanoke one name resonates in this way: that of Virginia Dare, the first English child born in the New World. From Jamestown we recall the bluff and courageous John Smith saved by the compassion of a trusting and loving Pocahontas. These are bedtime stories far more acceptable than the nightmare visions of the settlers who saw the Indians as savages and many of their fellow colonists as "Murtherers, Theeves, Adulterers, idle persons, and what not besides, all of which persons God hateth even from his very soule."[1]

Although what follows is ultimately an archaeological quest for what the 1585 Roanoke settlers called "the new Fort in Virginia" and for the palisaded site their 1607 successors first named James Fort and then James Towne, it also is a journey beyond the lost structures to the events that shaped their existence. To do that, we need to meet the people who built them, lived in them, died in them, and we need to know where they came from—both physically and historically.

So, where to begin?

In the shadow of London's St. Paul's Cathedral, between Shoemakers' Row and Puddle Dock Hill, and so close to the parish Church of St. Anne that the noise of its drums and trumpets disturbs the services, stands the Blackfriars Theatre. It is the summer of 1605, and under its roof a company of boy actors calling themselves the Children of Her Majesties Revels are in the third act of a new play from the quills of George Chapman, John Marston, and Ben Jonson, its title *Eastward Hoe*....

The Virginia Adventure

CHAPTER I

Whosoever Commands the Sea

THE SCENE is the taproom in a Thames-side tavern at Billings-gate Dock at the dawn of the seventeenth century. Through an open window we see a forest of masts and an apparent thicket of yards and spars of the fishing vessels berthed in the square recess of the dock. In the taverns and alehouses, amid the singing, laughing, and often brawling patrons frequenting the public rooms, merchants, captains, and crewmen negotiate terms for the next voyage. Enter two young London-ers, Spendall and Scapethrift, both ripe to be cozened by a rascally Cap-tain Seagull into buying passage to Virginia.

"Come, boys," he roars, "Virginia longs till we share the rest of her maidenhead."

Spendall asks: "Why, is she inhabited already with any English?"

"A whole country of English is there, man; bred of those that were left there in '79," Seagull assures him.

Whether the authors of *Eastward Hoe* intended to put a false date into the captain's mouth, or whether they themselves had their New World history wrong, one cannot say. Nevertheless, they were almost certainly referring to Roanoke's last colonists, who had been left there in August 1587 and were gone by the time a reconnoitering Spaniard stopped by in May 1588. The Roanoke settlers' disappearance was no well-kept secret, and we can assume that the better-informed members of the play's audi-ence knew that Seagull was lying. At the same time there must have been many who didn't and who, like Spendall and Scapethrift, were willing to swallow the promoters' propaganda and volunteer their savings and their lives in a new Virginia adventure.

Lest the prospect of encountering hostile Indians prove a deterrent, Seagull was quick to assure his gullible listeners that such fears were

Captain Seagull makes his pitch; after a seventeenth-century woodcut.

unfounded. The seventy-niners "have married with the Indians," he explained, "and make 'em bring forth as beautiful faces as any we have in England," adding that "the Indians are so in love with them, that all the treasure they have they lay at their feet."

For the London audiences of 1605, the word "treasure" was as riveting as it is today when television viewers are promised the sight of Spanish gold being plucked from a Florida reef. The eager Scapethrift pressed his host for details: "But is there such treasure there, captain, as I have heard?"

The bait had been taken; it remained only to plant the hook. "I tell thee," replied Seagull, "gold is more plentiful there than copper is with us; . . . and for as much red copper as I can bring, I'll have thrice the weight in gold. Why, man, all their dripping pans and their chamber-pots are pure gold; and all the chains with which they chain up their streets are massy gold; . . . all the prisoners they take are fetter'd in gold; and for rubies and diamonds, they go forth on holidays, and gather them by the sea shore, to hang on their children's coats, and stick in their children's caps, as commonly as our children wear groats with holes in them."

"And is it a pleasant country withall?" Scapethrift wanted to know.

"As ever the sun shined on," came the answer, "temperate, and full of all sorts of excellent viands; wild boar is as common there as our tamest bacon is here; venison as mutton. And then you shall live freely there, without sergeants, or courtiers, or lawyers."

"God's me!" gasped Spendall—and the audience doubtless roared.[1] It knew all about the "shoulder-clapping Sergeants" who hauled innocent yeomen into court, and about the arrogance of privilege and the dishonesty of lawyers. In short, in the earliest years of the seventeenth century the popular English vision of Virginia was of a Promised Land free of hierarchical authority, where nobody went hungry or shivered in winter, and where money grew, if not on trees, then around the necks of easily outwitted Indians. The playwrights' Captain Seagull painted his picture of Virginia exclusively in familiar European colors. But sailors who had crossed the ocean knew better, and before long the Virginia promoters' carefully fostered English perception of the benign American Indian would be drastically revised. He would join the ranks of the world's non-Christians as a subhuman species to be exploited, despised, and brutalized. In turn, and just as quickly, the English, who at first were seen by the Indians as gift-bearing demigods, were recognized for the cruel, avaricious, and duplicitous rabble that their own leaders said they were. As for the gold, it would remain as elusive as the dream that first sent Europeans over the western horizon in search of the East.

Most rural Tudor English families, unless called to war, traveled no more than twenty miles from their home villages, and although most knew that they lived on an island, few ever saw the sea. Consequently, the world beyond the water was thought none of their business or so incredibly alien that anything from the marvelous to the horrific was possible—and likely.

The insular English in the immediately post-medieval years were a far cry from their Continental counterparts, whose legacy of travel and cultural exploration went back to the classical days of the great Mediterranean empires and stretched from North Africa to the edges of the Orient. Long before the thirteenth century, when the Venetian Polos, father, uncle, and son, returned to tell of the wonders of Cathay and the court of Kublai Khan, trading contacts existed across the Asian continent via Samarkand to Persia, on to Baghdad, Damascus, and the Mediterranean shore at Acre.

The notion that sustained European trade with the Orient became possible only after Vasco da Gama had reached India by sea in 1497 confuses "to" with "from." Although a great deal of sand and hordes of allegedly devilish Arabs and Turks stood between European merchants and the markets of Cathay, trading routes going the other way were numerous. Indeed, by A.D. 1100 Asia Minor had become a cat's cradle of overland routes, with seaborne extensions from Ormuz in the Persian Gulf up the Red Sea to within camel's trot of El-Qahira and Alexandria. From Egypt goods traveled not only aboard Moorish galleys to Venice and Genoa but also along caravan routes that skirted the Mediterranean and crossed the Sahara to the Atlantic as far south as modern Ghana. Silk and porcelain from China, nutmeg and mace from the Moluccas, pepper, cotton cloth, and jewels from India, cinnamon from Ceylon, Persian carpets and Arabian perfumes all flowed steadily westward, earning fortunes for Arab and Eurasian merchants. However, most of such exotic Oriental goods as reached Scandinavia and Britain in the late medieval and Tudor periods traveled the Samarkand route to Riga on the Baltic, there to board ships of the Hanseatic League.

Land routes across Europe, even as late as the seventeenth century, were incredibly hazardous and problem-fraught. A plethora of dukedoms and small principalities extorted tolls for crossing their borders and using their ferries and bridges. Roads were appalling at best, and traders who traveled them unprotected by expensive and untrustworthy companies of mercenary soldiers were liable to wind up dead in a ditch. Those who escaped being robbed by brigands could expect to be cheated and over-charged by innkeepers, ostlers, wheelwrights, blacksmiths, and anyone else whose services they needed. Thus going by sea, regardless of its dangers both natural and Islamic, could be the safest and most reliable course.

Beginning in the 1480s, the quest for a route to the riches of the Orient that bypassed the hostile lands of Islam became Europe's greatest mercantile challenge. By then Bristol ships had almost certainly reached westward to the Azores. The Portuguese had found those mid-Atlantic islands by 1527, and the discovery there of Carthaginian coins suggests that the islands may have been known since the third century B.C. But England's entrée to the New World came in 1497, when John Cabot left Bristol and sailed past the Azores to rediscover Newfoundland and Cape Breton Island. Although many a British schoolboy has grown up seeing Cabot as a heroic son of the English soil, he was in fact Giovanni Caboto, a Genoese pilot and a naturalized Venetian. But no matter. He left from and returned to England to take his place as the first of the great British navigators.

Greenland was rediscovered in 1500, and in 1534 the French navigator Jacques Cartier made the first of three voyages to North America, exploring the St. Lawrence estuary as far upstream as Montreal. The immediate payoff for adventuring along these inhospitable northern shores of what Cartier dubbed "the land God gave to Cain" was whale oil. Recently discovered occupation sites and the remains of wrecked ships at Red Bay, Labrador, have revealed that Basque fishermen from northern Spain were setting up whale-processing plants there perhaps as early as 1540. Their fleets were soon joined by English and other Western European seamen who were discovering the scaly gold of the codfish harvest along New-foundland's Grand Banks.

The real gold, however, lay far to the south, across the differently dangerous waters of the Caribbean, and it was there that monarchs and city merchants looked for bankable returns. The voyages of Columbus, Amerigo Vespucci, Pedro Cabral, and other equally familiar south-sailing navigators are not in the mainstream of our present concerns. Suffice it to say that by 1580 Spain and Portugal had done an impressive job of planting their influence and themselves around the fringes of the best parts of the known world. With the blessing of the Catholic Church, whose Pope Alexander VI (he happened to be a Spaniard) had, in the 1494 Treaty of Tordesillas, exercised his divine right to split the globe between those two nations, Spanish possessions stretched uninterruptedly from present-day Chile to the Rio Grande, throughout the Caribbean, and up into Florida, while the Portuguese got a bit of Brazil, the whole of Africa and India, and everything else east to Japan. There was no place in this new world order for the likes of France or England.

Much, much later Napoleon dismissed the British as a nation of shopkeepers, but at the turn of the sixteenth century he would have called England a country of shepherds. Beginning in the twelfth century, English merchants recognized the profits to be made in shipping raw wool to the hungry looms of Flanders. Sheep as the way to wealth remained an English fixation for centuries to come, and it continued into the time when Spain and Portugal were dividing up both the resources and the markets of the hitherto unmapped world. That pleasurable task was virtually a fait accompli by the time Sir Walter Ralegh warned that "Whosoever commands the sea commands the trade; whosoever commands the trade of the world commands the riches of the world, and consequently the world itself."[2]

Although Henry VII has been called the father of the Royal Navy, and his successor, Henry VIII, continued to build new and better fighting ships (among them the now-salvaged *Mary Rose*), the notion that England should seek an empire beyond the security of her shores was not yet a serious proposition. Its first surfacing has been attributed to the lawyer and statesman Sir Thomas More, whose political essay *Utopia*, describing the mythical island of the Utopians and their idealistically communistic government, is believed in turn to have been inspired by the 1507 narrative of Amerigo Vespucci's South American discoveries. More's *Utopia*, which was printed in 1516, has been credited with prompting his brother-in-law, John Rastell, to fit out a fleet to plant a settlement in the New World, albeit in its northern expanses rather than its southern.

Rastell, a printer and publisher by trade, seems to have lacked any prior maritime experience. Nevertheless, he chose to command the fleet himself. That was a mistake. Supplied with a protective patent from the king dated March 5, 1517, and led by the ships *Barbara* and *Mary Barking*, his flotilla left London in the spring of that year, bound, as the patent put it, for "distant parts of world, remote from our Kingdom of England."[3] The parts proved less remote than expected, for the expedition got no farther than Cork on the southern coast of Ireland.

Little is known about the makeup of this first English colonizing effort beyond the fact that it was composed primarily of mariners and soldiers, augmented by a few craftsmen, specifically carpenters and masons. According to Rastell, seeds of dissension were deliberately sown between the sailors and soldiers, and by the time the fleet finally put out from Falmouth, any enthusiasm for settling the New Found Land had evaporated in favor of pirating or a trading voyage to Bordeaux. Rastell refused to be diverted and was put ashore at Waterford in Ireland while his ships went their several ways—none of them westward.

His belief in a New World settlement undimmed, Rastell returned to London and there wrote a play titled *A New Interlude and a Merry of the Nature of the Four Elements*. In it he vigorously promoted the merits of the continent which, with Cabot's exploits in mind, he claimed, "The moste wyse prynce the .vij. Henry [Henry VII] Causyd furst to be founde."[4] The landmass, said Rastell, extended for at least five thousand miles, and on its far side was another, narrower sea separating it from the Orient. His characters spoke of extensive resources of timber and copper, but not of iron. As for the inhabitants, they knew neither God nor the devil, and for "Buyldynge nor house they have non at all But wodes[,] cotes[,] and cavys small."[5]

This first English description of New World prospects was notably prosaic, for it held out no hope of gold, silver, or rubies on the seashore. News of Cortés's Aztec riches had not yet reached Europe. However, Rastell's *New Interlude* is important as a herald of things to come, and for containing the first-known English usage of the name America, which had been coined by the German cartographer Martin Waldseemüller; Waldseemüller had published a new map of the world in 1507 based in part on Amerigo Vespucci's narrative. Wrote Rastell:

> But this newe landes founde lately
> Ben callyd America by cause only
> Americus dyd furst them fynde.[6]

In 1527 Henry VIII sent "two fayre shippes," the *Samson* and the 250-ton *Mary Guildford,* on an American voyage "to seke straunge Regions," more specifically a northern route to Cathay, the *Mary Guildford* under the command of one John Rut.[7] The ships sailed out of the Thames on May 20, and on July 1 were parted in a storm, the *Samson* never again to be heard from. Rut sailed on and up into the ice and into the vicinity of what was later named Hudson Strait, then turned south along the coast of Labrador before anchoring at St. John's Harbor in Newfoundland, where he found two Portuguese and twelve French fishing barks at anchor. Three years earlier the Venetian seaman Giovanni da Verrazano, in the service of France, had explored the American coast from the Bahamas to Nova Scotia; now John Rut and the *Mary Guildford* were to follow much the same course in the opposite direction. There is, however, no record of where Rut may have landed, only that somewhere along the way his Italian pilot was killed by Indians.

In spite of these early English sorties—and there were others about which we know little or nothing—England's seafaring concerns focused less on the riches of the Orient than on opening up new markets for warm English woolens. Once Flemish weavers showed the English how to build and operate complex and efficient looms, the export of raw wool was banned, and remained so until the reign of Elizabeth. In the meantime, the cloth trade became Britain's staple export, and continued so in the early sixteenth century. As long as there were foreign merchants with open order books and foreign ships to crowd English ports with hatches open and holds ready, there was little incentive to look farther afield. Besides, Henry VIII's marital troubles and his resulting disenchantment with God's spokesman in Rome were being felt in every English home from castle to cottage. The ultimate breach with Rome and the dissolution of the monasteries created an upheaval in the ownership of land unprecedented since the Norman Conquest of 1066. Not only was it property that had to change, but men's minds as well. No longer, if wise, would one look to distant Rome for spiritual leadership; God's instrument was up the Thames at Hampton Court in the person of Bluff King Hal. This was an introspective concept that took some getting used to, one that kept the country physically and emotionally occupied while the monarchs and mariners of other countries, more secure in their faith and in their systems, were free to harness the wind.

Henry VIII died in 1547 with the Reformation firmly established in England, and in the hands of a new generation of leaders who felt com-

Seal showing Philip of Spain and Mary Tudor as partners on
the English throne; from John Speed's *Historie of Great Britaine*
(1632 edition).

fortable with the new religious doctrines and who particularly appreciated
the part where the monastic church lands were shared among the king's
friends. They looked to the new boy king, Edward VI, to keep it that way.
Unfortunately he died six years later, leaving the throne to his Roman
Catholic older sister, Mary, who in the course of her five-year reign
turned the system upside down. Disregarding the wishes of her Protestant subjects, she married the future Philip II of Spain, who thus became
king-consort of England and, albeit briefly, drew Britain into the expanding Spanish orbit. Initially cautious in the steps she took to ease the country back toward the Catholic fold, Mary eventually went the last yard and
formally returned an allegedly penitent England to the Holy Father.
Within weeks of that decision began the religious persecution that earned
the queen the sobriquet of Bloody Mary and in the space of four years
sent three hundred Protestants, from bishops to shoemakers, to burn at
the stake.

All this may seem a far cry from the arrival of three little ships in the James River fifty-two years later, but the reasons for their being there, the attitudes of the colonists, and no less those of the Indians who greeted them in their various ways, all had their genesis in the exploding European world of the mid-sixteenth century.

The Spanish and Portuguese, with no one to fear but the indigenous inhabitants of their conquered or treaty-secured real estate, moved rapidly to make firm their footholds, doing so with the point of Toledo steel and the balm of the Bible. Neither the French nor the English showed any interest in competing for the foreign lands or in seriously interfering with the Iberians' treasure-laden convoys. The world was an Hispanic oyster—or so it must have seemed until November 1558, when Bloody Mary died.

One of the men seized and imprisoned in 1555—on the ground that he was using magic to hasten the queen's death—was the London-born mathematician and astronomer Dr. John Dee, who, among his many scientific exploits, is remembered for having (so it was said) found in the ruins of Glastonbury Abbey a magic elixir which, when a grain was properly applied to a fragment of a warming pan, turned it to gold. Perhaps because his elixir was contained in a very small bottle, Dee was unable to repeat the feat, and he was still trying when he died in poverty at the age of eighty-one. In spite of his reputation as an alchemist and even as a sorcerer, his study of the mathematics of navigation was to prove a guide and inspiration to the great sailors who were to chart the course of history in the reign of Elizabeth. Although feared and shunned by many as an "invocator of divels," Dee served as an astrologer to the queen, who in 1580 sought his counsel on the scope of her titles to the world's newly discovered countries. Responding to the royal request, Dee presented his researches in two large vellum rolls, giving hydrographical and geographical descriptions which did much to promote the concept of a great British empire beyond the seas.

An abortive attempt by Sir Hugh Willoughby and his pilot, Richard Chancellor, in 1553 to reach China by sailing northeast around the Asian landmass had been sponsored by a stock company of London merchants who named themselves the Company of Merchant Adventurers of England for the Discovery of Lands Unknown. Their first president (called Governor) was John Cabot's son Sebastian, who had spent most of his maritime career working for the kings of Spain but had been given the post of inspector of the English navy by Edward VI. Sebastian, therefore, was the ideal choice to head a company seeking a royal patent when Prince Philip of Spain sat beside the English throne.

After the loss of Willoughby and two of his expedition's three ships, the seekers after lands unknown made several more attempts, the most far-reaching under the command of Stephen Borough, previously the pilot aboard the only ship to return from the first attempt. In 1557 Borough reached Nova Zembla (Novaya Zemlya) and the entrance to the Kara Sea before turning back, bringing home to his sponsors not silks and spice from Cathay but grim tales of fog and endless Siberian ice.

Thus thwarted, the merchant adventurers, renamed the Muscovy Company, turned their attention to testing overland routes which, in the great days of Kublai Khan, had been long and largely unmolested but now were anything but safe. Foiled yet again, the company listened to the advice of the all-seeing Dr. Dee, whose "shew stone" (a globe of quartz now in the British Museum) enabled him to know that beyond Nova Zembla and the Kara Sea would be found Cape Tabin and that once it had been rounded, the sailing would be simple. But it was not until 1580 that another English expedition accepted Dr. Dee's challenge, and it, too, failed.

Dee's crystal-enhanced vision was not restricted to the northeast; his navigational studies convinced him that there was also a northwest passage from the Atlantic into the Pacific somewhere north of the sixtieth parallel. This prospect brought to the fore a new name, that of Martin Frobisher, who in 1576 set sail with three ships westerly bound for Cathay. Shortly after reaching Greenland, the smallest of the three sank in a storm. The captain of the second, the *Michael,* decided he had had enough and returned to Bristol and, taking a chance on Frobisher's never making it back, reported that his "Generall captaine," too, had been lost at sea. He had not. Instead Frobisher aboard the ship *Gabriel* was able to satisfy himself that Dr. Dee was right.

On reaching Baffin Island, Frobisher discovered a deep inlet which he named Frobisher Strait. He believed that North America lay on the south shore of the strait and that the north shore represented the easterly horn of Asia. He found supporting evidence for that conclusion in the sealskin-wrapped inhabitants, who "bee like Tartars, with long blacke haire, broad faces, and flatte noses, and tawnie in colour,"[8] one of whom (lured by a tinkling bell) Frobisher enticed aboard and took home as a sample. Unfortunately, England's first Inuit caught cold on the way and soon died.

Queen Elizabeth reportedly had leaned out of her Greenwich Palace window to wave to Frobisher as his tiny fleet set forth, and on his return she welcomed and commended him "for the great hope he brought of the

Left: Dr. John Dee in a 1792 engraving. *Right:* Martin Frobisher, reengraved in 1849 from a 1620 original.

passage to Cataya."[9] But the voyage's real prize turned out to be neither the hope of Cathay nor a sickly Eskimo but a souvenir brought back by one of the sailors and described as a "blacke stone much like to a sea cole in colour, which by the waight seemed to be some kinde of metall or minerall."[10] Frobisher had considered it of no importance, but upon examination by an Italian alchemist, the souvenir was declared to contain gold, whereupon word spread through London that untold wealth, if not exactly at hand, was certainly within reach.

Frobisher's financial backers sent him off again but this time directed him more to the collecting of "this golde ore then for the searching any further discovery of the passage."[11] Provided with "one tall ship of her Majesties,"[12] named the *Aid*, to lead the smaller *Gabriel* and *Michael*, he returned to Frobisher Strait and discovered to his chagrin that it was only a bay extending deep into Baffin Island.[13] Nevertheless, Frobisher did find more of the black rocks, among them those his refiners reported as four sorts containing gold in good quantity. Returning with an estimated two hundred tons in his holds, Frobisher was greeted in London with uninhibited enthusiasm by his fellow investors, as well as by a prematurely grateful sovereign who gave him "a faire chain of gold" in recognition of his accomplishment. The chain proved to be the closest anyone actually got to gold. Assayers at the Royal Mint (adjacent to the Tower of

London, where part of the treasure had been deposited to ensure its safety) reported that they were unable to get their furnaces hot enough, and the commissioners charged with assessing the expedition's success reluctantly concluded that the quality of the second voyage's gold was not as high as that in the sailor's original black rock.

Unwilling to admit that the glittering crystals were not gold, the report tempered its negative conclusion by comparing the modest quality of the 1577 cargo with the superior ore to be expected from a third expedition. Pursuing gamblers' logic, the still-hopeful shareholding merchants of the newly founded Company of Cathay therefore dug deeper into their coffers to underwrite a much bigger enterprise carried aboard a fleet of fifteen ships. Frobisher sailed with them from Gravesend on May 27, 1578, and returned five months later laden with even greater quantities of worthless ore—to the financial undoing of everyone involved. Thus ended England's first euphoric episode in its effort to garner the riches of the New World.

Martin Frobisher's mining sites in the vicinity of Frobisher Bay entered Inuit lore, and the place where he established his base in 1578 became known as Kodlunarn (White Man's) Island. There, in 1862, the American explorer Charles Francis Hall found evidence of a European presence and concluded that the pottery, glass, and other relics he brought back had been left by Frobisher. Another American expedition in 1927 found more, and in 1990 a joint American and Canadian expedition, led by the Smithsonian Institution's Dr. William Fitzhugh, found others. Curiously, all three expeditions recovered fragments of green-glazed Germanic stove tiles which, though attributed to the Frobisher expeditions, were only beginning to be used in England ten years later. "As for stoves," wrote William Harrison in 1587, "we have not hitherto used them greatly, yet they do now begin to be made in diverse houses of the gentry and wealthy citizens. . . ."[14] By one of those coincidences that dapple the history of archaeology, discoveries made at the Fort Raleigh site in 1991 may help identify the kinds of Frobisher artifacts yet to be found on Baffin Island's bleak and frozen shores.

Although Frobisher's and other English attempts to fulfill Dr. Dee's northerly prophecies were useful exercises in hands-on education, they were halfpenny bids in the high-stakes game of European expansion. While English navigators' mandate was to go as far as they could and then try to get back, the Spaniards and Portuguese were going—and staying. Moreover, they had two and three generations' head start. Couple that fact with Spain's burgeoning power in Europe, which brought its military might almost in sight of English shores, and Protestant advisers to their Protestant queen had reason for concern.

Thanks to family inheritances, political scheming, and military adventures, the Habsburg empire in Europe pieced together by Charles V was the most formidable since the reign of Charlemagne, and in 1555 Charles turned it all over to his son Philip, who was then married to England's Queen Mary. In Central Europe the Habsburg holdings stretched from Silesia in the north through Austria to Croatia on the Adriatic. Charles had been king of Naples (which gave him half of Italy); he was duke of Burgundy, archduke of Milan, and master of Aragón, Sicily, Sardinia, Savoy, and Lorraine, as well as of Tunis in North Africa. But most disturbing of all, the king of Spain held key English Channel ports in the Netherlands.

As long as England retained its last French foothold at Calais, it could consider itself a participant in the European political and military game. But Mary, to please Philip, had allied England with Spain in its war with its chief rival for European supremacy, and as a result, in 1558 France overran Calais and thus drove England out of Europe. The blow to English national pride was tremendous, but in the greater scheme of things it freed England from a centuries-long fixation with Europe and paved the way for it to look elsewhere for pride-restoring successes.

Mary's return to Catholicism had not been well handled by her zealous advisers. The idea that the public burning of Protestant bishops and other heretics would prompt God to reward the queen with a healthy male heir resulted instead in a surge of anti-Catholic sentiment. Although the numbers who actually attended the burnings were small, the Protestant author John Foxe graphically recorded Mary's persecutions in a book that was at first rather dully titled *History of the Acts and Monuments of the Church*, but that enjoyed wider popularity as *Foxes Book of Martyrs*. First published in English in 1563, and embellished with numerous graphic woodcuts, it became second only to the Bible as approved reading, and throughout Elizabeth's reign it did much to keep the martyrs' memory alive and to foster hatred of both Catholicism and Spain.

All these events burned themselves into the Protestant psyche and prepared the English to cast aside the woolen cloak of the rustic island shepherd in favor of the sword and raffish plumes of the Elizabethan sea dog. The gold fever so quickly generated by the Frobisher expeditions and as quickly snuffed out; the failure to reach Cathay by either Arctic route; the loss of Calais; the religious turmoil of barren Mary's reign; and the proximity of a rich and powerful Catholic Spain basking in the yellow glow of Aztec and In $\ldots$ gold were all contributors to the sudden emergence of a generation of angry English sea soldiers. That is, of course, an exaggeration; the majority of the population continued its usual way of life. Nevertheless, a 1583 census of potential conscripts for the navy in the event of an attempted Spanish invasion listed 16,255 persons who were in some fashion "accustomed to the water."[15] Earlier in Elizabeth's reign only a few voluntarily took to the sea to defy the might of Spain, but like the "happy few" who stood against the French at Agincourt and the "first of the few" who flew against Hitler in the Battle of Britain, they were enough to make the difference.

With little but the weather to interrupt the flow of riches into Spanish and Portuguese treasuries, Iberian shipbuilders of the mid-sixteenth century continued to design and construct enormous galleons, floating castles to carry troops and settlers to faraway places, with holds big enough to house the returning loot. Although large ships with towering fighting platforms had been characteristic of Henry VIII's navy, by the third quarter of the sixteenth century English shipbuilders were constructing less top-heavy vessels with sleeker lines, and although still not able to turn on a groat, they were faster and more maneuverable than most Spanish warships.

Ironically, England's first, at least semiofficial entry into the Spaniards' sea-lanes and its first modest effort to play them at their own commercial game was launched aboard an antique built in Germany and bought from the league of Hanseatic merchants in 1545 for Henry's English navy. A large ship of seven hundred tons, the *Jesus of Lübeck* had all the attributes that the new English designers were discarding. However, she had one that overrode all others: The *Jesus of Lübeck* was a gift from Queen Elizabeth—her personal contribution to a London-financed slave-buying and -snatching expedition to the west coast of Africa. The captain of this enterprise was to be John Hawkyns, later the scourge of the Spanish Main.

Hawkyns was a Plymouth man and came from a seafaring family, his father having made three recorded voyages to Brazil between about 1528 and 1531. In several short voyages to the Canary Isles young John discovered that "negroes were very good merchandize in Hispaniola, and that they might easily be had on the coast of Guinea."[16] In 1562 he managed to trade a cargo of three hundred slaves for Caribbean hides, ginger, sugar, and pearls to the value of twenty thousand pounds. Although in doing so he fell foul of the Spanish authorities, his return to England was hailed as a commercial triumph, and London and Plymouth merchants needed no persuading that selling slaves to Spaniards was the way to wealth. The sooner Hawkyns mounted a second expedition, the richer everyone would be.

Such court luminaries as the earl of Pembroke and Lord Robert Dudley became leading shareholders in the new expedition and influenced the queen to contribute, as she did by providing that aging whale of a ship, the *Jesus of Lübeck*. With it as his flagship and as presumed evidence of royal blessing, Hawkyns left Plymouth with three other ships in October 1564.

Unlike the Portuguese, who had established an amicable trading relationship with the local African slave merchants, Hawkyns went about things more crudely. Once ashore, his rabble of a crew could be relied on to scatter about its own business of ransacking the villages in search of gold, thus making instant enemies of Portugal's friends. Nevertheless, after suffering disconcerting losses in both men and materials, Hawkyns corralled "so great a companie of Negros"[17] and set sail for the West Indies—but not before astute natives had cut the ozier hoops from around many of his water barrels, leaving him to cross the Atlantic on parlously short rations.

After Hawkyns's previous slave-selling visit (and probably because of it) unequivocal orders had been sent from Spain to its New World commandants that no such intercourse was to be countenanced. Indeed, when word reached the Spanish viceroy at Santo Domingo, he sent orders that not only was trading with the English forbidden, but they should be resisted with all available force. Hawkyns, however, was desperate to dispose of the worst of his thirsty and sickly Africans, and when cajoling and bluster failed to move the local authorities (pointing out that he had come there in "an Armada of the Queenes Majesties of England"),[18] he resorted to more direct persuasion. The sight of a hundred armored soldiers and a couple of cannon enabled Hawkyns to dispose of his entire supply, and to return to England in September 1565, laden (alongside more mundane merchandise) with "golde, silver, Pearles and other jewels great store."[19]

Complaints from Spain, and Queen Elizabeth's professed disavowal of her subjects' exploits, delayed a third expedition until 1567, when once again she lent Hawkyns the refitted *Jesus of Lübeck*. This time the squadron included the *Minion* (which had been with the second expedition) and four other, smaller vessels, one of which, the fifty-ton *Judith*, was commanded by a young man who may have been John Hawkyns's nephew, Francis Drake.

Following the by now familiar pattern, Hawkyns acquired his African cargo not through trade or diplomacy but by the slaughter and pillage of native villages and Portuguese vessels. The value of the haul in both slaves and goods was later set by the irate Portuguese at a sum in excess of seventy thousand gold pieces. With four to five hundred blacks aboard, Hawkyns sailed yet once more to the West Indies and their increasingly reluctant Spanish markets.

On September 16, after successfully disposing of most of his slaves, Hawkyns risked entering New Spain's principal continental harbor at San Juan de Ulúa (now part of Veracruz, Mexico). The decision proved to be the undoing of Hawkyns and most of his companions. Their arrival coincided with that of a fleet of thirteen treasure-laden Spanish galleons, aboard one of which was King Philip's new viceroy, Don Martín Enríquez de Almana, a man with few doubts about how to handle a ragtag bunch of piratical enemies of both God and Spain. In the ensuing battle only the *Minion* and *Judith* escaped. The latter, according to Hawkyns, "foresooke us in our great miserie"[20] and disappeared into the night—a strangely ignominious beginning to the dazzling career of her commander, Francis Drake.

In 1570 and 1571 Drake made reconnoitering sorties into the Caribbean, searching for points of Spanish vulnerability. Both he and Hawkyns concluded that successful attacks on the Spanish treasure fleets demanded large ships and plenty of them, and they knew that Elizabeth would not underwrite an enterprise that could end only in open war. Drake believed that the gold and silver umbilical cord to King Philip's treasury could effectively be severed on land, specifically where the gold-laden mule trains from Peru and the silks and spices from the Pacific *flotas* were carried across the Panamanian isthmus to the Caribbean port of Nombre de Dios. In May 1572, with two small ships and only seventy-three men, he set out to prove his point.

Although Drake's timing was off, and he was able to ambush only one Peruvian mule train, he successfully invaded Nombre de Dios, burned the town of Porto Bello and several Spanish ships, and was the first Englishman to cross the isthmus and see the Pacific. From his vantage point in a treetop Drake begged God to let him live to sail the new sea in an English ship. He returned to Plymouth on August 9, 1573, with loot to the tune of about twenty thousand pounds, not a great fortune by Spanish standards but nonetheless commendable in English eyes.

Four years later, inspired by his glimpse of the Pacific, Drake set out in the wake of Magellan to circumnavigate the globe, demonstrating—

the Treaty of Tordesillas notwithstanding—that the world beyond Europe was no longer a playground for only two nations, or, to be precise, *one* nation, for in 1580, the year of Drake's triumphant return, Spain annexed Portugal, combining their Catholic colonies both east and west into a single, intimidating global empire.

CHAPTER II

The New Fort in Virginia

A NY EARLY-sixteenth-century Englishman would have wagered
his last groat that his country's future would continue to be
shaped by the monarch and a circle of self-seeking advisers
drawn from the church and from the great landowning families. Instead
the impetus came from the courage and patriotism (leavened with no little greed) of a handful of outsiders—West Countrymen with tar in their
nostrils and salt in their beards. They were the ones who forged the Elizabethan spirit that was to steel Britain's empire-building backbone
through three hundred years. John Hawkyns's first and second voyages
had demonstrated that England possessed a future as a maritime trader,
albeit in black gold; his third set a course that led in 1588 to Spain's
attempted answer to the English problem, while Francis Drake's exploits
indirectly helped foster the notion that assaulting other nations' colonies
might in the long run be less productive than founding one's own.

In 1583 another Devon man, Sir Humphrey (or Humfrey) Gilbert, set
sail for Newfoundland with a fleet of five ships carrying 260 colonists and
crew to plant a permanent settlement in the New World, far, and relatively safely, removed from Spanish interference. It was his second
attempt at New World colonization, the first having come to grief after
an encounter with the Spaniards off Cape Verde. Gilbert had been
knighted for his military conduct against Irish rebels in Munster; he had
led English mercenaries against the Spaniards in the Netherlands, and he
firmly believed that he had been chosen by God to spread the Protestant
Gospel. In short, he was not an easy man to deal with, as the 1577 title to
one of the several advisory discourses he submitted to his sovereign suggests: "How Her Majesty might annoy the King of Spain by fitting out a

fleet of war-ships under pretence of a voyage of discovery, and so fall upon the enemy's shipping, destroy his trade in Newfoundland and the West Indies, and possess both Regions." No comment came from the palace, but perhaps because of his single-minded persistence, in 1578 Gilbert had received his queen's license to plant an American colony. It gave him the right "to discover, finde, search out, and view such remote, heathen and barbarous lands, countreys and territories not actually possessed of any Christian prince or people" and "to have, hold, occupie and enjoy to him, his heires and assignes for ever, with all commodities, jurisdictions and royalties both by sea and land. . . ."[1] Gilbert had been given carte blanche to claim whatever he could hold—provided he trod on no Christian toes in so doing.

A fleet of five ships left Plymouth on June 11, 1583: Gilbert's 120-ton flagship, the *Delight;* a larger bark, the 200-ton *Raleigh* belonging to his half brother Walter Ralegh; three much smaller vessels, the *Golden Hind* and *Swallow,* both of 40 tons; and the 10-ton *Squirrel.* For reasons never convincingly explained, the *Raleigh* quit the voyage after only two days' sailing, thus robbing the fleet of its "most puissant ship."

By July 27 Gilbert had reached the Newfoundland Banks, prompting Edward Hayes, the captain of the *Golden Hind,* to note that "The Portugals, and French chiefly, have a notable trade of fishing upon this banke, where are sometimes an hundred or more sailes of ships."[2] Thus by the 1580s the approach to the still-to-be-found Northwest Passage had become a pretty busy place. No longer were the transatlantic voyagers sailing alone into the vastness of an unknown sea. What remained unknown and generally unattractive to would-be settlers was the land beyond it, which Hayes described as an "uncomfortable coast, nothing appearing unto us but hideous rockes and mountaines, bare of trees, and void of any greene herbe."[3]

Just how many of Gilbert's settlers had been denied him as a result of the *Raleigh*'s desertion is unclear, but the record shows that the original company had been chosen with some care—their number twice that of the group that later sailed for Virginia to build James Towne. Hayes described Gilbert's team as having "every faculty good choice" and listed shipwrights, masons, carpenters, blacksmiths, along with the essential "Minerall men and Refiners" to identify and extract the expected supplies of gold. The majority of the settlers, however, were little more than warm bodies: sailors, useless on land, and landsmen, some of whom were useless anywhere, having been culled from English jails to work as servants.

Left: Sir Humphrey Gilbert, from an engraving of 1802. *Right:* Sir Walter Ralegh, the owner of Virginia "at all times for ever hereafter."

As if to demonstrate the quality of the help and as a foretaste of problems to come, the *Swallow* rejoined the fleet (after being lost in a fog two weeks earlier), its crew freshly resplendent in new clothing, having stopped and mugged a fishing bark, stealing her equipment and torturing her crew.

On August 3 Gilbert and his four ships assembled at the entrance to St. John's Harbor, where they found thirty-six English and other nations' fishing vessels at anchor. After a brief disagreement, and threats by Gilbert to force his way in, and after he had somewhat marred his impact by running onto a plainly visible rock "much above water faste by the shore,"[4] he was hauled off by the English fishermen and allowed to land. Two days later, in the name of England, his queen, and himself, Gilbert took formal possession of the harbor and the land around for a distance of two hundred leagues in every direction. He then announced three laws: The Church of England would be the mandated religion, anyone taking action to "offend" Her Majesty's right of possession would be executed, and anyone even talking about doing so would lose his ship, his fish, and his ears.

Although the expedition's officers professed to be satisfied with their accomplishment, the rank and file, having seen the New World, concluded that there was more to be said for old England. Some disappeared into the hinterland, awaiting an opportunity to hitch a ride on returning fishing barks, and others, less patient, stole one, dumped her crew, and took off on their own. More took sick, and several died. In the space of seventeen days England's first American colony came and went, leaving little behind but ill will and "the Armes of England ingraven in lead, and infixed upon a pillar of wood."[5]

Ordering the *Swallow* to take the sick home, Gilbert sailed south with the rest of his fleet to explore more of the American coast. In heavy weather the *Delight* ran aground and broke up, causing Gilbert to lose his cargo, his papers, and his ore samples. Distraught by their loss, Gilbert became increasingly irrational, and when, on September 9, his two remaining ships, the *Golden Hind* and *Squirrel*, ran into mountainous seas north of the Azores, he was last seen seated at the stern of the little ten-ton *Squirrel*, a book in his hand, shouting, "We are as neere to heaven by seas as by land."[6] Just how his words could be heard over the howling wind and pounding sea is anybody's guess; nevertheless, they remain among the legendary moments in the history of seafaring. Apocryphal or not, they were right. Around midnight the *Squirrel*'s lights went out, and when dawn came, not a trace of the ship was to be seen. A contemporary portrait at Compton Castle, the Gilbert family's home, is inscribed "Syr Humfrye Gilbert Knight dwowned in the discovery of Virginia. Anno 1584." The wording presumably was added later, hence the wrong place and the wrong date.

The battered *Golden Hind* reached the Devon port of Falmouth on September 20, 1583. Shortly afterward Walter Ralegh (whose ship's role in the Gilbert effort had been so short-lived and so curious) petitioned the queen to take over Gilbert's "to have and to hold" royal colonizing patent. He received it on March 25, 1584, thus securing a six-year open season on any lands not already occupied by Christians. Intent on choosing a location geographically more hospitable than Gilbert's Newfoundland, Ralegh fitted out two unidentified vessels of unspecified tonnage, one described as a ship and the other a pinnace (usually a small, two-masted vessel used to support a larger), under the command of Captains Philip Amadas and Arthur Barlowe. Not much is known about either, beyond the facts that Amadas worked for Ralegh prior to the voyage and that Barlowe (who wrote the surviving account of the voyage) had served as a soldier with him in Ireland. The fact is inescapable, however, that their mission was accomplished without a hitch.

The ships left an unspecified Devon port on April 27, 1584, dropped down to the Canary Islands, and then crossed the Atlantic. They took on water at Puerto Rico, where the crews found "the ayre very unwholsome"[7] and many took sick. After a ten-day layover the two ships sailed north up the Florida coast to a point at approximately 36° latitude, which would have put them abreast of the Outer Banks above Cape Hatteras. That information comes not from Barlowe's narrative but from intelligence gathered by the Spanish abbot of Jamaica, who reported that at that latitude "a great bay leads to where certain islands lie, and this is sweet water four leagues out to sea; and according to the Indians this is the best part of all that coast, and is a passage to the Pacific."[8]

The abbot's report mentioned that the entrance to the bay had been found by a Portuguese named Hernando, apparently an incorrect reference to Simon Fernández (or Ferdinando), master and pilot of the lead ship in the 1584 expedition and again the following year, when he was blamed for grounding the flagship at the entrance to Pamlico Sound. The Spanish report noted that "the savages ate 38 Englishmen" who had sought to land at one headland. Doubtless maintaining a similar level of inaccuracy, the report went on to relate that other Indians proved more friendly and, when asked for gold, gave the visitors "four pounds of gold and a hundred of silver and hides and many other valuable things."[9] The account was correct in adding that Amadas and Barlowe took home two Indians, but apparently wrong in saying that they left behind two Englishmen as hostages for the Indians' return.

The Amadas and Barlowe expedition penetrated what we now know as the North Carolina Outer Banks and, sailing their pinnace northward through Pamlico Sound, came to Roanoke Island. Reporting later to Walter Ralegh, Barlowe was enthused over its plants, trees, and wildlife but only once used the magic word his sponsors had been waiting to read. In describing the headband worn by Granganimeo, brother to the absent Indian King Wingina, Barlowe wrote: "upon his head a broad plate of golde, or copper, for being unpolished we knew not what mettal it should be."[10] This is a somewhat odd statement, for gold does not tarnish, whereas unpolished copper in the Outer Banks' salted air can be relied on to darken quickly or turn green. Nevertheless, the bottom line was clear: The islands and the coast beyond the sound held promise as a settlers' paradise—if not for gold miners.

That disappointment aside, Barlowe left no doubt that other, more mundane but commercially profitable resources were there in abundance, and that the climate and food supplies were ideal for a permanent settlement. Best of all, the natives were friendly. "We found the people most gentle, loving, and faithfull, voide of all guile and treason, and such as live

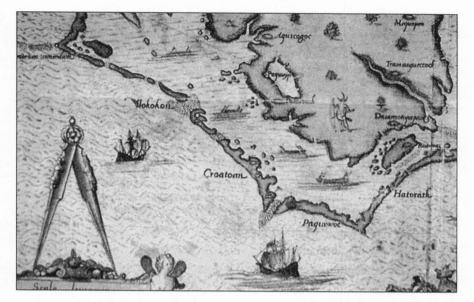

The North Carolina shores and sounds, from Théodore de Bry's 1590
edition of Thomas Hariot's *A briefe and true report of the new found
land of Virginia.*

after the maner of the golden age." A few lines later, Barlowe added that
"for a more kinde and loving people there can not be found in the
worlde."[11] These statements are in striking contrast with the rumored
thirty-eight eaten Englishmen and are important in the light of deteriorating relations between the Indians and later English arrivals.

Some authorities have contended that the Indians of Tidewater Virginia had had long experience of the white man, specifically of the
Spaniard, prior to the arrival of the James Fort settlers in 1607 and that
through intertribal grapevines the Indians had a fair knowledge of what
the colonizers were doing in Florida and the Caribbean. As is the case
with much else in these early pages of American history, one can cite evidence both for and against the grapevine theory. One nineteenth-century
school (citing "the painstaking and accurate historian John Fisk") claimed
that in 1526 a Spanish government official from Hispaniola, Lucas
Vásquez de Ayllón, had brought six hundred men and women, along with
a hundred horses, to establish a settlement near Jamestown Island which
he called San Miguel but that when Ayllón and many of the settlers died
of fever, the town was abandoned. The story remains intriguing, and perhaps because the six hundred included black slaves, it was given some

prominence during the 1907 Jamestown Tercentennial—showing that it was the Spaniards who deserved the dubious credit for introducing slave labor to America.

Part of the Ayllón story was true, though probably not the part that seated him near Jamestown Island. He did secure a patent from Charles V of Spain to colonize and Christianize on the American mainland between the thirty-fifth and thirty-seventh parallels, which stretched from the Neuse River in the south to Hampton Roads in the north, thus incorporating the entire area explored by Barlowe and by later Ralegh expeditions. Furthermore, Ayllón did found a major settlement named San Miguel de Gualdape. However, modern wisdom has it that the town was located somewhere between the mouth of the Savannah River and St. Helena Sound, where Ayllón and others in the early 1520s had rounded up Indians as slave labor for their Hispaniola sugar plantations. There is, however, another side to that coin. In 1609 a Spanish reconnaissance, led by Captain Francisco Fernández de Écija and sent to find out what the English were up to in Virginia, took back a remarkably accurate description of Jamestown Island provided by Indians of the Carolinas. They told him that the settlers had built a wooden fort and that the place was known to the Indians as Guandape—more or less as in San Miguel de Gualdape.

Charts and maps dating onward from 1500 clearly demonstrate that the Spaniards gradually expanded and refined their knowledge of North America's Atlantic coastline. By mid-century the Chesapeake Bay (Bahía de Santa María) was a familiar feature—if not to the English, who may at first have confused it with Pamlico and Currituck Sounds. It is true, too, that in 1570 Jesuits founded a short-lived mission somewhere south of the bay, probably on the James-York peninsula. Nevertheless, in spite of this actual settlement and at least two other exploratory visits in the seventies, to Arthur Barlowe's knowledge no Spanish ship had entered the sounds behind the barrier of the Outer Banks. Indeed, he was specifically told by the coastal Indians that the only white men they had ever seen had come from a ship wrecked twenty-six years earlier, men who had stayed no longer than three weeks before sailing away in borrowed canoes. The Indians could recall but one other wreck; it had been driven ashore crewless, and from it they had salvaged nails and iron spikes to shape into tools.

Barlowe's account, though confusing about time and distance, leaves the impression that the Indian King Wingina's subjects never traveled very far and lacked in-depth knowledge of the world beyond a six days' journey. Since many of the Indians encountered by the English had not been born when the first shipwreck occurred, it isn't surprising that "they wondred marvelously . . . at the whitenes of [their] skins, ever coveting to touch [their] breasts, and to view the same."[12] As Barlowe described it, these first English encounters with the Algonquian Indians were close to idyllic, and not even the announcement that the territory they called Wingandacoa had been annexed in the name of the queen of England elicited so much as a frown. To the time of their pale-skinned guests' departure the Indians looked upon them as generous friends with marvelous and magical gifts to bestow, and in return the English saw the yellowish-skinned Indians as easily manipulable savages.

After a stay of six weeks, their mission accomplished, Amadas and Barlowe hauled their anchors and set their sails for home, taking with them the two Indians Manteo and Wanchese, who were to learn enough English to play major roles in the white men's second coming.

Some authorities have claimed that Walter Ralegh edited Barlowe's account to make it sound more appealing to investors willing to help underwrite his intent to send a second expedition to Virginia and establish a permanent colony there. While the text's insistence on the friendliness of the Indians is almost certainly correct, modern visitors to North Carolina's Outer Banks and their relatively Spartan and sand-blasted vegetation may be forgiven for wondering what became of the Garden of Eden–style ecology that so entranced Arthur Barlowe. Nevertheless, it is evident in several passages that his account as later published had been expanded either by Ralegh or by editor Richard Hakluyt. Thus, for example, Barlowe's sentence naming the Indians' territory as Wingandacoa ends with the words "and now by her Majestie Virginia."[13] It was not until January 6, 1585, more than three months after the ships' return, that Ralegh was knighted by the queen, who then made him governor of the newly discovered American territory and permitted him to name it Virginia in her honor.

The royal mandate corresponded not at all with the limits of modern Virginia but extended "the space of two hundredth leagues"[14] north and south from Roanoke Island. Edward Phillips's *New World of Words* (1671) defined a league as "a certain proportion of ground in length only consisting of about two, or three miles," but even if one accepts the shorter distance, it carried the English claim south to Cape Fear and perilously close to territory that the Spaniards considered theirs.

Sir Walter Ralegh was not a gentle man; the seventeenth-century biographer John Aubrey began his essay upon him thus: "He was a tall, handsome, and bold man; but his blemish was that he was damnably proud."[15] A study in contrasts, he was, on the one hand, a scholar and poet and, on the other, a rough-and-ready countryman with a broad Devonshire accent, who became an awkward and brashly opportunistic courtier, approved of in London by few but the queen; yet on the quays, in the shipyards, and in the rural manor houses of his native West Country, he was loved, respected, feared. He was a close friend of most of the seafaring men who were about to transform England into the scourge of Spain, and his vision of his American mission almost certainly differed markedly from the opportunity for a kind and gentle coexistence with the Indians suggested by Barlowe's experience.

Weightily influential among Ralegh's friends was Richard Hakluyt, who (along with the wizardly Dr. Dee) is credited with doing most to put England in an empire-building vein. A confidant, too, of the accident-prone Sir Humphrey Gilbert, Hakluyt was an inland cleric fascinated by the sea and the lands beyond it. While studying at Oxford, he read everything he could find in any of six languages dealing with exploration, and in 1582 he published a volume, titled *Divers Voyages touching the Discovery of America*, in which he stressed the importance of spreading English sails. This publication, and others even more influential to be compiled later in his life, made Richard Hakluyt the accepted expert on expansionist cosmography. Consequently, his advice to Sir Walter Ralegh as the latter put together his second American venture, is of more than slight significance.

In a memorandum to an unidentified individual (who may have been Ralegh) the clergyman demonstrated a preference for Old rather than New Testament counsel, advocating that if the Indians should resist English demands, rather than turn the other cheek the settlers should smite them hip and thigh. "We will proceed with extremity," Hakluyt declared, "conquer, fortify and plant in soils most sweet, most pleasant, most strong and most fertile, and in the end bring them all in subjection and to civility."[16] They were words that planted the seeds of an Anglo-aboriginal policy whose legacy lingers still.

The number of men sent out (there were no women) in the spring of 1585 is uncertain, but David Quinn, the principal modern authority on the Roanoke voyages, has suggested that the intent may have been to land as many as five hundred. Of those, many were soldiers with all the support (such as armorers, blacksmiths, and gunsmiths) required to sustain them in both defense and offense. They would have opportunities to practice as the expedition made its way north from its first landfall at Puerto Rico and in its subsequent layover at Hispaniola. Most of the company were on salary and did not represent the kind of individual investment and commitment essential for a truly permanent settlement. They would stay for a year or two and go home, to be followed by new employees. A modern analogy would be the scientists, engineers, and company personnel working an overseas oilfield.

In addition to specialists ministering to the expedition's spiritual and medical needs, Ralegh's expedition included a scientific research team headed by his household tutor, Thomas Hariot (or Harriot), its task to assess the new territory's natural resources and profitability. Although only twenty-five years old, Hariot was already one of the true Renaissance men of Elizabethan England; astronomer, mathematician, surveyor, tinkering alchemist, and experimenter with lenses, he was an ideal choice to head the interdisciplinary Virginia survey. With him went a Jewish "minerall man" and, at the outset at least, John White, an accomplished watercolorist—the Tudor equivalent of today's project photographer.

Ralegh's fleet was commanded by an individual as fiery as himself, Sir Richard Grenville. Yet another son of the West Country (he was born in Cornwall), Grenville is best remembered through Tennyson's famous ballad "The Revenge" (1878), which begins "At Flores in the Azores Sir Richard Grenville lay . . . ," and tells how aboard his five-hundred-ton ship, Grenville fought a Spanish fleet of fifty-three galleons for fifteen hours before finally being overpowered and dying of his wounds. But that was six years into the future. The ship he was to sail to Virginia was the much smaller—140-ton—*Tiger,* another loan from Queen Elizabeth, who also contributed twenty-four hundred pounds of gunpowder—while still publicly denying involvement in anything that could be construed as hostility toward Spain.

The *Tiger* was described as a galleass, related in some respects to the Mediterranean galleys of Spain and drawing more water than would turn out to be good for her. The second vessel, the *Roebucke,* was of similar tonnage, but broad-beamed and shallow in the draft. Making up the rest of the fleet were the 100-ton *Lion* and the *Elizabeth* and the *Dorothy,* each of 50 tons, plus two pinnaces, seven ships in all. Philip Amadas from the previous voyage, now as naval second-in-command, was aboard the *Tiger,* as was the Portuguese pilot Simon Fernández, and Professor Quinn has suggested that Arthur Barlowe was master of the *Dorothy.* Then, too, the Indians Wanchese and Manteo were going home, though there is no knowing on which ship they were quartered. New to the leadership was Master Ralph Lane, a soldier steeled in combat in Ireland, who was

Sir Richard Grenville, first commander of the 1585
Roanoke enterprise, from an 1802 engraving.

second-in-command of Grenville's troops and was to remain in Virginia
as governor.

The enterprise got off to a poor start, running into a violent storm off
the coast of Portugal which sank one of the pinnaces and so scattered the
fleet that the *Tiger* found herself crossing the Atlantic alone. She had left
Plymouth on April 9 and on May 12 reached the southwestern coast of
Puerto Rico at Guayanilla Bay, where Grenville waited for the rest of his
fleet to rendezvous. While there, Ralph Lane directed the soldiers in constructing fortifications whose character should have much to say about
the tactics and methods he would employ on Roanoke Island and which,
by extension, might have a bearing on the nature of the triangular
defenses at James Fort. The unnamed historian of Grenville's voyage told
how Lane "began to fortifie very neere to the Sea side: the river ran by the
one side of our forte, and the other two sides were invironed with
woods."[17]

Without the benefit of plans or sketches, it would be reasonable to
deduce that the fort was triangular—one side facing the river and the
other two the woods. However, John White's drawing of the site shows
something entirely different. Interlocking entrenchments fronted the

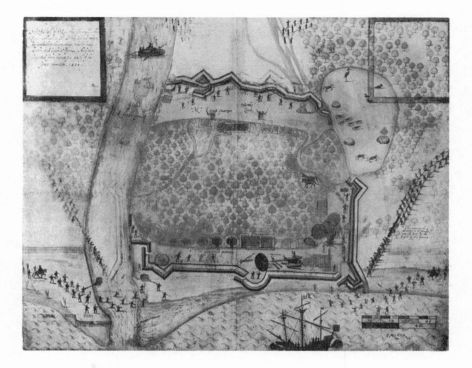

John White's rendering of Grenville's and Lane's defenses in Guayanilla Bay at Puerto Rico in May 1585. The ship in the foreground may be the *Tiger*.

ocean and turned inland until they reached a lake inhabited by cranes, ducks, and numerous seemingly duck-size crabs. Toward the extremity of the lake, the entrenchments resumed, turning left until they met the river. This last created the fourth side of a square which appears to have been unprotected by anything but the water. Several rectangular structures immediately behind the north entrenchments are marked as "Mr. Lanes Quarters," while another, larger structure against the south defenses is identified as "The Generalls Quarter." Adjacent to it are nine circular huts or tents, and behind them woods are interrupted only by paths and a corral for two horses. The woodland fills virtually the entire interior of what is really an encampment rather than a fort in the traditional sense of the word. Upriver to the left a boat returns with water barrels, while below, a column led by a mounted man (assumed to be Grenville) fires a signal shot as the soldiers begin to ford the estuary. Over to the right another column returns carting a large log, and behind the defenses still other men are building a pinnace in a location which almost certainly would have posed launching difficulties.

John White's extremely detailed watercolor drawing has acquired further but unintended oddities. In 1865 the only surviving collection of his work was sent to auction by its owner, the third earl of Charlemont. Before the sale at Sotheby's an adjacent warehouse caught fire, and in putting it out, firemen saturated the paintings. The Guayanilla Bay encampment view, being a page folded on itself, wound up with several elements duplicating themselves in retrograde, thus sending troops advancing into the sea and trundling their wheeled log into the river. But these confusions aside, the painting provides a clear impression of the kind of water-filled ditch and earthwork defense that Lane might build when he and his settlers reached their destination.

The pinnace under construction in White's painting was intended to replace the one lost off Portugal, making the important point that even single ships carried carpenters able to build fairly large craft from prefabricated parts, if not from scratch. However, as we shall discover, by the time Grenville was on his way home their efforts would suggest that their skills, their number, or their resources had diminished.

On May 23, after completing the pinnace and being joined only by the *Elizabeth,* Grenville prepared to move on. First he set fire to the neighboring woods (to pay back the Spaniards, who had promised to provide supplies but hadn't) and then he retired to the fort, "which the same day was fired also."[18] The question of how one fires a fort comes up later when we try to understand the extent of a fire at James Fort in 1608. John White's drawing suggests that the Guayanilla Bay defenses were no more than earthworks without wooden palisades, and if so, only the temporary buildings inside could have been burned. If, on the other hand, vertical log-walled palisades augmented the earthworks, how (short of jumping the centuries and dousing the timbers with gasoline) did one get them to stay alight?

On May 24, unaware that they were posing arcane questions for future archaeologists and historians, the *Tiger* and *Elizabeth* hoisted sail, quitting the inhospitable beachhead which someone (with good reason) had named Mosquito Bay. Heading north, the English ships attacked and seized two small Spanish frigates, one of them "with good and rich fraight, and divers Spaniards of account in her,"[19] whom Grenville subsequently ransomed. In the third quarter of the sixteenth century such incidents of unauthorized belligerence, though deplored by those at the sharp end of the sword, were recognized as standard travel hazards, just as brigandage was expected on European trunk roads.

Two days later, having learned from one of the Spaniards that there were valuable supplies of salt piled on a beach at Salinas Bay, Cape Rojo,

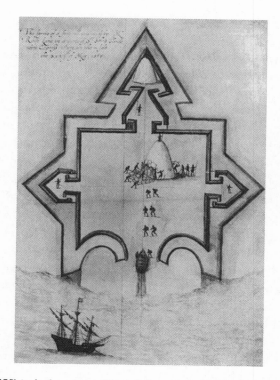

John White's drawing of Ralph Lane's defended salt pile near
Cape Rojo, Puerto Rico, in May 1585.

Puerto Rico, Ralph Lane took one of the captured frigates there and
loaded as much as he could carry. This additional assault on Spanish
property would be of no relevance were it not for the fact that Lane dug
and erected some highly elaborate defensive entrenchments around the
salt piles, defenses which (as at Mosquito Bay) were drawn by John
White. The system of redoubts and interlocking connections to protect
against lateral fire clearly attested to Lane's knowledge of military engineering. No great experience was needed, however, to recognize that
earthworks once thrown up not only defend against an enemy's missiles
but also prevent one from seeing that he is approaching. Consequently,
Lane posted lookouts atop the two conical salt piles while colleagues
chopped and shoveled away at their foundations. That forts and outposts
needed elevated watchtowers would be a point to remember when
one tries to reconstruct the appearance of forts on both Roanoke and
Jamestown islands.

The history of Grenville's continuing voyage through the West Indies
and up the coast of Florida to the Outer Banks need not concern us. Suffice it to say that on June 23 he arrived off the gap between Wococon and

Croatoan islands (the latter now part of Ocracoke and Hatteras islands, and probably the opening named Port Grinvil), and sent word up Pamlico Sound to Wingina at Roanoke. The Wococon gap was the widest into the sound, but it was also shoaled and shallow—and the *Tiger* was a deep-draft ship. With the Amadas-Barlowe expedition's Portuguese pilot, Simon Fernández, to guide her through, she went aground and flooded—to the chagrin of all and the embarrassment of pilot Fernández.

Fortunately the flagship could be refloated. Meanwhile, using a fleet of shallow-drafted boats, Grenville and most of the expedition's leaders passed through the shoals into the sound and spent several days exploring along the inner coastline south toward the Neuse River. Among the Indian villages encountered along the way was Aquascogoc, and while there, in one of American history's minor ironies, the English, who had come to take gold and silver from the Indians, found that the Indians had stolen a silver cup from them. Two days later Grenville gave the expedition's admiral, Philip Amadas, the unwise order to go back with eleven men to demand the return of the cup—or else. When it was not forthcoming, Amadas "burnt, and spoyled their corne, and Towne, all the people being fled."[20] He also spoiled the trusting relationship that had hitherto existed between English and Indians. Though in retrospect an incredibly foolish overreaction to a minor incident, it was entirely characteristic of the hair-trigger "take nothing from nobody" attitude of the English version of Spain's conquistadors. As for the Indians, the ability to smile while waiting to get even was as much an element of their culture as murderous impetuosity was of the English.

On July 18, with the damage done, the boats returned to the fleet anchored off the Wococon inlet (the *Tiger* by then pumped and caulked) and later sailed on up past Hatteras Island to the inlet of Port Ferdinando. There, after meetings with their last year's host, Granganimeo, they negotiated the placement on Roanoke Island of the first English settlement on Virginia soil.

In the days following the *Tiger's* ignominious arrival at Wococon inlet, Grenville was joined by at least two more of his fleet, whose masters had elected to bypass the Puerto Rican rendezvous and make their own way to the Outer Banks. These ships seem to have been the *Roebucke* and the *Dorothy,* the *Lion* having arrived earlier. Finding himself alone, the *Lion's* master, George Raymond, left several men on Hatteras Island and sailed on to Newfoundland. So, when Grenville decided that it was time to leave his settlers and go home, his flotilla probably amounted to four English ships and his two Spanish prizes. On August 5 Grenville dis-

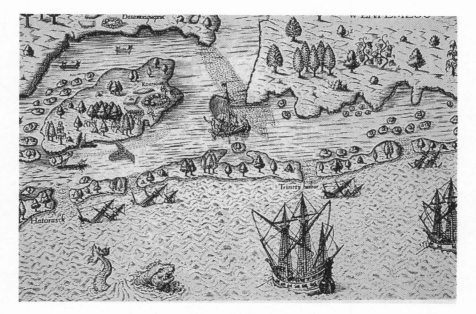

Théodore de Bry's 1590 engraving of an English shallop approaching Roanoke Island from the north, having passed through the broken barrier of the Outer Banks.

patched one of his officers, John Arundell, to England with the first report of the expedition's accomplishments, and Professor Quinn has deduced that the chosen ship was either the *Dorothy* or the larger of the two Spanish frigates. Besides the vessels still in the fleet, there would have been the pinnace built at Puerto Rico and several small boats, some of which are likely to have been left behind for the inshore use of the colonists.

Grenville finally weighed anchor on August 25 and about a week later sighted and boarded a straggler from Spain's homeward-bound treasure fleet, the three-hundred-ton *Santa María de San Vicente*, a ship gleefully described as "richly laden." It was only natural that finding her more commodious and doubtless in better shape than the refloated *Tiger*, Grenville should transfer himself to the prize and equally natural that he would do so to make sure that none of his notoriously unreliable colleagues should make off with it. Although this seizure emphasizes the Englishmen's increasingly blatant assaults on anything Spanish, its pertinence lies in a tiny detail—namely, the quality of the transportation used to board the Spaniard: "a boate made with boards of chests, which fell asunder, and sunke at the ships side, assoone as ever he [Grenville] and his men were out of it."[21]

That statement suggests one or both of two things: first, that Sir Richard Grenville had gone home with not so much as a longboat either in tow or on the *Tiger*'s deck, thus evidence that all the small boats had indeed been left behind, and second, that the skilled carpenters who had built the pinnace at Mosquito Bay were no longer aboard. If they were not, the presumption might be that they, too, stayed with the colonists to help them build their houses and fortifications on Roanoke Island. Indeed, this may explain an otherwise odd decision—namely, to delay the *Roebucke*'s departure by two weeks. When finally she sailed, she carried with her a letter from Ralph Lane to Richard Hakluyt, addressed "From the new Fort in Virginia, this third of September, 1585."[22] Although it does not follow that the "fort" had been completed by that date, the rehearsal in Puerto Rico had demonstrated that with sufficient manpower and with skilled artisans to do the tricky bits, much could be accomplished in relatively short order.

A key question that has to be addressed, even if it cannot definitively be answered, is what Lane meant by "the new Fort." Thanks to John White's drawing, we know that "our fort" beside Guayanilla Bay was not a castle but a fortified settlement, so it might appear reasonable to assume that the same would be true of Roanoke Island—but it also appears that it wasn't.

In spite of the fact that the English had burned cornfields and at least one village in the affair of the silver cup, Lane's September 3 letter to Richard Hakluyt reported only that "the people naturally are most courteous."[23] He may therefore have felt no pressing and immediate need to erect substantial defenses and instead "since Sir Richard Greenvils departure from us" spent more time exploring than in building. It is possible that when Grenville left ten days earlier, "the new Fort in Virginia" was more a location than a describable (or drawable) structure. Furthermore, in the absence of any on-island hostility, Lane concluded that rather than fortify his whole settlement, as would be done at James Fort in 1607, he would use the castle and village plan.

Sir Walter Ralegh's original intent, one still on line when Grenville and the fleet left Plymouth, was to follow them with a second supply of settlers to arrive once the pioneering bridgehead had been secured. Under Captains Amias Preston and Bernard Drake, the consolidators were to land in the late summer—about the time that Grenville left for home and Lane was building his fort and village.

In stark contrast with the speed of communications in today's world, throughout the centuries before pre-wireless telegraphy, vital news could take weeks and even months to reach the people who needed it. Thus Grenville had no way of knowing that ten weeks after he had sailed, deteriorating relations between England and Spain would cause the Preston-Drake expedition to be canceled. Instead they were dispatched to the Newfoundland fishing grounds to seize such Spanish vessels as they might encounter and to order English fishermen not to take their catches to Spanish ports.

There is no knowing whether Lane planned his Roanoke settlement to accommodate the expected new arrivals, but it is reasonable to deduce that if he intended to erect a palisade around its entirety, he elected to wait until he knew how large a space to enclose and until he had the men to man it. That he never built an encircling palisade is clear from his April 1586 description of a suspected Indian plot to destroy the settlement. In one stroke they intended, he said, to burn the English out "as well of them of the fort, as for us at the towne."[24] The latter referred to those of "the better sort," meaning the officers and gentlemen, suggesting perhaps that only soldiers lived in the fort. That, however, would have been the reverse of the normal practice, wherein the settlement leader's house would be in the fort (i.e., in the metaphorical "castle") while the lesser sort lived outside in the village.

In the same narrative, Lane feared that "In the dead time of the night they [the Indians] would have beset my house, and put fire in the reedes that the same was covered with . . . [and] would have knocked out my braines."[25] Clearly, therefore, Lane used the word "fort" interchangeably to mean both the settlement as a whole and the fortified part of it.

Nothing in the several contemporary narratives tells us anything about the fort's character or size. For these one must turn to the writing of later visitors and later still to the fuzzy findings provided by archaeology. A letter written by Virginia planter Francis Yeardley records that in 1653 a trader in beavers visited the island and was taken by the local Indians and shown "the ruins of Sir Walter Ralegh's fort, from whence I received a sure token of their being there. . . ."[26] Unfortunately Yeardley omitted to say what that token was. That there were artifacts to be found, there can be no doubt. About fifty years later the English traveler John Lawson reported that "the Ruins of a Fort are to be seen at this day, as well as some old English Coins which have been lately found; and a Brass-Gun, a Powder-Horn, and one small Quarter-deck-Gun, made of Iron Staves, and hooped with the same Metal; which Method of making Guns might very probably be made use of in those Days for the Convenience of Infant-Colonies."[27]

Although Lawson evidently knew little about the history of ordnance, he was right to assume that the iron gun was of that period. The medieval technique of building gun barrels from iron staves secured within multiple hoops continued for swivels and larger guns through much of the sixteenth century, but by its end had been superseded by cast-iron tubes. It is a pity that Lawson did not identify the coins (though he may not have seen them), for none has since been found on the site. But on private property not far from it an Elizabethan silver sixpence of 1563 has been unearthed from the roots of a tree. Carefully pierced for suspension, apparently by means of a steel drill, the coin was almost certainly given to the Indians by the English as a portrait of the Indians' new queen. As such, it is both the earliest surviving example of such a gift and the earliest known portrayal of Queen Elizabeth to be seen in America. Alas, regardless of its evident association with one or another of the Ralegh expeditions, the coin is not to be seen at the Fort Raleigh museum. The finder sold it to a New Jersey collector.

No one knows whether Lawson was shown other Elizabethan silver pieces (no copper small change was minted and circulated in Elizabeth's reign), but it is likely that he was confusing coins with brass counters known as jettons, three of which were found in the archaeological excavations that began in 1947. Made by Hans Schultes of Nuremberg, who was working between 1550 and 1574, the jettons are the most closely datable artifacts from the site. But they do more than that. Thanks to them, there is convincing evidence of a connection between the Roanoke fort and an Indian site forty miles away at Buxton near Cape Hatteras, where in 1938 an identical jetton was found. The Buxton site had been home to Indians of the Croatoan tribe, a name writ large in the final act of the Roanoke drama.

That later in the eighteenth century other visitors followed Lawson in pilgrimages to Ralegh's settlement site has been suggested by the discovery of two broken copper-alloy shoe buckles, one found seventy-four feet west of the reconstructed earthwork, and the other much farther away, at a distance of about six hundred feet. When I first examined these fragments some thirty years ago, I was content to dismiss them as relics of early tourists who burst their buckles clambering through the site's jungle of vines, but in 1993 I am convinced I was wrong. Renewed excavations west of the earthwork fort in 1983 yielded two fingernail-size ceramic fragments, one a sherd from an overglaze-decorated Chinese export porcelain plate and the other a tiny fragment of English creamware. In 1993 three more sherds were found together in the same area, two of them creamware and the third a fragment of transfer-printed pearlware that

Top, right and left: Obverse and reverse of an English silver sixpence of 1563. The finely drilled or punched hole above Queen Elizabeth's crown strongly suggests that the coin was given to an Indian as a necklace pendant to be worn as a portrait of his new monarch across the ocean. *Bottom:* Drawing of casting counter found in excavations at the Lost Colony site on Roanoke Island.

might date as late as 1810. None of these is likely to have been dropped by passing visitors; instead they point to potential buckle breakers living close to the fort in the last third of the eighteenth century and continuing into the early nineteenth century.

A map of North Carolina by John Collet published in London in 1770 shows seven dwellings on the northern half of Roanoke Island—plus a square enclosure with projections at each corner and labeled "Fort." On the same line as that word, but to the west of the island, is printed "Pain"—and John Paine is recorded on June 2, 1767, as paying one John Mann twenty pounds for fifty acres at the north end of the island and returning it to him in 1791. Five years later than the Collet map is another of 1775 assembled "From Actual Surveys by Henry Mouzon and Others," which shows the same seven dwellings as well as the fort, which is now identified as "PAIN FORT." The generally accepted and certainly the most

Detail from Henry Mouzon's 1775 map of the Carolinas,
showing a fort at the north end of Roanoke Island.

comfortable explanation has been that Mouzon's engraver incorrectly copied from Collet, who was only noting the site of Ralegh's settlement, and that neither mapmaker was suggesting that the fort was an operating eighteenth-century defensework. Indeed, both maps place the name "Walter Rawleigh" in what is now called Roanoke Sound.

That something purporting to be the remains of a sixteenth-century fort still existed in the early 1800s and had entered North Carolinian lore as such is beyond doubt. On the morning of April 7, 1819, President Monroe went ashore at the north end of the island from the steamboat *Albemarle* to inspect the historic spot. According to the *Edenton Gazette* for April 13, "traces" of Ralegh's fort were "still distinctly visible," and the possibility that like many a pilgrim through the ages, the president was shown a substitute relic may be a thought too unworthy to be countenanced. Nevertheless, it is necessary to ask how much of a sandy clay

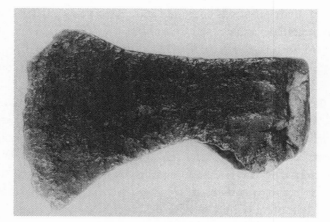

Iron ax found by treasure-hunting soldiers
digging on the Roanoke Island earthwork site
during the Civil War.

earthwork could be expected to survive amid the island's vines and woods
after more than 230 years of weathering.

Neither Yeardley's traders nor John Lawson provided any description
of any structural remains they found on the site, both being content to
classify them only as "ruins." More often than not, the word is (and was)
used to describe places and structures falling into decay, the word
"falling" most frequently being the prefatory adjective. Thus one might
think that because both visitors used the same word, they were more
likely to have been applying it to collapsing palisades and dwellings than
to the softening undulations of an eroding bank and ditch. Not until 160
years later does anyone tell us that the remains of a ditch were to be seen
on the site.

For that information we have to thank another pilgrim, Edward
Bruce, who wrote in *Harper's New Monthly Magazine* that "The trench is
clearly traceable in a square of about forty yards each way." He added that
one corner projected in the manner of a bastion, that the ditch was generally about two feet deep, and that "The whole site is overgrown with
pine, live-oak, vines, and a variety of other plants, high and low."[28] During the Civil War other forts were erected on the island, and soldiers
quartered there dug into the historic site and unearthed an ax now in the
collection of the University of North Carolina at Chapel Hill.

In the fall of 1895 an amateur antiquary named Talcott Williams
undertook limited excavations within the site, which by then was preserved by the Roanoke Colony Memorial Association, but he found very

little beyond charcoal and a corroded nail. Two years earlier the association had erected a substantial memorial to Virginia Dare (the first English child born in the New World) in the center of the ditched enclosure, its still-surviving foundation cutting into whatever archaeological evidence might have remained there. Further diminution of the fragile evidence occurred in 1921, when the North Carolina Department of Public Instruction made a movie, *The Story of the Lost Colony,* preparations for which involved reconstructing part of the defenses by digging a trench through one side of the historic ditch. Much more harm was wrought fifteen years later after the site had become a state historical park, at which time the whole fort was reconstructed with what might be termed "park palisadoes," complete with a central log blockhouse and, outside the fort, several log-built cabins and a chapel. Fortunately the stockade blew down in a 1944 hurricane, and shortly afterward the blockhouse was razed. Ironically, therefore, less than forty years of well-intentioned efforts to preserve and interpret the site had done more harm to it than had three centuries of neglect.

This, then, was the prior history of the site long known as Fort Raleigh when the United States National Park Service (which had acquired it in 1940) instructed archaeologist Jean C. Harrington to mount the first professional archaeological excavation. Harrington, whose work at Jamestown had made him America's premier historical archaeologist, was unquestionably the best man for a difficult job. His excavations on the Roanoke site began in 1947 and continued into a second season in 1948. The result: a sufficiently clear definition of the defensework's star-shaped trench pattern to permit its reconstruction. As a first step the remaining undisturbed stretches of the ditches were completely excavated, as was the entire interior, in search of traces of buildings that may have stood there. None were found perhaps because they had been eradicated by too much prior quasi-archaeological and patriotic hole digging, but perhaps because none had existed.

But surely, one may counter, Ralph Lane told us that there *were* structures inside the fort—structures in danger of being set afire by the Indian plotters. True, but was this star-shaped earthwork really "the new Fort in Virginia," as the casual visitor has been led to believe, or was it perhaps an outwork or a corner flanker for a much larger enclosure? The remains described by Bruce in 1860 were traceable "in a square of about forty yards each way,"[29] matching pretty closely the perimeter of the fifty-foot-square interior defined by Harrington. Build two modest cabins measuring twenty by fifteen feet (smaller than many a modern living room) in so small a compound, and there would scarcely be room to move around without climbing up onto the firing steps.

As Talcott Williams and J. C. Harrington quickly found out, the soil and subsoil of Roanoke Island are variations on an extremely sandy clay, easy to dig in but quick to erode in wind and rain, and Ralph Lane's men could secure their earthworks only with timber, a great deal of which would have been needed to support the weight of even relatively light cannon or to stop the shaped firing steps from crumbling away into a muddy scree. However, no traces of any posts to support such reinforcing timbering were found.

In its reconstructed form the Roanoke fort looks for all the world like a textbook exercise in cannon-dictated military engineering, a modified version of that illustrated 153 years later in Chambers's *Cyclopædia* as "A Hexagon Fortified with all the Kinds of Out Works Together with ye Manner of carrying on the Trenches of Approach." Using John White's drawings of the camp at Guayanilla Bay and the salt-pile defenses at Salinas Bay as evidence, historians have suggested that Ralph Lane had a penchant for earthworks. But what looked like overkill there looks like a lot too little here. Indeed, if structures had existed inside the Roanoke earthwork, any retreat of 108 colonists—even if fleeing only in their nightshirts—would have resulted in a hopelessly unmanageable and easily starved crowd. It made rather more sense, therefore, to interpret the structure as one of three or more bastions linked to one another by curtain walls of wooden posts or boards. But in this case, where were the remains of the other "forts"? Completed in 1950, the reconstructed earthwork remained a puzzle with no solution—until 1993, when a new and revolutionary possibility presented itself.

THROUGH the winter and spring of 1585–86 Ralph Lane, Thomas Hariot, and their assorted artisans, soldiers, and servants had done their best to explore the hinterland and assess its natural resources. In the process, in spite of the help of interpreter Manteo, they managed to alienate most of their Indian neighbors. Wanchese, the other ocean-traveled Indian, had returned to his people disenchanted with the Englishmen's brand of civilization and would use his knowledge to their disadvantage.

A single incident will suffice to establish Lane's idea of diplomacy. On an exploring voyage up Albemarle Sound into the Chowan River, he came to Chawanoac, where its old, paralyzed, but powerful chief, Menatonon, was holding a council meeting. At the head of about forty heavily armed and armored men, Lane invaded the village, seized the helpless chief, and then, presumably through Manteo, cajoled him into providing information about the tribes of the interior. Intending later to follow Menatonon's directions allegedly leading him to tribes rich with pearls and copper, Lane handcuffed the chief's favorite son and took him away as surety for his father's veracity. After the youth had the gall to try to escape, Lane had his legs immovably shackled and then threatened to cut off his head. Not surprisingly, the Indians told the English what they wanted to hear, some of it true and some false, while the colonists grew paranoiac trying to decide which was which.

Relations with their closest and once-friendly neighbor, Wingina, deteriorated during the winter. Wingina quit the island and moved to his mainland village of Dasemunkepeuc; this could have been the result of friction with the English, or it could have been no more than a normal, seasonal move. Lane evidently read the action in belligerent terms. On June 1, convinced that Wingina planned to attack, he entered the village, ostensibly to confer. Once inside, Lane gave the watchword, "Christ, our Victory!," whereupon his men assaulted and slaughtered any Indians they could catch—one of them Wingina himself.

In the context of its time there was nothing particularly outrageous about what Lane perceived as a preemptive strike. That he would, as he did on another occasion, behead a couple of captured Indians in full view of their brethren was a long-established method of discouraging potential opposition, one demonstrated again and again little more than a century earlier in England during the Wars of the Roses, when numerous nobles lost first their battles and then their heads. Others fortunate enough to be pardoned initially could expect as second-time losers to be hanged, disemboweled while still alive, and either skewered or quartered for display purposes. Indeed, until the eighteenth century, permanently installed iron spikes topped the Southwark end of London Bridge as mounts on which to exhibit the heads of malefactors and persistent questioners of the status quo.

Such European behavior came as no surprise to the Indians, who played their own power games by much the same rules—with one significant exception: Their mutilation of fallen enemies, by scalping or by dismembering, was motivated more by ritualistic tradition than by the Europeans' policy of intimidation coupled with the satisfaction of getting even. That is not to say, of course, that Indian witnesses to Lane's activities did not learn from them or that their memories were short. They had discovered to their cost that their fair-skinned erstwhile friends differed from other predatory neighbors only in the efficiency of their weaponry.

To understand what happened next, we have to go back a year to the event that had diverted Ralegh's second supply ships from Virginia to the Newfoundland fishing grounds. At the end of May 1585 Philip of Spain took his first overt step toward war with England: He seized all English ships then in Spanish ports in retaliation for Elizabeth's aid to the Protestant Dutch and her perceived encouragement of her subjects' New World piracies. It was a move considered particularly unsporting by the English, for many of the confiscated ships had carried corn to Spain at Philip's request to offset the previous year's failed harvest. When news of the seizure reached London early in June, warnings went out to all English merchant ships to stay clear of Spanish ports—hence the ordering of Captains Amias Preston and Bernard Drake to the Newfoundland fishing fleet.

Although one result of Philip's seizure was to deny the Virginia settlers their second supply fleet, another was to offer them salvation in the person of Sir Francis Drake. Knighted after his circumnavigation, he had tried in vain to interest his sovereign in mounting an army of sufficient size to seize the viceroyalty of New Spain by its Panamanian throat and thus throttle the flow of bullion that was the lifeblood of Philip's global ambition. For five years the queen would have none of it, fearing that it could push the equally irresolute Philip into a cross-Channel invasion. But after the Spanish king's seizure of the English ships, Drake's plan took on the aura of a really attractive idea.

The expedition left Plymouth on September 14, 1585, with Drake as general aboard the six-hundred-ton *Elizabeth Bonaventure,* one of two ships assigned from the queen's navy. The other, the *Aide* (almost certainly the ship she had lent to Frobisher eight years earlier), was less than half the size and probably not the second-largest in a fleet totaling twenty-five ships. Martin Frobisher sailed as vice admiral aboard the *Primrose,* and Francis Knolles as rear admiral on the *Leicester* galleon. Among the other vessels whose names are known was the *Sea Dragon,* which may have been one of the two ships Drake used when he made his first reconnoitering voyage to the Caribbean in 1570 or a newer vessel named in honor of Drake's Spanish sobriquet *El Dragón*—the sea monster, as well as Christianity's devil.

Be that as it may, Drake set sail with a formidable fleet carrying a complement of twenty-three hundred soldiers and mariners, his plan being first to capture the crucial southern Caribbean ports of Santo Domingo and Cartagena, next to strike at Panama before sailing north to invade the silver mines of Honduras. En route he paused along the Iberian coast to pilfer Spanish shipping and to make his presence felt at

Sir Francis Drake, who carried the first Roanoke colonists
back to England, engraved in the nineteenth century
from a contemporary painting.

the towns of Bayona and Vigo, with little more in mind than to let the
king of Spain know that *El Dragón* was again on the loose.

Sailing south to the island of Palma in the Canary Isles, where he
intended to take on water and other supplies, Drake was surprised to find
himself the target of so much Spanish heavy artillery that he thought better of it. Heading southward still, he found the island of S. Iago (São
Tiago) in the Cape Verde archipelago less troublesome and there landed
a thousand soldiers, more than sufficient to prompt any defenders to take
to the hills. The assault on S. Iago offered a valuable rehearsal for the
more serious business ahead, and Drake and his captains used the weeks
they remained there to convert an untrained rabble into a relatively well-
disciplined task force. Then, while a pall of black smoke from the burned
town still hung over the island, the fleet set its sails for New Spain and the
expected riches of the Main—blissfully unaware that the easy success at
S. Iago had silently and insidiously cost the army more casualties than in
any pitched battle to come.

The expedition's chronicler, Captain Walter Bigges, reported that "wee were not many dayes at Sea, but there beganne among our people such mortalitie, as in fewe dayes there were dead above two or three hundred men. . . . In some that died," he added, "were plainely shewed the small spots, which are often found upon those that be infected with the plague."[30] The wildfire ability of disease to spread through the cramped quarters of overcrowded transatlantic ships was already common enough to feature in most commanders' nightmares, and many a later Virginia colonist's hopes for a new life would end on a plank and with a splash.

In spite of mounting losses from the infection, Drake succeeded in seizing first Santo Domingo and then Cartagena. But in a surprising turnabout for a man of violent action, he called off his primary mission of taking Panama, on the ground that he considered his forces too depleted to assure success. Having failed also to wrest substantial ransoms from the Spanish governors of either Santo Domingo or Cartagena, *El Dragón* sheathed his claws, scrapped his plan to loot the Honduran mines, and headed north out of the Caribbean on his way home. However, he could not resist stopping first at Florida to harass the Spaniards at St. Augustine.

The town had been in existence for some twenty-two years, having grown out of a fort erected after a French colony at Fort Caroline some thirty miles to the north had been abandoned. This, the last French attempt to settle in Florida, has an ancillary bearing on the James Fort story in that among its three hundred men and four women had been one Jacques le Moyne de Morgues, a skilled artist whose drawings did for the indigenous inhabitants of Florida what John White's were to do for the Indians of Virginia. Besides ensuring the Florida Indians a modicum of immortality, Le Moyne made a careful drawing of the timber defenses of Fort Caroline, a structure triangular in shape and in a measure related to what John Smith and his colleagues were to erect in 1607 on Jamestown Island.

Although a competent artist himself, Drake had no draftsman of John White's caliber (at least that we know of) to draw what his expedition encountered. However, his lieutenant general and master of the *Tiger,* Christopher Carleil, had as his page a young Italian named Baptista Boazio, and he was to provide the expedition with its visual record, albeit more cartographic than pictorial. Indeed, when published two years later, Boazio's maplike views were embellished with natural history details provided by White. Be that as it may, these plats would be of little evidential use in searching out the background to Roanoke's or to James Fort's con-

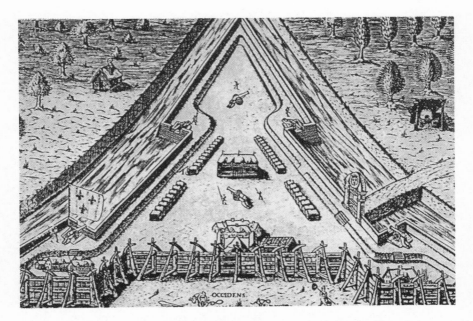

The post-and-plank-palisaded Fort Caroline, built by the French in
Florida on the St. Johns River in 1564; a de Bry engraving derived
from a drawing by Jacques le Moyne.

struction were it not for amplification provided by Walter Bigges's written description of the Spaniards' timber fort near St. Augustine. That
account provides important evidence of what the Spanish considered an
adequate defensework, and by extension it should fairly closely parallel
what English settlers could be expected to erect. "We found it [Fort San
Juan de Pinos], built all of timber," Drake's chronicler recalled, "the
walles being none other but whole Mastes or bodies of trees set up right
and close together in the manner of a pale." Those words will have significance when we try to determine what James Fort's eyewitnesses meant
in their descriptions of what they saw.

The St. Augustine account went on to note that no outer ditches had
been dug, though given time, the Spaniards evidently intended to do so.
The English, however, were not impressed by the existing structure, considering it "subject both to fire, and easie assault." The report went on to
describe how the fort's cannon platform was constructed—another factor
of value in trying to assess how James Fort's three artillery-supporting
flankers could have been built. At Fort San Juan the trunks of pine trees
were laid across one another, and the gaps between the latticework filled
with "some litle earth amongst." From this it can be assumed that the
platform was not elevated but was merely a firm bed to support the

tremendous weight of guns and carriages which otherwise would settle immovably into the ground.

As Drake's landing parties approached, the Spanish garrison fired two of its cannon before taking to its heels. One wonders why only two, for mounted on the single large channel-facing platform were "thirteene or fourteene great peeces of Brass ordinance"—later removed by the raiders along with "a chest unbroken up, having in it the value of some two thousand pounds sterling by estimation of the kings treasure."[31]

Although the English record lacked measurements for Fort San Juan, another contemporary source provided them for a newly built fort at Cartagena erected in the aftermath of Drake's visit. In 1587 its architect, and the king of Spain's surveyor, Baptista Antonio, described his structure as being "of timber fouresquare of 300. foote every way, and trencht, where wee may plant 15. or 16. peeces of ordinance, and keep 50. men in garison, and behinde the bourdes on the backside of the timbers, a Barricado of earth or muddle wall being foure foote in thicknesse, and behind the mud-wall, sand."[32] Antonio's statement that the 90,000-square-foot fort was garrisoned by only 50 soldiers suggests either that the Spaniards chose to spread themselves or that James Fort's original complement of about 104 souls was astonishingly cramped in its triangular "town" if, as was reported, it embraced only about 21,780 square feet.

After burning Fort San Juan as well as the wooden-housed and unprotected St. Augustine, pausing first to salvage such windows and architectural hardware as might be of use to Ralegh's Virginia colonists, Drake sailed north to pay them a visit. Clearly he intended to make the settlers aware of the growing Spanish threat and to provide them with not only builders' hardware but also captured armament and other supplies.

Aboard Drake's ships, along with his army of tired and sickly soldiers, was an incredible assortment of people whom he had freed from Spanish bondage, but for whom he had insufficient supplies to carry back to England. According to one doubtless overblown report, his passengers included twelve hundred Englishmen, Frenchmen, and Flemings, as well as eight hundred "of the countrey people."[33] Other sources named freed Moorish and Turkish slaves, runaway Indians, and blacks. Of these last, a report to Philip of Spain had this to say of Drake: ". . . he meant to leave all the negroes he had in a fort and settlement established at Jacan [Roanoke Island] by the English who went there a year ago. There he intended to leave the 250 blacks and all the small craft he had, and cross to England with only the larger vessels. . . ." The report went on to note that "This settlement and fort of theirs at Jacan are directly west of

Bermuda, 250 leagues from Santa Elena, from which position they can readily attack the fleets at any season. . . ."[34]

It was the beginning of June 1586 when Drake completed his destruction of St. Augustine. Because he had left Plymouth on September 14 of the previous year, he knew that Ralegh's second supply flotilla had been diverted to the Newfoundland fishing grounds, but he should also have known that another supply fleet would later be dispatched to Virginia. He therefore had reason to expect that by June 1586 Ralph Lane and his colonists should be well established, freshly supplied, and well able to absorb the 250 blacks, who thus were within days of entering United States history as the first African Americans to be settled there.

Just as Drake was unaware that the colony had received no reinforcement and was hard put to survive, let alone stand foursquare against the might of Spain, so Ralph Lane was ignorant of the fact that England was closer than ever to being at war with Spain and that Drake's hell-raising expedition had made certain that courtly diplomacy had run its course. When, on June 11, the two men exchanged their unsettling news, several truths became evident: Drake was not there (as the Roanoke settlers had first hoped) to resupply the colony; he was short of food himself and so was better able to provide guns than butter. Furthermore, Lane could not have had any desire or ability to house 250 blacks who would outnumber his white settlers by more than two to one.

With war perhaps already declared, the likelihood of Ralegh's being able to send reinforcements in response to a plea sent via Drake was too small to be gambled on. On the other hand, for all either Lane or Drake knew, Ralegh's second supply might have been delayed and could be only days or even hours from its safe arrival.

Faced with those standard communications problems which turned strategies and the fate of nations into games of chance, Lane and Drake reached a compromise. Drake would leave behind a cadre of skilled artisans, two pinnaces and several other small boats, and, more important, "the Francis, being a very proper barke of 70 tun,"[35] which would stay until August. This would allow more time for Ralegh's ship to arrive and, that failing, enable Lane to undertake an exploration of the Chesapeake Bay before heading home to England. With this agreed, Drake transferred his donated provisions to the Francis along with sailing masters for the pinnaces. At the same time Lane sent several of his senior people aboard—all this shortly before a storm of stunning ferocity bore down on the fleet.

By June 13 the hurricane season has scarcely begun, yet there can be little doubt that this storm, which raged for a full three days, belonged in that category. Hail the size of hen's eggs bombarded the anchored ships, and waterspouts momentarily linked sea and sky in violent embrace. It was enough to scare the tar out of Drake's crews, and many a master cut his cable and ran before the wind—among them the *Francis*, sending Ralph Lane's supplies and personnel pell-mell for England. As for the pinnaces and boats, they rode the Outer Banks surf in pieces the size of kindling.

June 16 found the seas still mountainous and the scattered fleet cautiously reassembling; the weather, as modern Devon fishermen still say, was fining away. But for Ralph Lane and his bedraggled colonists the storm had been the last straw, and regardless of Drake's offer to leave an even larger ship (too large to get through the inlet into the relatively calm waters of the sound), Lane and his officers decided they had had enough. They would accept Drake's alternative offer of passage to England. Two days later the fleet set sail, leaving Lane's hastily vacated fort and "towne" as rich pickings for the Indians—and to three unpleasantly surprised men who had happened to be away on the mainland when the evacuation decision was reached.

Although Drake had given instructions to his sailors to bring off the hundred or so colonists and ferry them out to the ships, no formal provision had been made for their baggage. The tides were fast, and the shoals treacherous, and in the pre-dredging sixteenth century, Drake's oarsmen can have had not only little enthusiasm for their assignment but doubtless a deep resentment toward the fleeing colonists who made it necessary. Consequently, much of their baggage never made it to the ships. Wrote Lane: "the weather was so boysterous, & the pinnaces so often on ground that the most of all wee had, with all our Cardes, Bookes and writings, were by the sailors cast overboord."[36] That statement has been much used to conclude that Hariot's and metallurgist Joachim Gans's records and samples were among the losses. It is curious, therefore, that in his description of the disaster, Hariot (Ralegh's handpicked scientist) says nothing about failing to return home with the all-important scientific evidence but mentions only a colleague's string of pearls intended as a gift to Queen Elizabeth "had wee not by casualtie and trough extremity of a storme, lost them with many things els in comming away from the countrey."[37]

The absence from the John White collection of any drawings of Roanoke Island and its new fort in Virginia is similarly explained: all cast overboard by Drake's scared and ignorant sailors. But if so, why did Hariot, who had the most use for the illustrations, mention only the scientifically worthless string of pearls? The answer may well be that White

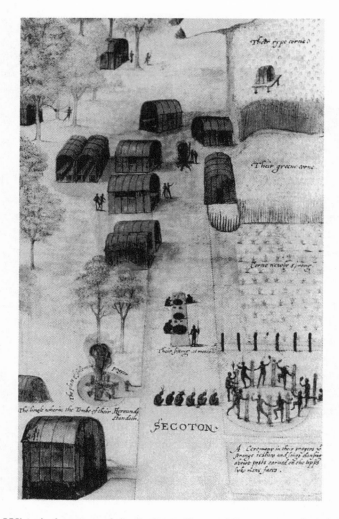

John White's drawing of the Indian village of Secotan, made while on tour with Sir Richard Grenville on July 15, 1585. The rendering is designed to inform rather than to convey pictorial accuracy. Thus, for example, the villagers' crop of corn is shown in three fields at as many stages: "newly sprong," "greene," and "rype."

wasn't there and hadn't been since Grenville sailed home on August 25, 1585—the year cited on the cover sheet of White's surviving drawings.

The name John White is absent from the list of Ralph Lane's colonists, though those of Hariot and Gans (Dougham Gannes) are there. Instead, the only documentary reference to White is his presence aboard one of the "ship-boate[s]" that accompanied Grenville in his July expedition through Pamlico Sound to the Indian settlements at Pomeiock and Secotan, both of which White drew, along with the wives of their chief men. Although two maps in the White collection include, in red, places visited by Lane's people in the months after Grenville had sailed, it is reasonable to argue that those were drawn later using cartographic information taken safely home by Hariot in 1586.

Much else remains open to speculation. The records tell us nothing about the fate of Drake's Africans. He did not mention them, nor did Lane, and although extant documents note the repatriation of a hundred Turks, only one "Negro with a cutt on his face that sayeth he came with Sir Francis Drak" is known to have survived—and he wound up in Paris.[38]

Had the 250 blacks been put ashore on the Virginia Outer Banks to fend for themselves, future arrivals would surely have mentioned finding them or learning about them. Perhaps, therefore, their fate is hidden in an eyewitness's single sentence: "Many also of our small Pinnesses and boates were lost in this storme."[39] Lane added that in the storm Drake "susteined more perill of wracke then in all his former honourable actions against the Spanyards."[40] Thus the hurricane of June 1586 may have ripped away the first page from the history of blacks in English America.

CHAPTER III

The Cittie That Never Was

"CONGRATULATIONS on your safe return" was about the level of enthusiasm Drake could expect as his battered fleet anchored at Portsmouth on July 28, 1586. He could report no real victory over the Spaniards. It was true that he had sacked several towns, but they had contained little of value, and though he left them in flames, their palmetto leaf–covered wooden houses were quickly rebuilt. He had failed to attack Panama or to loot the Honduran silver mines or even to capture a worthwhile treasure galleon. He did have the modest ransoms from Santo Domingo and Cartagena as well as the garrison pay chest from St. Augustine, but at best the return amounted to sixty thousand pounds sterling. Instead of chests of jewels and golden goodies to gladden the hearts of his investors, they had to be content with about 240 brass and iron cannon—acquired at a cost of 750 men, who included at least 8 land and sea captains, 4 lieutenants, and 8 gentlemen. No less distressing was the news that England's Virginia foothold had been abandoned.

That revelation must have been particularly galling to Sir Walter Ralegh, whose long-awaited supply ship reached Roanoke "Immediatly after the departing of our English Colony out of this paradise of the world."[1] Those were the words of the editor Richard Hakluyt, who, in spite of discouraging evidence to the contrary, was still promoting America as the new Eden. No records survive to name Ralegh's supply ship or to explain why if she was supposed to have sailed in the fall of 1585, she was still in port at Easter 1586. All we know is that she arrived too late, found the settlement deserted, and returned with her cargo to England.

About two weeks later seven more ships reached Hatteras Island. Sir Richard Grenville, unaware of all that had happened, was making good the original plan (the one thwarted by the Newfoundland diversion) to bring over sufficient reinforcements to withstand any Spanish attempt to dislodge the colony. According to the expedition's pilot, Pedro Diaz (a Spaniard captured in 1585), the fleet carried four hundred soldiers and mariners with sufficient supplies to last a year. As David Quinn has pointed out in his book *Set Fair for Roanoke,* the continuing emphasis on soldiers rather than on farmers, builders, and other nonviolent artisans, boded ill for any Indians who might at first have seen the English as nice neighbors. Two or three hundred uneducated soldiers with little to do but wait for a Spanish attack could be expected to become increasingly restless and prone to amusing themselves in unseemly ways. The Indians, therefore, had to think themselves lucky that on finding Lane's settlement abandoned, Grenville sailed away, leaving only fifteen or eighteen men, four cast-iron cannon, and (depending on whose account one accepts) supplies to last one to two years, metaphorically, if not physically, to hold the fort for England.

No eyewitness reports survive to describe the condition of Lane's fort and buildings when Grenville returned to Roanoke. Instead we have to make do with the comments of Pedro Diaz, whom Grenville had not allowed to land and see for himself. Diaz commented only that the fort was made of wood, of little strength, and located on the "inside by the water."[2] This last might be interpreted as meaning that the fort faced west toward Croatan Sound rather than north toward Roanoke Sound, where the earthwork remains have been found and reconstructed. Then, too, it is hard to equate the earthworks with a light wooden structure. One wonders, therefore, whether Diaz was describing another defensework constructed to face west toward an expected Indian attack from the mainland after Wingina had moved his village there in the winter of 1586.

Grenville made no mention of finding the three men left behind when Lane departed. Instead, according to Diaz, he came upon two hanging corpses, one white, the other Indian. The identity of this odd couple, and indeed that of their executioners, remains one of the smaller unsolved mysteries that beset the Roanoke chronicles. But as the weight of the decaying cadavers would have separated them from their heads in a few summer weeks, we have to conclude that they were the recent legacy of an event associated with Ralegh's supply ship.

Although Grenville spent two weeks searching for any trace of Lane's people and trying to make contact with Indians, friendly or otherwise, he saw only three, all of whom he seized and two of whom he lost. The third he carried back to England. There the Indian took the name of Ralegh

and was baptized in the parish church at Grenville's home port of Bideford in North Devon, where he died in 1589.

The question of who knew what pervades every tortuous step as one
strives to explain seemingly inexplicable decisions. With several hundred
or more soldiers under his command, we may ask why Grenville left fewer
than twenty to defend the foothold against untold numbers of hostile
Indians. The simplistic answer is that not knowing how badly Lane had
botched his Anglo-Indian relations, and with the Indians deliberately
melting into the landscape to avoid contact with the new arrivals,
Grenville might have assumed that the sun had not set on the halcyon
days described by Arthur Barlowe in 1584. That is, however, a tenuous
argument, as the dangling duo should have told him. Then, too, one
wonders what information was obtained from the captured Indian, who,
according to Diaz, spoke enough English to tell Grenville about Drake's
evacuation of the colony. Could he not also have told about the murder of
Wingina and the disenchantment of virtually every Indian community
within striking distance of Roanoke?

Whatever the explanation, a handful of men were talked into staying—perhaps enticed by the prospect of not having to remain aboard for
the round trip and of living well off the bountiful supplies being left with
them. It was a rationale that served them ill, for, left to themselves without any strong leader to maintain the military discipline needed in a hostile environment, the men probably settled into the kind of careless
existence that they must have dreamed of in England—until two seemingly unarmed Indians turned up. Twenty-eight more stayed hidden in
the woods. When two of the senior Englishmen went forward to greet
the smiling and gesticulating visitors, one was killed, and the other
escaped to retreat with his fellows into their supply building. Driven out
when the Indians set it afire, the garrison lost one man, who took an
arrow in his mouth, but the rest escaped to their boats and rowed away
toward Hatteras, never to be seen or heard of again.

John White obtained this account of what had happened from the
Croatoan Indians in 1587, and therefore, it lacks details from an English
point of view. However, it does include the statement that one of the
Indians had been wounded by a "wild fire arrow" and subsequently died.
Some authorities have cited this evidence to show that the settlers were
equipped with crossbows and incendiary arrows, as is perfectly possible.
On the other hand, this account comes from an Indian perspective, and it
is more likely that in the midst of the skirmish, which reportedly lasted
the best part of an hour, a defender returned one of the Indians' own fire
arrows.

Although Sir Richard Grenville's return to England with the news that he had reestablished the Virginia colony may have provided Sir Walter Ralegh and his investors with a little much-needed encouragement, Ralph Lane's earlier abandonment of the more populous and firmer foothold still rankled. Indeed, the whole idea of a Virginia adventure had received several blows below the waterline from disgruntled members of Lane's company. In his noble effort to correct the balance, Thomas Hariot began his *A briefe and true report of the new found land of Virginia* by denouncing the critics. "There have bene divers and variable reports, with some slanderous and shamefull speeches bruted abroad . . ." he wrote, "Which reports have not done a little wrong to many that otherwise would have also favoured and adventured in the action, to the honour and benefit of our nation. . . ."[3]

Had Ralegh been influenced by those who had "maliciously not onely spoken ill of their Governours, but for their sakes slandered the countrey it selfe,"[4] that might have been the end of his efforts to establish a Virginia colony. Instead, on April 26, 1587, he sent out three more ships under the command of the gentleman artist John White. The latter's account of the enterprise begins with the observation that Ralegh had assembled "one hundred and fiftie men to be sent thither."[5] In fact, the colonists included at least seventeen women and nine "Boyes and Children" for a total of 117 persons who actually reached Roanoke in late July.

John White's flagship (known as the Admirall) was the 120-ton *Lion*, a vessel of the same size as the *Susan Constant*, which twenty years later led a similar number of settlers to Jamestown Island. Accompanying the *Lion* were a flyboat and a pinnace whose names and tonnage are not known. Although early ship terminology is confusingly interchangeable, a flyboat was usually a fast-sailing vessel intended primarily for carrying bulk cargo. There is, for example, a 1698 reference to "A small fly-boat of 40 tunn . . . laden with Tobacco, Bacon, and Meal for Barbados."[6] However, they came much larger, and in 1688 John Clayton sailed to Virginia aboard the *Judith*, which he described as "Flyboat built" and of 200 or 250 tons. It is highly unlikely that John White's flyboat even approached that tonnage, for as a result of an accident at the beginning of the return journey, she wound up with only five able-bodied seamen to get her home. We can safely assume, nonetheless, that outward-bound she carried most of the stores needed to keep the colony alive and prospering through its teething months.

The presence of the women and children gave this venture a very different look from those before it and was much more in line with the pastoral ambience that Barlowe's first report had sought to reflect. These

Ship shapes of the late sixteenth and early seventeenth centuries.
1, bark; 2, galleon; 3, fluyt (flyboat?); 4, ketch; 5, caravel; 6, pinnace;
7, shallop; 8, shallop rigged for sailing.

people had come to stay and multiply, and they promptly demonstrated their ability to do so: On August 18 John White's daughter, the wife of his assistant, Ananias Dare, gave birth to a daughter, whom, with predictable originality, they named Virginia. Popular historians have been able to extract far less mileage from the fact that another child born later was listed only as Harvie. At least one infant was aboard when the *Lion* reached the West Indies, for White reported that some of his passengers had eaten wild fruit resembling small green apples (probably the poisonous fruit of the manchineel tree), and as a result, "a child by sucking one of [the] womens breasts, had at that instant his mouth set on such a burning. . . ."[7]

Because no prospectus survives to detail the incentives offered to would-be settlers, any more than does a copy of Ralegh's instructions to his Virginia governor, a passing reference at the tail of Thomas Hariot's narrative takes on tremendous importance. Stressing the generosity of his patron Sir Walter Ralegh, Hariot describes him as "so liberall in large giving and granting lande there. . . . The least that he hath granted hath bene five hundredth acres to a man onely for the adventure of his person."[8] Even if only half the men adventured at their own expense (the rest sailing as servants), and none got less than five hundred acres, and some considerably more, the Virginia land allocated to John White's first wave of settlers may have amounted to more than twenty-five thousand acres. In any area heavily populated by indigenous Americans, most of whom quickly learned to dislike the pale-skinned boat people, these grants could be honored only by the wholesale expulsion of the Indians. In making such a commitment, Ralegh must have known what it would entail (though the prospective settlers almost certainly did not), and so, too, must Governor White. He, however, would have known from experience that without horses or oxen to pull stumps or to drag plows, the average settler family would have had difficulty working five acres, let alone five hundred. Nevertheless, the intent to disenfranchise the Indians was clear enough.

As the result of both popular and scholarly modern writings, the fragile Roanoke settlement has assumed the name of the Cittie of Ralegh, but in truth, that never existed. Sir Walter Ralegh instructed his Virginia governor to establish his city to the north on the Chesapeake Bay, an area believed to be more accessible to shipping, of greater strategic importance, and possibly a gateway to the Orient. Consequently, White's return first to Hatteras Island and then to Roanoke was not to resettle but only to check on the well-being of Grenville's garrison.

It was while the ships lay off Hatteras that one of the most fateful and yet inexplicable events occurred. An unidentified "Gentleman," allegedly at the instigation of the *Lion*'s Portuguese pilot Simon Fernández, informed White that it was already too late in the year to sail on in search of a site for the city. The crews had decided that instead the colonists (with the exception of White and two or three others of his choosing) would be left at Roanoke. That White, commander of the enterprise with written orders to the contrary, should have meekly acquiesced to what amounted to a mutinous ultimatum, is extraordinary. But he did, and as a result, colonists looking to him for leadership could be forgiven if they held him responsible for whatever might befall them on Roanoke Island.

John White's knowledge of the 1585 expedition and of the shattered Anglo-Indian relationships left in its wake must surely have caused him to doubt that many, if any, of Grenville's greeters would be at dockside. If that was his fear, he cannot have been surprised to find the bones of but one man "which the Savages had slaine long before."[9]

On July 23 White, and "divers of his company, walked to the North ende of the Island, where Master Ralfe Lane had his forte, with sundry necessary and decent dwelling houses, made by his men about it the yeere before, where wee hoped to find some signes, or certaine knowledge of our fifteene men. When we came thither," White recalled, "we found the fort rased downe, but all the houses standing unhurt, saving that the neather roomes of them, and also of the forte, were overgrowen with Melons of divers sortes. . . ."[10]

That melancholy and brief description of Lane's settlement is both helpful and confusing—and hardly the words of a man returning to a place where he himself allegedly had dwelt for all of nine months. First White tells us that he found the houses "about" the fort, not beside it or extending in streets away from it, but around it, clustered perhaps like chickens around a hen. Then he says that the fort was "rased down." Because it takes considerable manpower or a mechanical grader to raze down an earthwork, we have to conclude that the fort's principal feature was a wooden palisade and not a particularly stout one, giving credence perhaps to Pedro Diaz's description of it as "a wooden fort of little strength."[11] What were the circumstances of its being razed down, and what exactly did it mean? By the mid-sixteenth century (and probably long before) the phrase "razed down" meant total destruction or obliteration, but "total destruction" can also be interpreted as being made useless. A palisaded fort could be so rendered by the wall's merely being breached in several places. Much, too, depended on how the palisades were con-

Trench dug adjacent to the Roanoke Island earthwork site by
J. C. Harrington in 1947, with the remains of 1936 palisade
posts in the foreground.

structed, and this is where knowing the truth about Lane's fort plays a
crucial role in interpreting the defenses at James Towne.

If, as the Spaniards had at St. Augustine, the Roanoke walls were built
from cut tree trunks set vertically side by side, the knocking down of a few
could cause long stretches to collapse sideways like a wall of playing cards.
If, on the other hand, the palisades were constructed in panels, either
between the still-rooted trunks of cut trees or between firmly seated
posts, damage would be fairly easily repaired and less likely to be
described as a razing down. Unfortunately J. C. Harrington's excavations
on the site of the reconstructed earth fort yielded traces of only one
straight-sided palisade trench, that of the bogus palisade erected in 1936.
He found no evidence of vertical posts in the contemporary silting of the
earthwork's ditches.

This is not particularly surprising, however, for it is more probable that any palisading associated with the dirt fort was set on top rather than beside it. When describing what he intended to accomplish if only he had more men and supplies, Ralph Lane told of his plan to explore the rivers and set up fortified outposts to protect his boats. He would have "raysed a sconce with a small trench, and a pallisado upon the top of it, in the which, and in the garde of my boates I would have left five and twentie, or thirtie men."[12] Had he used the same ditch-rampart-stockade combination on Roanoke Island, the ends of the posts would have been unlikely to reach to the subsoil to survive as archaeological dirty marks in the ground. Furthermore, being seated only in the rampart's soft and sandy clay, the vertical logs could easily have been loosened by rain and wind and caused to collapse. It is worth adding that as reconstructed, the Roanoke earth fort is scarcely large enough to house the "five and twentie" men whom Lane proposed leaving in one of his outpost sconces.

Although Harrington discovered no evidence of occupation within the fort, he did find traces of cooking fires as well as broken aboriginal pots in the silting of the ditches, apparently testifying to the presence of Indians on the site after it had been abandoned by the English, but how long after, he had no way of telling, for today's archaeomagnetic dating technique was not available when Harrington was digging. As for dating the pottery, the state of the art—and it was an art—was still expansively imprecise when his report on the pots ended thusly: "We can only conclude that both shell- and grit-tempered, simple-stamped wares of a fairly uniform shape, although varying considerably in vessel size, were in use by the Indians of this locality over an indeterminate period prior to and after the colonizing attempts of the late 16th century."[13] Nearly thirty years later, using radiocarbon dating, prehistorians can be more precise but scarcely more exact. Although they are able to place most of the pottery in the Late Woodland period of the North Carolinian Algonquian Culture between A.D. 800 and about 1750 and to identify most of it as "Colington Phase simple stamped," their brackets remain wider than the biggest barn door. Once in a while, however, historical archaeologists are able to come to the prehistorians' rescue. Renewed excavations in 1991 proved beyond all doubt that finding aboriginal pottery did not necessarily mean Indian occupation, for the 1585 colonists' scientific team had been using Colington wares and smoking Indian pipes.

John White's description of "the fort rased down" implies an act of man, ergo the Indians; but who is to say that it was not an act of God? Although the defenses described by Diaz evidently were still standing when Grenville departed in late July 1586, is it possible that they were blown down in a hurricane later that year? In weighing that possibility, one has to remember that in spite of the three-day hurricane that wrought such havoc amid Drake's fleet and helped precipitate Lane's departure in June, no one mentioned any damage to his fort or buildings. But it could have happened. As Harrington recalled, eight years after the North Carolina Historical Commission erected its palisaded reconstruction "the decaying stockade posts outlining the fort blew down during the 1944 hurricane."[14] Whatever brought about the collapse of Ralph Lane's 1585–86 fort, its vine-shrouded ruins clearly were useless, if not flat, when John White returned a year later.

White's continuing description of the settlement's structures as "all the houses standing unhurt, saving that the neather roomes of them, and also of the forte, were overgrowen with Melons . . ." seems to be saying two important things: first, that there were houses both outside and inside the fort, and second, that the houses had usable rooms over those of the lower, or "neather," floor. But like so much of the evidence, these "facts" have their problems. One has to question how it was possible for *all* the houses to be seen as structurally undamaged when we know that Grenville's men had been driven from their storehouse after the Indians set it afire. Regardless of what White meant by unhurt, we do know that he immediately gave orders that "that every man should be employed for the repayring of those houses, which wee found standing, and also to make other newe Cottages, for such as should neede."[15]

The distinction between houses and cottages is unclear, but in the general usage of the time a cottage was the humblest of dwellings for laborers and livestock. It is tempting to suggest, however, that Roanoke's houses may have had chimneys while the cottages had central hearths and smoke holes in the roofs. Be that as it may, we cannot doubt that the new arrivals' first impression of the place at least temporarily substituting for the "Cittie of Ralegh" had to be one of numbing disappointment. Shipboard visions of building a New World metropolis dignified with its own corporate shield of arms (which Sir Walter had purchased along with gentrifying heraldic arms for each of his lieutenants) and hyped up by everyone from Hakluyt and Hariot to Dr. Dee were replaced by a vine-covered reality that set the colonists to a hard-nosed assessment of their prospects.

White's hope to woo the Indians to renewed friendship with the help of Manteo (who had again returned with the expedition), got off to a rocky start. Within a day or so of the settlers' arrival, George Howe, one

Commemorative copy of the seal matrix granted to Sir Walter Ralegh for his Virginia colony in 1584. The matrix is here shown in retrograde to permit the inscription to be read.

of White's nine senior officers, went crabbing and unwisely "strayed two miles from his company," where he was found by an Indian hunting party. In what may seem a high level of overkill, the bowmen scored with sixteen arrows, "and after they had slaine him with their woodden swordes, beat his head in pieces, and fled over the water to the maine."[16] This attack is of archaeological interest in that White specifically describes the beating to pieces of the unlucky crabber's head *after* he had been killed, a sequence paralleling another encountered at Virginia's Wolstenholme Towne, which was attacked by Indians in 1622. There we found a hastily buried individual who had been felled by a blow to the forehead, then had been partially scalped, and finally, while lying facedown, had had the back of his skull smashed into poker-chip-sized pieces. Today such an incident is likely to be read simply as wanton savagery, but in the light of a deeper understanding of Indian culture, the skull-smashing and the scalping together must be recognized as ritualistic. What a 1622 account would describe as "a second murder" was necessary to ensure that an enemy could not rise again in the afterlife to accomplish what he had failed to do in this one.

Two days after George Howe's murder, Edward Stafford (captain of the anonymous pinnace), with Manteo and twenty armed men to back him up, sailed south to Croatoan Island on the Outer Banks chain, there to make contact with the hitherto friendly Indians of Manteo's tribe. From them Stafford learned of the flight of Grenville's remaining eleven men. He urged the Croatoan leaders to spread the word that the English wanted bygones to be just that and to invite the weroances (an Indian title bestowed on both great and lesser chieftains) of the neighboring settlements to gather for a peace conference at the English Roanoke settlement in seven days' time. The Croatoans said that they would see what they could do. The seven days came and went, but nobody showed up.

Having learned that surviving men from Wingina's village at Dasemunkepeuc had been responsible for the attack both on Grenville's men and on George Howe, and having decided that the weroances were not in the mood to talk peace, White sent Captain Stafford across the Croatan Sound to the mainland at the head of twenty-four men guided by the faithful, if somewhat out-of-touch, Manteo. Just before dawn on August 9 Stafford struck, not knowing that after killing Howe, Wingina's men had deserted their village of Dasemunkepeuc and that their place had been taken by Manteo's people from Croatoan Island. "Those Savages were our friends," White explained, but "it was so darke, that they being naked, and their men and women apparelled all so like others, wee knew not that but that they were al men: and if that one of them which was a Wiroances wife had not had a child at her backe, shee had bene slaine in stead of a man."[17]

With Manteo formally appointed lord of both Roanoke and Dasemunkepeuc and thus England's first vassal chief, and with the attack on the Croatoans papered over, the colonists supposed that they were under no immediate threat from their neighbors. Nevertheless, the next two weeks saw a growing edginess which generated into what White cryptically described as "some controversies" and into a ground swell of opinion both among White's "assistants" and among the colonists at large, that when the *Lion* and the flyboat returned to England, a spokesman for the settlers should go with them to urge "the better and sooner obtaining of supplies, and other necessaries for them."[18] On the surface, the proposal is difficult to explain. Since the majority of the colonists had arrived in relatively good shape and since none of their supplies had been lost en route, one wonders why they would be demanding more so soon.

After much debate and talk about who should go, and because none of the senior assistants wanted to now that the rigors of the voyage were behind them, it was agreed that Governor White should be the one to return. Like the rest, White was reluctant to leave his belongings to an uncertain future, particularly when it called for the group to leave the island and head north to the Chesapeake. But with promises still loud in his ears that his goods and purposes would be respected, John White went aboard the flyboat and on August 27 sailed for England. With him, too, went the unfinished history of the Third Colony.

Because White's is the only record of the last Roanoke settlement, little, if anything, is known about the character and competence of his deputies or about the colonists' response to finding themselves setting up shop on Roanoke Island when they were supposed to be devoting their energies to raising the Cittie of Ralegh somewhere else. Consequently, we can only guess at the rationale which concluded that managing without its appointed and most experienced leader was in the best interest of the colony. A possible explanation might be that although White undeniably was experienced, he had shown himself to be a weak and vacillating leader who could be more useful in England than in Virginia. If that was true, the debate among the assistants on who should go, and their slowly reached conclusion that White was their most persuasive spokesman, may have been an elaborate charade to get him off the island and onto the boat.

After a wretched voyage and a storm which blew the flyboat far off course, White and a starving crew finally made landfall at Smerwick Harbour on the western coast of Ireland on October 16, 1587. When he reached England three weeks later, White learned that the *Lion* had been towed into Portsmouth at about the time that he sighted the crags of Ireland. Thus, long before he could report to Sir Walter Ralegh, the latter knew that his city was not rising on the Chesapeake shore and that his flagship had limped home with no loot in her treasure chests and with so many of her crew dead or disabled that barely enough were left to bring her into Portsmouth Harbor.

Much had happened at home in John White's absence. War had been joined with Spain, and it was no secret that Philip II was building and massing an invasion fleet in many of his western ports. On April 2, 1587, Sir Francis Drake, armed with his queen's commission "to impeach the joining together of the King of Spain's fleet," sailed with a battle squadron to the coast of Portugal and audaciously entered the harbor at Cádiz to sink or burn thirty-three of Philip's biggest and best new ships. With that success and unaware that Elizabeth had once again gotten cold feet and countermanded her instructions, Drake sailed on to sink or seize a hundred more vessels, ending up off the Azores by capturing the treasure carrack *San Felipe* and her cargo of bullion, jewels, spices, silks, and Chinese porcelain, conservatively valued at £114,000, sufficient to cover the cost of building about forty-five fair-size galleons. This, then, was *El Dragón* at his best, and few of Elizabeth's counselors doubted that in spite of its losses, Philip's revenge-seeking invasion fleet would eventually put to sea.

The winter of 1587, therefore, was not a good time to be sending out a second supply to Virginia. Nevertheless, in consultation with his friend Sir Richard Grenville, Ralegh agreed to assemble another fleet at Bideford and in the meantime to dispatch a single pinnace with word that help would reach Roanoke by the summer of 1588. Although the pinnace never sailed, preparations for the departure of Grenville's fleet went forward, and by March it was ready to leave. On the thirty-first, however, an order of the Privy Council instructed Grenville to bring his ships around the tip of Cornwall to join the fleet being assembled by Lord Howard of Effingham and Sir Francis Drake at Plymouth, there to await the expected Spanish onslaught.

The intended Virginia fleet comprised as many as eight ships of varying size, most, if not all, of them armed and manned to play havoc with Spain in the Caribbean. The cost of outfitting such an expedition was more than any one man could bear, and invariably a consortium was put together with the aid of high-powered Captain Seagull–style salesmanship. According to John Aubrey, Ralegh cultivated a circle of young men with more money than sense, whom he could talk into footing the bills. Building a ship for a failed voyage to the Guinea coast, said Aubrey, cost one such protégé "the manor of Yatton Keynell, the farm at Easton Piers, Thornhill and the church-lease of Bishops Canning."[19] There being no immediate profit in supplying Virginia colonists, the prospect of privateering loot along the outward- and homeward-bound routes was what lured the investors. It took only the news of one *San Felipe* to offset the disappointments of a dozen crewless *Lions* and battered flyboats, and set the merchant adventurers once again reaching for their coffer keys. Thus the crews signing on at Bideford were much more interested in pillage than they were in the passenger business, as John White would learn to his cost.

In spite of the Privy Council's embargo on foreign sailings, White was able to persuade Ralegh and Grenville to release two pinnaces, the thirty-ton *Brave* and the twenty-five-ton *Roe*, neither considered fit to face the Armada. With fifteen new "planters" and fresh provisions for the Roanoke vanguard aboard, White left Bideford on April 22, 1588. However, the very next day, and before they were out of sight of the Cornish coast, the two ships were off in spirited and successful pursuit of four unidentified vessels. The following day they ran down two more. For the best part of two weeks the pinnaces pursued anything in sight, regardless of size. Eventually, however, the tables were turned, and the *Brave* was chased down off Madeira and boarded by a Frenchman after a battle which left the pinnace a shambles and many of her crew wounded or dead. Even White himself took head wounds from a sword and a pike, as well as a bullet in his buttock. Stripped of everything but her hull, the *Brave* limped back to England with, as White put it, "God justly punishing our former theeverie of our evil disposed mariners."[20]

Two months later, Spain's Invincible Armada of 132 soldier-crammed ships was sighted off the Lizard, and on July 31 began one of history's most famous sea battles. For a week the fate of Protestant England rode on the Channel wind, but when all was over, armed with scarcely more than a slingshot, St. George had slain Goliath. Girded in the shining armor of right, God, and their queen's virginity, the outnumbered English heroes had routed the Elizabethans' Evil Empire, and the stewardship of the world was changing hands. That, at least, is the simplistic mythology that would be taught to generations of wide-eyed British schoolboys—the empire-building scions of Drake, Frobisher, Grenville, Ralegh, and the rest. The reality, however, was less black and white than a muddy gray.

A battle had been won, but the war was far from over. In spite of his losses, Philip immediately began to patch his fleet together for a further invasion attempt, still mindful, no doubt, of the scathing comment made by Pope Sixtus V three years earlier, to the effect that it was odd to see the king of half the world defied by the queen of half an island. Even in the face of renewed harassment by Drake and other commanders, Spain was able to send two more armadas against England in 1596 and 1597 after having actually landed a mini-invasion force at Mousehole near Penzance in Cornwall in 1595. Spain invaded Ireland in 1601 and prepared another cross-Channel assault the following year. Not until 1604, after the death of Elizabeth and the accession of James I, was peace between Britain and Spain formalized. Thus to the end of Elizabeth's reign the Spanish threat remained paramount in the minds of the queen and her advisers.

The Armada of 1588 intruded into John White's efforts to resupply his Roanoke colonists. With the duke of Parma's army still threatening from across the strait of Dover, Elizabeth's prohibition on the dispersal of English ships remained in force. So for White, a year slipped by with nothing accomplished. The best he could record was membership on what amounted to a Virginia relief committee set up in London in March 1589. On paper, however, its intentions were more grandiose. It was to be a new corporation with hundred-pound shareholders to plant the Christian religion among the barbarous and heathen countries of America, for which Ralegh promised to secure a new enabling charter from the queen.

Having been burned by his small-scale venture aboard the *Brave* and *Roe* pinnaces, John White knew better than most what it would take to mount a successful expedition to Virginia. The new company needed both the funds and the fortitude of a major privateering enterprise. But 1589 was a bad year to be looking for it. Drake was preparing an armada of more than 140 ships and about eighteen thousand soldiers for an attack on the Spaniards at Lisbon, and with everyone focusing on that, concern for a hundred or so lost souls on a tiny Virginia island was muted at best. Nevertheless, early in 1590 William Sanderson (one of the new company's contributors) undertook to outfit a supply ship, the eighty-ton *Moonlight,* which was to be captained by White's old friend Edward Spicer, skipper of the previous expedition's flyboat.

Neither Sanderson nor Spicer was willing to send the *Moonlight* off into a war zone on her own, so it was agreed that she should sail in convoy with a three-ship privateering expedition being mounted by John Watts and associates, another London merchant syndicate. Its lead ship was to be the *Hopewell,* at 150 tons, which was captained by Abraham Cocke and would carry White and a "convenient number of passengers, with their furnitures and necessaries to be landed in Virginia."[21] The other vessels were the 100-ton *Little John,* commanded by the man who later led the first James Towne flotilla, Christopher Newport, and a pinnace, the *John Evangelist.*

The Watts ships were being fitted in the Thames, and Sanderson's *Moonlight* apparently at Plymouth, where they would rendezvous. But in late February, when it came time for White and his fresh colonists to board the *Hopewell,* he found to his dismay that Captain Cocke had arbitrarily decided that civilian passengers might compromise his privateering efficiency, and refused to let them board. "I was by the owner and Commanders of the ships denied to have any passengers, or any thing els transported in any of the said ships," said White, "saving only my selfe & my chest; no not so much as a boy to attend upon me."[22] Once again he meekly acquiesced, claiming that he had no time to complain to Ralegh and that had he tried, Captain Cocke would have sailed without him. One cannot help wondering why with the whole Virginia enterprise in jeopardy and knowing that the ships were to put in at Plymouth, which he could have reached overland in a couple of days, White made little effort to have Watts & Co. meet their contracted commitment. Instead he and his chest went aboard the *Hopewell* and remained a virtual prisoner there when the three-ship fleet left Plymouth—without waiting for Captain Spicer and the *Moonlight*.

The ships reached the island of Dominica at the end of April, and spent the whole of May and June playing at pirates in the Caribbean—with only modest returns for their efforts. On July 2 they were joined by the *Moonlight,* which, though loaded for Virginia, had no choice but to augment Captain Cocke's privateering fleet. Thus another summer month slipped away. Not until July 28 (well into the hurricane season) did Cocke decide to abandon the sport and head north for Florida and Virginia. One can guess at the unhappy John White's emotional state after five months of confinement in the company of quasi buccaneers who regarded "very smally the good of their countreymen in Virginia."[23]

Unlike modern crews, whose pay is their return for their labor, the crews of privateers relied on sharing the loot from anything that could be construed as an enemy vessel. Profits were split three ways: to the ship's owners, its outfitters, and the crew. In the back of John Smith's handy hints for young seamen (1627) is a listing of the company's shares, beginning with the captain at ten shares, all the way down to the boyes, "which is a single share or 1. and ½. or as they doe deserve."[24] Consequently, while the captain had a responsibility to his owners, the artificers and seamen working for their own profit could see none in risking their necks hunting for lost colonists across tricky shoals and among potentially hostile Indians.

The fleet reached Hatteras on August 15, and the next morning it anchored off the entry, then known as Port Ferdinando (close to modern Oregon Inlet), and sent two boats into the sound bound for Roanoke Island. However, a column of smoke to the southwest attracted the party's attention, and by the time they reached it and found no one there night was approaching. By the morning of the seventeenth, a northeaster was blowing up, and the seas were rising, and as the second of the two boats again entered the cut, it grounded on the bar, forcing the eleven men aboard to try to wade ashore. Seven, including Captain Spicer and the expedition's surgeon, failed to make it.

The disaster prompted the sailors (who didn't want to be there anyway) to demand that they forget the colonists and head home before the weather worsened. It says something for Captain Cocke that he refused to be persuaded. Setting out while it was still dark, the boats rowed toward the light of a fire in the woods near the north end of Roanoke Island. Once there, from the safety of the boats, White recalled that "we let fall our Grapnel neere the shore, & sounded with a trumpet a Call, & afterwardes many familiar English tunes of Songs, and called to them friendly."[25] That there had been Indians nearby to listen to this curious musicale is attested to by White, who recalled that when the boat crews went ashore after dawn, they saw fresh footprints in the sand. This, however, was as close as they came to finding any signs of life.

Carved on a tree at the crest of the sandy bank were the letters CRO, which, when they reached the settlement site, were expanded on a palisade post to read CROATOAN. White explained that he had left instructions that as the colonists were planning to "remove from Roanoak 50 miles into the maine," they should "write or carve on the trees or posts of the dores the name of the place where they should be seated" and, "if they should happen to be distressed in any of those places, that then they should carve over the letters of the name, a Cross."[26] He added that no such warning capped either inscription, and that is hardly surprising, for although the departing colonists could write where they were going (always supposing they knew), they could not report any problems they might encounter on arrival *until* they got there.

Some readers of the evidence have contended that the CRO that White found on the sandy bank tree was unfinished because the carver was disturbed and forced to leave in a hurry. No less logical, and on balance more probable, is the explanation that while loading the boats below the sandy bank, someone belatedly remembered White's instruction and ordered the letters carved. But someone else asked how they could be sure that when White returned, he would land at the same bank and tree. Would it not make better sense to carve the CROATOAN message on the fort gate, where no one could miss seeing it? "Good thinking, lad," said the officer, and ordered the carver to do just that.

Equally puzzling, of course, is why the inscription reported that the colonists had gone south to Manteo's friendly Croatoans when they were supposed to have gone north to the Chesapeake. Reports and rumors picked up by the seventeenth-century James Towne colonists strongly indicated that some had indeed gone north and that after their menfolk had been killed by the Indians, women and children survivors were absorbed into tribes living south of the James River. But White's about-to-be-lost colonists lacked ships large enough to carry all the equipment brought with them from England to build the Cittie of Ralegh. It seems likely, therefore, that some remained behind and over time moved most of the heavy equipment south onto Croatoan Island (also known as My Lord Admirals Island), there to await White's returning fleet. Located as the island is below the heel of Cape Hatteras, it would have provided advance sighting of ships sailing up from the Caribbean, a view impossible from the north end of Roanoke Island.

John White's account of what he and Captain Cocke found when they reached the abandoned settlement is the crucial and *only* documentary evidence of what archaeologists could hope to find there:

> . . . we passed toward the place where they were left in sundry houses, but we found the houses taken downe, and the place very strongly enclosed with a high palisado of great trees, with cortynes [curtains] and flankers very Fort-like, and one of the chiefe trees or postes at the right side of the entrance had the barke taken off, and 5 foote from the ground in faire Capitall letters was graven CROA-TOAN without any crosse or signe of distresse; this done, we entred into the palisado, where we found many barres of Iron, two pigges of Lead, foure iron fowlers, Iron sacker-shotte, and such like heavie things, throwen here and there, almost overgrowen with grasse and weedes.[27]

No melons this time, but evidently a wooden fortification far stronger than the structure mentioned by Diaz or the razed ruin that White's arriving colonists had found there in 1587.

Accepting the simple premise that White would first describe what he first saw, we would have to conclude that the taken-down houses were outside the palisade, just like those built "about the fort" by Lane's colonists, and that not until he had passed them did he see the Croatoan inscription. That makes no sense. Even if White had not been with Lane through the months of his increasingly crisis-ridden governorship, White had to know that the natives were no longer friendly. Besides, he had already lost one of his senior men (the crabbing George Howe) to Indian arrows, and he had learned that Grenville's ill-fated garrison had allowed the Indians to "convey themselves secretly behind the trees, neere the houses where our men carelesly lived."[28] It could happen again if the houses remained outside the palisade, and no commander in his right mind would let it. Therefore, in spite of White's chronology, we must assume that like the Fort Caroline settlement built by the French in Florida in 1565, the last Roanoke Island dwellings were clustered within the palisade of great trees.

The Roanoke colony's palisade evidently differed from that of Fort Caroline, where the defenses were built from posts, connecting rails, and planks. White's wording specifically describes "trees or postes," one of which needed to have its bark stripped to allow the carver to do his work. In short, the palisade he found standing in 1590 may have looked pretty much like the reconstruction erected on the earthen fort site in 1936.

White described a combination of flankers and curtain walls, meaning blockhouses or bastions projecting beyond the straight lines of the linking walls—a relationship similar to that discovered at Virginia's 1620 Wolstenholme Towne fort. Archaeologist James Deetz has noted that though this was a classic European means for the use of lateral (enfilade) fire to protect gates and the outsides of curtains, it had been employed on Indian sites in the Missouri river valley a thousand years earlier.

In 1959, while a utility line was being laid to the reconstructed earthwork that the National Park Service identified as Lane's fort, an area first described as a brick floor was discovered about thirty feet to the west. Six years later, J. C. Harrington returned to excavate fully what had been found. From his dig emerged the ground plan of a slightly sunken structure about nine feet six inches square with trees (described as "large tap roots") at its corners. Between them ran one-foot-wide trenches, which he concluded had contained laterally lying logs. Extending away from this square structure were more log trenches at angles of about thirty degrees. In his 1966 report Harrington correctly stated that what he was tentatively designating an "outwork to Fort Raleigh" was without known parallel.[29]

Eleven years later, after the Wolstenholme fort plan was published, Park Service historian Phillip Evans was the first to recognize that precedent did exist. Superimposing the Virginia fort's flanker onto that of Harrington's outwork showed that his taproots were almost precisely paralleled by its posts. Thus to continue to read Harrington's structure as being built around naturally growing trees became an act of faith of religious dimensions.

The supposed brick floor that had drawn Harrington back to Roanoke Island proved to be something else. Within his outwork he found three pits, one of them packed with discarded bricks as well as fragments from a stoneware flask made in Normandy in the late sixteenth century. The fragments helped date the bricks but did not then explain the bricks' idiosyncrasies, for these were no ordinary bricks. Several were unevenly burned, and some had been ground away to render one side deeply concave. Harrington conjectured that the grinding could have been the result of sharpening tools or swords or, less plausibly, of polishing armor.

That the bricks were of local manufacture there could be no doubt. An analysis of the clay proved it, giving credence to the testimony of Darbie Glavin (Darby Glande), an Irish soldier who had been with Lane and

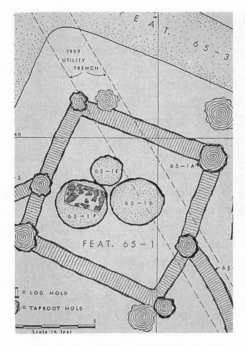

Left: Detail from J. C. Harrington's plan of his Roanoke fort "outwork," showing the three pits dug within it, one of them filled with bricks and brickbats.
Above: J. C. Harrington showing bricks found in a pit within the "outwork" structure he was excavating in 1965.

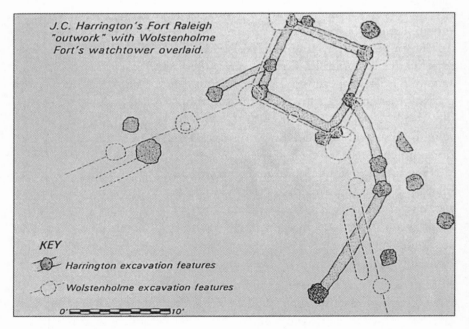

Plan of the Roanoke "outwork," found by J. C. Harrington in 1965, with the comparable plan of the 1620 watchtower at the Wolstenholme Towne fort shown in dashed lines.

Examples of reshaped bricks from the Roanoke fort outwork.

reported that upon arrival his people "began to make brick and tiles for a fort and houses."[30] Tile fragments were also found by Harrington, as they would be again in later excavations, but all were of English origin—this notwithstanding the fact that John White's son-in-law, Ananias Dare, had been in the tile-making trade.

Harrington's 1965 mandate had been to explain the "brick floor," and he had done so; but in the process he had uncovered an even greater mystery. His Wolstenholme-like outwork had been located so close to the reconstructed earthwork that it would have created an unacceptable obstruction into the defenders' field of fire. Although archaeologists and historians gathered at the site more than once in the decade and more after Harrington made his discovery, the meetings always ended as they began—with much headshaking and the airing of baseless conjectures. Nevertheless, out of these discussions began to emerge the iconoclastic possibility that the reconstructed earthwork might have been only *part* of Lane's fort. Nevertheless, to give Harrington his very deserved due, his 1962 report on his earthwork excavations had included hints that it might have been no more than a sconce erected at some distance from the main wood-built fort.

In 1982, inspired by Phillip Evans's Wolstenholme connection, National Park Service archaeologists, led by Dr. John E. Ehrenhard, carried out a remote-sensing survey of the area around Harrington's outwork. Using both magnetometers and soil resistivity meters, they identified several buried anomalies meriting test excavation. In the following year they returned to dig.

Contemporary examples representing the three types of science-related ceramic vessels found in excavations outside and within the Roanoke Island earthwork: Normandy stoneware flask, tin-glazed pharmaceutical pots, and metalworker's crucibles.

Hopes that the anomalies that looked so inviting on paper would turn out to hold the key to the Fort Raleigh site were not realized. But the digging did yield more ceramic evidence of Elizabethan occupation—thirty-eight sherds in all, among them fragments of crucibles, several pieces from tin-glazed pharmaceutical pots, and another sherd that looked as though it belonged to the Normandy stoneware flask Harrington had found in his brick pit within the square outwork.

On examining these fragments for the first time in 1989, I realized that this seemingly disparate group had two things in common: They weren't typical of domestic garbage, and they all came from objects commonly seen in paintings and engravings of alchemical laboratories where misguided metallurgists strove to convert base metal into gold. Independently, historian Phillip Evans and his Park Service colleagues had been looking again at Harrington's sharpening bricks and were wondering whether they had been shaped to serve as the arched entrance to a bread oven. Evans, I believed, was halfway to the truth. The possibility that other bricks hitherto dismissed as uninformative might now have something more to add sent us excitedly to the warehouse where Harrington's artifacts were stored.

Although originally fired at low temperatures, several of the bricks had been used as part of something that had caused them to become heavily fire-blackened. Some still retained traces of clay-based mortar and so could not have been discarded unused. If the bricks were related to the crucibles, pots, and flask in life as well as in the ground, then they almost certainly came from the furnace of metallurgist Joachim Gans.

The first known Jew to visit what is now English-speaking America, Gans was born into a family of scientists in Prague. He had traveled to England in 1581, and while serving there as a scientific adviser to Queen Elizabeth's antiquated mineral industry, he submitted to Secretary of State Francis Walsingham a proposal for an improved smelting process. Thus, when Amadas and Barlowe returned from Roanoke in 1584 with Indian copper ornaments, it was only natural to send a copper-working specialist with the next expedition. Such employment of a foreigner (the English called foreigners "strangers") was not unprecedented. On the contrary, it followed in the footsteps of Martin Frobisher in 1577, who had so unwisely put his trust in the German expert Jonas Schutz, and of Sir Humphrey Gilbert in 1583, who took with him as his "minerall-man and refiner" one Daniel, who was described as Saxon-born.[31]

Although no scientific instructions survive to detail what Ralegh and his backers required of their experts, the instructions given to Gilbert's artist, Thomas Bavin, made it clear that every detail of the newfound lands' animal, vegetable, and mineral resources was to be recorded, tested, and sampled. Ralegh's instructions to the Roanoke scientists doubtless were the same. Hariot was to help make maps and charts as well as keep the natural history and anthropological record, while Gans was to find and test the metals that were to make everyone's fortune.

The search for copper mines was high on Governor Ralph Lane's list of priorities, not only because copper was itself valuable but because it was also a source of silver. Consequently, late in March 1586 Lane and Gans with his team of miners were to be found edging their way up the Chowan River into hitherto unexplored Indian territory in search of minerals. It was there that Lane invaded the village of Chawanoac and fettered its already paralyzed king and from his son learned of the quantities of ore to be panned from the adjacent Roanoke River and mined in the mountains of the warlike Mangoaks, who possessed so much that they used copper plates to decorate their houses. But after two days' sailing and rowing up that river and with food supplies low (they had eaten their dogs' "porredge"), the zap and thud of incoming arrows advised against extending the trip. Gans returned to base with samples only of already worked copper acquired from the Chowan Indians. Nevertheless, we do know that he was able to make quality tests from such material, Hariot noting that from "diverse small plates of copper . . . wee also founde by triall to holde silver."[32]

Hans Holbein's 1537 satirical woodcut of a German alchemist at work in a laboratory as chaotic as his mind. Holbein's glassware and crucibles are paralleled by fragments found on the 1585 science center floor at Roanoke Island.

J. C. Harrington's excavations on the site of the later reconstructed earthwork yielded two sizable lumps of copper waste, one in the silted filling of the ditch and the other from the land surface *under* the dirt thrown up to build the rampart. From that same sealed land surface came fragments of a Spanish olive jar, whose neck lay at the bottom of the ditch, and a cluster of large iron nails. Assuming that the earthwork was Lane's original fort, Harrington had cause to scratch his head. Unable to explain convincingly the presence of worked copper before the fort was built, he wrote: "Their position, therefore, is not conclusive as to origin, but does show that they are not recent."[33] Addressing the equally vexing problem of the jar fragments, Harrington could only conclude that "the vessel had been broken and discarded while the fort was under construction."[34]

In the light of Pedro Diaz's statement that Lane's fort had been of wood and of little strength, the artifacts under the earthwork's rampart suggested another explanation. The reconstructed fort was not Lane's at all; instead its ditch cut through and its dirt rampart overlay the ground where Joachim Gans had had his worksheds and furnaces.

Only renewed digging could prove or disprove that thesis, but the Park Service gave it sufficient credence to allow it to be tested—even if the result might show that for forty years its staff had been interpreting the wrong fort. In the fall of 1991, therefore, with major funding from the National Geographic Society and the help of both patriotic societies and private foundations and individuals, we reopened Harrington's outwork excavation as well as the artifact-yielding area explored by Ehrenhard in 1983. And in what must rank among archaeology's major miracles, part of Gans's lab floor survived undisturbed. Ehrenhard had stopped two inches above it, and Harrington, whose drawings showed the entire area dug out, had left a three-foot strip undisturbed along one of his survey lines. From that narrow strip came more than sixty diagnostic artifacts, among them fragments of chemical glassware, Indian pottery that had been used in distilling, more fragments from French stoneware flasks, many crucible sherds, antimony used in assaying, chips of coal and flint, iron scale reportedly used in making a cement to hold the parts together, and much pine charcoal. Equally exciting was the discovery of nut fragments and seeds, suggesting that Gans may have shared his lab and equipment with Hariot. Another small undisturbed area close by yielded an Elizabethan iron fishhook—a most appropriate artifact to recover on an island whose principal industry has for centuries been fishing.

Although there seemed little doubt that the workshop floor had yielded debris from Joachim Gans's activities, we needed proof that he really did melt copper in his crucibles. Hariot's previously cited statement that "The aforesaide copper wee also found by triall to holde silver" meant that the Indians' copper was melted in crucibles and separated from trace silver, in which case cuprous residue should be found attached to the fragments. But when crucible sherds believed to contain such residue were submitted to the University of Virginia for analysis, the answer came back that the tested sample seemed to hold nothing but dirt. A tiny drop of decayed copper oxide from the floor was equally uninformative. It could have come from anything. Eventually, however, a single crucible fragment, scarcely an inch long and half an inch wide, revealed, gripped amid the blisters of usage, a pinpoint-size speck of orange-red copper.

A second season in 1992 to complete the clearance of the Hariot-Gans workshop area yielded more copper-encrusted crucible sherds and, most surprising of all, a small lump of copper oxide that may be slag derived from an attempt to smelt copper ore obtained from the Indians. It is hoped that further analysis will determine whether this is so, or whether the oxide is instead residue from melting copper objects. Either way, this is firm evidence that European metallurgical technology was being employed on the Roanoke site.

An aboriginal bowl used by the 1585 Roanoke Island expedition's scientific team and found on its research center floor, here being pieced together by Audrey Noël Hume.

The renewed excavations were expanded to redig part of the fort's interior, seeking evidence of structures or activities that had escaped Harrington's notice and had not been destroyed while the 1950 reconstruction was built. Although we held out little hope for this phase of our work, we needed to be sure that nothing significant survived. As feared, the interior proved to be riddled with modern disturbances, but one large hole whose fill included twentieth-century nails and bottle glass also yielded fragments of Gans's crucibles and part of a Normandy flask—sherds similar to those we had been finding embedded in the 1585 workshop floor. From a root hole at the edge of the modern hole (but predating the 1936 blockhouse reconstruction) came more crucible sherds and an Elizabethan lead seal from a bale of cloth bearing a merchant's initials—the first lettered message to be found since John White read CROATOAN on the palisade gate.

Unless dirt from outside the dirt fort had been hauled into it prior to 1936—and there was no documentation to suggest that it had—it followed that the Gans-related artifacts had been there since 1586. That

The interior of Roanoke Island's reconstructed earthwork was partially
reexcavated in 1992. The Gans-Hariot workplace area lies beyond
the rampart in the right background.

there were no other artifacts of the kind you would expect to find around
the houses that Lane said were inside his fort was further evidence that
this was *not* that fort. Instead, as we had suspected, the diggers of its ditch
had sliced through ground strewn with the artifacts left there by Ralegh's
scientists when they evacuated the island to join Drake's fleet.

The expanded digging on the Hariot-Gans workshop site in 1992
revealed many more post and tree holes than had been found by J. C. and
Virginia Harrington in 1965. While it was remarkable how accurate their
recording had been, their time had been limited, and their helpers largely
unskilled. It was only natural, therefore, that with a highly skilled crew at
every level, and in the light of thirty years' additional experience, much
more should be found. And it was. The problem, however, was that so
many additional structural holes were found that the straight lines of
Harrington's supposed log walls extending away from his central blockhouse became far less defined and may not have existed. Instead it could
be argued that his square structure was freestanding (p. 74). If so, its tree-
hole similarity to the Wolstenholme fort's watchtower could be coinci-
dental. After all, it is less than surprising that two structures measuring
approximately nine feet six inches by nine feet six inches should have corner posts in matching places.

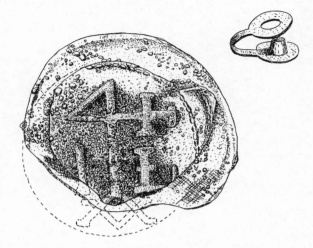

A cloth merchant's incomplete lead seal found within the Fort Raleigh
earthwork in 1992. The small sketch at right shows how seals were
shaped and folded before being squeezed and impressed. The dotted
lines complete the Roanoke seal's central motif as well as the beaded
border surrounding the initials. The resulting space to the left
allowed room for the first letter to be an H. That to the right
is a crossed L. Surviving width ¾ inch.

That Harrington's outwork had been built with posts, not with conveniently located growing trees, was explained in 1991, when we uncovered
a section of the 1936 palisading that had been sawed off in 1944. One of
the surviving post stubs was in the grip of living roots from a nearby cedar
tree. The local soil being short of nutriment, new roots would be drawn
to any decaying organic matter, be it old roots or old posts. In time the
growing root system would totally consume a post and expand beyond the
originally dug hole to create precisely what Harrington had recorded: tap-
root holes where posts first had stood. Here was a classic archaeological
object lesson, for although all of us believed that this could happen, none
of us had ever seen the physical proof.

Knowing, as we now did, that Harrington's structure was unrelated to
the earthwork, we were left with the task of providing our own alternative
identification. It was a task made the more difficult by the fact that in
backfilling Harrington's 1965 excavations, Park Service engineers had
used mechanical equipment that dug deeper than he had and thus
destroyed most of the traces he had carefully recorded. Indeed, when he
visited the site in 1991, he was no better able to interpret what we were so
glumly examining.

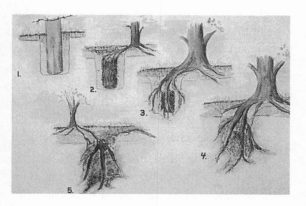

Left: A 1936 palisade post at Fort Raleigh in the process of being "eaten" by living tree roots converting its context from a posthole into a tree hole. *Right:* Diagrammatic devolution of a post and its associated man-dug hole into a tree root and its naturally created hole: 1, the post as installed; 2, the post's decaying stump attacked by young tree roots; 3, roots expand to change the shape of the hole; 4, mature roots destroy both post and hole; 5, the first tree dies and its roots become food for another, further disguising the original posthole.

By no means does it follow that a nine-foot-six-inch-square structure had to be as tall as a watchtower. Then again, it could have been, perhaps to provide Hariot's and Gans's workers with visual contact with Lane's fort and settlement some distance away. When we remember that the shaped bricks were found inside it, its identification as a building housing the scientists' furnaces seems equally, if not more, logical (p. 74).

In 1947 Harrington's preliminary trenching had encountered a pit containing quantities of charcoal which he believed had been burned in it. Although the pit is some 125 feet from the Hariot-Gans workshop area, the presence of much charcoal on the latter's floor prompted us to return to the pit in the hope of finding charcoal still there that could be subjected to carbon 14 dating. In 1947 such techniques were unavailable, and consequently, finding no man-made artifacts in the pit, Harrington had been unable to determine how old it was. It turned out that the charcoal had been burned elsewhere and dumped into the pit, whose fill continued beneath it to an unknown depth. An auger brought up dirty brown soil at about seven feet—strong evidence, I thought, that the hole could be the top of a backfilled well shaft. If so, and if the charcoal could be dated to the Ralegh period, its lower depths might yield domestic artifacts that would prove its close proximity to the lost settlement site, or alternatively, the presence of science-related items could link it to the Hariot-Gans operation. Alas, because we were out of time and lacked the manpower and materials to dig down safely fifteen or more feet through unstable sand, the season ended with the hole backfilled and its secrets withheld.

My first decision had been to consider our mission complete and leave the tricky, perhaps dangerous task of digging below Harrington's pit to the next generation of Fort Raleigh investigators. But when the charcoal's carbon 14 dates came back, I changed my mind. The process provides brackets of approximately a hundred years on either side of a mean date, and in this instance they opened at about 1450 and closed around 1660, putting the Ralegh years squarely and tantalizingly in the middle.

Believing that a major discovery might be within our grasp, the same blue-ribbon crew returned to the site in April 1993 and again began to dig. But the previous year's hopes slowly faded in tandem with the disappearing "well." The dirty soil brought up by the auger had been the product of natural seepage. It seemed that we were no closer to explaining Harrington's charcoal pit or to locating the Elizabethan colonists' village.

But while taking the final record photographs, I noticed a pale brown stain in the sand close to the pit. Scraped with a trowel, it began to look like yet another posthole, but this one was different. In its fill we found quantities of charcoal and a large lump of bog iron—a combination that could point to experimental iron smelting on the site by Hariot's artisans in 1585. He had reported finding rocks near the waterside which, "by the triall of a minerall man, [were] founde to holde Iron richly."[35] The 1993 excavation ended therefore with yet another tantalizing clue—a magnet to justify yet more digging, this time in search of the place where that mineral man made his iron trial.

Although collectively the evidence of 1585–86 metallurgical research could justifiably be claimed as one of the most important discoveries since archaeological digging at Fort Raleigh began, the aim of the 1991–92 excavations had been to test and, one hoped, prove the theory that the earthwork cut through the Hariot-Gans workshop area and so was of later date. It did, and it was. The next questions, therefore, were two that history, not archaeology, would have to answer—namely, Who built the earthwork, and when?

We had three Elizabethan possibilities. First, Lane had the earthwork erected after Gans had finished his work and vacated the site. But to counter that, we know from the records that the aborted expedition in search of mines whose copper ore could be assayed did not take place until March or early April 1586, perhaps a mere six weeks before Drake arrived to take his colonists home. Furthermore, when Grenville arrived shortly thereafter, he found the fort to be of wood. Clearly, therefore, Lane did not build the earthwork. The second major candidate is White's group of 1587–88. However, when they arrived, they found Lane's fort razed, and at some time after White returned to England, they erected a James Fort–style palisade around the entire village that was still standing when White returned in 1590. The documentary evidence therefore weighs against the "Lost Colonists" having built the earthwork. That leaves only one other sixteenth-century candidate: Grenville's tiny and doomed garrison left on the island in the summer of 1586.

Like Harrington before me, I remained locked into the belief that the earthwork *had* to be Elizabethan: because it stood on the site where Elizabethan artifacts had been found and, more convincingly, because Harrington had found Indian cooking fires in the partially silted ditch. I therefore argued that Lane's "wooden fort of little strength" would have been too large for fifteen men to defend, and so, as White discovered, it was razed, perhaps with the intent to chop up its timbers and use them to build a breastwork on the top of an earthen sconce constructed by Grenville's soldiers and sailors before they sailed home. To demonstrate how much better suited the earthen fort was to house Grenville's garrison than Lane's hundred-plus colonists, I went so far as to photograph fifteen members of our archaeological crew standing self-consciously inside it.

Like arguments that demolished the candidacies of Lane and White, those rebutting the "it had to be Grenville's men" argument were no less persuasive. Grenville never mentioned building an earthwork, and when in the following year White's group arrived, he mentioned only a fort that had been "rased down"—and nobody would have done that to an earthwork. Even more damning is the fact that when Grenville's men sought safety from Indian arrows, they retreated into their storehouse, not into a fort. I tried to refute both negative arguments by contending that the earthwork was unfinished when Grenville departed and therefore provided inadequate protection—hence, perhaps, the fact that Harrington found no traces of gateposts. I explained White's failure to mention any dirt fort on the ground that by the time he arrived, it had eroded to such a degree as to be unworthy of comment.

Because so much in archaeology is rooted in trying to prove what one wants to prove, we frequently are guilty of clinging to untenable flotsam as though our reputations were in danger of drowning. My "Grenville's men" theory was no exception. Nevertheless, from time to time, usually in the dead of night when waking from some unpleasant dream, I dared think the unthinkable: Was it possible that the earthwork was not Elizabethan at all? Could we really justify ignoring the fact that a fort was drawn on approximately the right site on the John Collet map of 1770 and on the Henry Mouzon version of 1775 in lettering as large as any on the map? The conventional Park Service wisdom had it that both maps were depicting the historic site. But if true, why inscribe "PAIN FORT" beside it in easy-to-read capitals and engrave "Walter Rawleigh" away in the sound to the south in tiny lowercase lettering? Furthermore, in a second edition of Mouzon's map the historical reference is omitted while the bold definition of the fort remains. The Mouzon map shows a second fort using the same device (but with a building inside it), this one on the Neuse River and labeled Fort Barnwell—built by Colonel John Barnwell during the Tuscarora War of 1711–1713. Couple all this with the fact that John Paine had bought fifty acres at the north end of the island in 1767, and the evidence is strong that Collet and Mouzon were more interested in contemporary fact than in ancient history.

The 1775 map shows the shipping channel passing through Roanoke Inlet and by Pain Fort, the closest and only land point before reaching the vulnerable port of Edenton, which in that period was the principal outlet for the colony's tobacco. Although shipping passing the fort might not have been in range of its guns, they certainly would have discouraged any invasion of the island from that direction. But invasion by whom and for what purpose?

England's war with Spain and France known in Europe as the War of the Austrian Succession (1739–48) and in America as King George's War had seen a major Spanish attempt to invade South Carolina in 1742. Common sense would have dictated the need to defend Roanoke Island, for he who controlled the Pain Fort site held the key both to Edenton and to the back door to Virginia. The same was true during the French and Indian War (1756–63). There is every reason to expect, therefore, that during either or both wars the local militia would have thrown up an artillery emplacement just to be on the safe side. Nevertheless, in an unpublished 1982 report for the Park Service on the historical geography of Roanoke Island, historian Bruce Cheeseman stated that no records exist of fortbuilding there in the eighteenth century. One might counter that the Collet and Mouzon maps are indeed such a record and that conversely no record exists, either written or cartographic, to document earthwork construction in the sixteenth century.

Because the earthwork occupies the place where Williams, Harrington, and his successors found Elizabethan artifacts, the long-held

Restored Indian pots whose fragments were recovered by J. C.
Harrington during his 1950 excavation of the earthwork's ditch.

assumption is that this is the site that naturalist-historian John Lawson
visited in 1701, on which he found cannon and other scattered artifacts,
and is therefore the site of the 1585–88 village. But we now know that all
the artifacts found in the vicinity of the earthwork are associated with the
"industrial park," not with the domestic dwellings of the Lane and White
settlement. Equally important was the very reasonable assumption that
because the earthwork's entrance faced west, the Lane-White village had
to extend in that direction. Eliminate the fort, and that directional focus
disappears.

There remains, nonetheless, Harrington's assertion that he found
Indian cooking fires in the fort ditch, meaning that the fort had to be in
existence before the last Indians left the island in the early eighteenth
century—before King George's War began.

Looking again at the three broken pots found in the ditch, one is
struck by the fact that not all the fragments are there. Gravity being what
it is, if the pots really were broken in the ditch, why were all the pieces not
found? In the 1992 excavations inside the fort, several joining sherds from
another Indian pot of the same period were found in a pit containing
modern bottle glass, but no archaeologist would claim that the glass had
to have been dropped there when an Indian broke his pot. On the contrary, the weight of evidence points to Gans, Hariot, and their people
using—and breaking—Indian pots that remained on the site, were disturbed during the fort building, and, when the earthwork decayed, were
redeposited into the partially silted ditch or into much later dug pits.

But Harrington found evidence of fires—Indian fires—in the ditch
silt. How, one might ask, can those be explained in any other way?

We know from the English domestic potsherds found immediately west of the earthwork in 1983 and 1993 that somebody was living there in the late eighteenth and early nineteenth centuries. It seems reasonable to argue, therefore, that that person would have cleared brush and burned it in the confines of the still-hollow ditch. Then, again, we know that in 1819 President Monroe was taken to a site where he was shown "the remains of the Fort, the traces of which are still distinctly visible," a viewing that might have called for some prior clearing and hasty brush burning. If, therefore, one or more fires were lit in the partially silted ditch, and the Indian pottery found in their vicinity was deposited in the next and final phase of the rampart's erosion, the association recorded by Harrington might have been misleadingly created.

The story of Sir Walter Ralegh's settlements had long been a cornerstone of American colonial history. Indeed, the Raleigh Tavern in Williamsburg with his bust over its front door was a constant reminder of Virginia's roots through much of the eighteenth century. Nevertheless, it seems clear that the historic site's location was remembered only in general terms, and although *a* site was shown to President Monroe, it was no long-established shrine and was of insufficient interest to be marked on any of the surviving maps and charts of the island drawn before 1770 or between 1820 and the founding of the Roanoke Colony Memorial Association in 1894. Although detailed maps drawn in the aftermath of the Battle of Roanoke Island on February 7 and 8, 1862, show nothing on the site but sand hills, victorious Yankee soldiers knew the "Monroe" location well enough to dig holes there in search of treasure.

If the local dignitaries who led President Monroe to the historic site knew that the earthwork had been constructed by their grandfathers, they certainly were not about to admit it. And once officially—presidentially—accepted, the fort site became "Ralegh's fort" through the rest of the nineteenth century, eventually to be scientifically validated by archaeologist Talcott Williams and all who came after him—until 1992.

If I am right in claiming the earthwork to be an eighteenth-century red herring, then we no longer need look west from its entrance in search of the Elizabethan village. Instead future archaeologists are freed to search east, south, and north—anywhere but the immediate vicinity of Thomas Hariot's and Joachim Gans's science center, for as in English medieval and later communities, noxious and potentially dangerous industries were kept outside the city walls.

In 1982, while walking the beach at low tide below the eroding cliff northeast from the fort, historian Phillip Evans found a barrel and a hol-

The standard nineteenth-century log-cabin concept of the Roanoke settlement in a hand-colored wood engraving of 1851.

lowed log seated in the bed about fifty feet offshore, both evidently the bottoms of old well shafts—precisely the kind of discovery we had hoped to make below Harrington's charcoal pit. Carbon 14 dating for one barrel provided brackets of 1285–1660, and for the other 1340–1665. Although these dates demonstrated that both liners could have been made in the 1580s, their location made little sense when everyone *knew* that the village lay way off to the west beyond the fort's entrance. Now, however, we are free to speculate that these liners were the bottoms of wells dug within the village or inside Lane's weak wooden fort. If correct, this interpretation provides a marker—a vanishing point—on which future excavations should focus.

The new evidence was presented at a symposium of historians, archaeologists, and National Park Service officials in May 1993, at which time I expected to be run off the island on a rail. Instead, after I had departed, anthropologist Dr. David Phelps observed in a generous oversimplification, "We have lost the fort and found the colony." Time and more digging may prove him right.

Although the 1991–93 excavations did much to define the historical sequence at Fort Raleigh, they failed to find the hoped-for parallel to palisade construction at James Fort in 1607, nor did they find a trace of John White's Lost Colonists. To complete that story as far as it goes, one has to return to 1590 and to White's description of what he saw when he entered the palisado: bars of iron, a couple more of lead, four small iron cannon (fowlers), iron shot for larger guns called sakers, and other heavy but unidentified objects, all "throwen here and there."[36] The fowlers were light guns commonly swivel-mounted on ships and, when loaded with small shot, nails, and even gravel, were an effective defense against enemy boarders. Charged in that way, they would be equally damaging to Indians—far more so than the five- to six-pound balls fired from powder-hungry sakers. White had described all four fowlers as iron, but when John Lawson was there more than a century later, what he saw were a "Brass-Gun" and "one small Quarter-deck-Gun."[37]

Historians have had difficulty equating any of White's "foure iron fowlers" with Lawson's brass gun, arguing that brass, or rather *bronze,* guns were not made at swivel size and that had any of the fowlers been of yellow metal, John White would have mentioned it. In truth, swivel guns did come in bronze and in the right period. Thus, for example, a breech-loading swivel gun dated 1563 was recovered in 1905 from the Armada wreck of the *San Juan de Sicilia* in Scotland's Tobermory Bay. More recently another 1588 Armada wreck, the *Trinidad Valencera,* which went down off Northern Ireland, has yielded what is believed to be a Venetian swivel gun (*falcón pedrero*), whose barrel is of bronze and its breech is iron. Such a metal combination lying on the wet Roanoke earth for three years could almost certainly lead to bronze being mistaken for iron. But even without the iron component, under the right climatic conditions, copper alloys will darken to brown rather than turn green. That being so, we should not too quickly dismiss the possibility that regardless of Lawson's finding only two guns, he and White had been viewing the same scene at different stages of its devolution.

Because in 1586 Lane's people had departed in too great haste to try to ship out heavy artillery, their guns should have been still there when White returned in 1587. We know, too, that regardless of the guns left behind in June 1586, when Grenville landed his small garrison, he provided it with four iron guns of unspecified caliber. Why those were needed when Lane's guns should still have been there is unclear. Then, too, it is highly probable that not knowing what to expect, White's 1587 settlers would have brought their own artillery, for these were the people who were to establish Britain's military foothold on the Chesapeake. All in all, therefore, the Roanoke settlement site should have been replete with hard-to-heave artillery, yet when White returned in 1590, he found only the light guns and only the shot for the massive sakers. Looking, he said, "for any of the last Falkons [weight eleven hundred pounds] and small Ordinance which were left with them," he walked to the northeastern shore of the island "toward the poynt of the Creeke," searching, too, for "any of their botes or Pinnisse."[38] He found nothing. But that White went looking is significant, for there evidently had been a developed landing place where the pinnace docked and heavy goods were brought ashore and carried to the fort and settlement.

To what extent the northern end of the island has been eroded by tide and wind since the sixteenth century remains an important but unresolved question. Nevertheless, one has only to examine the existing escarpment to see how vulnerable it is. Indeed, Phillip Evans's discovery of one or more wood-lined wells fifty feet out into the sound is clear evidence of heavy erosion.

Lining well shafts with bottomless barrels was a practice in England at least as early as the first century A.D., and, more pertinent, it was employed in the vicinity of Roanoke Island before June 1588. How do we know this? Because a visiting Spaniard said so.

Captain Vicente Gonzáles had been sent north from St. Augustine in a bark carrying thirty soldiers and sailors, their mission to find the English settlement which Philip of Spain believed to have been established on the Chesapeake Bay. On his way back, having failed to find any trace of the English or their Cittie of Ralegh, Gonzáles faced strong contrary winds off the Outer Banks and had to strike his sails and use oars to carry his ship through an inlet into the safety of Pamlico Sound. Although the summary of his voyage is imprecise, it seems likely that he proceeded north past Roanoke Island and departed through another unidentified opening that took him back into the Atlantic, where he deduced the latitude to be 30°50′N and approximately level with the modern village of Salvo. Somewhere along the way, "on the inside of a little bay," Gonzáles came upon a "slipway for small vessels, and on land a number of wells made with English casks, and other debris indicating that a considerable number of people had been here."[39]

Try as one may to equate the cask-constructed wells with the barrels found by Evans in 1982, logic insists that if the Spaniards landed on the north end of Roanoke Island and examined the ground with sufficient care to look down the wells and to identify their linings, not just as casks but as *English* casks, it is inconceivable that they would have failed to notice something as big as a palisaded fort. The explanation has to be that Gonzáles found the boat slip and other evidences of English occupation on the sound side of the Outer Banks adjacent to one of the inlets. Less arguable, however, is the conviction that by the time Gonzáles entered Pamlico Sound in the spring of 1588 White's colonists had gone both from Roanoke Island and from the Outer Banks.

In 1590 John White knew nothing of Gonzáles's visit and had to try to figure out for himself how much time had elapsed since his people had departed. Returning to the fort from his search for boats, he was met by several sailors who reported having found "where divers chests had bene hidden, and long sithence digged up againe and broken up."[40] When they showed him the spot, this is how White described the scene:

> Presently Captaine Cooke [Cocke] and I went to the place, which was in the ende of an olde trench . . . wheere wee found five Chests, that had bene carefully hidden of the Planters, and of the same chests three were my owne, and about the place many of my things spoyled and broken, and my bookes torne from the covers, the frames of some of my pictures and Mappes rotten and spoyled with rayne, and my armour almost eaten through with rust; this could bee no other but the deede of the Savages our enemies at Dasamongwepeuk, who had watched the departure of our men to Croatoan; and assoone as they were departed, digged up every place where they suspected any thing to be buried: but although it much grieved me to see such spoyle of my goods, yet on the other side I greatly joyed that I had safely found a certaine token of their safe being at Croatoan. . . .[41]

White was almost certainly correct in assuming that the Indians had looted the settlement just as soon as its inhabitants were out of musket range. The likelihood that months or years would elapse before they dug up the chests makes no sense. Indeed, once a season's weeds grew over the burial place, it would have been extremely hard to find. The crucial question, therefore, is how long would it take the paper of White's books, maps, and pictures to decay. Modern paper turns brown in the sunlight within days and becomes brittle in a matter of weeks, and in a few months wind and rain would cause the outer leaves to disintegrate. But that was not true of rag paper or vellum, both of which were much more durable.

We have to remind ourselves that John White the 1587 governor was almost certainly John White the artist who had accompanied Grenville and Lane in 1585 and whose renderings of Virginia Indians and wildlife are among the surviving glories of Elizabethan watercoloring. Now he had returned to find the frames of his pictures and maps "rotten and spoyled with rayne." It is curious, therefore, that he fussed over the damaged frames but said nothing about the effects of time and rain on the paintings and maps themselves. Was he perhaps referring to painters' frames for stretching canvases rather than to standard mounts for finished work? But since White was a watercolorist, not a painter in oils, this explanation seems farfetched. Another explanation might be that he was referring to the stringed frames called *reticula* that are used by artists to reduce and enlarge their subjects. But here again the contextual language speaks against it.

Several other pieces of slightly less questionable information can be culled from White's description of what he found in the violated chests. First, the chests themselves: Assuming that he had taken one chest home with him in 1587, we can conclude that the possessions of someone as senior as the governor of the Cittie of Ralegh were limited to the cubic capacity of four chests. Then the maps and paintings: If we accept the premise that they were to be displayed in frames, it follows that White expected to embellish his Virginia home with the cultural niceties of Elizabethan England. Finally, the armor: He found it almost eaten through with rust. Steel is slower to rust than is less-tempered iron, so to reach the stage of being eaten through would take at least a year and probably much longer. The presumption, however, would be that the linings and connecting leathers would decay first, though White makes no reference to those. No less curious is the fact that looting Indians (who previously had salvaged nails from shipwrecks) would have found neither ornamental nor practical uses for the parts of plate armor.

Regardless of the inconsistencies, one is forced to conclude that on the evidence of the rusted armor, John White's chests had been looted at least a year before he found them. On the other hand, the survival of his books after their covers had been ripped off (possibly because they were embellished with stamped metal corners and clasps attractive to the Indians) makes it unlikely that they would have survived in any booklike condition for more than two years. The evidence thus points to the colonists' departure in the spring of 1588 or at least before Vicente González stopped by in June or July.

While White stood at trenchside, bemoaning the fate of his possessions, sailors were nervously watching the scudding clouds, listening to the rising wind, and forecasting "a foule and stormie night." They were right, and the next morning the fleet left Port Ferdinando to drop down to Croatoan Island. But the weather grew worse, anchors were lost, and Captain Cocke decided that trying to go ashore at Croatoan was out of the question. Having been unable to take on freshwater before the storm broke or to set out on an Atlantic crossing without it, Cocke proposed to return to Puerto Rico and winter in the Caribbean, a proposal White accepted (he really had no choice), while demanding an assurance that come spring they would return to resume the search. Cocke agreed, but the acting captain of the supply-carrying *Moonlight* decided that his ship was leaking too badly to stay over and headed home. John White had to know that in the privateering business neither promises nor contracts stood much chance in the face of a fair wind and a Spanish sail; nevertheless, if he wanted to see Croatoan again, he had to sit out the winter in the hope of rejoining his people albeit three years late and without the help they had sent him to obtain.

The plan lasted all of two days. Sailing south into contrary winds proved too much, and Cocke changed his mind and decided to head for the Azores, take on water, then double back to the Caribbean. Although he had left England with a three-ship flotilla and reached Virginia with three, they were not the same vessels. Those that dropped anchor off the Outer Banks were Cocke's *Hopewell*, Spicer's *Moonlight*, and a prize picked up in the Caribbean. Left down there chasing more and bigger quarry were William Lane on the *John Evangelist* and the expedition's Vice Admiral Christopher Newport aboard the *Little John*. When Cocke reached the Azores, both ships were already there, along with their only prize, a sixty-ton Spaniard, the *Trinidad*, carrying a valuable but dull cargo of hides, ginger, and the like. The news from Captains Newport and Lane was not good, as Cocke could plainly see. Newport was missing an arm. He had lost it in a costly battle with a Spanish galleon of the silver *flota* which, though taken, was so badly damaged that she sank before her cargo could be transferred. A second target went aground, and she, too, sank with her cargo unsnatched. With twenty-four men dead, and both the English ships in bad shape, Newport and Lane had headed for home by way of the Azores.

On learning all this and being without his supporting privateers, Captain Cocke agreed that it was indeed time to go home, though he was briefly dissuaded by the presence of a large English squadron commanded by Sir John Hawkyns lying in wait for the annual Spanish treasure convoy. The opportunity to share in the fun prompted Cocke to join the fleet, but on October 1, 1590, after word arrived that they had missed the Spaniards, Cocke set his course for Plymouth.

So ended John White's search for his Lost Colony. Since Cocke's ships had fired their heavy guns to attract attention as they lay off the

Outer Banks, we can reasonably suppose that had the settlers been on Croatoan they would have recognized the vessels as friendly and would have lit signal fires or answered with their own guns.

The mystery of Virginia's Lost Colony soon became perennial—hence Captain Seagull's misdated claim that "A whole country of English is there, man; bred of those that were left there in '79."

To the first James Towne settlers the fate of their predecessors was of more than passing interest, and as we shall see, the Indians naïvely or perhaps deliberately provided tantalizing hints that the 1587 colonists were still alive and living in the interior. The clues proved sufficiently intriguing that in December 1608 John Smith, who was then in command at James Towne, sent "Michael Sicklemore, a very honest, valiant, and painefull souldier, with him two [Indian] guids, and directions howe to search for the lost company of Sir Walter Rawley."[42] Sicklemore found no trace, nor did two other James Towne colonists who were sent out some months later on the same errand. A subsequently published account (for which the original documentation does not survive) did its best to put an end to speculation, claiming that Powhatan, overlord of the Tidewater Virginia tribes, had confessed to having "bin at the murther of that Colonie: and shewed to Captain Smith a Musket barrell and a brasse Morter, and certaine peeces of Iron which had bin theirs."[43] It was not the first time that Powhatan had been charged with the murders. In 1609 the Virginia Company's instructions to Sir Thomas Gates noted that he might yet find "foure of the englishe alive, left by Sr Walter Rawely wch escaped from the slaughter of Powhaton of Roanocke. . . . "[44]

Nonetheless, the legend survived these claims. Rumors persisted that four of John White's men were living with the Indians, and almost a hundred years later traveler John Lawson effectively kept that onetime possibility alive. The Hatteras Indians, wrote Lawson,

> . . . tell us that several of their Ancestors were white People and could talk in a Book as we do; the Truth of which is confirmed by gray Eyes being found frequently amongst these Indians and no others. . . . It is probable that this Settlement miscarried for want of timely Supplies from England; or through the Treachery of the Natives, for we may reasonably suppose that the English were forced to cohabit with them for Relief and Conversation; and that in process of Time, they conformed themselves to the Manners of their Indian Relations; And thus we see how apt Human Nature is to degenerate.[45]

Lawson's final thought on the subject is graphic proof that English arrogance and disdain for the Indians and their culture had not changed an iota in a century of opportunities to do so. He, on his dying day, however, would have considered his point amply proved. In 1711, while exploring in the same Neuse River area where Grenville and Lane had found the natives hostile, Lawson met his death at the hands of the Catechna Indians, his tortured body reportedly pierced by countless pine bark splinters which when lit turned him into a living torch.

CHAPTER IV

West from the Azores

J OHN WHITE'S empty-handed return put Virginia on the back burner for a decade and more, but it did nothing to dissuade the English from the notion that the Spanish Caribbean had become a privateer's playground, and in the years immediately after the 1588 routing of Philip's first Armada, more than a hundred quasi-piratical expeditions left English ports. Among the men in command were the one-armed Christopher Newport and George Somers, later admiral of the ill-fated Third Supply to Jamestown in 1609. Because Newport led both the first and second fleets to Virginia, the scope of his previous exploits has relevance insofar as they convinced the patentees of the Virginia Company of London (of whom Somers was one) that Newport was a man well practiced in American waters.

Leaving the Thames in January 1592, Newport took a fleet of three ships and a pinnace on a West Indian tour which, in the space of seven months, claimed the destruction of four Spanish towns, the sinking of seventeen Spanish ships, and the bringing home of two more. One of the seventeen proved to be a three-hundred-ton Lisbon slaver carrying as many "Negros young and olde" to Cartagena.[1] This being a cargo for which Newport had no use, he set the Portuguese merchant ashore about three miles from San Juan, Puerto Rico, and told him to find a buyer. To Newport's surprise the merchant preferred to cut his losses and failed to return. After waiting all day, the fleet sailed on up the coast a distance of thirty miles, released the blacks ashore to fend for themselves, and then burned their ship. Apologists for subsequent slavery in Virginia have pointed out that (Drake's lost passengers notwithstanding) it was the Dutch, not the English, who in 1619 first introduced blacks into the colony. But as we have seen, English merchants had been in the Guinea trade for decades. Men like Newport had had ample opportunity to weigh the merits and disadvantages of black labor and would not have thought twice about using it if need and profit had coincided.

Of more immediate significance to promoters of the notion that gold and silver waited to be wrested from other New World inhabitants besides the Incas and Aztecs was Captain Newport's reported experience at the end of his Caribbean foray. On one of "certeine islands within the point of Florida," probably somewhere in the Bahamas, Newport sent his pinnace ashore in search of freshwater. Although the sailors failed to locate it, they "found the Savages very courteous unto us, who came brest high into the sea, and brought us a line to hall in our boat on shore, and shewed us that up into the land Northward was fresh water, and much golde."[2] Here were the basic ingredients for the happy privateer: water and gold. One may wonder how the crew managed to get that idea across to the alleged savages, who were unlikely to have rated gold on a par with water among life's primary necessities, yet Newport's men did so and quickly discovered a buyer's market. The boatswain's mate gleefully traded "an olde rusty hatchet" for a piece of gold worth about ten English shillings (probably sixty times the value of the hatchet) and worn at the knee of one of the Indians.[3]

Stories like these did much to restore the confidence of investors who may have vainly combed the reports of Lane and White for similar encounters with the locals. If the Indians of offshore Florida wore gold as garters, would the Virginia savages be as forthcoming?

Other, more farsighted commercial adventurers could see beyond pillage and the checkmating of Spain, and had done so for years. In 1583 Sir George Peckham, principal backer of Humphrey Gilbert's Newfoundland fiasco, saw a variety of benefits, not the least of them an opportunity to assist the depressed English cloth trade by selling haberdashery to the Indians. It was well known, he claimed, that the Indians, "so soone as they shall begin but a little to taste of civility, will take marvelous delight in any garment, be it never so simple; as a shirt, a blew, yellow, red, or greene cotton cassocke, a cap, or such like, and will take incredible paines for such a trifle." Although Sir George failed to stipulate how the Indians would pay for the goods, he was convinced that England's ailing cloth trade towns and villages "shal by this meanes be restored to their pristinate wealth and estate."[4]

Peckham had other ideas that would have been more convincing to some elements of the population than to others. America, he said, would be a good place to dump undesirables "which do now live idly at home, and are burthenous, chargeable, & unprofitable to this realme. . . ." The same, he claimed, applied to children aged twelve to fourteen and to "idle women which the Realme may well spare,"[5] all of whom could be put to work in the New World for the betterment of the Old. It was an idea whose time had almost come, and one that would persist until the mid-nineteenth century, when, in the face of rising Australian protest, the transportation of felons was abolished by means of the Penal Servitude Acts of 1855 and 1857. Peckham's proposal was to be activated first in 1619, when, by royal warrant, a hundred "dissolute persons" were shipped to Virginia. The City of London's Common Council saw this as an opportunity to get rid of a hundred children out of its "superfluous mulititude" but quickly ran into a problem, reporting that "Now it falleth out that among those Children, sundry being ill disposed, and fitter for any remote place then for this Citie, declare their unwillingnes to goe to Virginia: of whom the Citie is especially desirous to be disburdened; and in Virginia under severe Masters they may be brought to goodnes."[6]

But 1619 was a long time into the future. Sir George Peckham did not live to see his propositions put into practice, dying in penury in 1608, unable to contribute to the ultimate Virginia adventure. However, one of his contemporaries with similar ideas stood front and center as the new plans to plant English in America took shape. He was Sir John Popham, lord chief justice of England, remembered by John Aubrey, albeit incorrectly, as the man who "first set afoot the Plantations—e.g. Virginia—which he stocked or planted out of all the gaols of England."[7] He had, nonetheless, been part author of an act of Parliament authorizing banishment "into such parts beyond the seas as shall be at any time hereafter for that purpose assigned" simply as the punishment for vagrancy.[8]

Popham played a major behind-the-scenes role in persuading James I to grant several of his "loving and weldisposed subjects" the first Virginia charter, among them his kinsman George, who, along with Sir Walter Ralegh's cousin Raleighe Gilberde (Gilbert), was to lead a northerly colonizing expedition to parallel the James Towne enterprise. Although this Sagadahoc Colony was destined to fail, its brief occupancy at the mouth of Maine's Kennebec River is of great importance in that it bequeathed us a plat of the township called Fort St. George. Because, through either ill luck or negligence, the James Towne settlers left no plan nor even a single sketch of anything they built, the Popham drawing becomes a pearl of no little price.

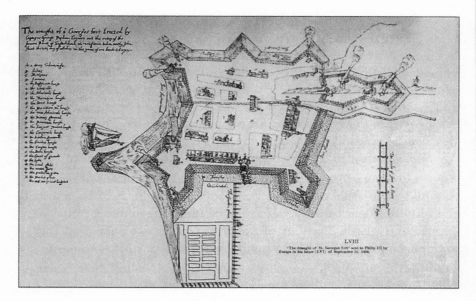

Plan of Fort St. George on the Kennebec, 1607; forwarded from
London to Philip III of Spain in September 1608.

Although the North American coast had been poked and prodded
with increasing frequency during the second half of the sixteenth century,
nobody, Spaniard, Frenchman, or Englishman, had shown any enthusiasm for probing to any depth the rocky shores which by the turn of the
century were known to the English as the northern part of Virginia.
Basque, French, Portuguese, and English fishing fleets had long crowded
the codfish banks and thus become familiar with the shores and inhabitants of Newfoundland, and Spanish God-promoting sorties had carried
missionaries and their protectors north from St. Augustine to the Chesapeake; but although ships of many nationalities sailed from the Caribbean
up the New England coast, few found the forests behind its jagged shore
and treacherous reefs worth the risk of more than spyglass inspection.
What excuse mariners offered for passing up New Jersey seems to have
gone unrecorded.

Both generalizations and summaries can get their authors into deep
trouble, and in focusing on events bearing on the James Towne settlement, I have been negligent of the French, save for a passing reference to
their 1565 Fort Caroline in Florida. Unlike the Spaniards, the French were
not seen as a threat either to the Roanoke colonists or to their James
Towne successors; but to Englishmen whose eyes turned northward, the
French were the chief competitors. Since the 1580s it was there that the
French looked for fish and furs rather than compete with Spain for bul-

lion in the Caribbean. France's interest in the New World was, however, more venerable than that, dating back to 1523, when the Florentine navigator Giovanni da Verrazano, on behalf of Francis I, mapped and described the American coast from Florida to New England. Eleven years later Jacques Cartier began the series of voyages to the Gulf of the St. Lawrence that were to inscribe "Nova Francia" on future maps of North America, though it was not until the entry of Samuel de Champlain and his founding of Quebec in 1608 that New France became a formidable reality. For our purposes, however, the French remain only an *éminence blanc* far off in the inhospitable north—at least until 1611, when Louis XIII somewhat presumptuously granted to the French Jesuits everything from the St. Lawrence to Florida.

In March 1602 two almost simultaneous expeditions departed England, one sponsored by Sir Walter Ralegh, leaving from Weymouth and going south under the command of Samuel Mace in yet another attempt to locate the Lost Colony, and the other with thirty-two men aboard the "good ship the Concord" sailing out of Falmouth north to the vicinity of the forty-third parallel. Whereas virtually all previous voyages had taken either the northern route down from Newfoundland or the southerly up from the Caribbean, the *Concord* went out the way others came back: via the Azores directly across to the continental coast—and the vicinity of Concord, New Hampshire. The first landfall, however, has been estimated as somewhat farther north, around Maine's Casco Bay.

Sponsoring the *Concord* expedition was Shakespeare's wealthy and influential friend Henry Wriothesley, third earl of Southampton, and commanding it were the highly experienced ex-privateer Captain Bartholomew Gosnold and his goldsmith cousin Bartholomew Gilbert. That the New England Indians had had previous encounters with Europeans was immediately apparent. Coming out in a sail-driven Basque shallop, six Indians boarded the *Concord,* one of them wearing a waistcoat, breeches, stockings, and shoes, acquired from the same source as the boat. Though he was somewhat overdressed by comparison with his five naked companions, the Indians impressed their visitors as being "a people tall of stature, broad and grym visaged."[9] That impression was to be neither tested nor cemented, for Gosnold could find no safe harbor and headed south to add two names to the American map: Cape Cod and Martha's Vineyard.

After exploring the islands of Nantucket Sound, Gosnold chose the one he called Elizabeth Island (now Cuttyhunk, the most southerly in the chain forming the tail of the Barnstable peninsula) and there proposed to

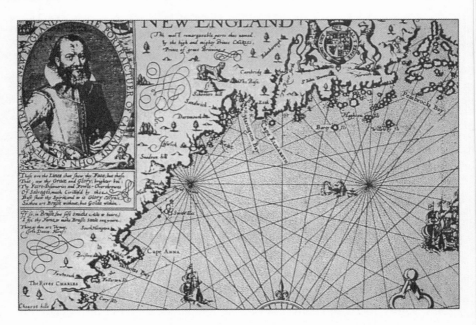

John Smith's map of New England, 1616.

stay. He sowed trials of wheat, barley, oats, and peas and saw them sprout nine inches tall in two weeks. Food was plentiful, the grass was green, and the natives were friendly and ready to trade—too ready, as it turned out.

Gosnold's plan was to remain with eleven volunteers while Gilbert sailed the *Concord* home to report the discovery of this earthly heaven and to return in the spring with more people and fresh supplies. To that end the crew spent three weeks building a large house for the dozen who were to stay, as the Indians continued to bring in an ever-growing variety of furs from beaver to seal, all in exchange for "knives, babies' beades, and such toyes."[10] As they watched the bales being loaded aboard the *Concord* and estimated the profit to be shared among the returnees, the eleven volunteers changed their minds. Home, they concluded, was where the hides were, so Gosnold had no choice but to sail away, leaving his new house to the doubtless puzzled Indians.

Besides the furs, Gosnold filled his holds with cedarwood and sassafras roots (selling at three shillings a pound, it was considered just the thing for curing the *lues venerea*) and expected to be received in England with unbridled delight. Not so, at least not entirely. Although one report suggests that Sir Walter Ralegh had authorized, if not contributed to, the voyage, he clearly did not recall it when he turned up at the port of Weymouth to see one of his own ships come in. There he found Gilbert unloading twenty-two hundred pounds of sassafras, this being the residue after his investors had carted their share away to London. Assuming that any bits of America not controlled by other Christian princes were part of Virginia and therefore his by royal patent, Ralegh promptly confiscated the sassafras. He not only charged Gosnold and Gilbert with poaching on his territory but damned them for bringing in so large a supply that they were ruining the market for himself and everybody else. Not content with grabbing the sassafras, on learning that twenty-six cedar trees had been off-loaded at Dartmouth, Ralegh wrote to the secretary of state seeking the right to seize those, too. Nevertheless, in spite of Ralegh's unexpected preference for putting profit before patriotism, the voyage of the *Concord* was widely hailed as another successful step toward planting England in America.

Samuel Mace's Lost Colony search, on the other hand, proved less successful. He reached the American coast closer to Cape Fear than to Cape Hatteras and spent a month trading with Indians who knew or professed to know nothing of the English colonists. Having taken on a cargo also largely devoted to sassafras, Mace made no effort to land at Croatoan or Hatteras Island and instead returned to England, claiming that bad weather and lost anchors had kept him from his mission.

Although gold glittered best in the imagination, sassafras had its own appeal, and in April 1603 a consortium of Bristol merchants sent out an expedition specifically designed to import its root and bark. Two ships, the fifty-ton *Speedwell* and twenty-six-ton *Discoverer,* were commanded by Captain Martin Pring, a man remarkable, at least in modern eyes, for assuming so great a responsibility at the age of only twenty-three. Of particular interest is the listing of the "slight Merchandizes" that Pring took with him to trade with the Indians: "Hats of divers colours, greene, blue and yellow, apparell of coarse Kersie and Canvasse readie made, Stockings and Shooes, Sawes, Pick-axes, Spades and Shovels, Axes, Hatchets, Hookes, Knives, Sizzers, Hammers, Nailes, Chissels, Fish-hookes, Bels, Beades, Bugles, Looking-glasses, Thimbles, Pinnes, Needles, Threed, and such like."[11] The popular notion that all one needed for the Indian trade was beads and hatchets clearly had not taken root (if it ever did) when Pring's sponsors were getting their kit together. Excavations of a Wampanoag burial ground at Burr's Hill in Rhode Island and another of the neighboring Narragansetts near Jamestown on Conanicut Island both have yielded European metal and some textile artifacts closely paralleling Pring's inventory.

Following Gosnold's course, Pring struck west from the Azores and reached land more or less where his predecessor had. After sailing a short distance up two rivers (one of them undoubtedly the Kennebec), Pring headed south into what he named Whiston Bay (now Cape Cod Bay) and went ashore to set up a palisaded encampment. Its site is traditionally thought to have been on the secondary bay later to enter history as Plymouth Harbor; but more recently the theory of an entirely different location at the tip of Cape Cod in the vicinity of present-day Provincetown has gained supporters. Indisputable, however, is the fact that Pring erected a fortified compound and remained for seven weeks, planting the mandatory wheat, barley, oat, and pea seeds and watching them obligingly pop up.

Pring's account of his now-questioned "Plymouth" habitat was full of enthusiasm for the promise of this northern part of Virginia. It also included a passing observation which reveals much about the hard-to-appreciate juxtaposition of delicacy and crudity that was characteristic of life in the colonizing years. One sees it in the fragility of drinking glasses found in the garbage pits of rude James Towne period homes, in the contrast between the splendid gilded, decorative woodwork aboard even modest ships and the appalling belowdecks conditions experienced by their crews, and in the lace collars and golden garters of soldiers with beer on their breaths and blood on their swords. Pring's company included two huge mastiffs capable of carrying eight-foot pikes in their mouths (to scare the wits out of threatening natives) and a boy who played a fragile stringed instrument called a gittern—and used it to set nonthreatening Indians to dancing. A gittern (or cithern) was an elaborately crafted instrument akin to a guitar and more suited to accompanying love songs than rowdy sailors' shanties. Nevertheless, I was reminded of Pring's musician when I was cataloging artifacts brought up from the 1619 wreck of the *Warwick* at Bermuda, for among them was the boxwood bridge from a multistringed instrument—testimony to gentler moments in a violent age.

Pring's was not a colonizing mission, and having loaded his ships with sufficient sassafras to satisfy his sponsors, he was ready to sail for home. Not having experienced the hardships of winter in New England, he returned filled with enthusiasm for the trading and settling potential of the coastal region north from Cape Cod to Casco Bay. There was, however, no immediate rush to pursue it.

At least three more English attempts to settle dissenters from both ends of the religious spectrum in the New World preceded the granting of a royal charter to the Virginia Company of London. Two were led by the merchant and sailor Charles Leigh, who first tried to plant Puritan

A 1706 Dutch engraving of Martin Pring's encampment in
Massachusetts in 1603. Note mastiff kennels flanking the entrance
and Indians dancing to the music of a gittern.

separatists on the Magdalen Islands in the Gulf of St. Lawrence, only to
be driven off by Basque and Breton walrus hunters. He and Martin Pring
then took another group to a no more hospitable region—the jungled and
fever-ridden Guiana coast of South America, an ill-starred enterprise
that cost Leigh his life.

Underwritten by the earl of Southampton and Sir Thomas (soon to be
Baron) Arundell and commanded by Captain George Waymouth, the
third voyage had been designed to establish an American colony for
English Catholics, but when men prominent among them saw the
expected exodus as a betrayal of British Catholicism, the voyage became
no more than another probe to locate the right place to found a later settlement. A single ship, the *Archangel,* with a company of only twenty-
seven men left Ratcliffe on the Thames on March 5, 1605. Aboard was a
Catholic scholar, James Rosier, a veteran of the 1602 Gosnold exploration, and it was he who wrote the necessarily upbeat account of the new
enterprise.

Fortunately for Rosier, he did not have to stretch his imagination, for
all went relatively well—with the possible exception that the wind blew
the *Archangel* north of Cape Cod when Waymouth had intended to
explore to its south. Thus another English expedition found itself stand-

ing off the Maine coast near the mouth of the Kennebec River. Way-mouth and his crew went ashore on what is now Allen's Island and there planted their sample barley and pea seeds, which sprouted a commend-able eight inches in sixteen days. They also assembled their pinnace (which they had brought over as a kit) and used it to explore the neigh-boring islands and estuaries. That the Waymouth expedition had a dis-tinctly Catholic bias is suggested by Rosier's note that "The Iland where we watered is named Insula Sanctae Crucis, because there wee set our first Crosse."[12] Apart from confirming that summer in Maine was a pleas-ant experience and that virtually any promontory or bay around the Ken-nebec would be a good place to build, the Waymouth reconnaissance's principal achievement proved to be the hijacking of two canoes and five Indians.

If Rosier is to be believed, the captives accepted their predicament with surprisingly good grace. On the voyage back to England they learned enough English to provide information about their crafts and cul-ture, and on arrival they conducted themselves in what was recognized as a commendably civilized manner. The five were by no means the first to have been stared at in England. Manteo and Wanchese had been followed by others brought back by later expeditions, and in September 1603 a number of Indians gave a demonstration of canoe paddling on the Thames for the edification of antiquary Sir Walter Cope and others with a growing interest in doing business in America. Those Indians were given nine shillings for their trouble and thus earned their otherwise face-less place in history.

While English entrepreneurs gauging the waters of profit in America looked at the Indians either as potential opponents or as markets, schol-ars were eyeing them as clues to their own European ancestry. Was it possible, antiquaries were asking themselves, that just as the newly dis-covered Americans were still using stone and wooden tools and weapons, so there had once been a pre-Metal Age in Europe? Might this not explain the similar stone axes and tools that turned up from time to time in English fields? Such questions had begun to be asked early in the six-teenth century, notably by the father of palaeontology, Michele Mercati (1541–93), longtime superintendent of the Vatican's botanical gardens, who had the opportunity to study the growing collection of American curiosities presented to the popes by Italian, Portuguese, and Spanish explorers.

By 1590, when Théodore de Bry illustrated Thomas Hariot's account of the Roanoke experience based on John White's paintings, de Bry

John White's watercolored drawings of ancient Picts, male and female, were used by de Bry as an appendix to Hariot's report to make the point that the British had once been as "savvage" as the sixteenth-century inhabitants of Virginia. Variations on these images were to become the standard interpretations of ancient Britons, here on a page from John Speed's *Historie of Great Britaine* (1632 edition).

appended five very similar-looking engravings "for to showe how that the Inhabitants of the great Bretannie have bin in times past as savvage as those of Virginia."[13] However, he avoided the mistake, later made by Isaac de la Peyrère of Bordeaux, of defining the times past. De la Peyrère rashly published his belief that European stone objects popularly identified as thunderbolts were relics of an ancient race preceding Adam and Eve, a proposition so theologically unacceptable that in 1655 he was seized by the Inquisition and was lucky to escape joining his books on the bonfire. "I doubt not but that you have often seen these Arrow-heads they ascribe to elfs or fairies," wrote British antiquary Edward Lloyd in 1699; "they are just the same chip'd flints the natives of New England head their arrows with at this day: and there are also several stone hatchets found in this kingdom, not unlike those of the Americans."[14]

Such arcane interests were shared by few of the hard-nosed businessmen of London and Bristol who met in 1606 to plan a future for the flint-chipping Americans. Sir Walter Ralegh, a founding member of the Society of Antiquaries and one who undoubtedly was interested in the potential relationship between English and American prehistory, was no longer at the forefront of Virginia voyaging. Instead he was a prisoner in the Tower of London, condemned for allegedly plotting the death of James I, his sentence pronounced by another key figure in the Virginia story, Lord Chief Justice of the King's Bench Sir John Popham.

George Waymouth returned from his March 1605 expedition in July, whereupon James Rosier's account was rushed into print to add documentation to the word-of-mouth plaudits, all of which prompted another player to join the game to replace an old one who had dropped out. Sir Thomas Arundell, since elevated to Lord Arundell of Wardour, had lost interest in founding a colony of Catholics in America and had turned his attention to raising an English Catholic regiment for service in the Netherlands. Thus the way was opened for another suspected Catholic sympathizer to step forward. In October 1605 Sir John Zouche of Codnor Park in Derbyshire entered into an agreement with Waymouth to set up a northern Virginia colony with Zouche as "Lorde Paramount" and Waymouth in "the next place of Commaunde unto himselfe aswell at sea as at land."[15] The prospect of such a private princedom being set up as part of the English realm did not sit well with the new administration, and it was Sir John Popham who led the charge to transform the practice of private adventuring with royal blessing, characteristic of the previous reign, into a more businesslike and unified arrangement operating as a controlled element of the nation's foreign policy. Popham proposed an amalgamation of the West of England interests, centered on Plymouth, Exeter, and Bristol, with those of London, the former focusing on northern Virginia and the latter on the south.

After several meetings a draft proposal was submitted through Lord Salisbury, the king's principal secretary of state, and it eventually became the charter that received royal approval on April 10, 1606. The company was to have two branches, the First (London) to form the southern colony and the Second (Plymouth) to establish the northern. In the words of the first charter, the king commended "soe noble a worke" as an instrument tending to the glory of God in "propagating of Christian religion to suche people as yet live in darkenesse. . . ."[16] The territorial scope of that darkness was defined as follows:

> . . . a colonie of sondrie of our people into that parte of America commonly called Virginia, and other parts and territories in America either appartaining unto us or which are not nowe actuallie possessed by anie Christian prince or people, scituate, lying and being all along the sea coastes between fower and thirtie degrees of

northerly latitude from the equinoctiall line and five and fortie
degrees of the same latitude and in the maine lande betweene the
same fower and thirtie and five and fourtie degrees, and the ilandes
thereunto adjacent or within one hundred miles of the coaste
thereof.[17]

The Company's London and Plymouth branches were instructed to be
separated from each other by a hundred miles, but at the same time the
areas decreed as being under the control of each overlapped by three
degrees of latitude. The London Company's territory would stretch from
the thirty-fourth to the forty-first parallel, and the Plymouth from the
thirty-eighth to the forty-fifth. In modern terms the overlap extended
from the Virginia-Maryland state line on the Eastern Shore up almost to
the northern tip of Long Island. As for the unknown interior, the 1606
charter gave both companies the first hundred miles, plus the assurance
that no other Englishmen would be allowed to "plante or inhabit behinde
or on the backside of them"[18] without Privy Council approval.

In real estate terms the charter's wording annexed the entire continental coast from Cape Fear north to Eastport, Maine, on the modern Canadian frontier. Time, however, would show that just as the Spaniards were
unprepared to be told that Cape Fear was not part of La Florida, so the
French would not easily be persuaded to tear up any maps showing Nova
Francia reaching south to the forty-fourth parallel. Indeed, in 1605,
Samuel de Champlain had sailed as far south as Cape Cod looking for a
place to settle, went again the following year, but didn't stay. So it
remained an undeniable fact that for the English, the coast between the
thirty-fourth and forty-fifth parallels was conveniently devoid of Christian princes and thus anybody's for the asking—or taking.

The men named as grantees for the London Company were Sir
Thomas Gates (soon to be governor and a formidable administrator for
the Virginia colony); the newly knighted Sir George Somers (then mayor
of Lyme Regis and later admiral of the Third Supply); Richard Hakluyt,
editor of the *Principal Navigations;* and Edward Maria Wingfield, who
was to be elected first president of the council in Virginia. A matching
but less well-remembered foursome was named for the Plymouth Company: Thomas Hannam, recorder of Plymouth and Chief Justice Popham's
grandson; Raleigh Gilbert, Sir Walter's nephew; William Parker, ex-
privateer and mayor of Plymouth; and Popham's kinsman George.

In the summer of 1606, encouraged by Waymouth's report, Sir John
Popham financed something short of a shipload of planters to "settle a

plantacion in the river of Sachadehoc" (now a branch of the Kennebec), thus the first enterprise launched after the creation of the Virginia Company, whose planning preceded the London stockholders' James River–bound fleet by as much as six months. According to William Strachey, who later served as secretary at James Towne, Popham's ship sailed in "about Maye" with one Haines as master and Martyn Pryn (Martin Pring) as captain but was captured by a Spanish fleet off Graciosa Island in the Azores.[19] Other, more reliable deponents, who make no mention of Pring's involvement, name Henry Challons as captain, identify the master not as Haines but as Nicholas Hind, put the sailing date as August 12, and the encounter with the Spaniards in the vicinity of the Bahamas.

Such wide discrepancies among relatively contemporary accounts of the same incident demonstrate that any attempt to summarize events occurring four hundred years ago is akin to skating in lead boots on melting ice. Just how Strachey came to make so many mistakes will soon become evident. Nonetheless, Popham and his Plymouth associates did send out a small ship, the *Richard*, in August 1606, bound for Pemaquid on the Maine coast north of the Kennebec. Although Strachey called it a colonizing venture, the intent was less clear. Challons's instructions were that "if any good occasion were offered, to leave as many men as wee could spare in the Country."[20] The number available for sparing was quite small, for the total company amounted to only twenty-nine men, plus two of five Indians (Mannido and Assacomoit) brought to England in the previous year by George Waymouth.

With the direct Azores route well established, it is hard to understand why an exploratory and colonizing expedition bound for Maine should take the long southern route—unless old privateering blood still flowed in the veins of Captain Challons and his crew. But England had been at peace with Spain for the past two years, and the days of authorized piracy were suspended, if not past. As members of the *Richard*'s company told it, the ship had crossed on the usual southern course from the Canaries to St. Lucia, and from there sailed up past several West Indian islands, minding her own business (pausing only to rescue a Spanish priest), until caught in a hurricane about 180 leagues from Puerto Rico.

When the storm abated, the crew found themselves in a thick fog and in the middle of a Spanish fleet variously reported as eight or eleven merchant galleons. Lest there should be any misunderstanding of the *Richard*'s peaceful intent, Challons quickly raised the now officially friendly English flag. To his amazement, the response was a barrage of

James I, a painting by Marc Gheeraedts.

cannonballs that ripped his sails to shreds. The Spaniards' lead ship then closed with the *Richard* and boarded her. Although the English claimed to have put up no resistance, the Spaniards attacked them with rapiers, swords, and short pikes, severely wounding two of the crew and one of the Indians. The latter made the mistake of using his newly acquired English to explain that this was "King James his ship," a revelation that did nothing to discourage his attackers from stabbing him six times. A side note to the testimony highlighted the obvious: "King James his name little respected by Spaniards."[21]

The report claimed that the entire crew was beaten, stripped almost naked, and transferred to several of the Spanish ships, and after a voyage to Spain, during which they were given little water and only maggot-ridden food, most of the English were thrown into prison, accused of violating the territorial waters of the Spanish Empire. The affair of the *Richard* had created a nasty international incident with all sorts of equally nasty implications.

Since the peace with Spain in 1604, England had taken for granted that the major nations at least tacitly agreed to a global policy of freedom of the seas. In the same year the youthful jurist Hugo Grotius began work on behalf of the Dutch East India Company on a legal brief to that effect, a document which five years later was published as the famed *Mare liberum* and remains the cornerstone of international law governing the rights of passage on the high seas. Unfortunately no wording of that kind figured in James I's peace treaty with Spain. It allowed for unrestricted trade between English merchants and Spanish Europe, but it said nothing about the Elizabethans' claim to free trade and intercourse with Spanish America or the Portuguese colonies in Africa and Asia, and James had no desire to push for it.

Through the first years of his reign James I did little to suggest that he would be a champion and ally of the westward-looking merchant adventurers or that he would gird on the armor of Elizabeth to keep Spain on the defensive. James had seen enough bloodshed in his youth and had come south to England a pacifist, dourly suspicious of the remnants of Elizabeth's old order. Born to a kingdom with no seafaring history, he had no feel for the importance of sea power, and throughout his reign he allowed the navy that had been the nation's savior in 1588 to decline into impotence, thus weakening his position in dealings with Spain. Then, too, there was his almost paranoid hatred of tobacco—America's gift to mankind, the weed that led to "the horrible Stygian smoke of the pit that is bottomless."[22]

All in all, the steam had gone out of the Elizabethan Age, and where once the seizure of the *Richard* would have sent the likes of Drake and Frobisher out to pay the Spaniards back in spades, now the pros and cons were to be carefully and protractedly debated. With the Virginia Company charter granted, no one hoping to benefit from it was anxious to argue with Spain over whether or not Virginia was part of the "Indies," as the Spaniards claimed. Indeed, there were some who advised "that it were better to leave these prisonners [Challon and his crew] to their fortune, then by bringing it in question to stir up some greater inconveniences that might ensue of it."[23]

In Spain the British ambassador, Sir Charles Cornwallis, was doing his best to get Challons's men released, but he got nowhere with the Conde de Lemos, president of the Council for the Indies, and indeed was left with no doubts whatever on the Spanish view of foreign trade in the Caribbean. From their experience in the Netherlands, de Lemos explained, the interference of French, Germans, Dutch, and English only upset and confused people newly seasoned with the Catholic faith. Furthermore, the Spanish Empire in America was not yet sufficiently fortified and secure that it was ready to allow "hungry, or Curious eyes" to inspect so precious and desirable a jewel. And if that wasn't reason

enough, the Spanish considered that "the Dominion, Right, and possession, was theirs, and therefore Lawfull, both by rule of nature, and
nations, to appropriate it to themselves, and exclude others."[24]

This, then, was the atmosphere developing when the Plymouth and
London companies were bracing themselves to make major investments
in Virginia, and in the end it forced the king to commit himself to a
firmer stand in support of their right to pursue their colonial aims. In
doing so, he had the support of the average Englishman, for anti-
Catholic sentiment had hardened in the aftermath of the botched 1605
Gunpowder Plot, an allegedly papist conspiracy to dispose of both king
and Protestant Parliament in one big bang. Perhaps to make sure that the
English public got the point, Parliament ruled that the date should be "a
holiday for ever in thankfulness to God for our deliverance and detesta-
tion of the Papists."[25] Sir John Popham, incidentally, had been the presid-
ing judge at the conspirators' trial and was responsible for ordering the
torture that reduced Guido Fawkes to a shattered wreck before he finally
stumbled to the scaffold.

By the time the James River and Kennebec convoys sailed in their
respective directions, any illusions about treaty-created Spanish goodwill
had been dispelled. The papists were the sworn enemy of the English
Crown, and Spain was the pope's bloody instrument and, as far as the
London Company was concerned, the only real threat to its Virginia
enterprise. The "wilde, godlesse, and slavish Indian,"[26] as the king
described him, was more a nuisance than a menace.

The London Company's three ships sailed from the Thames on
December 20, 1606, took the southern route, and reached Martinique in
the West Indies on February 23, 1607. The Plymouth Company, however,
got off to a slower start (in the wake of the *Richard* debacle, which the
adventurers estimated had cost them five thousand pounds), and its full-
scale colonizing expedition did not depart on the Azores course until
June 1—nine days before Sir John Popham died. Two ships were involved,
the *Gift of God* (which Strachey called a flyboat), commanded by George
Popham, and the *Mary and John,* under Raleigh Gilbert; together they
carried 120 persons, but only 65 were destined to remain. This time the
leaders had very little doubt about where to settle.

Within days of the *Richard*'s sailing, Sir John Popham had sent out a
backup supply ship, captained by North Virginia patentee Thomas Hannam and with Martin Pring as master—hence Strachey's confusing the
latter with Henry Challons and, indeed, the whole *Richard* affair with
this Hannam-Pring supply. The ship (for which we have no name) took

the northern route, expecting to meet the *Richard* "at the place appointed," and when she failed to show up, Hannam took another good look at the coastline at the mouth of the Kennebec and returned with the conviction that it was not only a nice place to visit but a good place to stay. So Popham and Gilbert made for the same area. They got there on July 3 but then spent until August 18 exploring the neighboring islands and estuaries before they "mad Choies of a place for our plantation," the site "beinge almoste an Illand of a good bygness."[27] Although over the years historians have suggested various locations for its placement, today most agree that Popham and Gilbert chose what is now Sabino Point at the confluence of the Kennebec and Sagadahoc Rivers in the country of the Mawooshens, three of whose canoes paddled by at a safe distance while their new neighbors inspected the site.

As it was now late summer, one might have expected instant action from the crews. Instead August 19 was devoted to modified pomp: sermonizing from the preacher and the ceremonial reading of the Plymouth Company's patent "with the orders and Lawes thearin prescrybed." That done, everybody went back to the ships. Not until the next day did George Popham set spade in the ground to turn the first symbolic sod, whereupon—and this is where archaeologists' noses begin to twitch— "after hem all the rest followed and Labored hard in the trenches about ytt."[28] Unlike fortifications and buildings whose foundations may be laid on the earth's surface, trenches cut into the earth create scars much harder to eradicate and should survive to be revealed by excavation.

For the next several days all hands (with the exception of the ships' carpenters, who were building a shallop) continued to dig trenches and erect both the fort and a building in which to store the settlers' supplies. They were still at it twenty-two days later. Unfortunately we have no detailed eyewitness description of either fort or storehouse, nor do we know when they were completed. One version of the anonymous narrative ends on September 26, and another on October 6, the day that the *Mary and John*, captained by Robert Davies, set sail for England. The log of the extra days tells us only that between September 30 and October 2 everyone was "busye about the fort" and that on Sunday, the fourth, George Popham took five Indians as his guests "to the place of Publike prayers" for both morning and evening services.[29] Thereafter the published versions of the Sagadahoc story slip into the third person, and it is unclear who wrote what or when. Consequently, the all-important description of the settlement written after the ship sailed is of uncertain credibility. But this is what it says:

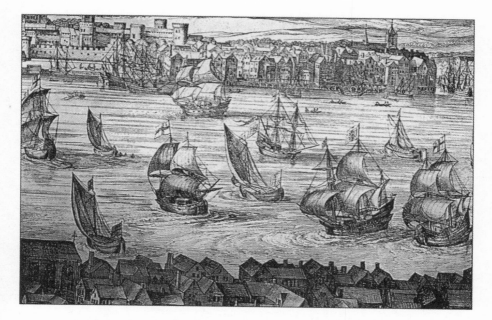

Oceangoing ships at anchor and under sail in the River Thames opposite the Tower of London. A detail from Claes Visscher's 1616 panorama.

After Captain Davies' departure they fully finished the fort, trencht and fortefied yt with twelve pieces of ordinaunce, and built fifty howses therein, besides a church and a storehowse; and the carpenters framed a pretty Pynnace of about some thirty tonne, which they called the *Virginia*. . . .[30]

Did they really build fifty houses inside their fort—to house a maximum of 65 people, 20 of whom were to go home in December? These are numbers of considerable relevance when we try to assess the needs of a maximum of 102 people at James Towne in the same year. Of even greater pertinence is the plan of Fort St. George dated October 8 and drawn by John Hunt, of whom absolutely nothing is known.

The plan fell into the hands of one of the more sinister figures lurking in the background of English-American history in the early seventeenth century: Pedro de Zúñiga, Philip III of Spain's ambassador in London. Along with other information he collected from spies and agents, Zúñiga sent the Hunt plan to his master in Seville and thence into the Royal Archives, where it was found in the 1890s by J. L. M. Curry, United States minister to Spain. Was Hunt among the sixty-five settlers who waved good-bye to the *Mary and John* on October 6, 1607, or was he perhaps looking the other way to watch the land recede? If the latter was true, did he spend the second day out making a finished copy of a measured plan he had drawn before he left, or was he sketching from memory before it faded and rendered his recollections even more inaccurate? If, on the other hand, Hunt remained behind, was he recording what had actually been built or was he stylizing the details so that viewers at home would recognize a church or a gate when they saw it marked? There can be no doubt that both a castellated and tower-flanked "water gate" protected by cruciform medieval archery slots and a "land gate" with corbeled turrets were far beyond the capabilities or needs of the colonists. That being so, how much more artistic license did the helpful Hunt exercise?

Even if we assume the worst, the placement of the artillery (one demiculverin, two sakers, two minions, and four falcons), the number and identification of the buildings, and the curious configuration of the enclosure all have the ring of authenticity—although the number of drawn cannon is three short of that given in Strachey's narrative.

Scholars who accepted that the fort stood at Sabino Point did so with the proviso that to fit the geography, one had to assume that Hunt greatly exaggerated the enclosure's size. However, in 1986, after studying all the surviving maps, National Geographic Society cartographer Andrew J. Wahll concluded that "the shoreline of Sabino Head changed more between 1857 and 1891 than between 1607 and 1857,"[31] and he was able to demonstrate that when the Hunt plan is superimposed on the 1857 map, it fits with impressive exactitude. In two seasons of very limited excavation in 1962 and 1964, the Maine State Parks and Recreation Commission found no traces of trenches, houses, or fortifications, but it did find a few European artifacts, most significant among them being several fragments of North Devonshire earthenware jars which have since been paralleled on Roanoke Island's 1585 science center site and aboard the wreck of the *Sea Venture* at Bermuda. That ship went down two years after the Popham colony was founded. Thus there is little doubt that such jars were available to Popham and Gilbert, who provisioned their ships at Plymouth in the county where the jars were made.

In the continuing search for what can best be described as the *character* of the Virginia Company's James Towne, no archaeological site ranks higher on the list of things needing to be completed than does the excavation of Sabino Point. But in the absence of renewed digging the written reference to Popham's fifty houses and the array of buildings shown on the Hunt plan remain as much at odds as do the palisades and houses on Roanoke Island. Far from drawing fifty houses, Hunt showed nine assigned to officers and key craftsmen, yet he specified none as quarters for the rest of the settlers. But since he showed six window openings in the attic of the store (a detail present in no other building), the presumption has to be that people of the lesser sort were housed there. The luckier ones were accommodated as follows:

President's house (Popham)   Sergeant major's house
Admiral's house (Gilbert)   Corporal's house
Munition master's house   Blacksmith's house
Vice admiral's house   Cooper's house
Provost's house

In addition to these living quarters, several other buildings are listed, most eventually having parallels at James Towne:

Munition house   Court of guard
Buttery general   Chapel
Kitchen general   Storehouse
Bakehouse

The Hunt plan also showed an elaborately laid-out garden outside the fort, protected on one side by a cliff, on another by the fort ditch, and on the two others by a highly fanciful fence with alternating tall and short posts, each capped by an elaborate finial. The gateway, as drawn, was even more grandiose and complemented at the corner by something that might be a garden house topped by a flag or weather vane. Nonsense though this rendering almost certainly was, the decision to lay out the garden beyond the protection of the fort speaks to the settlers' assumption that their Indian neighbors were not a problem—even though rumors circulated that not too far away lived a tribe of monstrous and cannibalistic Indians whose teeth were three inches long.

It turned out that the colony owed its undoing not to long-toothed neighbors but to the enemy within. Once the initial creative euphoria had worn off, internal disputes fostered the kind of glum disenchantment that slowly saps the strength of any organization. At Fort St. George the cancer grew from the top down, and from the several postmortems we learn its cause. President George Popham is described as "an honest man, but ould, and of an unwildly [unworldly] body, and timerously fearful to offende, or contest with others that will or do oppose him." His second-in-command, Raleigh Gilbert, on the other hand, was the opposite:

"desirous of supremasy, and rule, a loose life, prompte to sensuality, litle zeale in Religion, humerouse, head stronge, and of small judgment and experience. . . ." Collectively the settlers were riddled with "Childish factions" and with "ignorant timerous, and ambitiouse persons [who] hath bread an unstable resolution, and a generall confusion, in all theyr affayres."[32] The sad truth, of course, was that the kinds of stable, hardworking, and reliable people needed to ensure colonizing success were those least likely to volunteer.

The *Mary and John* reached Plymouth on December 1, 1607, and at once Sir Ferdinando Gorges (previously chief partner to the now-deceased Sir John Popham), eager to view the expected cargo of Virginian commodities, hurried aboard. Back onshore and writing to Secretary of State Lord Salisbury, he made no effort to hide his disappointment. Although his letter opened with "greate newes" of a fertile country with great rivers, excellent harbors, and tractable inhabitants, Gorges grimly ended the short catalog of pluses with the damning words "but no returne, to satisfy the expectation of the Adventureres."[33] Two days later, presumably after Captain Davies's more thorough debriefing, Gorges wrote again to the secretary of state giving his depressing assessment of the Popham personnel.

Meanwhile, at Fort St. George, glorious summer had given way to a winter of icy discontent. Rumors of an impending attack by the French from Canada had kept the expedition's second ship, the *Gift of God*, moored in the Kennebec longer than was good for her. The ice was thickening, and if she remained much longer, she would be imprisoned until the spring. She eventually left on December 16 with 50 men and boys aboard, an enormous number from an enterprise that had begun with only 120. Some, of course, were the *Gift*'s crew, who expected to leave anyway, but others evidently included many, like the cooper, who were still needed.

Providing food and drink for the entire Atlantic crossing and for so lengthy a departing passenger list was virtually impossible without endangering those who were to stay, so the council agreed that the ship's captain, John Elliott [Eliot], and its master, John Havercombe, should be free to sell their cargo of thirty-three masts to buy victuals when they reached the Azores. This they did, along with a cannon of saker size, and thereby refurbished, the *Gift of God* reached Plymouth on February 7, 1608. Three months later Havercombe was in jail, charged in the High Court of the Admiralty with having sold the masts which Sir John Popham's heirs claimed belonged to his estate. This mean-minded and picayune treatment is the clearest proof that the whole Popham enterprise had been funded, both monetarily and psychologically, at the nickel-and-dime level. Thus, after the return of the second profitless ship, Sir Ferdinando Gorges wrote to the secretary of state in even more disgusted terms. Only with new, on-site management, he contended, could the investors hope to reap the profits that the old leadership continued, fruitlessly, to promise.

If George Popham was aware of his failures and how his empty ships would be received by the Plymouth backers, he gave no hint of it when he sealed his letter to the king on December 13. His Majesty would be enraptured to know that on account of his "admirable justice and incredible constancy,"[34] wrote Popham, there was no one in the world more admired by the Indians than the king of England. Furthermore, they were confident that his God was better than theirs. Popham's letter points either to craven crawling to his king or to an astonishing level of naïveté in his acceptance of the Indians' assurances.

Popham was sure that His Majesty would want to know that the Indians had told him of a sea only seven days' march inland, "a sea large, wide and deep, of the boundaries of which they are wholly ignorant; which cannot be any other than the southern ocean, reaching to the regions of China, which unquestionably cannot be far from these parts."[35] We may wonder whether Popham might not have expected his royal reader to ask why, if the door to the Orient was only seven days distant, he hadn't sent somebody out to open it. Nevertheless, the statement is important as a reminder that the search for a western passage to the East was still the ultimate commercial prize.

To give the Indians their due, if Popham's explorers could have traveled about 280 miles west in the prescribed seven days, they would indeed have reached a sea large, wide, and deep. We know it now as Lake Ontario.

Sir Ferdinando Gorges's relief ship, commanded by the returning Captain Davies, did not reach the Kennebec until the summer of 1608, by which time George Popham was dead, and the settlers had survived a harsh Maine winter and were in no mood to face another. Davies had brought Raleigh Gilbert a letter telling him that his older brother, Sir John Gilbert, had died and that he, Raleigh, had inherited the estates. On reading the good news, Raleigh Gilbert took a very short time to conclude that there was more to be said for being a wealthy English country squire than the admiral or president pro tem of a godforsaken outpost of empire. When Gilbert announced his intention to quit and called for a volunteer to take his place, no one stepped forward. Instead everyone began packing.

The relief ship, accompanied by the thirty-ton pinnace *Virginia* (the first British ship built in America and thus perhaps the settlers' only praiseworthy accomplishment), took the last of the Popham people aboard on September 30, 1608. The next day the deserted Fort St. George began its slow process of vanishing into the earth. When the traveler Samuel Maverick visited the site in 1660, he "found Rootes and Garden hearbs and some old walls there . . . which shewed it to be the place where they had been."[36] So ended the story of the Popham Colony, and with it the future of the Plymouth branch of the Virginia Company.

CHAPTER V

Most Welcome and Fertile Place

"ON SATURDAY the twentieth of December in the yeere 1606. the fleet fell from London. . . ."[1] So began the story of James Towne and the first chapter in the history of modern Virginia. But for most of the passengers aboard the three ships it was as much an end as a beginning, the end of lives which henceforth would become increasingly distant in both miles and memories. In truth, the emigrants had only to look around at their fellow voyagers to recognize that many of the problems of the life they were leaving were sailing with them; but few, if any, believed that the future promised worse than the past. Whether or not it would do so depended in large measure on each person's aspirations, and those derived from (and were judged against) his previous experience. Furthermore, there were no women among the passengers, and that in itself had a bearing on the kind of world these first Virginians were about to create.

The England they were leaving inevitably was remembered differently by each according to his station. Much has been made of the charge that among the colonists were too many "gentlemen" and too few workers. But the disparity was not as marked as it has been drawn. It is true that of the known names, the gentlemen added up to forty-two by one count and fifty-four by another, while the rest, made up of craftsmen and laborers, accounted for only twenty-eight or thirty-one. To these, however, one must almost certainly add most of the people whose names appear on neither list and are simply thrown in at the end as "divers others," numbering either eighteen or thirty-eight.[2] By this reckoning the total of gentlemen and others would be split more or less evenly.

No less important is to interpret correctly what was meant by a gentleman, for even into the present century the word has retained a legal, hierarchical meaning: a person entitled to possess heraldic arms but not a member of the nobility. Besides its official interpretation, in the seventeenth and eighteenth centuries the term was very loosely used and did not necessarily embrace qualities given in the *Oxford English Dictionary* definition: "a man of chivalrous instincts and fine feelings." Gentlemen stood on the first rung of society's leadership ladder, and as playwright Ben Jonson noted in 1600, many still had mud on their boots. "I have lande and money, my friendes left mee well," declared one of Jonson's characters, "and I will be a gentleman whatsoever it cost me."[3]

Although these scions of the lesser gentry were socially far removed from those of their fellow passengers who were listed as laborers, and measured comfort and success against a different yardstick, they shared much, knowing both the beauty and rough tranquillity of rural England and, albeit briefly, the contrastingly chaotic excitement of the nation's one big town. Because their ships sailed from the Thames, all must have had at least a treading acquaintance with London's narrow streets.

For both poor and rich, emigrants' expectations and their hopes of fulfilling them were dependent on the quality of life they were leaving. The jobless laborer who had forsaken rural poverty for city squalor would be delighted with a ten-by-twelve-foot one-room Virginia house he could call his own, but a gentleman who had left the comforts provided by wealthy parents would find an amateurishly constructed dwelling thrice that size a disappointment sufficient to sour his judgment and render him an intolerant master and a troublesome neighbor. We have to bear in mind, too, that there is no sure way of knowing how many of the 102 first James Fort settlers really intended to live out their lives in Virginia. Those who expected to find gold almost certainly planned to return to England to spend it, and when they learned that their glittering ore was only "fool's gold," melancholia must have become a communicable disease.

As the passengers boarded the open boats that were to carry them downstream to the waiting fleet on that drab December day in 1606, most must have drawn their cloaks tighter around them and longed for the imagined warmth of Virginia. Those among the crew and leadership who knew what awaited the settlers almost certainly kept it to themselves. Even so, the emigrants' excitement must have been tempered with fear of the unknown. They really believed that behind the next hillock there could be savages with three-inch fangs, two-headed lions, and dragons with very bad breath. But their most monstrous expectations were reserved for the ocean depths, out of which giant serpents could rise to snatch sailors from the rigging. Multi-tentacled monsters could grip whole

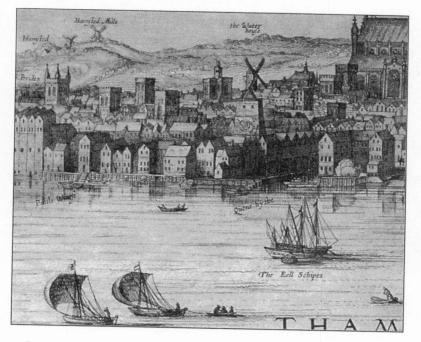

London's riverside tenements; a detail from Claes Visscher's 1616
panoramic view of the city.

ships and drag them down, and in the shallows lurked crabs so large that
their jaws could bite off a man's leg. On the basis of mariners' reports,
these fabulous creatures became real in contemporary engravings, and
throughout the seventeenth century few printed maps and charts lacked
mermaids or monstrous fish to break the surface in mid-ocean.

Even if, in 1606, fear of fabulous fish was not universal, fear of the elements was shared by all. Passengers, most of whom had never before seen
either the sea or a ship, well understood the violence of storms that could
send castle battlements toppling, rip roofs from cottages, and burn down
the spire of St. Paul's Cathedral. The prospect of facing such furies on the
open sea must have given pause to every landsman when he saw, for the
first time, just how small his floating house was to be.

The voyagers' flagship (the admiral) was the 120-ton *Susan Constant,*
with a waterline length of about seventy-six feet; the second vessel, the
Godspeed, had a burden of 40 tons and a length around forty-eight feet,
while the little two-masted pinnace *Discovery* had a capacity of only 20
tons and measured barely thirty-eight feet at the water. Aboard these,
along with baggage, food and drink, spare parts for the ships, at least one

The reconstructed *Susan Constant, Godspeed,* and *Discovery,* moored at the Jamestown Settlement in 1989.

dismantled boat, and undetermined livestock, were distributed 144 passengers and crew, 71 on the *Susan Constant,* 52 on the *Godspeed,* and 21 crowded aboard the *Discovery.*

Although the surviving accounts of the voyage say that the fleet sailed from London, the statement is somewhat misleading. Were it true, Sir Walter Ralegh would have been able to watch from his prison exercise walk along the battlements of the Bloody Tower as the ships sailed past. Much could have been made of his thoughts as the new vessels and new people set out to claim the Virginia that once had been his. The truth, however, is that anchorage in the city reach between London Bridge and the Tower was always crowded, and maneuvering difficult. Consequently, most convoys assembled below the city, lying off the villages of Wapping and Ratcliff, the latter the point of departure for several exploratory voyages, including those of Willoughby in 1553 and Frobisher in the 1570s. Even there, however, maneuvering could be tricky. Indeed, so busy were these lower reaches that in 1669 a foreign visitor, Count Magalotti, recorded that "it is said that there are more than one thousand four hundred [ships] betwixt Gravesend and London Bridge . . . to which are added the other smaller ships and boats, almost without number, which are passing and repassing incessantly, and with which the river is covered. . . ."[4] There may be some excuse, therefore, for the *Susan Constant*'s getting into trouble even before the passengers boarded.

So charitable a view was not shared by the owners of the ship *Philip and Francis*, which wound up with a broken bowsprit, prow (called the beakhead), and sheet anchor. On the night of Sunday, November 23, the *Susan Constant*, after being loaded upstream, was brought down to Ratcliff Cross and moored close to the *Philip and Francis*—too close, according to the latter's crew. When the tide turned, the heavier and lower-riding *Susan Constant* swung on her moorings and slammed into the bow of the other ship, while her skeleton crew "sate tiplinge and drinkinge and never looked out or endevored to cleare the ships."[5] When the *Philip and Francis*'s owners brought suit against their opposite numbers in the High Court of Admiralty, one of the key questions was whether or not the *Susan Constant*'s crewmen were drunk on the job. They, of course, took umbrage, one of their witnesses insisting that "there was no other beare but four shillinges beere on borde at that tyme."[6] It is worth noting that none of the three *Susan Constant* witnesses was sufficiently educated to sign his name.

When the three Virginia-bound ships hauled their anchors and slipped with the tide downriver toward Greenwich and the sea, they must have passed Sir Francis Drake's famous circumnavigating *Golden Hind*, a ship which, above all, symbolized the glory days of Elizabethan derringdo. Now, like Ralegh in the Tower, a relic of a fading past, she lay among the many other hulks rotting in the mud along the Deptford shore. The future sailed with the *Susan Constant*, *Godspeed*, and *Discovery*.

The fleet's commander, Admiral Christopher Newport, was one of the most experienced seamen left from the old era. The same can be said of the *Godspeed*'s Bartholomew Gosnold, but not of the *Discovery*'s captain, John Ratcliffe, who turned out to be a mysterious somebody else. Promoters of the 1985 voyage of a reconstructed *Godspeed* made much of these commanders' East Anglian origins, and it is true that they came from England's eastern counties, but there seems to have been no regional bond of the strength that tied Devonshire's Ralegh, Gilbert, Frobisher, Drake, and other Elizabethan sea dogs. Indeed, Newport, who was born at Harwich in Essex, has been described as "Christopher Newport of Limehouse, Mariner."[7]

Who would be in charge when the settlers set foot on land remained unknown throughout the voyage, as Newport, Gosnold, and Ratcliffe each had sealed instructions from the London Company to be opened "Within four and twenty hours next after the said Ships Shall arrive upon the said Coast of Virginia and not before. . . ."[8] The procedure made sense, even if it did not suggest total confidence in the voyagers. Had the intended James Towne hierarchy been revealed at the outset, there would

Portrait of Captain John Smith used to decorate
his map of New England.

have been endless time for analysis and second-guessing by gentlemen
whose names were not elevated to the top of the list, with the possibility
of the leadership's being rearranged at the point of a sword. In any case,
one of those destined to head the ticket had indulged in an allegedly
mutinous dispute with Newport and as a result spent most of the voyage
under arrest. That characteristically contentious entrance notwithstanding, Captain John Smith survives in the literature of his own creation as
the most colorful figure in early Virginia history.

Born in 1580 at Willoughby in Lincolnshire, and after a spotty education and a brief apprenticeship to a King's Lynn merchant, Smith joined
a troop of English mercenaries fighting in the Netherlands for Dutch
freedom from Spain. By the time he was twenty Smith was aboard a merchant ship in the Mediterranean and profited when its captain (in a
momentary lapse into piracy) seized a rich Venetian vessel. Thus set up,
Smith moved onward and eastward, joining Austrian forces in their war
with the Turks in Hungary, where, according to his own narrative, he performed amazing feats of valor but finally met his match (he was very
short) and was captured, then sold as a slave to a Turk who gave him as a
present to a girlfriend in Constantinople. She fell in love with Smith and

sent him to her brother to "learne the language, and what it was to be a Turke." But the brother treated him as an infidel slave and within an hour of Smith's arrival had him stripped and his head shaved, and a "great ring of iron" riveted around his neck.[9] His education limited to learning the art of dehusking grain, Smith eventually killed his captor with a threshing bat and escaped. After several other adventures of no relevance to the Virginia story, we find him back in England in the winter of 1604–05. By then a soldier with the dash of a latter-day Elizabethan, Smith made himself loudly familiar in circles promoting the development of the Virginia Company and thus got his name onto the sealed list of councillors locked in the voyage commanders' chests.

When the orders were opened, and the names for a seven-man council read out, the principal surprise must have been the list's brevity—particularly for those who weren't on it and who remembered that the Company's charter called for thirteen. Besides Newport, who would stay for only six weeks before taking the *Susan Constant* back to England, two of the listed names were a foregone conclusion: Captains Gosnold and Ratcliffe. The others were Smith, Captains John Martin and George Kendall, and Master Edward Maria Wingfield, plus an ex officio adviser in preacher Robert Hunt. John Martin had influential relatives, being the son of Sir Richard Martin, master of the mint, and the brother-in-law of Sir Julius Caesar, master of the rolls. Beyond those credentials he is known only as a quarrelsome individual and therefore a poor choice. George Kendall turned out to be not much better. Probably owing his appointment to having been an employee of Secretary of State Lord Salisbury and a cousin of the Company's influential Sir Edwin Sandys, Kendall would become embroiled in political intrigue at James Fort and earn himself his place in history as the first Virginia gentleman to be executed for mutiny. Selecting Wingfield, on the other hand, required no string-pulling on his behalf; he was, after all, one of the four original patentees of the Virginia Company's London branch. In addition, he had had some military experience both in Ireland and in the Netherlands, and although one historian has defined that as "gallant service," and another as "brief and inconsequential,"[10] it led to a useful serving association with Ralegh's partner Sir Ferdinando Gorges, who, in turn, was a close associate of Lord Salisbury's. Wingfield's age is uncertain (he is said to have been born around 1560), but since he was the only patentee to put his life where his money went, there can be no doubting his seniority or the expectation that he would be chosen to govern the new colony.

The choosing was done in a naïvely democratic manner that was the least likely to ensure success. Rather than the Company's King's Council for Virginia appointing the governor and giving him full authority in all matters concerning the operation, safety, and expansion of the colony, the seven councillors in Virginia were ordered promptly to "proceed to the Election and nomination of a President of the said Council," who was to hold office for only one year but whose authority in "matters of Controversy and Question" would depend on his having two votes "where there shall fall Out to be Equality of Voices."[11] In short, if four voted against him, the president was overruled.

Had Wingfield been a forceful, wise, and popular individual, the power of his personality might have kept the councillors in line; instead he is remembered as "an arrogant man of no special capacity" and as "self-confident, pompous, and puffed up by his own sense of superior birth and position, and unable to co-operate with common men and unfit to rule them."[12] Because Wingfield lacked any of the attributes necessary to govern, his weak yet contentious presidency provided a spawning ground for dissension, which further contributed to his problems. These were not helped by the antipathy which quickly developed between him and the equally opinionated, and allegedly mutinous, John Smith, who from the start smarted under Captain Newport's refusal to let him take his prescribed place on the council. Thanks in part to the reasoned intervention of the Reverend Hunt, Newport and Wingfield eventually allowed Smith to take his seat on June 14. But this was not a man with a short memory for indignities endured, and Captain John Smith was destined to become both the colony's savior and a contributor to its near-disintegration.

Two incomplete lists of the settlers survive, both published in the works of John Smith, one giving sixty-seven names and the other eighty-two. Neither list is in alphabetical order, but each places Preacher Hunt immediately after the six staying council members, followed by gentleman George Percy, who could with reason have expected to be appointed to it. Percy was a younger brother of Henry Percy, ninth earl of Northumberland, an early supporter of James I, whose subsequent disenchantment landed him in the Tower and cast a shadow across all the Percys. George had served as a volunteer for the United Netherlands in its war with Spain, and when he reached Virginia at the age of twenty-seven, he could claim both noble birth and military experience. He also was well educated, having studied at Oxford and the Middle Temple. Though passed over by the Company, he was destined to make his mark both in the colony and in history as the author of the most detailed account of the voyage of the *Susan Constant* and of the tribulations besetting the colonists once they got there, a report titled *A Discourse of the Plantation of the Southern Colonie in Virginia by the English, 1606.* Much later, in 1624 or 1625, apparently in response to charges made by Smith, Percy wrote another, long-unpublished treatise notable for its interminable title and creative spelling: "A Trewe Relacyon of the Procedeinges and Occurentes of Momente w^{c}h have hapned in Virginia from the Tyme s^{r}Thomas GATES was shippwrackte uppon the BERMUDAS an^o 1609 untill my depture outt of the Country w^{c}h was in an^o Dni 1612." Rich in human interest and steeped in personal bias, Percy's "Trewe relacyon" has been described as "a masterpiece of disagreeable detail."[13]

Several other gentlemen are also likely to have had great expectations, among them Anthony Gosnold, the younger brother of council member Bartholomew Gosnold, and Captain Gabriel Archer. The latter had been a partner with Gosnold in the 1602 voyage of the *Concord* to New England and had written an account of that enterprise which was circulated at the time and republished in 1625. In Virginia he was to join the several individuals who are known to have penned descriptions of the country and its people, as well as the growing list of colonists who could not get along with John Smith. Of the rest of the gentlemen passengers very little is known. Some undoubtedly were as useless and profligate as they have been painted, but others must have had guts, if not brains, and guts were a valuable attribute among men who faced an unknown from which there could be no quick retreat.

Besides the gentlemen and twelve men described as laborers, the technical side of colonization was served by four carpenters (among them Anas Todkill, who was to keep a journal, a version of which survives in John Smith's collected works); James Read, the blacksmith; a couple of bricklayers, John Hurd and William Garrett; Edward Brinto, a mason; a tailor named William Love; and Thomas Couper, the barber. Read probably doubled as a gunsmith, and if Hurd and Garrett were not to be singularly short of work, one or both of them needed the skills of a brickmaker. The company included two surgeons but no apothecary and no listed mineral man to identify and assay the gold. Even more surprising, nobody was listed specifically as a farmer or husbandman, the presumption perhaps being that anyone could plant, weed, water, and harvest. Although the colonists expected, at least at the outset, to be supplied from England, it is evident from the experimental plantings recorded from previous American voyages that raising sustenance crops of wheat, barley, oats, and peas was recognized as an essential activity.

To the lay eye, the terms "plantation" and "planter," both much used in the seventeenth and eighteenth centuries, suggest an agricultural unit (as in cotton or tobacco plantation) and a person in the business of setting seeds and plants in the ground. That, however, was not the early colonial meaning: The planters were planting themselves, and the chosen place was the plantation. Nevertheless, following London's instructions, Captain Newport (who, as admiral, remained in command until his departure) divided his personnel into three groups of equal size: explorers, builders, and agriculturalists. Of these three, only the exploration unit had much appeal for the gold-hungry gentry, and while the building group had four staff carpenters augmented by others from the ships, the agronomy team's subsequently dismal performance seems proof enough that it was woefully short of land management skills and experience. Indeed, when reviewing the agricultural lessons learned in the first weeks of settlement, Gabriel Archer wrote that "the thing we crave is some skillfull man to husband sett plant and dresse vynes, sugar canes, olives rapes hemp flax, lycoris pruyns, currantes, raysons, and all such thinges, as the North Tropick of the world affordes. . . ."[14] For the purposes of our investigation, however, the key question is this: Who and how many among the settlers had the skills and experience to build James Fort? But first they had to decide where to put it.

Captain Newport had opened his orders and revealed the names of the council within a day of reaching the Chesapeake. Although they would not be sworn in until they landed at the chosen settlement site, it is clear from the detailed written instructions provided by the London Virginia Company that decisions relating to the choice were to be a committee responsibility. The principal criteria would be these:

1. Find a location as much as a hundred miles up a navigable river, preferably one bending to the northwest "for that way you shall soonest find the other sea" and thus access to Asia.
2. Choose a place where the river is narrow so that enemy boats are in musket range from both banks.
3. Select "the strongest, most wholesome and fertile place."
4. "In no case suffer any of the native people of the country to inhabit between you and the sea coast."[15]

Seventeen days' reconnoitering finally led thirty miles up the Powhatan River (quickly renamed the James) to the low-lying, marsh-embraced three-mile-long peninsula today known as Jamestown Island, which was then attached to the north shore by a thirty-yard-wide isthmus that flooded at high tide. With the company's criteria in mind, it is hard to imagine a less appropriate location to plant a settlement—even if in succeeding centuries erosion fundamentally changed the shape of the island, and surviving maps of the time indicate that it has not.

Apologists have argued that the site was chosen for military reasons and that the first consideration "was its possibilities for defense against a foreign foe,"[16] but clearly it met none of the company's strategic criteria. It was not sufficiently far upstream to hamper an enemy's approach or to provide a hundred miles' worth of warning time, and instead of being of musket-straddling breadth (about sixty yards), the river at Jamestown Island was more than a mile wide. In reality, such defense as the site offered would have been limited to its remaining hidden from an enemy until he was virtually broadside to the settlement. Indeed, if that was the idea, a lurking strategy could have been better applied at numerous other points on either side of the river where higher ground afforded significantly greater protection. As European coastal defenders well knew, the ability to fire down on ships whose artillery was mounted only to batter other ships gave the landsmen an immense advantage. At Jamestown Island, however, a Spanish fleet could have brought its starboard ordnance to bear on the settlement with devastating effect, and as we shall see, James Fort's own guns were deployed in such a way that only a few were trained on the river.

John Smith's first brief account of the choice says that it was "a verie fit place for the erecting of a great cittie," then adds "about which some contention passed betwixt Captaine Wingfield and Captaine Gosnold."[17] It is unclear how much influence the council members actually exercised in the site selection, for as we have seen, they were not sworn (and thus officially active) until they went ashore on the morning of May 14. Smith, of course, was still in Newport's doghouse and unable to vote. George Percy, whose opinions would have been equally helpful to the council, recalled that two days earlier they had "discovered a point of Land, called Archers Hope [named for Captain Gabriel Archer, who presumably favored it], which was sufficient with a little labour to defend our selves against any Enemy. . . . [I]f it had not beene disliked, because the ship could not ride neere the shoare, we had setled there to all the Collonies contentment." Percy noted that the Archer's Hope site lay eight miles from the Jamestown Island location "where our shippes doe lie so neere the shoare that they are moored to the Trees in six fathom water."[18]

Much reliance has been placed on Percy's measurement, but a fathom measured six feet or the spread of a man's arms, and six of them made an inshore depth of thirty-six feet. Although it is true that the modern dredged channel drops to that depth, and more, about a tenth of a mile from the Jamestown shore, the inshore depths range from two to fourteen feet. Although a far cry from six fathoms, fourteen feet would be sufficient to harbor the *Susan Constant* and *Godspeed,* whose reproductions draw little more than nine and six feet, respectively. If, on the other hand, Percy's measurement is right, then drastic changes must have occurred along the island shore since 1607. The possibility that he was exaggerating (or had mislaid his notes when he wrote) is suggested by the fact that Archer's Hope lies scarcely five miles downstream from Jamestown rather than the eight that Percy cites.

Although it is possible that the councillors had difficulty telling a fertile from an infertile location, they nevertheless had London's instruction to find just that, likewise one that was "wholesome," meaning healthy. Jamestown Island was neither. Geologically it comprises a bed of fine sand capped by several feet of clay merging into a few inches of topsoil whose maximum surface elevation is less than twenty feet above mean low tide. This means that wells driven through the loam and clay would be drawing on brackish river water percolating through the sand. Couple that with the fact that almost half the island is, and was, swamp wherein malaria-carrying mosquitoes bred, and you have a locale as unwholesome as they come.

The estimated 800 acres of mud and marsh grasses are not restricted to one area but stretch in two groups of channels reaching into the high ground from the north and east. Professor Lyman Carrier in his study of Virginia agriculture in the seventeenth century has stated that the remaining 850 acres comprised "heavily timbered forest" and that "the fact that the Indians had never cleared any of the land indicates that they did not consider it of the best quality."[19] If this is true, it follows that the colonists found no open ground on which to build their fort and first had to clear a sufficient area of the forest, but as Dr. Carrier has noted, "Clearing forest lands even with modern tools and equipment is a slow laborious process,"[20] and felling trees is only the beginning. While a forest of stumps outside the fort may have been temporarily acceptable, their presence inside it would have created innumerable problems for the inhabitants, yet because the planters lacked horses or oxen to pull the stumps, the only alternatives were to dig them up or burn them out. One demanded an enormous amount of backbreaking labor, and the other

Top: Typical pitch and tar swamps on Jamestown Island. *Bottom:* The Jamestown Island marshes looking downriver. Hog Island on the south shore of the James is visible in the upper right distance.

posed an unacceptable fire hazard. Had either been employed, some-body's account of the first days' efforts should have mentioned it, but none does.

Then, too, one has to question Dr. Carrier's assertion that the Indians had never cleared any of the land, for Dr. John L. Cotter, who directed the National Park Service's archaeological excavations on the island between 1955 and 1957, reported that aboriginal artifacts and soil indica-tions pointed to Algonquian "occupation within 100 years previous to 1607."[21] A century is not a long time in the growth of a tree. If, as Dr. Car-rier asserts, most of the island was covered by primeval forest, and Dr. Cotter is right in detecting Indian occupation as recently as the beginning of the sixteenth century, tree growth overlying the Indian sites would have been comparatively light and easily cleared.

Disagreement persists about the appearance of primeval forest land in Tidewater Virginia, some contending that the thick foliage of ancient trees would have prevented new growth below and so permitted easy pas-sage between the trunks, while others envisage the trees swathed in a jungle of vines and creepers rising out of dense underbrush. The truth may lie somewhere in between. Because the records for May 13 describe no prolonged exploration of Jamestown Island before the fort site was selected, the presumption must be that it was easily seen and decided on. Furthermore, in their previous days of exploration Newport and the lead-ing colonists had had firsthand experience of the welcome they could expect from the Indians and the tactics they employed: As Gabriel Archer put it, "their feight is alway in the wood with bow & arrowes."[22] Archer was particularly well versed in this subject, having been wounded in both hands on April 26, his first night ashore.

The three ships had followed in the intended path of Ralegh's 1587 colonists, making landfall on the south shore of the Chesapeake Bay, where George Percy declared himself "almost ravished" by the sight of the streams of freshwater and the "faire meddowes and goodly tall Trees."[23] The local Indians, on the other hand, were less entranced by the sight of their visitors, and attacked them as they were returning to the ships. "There came the Savages, creeping upon all foure, from the Hills, like Beares; with their Bowes in their mouthes," who, according to Percy, "charged us very desparately in the faces." They were soon driven off by musket fire, but not before Archer had been wounded and a sailor had been hit "in two places of the body very dangerous[ly]."[24]

This first encounter with the indigenous Americans must have been alarming to the rank-and-file English; unlike their leaders, who undoubtedly had read Ralph Lane's and John White's sobering reports, they were more likely to have swallowed the lovable-savage line being peddled by the London promoters. Four days later the fainthearted may have been somewhat reassured, for after setting up a cross at the point they named Cape Henry, Captain Newport made contact with five nervous but eventually friendly Indians, who invited a delegation to their town at Kecoughtan. There, said Percy, they were entertained by "the chiefest of them" and their retainers "very kindly."[25]

The Kecoughtan Indians were a small tribe, said to number only about seventy-five, but they were strategically located at the mouth of the James River and were destined to be the cause of future unpleasantness. Their young weroance named Pochins was one of several sons of Powhatan, the paramount chief (often referred to by the English as the emperor) of the Algonquian tribes of Tidewater Virginia. Pochins's hospitality gave his guests their first exposure to the culture of the Virginia Indians, and as has been the case throughout history whenever different civilizations met, the more technologically advanced looked on the other less with admiration than with amusement. Percy, who at the next stop admitted that "we knew little of what they meant," had noted first that the Kecoughtans hung chicken legs through their ears.

> They shave the right side of their heads with a shell, the left side they weare of an ell long tied up with an artificiall knot, with a many of Fowles feathers sticking in it. They goe altogether naked, but their privities are covered with Beasts skinnes beset commonly with little bones, or beasts teeth.[26]

In turn, the Indians saw the English as overdressed and commonly called them the Coat-wearing People and, when they got to know them well, the Cutthroats.

Because the written history of the Virginia Indians began with, and was seen through the eyes of, seventeenth-century foreigners, our knowledge of the millennia that went before is woefully sketchy, and even what we are told about Indian tribal relations of the time is imprecise and unedited by the participants. It seems, nevertheless, that the history of the Algonquian and other eastern American tribes had, for several centuries at least, been one of alliances and confederations, smaller tribes content to be ruled or influenced by larger and more charismatic and powerful weroances. Of these, Powhatan was close to the last in the line, and he was the ruler, at least in name, of a confederacy that reached inland to the falls of the James River at modern Richmond, north to the Potomac River, and south into coastal North Carolina.

Although Powhatan had inherited dominion over only six tribes, by the time the English landed in 1607 he ruled or had influence over as many as twenty-eight, encompassing an estimated two hundred towns and villages. By then he was in his seventies and mellowing. Describing his appearance some four years later, the colonist's secretary, William Strachey, remembered him like this:

> He is a goodly old-man, not yet shrincking, though well beaten with many cold and stormy wynters. . . . Of a tall stature, and cleane lymbes, of a sad aspect, rownd fat visag'd with gray haires, but playne and thyn hanging upon his broad showlders, some few haires upon his Chynne, and so on his upper lippe. He hath bene a strong and able salvadge, synowie, active, and of a daring spiritt, vigilant, ambitious, subtile to enlarge his dominions. . . . Cruell he hath bene, and quarrellous, as well with his owne Weroances for triffles, and that to stryke a terrour and awe into them of his power and condicion, as also with his neighbours in his younger dayes. . . .

Strachey added that the old king now delighted in security and pleasure and was at peace with "all the great and absolute Weroances about him, and is likewise more quietly settled amongest his owne."[27]

The name Powhatan recalled his birth into the tribe who lived at the falls of the James River, but his ceremonial name (and the one by which he was addressed by his priests and advisers) was Wahunsenacawh. When the English arrived, Powhatan's capital was located at Werowocomoco (meaning "the king's lodge") on the north bank of the river that the Indians called the Pamaunk and that the colonists named first Prince Henry's, then the Charles, and finally the York.

By 1607 Powhatan had controlled the region for at least nineteen years—if his claim to have "bin at the murther" of John White's Lost Colony is to be believed. Just how tight his control was is hard to say, for there were several occasions through the years when individual tribes were independently at war with the English while Powhatan was officially at peace with them. On the other hand, some like the formidable Chickahominies considered themselves sufficiently independent to make their own peace treaties with the colonists on terms evidently not first referred to Powhatan for approval. There would also be occasions when he would be in conflict with the colonists, while tribes such as the Patawomeke would be trading with them and declaring undying friendship. Comparable differences developed among the colonists, some anxious to coexist with their Indian neighbors, to live among them, and even to marry them, while others saw them as the devil's brethren and good only when dead. In short, nothing in the Virginia colonists' relationships with the "naturals" was to be neatly cast in "us versus them" terms. Each would learn to play the game from day to day according to the cards being dealt.

Before setting up their cross at Cape Henry, Captain Newport's men had assembled the large open boat which they had brought from England as a kit. Called a shallop, it was propelled by seven pairs of oars and a single bow-mounted sail and could carry about twenty-four men and their baggage. Using the shallop as a tender to support their three ships, Captain Newport, George Percy, Gabriel Archer, and other senior settlers left Kecoughtan and explored as much as forty-five miles up the river to modern Hopewell. On the way they stopped first to be received by Wowinchopunck, king of the Paspaheghs, who lived at Sandy Point near the mouth of the Chickahominy River about seven miles above Jamestown Island. Although the Paspaheghs could muster only about forty warriors, Wowinchopunck was considered one of Powhatan's most formidable leaders, and in spite of his warm welcome, the explorers soon learned he was not to be trifled with.

Drawn, no doubt, by the sight of the three strange ships lying in the river, the weroance of the Quiyoughcohanocks, who lived on the opposite bank, crossed in a canoe to find out from the Paspaheghs who their visitors were and to invite them to his village. When Newport declined on the ground that it was too late in the day, the king renewed the invitation the following morning and sent a guide to escort him. Perhaps because the weroance had shown his irritation that the strangers had gone first to the Paspaheghs, Newport may have been overly cautious, but whatever the reason, he elected to man the shallop with musketeers and shield-protected swordsmen. He may, therefore, have been somewhat taken aback to be greeted by the now flute-playing weroance whose primary concern was to demonstrate his importance as well, presumably, as his musical talent. Percy clearly was impressed both by his demeanor, "as though he had beene a Prince of civill government," and by his regalia:

> ... with a Crown of Deares haire colloured red, in fashion of a Rose fastened about his knot of haire, and a great Plate of Copper on the other side of his head, with two long Feathers in fashion of

Detail from John Smith's map of Virginia, showing the James River
from Point Comfort to the falls at modern Richmond.

a paire of Hornes placed in the midst of his Crowne. His body was
painted all with Crimson, with a Chaine of Beads about his necke,
his face painted blew besprinkled with silver Ore as wee thought;
his eares all behung with Braslets of Pearle; and in either eare a
Birds Claw through it beset with fine Copper or Gold.[28]

Although more than six months passed before any colonist set eyes on
the great Powhatan, Captain Newport's eight-day reconnaissance had
enabled the newcomers to get to know the neighbors—and, although not
to be afraid, certainly to be wary of them.

The expedition's main purpose had been to find a suitable place to settle, but in spite of encountering on the river's south shore what Percy

described as fine paths, pleasant springs, and "the goodliest Corne fieldes that ever was seene in any Countrey,"[29] the council preferred Jamestown Island, which was singularly short of pleasant springs. Making no more sense was the decision to put ashore the entire settling complement, as was done on May 14, without creating sufficient defensible space between themselves and the forest, for as Percy reveals, they knew very well that they had chosen their "seating place in Paspihas Countrey."[30]

Of all the available Englishmen, the forty sailors aboard the ships are likely to have been the best able to cut lumber and build defenses, and while the enterprise remained under Admiral Newport's supervision, they could be employed as he saw fit. Although sailors, particularly the crews from later supply fleets, considered themselves there to sail the ships, not to apply their skills and brawn on behalf of incompetent landlubbers, Newport had no choice but to conscript them, there being no way that fifty or so gentlemen used to watching others work could have turned themselves into lumberjacks overnight. Neither they nor the rest of the settlers could have opened a large enough clearing in an ancient forest without help from every available hand—or perhaps even with it.

That trees were cut is undisputed. The crucial questions, however, are how many and how large they were. On balance, it seems likely that growth in the chosen area was less than a century old and that felling to stump level posed no insurmountable problem. Unfortunately, no step-by-step account survives to tell us who did what during the first two or three days on the island. The best chronology we have allegedly comes from the quill of a now-unidentifiable settler later published by Smith:

> Now falleth every man to worke, the Councell contrive the Fort, the rest cut downe trees to make place to pitch their Tents; some provide clapbord to relade the ships, some make gardens, some nets, &c. The Salvages often visited us kindly. The Precidents overweening jealousie would admit no exercise at arms, or fortification, but the boughs of trees cast together in the forme of a halfe moone by the extraordinary paines and diligence of Captaine Kendall.[31]

This information clearly is telescoped in time, for it is hardly likely that people would have been splitting clapboard with which to cargo the ships before their immediate protective and housing needs had been addressed. It is surprising, too, that the settlers would be making nets, a task to which they could usefully have applied themselves during the voyage. But with these red herrings set aside, the wording does say significant things about the fort, albeit tainted by somebody's (probably Smith's) antagonism toward President Wingfield. We are told that the council "contrived" it. Today the term has a deceitful ring, but the usage here has to be the *Oxford English Dictionary*'s third meaning: "To devise, invent, design a material structure." However, that piece of information becomes less straightforward when we are told in the statement that Wingfield prevented the erection of fortifications beyond any that could be constructed from the boughs of trees, the inference being that Jamestown's first defenses were little more than brushwood. Why did Wingfield prevail in this decision when the rest of the council had the right and the numbers to outvote him? And where does Captain Kendall fit into the equation? Though a member of the council and in a position to have had much to say about the character of the fort, he earns praise for his diligence in building an inadequate structure.

Careful examination of the quoted statement yields two more items of somewhat muddy data: While the council was contriving the fort, "the rest cut downe trees to make place to pitch their Tents." This tells us that the tents were not being erected inside the fort, which therefore did not need to be big enough to encompass them. The second clue relates to the shape of the tree-bough defenses "cast together in the forme of a halfe moone." The term "half-moon" had a specific meaning in the lexicon of fortification, though frequently cited in its French form: *demilune*. With typical Gallic perversity, such structures were shaped not like a partial moon but like a triangle having a semicircular indentation in the back of it—hence the half-moon. The 1738 edition of Chambers's *Cyclopædia* described it thusly: "HALF-MOON, *Demi-lune*, in fortification, an outwork, consisting of two faces, forming together a salient angle, whose gorge is turned like an *half-moon*. . . . The gorge of an *half-moon* is made bending in like a bow, or crescent." (See p. 147.) The important point here and in virtually every available source, is that half-moons were outworks, projecting beyond the bastions of the fortification proper. They were not the fort itself, as Smith's narrative indicates was the case when the first defenses were erected at Jamestown Island on May 14, 1607. What monumental stupidity, we may ask, could persuade the council to conceive a fort shaped like an outwork rather than a fort?

To this Kendall and his fellow councillors might angrily have retorted, and with some justification: The stupidity was not ours but yours, the historians', for not understanding what we've been telling you—and will continue to tell you as the story unfolds.

CHAPTER VI

Arrows of
Outrageous Fortune

&

WITHIN a week of the colonists' arrival, work on James Fort was sufficiently advanced for Captain Newport to depart on an exploratory trip upriver in search of minerals and the East India Sea. With him went nineteen good men (or twenty-one, depending on which account you prefer), including Smith, Percy, and Archer, who subsequently wrote the most detailed account of "the Discovery of our River, from James Forte into the Maine."[1] Unfortunately, neither Archer nor any other chronicler whose words survive gives a clue to *how* advanced the James Fort works actually were. Newport was intending to take the *Susan Constant* and *Godspeed* back to England in June, but the instructions from the London Company were that he should spend two months exploring upriver while Bartholomew Gosnold took twenty more men and six pickaxes to inspect high ground and dig for minerals. So, ready or not, the third of the company defined in London's instructions as the "forty discoverers" had to get on with it.[2] As it turned out, Newport did not need two months to find the navigable extremity of Powhatan's river. In four days he reached what Percy called the "head of this River"[3]—the falls at modern Richmond—in the territory of the Powhatan tribe, the birthplace of the great Powhatan, and then ruled by his son Parahunt, whom Newport called Pawatah.

After several friendly meetings with Parahunt and the neighboring Indians, Newport set up a cross on one of the small islands at the foot of the falls and ordered two names to be inscribed on it: his own and that of Iacobus Rex, plus the date 1607. According to Archer, the assembled company then said a prayer for James and the project and thereafter "proclaymed him kyng, with a greate showte."[4] The English had wisely waited

A detail from John Smith's map of Virginia, showing James Towne
and its environs as well as Powhatan's base at Werowocomoco (right).

until Parahunt and his entourage were out of sight; nevertheless, the great
shout evidently puzzled the remaining Indian guide, and Newport
thought it best to explain that the two arms of the cross signified on the
one hand the great king Powhatan, and on the other himself, and that the
point of intersection represented their united league. As for the shout,
that was an expression of the English reverence for Powhatan. Newport
may have thought it unnecessary and unwise to mention Iacobus Rex and
the fact that the visitors had just made him king of everywhere they trod.

Contacts with the Indians remained friendly throughout this exploratory trip, and for the first time the English had an opportunity to
visit their villages and be received by their weroances, to whom they gave
"penny knyves, sheeres, belles, beades, glasse toyes &c."[5] They also provided their hosts with their first taste of aqua vitae—unrectified alcohol—
which went down well at the start, but later the king of Arrohattoc, who
lived on the north bank of the river about twelve miles below modern
Richmond, was taken ill and blamed his "greefe" on his guests' "hott
Drynckes."[6]

Having reached the navigable extremity of the river and having
renamed it the King's River, Newport had fulfilled the letter of his instructions, if not their intent, and so after an absence of only seven days the

Susan Constant returned to Jamestown. What the discoverers found when they got there was in striking contrast with the impressions they had garnered on the trip. Because the colonists' premier chroniclers—Smith, Percy, and Archer—were with Newport, we have only secondhand knowledge of what had happened in their absence, but its bones were these:

On May 26, the day before Newport's men returned, a force of more than two hundred Indians, led by "their kyng," assaulted the fort and shot arrows through the tents, wounding ten and killing one man and a boy. In return the colonists killed "Dyvers of them," but since the Indians dragged their dead and wounded off into the woods, no estimate of their casualties was recorded. Gabriel Archer wrote that "ffoure of the Counsell that stood in front were hurt in mayntayning the fforte, and our president Master Wynckfeild (who shewed himselfe a valiant Gentleman) had one shott cleane through his bearde, yet scaped hurte."[7] Had it not been for cannon firing what Archer described as "small shott" from the moored *Godspeed,* the Indian attack might have succeeded in bringing England's latest Virginia adventure to naught.

John Smith's account put the defenders in equal jeopardy but described their redemption somewhat differently. "Had it not chanced a crosse barre shot from the Ships strooke downe a bough from a tree amongst [the Indians], that cause them to retire," Smith wrote, "our men had all been slaine, being securely all at worke, and their armes in drie fats."[8] A bar shot was formed from two halves of a cannonball separated by an iron rod averaging a foot long and was used for shearing an enemy ship's rigging—very different from the small shot cited by Archer. Smith's reference to the arms being in "dry fats" meant that the weapons were stored in large boxes or barrels unsuitable for liquids, known as dryfats or dryvats. His point reinforced his previously cited statement that President Wingfield "would admit no exercise at armes," leaving the men untrained to use them.[9] Now he was adding that after two weeks ashore the arms still had not been unpacked. Archer, though belonging to the anti-Wingfield faction, had given the president credit, if not for his foresight, at least for his courage. Smith's account differed, too, in that he listed seventeen wounded and only the boy killed. Percy, the third source, said nothing about this, the most critical event since the landing.

If one reads between Archer's lines, it appears that the half-moon fort built from tree limbs had been neither reinforced nor enlarged in Captain Newport's absence and that it was, indeed, very small. Thus four council members could stand in front to defend it. Had all the available defenders been inside the fort, the odds against four out of five councillors' being hit (in a total of twelve or even eighteen casualties) would have been appreciably longer.

More informative—as far as the fort is concerned—than the accounts of the attack are those describing what happened next. Wrote Archer: "We settled our selves to our owne safety, and began to fortefye; Captayne Newport worthely of his owne accord causing his Sea men to ayde vs in the best parte therof." His entry for the next day, May 28, reads: "Thursday we laboured, pallozadoing our fort."[10] Smith said much the same thing:

> Hereupon the President was contented the Fort should be pallisadoed, the Ordinance mounted, his men armed and exercised, for many were the assaults, and Ambuscadoes of the Salvages, and our men by their disorderly stragling were often hurt, when the Salvages by the nimblenesse of their heeles well escaped.[11]

Both witnesses make it clear that the first effort to build a substantial palisaded fortification on Jamestown Island did not commence until the settlers had been there for two weeks and that hitherto their defenses had been limited to the light wood half-moon. Furthermore, it was not until the palisaded structure was built that the settlers' artillery was mounted, thus explaining why it fell to the ships' ordnance to save the day when the massive Indian assault was on the edge of succeeding.

Extracts from Gabriel Archer's journal entries through the next few days provide important clues to the character of the terrain in the fort's immediate vicinity. At the same time they dramatize the threat posed by the Indians and the inevitable nervousness of the settlers sensing unseen eyes fixed upon them from the woods, when even a colonist intent on "naturall necessity" had to listen for the twang of a bowstring.

> May 29.   Fryday the salvages gave on againe, but with more feare, not daring approche scarce within musket shott: they hurt not any of us, but finding one of our Dogges, they killed him: they shott above. 40. arrowes into, and about the forte.
> 30. Satterday, we were quyet.
> Sunday they came lurking in the thickets and long grasse; and a Gentlemen one *Eustace Clovell* unarmed stragling without the ffort, shot. 6. Arrowes into him, wherwith he came runinge into the ffort, crying Arme, Arme, thes stycking still: He lyved. 8. Dayes, and Dyed. The Salvages stayed not, but run away.

June 1. Monday some. 20. appeared, shott Dyvers Arrowes at ran-
dome which fell short of our fortte, and rann away.

2. Tuesday ⎫ quyet and wrought upon fortification, Clap boord,
3. Wednesday ⎭ and Setting of Corne.

4. Thursday by breake of Day. 3. of them had most adventurously
stollen under our Bullwark and hidden themselves in the long
grasse; spyed a man of ours going out to doe naturall necessity,
shott him in the head, and through the Clothes in two places
but missed the skynne. . . .

8. Monday, Master *Clovell* Dyed that was shott with. 6. Arrowes
sticking in him. This afternoone. 2. salvages presented themselves unarmed a farr of[f] Crying *Wingapoh;* there were also
three more having bowe and arrowes: these we Conjectured
came from some of those kinges with whom we had perfect
league: but one of our Gentlemen garding in the woodes and
having no Comaundement to the contrary shott at them. . . .

13. Satterday. 8. salvages lay close among the weedes and long
grasse: and spying one or two of our Maryners Master *Ihon
Cotson* and Master *Mathew Fitch* by themselves, shott *Mathew
Fytch* in the somewhat dangerously, and so rann away this
Morning.[12]

The next day two Indians whom Newport and his companions had met on
their upriver exploration arrived at the fort with word from the kings of
their region that they would assist in making peace with the Paspeheghs
(in whose hunting territory the English had chosen to settle) as well as
with their neighboring allies, the Quiyoughcohanocks, Weanocs, Appomattocs, and Chiskiacks, who, presumably, had assisted in the May 26
assault. One of the messengers advised the settlers "to Cutt Downe the
long weedes rounde about our Forte, and to proceede in our sawing."[13]

It may seem extraordinary that having several times been shot at from
the long grass, the English would need an Indian's advice to promote the
notion of cutting it down, but such was the case. What is significant,
however, is the fact that there *was* long grass as well as thickets "rounde
about" the fort, indicating that the forest lay at some distance from the
defenses—indeed, sufficiently far removed for the arrows fired on June 1
to fall short. Grass sufficiently long to hide in does not grow in forests,
and it would in any case have been trampled flat had it been uncovered by
felling the trees. These references to the weeds and long grass have been
interpreted as evidence that on at least one side the fort lay close to the
edge of one of the island's several tongues of marshland. If this is true, as

Archer's entry for June 4 makes clear, the marsh and its grasses reached right up to the bulwark, meaning either the new palisade or the old half-moon. Either way this makes no sense. Furthermore, had the Indians waded through a swamp to launch their attacks, Archer, Smith, or someone would surely have mentioned it. Much more logical, therefore, is the conclusion that the fortifications were erected in an area earlier stripped and cultivated by the Paspaheghs and sufficiently lightly wooded when the English arrived for thickets and tall grasses to grow under and between the trees.

The term "bulwark" can be interpreted in about as many ways as can the word "palisade." In its strict sense the *Oxford English Dictionary* favors a Scandinavian origin created from words translated into English as "bole," meaning "tree," and "work," meaning exactly that—i.e., a work constructed from tree trunks, which, just to confuse things, can also be applied to a palisade. However, the same dictionary gives the primary definition for "bulwark" much more loosely: "A substantial defensive work of earth or other material; a rampart, a fortification." Thus the term "bulwarke" had been used in 1578 to describe the entirety of the "new found fort" built by men of Frobisher's last Baffin Island expedition. In 1738, however, Chambers's *Cyclopædia* compared "Bulwark" with "*propugnaculum* in the ancient fortification," adding that it "amounts to much the same thing with *bastion* in the modern." Chambers devoted half a page to bastions of ten types, but made it clear that collectively they formed projections standing out from a rampart or curtain wall and comprised two faces and two flanks. Similar flankers were common in sixteenth- and seventeenth-century fortifications, so it is reasonable to argue, if not to conclude, that Archer used "bulwark" in that sense. Percy, as we shall see, certainly did so.

With this reasoning in mind, we need to go back to the day of the landing and recall who was doing what: Some were cutting trees to make way for tents, others were making clapboard, digging gardens, weaving nets, while the council toiled to "contrive the Fort." If all the councillors were doing was drawing up a plan for one half-moon-shaped fortlet, they were overstaffed and underworked. If, on the other hand, they were designing fortifications for the entire settlement—of which the half-moon was but the first component—then they had much to discuss and plenty to keep them busy pacing and marking.

Here, and always, the modern interpreter is faced with the difficulty of distinguishing between the way in which we understand words and the way that they, *any* they, meant them. George Percy is credited with nam-

A composite plan illustrating the various features of fort construction
used by military engineers in the seventeenth and eighteenth
centuries. From Ephraim Chambers's *Cyclopædia*, 1738.

ing the embryonic settlement James Fort, and it would seem that he did
so before any real fort existed. In view of the fact that the London Company's instructions did not call for the fortification of the entire settlement, perhaps one can draw an interpretive parallel to the Hudson's Bay
Company's much later usage of "fort" to mean a trading settlement.
Doubtful though that connection may be, the surviving documentation
for James Fort's first days leaves little doubt that the name was being used
in advance of reality. Thus, when Percy noted that on the sixth day the
weroance of Paspahegh sent forty of his men who "faine would have layne
in our Fort all night,"[14] we have to choose between believing either that
the Indians wanted to stay inside the half-moon or that they wished to
camp among the adjacent tent-housed English. On balance, the latter
interpretation seems the more logical.

Throughout recorded history there had been two ways in which urban
populations, large or small, could be protected. The leader either erected
a defensible wall around them and their homes or else built himself a supposedly impregnable castle and, when attacked, invited the neighbors in
before their houses turned to ashes. The latter way, of course, was cheaper
and more appealing to leaders, and in medieval England this was both the
physical and the societal relationship between lords and tenants. After the

Wars of the Roses ended in England in 1485, aging castles gave way to manor houses moated more for show than for defense. But in Ireland fighting between English and Scots settlers, on the one hand, and the so-called Wild Irish, on the other, perpetuated the necessity for defensive planning, and while major cities like Londonderry and Coleraine were walled around, most of the smaller settlements, which (as in the New World) were called plantations, relied on nearby forts for the protection of lives and livestock.

Some of the forts began as mere earthworks used by the indigenous Irish for the nocturnal protection of their cattle and were defined by the word "bawn," from the Gaelic *baahün*. Others were built from scratch in stone, complete with corner towers and flankers, and the walls between parapeted or pierced for musketry. The villages built by the English between 1610 and 1620—much the same period when the English in Virginia were putting down roots—are known as bawn villages, their houses usually laid out either in a single wide street or in two streets in a cruciform pattern intersecting on a marketplace or village green. At one end stood the bawn, and within it was the home of the settlement leader. Instructions printed in 1610 for the guidance of English developers in Ulster (much the same cast of characters as was involved in the Virginia ventures), there called "undertakers," summarized the bawn village concept: "Every of the said Vndertakers shall draw their Tenants to build houses for themselves and their families, not scattering, but together, neere the principall house or bawne, as well for their mutuall defence and strength, as for the making of Villages and Towneships."[15] Though varying from place to place, the basic Anglo-Irish village plan is reflected in the London Company's 1606 instructions to Captain Newport:

> And seeing order is at the same price with confusion, it shall be adviseably done to set your houses even and by a line, that your streets may have a good breadth, and be carried square about your market place, and every street's end opening into it; that from thence, with a few field pieces, you may command every street throughout, which market place you may also fortify if you think it needfull.[16]

It would be left to the much later settlers of Plymouth, Massachusetts, to erect a blockhouse at the hub of their settlement; but as with Ralph Lane's 1585 settlement on Roanoke Island the Virginia Company's instructions for its yet-to-be-named town were clearly along bawn village lines. Within that framework, therefore, building the first tree bough half-moon to represent the bawn, and letting the settlers' tents stand in for the village, made good sense—provided the natives were friendly. And according to Smith, in the first days of settlement "The Salvages often visited us kindly."[17] George Percy, on the other hand, was less sanguine and feared treachery at every turn. But apart from a quickly ended contretemps over a stolen hatchet, no violence was reported. On the contrary, the visiting weroance of the Paspaheghs, Wowinchopunck, gave his personal assurances that he would give the English as much land as they cared to take. Not until the attack of May 26 did Wingfield and the council discover just how unkindly the Paspaheghs could be.

Perhaps, therefore, carefully sown complacency had caused President Wingfield to neglect the furtherance of defenses or to deviate from the original intent to build a residential village separate from, but contiguous to, the fort. If the latter was to be of the bawn variety, the preliminary design could have limited it to an enclosure having but one projecting flanker and containing only the storehouse. Curiously, however, in spite of the Company's explicit instruction that "all your carpenters and other such like workmen . . . do first build your storehouse and those other rooms of publick and necessary use before any house be set up for any private person,"[18] no mention is made of the storehouse's being erected. Nevertheless, decisions on its planned size and location would have a bearing on the dimensions of the fort.

Although thirteen years later in its construction, the bawnlike fort farther down the James River at Wolstenholme Towne provides the only clearly defined character and size of the kind of fort the London Company may have envisaged. Discovered in 1977 at Carter's Grove, Wolstenholme Towne was fully excavated by archaeologists from the Colonial Williamsburg Foundation, who revealed a classic bawn village with a palisaded fort at the landward end, containing one major building (the governor's residence?) and two smaller, the fortified enclosure measuring 121 feet 6 inches by 85 feet 6 inches. Considering that the Wolstenholme venture was supposed to accommodate more than two hundred settlers—at least twice the number landed at Jamestown in 1607—a bawn fort of Wolstenholme proportions could well have been on Wingfield's drawing board.

Continuing study of the Wolstenholme Towne discoveries has established beyond all reasonable doubt that the main settlement was defended not only by the rear-protecting fort but also by a much smaller mini-bawn closer to the river. It was in this heavily palisaded enclosure with its projecting flankers predating the fort, that the settlers' only cannon is

Wolstenholme Towne (1620–22) as partially reconstructed at Carter's Grove on the James River below Jamestown Island. The outlined fort stands in the background beyond another compound containing a multiple dwelling and a store building.

believed to have been mounted to fire on approaching enemy shipping. One may wonder, therefore, whether Wingfield and his colleagues were considering building additional bulwarks or fortlets at strategic points at the perimeter of the village, one perhaps farther up or downstream from the first and another, say, to the rear, knowing that the peninsula was vulnerable to assault up or across the waterway today known as the Back River. One thing is certain: By mid-June, James Fort *did* possess three bulwarks. George Percy described the fort thus: "The fifteenth day of June, we had built and finished our Fort which was triangle wise, having three Bulwarkes at every corner like a halfe Moone, and [with] foure or five pieces of Artillerie mounted in them we had made our selves sufficiently strong for these Savages. . . ."[19]

Here, then, we have a fortification comprising three bulwarks linked together by palisade walls to create a triangle of unspecified proportions. It is significant that Percy used Gabriel Archer's word "Bulwarke" when numbering the flankers and Smith's "halfe moone" to describe their character, thus clearly establishing a design link between the three palisaded bastions and Captain Kendall's first tree bough structure.

Percy's only clue to the size of the fort has to be drawn from his comment about the artillery—a strangely imprecise accounting that can be read in either of two ways: There were four or five pieces distributed between the three bastions or four or five mounted in each. And why "foure or five"? Surely, we may ask, knowing how difficult heavy guns were to bring ashore and set up, Percy should have known whether there were four or whether there were five. And what size guns were they, and how were they mounted? The most logical interpretation must be that no flanker had more than five pieces of ordnance and none fewer than four, which is, no matter how you slice it, a fierce display of artillery.

Artillery came in two basic varieties: naval and military. Although the same barrels were used for both, the carriages were very different. Naval carriages were short and boxlike with two or four sometimes unshod wheels big enough only for the back-and-forth loading movement necessary aboard ship. Land artillery, in contrast, had much larger carriages with huge iron-shod wheels, capable of being hauled by men and horses over the roughest terrain. And it was "field pieces" that the Company's instructions cited as needed to command the streets of bawn villages. Ergo field artillery was carried aboard the first fleet, and field artillery meant guns and carriages as much as fifteen feet long to be mounted inside the three bastions.

Even in the most conservative interpretation of Percy's "foure or five pieces," two field cannon in two of the flankers and one in the third called for emplacements of considerable size. His statement tells us that the guns' presence convinced the colonists that they were "sufficiently strong for these Savages"—confidence presumably born of the belief that the success of the ship-mounted artillery against the attack of May 26 would be repeated whenever the fort's guns were fired. But as John Smith made clear, the salutary effect on the attackers had been achieved by the surprise of seeing a bar shot drop a tree limb. That novelty would soon wear off, to be replaced by the realization that cannon were more damaging to trees than to Indians.

Contrary to popular belief, sixteenth- and seventeenth-century cannon rarely, if ever, fired explosive balls, and rather than burst with photogenic flashes and puffs of smoke, their projectiles landed with anticlimactic thuds. When cannon fired ship to ship, injuries to personnel came largely from wood splinters caused by heavy shot breaching a hull's wall or from spars felled by bar or chain shot. On land, because armies marched toward each other in tightly massed ranks, balls did as much damage by the lateral propulsion of people parts as by direct contact. Spread the targets apart, therefore, and cannonballs became virtually useless.

In 1626 John Smith published a guide to would-be ship owners and mariners, entitled *An Accidence; or, The Path-Way to Experience,* in which he provided a statistical chart for shipboard ordnance, the largest being a cannon weighing about 8,000 pounds and firing a 63-pound ball, down to a falconet weighing only 500 pounds, and propelling a 1¼-pound shot only two inches in diameter. Between those poles downward ranked the demicannon, culverin, demiculverin, saker, minion, and falcon. Of these, the most widely used "big guns" were the culverin and saker, the former firing a five-inch ball and the latter one of three and a quarter inches. According to Smith's table, the culverin could be relied on to propel its ball with aimed accuracy a distance of about 1,300 yards, while the saker had a point-blank range some 434 yards shorter. More important, at a time when sending home for more gunpowder could take six months, commanders needed no reminding that every culverin shot used up 14 pounds of powder and that each saker firing expended 5¼. When one considers that firing a musket ball required less than an ounce of powder, it takes no computer-equipped military genius to recognize that there is more to be said for firing 224 musket bullets at moving Indians than trying to hit them with one five-inch 18-pound ball. Admittedly, ordnance of most sizes could be loaded with any sharp or lumpy trash that came to hand and could be more effectively used as antipersonnel blasters at short range; but even so, such tactics expended the gunpowder supply at a prodigal rate.

In spite of Percy's confidence in the artillery as a defense against the Indians, the fact remained that the guns were really there to beat off Spanish warships. Consequently, regardless of whistling arrows to identify the colonists' real and present enemy, one has to suppose that when the council designed James Fort, it located the ordnance emplacements to defend against shipborne European attackers. Elevation had to be a factor. Standing the guns on the ground behind a wall sufficiently high to protect their crews was a quick and easy solution adequate for use against the Indians. But if the shots were to be fired at distant ships, every inch of elevation helped, and Jamestown Island itself provided very little. The question, therefore, has to be whether James Fort's bulwarks were raised platforms filled with dirt or even perhaps raised decks with storage space beneath. Although a case for the latter will be made in the light of later events, the early evidence (as we shall see) will testify against it. Building platforms to support artillery, any piece of which could weigh from thirty-five hundred to fifty-five hundred pounds, posed a formidable engineering problem, although we have to remember that ship's carpenters were accustomed to working aboard structures designed to do just that.

Elevated or not, the guns certainly needed to stand on wooden platforms or mattresses; otherwise their dead weight, coupled with their recoil movement, would bog them down in the Jamestown clay. Théodore de Bry's engraving from Jacques le Moyne de Morgues's 1564 drawing of France's Fort Caroline in Florida shows its ordnance standing on planked bibs, wedge-shaped to increase elevation (p. 48). Thus, by rolling the guns backward, the gunners could depress their muzzles to the horizontal, a process achieved on naval carriages by means of wedges beneath the breech.

Installing the guns to their best advantage, and even siting the bulwarks to house them, required a knowledge of gunnery, not just an ability to manhandle the parts. That responsibility almost certainly fell to Captain Newport's gunner, Robert Tindall, whose business card (had he had one) would have read "Gunner to Prince Henry"—James I's son and heir who was to die in 1612. Although little is known about Tindall, he styled himself in that way in a letter to the prince written from "Iames Towne in Virginia this: 22 of Iune 1607."[20] The letter was accompanied by a now-lost journal and a surviving chart showing the deep water in King James's and Prince Henry's (later the York) rivers. That in the first days of the landing the settlers had done little or nothing with their artillery can be explained by the fact that Newport took Gunner Tindall with him on his exploratory probe to the falls of the James. After returning, and when the artillery installation was complete, Tindall went back to England with Newport, but he returned as ship's master under another captain in 1609, by which time his artillery was in shabby shape.

No documentation survives to make certain that the James Fort ordnance was mounted on field rather than naval carriages, but we do have the sketch of the Popham settlement on the Kennebec showing all its nine pieces on field carriages (p. 100). Then, too, there is John Smith's published drawing of the various later forts and watchtowers on Bermuda. The island is shown defended by fifty-one pieces, only four of them on naval or garrison carriages. The same evidence has something to say about the questionable likelihood that the James Fort settlers would or could have hauled guns on field carriages up onto platforms sufficiently elevated to permit usable space beneath. After all, rolling the guns up to the flat top of an earthen ramp was one thing; lifting them with blocks and tackle to a second-story deck was quite another. If, however, Smith's Bermudian engraving has any credibility, it demonstrates that at least four forts had cannon atop their battlemented roofs, three of them mounted on field carriages.

Top: A vignette from John Smith's map of Bermuda, showing cannon
mounted on field carriages. *Bottom:* A reproduction cannon of saker
bore mounted on a naval carriage and standing on an elevated
flanker platform at Wolstenholme Towne. The original
barrel is dated to 1601, and the carriage to 1628.

Although it is likely that once Captain Newport and the *Susan Constant*'s ship's carpenters left for home, the pace and quality of James Fort construction would both slow and simplify, we can reasonably expect that work on the defenses would continue—regardless of George Percy's declaration that on June 15 the fort was finished. At the same time, of course, much else had to be done. The London instructions had called for the immediate erection of the storehouse, and although neither Percy nor Gabriel Archer has anything to say about it, the latter's journal notes that on June 9 a felled oak emitted a substance akin to vinegar, adding (and this is the point) that the tree was being cut to make clapboard. Archer, unfortunately, does not tell us whether all these short wall-covering boards were intended for Newport to take home as cargo or whether some were destined for the storehouse and other community buildings.

On Thursday, June 11, Archer recorded that "Articles and orders for Gentlemen and Soldyers were upon the Court of Garde. . . ."[21] The term is a corruption of *corps de garde* and here refers to a guardhouse or at least to a place where the guard assembled and where, presumably, the orders were posted. The building so described on the Popham plat stood in the middle of the settlement's central square, was three bays long, and appears to have had a belfry at one end. In short, it was a building of both prominence and substance. In addition, the Fort St. George settlement is shown to have had a smaller structure within one of the flankers marked as "the Munition house" (p. 278). It made good sense, and it certainly was true of later forts, that the gunpowder magazine should be located away from the central dwelling area and within a tightly walled space where an accident would do the least damage. There initially being no reference to a munition house at James Fort, we can only speculate that most of the powder remained on the ships as long as they stayed and that thereafter it was transferred into the fort, perhaps into the *corps de garde* or into the general store.

Little information is available to describe the settlers' developing living quarters; we know only that when the Indians attacked on May 26, they were able to shoot through the tents, as perhaps they could not have done had the tents been inside the first brushwood half-moon. Two days later the work of palisading was in high gear, and one may reasonably conclude that thereafter all dwellings were within the walls. James Fort had become the walled James Towne. However, as previously suggested, had the natives proved friendly, it is fair to argue that the settlement would have developed on the more open plan of the Irish bawn village, as represented later in Virginia by Martin's Hundred's Wolstenholme

The 1607 James Fort as interpreted in the 1950s, showing vertical poles abutting to create the palisades. Interior dwellings are correctly shown as a mixture of canvas tents and low, A-framed "cabins."

Towne—and doubtless by other comparable communities whose remains have yet to be found.

John Smith provides two descriptions of early living conditions within the fort, but since neither is precisely dated, one has to conclude that he was describing the situation in the days before and after Captain Newport's departure. If true, it would appear that Newport left the settlers inadequately housed and that they were incredibly slow to improve their lot.

> When I went first to Virginia, I well remember, wee did hang an awning (which is an old saile) to three or foure trees to shadow us from the Sunne, our walls were rales of wood, our seats unhewed trees, till we cut plankes, our Pulpit a bar of wood nailed to two neighbouring trees, in foule weather we shifted into an old rotten tent, for we had few better, and this came by way of adventure for new; this was our Church, till wee built a homely thing like a barne, set upon Cratchets, covered with rafts, sedge, and earth, so was also the walls: the best of our houses of the like curiosity, but the most part farre much worse workmanship, that could neither well defend [against] wind nor raine. . . .[22]

That description culled from an aging memory was published many years later, in 1631, yet it differs little from Smith's summary written in 1608, while the misery was fresh in his mind. His comment on the tents coming "by way of adventure for new" was one often heard in the first years of colonization. He was saying that the adventurers (the expedition's backers) had bought old equipment and had shipped it as new. "As yet we had no houses to cover us," said Smith in 1608, "our Tents were rotten, and our Cabbins worse than nought: Our best commoditie was Yron which we made into little chissels. . . ."[23] The last line is hard to explain unless a chunk is missing from Smith's text, but even so, the notion that a settlement so well supplied with tools that it was able to trade knives to the Indians should be spending its time manufacturing small chisels makes very little sense.

Later, both in his *Proceedings of the English Colonie in Virginia* (1612) and in his *Generall Historie* (1624), Smith allowed himself to be promoted as the architect of James Towne's survival, claiming that "by his owne example, good words, and faire promises, [he] set some to mow [the reeds and grasses needed for roofing], others to binde thatch, some to build houses, others to thatch them, himselfe alwaies bearing the greatest task for his own share, so that in short time, he provided most of them lodgings neglecting any for himselfe."[24] There probably was truth in the claim, but it's also a fact that in late August Councillor Bartholomew Gosnold died in a tent, and on September 10 his dissident colleagues "Came to the Presidentes Tennt with a Warrant."[25] Clearly, therefore, eleven weeks after the *Susan Constant* and *Godspeed* left Wingfield and the colonists to fend for themselves, even the president was still living in a tent—this in spite of the fact that on June 22 the council in Virginia had reported to the Company that it had already built several houses.

Just as attempts to translate accurately from a foreign language can lead to distortions if one does not understand the writer's intent, the same is true of interpreting seventeenth-century English. To the Virginia colonists a tent need not always have meant a portable structure made from poles, lines, and canvas. It could also mean a temporary hut, in which case Wingfield could have received the warrant in a tent-shaped structure roofed with brushwood and reeds.

Everyone had known from the outset that the ships would leave once the James Fort settlement was established, but as the day of departure drew near, there must have been many among those who had committed to stay who now wished they hadn't. The dissension that had simmered ever since the expedition left England had taken factional root once the names of the council were revealed. Opposition to the luckless President Wingfield blossomed, and even the council members themselves were divided, Captains Martin and Kendall jockeying for position, and Gabriel Archer at the top of the gentlemanly heap stirring the pot—or so Wingfield asserted when he returned, unseated, to England.

To give him his due, Christopher Newport was all too aware of the explosive situation he was leaving behind, and before departing, he questioned President Wingfield on "how he thought himself setled in the gouernment," to which Wingfield answered that he feared nothing but the objectives of Captain Gosnold and Gabriel Archer. The former, he said, was "strong with freinds and followers, and could [cause disruption] if he would; and the other [Archer] was troubled with an ambitious spirit, and would if he could." It was a clever line, but unwise. In an effort to remove the real or imagined threat, Newport took the two men aside "and mooved them with many intreatyes to be myndefull of their dutyes to his Majestie and the Colonye."[26] Newport may have scored marks for good intentions, but none for diplomacy. Gosnold and Archer now knew where they stood in the mind of their elected leader, and neither was comfortable with the knowledge. Three days later, on the evening before the *Susan Constant* and *Godspeed* were to leave, Newport came ashore to host a last supper with the council and senior gentry, thereby seizing his final opportunity to plead for loyalty and amity.

On Monday, June 22, Newport sailed from what George Percy described as James Port.[27] One day before or three days afterward (depending on whose account you prefer) an envoy from paramount Chief Powhatan arrived with a message. We have to remember that no Englishman had yet met Powhatan, yet his was a larger-than-life shadow stretching across every Indian village and into every political conversation. That his message was one of friendship must have been cause for relief, as was his assurance that if Wowinchopunck and his allies did not cease their harassment, Powhatan would join with the English to defeat them. This was the best possible news, for it meant that the settlers could "sowe and reape in peace."[28] A month later the weroance of the hitherto antagonistic Rappahannocks (a tribe living on the north bank of the Rappahannock River) promised with hand on heart that henceforth he would be the pale men's friend.

But if the enemy without professed to seek peace, the enemy within was less easily wooed. As the colonists' supplies dwindled, charges and countercharges of graft and mismanagement flew as damagingly as Indian arrows. By the beginning of August not only were the traumas emotional, but many of the settlers were physically ill—and getting more so.

The sixt of August there died John Asbie of the bloudie Fluxe. The ninth day died George Flowre of the swelling. The tenth day died William Bruster Gentleman, of a wound given by the Savages. . . .[29]

So began George Percy's doleful litany of mortality. Some like Jeremy Alicock, the standard-bearer, died of wounds, others, like gentleman Corporal Edward Moris, simply "died suddenly" of unspecified causes. Edward Browne, Stephen Galthrope, Thomas Gower, Thomas Mounslic, Robert Pennington, John Martin: the list stretched out from day to day. Experience would teach that Europeans arriving in Virginia in the spring lacked the conditioning necessary to see them through the hot and humid summer, and for that reason sailing schedules were later adjusted to bring newcomers ashore in the late fall and winter. But even these faced what would be called a seasoning, and many continued to die of dysentery and malaria within six months of their arrival.

Summarizing various symptoms (several of them characteristic of typhoid), Percy graphically described the misery of life and death at James Fort in the weeks after Captain Newport sailed and the lifeline to England was severed:

Our men were destroyed with cruell diseases as Swellings, Fluxes, Burning Fevers, and by warres, and some departed suddenly, but for the most part they died of meere famine. There never were Englishmen left in a forreigne Countrey in such miserie as wee were in this new discovered Virginia. Wee watched every three nights lying on the bare cold ground what weather soever came warded all the next day, which brought our men to bee most feeble wretches, our food was but a small Can of Barlie sod in water to five men a day, our drinke cold water taken out of the River, which was at a floud verie salt, at a low tide full of slime and filth, which was the destruction of many of our men.[30]

According to Percy, the colonists continued in this parlous state throughout the five months until Newport returned with fresh supplies. So weakened were the survivors that at no time could more than five able-bodied men be found to mount guard on the bulwarks. The others lay "groaning in every corner of the Fort most pittifull to heare." As the death toll climbed, the civilities of mourning crumbled in the face of practical reality, and with three or four dying in a single night, the dawn saw "their bodies trailed out of their Cabines like Dogges to be buried. . . ."[31]

Percy's grim narrative contains several pieces of important, if somewhat contradictory and even inexplicable, information. On the one hand, he cites the discomfort of lying on cold, wet ground while on guard duty, but then he says that at no time could more than five fit men be found to man the bulwarks. With three bastions to guard, it is difficult to imagine how five men could have rotated through the several watches. Nevertheless, John Smith told much the same story, blaming the settlers' plight in part on insufficient good food and in part on "continuall watching, foure or five each night at three Bulwarkes."[32] In the light of Percy's statement Smith has to mean a total of five and not five at each post. Regardless of the numbers, the question remains: Why, if some were sleeping between watches, were they not provided with straw mattresses and some kind of cover? After all, they weren't away in the woods. What the account does reveal, however, is that if the guards were mounted in or on the flanking bulwarks and were lying on the ground while so doing, it follows that the structures either were internally at ground level or were filled with dirt—not elevated on wooden platforms. Out of this conclusion another emerges: At this early stage in the fort's evolution, with the night watch on duty at earth level, there can have been no elevated watchtowers of the kind encountered by Drake at St. Augustine.

The James Fort colonists' unwillingness or inability to work toward their own salvation remains one of American history's major mysteries. Percy speaks movingly of the daily ration of a small mug of barley soaked in water and shared between five men—while they camped beside a river brimming with fish. We know that at the outset some of the men were ordered to make nets, and that on June 13 crewmen from the *Susan Constant* caught a giant seven-foot sturgeon which Captain Newport gave to the onshore settlers. The smallest of the three ships, the pinnace *Discovery*, remained with the settlers and could perfectly well have been used for fishing. John Smith noted that at least until mid-September young sturgeon two to three feet long were there for the netting, seven or eight at a time, "often more, seldom lesse. In the small rivers," he added, "all the yeare this is good plentie of small fish, so that with hookes those that would take paines had sufficient."[33] Writing specifically of the time when Percy was describing the mugs of sodden barley, Smith stated that "onely of Sturgion wee had great store, whereon our men would so greedily surfet, as it cost manye their lives."[34]

Percy's recognition that bad water was the cause of many deaths leaves one asking why, then, nothing was done to combat its dangers. That foul water was bad for you had been known for centuries, and there is ample evidence that in late Tudor England, communities had become increasingly conscious of the need to replace dirty wooden water pipes with new lead ones—not, we now know, a very good idea, but evidence of the recognized need for hydro-hygiene. Thus, for example, in 1612, an indenture relating to London's New River forbade contaminating its water with "anie earth rubbish soyle gravell stones dogges Catts or anie Cattle Carrion or anie unwholesome or uncleane thing. . . ."[35] There was no way, of course, that the James Fort settlers could change the content of the river, but they could at least have boiled its water. Although considering the geology of Jamestown Island, it would have been fruitless to try to reach sustained freshwater by digging wells, they were not to know that—but nobody even tried! Nor, for that matter, did anybody leave the island in search of a freshwater spring whose water could be brought into the fort in barrels. The solution to all these enigmas may lie with the river water and the possibility that a creeping and debilitating lethargy resulted from drinking it.

If the water, rather than inherent laziness, was to blame for the settlers' self-defeating slothfulness, it seems not to have been manifest by the time Christopher Newport left for England. At that time, according to Smith, Newport left "all our men in good health and comfort, albeit, that throgh some discontented humors, it did not so long continue. . . ."[36] The discontented humors did not refer to sickness of the body but rather of the mind as generated by the hostility between the weak and therefore vulnerable President Wingfield and the scheming members of his council.

As Wingfield had confided to Newport, Wingfield's distant cousin Bartholomew Gosnold had sufficient supporters to be a threat if he wanted to be. But in spite of disgreements over where to locate the colony, Gosnold gave no hint of mutinous intent. On the contrary, he was a stabilizing influence on his more volatile colleagues. Thus on August 22 it was to Wingfield's dismay that he learned that Gosnold, who had been ill for the best part of three weeks, had died. With the voice of reason and caution silenced, the dissidents quickly made their moves. On or about August 28 Councillor George Kendall was accused of sowing discord between president and council and was confined aboard the *Discovery* to await trial. With Gosnold and Kendall out of the way, only three of the Virginia Company's original councillors remained, and on September 10 all three—Smith, Martin, and Ratcliffe—signed a warrant deposing Wingfield from the presidency and naming Ratcliffe to the job. At the same time Wingfield's enemy Gabriel Archer was given the post of recorder of Virginia, making him chief magistrate at Wingfield's trial.

James Fort's blacksmith had a noose around his neck and was about to
be pushed off a ladder when Governor Ratcliffe decided that no
matter what his crime, James Read was more useful alive than dead.
A contemporary woodcut illustrates the procedure.

Wingfield now joined Kendall aboard the *Discovery* to await his day in
court to answer to a long list of various and paltry charges, ranging from
the concealing of communion wine (which the councillors preferred to
imbibe on temporal occasions) to the misappropriation of a tin whistle of
the kind used in trade with the Indians. Two weeks after his arrest
Kendall was released but denied the right to bear arms. In the absence of
evidence to the contrary, one may conjecture that the name of the game
had been to remove him from the council simply to close the shortened
rank against Wingfield, and with that accomplished there was no point in
going to the trouble of keeping him confined.

But that was not the end of the Kendall affair. For reasons no more
clear, the new president, John Ratcliffe, struck James Read, the colony's
blacksmith. And the blacksmith smote him back. Hitting the boss is
never a particularly stellar idea, nor was it for Read. Ratcliffe ordered him
hanged. One can argue, however, that killing the man who mends your
guns, makes your nails, repairs your chisels, and fixes your locks, not to
mention shoes your horses (if you have any), might not be the wisest of

responses. That thought may have been put into the president's ear by his colleagues, thus making him attentive when Read, with the rope around his neck and within moments of being pushed off a ladder, proposed trading his life for revealing a plot against the administration.

The plotter, according to Read, was the previously accused and therefore vulnerable George Kendall, whose alleged plan involved the crew of the *Discovery*, which he proposed to divert from a fishing expedition and send to England. If this was true, it remains unclear whether Kendall meant to go too, or whether he intended the pinnace to carry unauthorized letters of complaint against the leadership. That possibility immediately raises the question: To whom would the letters have been addressed?

The only clue is provided by one of Newport's sailors, an Irish Catholic named Francis Magnel, who spent eight months in Virginia and was there during Kendall's trial. Magnel later became involved with Irish and disloyal English exiles in Spain, and while in Madrid in 1610 he was interviewed by the archbishop of Tuam. Magnel reported that Kendall was a Catholic English captain who was executed "because they knew that he wanted to come to Spain to reveal to His Majesty what goes on in that land. . . ."[37] Was he, therefore, a spy in the pay of English Catholics in Spain, or on the contrary, as a past employee of Lord Salisbury was he the eyes and ears of England's secretary of state? Salisbury had both a personal and a national interest in the fate of the colony and from past experience had good reason to question the reliability of the upbeat official reports he could expect when the *Susan Constant* returned.

Regardless of whether Kendall's letters would have been bound for England or Spain, they would not be to the new council's advantage. Besides, it was a standing rule in the colony that no private letters would be dispatched without first being read and approved by the council.

According to John Smith, who, since the removal of Wingfield, claimed to have been given military command of the colony, he now dealt with the Kendall matter by training several small cannon and more muskets on the *Discovery* and ordering the crew to "stay or sinke in the river."[38] They stayed. Kendall was charged with "a dangerous conspiracy,"[39] tried, condemned, and shot. At his trial Kendall had tried to escape on a curious technicality, claiming that President John Ratcliffe had no legal right to pass sentence because he wasn't really John Ratcliffe, but John Sicklemore. This revelation (if such it was) caused only a momentary glitch in the proceedings against Kendall. Council member John Martin pronounced judgment instead. We are left, nonetheless,

Robert Cecil (1563–1612), secretary of state, lord high treasurer, earl of Salisbury, and principal adviser to James I. An 1836 engraving from the portrait by Federigo Zuccaro.

with the unsolved question of the president's identity. He had been appointed to the council in London as John Ratcliffe, and under that name he had commanded the *Discovery* in its Atlantic crossing, and now, still John Ratcliffe, he was chief executive officer of the Virginia enterprise. Sometime afterward, perhaps as a result of Kendall's having blown his cover, the president changed his name. In a letter written a year later, John Smith stated with obvious contempt that "Cap. Ratliffe [*sic*] is now called Sicklemore, a poore counterfeited Imposture. I have sent you him home, least the company should cut his throat."[40] So why the alias? What did he have to hide?

No historian has yet solved this mystery, though it has been suggested that Ratcliffe may have been another of the earl of Salisbury's secret agents, thus explaining the appointment of so shadowy a figure to the council. It may also explain how Kendall came to know Ratcliffe's real name. Smith certainly suggests such linkage between Ratcliffe and the secretary of state, for in the same letter he mentions an "idle Letter sent to my Lord of Salisbury, by the President and his confederats." Unfortunately Ratcliffe alias Sicklemore's letter has not been found, so there is no proof that there was anything secret in its contents. Besides, had both Ratcliffe and Kendall been in the secretary's employment, it is unlikely that Ratcliffe would have had him shot—unless, of course, the espionage game was being played within an even more Machiavellian scenario than we have reason to suppose.

Regardless of John Ratcliffe's secret life, there was no hiding the fact that the new president was no more effective a leader than the aging Wingfield he had helped depose. Furthermore, the triumvirate of Smith, Martin, and Ratcliffe remained in accord scarcely longer than it took to make the change and be rid of Kendall. As the weeks slipped by, and as the food supplies shrank and the number of fresh-capped graves grew, the surviving settlers looked more and more to the only man with new ideas and the will to implement them. John Smith was by no means the best officer one might wish to serve under. He was short on both temper and stature, and like many small men, he had a compensatingly big ego and a tongue to match it. But he did get things done, he was undeniably courageous (many would call him foolhardy), and when decisions needed making, he would make them—right or wrong.

From a distance of close on four centuries, it is extremely difficult for us to put ourselves in the shoes of those who first limped through the dust and then the mud of James Fort in the autumn of 1607. About a hundred men and boys were left behind after the *Susan Constant* and *Godspeed* departed—a hundred to hold disputed title to territory more extensive than the whole of England. For starters one needs to have a mental image of what a hundred people look like. Imagine them sitting in the stands of a football stadium having an eighty-thousand-person capacity; consider them traveling in a two-thirds-empty jumbo jet or failing to fill three school buses. Then watch them die two or three at a time, reducing the number to barely forty. Although we may successfully understand how small a group they were, comprehending their isolation when we live in a world overflowing with people is much harder. For the colonists there was no quitting, nowhere to go, no escape but the grave. If they had had a productive job to do, its completion would have been something to work toward. Instead their goal was merely survival. Couple that with fear—fear of the Indians, fear of the unseen enemy that sapped their strength, and, perhaps most unnerving of all, fear of one another—and you have a blueprint for failure. An indecisive leadership and the suspicion that any one of your tentmates might be somebody's spy promoted, on the one hand, opportunities for mutiny and, on the other, a reluctance to do or say anything that might be distorted and reported. The trials of Read and Kendall were reminders that the power of an unstable and fractious leadership could be as deadly as any other peril the settlers faced.

The long-established and simplistic explanation for the James Towne colonists' early failures—namely, that there were too many who called themselves gentlemen and too few laborers—simply won't wash. As much of the blame belongs elsewhere: to bad water, to bad planning in London and to resulting bad leadership in Virginia, and ultimately to the timeless frailty of sick and frightened people.

The message that went to England was entirely different. The *Susan Constant* and *Godspeed* got there on July 29, and Newport immediately wrote to Lord Salisbury with what he termed "gladd tidings" from a country "verie Riche in gold and Copper."[41] He had brought samples of the gold, he said, and looked forward to showing them to the king. An official letter from the council to the Company in London made no mention of the sample but spoke of the need for reinforcements "leaste that all devouringe Spaniard lay his ravenous hands upon theas gold showing mountaines."[42] Merchant adventurers who had listened to too many Captain Seagulls rejoiced with caution. On hearing the news, Sir Walter Cope, antiquary, politician, and Virginia Company shareholder, wrote as follows to his friend Lord Salisbury:

> If we may believe, either in words or letters, we are fallen upon a land that promises more than the Land of Promise. Instead of milk we find pearl and gold instead of honey. Thus they say; thus they write. But experience [being] the wisest school mistress must lead your Lordships, whose wisdom teaches to be of slow belief.[43]

Having delivered this opening caveat, Cope went on to say that if the gold turned out to be real, it would take little prompting to get more London citizens to underwrite the next Virginia voyage. He even went so far as to wager that with a little persuasion from the king, fifty citizens who had already subscribed five hundred pounds a head in the forthcoming East India Company voyage to the Orient would be willing to divert their money westward.

Alas, within ten days of Newport's arrival, the bubble burst. A preliminary examination of the samples "appeared at sight so suspycyous" that four independent assayers from different parts of London were commissioned to test them. "In the ende," sneered Cope, "all turned to vapore."[44]

Most historians have concluded that the samples were iron pyrites, appropriately known as fools' gold. This, however, seems unlikely, for a man like Richard Martin (who had collected the samples) must have been well acquainted with iron pyrites, lumps of which were used in the ignition of wheel-lock firearms. It is much more probable that the material was mica, flecks of which are found in estuarine clays. Cope, who evidently had a low opinion of Richard Martin, accused him of deliberately deceiving not only Newport but also the king, the state, and his own father, "Seeking by thys temptation to have drawn hys father to have made over unto him somm Supplyes, which otherwyse he dowted never to procure."[45]

With the dreams of instant wealth tarnished, Newport's cargo of clapboard was seen as very dull indeed. And there was more bad news: If the Virginia council's sealed letter to the Company was to be believed, Newport's sailors had spent much of their time digging up sassafras roots to ship home for their own private sales. "I beleeve they have the thereof two tonnes at the leaste," Wingfield complained, "which if they scatter abroad at their pleasure will pull downe our price for a long time."[46] Given the reaction to the Gosnold and Gilbert cargo from New England in 1602, and the furor created by Sir Walter Ralegh over twenty-two hundredweight, the prospect of two tons must have sent shock waves through the sassafras market. On the other hand, just as they can today, skilled lobbyists were adept at finding silver linings. A surfeit of sassafras might be an immediate problem, but in the long run it simply demonstrated the potential bounty of Virginia and thus could be used as a powerful incentive to investors. As for the embarrassed Christopher Newport, he assured the Company that gold *had* been found but that through an unfortunate slipup, he had brought the wrong sample. He was ready, he said, to go back and "resolves never to see your Lordshippe before he bringe that with hym which he confidentlie beleeved he had broughte before."[47]

At a full meeting of the Company on August 17, the members agreed to let Newport command the supply ship and to add a "nymble pynnace" to accompany it.[48] Together they would transport another hundred men along with all supplies needed both for them and for those already at James Fort. But the Company's generosity went hand in hand with its parsimony. John Smith had complained that tents sent with the original colonists were rotten. Now it was sending a supply of cloth and a quantity of trade beads bought cheaply as leftovers from the East India Company's 1603 voyage, regardless of the fact that they knew the cloth to be "very much motheaten."[49]

Watching and listening through every available keyhole were the spies of Don Pedro de Zúñiga, the Spanish ambassador, who reported to his king that he had found "a trustworthy person through whom I can learn everything that goes on in the [Virginia Company's] council."[50] In the same letter to Philip III, Zúñiga assured his master that the council members were "frightened to death that Your Majesty will throw them out" of Virginia. In an apropos but unconscious allusion to Virginia's future prime crop, Zúñiga urged the king "to root out this noxious plant while it is so easy."[51]

Zúñiga was right to claim that the English feared and expected a Spanish attack on the Virginia settlement. Ever since the Gunpowder Plot of 1605, Protestants had seen Spanish spies and Catholic turncoats lurking around every corner. Early in August Captain George Waymouth, who in 1605 had explored for a suitable site to plant a colony of English Catholics, was arrested at Deal in Kent "with intent as is thought to have betraied his frends and shewed the Spaniards a meanes how to defeat this Verginian attempt."[52] The writer added that Waymouth was a special favorite of the doubting Sir Walter Cope.

Waymouth was undeniably a Catholic, but it by no means followed that he was also a friend of Spain. In a later report to King Philip, Zúñiga stated that the Virginia-bound ship and pinnace were to carry 120 men, each of whom had been required to take the oath of supremacy. This English oath of allegiance was intended to separate those who were loyal to James I from those whose first responsibility was to Pope Paul V, who had forbidden English Catholics to swear it. Whether Waymouth had or would so swear has not been determined, but the fact of his arrest is clear evidence of the nervousness and suspicion that Catholicism generated, coupled with the fear that its New World champions were intent on evicting their new Protestant neighbors.

Had Philip followed the feisty Pedro de Zúñiga's advice to destroy the colony before it could take root, the history of North America might have taken a very different course. According to the ambassador, the fact that the original colonists, and now their first reinforcement, were all men was unequivocal proof that the English were less interested in colonizing than in practical piracy. Although that may well have lurked in the minds of Sir Walter Ralegh and the first Roanoke adventurers, the 1607 operation was truly what its charter claimed—namely, the plantation of England in America.

The Spanish king was proving to be a very thin chip off his father's formidable block. An indecisive pedant reluctant to take responsibility for anything, he left governmental policy to his favorite, the duke of Lerma, while he enjoyed the extravagant but pious privileges of monarchy. Consequently, Zúñiga's impassioned pleas for instant action resulted only in vaguely encouraging replies. Ironically, however, the ambassador's bird dog efforts proved more helpful centuries later to British historians than to 1607 Spain. His reports languished in the Spanish archives until the late nineteenth century, when they were discovered and decoded to provide more, albeit slanted, information about the Virginia project than survives in known British sources.

The ever-frustrated Pedro de Zúñiga earns high marks for trying, for in addition to his covert recruitment of spies and his shipping their reports home to Spain, he did his overt damnedest to scuttle the Virginia adventure at the Court of St. James's. At two o'clock on Sunday, October 7, and only after several delays—the king had only just got back; the king was away hunting; the king had a fever; the king was expecting his council—Zúñiga secured an audience with James I. With the usual obsequious pleasantries behind him, the ambassador told the king in clear (but still diplomatic) language that his Spanish master was not at all amused by Englishmen meddling in America "since it is a part of the Indies belonging to Castile." Failure to recognize that geopolitical fact, Zúñiga added, could have "inconvenient results"—diplomatic doublespeak for the direst military consequences.[53]

James, the son of Mary Queen of Scots and Lord Darnley, who has been described as the comic offspring of a tragic union, firmly believed that the pen was mightier than any number of claymores and that rattling one at him was unsporting and unsettling. His initial response to Zúñiga, therefore, was to claim that he knew nothing of the details surrounding the Virginia voyages and so was in no position to comment. He also didn't know that Spain laid claim to Virginia, and furthermore, he didn't consider it part of the Indies. He did allow, however, that the treaty of 1604 had given Spain restricted access to the Indies proper and stated that if Englishmen went there, they did so at their own risk and, if caught, could expect to be punished. To this Zúñiga replied that it would be better for Anglo-Spanish relations if they were prevented from setting out. Warming to his work, Zúñiga focused again on the Virginia foothold. Reporting afterward to Philip, he claimed to have told James "that this scheme of going to settle in Virginia was exposed [by] the shabby deceit with which it is carried out; for the land is very sterile, and consequently there can be no other object in that place than it seems good for piracy, and that should not be permitted."[54]

James allegedly replied that he was inclined to agree with Zúñiga that the Virginia land was unproductive, adding that those who hoped to find great riches there were deceiving themselves. As for the piracy charge, James would have it looked into. For his part, the king reportedly insisted that he was reaping no personal benefits from the venture. Although Zúñiga did not comment on the point, James's opinion of Virginian productivity belied his opening assurance that he knew no details.

Zúñiga wrote his summary of his audience with the king on October 8, the same day that two vessels, the ship *John and Francis* and the pinnace *Phoenix,* sailed from Gravesend. Virginia's First Supply was on its way.

Ten days later, having received no official reply to his submission, Zúñiga managed to corner Secretary Salisbury and was told (or so he said) that if Englishmen went where they were not allowed, they could expect to be punished, and on reflection he (Salisbury) agreed that Virginia was one of those places. If he did make such an unlikely admission, it was immediately contradicted by James's refusal either to call back the first settlers or to prevent more from sailing, this on the ground that to do so would confirm the king of Spain's claim to be "Lord of all the Indies." Thus was his ambassador returned to square one. An exasperated Zúñiga reported that before the year's end, and with no legal restraints to deter them, five or six ships would be Virginia-bound from London and Plymouth. "It will be a service to God and Your Majesty," Zúñiga asserted, "to expel those rogues from there, hanging them while so little is needed to make it possible."[55]

That letter reached Spain on October 28, and the same day Philip answered it, commending Zúñiga for "converting the Earl of Salisbury to my service"—a conclusion which would have astonished the intensely loyal secretary. Beyond that the king limited his response to what Zúñiga saw as the Virginia crisis by telling him to keep up the good work of sending reports on which ships were leaving. Clearly Philip and the duke of Lerma failed to share their ambassador's sense of urgency. Two weeks later still the Virginia question came up at a meeting of the Spanish royal council, at which Spain's negotiator for the 1604 treaty admitted that he had sidestepped the issue, in part because the English had been in Virginia (albeit off and on) for thirty years and in part because admitting England's right of possession would open the gate to further encroachment. He had thought it better to let there be a tacit agreement that England would be excluded from navigating in the Indies. If asked, of course, the English would have read the treaty's wording as a tacit agreement to do the opposite. Ignoring that point and pursuing their own, the Spanish council now concluded that the tacit agreement gave Spain the right to throw the English out of Virginia before they could receive further reinforcements. To this end the council unanimously proposed ordering Spain's Caribbean fleet to get on with it. The minutes of that meeting bear Philip's characteristically vague endorsement: "Let such measures be taken in this matter as may now and hereafter appear proper."[56]

Meanwhile, at James Fort the frail subjects of all this international diplomatic posturing and indecision had continued on their course toward self-destruction—without any Spanish assistance. Although only about forty colonists had survived the summer, thanks to John Smith's having taken the initiative and embarking on an aggressive policy of trading with the Indians (by force if necessary), the colonists' food supplies were improving, and so were their health and morale. Again Smith talks about the building of houses, but although he tells of his taking over the duties of cape merchant (the supply officer), the original incumbent, Thomas Stoodie, having died at the end of August, Smith makes no reference to building the store in which to house the supplies—the structure which the Virginia Company had ordered to be the first erected. We are left wondering, therefore, where the supplies were kept and how they were distributed or, for that matter, how they were protected from clandestine distribution.

Cooler weather, improved health, and the confidence stemming from the Indians' willingness to trade encouraged the settlers to become more adventurous. Smith led several exploratory expeditions, each expanding their knowledge of the new world around them. In early or perhaps mid-December the council agreed that Smith should try to discover the source of the Chickahominy River, which flows into the James about five miles above Jamestown Island. Smith evidently hoped that it might lead to a great lake which in turn would lead to the Orient and that by finding it, he could upstage Newport, whose similar quest had come to naught at the falls of the James. The omens were not propitious. The weather had turned bitterly cold, ice was beginning to crackle at the river's edge, and icicles were forming on the dead branches of old trees protruding from the shallows—harbingers of a no less chilly reception awaiting Smith and his companions. The oft-told story of that trip and its aftermath survives as perhaps the most celebrated legend in early American history. It goes something like this:

With nine companions, six of them oarsmen, Smith set out in a boat which he described as a barge and made his way about twenty-seven miles up the Chickahominy until his passage was blocked by too many fallen trees. Leaving the boat with seven of his men aboard and instructing them not to go ashore, Smith rented a canoe and two Indian guides allegedly to take him duck hunting but in reality to continue his exploration up the narrowing river. With him went his other two men: gentleman John Robinson and carpenter Thomas Emry. After traveling about twelve miles, they stopped to make a fire and prepare a meal, and Smith, ever anxious to be doing something productive, left Robinson, Emry, and one Indian boiling the food, while he took the second Indian on a short reconnaissance. The two Englishmen were left with their muskets loaded and their matches burning and with instructions to fire a warning shot into the air at the first sight of an approaching Indian. No shot was ever fired.

A quarter of an hour later, Smith heard Indians shouting, and, fearing that Robinson and Emry had fallen victim to a surprise attack, he put his pistol to his guide's head and tied the man's arm to his own hand with the only string available—one of Smith's garters. The guide insisted that he had nothing to do with whatever was going on, and while this strangely bonded couple was arguing, an arrow nicked Smith on the thigh. Spotting two Indians about to try again, Smith swung his guide in front of him as a shield and fired several shots from his pistol, causing his attackers to retreat. Just how he managed to perform the two-handed task of reloading with a reluctant Indian tied to one of them is conveniently ignored.

Smith wrote three versions of this story. In one he merely shot at his attackers, who fell down and fled; in another he killed two of them. In one Robinson and Emry were left sleeping by the fire, and in another they were cooking and watching with matchlocks poised. In two of the accounts Smith left his companions to go bird-hunting for their meal, but in the first he went off "to see the nature of the soile."[57] If, however, we accept the hunting explanation and remember that he shot at his attackers with a pistol (which he identifies as a French pistol), what, we may ask, had become of his nine- or ten-pound hunting musket? In trying to reconstruct what happened, all one can do is to select the most reasonable scenario—unreasonable even though much of it may appear.

Although other chroniclers attested to the skill of Indian bowmen, those who attacked Smith appear to have been uncharacteristically inept. According to his first account, they loosed off twenty or thirty shots as he crouched hiding behind his garter-tied Indian, all of which either missed or fell short. In a later version he "had many arrowes that stucke in his cloathes but no great hurt."[58] No mention is made here of the impact on his unclothed shield. That the arrows should fall short suggests that at least some of his attackers were content to pepper him from long range while others, more courageous, approached close enough to provide Smith with an opportunity to kill two with his pistol. He tells us that the accurate point-blank range of Indian archers was about 40 yards and that elevated "random" firing could do damage up to 120 yards. Although the pistol had a carefully aimed range of perhaps 100 yards, loading it was a woefully slow business, and, one might think, almost impossible with freezing fingers and an appended Indian. Whereas Smith and his living shield were a static target, the Indians were free to move between the protecting cypress trees at the edges of the swamp. It is possible, of course, that they intended to miss, for in the next episode, when Smith was trying to face down two hundred, their leader ordered them not to shoot for fear of killing the guide.

Little doubt exists that the train of events began as the result of the men on the barge ignoring Smith's orders to remain in the safety of midstream. Several went ashore, and one of them, laborer George Cassen, was seized by Indians. His fate at their hands was destined to become an oft-recalled stereotype for Indian savagery. He reportedly was "sacrificed, as they thought, to the Divell [the English interpretation of the Indians' god], being stripped naked, and bound to two stakes, with his backe against a great fire: then did they rippe him and burne his bowels, and dried his flesh to the bones, which they kept above ground in a bye-roome."[59] Under torture the hapless Cassen had revealed that the short and noisy English trader with the bushy beard had gone paddling upriver into the Indians' midst.

The trail led first to Robinson and Emry, who were quickly dispatched in a hail of arrows. The number of attackers is given once as 300 and twice as 200, but either way the number is very large in view of the fact that the Paspahegh tribe, for example, numbered only about 160. But these were not Paspahegh; they belonged to the much larger Pamunkey tribe, which lived in modern King William County at the confluence of the Mattaponi and Pamunkey rivers and had a population of more than 1,000.

Attempting to flee, Smith dragged his doubtless terrified guide with him into the Chickahominy swamp, and there became inescapably stuck. None of the Indians made a move to dispatch him. They simply stood and waited as mired limbs became numb with cold and Smith grew slowly shorter. His no less chilled guide attempted to negotiate, asking that Smith be allowed to rejoin his men at his boat. The Indians saw no merit in that and told Smith that his men were dead. Although the Indians reportedly used the words "the rest . . . were slaine," suggesting more than two, Smith evidently was referring to the canoe, not to the boat on which he had left his seven men. The survivors of that attack had managed to push the boat clear and eventually returned to the fort with the news that Smith almost certainly was lost.

Onto the stage had stepped the Pamunkeys' weroance, a figure ultimately even more formidable than his older half brother, the great and still-unseen chief Powhatan. Smith found himself face-to-face with the sixty-year-old future scourge of the English, Opechancanough. Told that his life would be reserved (not necessarily synonymous with "preserved"), Smith finally gave up, surrendered his pistol, and was hauled out of the mud.

Smith's first version of the story was published within a year of the event; the last became part of his *Generall Historie,* which went to press in 1624 and included a small map of "Ould Virginia" that inexplicably shows only the Roanoke-related section of North Carolina. The caption, however, makes it clear that the plate is intended to illustrate "part of the adventures of Cap: Smith in Virginia." Surrounding the map on three sides is a comic-book series of panels by the engraver, Robert Vaughan, shamelessly borrowing Indian scenes from de Bry's 1590 illustrated edition of Thomas Hariot's Virginia report. Smith is shown in each of six vignettes, and lest readers had difficulty identifying him, the large initials C.S. (Captain Smith) were printed beside him.[60]

The first in the series (though not in placement) shows Smith firing at his attackers with a musket—not a French pistol—with an extremely small Indian tied to him by what must rank among the world's longest garters. The caption reads "C. Smith bindeth a salvage to his arme, fighteth with the King of Pamaunkee and all his company, and slew three of them"—three, not two. True to the caption, the engraving shows Smith's shield tied to his upper arm, not to his hand, as he stated in 1608. One may be forgiven for wondering whether when he was telling his tale—as he doubtless did innumerable times—someone questioned Smith's ability to load with with one hand tied, thus prompting story modifications for the 1624 printing.

The next illustration shows "How they took him prisoner in the Oaze," which is, of course, where we left him.

Safely extracted from the swamp, Smith proceeded to present Opechancanough with a compass and was allowed time to explain how it worked. That led Smith into what he described as "a discourse of the roundnes of the earth, the course of the sunne, moone, starres and plan-

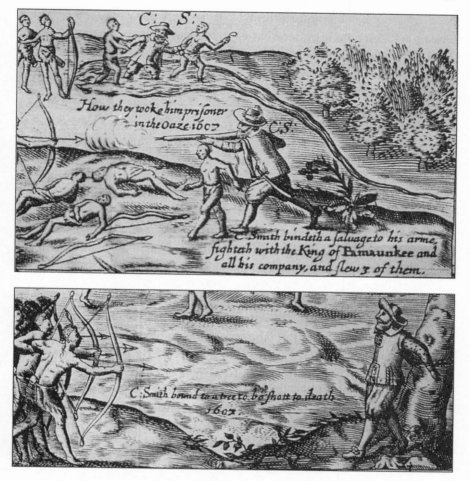

Top: Smith caught in the Chickahominy swamp and using a garter-fettered Indian as his shield. *Just above:* Smith tied to a tree and about to be shot. From his *Generall Historie,* 1624.

nets."[61] With this short course in astronomy behind him, he was escorted back to the rented canoe, where he saw the body of Robinson shot full of arrows. Emry was nowhere to be seen. It is hard to imagine Smith plucked from the mud and being in a position immediately to produce the compass and lecture his captor on why the earth wasn't flat. Perhaps this was why, in his *Generall Historie,* Smith decided to rewrite. In this he kills three attackers and wounds "divers others" and starts back in the direction of his boat only to slip "up to the middle in an oasie creeke." After being pulled out, he is taken back to his own campfire, where the Indians helpfully "chafed his benumbed limbs." It is only now, after Smith has demanded to see their leader, that Opechancanough appears and is given "a round Ivory double compass Dyall," Smith's opening gambit leading to a playing-for-time lesson, not only in astronomy but in world geography, racial differences, "and many other such like matters." This leaves his audience "amazed with admiration"—but only temporarily.[62] An hour later his immediate captors tie him to a tree and prepare to shoot, but even as the bowstrings stretch, Opechancanough steps in with compass held aloft and saves him. This, then, is the *Generall Historie*'s version of Smith's capture, and although it still contains much that is hard to believe, the sequence of events is more logical than was the original *True Relation.*

Through the next several days Smith was extravagantly fed (he thought he was being fattened to be eaten) and carried up and down the rivers from tribe to tribe to be paraded as the ultimate trophy. In the course of these travels Smith had several conversations with Opechancanough, ranging from handling sailing ships to Christianity—though in what language is unstated. In return the weroance explained the extent of Powhatan's empire. Talking about nations beyond it, he mentioned Ocanahonan, a place which historian Philip L. Barbour locates somewhere on the Virginia-Carolina border west of the Chowan River. The people living there, Opechancanough told Smith, wore clothes just like his. Although Smith drew no immediate conclusion from that surprising revelation, one cannot help wondering whether the inhabitants of Ocanahonan included survivors from the Lost Colony or alternatively whether the Indians knew enough about the settlers' fate to be wearing their clothes. Smith, however, was too much in fear for his own life to be bothering about Ralegh's people. Every hour through his long imprisonment, he confessed, he was expecting "to be put to one death or other."[63]

While he was held prisoner at Opechancanough's hunting camp at Rasaweack on the north bank of the Chickahominy, the Indians, believing that English medicine was superior to theirs, called on Smith to cure a man he had wounded with his pistol. Back at the fort, Smith told them, he had a water which he knew would do the trick—if his captors would let him fetch it. But although the Indians had high regard for English medical skills, they held English veracity in less esteem: they would send their own messengers to collect the curative. Though Smith was disappointed that his escape ploy had failed, the incident provided him with an opportunity to let his compatriots know that he was alive. Using pages from a pocket notebook, "he write his minde to them at the Fort,"[64] and in three days the couriers returned with the supplies he had requested—

more important, demonstrating a new level of English magic: thought transference with the aid only of marks on paper.

Smith eventually was taken to Powhatan's capital at Werowocomoco on the York River and thus became the first Englishman to come face-to-face with the great leader—or possibly face-to-foot because Powhatan received him lying on what Smith called a bedstead under a cover of raccoon skins. Flanking him on mats sat his "chiefe men," and behind them attendant young women, their heads painted red and their shoulders draped with chains of white beads. What else they wore is unclear, though Smith refers to Powhatan himself as a "naked Salvage." Earlier the letter carriers had gone to the fort "in as bitter weather as could be of frost and snow,"[65] leaving no doubt that this was already goose bump time in Virginia.

In the first of Smith's accounts of what happened next, he records nothing beyond a dialogue between Powhatan and himself wherein the former tries to find out why the English have come to his country (Smith blames it on storms and ship damage caused by Spanish attackers), and in return Smith tries to discover what Powhatan knows of American geography. At the end of these exchanges Powhatan releases him and sends him home with four men to guard and guide. Any reader with prior knowledge of the Jamestown Story will have recognized that something is missing: Not a word has been said about the famous Pocahontas rescue.

In the *Generall Historie* the sequence begins with Smith being brought into Powhatan's palace-hut, whereupon all the assembled Indians give "a great shout." Then a senior female, Oppossunoquonuske, sister to the weroance of the Appomattocs, whom Smith had met while on his James River exploration with Newport, brings him water to wash his hands. Another woman brings feathers to dry them; then he is fed "after their best barbarous manner."[66] To this point (and probably beyond) one can detect a carefully orchestrated ceremony.

Smith had been in Indian hands for perhaps two weeks, held by Powhatan's younger half brother, who knew that he had stumbled on the most desirable of English prisoners. Opechancanough's long interviews with Smith (somehow overcoming any language barrier) must have left the weroance confident that he had milked the bombastic Briton of everything he had to tell. Furthermore, he almost certainly had received instructions from Powhatan on how to treat the prisoner and in which villages to parade him before bringing him to Werowocomoco.

We cannot doubt that Powhatan, therefore, had had time to weigh the information, review his options, and ponder the advice of his assembled "chiefe men" before deciding what would be done when Smith was finally

The emperor Powhatan with tobacco pipe in hand and enthroned in his lodge; vignette embellishing Smith's map of Virginia (second state incorrectly dated 1606). Disagreeing with Smith's text, the caption notes that Powhatan "held this state & fashion" when Smith was brought before him. The map was first published in 1612.

brought before him. With the cast assembled, the roles defined, and the script explained (if not rehearsed), it is unthinkable once the performance began that any mid-scene glitch would be allowed to mar its dramatic conclusion.

According to Smith, a long consultation followed the feasting, but as he does not elaborate, the chances are that either he failed to understand what was being said or it was conducted out of his hearing. At its end two large rocks are brought in, Smith is seized and forced to place his head on the stones as though on a block. With clubs raised, several executioners await the order "to beate out his braines."[67] Enter Pocahontas, Powhatan's favorite daughter, a child no more than ten or twelve years old; she rushes

Pocahontas intercedes for Smith's life, a mistake which, according
to the caption, led to his subjecting "39 of their kings." To find
out how, it advises "reade y^e history." An illustration from
Smith's *Generall Historie*, 1624.

forward, takes Smith's head in her arms, and lays her head on top of his
to receive the blows. Powhatan relents, spares Smith's life, and announces
to the assembled company that henceforth the Englishman shall live to
make hatchets for him and bells for his daughter.

I hasten to add that my intent is not to make light of this treasured
American legend, but to suggest the admittedly heretical possibility that
what Smith later (perhaps *much* later) chose to interpret as Pocahontas's
instinctive gesture on his behalf was in reality a piece of carefully staged
theater. Through the affair of the wounded warrior and Smith's message
to the fort, its inhabitants knew that he was in the hands of Powhatan's
kinsman. Consequently, to have executed Smith would have been to
bring down on Powhatan and his confederacy the wrath of the English,
and as Smith had emphasized to Opechancanough, there were plenty
more across the water where these came from. It made much better sense
to spare him and to try to turn him into an ally. To that end, what better
way could the idea of benevolence be transmitted than through a response
to the universal language of a child's tenderness? The king's power had

been demonstrated, as had the impotence of his captive—dramatized by his being saved not by strength but by the weakness of a female child.

No matter how one reads the evidence, the Pocahontas-Smith legend—as told in Virginia from the eighteenth through the nineteenth century, and embodied in the buckskinned beauty in bronze who still greets visitors at Jamestown—stands at some distance from the truth. Pocahontas (Powhatan's pet name for the daughter whose real name was Matoaka) seems to have been born in 1595, making her no more than a child of barely twelve when she "saved" the bearded, battle-scarred twenty-seven-year-old John Smith, whom, as far as we know, she had never before set eyes on. That she later became attracted to the English to the extent of eventually marrying one of them and going to England is firmly established, but her relationship with Smith never extended beyond mutual respect, or so he said. When others suggested that Smith could have secured the country by marrying her himself, he insisted that the thought never crossed his mind, and that in any case marriage to Pocahontas "could no way have intitled him by any right to the kingdome."[68]

Two days after sparing his prisoner, Powhatan came to the place where Smith was confined and told him that they were now friends. If Smith would go to James Fort and send him "two great gunnes, and a gryndstone,"[69] Powhatan would make him weroance of Capahowasic, a few miles downstream on the York River from Werowocomoco, and accept him as a son to be named Nantaquoid. Smith said he was honored, and off he went to James Fort accompanied by a dozen guides (or four, depending on which of Smith's narratives one prefers) who presumably intended to carry home the two pieces of ordnance and the grindstone. Among the guides went Rawhunt, one of Powhatan's most trusted servants.

On or about January 2, 1608, John Smith finally returned to base and there showed Rawhunt and the others two demiculverins, which he said were theirs for the taking—all nine thousand pounds of them. In a wry understatement, Smith noted that "they found them somewhat too heavie." Instead Smith gave a demonstration of a demiculverin's firepower, loading one or both with stones and discharging them at a "great tree loaded with Isickles, the yce and branches came so tumbling downe, that the poor Salvages ran away halfe dead with feare."[70] Later they returned, were given a miscellany of more portable gifts for Powhatan, his women, and his children, and departed relatively well satisfied. What Powhatan had to say to Rawhunt when he learned that his new son had sent him trinkets instead of great guns and the grindstone can only be imagined. However, if blame was to be laid, it cannot have been at

Smith's door, for several days later Pocahontas and her attendants were sent to the fort bearing supplies of food for the colonists.

The demiculverin saga is of interest on several counts, not the least being the description of the hardness of the weather in December 1607. In modern times daytime temperatures rarely drop into the teens, and the frost quickly disappears when the sun gets up. Indeed, those of us fortunate enough to live beside the river in sight of Jamestown Island are often able to sit on patios without coats as late as the first week in January. However, as described by Smith throughout the weeks of his captivity, the weather remained as bitter as anything experienced today in late February and March. Pertinent, too, is the reaction (or lack of it) from the fort-bound colonists when Smith turned up with twelve Indian companions for whose entertainment he proceeded to waste as much as eighteen pounds of gunpowder.

Smith returned to find conditions in the fort no less explosive; he described them as in a state of combustion. With the ground frozen, with no opportunities for fishing or hunting, and with food supplies almost exhausted, the few settlers still strong enough to take a stand on anything were preparing to board the *Discovery* and abandon the colony. That, however, is one version. Another has Smith arriving shortly after dawn to be greeted by "each man with the truest signes of joy"—with the exception of Gabriel Archer "and some 2. or 3. of his."[71] No mention is made of the planned departure, and in the account which does speak of it the men promoting the abandonment are not named.

In Smith's absence President Ratcliffe had used his two votes to override the ever-sick John Martin's nay, thus to elect his friend Archer to the council. One is tempted to conclude, therefore, that Ratcliffe and Archer were leading the exodus. Be that as it may, Smith arrives in the nick of time, trains sakers, falcons, and muskets on the pinnace, and threatens to sink it if it tries to cast off—a rerun of the Kendall standoff. Just as we do not know who was aboard the *Discovery*, so there is no knowing who rallied to Smith to be his gun crews and musketeers. According to the deposed President Wingfield (who remained a prisoner on the ship), Archer, in the powerful dual roles of councillor and recorder, indicted Smith for causing the deaths of his Chickahominy companions Robinson and Emry, had him deposed from the council, tried, and condemned—all within hours of his return. Smith was to hang the next day, said Wingfield, "so speedie is our lawe thear."[72] Thus, with Smith gone for good, Ratcliffe's two votes could legally be used to confirm Archer to the council over Martin's one-vote opposition.

But even as Smith's enemies congratulated themselves, and while he contemplated his last dawn, help was sailing up the James River. Just as darkness fell on this tumultuous day, the returning Christopher Newport dropped anchor off Jamestown Island. With him aboard the *John and Francis* came at least 60 of the 100 (or 120) new colonists, most of them relatively healthy and quickly shifting the numerical balance away from the island's 40 survivors. Smith was freed, the long-imprisoned Wingfield was taken ashore and allowed to live in the fort, Archer's plans to create a parliamentary system at variance with the Company's instructions were scotched, and something akin to the status quo was restored.

To many who welcomed Newport's return with the First Supply, this may have seemed like the kind of happy ending familiar to London theatergoers, the euphoria marred only by the news that the *Phoenix* with forty more settlers and some of the supplies had disappeared into a fog on Christmas Eve, not to be seen again. The *John and Francis* arrived on Saturday, January 2, 1608, and Captain Newport probably spent Sunday sorting out the political mess and conferring with Smith and others about housing the new arrivals, most of whom remained aboard until Monday.

Three days later, on January 7, there rang out from within the fort the cry which, from the beginning of time, has struck terror into every human heart: Fire!

CHAPTER VII

Alarums and Excursions

❧

"CAPTAYNE Newport haveing landed, lodged, and refreshed his men, ymploied some of them aboute a faire stoare house, others about a stove, and his Maryners aboute a Church, all which workes they finished cherefully and in short tyme." Thus wrote the deposed President Wingfield, clearly suggesting that until Newport's return no adequate storehouse, communal kitchen (the stove), or church had been built under either Ratcliffe's or Wingfield's regime. The latter's next sentence begins "The 7 of Ianuary, our Towne was almost quite burnt, with all our apparell and provision. . . ."[1] If this statement is taken at face value, one should conclude that between Monday and Thursday Newport's men erected all three public buildings. Considering that the trees had to be felled; the timbers dressed, laid out, and morticed; postholes dug; roofing materials assembled; and wattle walling created, all by people who were not really housewrights, one is left wondering whether Wingfield really meant what he implied.

As noted earlier, John Smith was to claim that in the fall of 1607 he had set the survivors to "binde thatch, some to build houses, others to thatch them"[2] so that he quickly provided durable accommodation for most of the settlers. In that 1612 report, of which Smith was only part author, no mention is made of his building a church. Nineteen years later, however, he recalled that when he "went first to Virginia," in fair weather services were held in the open, and in foul weather under a rotting tent. "This," said Smith, "was our Church, till wee built a homely thing like a barne, set upon Cratchets [forked poles], covered with rafts [rafters], sedge, and earth, so was also the walls."[3] He went on to suggest that Sunday sermons were read there until the minister died—this a reference to

Robert Hunt, previously vicar of Heathfield in Sussex, surrogate in Virginia for his friend the great Virginia publicist and editor the Reverend Richard Hakluyt.

In November 1606 King James had issued a series of articles and instructions to the men named in the First Virginia Charter, and on the twenty-fourth of the same month he set his seal to a dispensation provided jointly to Hakluyt and Hunt, authorizing them to go with the expedition to preach the word of God and thereby to absent themselves from their respective English parishes. At fifty-four Hakluyt was a relatively old man and did not go; thus it fell to the thirty-seven-year-old (or thereabouts) Hunt to carry the Protestant banner into the heathen wilderness. He was to earn the respect of all sides in the James Towne disputes, and his death in 1608 would be an incalculable loss.

Most authorities, from Lyon G. Tyler onward, have concluded that James Towne's first church was built before the January 1608 fire, but if so, it is curious that neither in his *True Relation* (1608) nor in the *Proceedings* (1612) did Smith make any reference to that pious accomplishment. With the leadership still living in tents through the summer of 1607, logic dictates that the rotting tent served until ill health discouraged anyone from building anything, and this moves us into the period when Smith took charge and supervised the building of houses. One might argue, therefore, that if he did not build a church then (had he done so, he would have said so), at no prior time were the circumstances right for such construction.

Though simple and rustic, the cratchet church was considered of better construction than the best of the settlers' houses, which Smith described as being "of the like curiosity, but the most part farre much worse workmanship, that could neither well defend [against] wind nor raine."[4] Were these, then, the houses built in the fall of 1607 for which Smith chose to take credit? These problems, here and throughout the Roanoke and James Towne narratives, result from the testimony of sometimes incoherent witnesses often recorded years after the events they were describing and not infrequently "helped" by an incompetent seventeenth-century editor.

Wingfield had seemed relatively pleased with the construction capabilities of Newport's men, referring to a "faire stoare house," and in those days "fair" was the antonym of "foul" and meant "pleasing to the eye, good-looking." Although he provided no descriptive adjective for either the stove or the church, the context presumes satisfaction with all three. Sixteen years later, in a bitter attack on the avarice and incompetence of

Newport's mariners, John Smith charged that "they did helpe to build such a golden Church that we can say the raine washed neere to nothing in 14. days."[5] That may be a wild exaggeration, but it would seem that the postfire store and church were not the best, for in September the church was repaired and the store reroofed, work which had begun in April— only three months after they were built. But first came the fire.

How it started no one knows, but where it began can be deduced. Smith stated in his usual elliptical style, "Where this new supply being lodged with the rest, accidentally fired the quarters, and so the Towne."[6] Thus the fire began in the place where the new supplies were quartered or housed. Because public buildings of this kind were usually adjacent to the central square (as was the case at Fort St. George on the Kennebec), it is fair to assume that the same was true of James Towne, and on that basis we can attempt to reconstruct how the flames spread. To do that, we need to consider the testimony of eyewitnesses, beginning with a man new to us.

Francis Perkins (or Perkin) had just arrived aboard the *John and Francis.* Smith in his *Proceedings* listed him as a laborer, but clearly Perkins did not see himself as such. On the contrary, he would write seeking help from members of the Virginia Company in London to get him elected to the council at James Towne. With minimal modesty he explained that some of its members "understand affairs of state no better than I do, and whom I equal in business [acumen]."[7] By the time Smith published his *Generall Historie* in 1624, he had upgraded Perkins to the rank of gentleman, which was almost certainly where he belonged. He was therefore a witness with educated eyes and one who wrote his recollections of the fire within three months of the catastrophe: "After we disembarked, which was on Monday, the following Thursday there was a fire that spread so that all the houses in the fort were burned down, including the storehouse for munition and supplies, leaving only three. Everything my son and I had was burned, except a mattress which had not yet been taken off the ship."[8]

We could have wished for much more, but Perkins provides several pieces of important information: He gives us the day of the blaze (Thursday); he says that the munitions were in the store and that only three buildings survived. Wingfield's account, though providing the date (January 7), was briefer still. "Our Towne," he said, "was almost quite burnt, with all our apparell and privision."[9] Then comes Smith, in three versions. In 1608: "Within five or six dayes after the arrivall of the Ship, by a mischaunce our Fort was burned, and the most of our apparell, lodging and private provision, many of our old men diseased, and of our new for want of lodging perished."[10] In 1612 Smith added some more specific information: ". . . the Towne, which being but thatched with reeds the fire was so fierce as it burnt their pallizadoes (though 10. or 12 yardes distant) with their armes, bedding, apparell, and much private provision. Good Master Hunt our preacher lost all his library, and al that he had (but the cloathes on his backe,) yet none ever see him repine at his losse. This hapned in the winter, in that extreame frost, 1607."[11] In 1624 Smith's *Generall Historie* repeated the same passage but changed the distance between buildings and palisade from ten or twelve yards to eight or ten.

We know that the fire occurred at a time of an incredibly hard frost— only a week earlier, Smith had shot icicles out of a tree. No one mentioned snow, so it would seem that there was none on the thatched roofs. Had there been, the roof of the first building might well have collapsed inward, trapping the fire within the walls and quenching it as the snow melted. Consequently, sparks rising into the first burning roof would not have ignited others had they been protected by even an inch of snow. The presumption must therefore be that a late December ice storm had been followed by a period of dry cold, freezing the river well beyond the shore, making the efforts of a bucket brigade so slow as to be useless.

Experiments carried out in Serbia by anthropologist Dr. H. A. Bankoff of Brooklyn College, New York, have demonstrated what happens when an earthfast wattle-and-daub cottage burns. A fire started in the room below the floored attic takes twenty minutes to burn through the thatched roof. That initial blaze sends tremendous heat upward, causing the burning thatch to blow dangerously away, but then the fire dies down and can be extinguished without irreparable damage to the clay-covered walls. Left to itself, however, the caved rafters continue to burn, the flames running up them to ignite the wall posts. Slowly, in the course of about six hours, some (but not all) of the framing posts burn down through the walls, igniting wattles as they go. Similar destruction patterns were discerned at the Wolstenholme Towne site, which the Indians burned in 1622. While some posts had charred all the way down into the ground, scorching the clay around them as they went, others in the same building showed no signs of burning. With this in mind, we have to ask how total was the destruction at James Fort, and if it really was complete, why did more than a hundred people fail to halt it at the end of the first phase?

That question promptly poses another: Did the fire break out in the daytime or at night? The only evidence, oblique though it is, comes from Perkins, who tells us that of all his possessions, only a mattress was still safe aboard the *John and Francis*. Although he does not say so, it is possible that while his lodgings were being prepared ashore, he continued to sleep on the ship. If that were so and he was actually asleep on the mattress at the time, he probably would have said so. There are obvious flaws in that reasoning. If the mattress was Perkins's bed, why did he not say that other associated bedding survived?

Any thesis built on what people did *not* say has an inherently weak foundation, but for reconstructing the James Towne fire one has little else. If the fire swept the fort at night, the sight of the flames leaping from roof to roof, and of the showers of sparks flying up into the black sky to be reflected on the river's icy mirror, would have been so terrifying and at the same time so beautiful that someone *surely* would have mentioned it. In daylight fire loses its majesty and thus some of its terror, and for those close to it the smoke shrouds the scale of the disaster. Not until it is over, and one sees the extent of the wreckage, is the lasting impression registered. Thus, in each of the surviving descriptions, the results of the fire are described and not the blaze itself.

Assuming that the fire did occur during the day, we ask again: Where were the thirty-eight or forty surviving original settlers? Where were the sixty or eighty new arrivals? Where were Newport's sailors? And where, for that matter, was John Smith, who in most of his accounts leaps into the forefront of the action?

The usual practice when one was faced with an urban fire was to tear down or even blow up buildings in its path. Although the James Fort structures evidently were so poorly constructed that gunpowder would have done more harm than good, one might think that with more than a hundred men on hand, the blaze could have been quickly isolated, and that sentinels on the roofs of adjacent houses could have smothered falling sparks before they could do real damage. Wind always plays a significant role in the direction in which a fire spreads and at the same time saves whatever lies in the wind's path before the blaze reaches it. In theory, therefore, if the fire started in the centrally located storehouse, at least half the settlement should have been spared. Instead it seems that the flames spread in every direction at once and so quickly that the settlers could do nothing but run for their lives.

The explanation may lie in Perkins's testimony, in which he tells us that save for three houses, everything burned, including "the storehouse for munitions and supplies." It is true that in the seventeenth century the word "munition" embraced all the equipment of war, not merely ammunition, but in Perkins's context, gunpowder can certainly be presumed to be at least part of the cited munitions. If, therefore, the colony's gunpowder was kept in the place where the fire broke out, the barrels would have exploded, propelling blazing pieces up into the air to rain down on roofs in all directions. The fire would have started everywhere at once and would have taken hold on the thatched roofs before anyone could have done anything about it. An obvious flaw in this script, however, is that nobody said anything about an explosion. Indeed, neither Smith nor Wingfield made any specific reference to the loss of munitions.

The plan of Fort St. George on the Kennebec shows the powder magazine located at one far corner and within a flanker whose walls would diminish the impact of any accident. Then again, Robert Barret's 1598 *The Theorick and Practike of Moderne Warres* shows in detail how any army commander should lay out his camp: placing "the munition of the artillery" at one corner within a separating earthwork. In short, it would be an incredibly foolish or lax commander who stored his gunpowder in the middle of the camp, fort, or town. But if that is what the James Towne leaders did, they would almost certainly say as little about it as possible. The resulting cover-up could explain why so little information reached London to describe what long remained one of the most spectacular catastrophes in early British colonial history.

In the midst of a freezing winter, the loss of clothing must have been particularly disastrous, and each of the three witnesses cited the loss of "apparell." Perkins became specific when pleading for replacements, asking that his friend Sir William Cornwallis send him "ten pounds worth of discarded clothing, be it [outer] apparel, underwear, doublet, breeches, mantle, hose, or whatever he likes, for we need everything because the fire burned all we had, and anything will be of use to us."[12] For this information we have to thank Spain's bird dog in London, the ever-probing, ever-hunting Ambassador Pedro de Zúñiga, who acquired a copy of Perkins's letter, had it translated into Spanish, and shipped to Philip III on June 26, 1608. Thus the bothersome reference to Perkins's "underwear" (a term not in general use until the late nineteenth century) is evidently a product of the modern retranslation. More important is the reminder that Spain was watching and, if Zúñiga had his way, preparing to accomplish what the fire had failed to do.

Burning the settlers' shelter and sustenance was blow enough, but according to Smith, the fire also burned the palisades—regardless of the fact that the houses had been set back on lines separating the buildings from the palisades by a minimum of thirty feet. To take effective hold, fire has to burn upward and feed from underneath. But the vertical walls of a palisade have no underneath. Three explanations are possible: first, that Smith was deceiving when describing the set-back building line and that sheds were actually built directly against the palisades; second, that the bulwarks' cannon were mounted on raised platforms; and third, that elevated board-floored walkways were attached to the inside of the palisades to enable musketeers to fire over the top. This last calls for a level of construction that no one mentioned at any time in the history of James Fort. But as a way of defending walls too long to be enfiladed, such a platform is by no means unlikely. There were only two others: The palisades were breast-high and one fired over the top (hence the term "breastwork"), or vertical slots were cut between the posts or pales to serve as musket ports. In 1630 a plan for a major Anglo-French settlement in what later became South Carolina instructed that "in the paile make loope holes for Muskett shott."[13]

Unfortunately the most detailed description of James Fort was not to be written for another two years, and as its author would not see the fort for the first time until May 1610—by which time many changes could have been made—such testimony could be misleading. Consequently, the search for James Fort's appearance must be suspended at this point. Suffice it to say that April found the settlers "rebuilding our towne, the repairing our pallisadoes, the cutting downe trees, preparing our fields, planting our corne, and [working] to rebuild our Church, and recover our store-house; al men thus busie at their several labours. . . ."[14] Why, or if, they delayed from January 7 until April to embark on this work remains a mystery. It is no easier to explain the constructional chronology. The above-cited passage from Smith's *Proceedings* begins with the words "The spring approching, and the ship departed," thus describing activity after April 10, when Christopher Newport and the *John and Francis* sailed for England. The *Proceedings* unequivocally tell us that *after* the ship sailed, the men rebuilt the church. But ex-President Wingfield had told us that it was Newport's mariners who built it—at the same time that others of his men were putting up the fair storehouse and the kitchen. Remembering that Smith later dismissed the sailors' structure as so poor that in two weeks the rain virtually destroyed it, there remains the possibility that an extremely rough church, store, and other buildings were quickly erected in the immediate aftermath of the fire and that by April they were in need of extensive repairs.

Difficult though it is to believe, no laborers were put to work digging a well inside the fort for a full year *after* the fire. Until then the colonists continued to draw their water from the river, which, as George Percy noted, "was at floud, verie salt, at a low tide full of slime and filth, which was the destruction of many of our men."[15] With Percy aware that drinking bad water could cause death, one must suppose that everyone else knew it. If so, we have to wonder why they were not clamoring for a well or at least for water to be brought from mainland springs and housed in barrels in the fort.

Between the January fire and Newport's departure in April much happened to shape both the colony's administration and its relations with the Indians, most of it the product of greed.

The loss of the First Supply's foodstuffs meant that after three days of feasting and rejoicing, the ill-fed old survivors found themselves hosts to as many as eighty new mouths, all of them with teeth chattering and in need of shelter. In short, James Towne was now infinitely worse off than it had been before, as Smith admitted in his reference to many of the old men dying through the loss of provisions and the new perishing for want of lodging. If they had been left to themselves, there might have been nobody to greet the spring. That some survived was due primarily to the hard-to-justify generosity of Powhatan, who twice a week sent gifts of bread, venison, and other foodstuffs as personal gifts to Smith. Popular legend has it that Pocahontas was often the carrier of these gifts, but in his first narrative, the *True Relation,* Smith introduces her later in another context, having omitted any mention of her or the famous head-on-the-block scene at Werowocomoco.

As Powhatan's prisoner Smith had not only lectured his captors on everything from world politics to astronomy but also propounded on the omnipotence of his "father" from across the sea, Christopher Newport. Consequently, when Newport returned, Powhatan was anxious to meet him. But Newport was wary of Smith's relationship with the Indian leader and at the same time was enamored of his own management skills. Savages, however important, should be made to wait.

Instructed by the Company to make a real effort to find Ralegh's 1587 colonists and reacting to Indian reports of people wearing European clothes living to the south of Roanoke Island, Newport had arranged with the king of the Paspaheghs to serve as guide to two of his men. But they got no farther than Warraskoyack on the south side of the James River before the Indian tricked and cheated the Englishmen in some unspecified manner and left them. For the time being, therefore, the quest for the Lost Colony was called off. Nevertheless, the rumors persisted, the most specific being that inland to the southwest "the People have howses built with stone walls, and one story above another, so taught them by those English who escaped the slaughter at Roanoak." According to the Indian

Left: Fragment from a bronze candelabrum dating from the first half of the sixteenth century and found on an Indian site in King William County. Height 4½ inches. *Right:* A bell metal mortar dated 1590 and found in King William County; probably Dutch. Height 3½ inches.

report, there had been seven survivors—four men, two boys, and "one young Maid"[16]—who had fled up the Chowan River and were lodged at the town of Ritanoe, where they were working copper for its weroance.

No one has yet proved the truth of this or any other Lost Colony survivor story, but over the years the chance discovery of several eye-catching metal artifacts have helped keep alive the legend of these and other lost Europeans. Among them are a part of a German bronze candelabrum dating from the first half of the sixteenth century and dug up in King William County and an elaborately decorated bronze mortar inscribed in relief LEEITE VERWINT AL DINCK ANNO 1590, found in a field near Richmond. The most recent was shown to me even as this chapter was being written: a Renaissance-style Catholic bronze seal matrix found near Smithfield and, like the candelabrum, datable to the first half of the sixteenth century. Whether this latest treasure is a relic of a Spanish presence in Virginia prior to 1607 or all these relics were subsequently traded as "toys" to the Indians remains anybody's guess.

Impression from a copper-alloy seal matrix of a kind associated with a Catholic order and dating from the first half of the sixteenth century. Found near Suffolk, Virginia. Length about 3¼ inches.

In February 1608, with the James Fort settlers almost entirely dependent on the Indians for food, Smith and Newport made the long-promised visit to Powhatan. With them went a new member of the council, Mathew Scrivener, who had arrived on the *John and Francis* and quickly showed himself to be Smith's loyal supporter. Rather than march and canoe to Werowocomoco, they sailed down the James and up Prince Henry's (York) River aboard the *Discovery* and an oar-propelled barge, together transporting a company of forty men. Twenty of them went ashore in the barge with Smith, all wearing quilted armored vests called jacks and armed with swords and muskets. Smith was taking no chances.

Powhatan's desire to meet Newport was in part curiosity to see what manner of man it was whom Smith in Indian parlance called father, but also to let him know that he, Powhatan, was no less a father to his people.

Considerable care, coupled perhaps with a degree of cynicism, had there-fore gone into preparing the reception. Knowing how much the English needed his food, Powhatan had forty or fifty large platters of bread set outside his house as gifts. For his part, Smith gave the king a white grey-hound, a suit made of red cloth, and a hat. This might seem an irrelevant detail, having nothing to do with our search for the shape and character of early James Towne, until one remembers that only a few weeks earlier the fire reportedly had cost the settlers all their clothing, munitions, and other supplies. Evidently much must have escaped by being aboard the *John and Francis,* for Newport was later able to give Powhatan twenty swords, a gift of which Smith vehemently disapproved. As for the jacks worn by his escort, these may well have belonged to the ship, for such coats were most widely used as light and flexible armor by fighting men at sea. Indeed, the wearing of jacks might be evidence that the colonists' plate armor corselets had lost their straps and linings in the fire.

In spite of the fact that Smith had been in Powhatan's court before, albeit under different circumstances, he declared himself vastly impressed by "this proude salvage," enthroned among "his finest women, and the principall of his chiefe men," and confessed that he was in the presence of "such a Majestie as I cannot expresse, nor yet have often seene, either in Pagan or Christian."[17] Opposunoquonuske, the weroansqua (queen) of the Appomattocs who had brought the prisoner Smith water to wash his hands and who, historian Philip Barbour notes, had no love for the English,[18] now did it again. This time Smith, no longer in immediate fear of death, had time to note that she was "a comely yong Salvage."[19]

Powhatan did not disguise his disappointment that he and his people were all dressed up to greet Father Newport and were getting instead only the already familiar Smith; but he evidently did his best not to see it as a snub. Forced to wait until the next day, Powhatan invited Smith to sit beside him, while announcing to the assembly that he had named Smith a weroance of the Powhatans, that in consequence, all corn, women, and land should be to the English as to Powhatan's own people, and that thenceforth no man should call them strangers. These expressions of friendship, coupled with interminable "orations of protestations" and "pretty Discourses"[20] (most of which Smith's companions cannot have understood), evidently took awhile, as did their repetition to the throng of about five hundred assembled outside. By the time the speeches were over, the mandatory feasting was concluded, and Smith able to leave, the tide had gone out, leaving his barge stranded in the mud. Though fearing a trap, he had no alternative but to accept Powhatan's offer of overnight accommodation and renewed feasting. Those of his escort who possessed wheel lock or snaphaunce pistols no doubt slept with them primed and within reach.

There was no trap, and the next morning Newport, Scrivener, and the rest of the company arrived to begin their meeting, opening with a pre-arranged ceremony at which both sides played their hands with equal caution. Smith had told Powhatan that to prove his friendship, Newport would give the Indian king his son as hostage and asked that in return Powhatan surrender his own son. Newport's "sonne" turned out to be a thirteen-year-old boy laborer named Thomas Savage, perhaps jokingly selected for the appropriateness of his name. In turn, Powhatan's "son" proved to be a trusted servant named Namontack, described as "one of a shrewd, subtill capacitie,"[21] who was to be taken back to England by Newport and touted as a genuine Virginia prince.

No surviving accounts have anything to say about Powhatan's reaction to meeting Smith's "father," and in any case the Indian leader was too wily a player to show what he was thinking. However, he may quickly have concluded that the best the white men could produce was no better than many another, and somewhat less so in that, having lost one hand to the Spaniards in 1590, Newport could not now draw a bow. The English might have guns and sharp swords, and Smith might be able to transmit his thoughts on bits of paper, but when it came right down to it, they starved and died like anyone else. In trading with them, Powhatan concluded that he held most of the cards.

"Captain Newport," he said, "it is not agreeable to my greatnesse, in this pedling manner to trade for trifles; and I esteeme you also a great Werowance. Therefore lay me downe all your commodities together; what I like I will take, and in recompence give you what I thinke fitting their value."[22]

Had Smith been the negotiator, not merely the interpreter, he would have found a polite seventeenth-century way of saying, "Not bloody likely!" But although he warned that Powhatan intended to cheat, Newport was so anxious to exhibit his own greatness that he refused to haggle. Smith was later to say that they could have gotten a better deal in Spain! Instead of trading their English goods for an expected twenty hogsheads (about 160 bushels) of corn, they got scarcely 4 bushels. Fortunately for all concerned, after noticing Powhatan's interest in blue beads, Smith was later able to strike a much more satisfactory deal. These beads, he said, were made from a rare material the color of the sky and were worn only by the world's greatest kings. The pitch made Powhatan, like many a

Left: Through trade and by stealth Powhatan acquired several hundred swords. Found by a Civil War relic collector in Henrico County, where Powhatan and his immediate followers lived during the latter years of his life, this broadsword may have been one such Indian trophy. Surviving length 19¼ inches. *Right:* John Smith trading with Indians in New England; detail from a de Bry engraving. The proffered knife is drawn with sufficient accuracy to show what appears to be the mark of the London Cutter's Company on its blade.

modern used-car customer, "halfe madde to be the owner of such strange Jewells,"[23] mad enough in fact to exchange 300 bushels of corn for a couple of pounds of beads.

With Newport, on the one hand, wanting to be seen as regally generous and Smith, on the other, equally anxious to get the best for his buck, it was inevitable that relations between the two men should grow strained. Neither could have forgotten that it was under Newport's orders that Smith had traveled to Virginia as a prisoner and that with Newport's concurrence, too, he had at first had been denied his seat on the council. Consequently, there developed increasing competition to show the settlers, new and old, who was the more successful in meeting their needs. The corn-getting visit to Powhatan clearly ended with a score for Smith.

If Smith's own, admittedly self-serving writings are to be believed, the James Towne fire had virtually negated the good that the arrival of the *John and Francis* had promised. Worse, a bad decision made in the euphoria of that arrival had wrecked trading values. To keep the ship's sailors happy, the council had agreed that they should be free to trade privately with the Indians on any terms they liked. Before long, Indian goods that had hitherto been bought for an ounce of copper were selling for a pound. "Thus," wrote Smith, "ambition and sufferance cut the throat of our trade."[24] And then came the gold fever.

To understand how this madness developed, we have only to recall *Eastward Hoe* and Captain Seagull's promise that "for as much red copper as I can bring, I'll have thrice the weight in gold."[25] The play's wide-eyed and impressionable adventurers, Spendall and Scapethrift, were but a reflection of the hopes of virtually every man who risked his life and savings to make a fortune in Virginia. Mariners who otherwise would have preferred to sign on for a tour of Caribbean piracy put their money into copper, beads, tools, mirrors, bells, and penny whistles in the expectation of trading them for gold. Instead what they were able to take home more closely paralleled the gifts that Francis Perkins was able to send back to his friends and benefactors.

"I have sent to my Lady your wife," he wrote, "a pair of turtle-doves, others to my Lady Catherine, and others to Sir William Cornwallis, hoping that when our [ships] make another trip I will have better things to send you. I am sending an ear of the native wheat, with two pots of our ordinary earth, and two more to my Lady Catherine. . . ."[26] Turtle doves and Indian pots were not at all what Newport's sailors had in mind, and when it became apparent that the Indians had no gold, the crew's willingness to help the settlers faded. As their admiral Newport should have kept his men in line, but he was as eager as they to find gold. He could not have forgotten his embarrassment at having returned from the first voyage with the wrong samples or his promise not to come home again until he could "bringe that with hym which he confidentlie beleeved he had broughte before."[27] To make sure that there were no more silly mistakes, the *John and Francis*'s passenger list had included two goldsmiths, a jeweler, and a pair of metallurgical refiners, William Dawson and Abraham Ransack, the latter a name straight out of a Ben Jonson play.

These two became the colony's Pied Pipers. Following a claim apparently first made by Councillor John Martin, they declared that gold was to be found in the mud along the tidal north shore of the James River. With the experts to lead the way, there was no shortage of volunteer diggers. As one eyewitness quoted by Smith put it, they "made all men their slaves in hope of recompense; there was no talke, no hope, no worke, but dig gold, wash gold, refine gold, load gold."[28] What they eventually loaded was not gold, but it shone and sparkled sufficiently to keep the myth alive, and in consequence, Newport and the *John and Francis* remained off Jamestown Island for fourteen weeks when, as Smith bitterly noted, "shee might as well have been gone in 14. daies."[29]

Throughout those weeks the crew devoured food supplies which should have been left for the settlers, and when the ship finally departed, she took with her the best of the remaining stock to be consumed on the homeward voyage. Members of the crew who had food of their own or who had bought corn in inflationary trade with the Indians sold it at fifteen times its worth, taking in return gold rings, furs, and anything else of value. To the luckless colonists ashore the ship's company was seen as "vile commanders," and the vessel itself as "this removing taverne."[30] Had the damage been limited to the antagonism that had grown up between ship and shore, Newport's departure would have seen the end of it. In spite of the fact that two of the council's problem people, Wingfield and Archer, went with him, newly rooted factionalism gnawed at the top. Ostensibly in command remained the ineffectual President Ratcliffe (alias Sicklemore), made the more so by his sickness resulting from a hand severely damaged when a gun exploded in it. Ratcliffe had been content to applaud Newport's lordly lead, and so, too, had the ever-ill John Martin. On the other side stood the blustering but pragmatic John Smith and his ally, the newly arrived and appointed Mathew Scrivener, both of whom could blame Ratcliffe for having helped Newport render the Indians infinitely more difficult to handle.

At Newport's departure, Powhatan had sent him twenty turkeys and asked for as many swords in return, so Newport, in a last grandiloquent gesture, gave the turkey-bearers the weapons. Needless to say, shortly thereafter Powhatan sent Smith a similar gift with the same request, and when Smith made it clear that there would be no more weapons-for-turkeys deals, their paper-thin friendship buckled. Furious, Powhatan ordered his people to take the weapons by whatever means they could. In their several efforts to do just that, the Indians ran afoul of Smith, who, according to his *Generall Historie*, hunted them up and down Jamestown Island, taking and whipping seven prisoners, who were held hostage inside the fort. In reprisal, the Paspahegh Indians seized two "foragging disorderly souldiers"[31] and, using them as pawns, demanded the release of the seven—or else. So accustomed had the Indians become to President Ratcliffe's policy of at all costs being nice to the natives that they were taken completely by surprise when Smith and his musketeers sallied out from the fort. In less than an hour of skirmishing he so demoralized them that they meekly handed over their two Englishmen and decided to say no more about the seven captive Indians.

The seven, however, had plenty to say when each separately heard musket shots and was told that his fellows were being executed for their failure to cooperate. Powhatan, they confessed, was behind the ambushes, thefts, and threats and had urged his vassal weroances to cut the English throats. Now, however, Smith's impressive show of force not only chastened the Paspaheghs but prompted Powhatan to review his options and decide that once again it was time to smile. And who could be more persuasive in gaining acceptance for his honeyed words than the daughter who had saved John Smith's life?

It is in this context in his 1608 *True Relation* that Smith first introduces Pocahontas to his English readers, describing her as "a child of tenne yeares old, which not only for feature, countenance, and proportion, much exceedeth any of the rest of his people, but for wit, and spirit, the only Nonpariel of his [her father's] Country."[32] To twentieth-century eyes, the notion of a ten- or even twelve-year-old Iranian envoy negotiating the fate of hostages with the secretary of state would be absurd, and so also would it have been thought in 1608. With that said, however, we need to remember that until the late Victorian era adult attitudes toward children differed from our own. In England, for example, the age of marital consent was twelve until 1875, when it was raised to thirteen.

Although Pocahontas enthusiasts have put Powhatan's words into her mouth, in reality she was sent along only as a none-too-subtle reminder of the day when Smith's own life had been forfeit. Powhatan's distress and regret at the behavior of "some rash and untoward Captaines" were voiced not by Pocahontas but by his "most trustie messenger, called Rawhunt, as much exceeding in deformitie of person, but of a subtill wit and crafty understanding."[33] Opechancanough also sent emissaries saying that two of the prisoners were his friends, but that was an argument hardly likely to win him any points. Smith, in making his decision—presumably after consultation with Ratcliffe and the council—informed the messengers that in agreeing to spare the lives and to release all seven prisoners, he did so only for the sake of Pocahontas. Although Smith nowhere says it, we can reasonably assume that his decision had less to do with Pocahontas's winning ways than with his desire to clear his life-for-a-life slate with Powhatan.

With some ceremony Smith had the prisoners escorted under guard to the church to hear the Reverend Hunt lead them in prayer. Then Smith fed them, gave them back their bows and arrows, and, in his words, "with much content, sent them packing."[34] If he had ever been tempted to trust Powhatan's promises of friendship, he would not do so again. Nevertheless, the role played by Pocahontas in the prisoners' release led to a strange and one might think inexplicable attraction on her part for the English who meant her civilization so little good.

The foregoing summary of the confrontations stemming from Christopher Newport's unwise weapons trading may well have been spread over more time than I have suggested. Indeed, historian Philip Barbour places the date of the prisoner release somewhere between April 20 and June 2. As previously noted the problem of determining the order of events is made the more difficult by Smith's having published three versions of just about everything he did, the shortest being the most immediate (1608). What is needed is a continuation of the kind of dated journals penned during the first months of settlement by Gabriel Archer and George Percy. Archer, of course, had been sent home, as the *Proceedings* put it, "to seeke some place of better imploiment,"[35] but Percy was still there and still writing. This brings us to the Reverend Samuel Purchas.

Although he never came to Virginia or held any prominent place in its affairs, Purchas was to play a crucial role in determining what we know, and indeed what we do *not* know, about early James Towne. He was an English cleric whose ecclesiastical prominence peaked in 1614, when he was made chaplain to the archbishop of Canterbury. Born in 1575 and educated at St. John's College, Cambridge, Purchas devoted his spare time to becoming a latter-day Richard Hakluyt, from whose estate Purchas obtained numerous travel-related manuscripts. Then, too, perhaps as the result of his friendship with John Smith, Purchas became the custodian and editor of many early Virginia manuscripts, which he included in the mammoth four-volume publication he titled *Haklutus Posthumus, or Purchas his Pilgrimes, contayning a History of the World in Sea Voyages and Land-Travells by Englishmen and others . . . &c.* Invaluable though Purchas's *Pilgrimes* has become as the only surviving version of immensely important literary sources, its worth derives less from his accomplishment than as compensation for his appalling negligence as both editor and custodian. His biographer, John Knox Laughton, was to declare that a "comparison of what he has printed with such originals as remain shows that he was neither a faithful editor nor a judicious compiler, and that he took little pains to arrive at an accurate knowledge of facts."[36] Although today Purchas has his apologists, who consider that assessment overly critical, the fact remains that his failure to catalog or to return many of the manuscripts entrusted to him ensured that at his death in 1626 many disappeared, along with priceless unpublished maps and drawings.

Rev. Samuel Purchas, whose major contributions to Virginia
history were marred by sloppy resource management.
From an undated nineteenth-century engraving.

Because Purchas often tinkered with the texts he published, historians
have been compelled to work with what often amounts to secondhand
data, and therefore always of uncertain validity. Among the losses
attributable to his carelessness is the whole of Percy's *Discourse*, which, in
the published text, ends on or about September 19, 1607, with Purchas's
note that "The rest is omitted, being more fully set downe in Cap. Smiths
Relations."[37] The rest—which was never seen again—may well have contained a detailed chronology of the middling months of 1608. This was a
crucial period for which we have no firsthand accounts, Smith's *True
Relation* having ended sometime before June 2, when he set out on an
expedition up the Chesapeake in search of the South Sea, an adventure
from which he did not return until July 20.

Three months earlier, on April 20, while the settlers were at work
around the fort, felling trees and planting corn, an "alarum" sounded,
sending everyone running for their weapons, fearing another Indian
attack. It proved, however, to be an unidentified sail approaching upriver,
raising the possibility that the Spaniards were coming. It turned out to be
the lost-in-a-fog and given-up-for-sunk *Phoenix* with her forty settlers
and a hold laden with supplies. A diversion that may have begun in fog

had apparently evolved into "many perrills of extreame stormes and tempests,"[38] which had carried the *Phoenix* back to the West Indies, where she remained to refit and take on fresh supplies of food and water. Consequently, when finally she reached James Towne, Captain Francis Nelson brought relatively healthy passengers, and supplies not appreciably depleted by the extended voyage.

Important though the arrival of the *Phoenix* was to the colonists, to us the circumstances of her sighting are equally pertinent in that they have something to say about the fort's early-warning system. An "alarum" had warned the choppers and planters of an impending attack; the question is: What kind of alarum? It could have been the ringing of a bell, the sounding of a trumpet, the beating of a drum, or even a gunshot. The word "alarum" itself has become the modern "alarm," but in the sixteenth and seventeenth centuries it was often written in its literal form: *al'arme*, meaning exactly what it says: "All arm!" On April 20, at James Fort, the alarm evidently went out without explanation; otherwise the settlers would have known whether to expect Indians or Spaniards.

If we only knew how far away the approaching ship was when first sighted, and by whom, we might well be within inches of solving the mystery of James Fort's location. No evidence exists to suggest that the settlers had yet built blockhouses or lookout points elsewhere on the island, so one has to conclude that the *Phoenix* was first seen either by a fisherman out on the river or by someone within or close to the fort. The traditionally accepted location for the fort site (in the vicinity of the brick church) would ensure a view of at least two nautical miles downriver, making it reasonable to argue that without the aid of a spyglass, the ship's identity could not immediately be determined. If, on the other hand, the fort stood in the lee of the island, the ship would have been broadside to it when it first came into view at a distance of only a few hundred yards. At that range its St. George's Cross ensign should easily have been recognized. This, then, would seem to be a damning argument against our accepting the lee location theory—until we recall that when captains were unsure of their reception, they commonly ran without their colors displayed. For all the overdue Captain Nelson knew, the current occupants of James Fort might be flying the red and yellow of Spain.

After the *Phoenix*'s felicitous arrival, President Ratcliffe instructed Smith and Scrivener to lead an expedition up the James into the territory of the Monacan Indians, broadly a confederacy of Siouan tribes, enemies of Powhatan, living above the falls (at modern Richmond) and west to the Blue Ridge. It was to be a major undertaking involving sixty to seventy men, who, to prepare themselves, spent a week training to "march, fight, and scirmish in the woods."[39] The plan was to use the *Phoenix* and her sailors to transport the expeditionary force as far as the falls, but Captain Nelson had second thoughts and demanded that he be paid for the hire of his ship and his men. With that wrench firmly in the machine, other issues surfaced. What was the expedition's purpose, and who should profit from it? Then, too, there was resentment that President Ratcliffe should order it but would not lead it himself. In the end, it seems, the project was called off, freeing the settlers to plant and tend their crops and to fell and cut cedar to load the ship.

One useful piece of ancillary information can be culled from the aborted Monacan expedition. Describing the little army's instruction in woodland warfare, Smith noted that amid the trees "Thicks there is few,"[40] meaning that the absence of underbrush made movement easy. This is in marked contrast with much of the modern Tidewater's woodland, whose young and light forest permits undergrowth to flourish. Looking at such woodland and assuming that it was ever thus, one wonders how in later years, in the absence of cut roads, horsemen could ride from place to place or even how Indians could hunt or attack through forest without getting their breechclouts snagged in the brambles. Smith's answer: Thickets were few.

From the first days of landing in May 1607 the settlers had been put to felling trees, initially to build the fort, then to provide clapboard to send home as cargo, and thereafter to build and rebuild houses and to clear ground for planting. One has to suppose that the felling process was undertaken in a planned manner designed to open vistas around the fort and to deny the Indians cover in bowshot of it. Sensible defense would have required that any field crops raised beyond the fort should have been surrounded by a pale at least breast high to discourage both deer and Indians. Indeed, you may remember that at the start, helpful Indians had advised cutting down "the long weedes rounde about our fforte."[41] Now, however, the settlers had planted corn outside it—corn grown sufficiently high to enable two red-painted and cudgel-wielding Indians to come up on Smith with malice in mind.

It is not clear what happened next, but it seems that once spotted and unable to take Smith by surprise, the two Indians decided that they were no match for him and sheepishly assured him that they meant no harm. The point, however, is that although the colonists were daily working beyond the safety of their palisades, they did so in constant fear of a snapping twig or a sudden flight of doves. In such an atmosphere it is hard to imagine anyone's deciding to go off on his own or to build a home beyond the protection of the fort—least of all President Ratcliffe, who, in the case of the Monacan expedition, had made it clear that he preferred to stay in the fort. Nevertheless, there is evidence that while the *Phoenix* was at James Towne, Ratcliffe began using men (possibly carpenters from the ship) to build him what was later described as an "unnecessary building for his pleasure in the woods."[42] Construction cannot have gone on all summer, but the work evidently was not finished by September 10, when the president was deposed and "the building of Ratcliffes pallas staide as a thing needlesse."[43]

Little more than a century later administration critics used the term "palace" to describe the mansion being built for Virginia's royal governor in Williamsburg. Applied literally, however, the word was used in both centuries to mean an official residence. Whether or not palatial splendor was implied in the clearly critical assessment of Ratcliffe's character and performance, we can only learn when somewhere in the Jamestown Island woods archaeologists come upon the remains of a large, early, and isolated dwelling. Even without our laying bare its postholes, Ratcliffe's "pallas" is proof of expansion beyond the palisades at a time when armed Indians still lurked in the corn and sentries stood guard through the night on the fort's bulwarks.

With President Ratcliffe's upriver exploration in force postponed, John Smith set about preparing a more modest but no less important venture—to wit, a voyage in a boat much smaller than the *Phoenix,* up the Chesapeake Bay in search of the South Sea. Captain Nelson no doubt was pleased not to be asked to participate. His job had been to bring his forty settlers to James Towne; he had done it; he was months overdue, and he wanted to get home. That he remained for six weeks was due in part to the sickness (perhaps in mind as well as body) of Councillor John Martin, who continued to involve himself in the gathering of gold-laden clay to be loaded aboard the *Phoenix.* To Smith's no little relief, Martin sought the council's permission to go with it. As his servant Anas Todkill none too delicately put it, "being alwayes very sickly, and unserviceable, and desirous to injoy the credit of his supposed Art of finding the golden Mine, [he] was most willingly admitted to returne for England."[44]

The *Phoenix* finally departed on Thursday, June 2, her hold loaded with cedarwood. Captain Nelson could not have known that his most important cargo would prove to be a small packet of papers handed to him by John Smith just before he sailed. It was a long letter, perhaps as many as forty pages of it, describing Smith's version of the colony's first

year. Although written to a now-unidentified individual, Smith evidently
intended it to be circulated, for his hastily penned final paragraph (always
supposing that it was he who wrote it) has to have been designed as
quotable copy for the London investors:

> . . . wee now remaining being in good health, all our men wel con-
> tented, free from mutinies, in love one with another, and as we
> hope in a continuall peace with the Indians, where we doubt not
> but by Gods gracious assistance, and the adventurers willing minds
> and speedie furtherance to so honorable an action in after times, to
> see our Nation to enjoy a Country, not onely exceeding pleasant for
> habitation, but also very profitable for comerce in generall, no
> doubt pleasing to almightie God, honourable to our gracious
> Soveraigne, and commodious generally to the whole Kingdome.[45]

If, indeed, those were Smith's words, he should have wondered whether
almighty God really wanted to be associated with such a travesty of the
truth. But the passage is as likely to have been supplied by someone in
London, perhaps by "I.H." (probably John Healey), who, without Smith's
knowledge or permission, was hired to edit the manuscript for publication. As I.H. explained in his introduction addressed to his "Courteous,
Kind and indifferent Readers,"[46] the letter had passed through two or
more hands and come to him without an identified author. The absence
of any such tail as "Your loving friend, John Smith" supports the argument that his last words were removed and the hyping paragraph added.
Whatever the truth may be, it is clear that the text of what finally reached
the public as *A True Relation of such occurences and accidents of noate as hath
hapned in Virginia since the first planting of that Collony, which is now in the
South part thereof, till the last returne from thence* had been so heavily edited
or censored that some of it made not a whit of sense. Nevertheless, for all
its faults, Smith's letter was the first detailed account to be sent back by a
member of the council and was avidly read by everyone with a stake in
Virginia.

With the letter went a roughly drawn map of Tidewater Virginia
showing the known Indian villages along the rivers and in several instances
the trails leading to and from them. Most important, however, are its rendering of Jamestown Island and on it the only surviving sketch of James
Fort. I shall return to this map in detail anon; at this point it's enough to
note that it existed, was sent to London—and lost. Once again we have
Don Pedro de Zúñiga's secret and treacherous contacts to thank for its

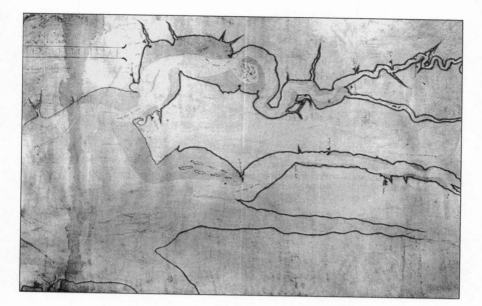

Detail from Robert Tindall's 1608 "draughte of virginia," marking the location of James Towne on a broad and bayless side of the island, and with deep water along that frontage.

survival, for he secured a copy and sent it to Philip III, in whose archives it remained. Though it is now known as the Zúñiga Map (p. 406), its wording is in English and thus is the work of an English copyist—certainly not of Zúñiga himself, who, since he always conversed with James I in French, may not have spoken English.

There's no knowing how many other amateur cartographers sent home sketches that haven't survived. One that did was drawn by the gunner Robert Tindall and sent to his patron the prince of Wales along with a journal that hasn't. What Tindall described as a "draughte of our River" is really a simplified navigational chart of the river and its shoals, unfortunately drawn to so small a scale that the outline of Jamestown Island and the location of the settlement, though shown, serve only to place the latter toward the northern end of the island. The Tindall chart is dated 1608, but it or another Tindall "draughte of our River" accompanied a letter of June 22, in the previous year, the day that the *Susan Constant* and *Godspeed* returned to England. The presumption has to be that the 1608 date was added later by a well-intentioned but historically unhelpful clerk. Only if Tindall's letter missed the post and had to wait until April 10, 1608, when Newport went back for the second time, could the date be valid.

What we know of London's responses to news from James Towne comes largely from peripheral sources, not from the primary participants in the Virginia adventure. The Company's meeting minutes, depositions, and correspondence, collected together in what are called the Court Books, are missing prior to 1619, a loss far more disastrous than the incompetence of Samuel Purchas or his executors. Consequently, much of the Company's decision-making can only be surmised on the basis of the results. For example, in spite of Christopher Newport's anticlimactic return in July 1607, the Company had almost immediately sent him back with the First Supply, and the same was to be true of the Second, which left soon after the *Phoenix* had reached England early in July 1608. The latter's arrival was not received with much enthusiasm by Company investor John Chamberlain, who told a friend that "I heare not of any novelty or other commodities she hath brought more than sweet woode,"[47] thus confirming Smith's statement that her cargo was primarily cedar.

When the *Phoenix* hoisted sail and slipped away down the James River on June 2, she was accompanied by Smith and fourteen others on the first leg of their expedition to the Chesapeake. They were traveling aboard an open vessel described first as a two-ton and later as a near-three-ton barge propelled by both sail and oars, whose only cover from sun and rain was a stretched tarpaulin. The barge was almost certainly the one that had accompanied the *Discovery* on the February visit to Powhatan and had been brought disassembled aboard the *Susan Constant* or the *Godspeed.* When Newport returned with the Second Supply, he would be bringing with him another barge, this one in five pieces, which he expected to be carried over the mountains to the South Sea.

Smith's expedition sailed up the Eastern Shore and reached into the Potomac River, visiting Indians of varying levels of conviviality, none of which exploits has a bearing on the development of James Fort. It was nevertheless a fishing expedition both figuratively and literally, and to the latter end the party included Jonas Profit, identified as a fisherman, and Richard Keale, a fishmonger. We may assume that Profit was to catch fish, and Keale to determine their food value and marketability. However, in the *Generall Historie* both men are listed only as "Souldiers," which may explain the team's farcical behavior when confronted by the bounty of the Chesapeake. "In diverse places," wrote Smith, "that abundance of fish lying with their heads above the water, as for want of nets (our barge driving amongst them) we attempted to catch them with a frying pan." In case it helps, I should note that unlike modern frying pans, which have handles no more than nine inches long, those of the seventeenth century measured as much as three feet. But short or long, it made no difference. As Smith admitted, "we found it a bad instrument to catch fish with."[48]

Later, when the netless fishermen encountered large numbers of fish in very shallow water, Smith set everyone to spearing them with their swords. "By this devise," he added, "we took more in an houre then we all could eat."[49] One of those impaled by Smith proved to be a flat fish with a long tail which promptly demonstrated that some fish are nice and others aren't. It was a stingray, and it drove its barb an inch and a half into Smith's arm. The result proved so painful, and the swelling so alarming, that Smith ordered his own grave to be dug; but thanks to a "precious oile" provided by the expedition's doctor, the swelling receded, and Smith, in a characteristically macho gesture, elected to eat the fish for supper. Nevertheless, he remained sufficiently ill for the trip to be called off.

Either as a practical joke or to test James Fort's preparedness, Smith had the returning barge decked out with streamers to resemble a Spanish frigate. To a modern lookout used to seeing a frigate as larger than a destroyer and smaller than a cruiser, the idea that a rowed barge with one small sail could be mistaken for a frigate may be hard to accept, but in the early seventeenth century frigates were small support craft and similarly propelled. More valid, however, is the question of why Smith's barge was equipped with Spanish streamers. The answer may be that they were carried aboard to replace the St. George's Cross quickly in case the expedition should be sighted by a Spanish warship.

If by hoisting the red and yellow banners Smith was playing games, on landing he found nobody in the mood for jokes; all the hitherto healthy new arrivals from the *Phoenix* were now sick, and so were many who had been there longer, "al unable to do any thing, but complain of the pride and unreasonable needlesse cruelty of their sillie President."[50] Even Smith's friend Mathew Scrivener lay delirious with what Smith described as a "callenture." He probably meant only a fever resulting from sunstroke, but in its primary usage the word meant a tropical fever contracted by sailors and characterized by the victim's fantasizing that the sea was a green field into which he wanted to run. What effect it had on sailors already on land is not recorded.

Without undue arrogance, John Smith could conclude that every time he turned his back the place fell apart. So, responding to what he concluded to be the will of the people, Smith deposed Ratcliffe and appointed himself president. But because the Indians he had met on his first trip up the Chesapeake Bay had led him to believe that it eventually opened into the South Sea, Smith was eager to try again. Consequently, he appointed the still-fevered Scrivener deputy president, and on July 24, after a stay at James Towne of only three days, he set out again with a slightly smaller but otherwise much the same company. A significant change, however, was that the doctor, Walter Russell, remained behind, presumably to help the James Towne sick, his place taken by a surgeon. In contrast with Russell, who headed Smith's cast list as "Doctour of Physicke" in both the *Proceedings* and the *Generall Historie,* surgeon Anthony Bagnall ranked in the former at the bottom of the list of gentlemen and in the latter among the "Souldiers." In both the seventeenth and eighteenth centuries physicians were considered scientists and gentlemen, whereas surgeons rated with butchers. The distinction was practical as well as social. Had Bagnall been in charge of health when Smith speared the stingray and the stingray speared him, the chosen remedy could have been amputation rather than the application of a precious oil.

Fortunately for all involved, and in spite of a good deal of belligerence on Smith's part, no one was wounded enough for Bagnall to unpack his knives and saws. That is not to say, however, that Smith's second excursion into the Chesapeake Bay was without its dramas. His meeting with a sixty-strong representation from the Susquehannock Indians, whom Smith described as a "gyant-like people,"[51] must have made a lasting impression on that short man. Not only was their size a surprise, but so, too, was the fact that they were equipped with European hatchets, knives, and other tools acquired in indirect trade with the French in Canada. With English fears focusing myopically upon the Spaniards, here was a reminder that there were other Europeans to be reckoned with in this dangerous New World. But even more disturbing must have been the English settlers' growing awareness of the vastness of the land around them and the fact that wherever they looked there were Indians, not necessarily in large numbers but living in scores of villages in alliance one with another, and all capable of living off the land and manufacturing the arms needed for their security. Contrastingly, an English soldier had only to empty his powder flask or run out of lead to be left with an utterly useless musket. Even with the benefit of John Smith's training course in guerrilla warfare, wearing a heavy helmet and at the very least an iron breast- and backplate, he remained the equivalent of a tank in the jungles of Southeast Asia. Unused to the climate and only slowly becoming aware of the land's potential, he owed his future to a fragile transatlantic supply line. And what sort of future was it to be? Was he fated to end his days splitting clapboard and searching ever farther afield for food-providing Indians who had no bones to pick with him? Did John Smith allow such thoughts to burden him? Probably not. A pragmatist always ready to take today's problems head-on, leaving the outcome to be tackled no less forthrightly tomorrow, he was a man in the mold of Pizarro and Cortés, ready to con or kill the savages by whatever ignoble means might be necessary to do his country's work.

On the return from the Chesapeake, a storm blew Smith's barge across the James estuary into the Nansemond River. Exploring several miles up it, the party came to several groups of Indians who beguiled them with friendly words and entertained them at a lodge on what may have been Dumpling Island. Other Indians added their invitations to visit farther up the river, but when Smith followed, his barge was ambushed by two or three hundred warriors shooting from both sides of the narrowing channel. Most of the arrows stuck in the Englishmen's shields, though as Smith put it, surgeon "Anthony Bagnall was shot in his Hat."[52] The outcome of this now-we-like-you, now-we-don't behavior was that Smith retreated, burning the Indians' cornfields and chopping their canoes in pieces. He would desist, he said, if the Nansemonds would surrender their king's bows and arrows, hand over a chain of pearls, and buy peace with four hundred baskets of corn. In the end, loaded with as much corn as their barge could carry and departing as "good friends,"[53] the explorers returned to James Towne. The point, of course, is that by no stretch of imagination could the two sides have parted good friends. Regardless of who was to blame—and we have only Smith's side of the story—he had encountered a new group of Tidewater Indians and left them humiliated and thirsting to get even.

With the Nansemond diversion astern, the expedition reached James Towne on September 7 to receive the good news that Mathew Scrivener was much recovered, the crops had been harvested, and Ratcliffe was in custody and charged with mutiny. Then the bad news: Many of the settlers were reported dead, and others sick, and supplies housed in the store had been spoiled by rain.

After fifteen months of colonization, and all too often having to gauge the numbers of living and dead with the aid of records which say only "many dead," we are left with a very uncertain tally of the living. If, however, fewer than 40 had survived to greet the *John and Francis,* which had brought a maximum of 80 new settlers, to be followed by 40 more aboard the *Phoenix,* we have a total of 160 from whom to deduct deaths occurring in the first eight months of 1608. Supposing the latter figure to be in the neighborhood of 40, we have a living total of about 120. Smith, in 1624, put it at 10 more.

Either estimate raises two significant points. First, the fort's palisades were now embracing more people than it had protected when first built, and second, as many as one hundred graves are thought to have already

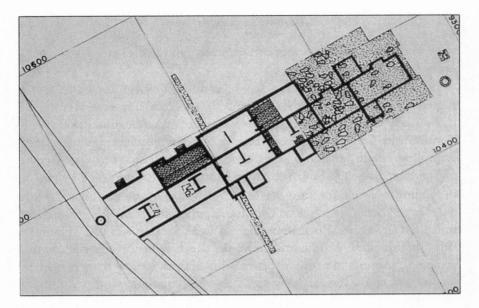

Detail from the National Park Service's archaeological plan of
Jamestown, showing the Ludwell-Statehouse complex (ca. 1666–98)
and at its landward end some of the graves that predated it.

put their archaeological imprint on Jamestown Island. In addition to the
graveyard associated with the brick church (whose first wooden manifestation on the site may date from about 1617), two others have been found,
one containing about sixty-two burials and located to the northeast of
later James Towne's "New Towne" and the other to the northwest
beneath the foundations of the Ludwell-Statehouse structures, which
were erected in or about 1665. Test excavations in 1955 revealed seventy
graves lying on a rise geographically identified as the Third Ridge and
reaching to the river's edge. Had the entire cemetery been uncovered,
archaeologist John Cotter guessed that as many as three hundred interments might have been found, and for him this was proof that James Fort
had stood close by on the supposedly eroded projection into the river
called Church Point. Unfortunately the excavations uncovered only ten of
the burials, and Dr. Cotter's published report says nothing about their
sex, ages, or cause of death, commenting only that "Evidence here indicated hurried interment, probably without coffins in most cases."[54] Readers are left to guess for themselves just how many of the uncovered ten
were "probably" buried without coffins, whose nail traces should have survived. In short, none of the questions of who, why, when, and how, crucial to determining the cemetery's place in the James Towne story, were

answered. Nevertheless, as the later chapters unfold, the body count needs to be kept in mind.

In the fall of 1608 the count of the living was of more immediate concern. If, as seems likely, there were about 120 men dwelling within the compound, we can guess that they would have needed a minimum of about twenty houses, thus an average density of 6 to the house. Taking the Popham Colony at Fort St. George on the Kennebec as a guide to housing a similar number, we find that they occupied and used about twenty-five buildings, nine of them assigned to single individuals and their servants, ranging downward from president to blacksmith, but with few, if any, drawn structures left over to accommodate the majority of the lesser people. However, as I noted earlier, it is possible that some of them were quartered in the attic over the store. In making the comparison, we have to remember that the Popham Colony differed from that at James Fort in that the latter was less militarily structured and heavier on gentlemen, 51 of them among the original 104 and 33 more from aboard the *John and Francis*. Although death whittled at their ranks as evenhandedly as it did those of the "other sort," gentlemen almost certainly were less willing to live half a dozen to the house. And 28 more were on their way.

The need to prepare for a third ingestion of settlers aboard the Second Supply was much in Smith's mind when he returned from the Chesapeake. The next day the council, supposedly at the request of the Company, formally elected Smith to the presidency. Immediately he ordered repairs to the church and particularly to the store whose leaks had wrought havoc with the materials it was supposed to protect. At the same time he made sure that "buildings [were] prepared for the supply we expected."[55] If, as I have tried to demonstrate, the fort was already too small to contain James Towne, it seems reasonable to deduce that it could best be made bigger by pushing out its most easily rebuildable elements—namely, the palisade curtains between the heavily constructed bulwarks or flankers. If the builders recognized the need to keep the river-facing wall straight, the obvious enlarging step would be to push out the other two sides of the triangle to create a five- rather than a three-sided enclosure.

In his *Proceedings* (1612) Smith made it clear that he did something, though exactly what is open to debate. "The fort," he wrote, "reduced to the forme of this figure . . ."[56] and then to historians' dismay, he or his publisher left the figure out! Even Purchas was aware of the loss, but before he reprinted Smith's *Proceedings* in his *Pilgrimes* in 1625, he apparently never bothered to ask Smith what had become of it. As for Smith himself, when he issued his *Generall Historie* in 1624, he made amends for the omission (after a fashion) by changing the *Proceedings'* text to read: "the Fort reduced to a five-square forme."⁵⁷ To modern eyes the word "reduced" reads as a diminution rather than an expansion, but in seventeenth-century usage it often meant to "bring back" or change in shape, in this instance to change the lines of two of the three palisades to create a five-sided plan—or so it would seem on the basis of the testimony describing the fort as it was in September 1608. As we shall see later, subsequent evidence will be unsupportive.

Smith had been president for scarcely three weeks before Newport arrived with the Second Supply and its seventy new faces, two of them female: "Mistresse Forest and Anne Buras her maide,"⁵⁸ the first Englishwomen to call James Towne their home. Mistress Forest accompanied her husband, Thomas, who was listed among the passengers as a gentleman, but Anne Buras (or Burrows) was unmarried and thus an arrival of promise. No record recalls whether she was young or fair of face, but even if she had been as ugly as sin she would have been warmly welcomed by the men of James Fort. Two months later, in James Towne's first wedding, she married carpenter John Laydon, bore him four daughters, and was still alive in 1625. Mrs. Forest, on the other hand, disappeared from the record as soon as she arrived, as did her husband, though he may be the Thomas Forrest who had fifty pounds invested in the Virginia Company in 1620.

John Smith evidently reacted with less enthusiasm to two more of the fresh arrivals—namely, a pair of new appointees to the council, Captains Peter Winne and Richard Waldo, described as "auncient Souldiers and valiant Gentlemen, but yet ignorant of the business."⁵⁹ We can little doubt, however, that they were fully versed in the Company's wishes and knew that it put its trust in its admiral, Christopher Newport. Nor could they fail to notice that the deposed and imprisoned President Ratcliffe was quickly released and "permitted to have his voyce."⁶⁰ Lest there be any doubt about the way the wind was to blow, Newport brought with him a letter from the Company berating the administration, and Smith in particular, for their inability to act in unison and chiding the settlers in general for their "idle conceits."⁶¹ The seeds of Newport's and Smith's antagonism, which had been germinating in the days before the *John and Francis* sailed for home in April, were in full flower by the time she docked in England. Unfortunately for Smith, he had no advocate to speak on his behalf when Newport and Archer addressed the Company's council. Its conclusion, therefore, was that Smith was a loose cannon, unwilling to follow orders, and prone to treat the Indians with steel gloves to the detriment of good Anglo-savage relations.

London's views on dealing with the natives were uneasily ambivalent. On the one hand, it considered those it saw as savages to be the devil's children whose only salvation lay in being won for Christ (much the same thinking that governed Spanish colonial policy); on the other hand, as long as the Indians had the power to be difficult, one should avoid being nasty to them. When in 1629, for example, a Frenchman sought English backing to plant a two-thousand-strong settlement south of the thirty-fifth parallel in what the Spanish still called Florida, he was instructed: "Be sure you trouble not the Indians in their plantations or any other thing of theirs; but live in quietness with them as you shall see fitting."[62] For their part, the Indians from Florida to Canada knew enough by now about Europeans, whether French, Spanish, or English, not to be lured passively into slavery or oblivion.

The Virginia Company both received and delivered much advice on how best to handle Powhatan and the tribes of his confederacy. Any disposition to righteous belligerence, however, was tempered by a reluctant awareness that the James Towne colonists seemed incapable of surviving without the indigenous Americans' help. To better secure that help, Newport returned to carry out one of the most ludicrous decisions ever to come out of a committee. With the aid of a cheap copper crown, and in the name of James I, king of England and Scotland, Newport would crown Powhatan king of whatever he thought he already possessed.

CHAPTER VIII

Crowning and Other Achievements

THE ARRIVAL of the Second Supply appreciably increased the infant colony's stock of gentlemen. To these twenty-eight were added at least a dozen laborers and fourteen tradesmen whose crafts unfortunately are not recorded. Those who had come on the *John and Francis* and the *Phoenix* had included six tailors, a tobacco-pipe maker, a jeweler, and a perfumer, and we have to assume that the later arrivals were an equally motley lot. In a highly impolitic letter to the Council of Virginia in London, John Smith asked that "When you send againe I intreat rather send but thirty Carpenters, husbandmen, gardiners, fisher men, blacksmiths, masons, and diggers up of trees, roots, well provided; then a thousand of such as we have."[1] For the pragmatic and short-fused Smith the arrival of Captain Newport and his supplies was a very mixed blessing. On the one hand, Smith knew that the settlement could not survive without injections of new blood, food, clothing, and munitions, but on the other, the ship's company, from its admiral down, could be relied on to cause him trouble for as long as it remained.

Although not named in Smith's writings, the ship has been identified as the *Mary and Margaret*,[2] her tonnage unknown but large enough to carry the seventy settlers, their baggage, Namontack, the repatriated bogus Indian prince, a crew of maybe fifteen, a complete Elizabethan-style bed as a gift for Powhatan, and Newport's five-piece barge, which he was to carry on the colonists' frail backs over the falls to deep water en route to the gold mines and the South Sea. Smith shared his thoughts on this, too. If Newport "had burnt her to ashes, one might have carried her in a bag," he wrote, "but as she is, five hundred cannot."[3]

Like that of many a modern business, the Virginia Company's London management had only the vaguest understanding of life and labor on the shop floor—in this case, on the ground in and around James Fort. The managers, the trustees, and the shareholders looked first to the bottom line, and what they saw was writ large in red ink. Cargoes of cedar, clapboard, sassafras, and John Martin's sparkling mud were not at all what the front office had in mind; hence its renewed demand that Newport use the settlers to keep exploring until they found the gold mines. If Ambassador Zúñiga is to be believed, the Company continued to be guided by Sir Walter Ralegh, who provided it with helpful memos from his cell in the Tower of London, one of which fell into Zúñiga's hands. "It is here, being translated," the ambassador told his king, "because it is his original, and when that is finished we will compare it with the chart which they have made."[4] Ralegh's continuing influence almost certainly explains the Company's further instruction to Newport to redouble his efforts to find survivors of the Roanoke colony, for with John White dead in 1593, nobody else had much reason (beyond curiosity) to care what had happened to them.

To broaden the range of saleable commodities, the Company had sent out specialists in the garnering of pitch and tar, the boiling of soap ashes, and the manufacture of glass, a singularly inappropriate product to pack and ship. But a chronic shortage of window glass in London coupled with a declining Surrey glass industry resulting from the curtailment of wood as furnace fuel in the closing years of Elizabeth's reign, prompted glass merchants to look to America as a wood-rich site for a waning industry. Besides, Robert Mansell, one of the key figures and eventual sole patentee of English glass production in the early seventeenth century, was also on the Virginia Company's council. It is fair to conclude, therefore, that it was at Mansell's instigation that a trial glass factory was set up in the autumn of 1608 on a site described as "in the woods neere a myle from James Towne."[5] In 1931 Jesse Dimmock, owner of property long known as Glass House Point, discovered pieces of glass slag lying in the sandy soil not far from the river's edge. An amateur antiquary, he conducted his own excavations and soon found the remains of three rock-built furnacelike structures. Having gone that far, Dimmock wisely desisted, fenced the site around, and left it to the National Park Service to embark on its own, professionally led excavations sixteen years later.

The twenty-four acres at the northern end of the causeway linking Jamestown island to the mainland was recorded in 1654 as being "commonly knowne by the name of the Glasse House"[6] But on that evidence alone, and in the absence of any closely datable artifacts from the Dimmock excavations, there was no knowing whether this name linked the land with the 1608 venture or with a second glassmaking attempt that began in 1621. Fortunately there was another eyewitness to identify the first site more closely. The operation was manned by some of the Dutchmen (really Germans—i.e., Deutschmänner) and Poles brought over with the Second Supply, and by 1610 they had set up what was then described as a "goodlie howse . . . with all offices and furnaces thereto belonging" and situated "a little without the Island where James towne standes."[7] There being no other nearby location "without the Island" than the "Glasse House" tract, there is no doubt that Jesse Dimmock did find the site of British America's first, and possibly also its second, industrial enterprise. As we try to understand the evolution of James Fort into James Towne and later into James Cittie, what's important is John Smith's statement that the first glasshouse was built in the woods nearly a mile from the protection of the fort, for here is solid evidence of the settlers' willingness to expand beyond the safety of their palisades—regardless of the dangers.

In addition to glass, pitch and tar, and soap ashes, the Company called for more clapboard, ignoring the amount of heavy labor involved in cutting and splitting it. In his wide-ranging letter to the council Smith pointed out that London merchants would be better advised to buy clapboard from Russia or Switzerland, where labor forces were trained to harvest it and where the right forests were plentiful. Virginia's amateur woodsmen are "ignorant miserable soules, that are scarce able to get wherewith to live, and defend our selves against the inconstant Salvages," Smith declared. Not only that, but in the Virginia forests it was hard "finding but here and there a tree fit for the purpose,"[8] so hard, in fact, that it was sometimes necessary to venture as much as five miles from the fort. When Smith did so, he did it in force. One of its members described his taking a party of thirty of his gentlemen tree-felling and getting the work done in the guise of healthy recreation. Within a week they became masters of their craft, "making it their delight to heare the trees thunder as they fell, but the axes so oft[en] blistered there tender fingers, that commonly every third blow had a lowd oath to drowne the eccho."[9]

Smith made it clear in his letter that he was dutifully complying with the Company's demands, but he made it equally clear that he considered most of them at best unrealistic and at worst plain stupid. The supply, which, by the Company's reckoning, had cost about two thousand pounds sterling, was worth scarcely a hundred in actual help, he said. Even if true,

Top: The Jamestown glass factory as first reconstructed.
Bottom: The glass factory site near Jamestown, as uncovered by
J. C. Harrington in 1949.

this was not the way to win friends in London. But warming to his work, Smith saved his sharpest barbs for the great public relations ploy. "For the Coronation of Powhatan," he wrote, "by whose advice you sent him such presents, I know not; but this give me leave to tell you, I feare they will be the confusion of us all ere we heare from you againe."[10] The problem was the same that Smith had inherited from Newport's last visit when he had traded swords for turkeys. Were it not for "this stately kinde of soliciting" which made Powhatan so overvalue himself, his goodwill could have been purchased for a "playne peece of Copper."[11] Instead he was to be given gifts of a basin and ewer from James I himself, as well as the bedding and bedstead, miscellaneous clothing, and what were collectively described as "costly novelties," plus, of course, the trappings of kingship—the red robe and the cheap crown.

In view of Smith's volatile disposition, Newport almost certainly was aware that he considered the coronation idea one of the worst the Company had devised, and it must have given Newport some silent satisfaction that the most appropriate messenger to take Powhatan the good news was the colony's president, Captain John Smith. For his part, however, Smith saw the visit to Werowocomoco as an opportunity to try to persuade Powhatan not to be too carried away by Newport's gifts and flattery. In his *Generall Historie* Smith pointedly noted that in spite of his hard-line policies toward the Indians, he could safely make the trip with only four companions "where Newport durst not goe with lesse than 120."[12] Going was one thing, however; getting Powhatan to come to James Towne to be crowned was another.

"If your King have sent me Presents," Powhatan told Smith, "I also am a King, and this is my land: eight dayes I will stay to receive them. Your Father [Newport] is to come to me, not I to him, nor yet to your Fort, neither will I bite at such a bait."[13] Like it or not, Muhammad would have to go to the mountain.

Powhatan had agreed to wait only eight days before leaving for another of his progresses among his vassal tribes, so the English had little time to get ready. The bed and the rest of the gifts were loaded onto three barges and shipped down the James and up Prince Henry's rivers to Werowocomoco, while Newport and the fit council members, guarded by fifty musketeers, set out overland. Arriving at the Prince's River shore, they boarded the barges for the crossing, thus providing us with the first evidence that the colony now had three and not two barges.

Although it is unlikely that any of the English (with the possible exception of George Percy) had attended James I's coronation, the first in forty-five years, they undoubtedly had a rough idea of the drill. The new monarch processes into Westminster Abbey and kneels on the altar steps to receive the Holy Sacrament, to take the coronation oath, and then to receive the crown from the archbishop of Canterbury. Somewhere in the proceedings the monarch receives the orb, scepter, spurs, and several symbolic swords, but since none of these (with the possible exception of a scepter) was part of the Virginia kit, all that Newport had to do was to get Powhatan down on his knees, while he, Newport, played the archbishop. It turned out, however, that had Newport and his secondary bishop substitutes had a better grasp of the procedure laid out in the *Liber Regalis,* the ceremony might have gone a mite more smoothly, for in the centuries-old English ritual the king was already enthroned, already holding the orb and scepter, and sitting bolt upright to receive the crown.

Upon their arrival, several of Newport's men were ordered to unpack the heavy wooden bed and its hangings and to assemble them within Powhatan's mat-covered longhouse, where the coronation ceremony was to take place. Beyond that, nothing is known about the bed. Whose idea was it to give him this massive gift? Had he received reports of such a bed at James Towne and asked for one for himself? On the whole, it seems unlikely that anyone living there in 1608 would have brought over anything so space-hungry. The chances are, therefore, that this was another bright idea on the part of the Company's council.

With some reluctance Powhatan was persuaded to put on the "scarlet cloak and apparel," a process achieved "with much adoe" and accepted only after Namontack assured him that English kings really did wear such things. To Powhatan, the ruler of a formidable empire with customs entrenched deep in antiquity, respect and dignity were no less important than to any European monarch. Thus to ask him to put on the cloak and other alien apparel was on a par with asking King James to appear at Westminster wearing nothing but beads and a breechcloth. But dressing Powhatan up was only the beginning; when it came time to get him to kneel to receive the crown, "a fowle trouble there was." A prolonged litany of persuasions, examples, and instructions got Newport nowhere, for Powhatan was not about to kneel to any man. "At last by leaning hard on his shoulders, he a little stooped, and three having the crowne in their hands put it on his head."[14] Smith's *Proceedings* put it somewhat differently, saying that Newport alone placed the crown on Powhatan's head. But whether one did it or three, the only European coronation ever to be performed in America had all the dignity of a shotgun wedding.

The shot came next. Someone fired a pistol, causing near-panic among the Indians, who had not been warned that this was a signal that the king was crowned and the cue for spontaneous rejoicing. Just as royal moments in London were celebrated with the ringing of church bells and the firing of cannon aboard ships on the Thames, so Newport's public events director had arranged for guns on the barges to be fired in such a barrage that "the King start[ed] up in a horrible feare." After he and his attendants were calmed down, Powhatan presented Newport with his "old shooes and his mantell,"[15] both of which he presumably had been persuaded to remove during the enrobing. It has long been supposed that a shell-decorated deerskin sheet which entered the new Ashmolean Museum at Oxford in 1683 was Powhatan's cloak, taken home by Newport, and originally in the collection of John Tradescant, father and son. The latter's 1656 catalog listed it as "Powhatan, King of *Virginia's* habit all embroidered with shells, or Roanoke."[16] The mantle is still to be seen at the museum, but current scholarly thinking concludes that, although undoubtedly of Virginia Indian manufacture, the Tradescants' treasure was neither Powhatan's nor a mantle.

One of the principal duties of a vassal or subordinate king is to do what he is told; consequently, Newport's first demand of the newly crowned King Powhatan was that he supply men and guides to assist in the great expedition above the falls into the lands of Powhatan's enemies the Monacans. Powhatan, however, seems not to have been properly briefed on his new status and responsibilities, and so declined to provide any support other than Namontack, who would keep Powhatan apprised of anything worth knowing. The coronation enterprise therefore ended with Powhatan enriched by a miscellany of gifts for which he gave in return about eight bushels of corn, a used mantle, and a pair of old shoes. With these souvenirs and some more corn bought on the open market at Werowocomoco, Newport and his retinue returned to James Towne. They had done as the Company instructed, and that had to be the measure of their success.

With the coronation behind him, Newport set off on the great expedition, taking with him 120 men, including William Callicut, the gold refiner. John Smith, as president, stayed behind at the fort with the remaining eighty men (many of them sick and otherwise below par) with instructions to make glass, boil soap ashes, cut timber, and load the ship for its return to England. These were not the kinds of chores to which Smith warmed. He would have much preferred to be out on the cutting edge of discovery, so it is safe to guess that the abrasive letter he wrote to

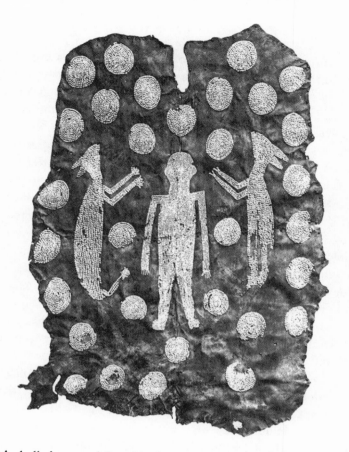

A shell-decorated deerskin "mantle" said to have belonged to
Powhatan. Presented to John Tradescant, father and son,
perhaps by Captain Christopher Newport, and listed in
the Tradescant catalog of 1656.

the Company in Newport's absence was the product of this and many
other frustrations.

Winter was fast approaching, and the settlement's food supplies were
dwindling. Unwilling to rely on Newport's ability to return laden with
corn, Smith took a chance and sallied out from the fort to persuade the
Chickahominies to part with some of theirs. When his first overtures
were repulsed with what he described as "as much scorne and insolency as
they could expresse,"[17] Smith explained that he had not really come to
trade but rather to pay them back for his capture the previous December
and for the murder of his men. When the Chickahominies decided that
Smith wasn't bluffing, their envoys assured him that all they wanted was
peace, and as proof they provided him with fish, fowl, and two hundred

bushels of corn, which, they said, because of the poor harvest, they could ill afford. In that admission lay the germ of problems ahead, but it seems to have been shrugged off, probably in the belief that reluctant taxpayers always plead poverty. What mattered was the haul. Delighted with its size, the English sheathed their swords and "parted good friends."[18] It remained to be seen whether Newport's 120-man expedition could top that.

If Smith secretly hoped that Newport would fail, he was not disappointed. On reaching the falls, the expedition marched inland about forty miles. No one has recorded whether or not they were carrying the five-part barge on their backs, but a now-anonymous member of the party (later quoted by Smith) reported that they discovered two Monacan villages, "the people neither using us well nor ill."[19] To be on the safe side, however, Newport chose to seize one of their lesser weroances, shackle him, and force him to serve as a guide. Once again the English seem to have been indifferent to the seeds of hatred they were leaving in their wake.

The search for gold mines proved as fruitless as before, but refiner Callicut claimed to have extracted a small quantity of silver from his earth samples, and with that dubious success Newport returned to James Towne. "Where," Smith may have asked, "is the Indians' corn?"

The unidentified expedition chronicler answered, "Trade they would not, and finde their Corne we could not; for they had hid it in the woods: And being thus deluded," he went on, "we arrived at James Towne, half sicke, all complaining, and tyred with toyle, famine, and discontent, to have onely but discovered our guilded hopes, and such fruitlesse certainties, as Captaine Smith fortold us."[20]

Throughout all this Newport's ship remained idly in the river with its metaphorical meter running on behalf of its owners and its crew answerable only to their absent admiral. If Smith is to be believed, Newport's insistence to the Company that Virginia's resources could sustain any number of settlers led the council to send out the new people without the foodstuffs to support them. Only the ship's crew was well supplied, and with little to do the sailors grew fat while the settlers in the fort languished. Having traded away their own possessions, the more enterprising settlers took to robbing the store and trading axes, pickaxes, hoes, chisels, pike heads, and even gunpowder to the sailors in exchange for butter, cheese, beef, pork, biscuits, oatmeal, oil, beer, and alcohol—which gives some idea of what that forbidden commissary had to offer. In turn the sailors traded the tools to the Indians for furs. Within the space of seven weeks the colony's store of two or three hundred iron tools had been whittled down to a point where "scarce twentie could be found."[21] That such looting could have gone on without the storekeeper (the cape merchant) noticing is hard to believe. But the fact remains that in spite of Smith's threats, the settlers knew that once the ship sailed so did their last chance to obtain good food.

The date of Newport's departure is not recorded, but it would seem to have been between November 27 and December 3. He left behind a colony numbered by Smith at about two hundred, few of whom could expect to survive the winter unless strenuous and immediate measures were taken to stock the fort's granaries. Mindful of his recent success in frightening food out of the Chickahominies, Smith decided to have another go at the Nansemond Indians. The same "Give us what we want or we'll take the lot" diplomacy yielded another hundred bushels of corn, but other Indian communities quickly learned what was happening and contrived to vanish along with their corn before Smith's extortionists arrived. Although the Chickahominies, the Nansemonds, Weanocs, Appomattocs, and other visited and intimidated tribes all were part of the Powhatan Confederacy, lines of communication between the English and the emperor remained open, at least to the extent that he was still sending requests for things he fancied—like a house to put his bed in.

If his "good friend" and appointed weroance John Smith would send him men to build the house, Powhatan would appreciate their bringing with them one grindstone, fifty swords, some muskets, a cock and a hen, plus a gift of copper and beads. In return Powhatan would fill Smith's ship with corn. Or would he? Smith was not yet so desperate as to be willing to reverse his "no weapons for food" policy, but if Powhatan had that much corn to trade, he had that much which could, if necessary, be taken by force. To lull Powhatan into complacency, Smith sent four of his Dutchmen to start building the house. With them went two Englishmen, one of them the previously hostaged and now native-speaking Richard Savage. They traveled overland, Smith allowing them time to get started before embarking his troops on one shallow-draft barge and an unidentified deeper-water pinnace.

The plan did not sit well with Smith's erstwhile supporter Mathew Scrivener, who now seems to have thrown his support behind Newport as a straight-line Company man. Indeed, Scrivener and fellow council member Captain Winne had accompanied the departing Newport as far as the mouth of the James. Meanwhile, Smith called for volunteers. Of the pool of 198 or so, only about 38 stepped forward, the rest figuring that since Smith usually succeeded in his ventures, there was no point in their risking their necks when they could stay behind and wait for the corn to come in. Smith put Scrivener in charge of the fort in his absence, detailed Captain Waldo to stand by to lead reinforcements should they be needed, and set out with himself and a dozen men in the barge, and the rest (plus a crew of 3 sailors) aboard the pinnace. The roster of the alleged volunteers by itself raises questions about the wisdom of the enterprise, for its names included the cream of the colony's crop: Lieutenant George Percy, brother to the earl of Northumberland; Francis West, brother to Lord De La Warr (now spelled Delaware); William Phettiplace, captain of the pinnace; Robert Ford, clerk to the council; six or seven other gentlemen; and surgeon Anthony Bagnall—all people the colony could ill afford to lose.

Like the icicled December of 1607 (which in Europe, too, had been one of the coldest in living memory), this one was no better. The expedition therefore set out into a river already partially frozen and made its way down the James, around Point Comfort, and up into Prince Henry's River (York), stopping along the way to be the unexpected guests of the Indians at Kecoughtan, where they remained through Christmas week as a blizzard blew in from the bay. Not until January 12, 1609, did the two-vessel fleet reach Werowocomoco, where they found the river frozen half a mile from the shore. Undaunted, Smith used the barge as an icebreaker, and when the receding tide left it stranded, he led his advance party ashore by wading waist-deep through the freezing mud. They were still some distance from Werowocomoco, but Powhatan sent bread, turkey, and venison while Smith's team sheltered in abandoned Indian lodges. The next day Powhatan visited and told Smith that he had no corn to spare, and neither did his people. However, for forty swords he might rustle up forty filled baskets.

On their first night out from James Fort the boats had stopped on the south side of the river at Warraskoyack, where the old king, Tackonekintaco, whom Smith described as "this kind savage," had warned that Powhatan was not to be trusted. "Bee sure hee hath no opportunitie to seaze on your armes," advised the chief, "for hee hath sent for you only to cut your throats."[22] In truth, as Powhatan later pointed out, he had sent not for Smith but only for the house builders. Three centuries too soon to have heeded the British adage "Never trust the Germans," Smith was unaware that his "Dutch" craftsmen had concluded that they were better off on the side of the Indians and so had warned Powhatan of Smith's intentions. Thus both sides had seen the other's hand, and for the next several days of negotiation each jockeyed for striking position as construction of Powhatan's house went on.

Through the nineteenth century Werowocomoco was thought to have been located near Timberneck Creek, where a massive rock-built kitchen type of chimney (now reconstructed) is still known as Powhatan's Chimney. In reality, it can be nothing of the sort, for most modern authorities put the site more than nine nautical miles farther upstream, in the vicinity of Purtan Bay. This, by no means incidentally, is pretty much where Smith showed Powhatan's capital on the Zúñiga Map (p. 406).

Smith's attempts to maneuver Powhatan into either a deal or a defeat were thwarted by the latter's prior knowledge, while a Powhatan plan to slaughter Smith and sixteen of his men as they sat at their supper was scotched by his "dearest jewell and daughter," Pocahontas. Regardless of the freezing cold, she came in the "darke night" and "through the irksome woods"[23] to warn of her father's intent. This important story appears both in Smith's *Generall Historie* and in the section of his *Proceedings* attributed in part to William Phettiplace, who captained the pinnace on that expedition and therefore cannot have been a later embellishment.

With Smith's attempts to win a major corn supply from Powhatan going nowhere, and with the danger of a fumble or an interception increasing as the game wound down, Smith decided to try his luck farther up the Prince's River at the Pamunkey village of Powhatan's half brother Opechancanough. There's no doubt that Opechancanough had been fully briefed on what had happened at Werowocomoco and intended to repeat the same maneuvering, beginning with affability and promises and continuing with prolonged and tiresome bargaining designed to make the English focus more on business than on defense. After several days of this, Smith and his fifteen men walked into Opechancanough's trap. Arriving at the king's house (apparently somewhat removed from the main Pamunkey village), Smith expected to strike a major deal. Instead he found the place deserted, as seven hundred warriors waited out of sight in the fields around it.

Meanwhile, Powhatan was taking advantage of Smith's absence from James Fort to try a new ploy to obtain the weapons he had been refused. Using his new German secret weapon, Powhatan sent two of the Dutchmen to the fort to report that all was well with Smith and the expedition but that he needed additional tools and fresh clothing. The Dutchmen, whose names live in infamy only as Adam and Francis, at the same time contrived with the help of other treacherous colonists to steal three hundred hatchets, fifty swords, eight muskets, and as many pikes, all of them handed to a party of Indian bearers waiting in the woods near the glasshouse. The Dutchmen's new English confederates were promised a good life if they, too, would join Powhatan and thus escape the starving death that was sure to befall the rest of James Towne's inhabitants. That promise not only lured them into stealing the equipment but later sent several renegades sneaking off into the woods en route to Werowocomoco.

The weapons loss was not the only disaster to strike James Towne in Smith's absence. Although Captain Richard Waldo had been told to remain in the fort to be ready at a moment's notice to bring up reinforcements, he decided to (or was ordered to) accompany his temporary commander, Mathew Scrivener, on a trip across the James River to Hog Island. The boat was described as a skiff but has since been termed a canoe by some historians, this in spite of the fact that Smith in his *A Sea Grammar* (1627) explained that large ships towed or carried small boats "called Shallops and Skiffes, which are with more ease and lesse trouble rowed to and againe upon any small occasion."[24] This small occasion presumably involved hunting hogs which the colonists left to breed on the island, though why it took the fort's senior officers to do it remains a mystery. Along with Scrivener and Waldo went the late Bartholomew Gosnold's brother Anthony and eight other men of unspecified rank. No one ever discovered whether the boat was on its way over or coming back laden with hogs, but those who saw it set out said that with eleven men aboard it was already overloaded. Furthermore, "so violent was the wind [in] that extreame frozen time"[25] that they doubted whether the boat could have survived had it been empty. But it wasn't, and it didn't. The skiff sank, drowning everyone aboard. Not until Indians found the bodies washing ashore did the settlers in the fort learn of the disaster.

Captain Peter Winne would seem to have inherited command, and he or a committee was faced with the task of finding a way to let Smith know what had happened. The usual call for volunteers was greeted with glum silence; "none could bee found would undertake" the mission.[26] Eventually Richard Wiffin, who placed number six among the gentlemen who had arrived with the First Supply, agreed to carry the bad news alone. On reaching Werowocomoco, he found Smith gone, but the village in a turmoil of war preparation. The Dutchmen were still there, as were Richard Savage and Smith's boy page, Samuel Collier, who had been left to learn the language, plus another Englishman, Edward Brinton, who Smith had agreed should stay with the others to help Powhatan hunt birds. When the Dutchmen returned with the stolen tools and weapons, Savage and Brinton left Werowocomoco to warn the fort's officers that they had been duped, but they were apprehended before they got very far and brought back to Powhatan as prisoners. According to a textual addition to the

Generall Historie, Wiffin was hidden by Pocahontas and then helped on his way to catch up with Smith as he prepared to do battle with Opechancanough's massed warriors.

Although Smith had called on his fifteen companions to "fight like men, and not die like sheepe,"[27] the battle did not take place. Instead Smith contrived to seize Opechancanough and, gripping him by his hair with one hand and holding a pistol to his chest with the other, ordered the chief's men to throw down their weapons. This doubtless became one of Smith's favorite dinnertime stories and grew more colorful with each telling, so by the time he wrote the *Proceedings* in 1612 Opechancanough had become a "trembling King, neare dead with feare,"[28] whom Smith paraded in front of his disheartened warriors. The resulting standoff produced gifts of corn and other foodstuffs, but with the entire countryside in arms against Smith, it was a Pyrrhic victory. Consequently, when Wiffin arrived with all his bad news, Smith decided to retreat from the Pamunkeys and to head home, pausing on the way to surprise Powhatan at Werowocomoco and to get even with "those damned Dutch-men."[29] But he was too late. Powhatan had evacuated the town, taking all his supplies with him.

The great expedition to obtain a major corn supply from Powhatan while teaching him the lesson he would long remember had not gone well. Powhatan had learned lessons all right, but not of the kind Smith had in mind. As for the corn supply, the total haul amounted to only 279 bushels, though admittedly the figure looked better by the time Smith wrote the *Generall Historie* and jacked the figure up to 479 bushels—plus 200 pounds of deer fat. Whatever the true figures, the supplies were at least fresh—in contrast with those in the store at the time of Newport's departure, which were described as "so rotten with the last Summers rayne, and eaten with Rats and Wormes, as the Hogges would scarcely eate it."[30] That, nonetheless, was the diet enjoyed by the fort's inhabitants until the return of Smith's expedition.

As usual in his absence, nobody had accomplished anything useful, so Smith immediately set about whipping his people into some semblance of shape. One of his many problems was to know who could be trusted. Four of the thieves who had looted the store and fled to Powhatan had been encountered on the way, and their explanation that they were simply lost in the woods, surprisingly enough, was accepted. Powhatan, however, had been assured that these men would be joining his Dutchmen (who, owing no allegiance to Britain, were busily instructing the Indians in the use of their new weapons), and no doubt he had visions of creating a renegade

C Smith taketh the King of Pamavnkee prisoner 1608

Smith avoids Opechancanough's trap and instead takes the king
prisoner. It is likely that Smith had some say in the rendering of this
illustration for his *Generall Historie*. If so, the treatment of his
falchion sword and pistol may be relatively correct.

troop to fight against the English. Consequently, when the recruits failed
to show up, Powhatan sent the Dutchman Francis to find out what had
become of them.

It seems that at this time other Dutchmen and perhaps the two Poles
were working on the mainland at the glasshouse, for this was the place
described by Smith as the "Rendezvous for all their unsuspected vil-
lany."[31] Someone told him that the renegade Dutchman was there, but
not that Wowinchopunck, king of the Paspaheghs, and forty bowmen
were lying in wait. Although the details are unclear, it seems that when
the would-be ambushers saw Smith approaching with twenty of his men,
Dutch Francis and the Indians retreated into the woods. Leaving his
twenty to go after them, Smith set out for the fort alone. But he had gone
only a short distance before Wowinchopunck stepped out of the bushes
with bow drawn. Since Smith was armed only with a sword described as
a "faucheon," he rushed the Indian before he could shoot. The king, in
turn, held Smith so that he could not draw his weapon, and locked

C: Smith takes the King of Paspahegh prisoner. A° 1609.

Smith, with falchion drawn, captures Wowinchopunck, king of the
Paspaheghs. Another illustration from the *Generall Historie*.

together, the two men staggered into the river, where each tried to drown
the other. Eventually Smith was able to get his hands around the king's
throat and force his head under the water. Then, stepping back and drawing his sword, he was about to sever the Indian's head. At the last minute,
however, he thought better of it and instead dragged him prisoner back to
the fort.

The capture of the king of the Paspaheghs provided one of the highlights of Smith's history and was chosen for inclusion in its previously discussed comic-book illustrations. So, too, however, was his capture of
Opechancanough, its caption reading "C. Smith taketh the King of
Pamaunkee prisoner, 1608." That, of course, was the date by the Julian
calendar, which began the new year on March 25, not the Gregorian calendar's January 1, which would not be implemented in England and
America until 1752. Thus Smith's capture of Opechancanough took place
in mid-January, in what the caption correctly said was still 1608. However, the caption illustrating the affray near the glasshouse reads "C.
Smith takes the King of Paspahegh prisoner, A° 1609," thus putting the
fight at some time after March 25. From the *Generall Historie*'s text alone
(which cites no date) one might suppose that the return of Francis, the
devious Dutchman, occurred within days of Smith's return from his great

expedition, but evidently the described events, though in sequence, stretched across weeks and even months.

The engraving of the fight with the Paspaheghs' weroance has value for another, entirely different reason. It shows the two men standing in shallow water with Smith wielding a single-edged sword with a slightly curving blade akin to that of a Turk's scimitar. Though popular among northern European soldiery in the fourteenth and fifteenth centuries, by the seventeenth century this was a relatively uncommon sword type (no examples of which have been found on seventeenth-century sites in Virginia), tempting one to dismiss it as no more than the artist's fantasy. But twice in the text Smith's weapon is identified as a "faucheon," the common seventeenth-century spelling for a falchion, which is the correct terminology for a blade of that shape. Although surviving examples often are Venetian, an English specimen in London's Wallace Collection is attributed to the right period: 1600–20.[32] Nevertheless, there's no denying the sword's Islamic character, raising the possibility that because Smith's previous military adventures had been in wars with the Turks, his flamboyant character prompted him to arm himself with this flashy, cutlasslike weapon. One thing at least is certain: If, as he claimed, he was about to strike off the king of the Paspaheghs' head, he could have done the job with no better blade than that of a falchion.

The pre-spring months of Old Style 1608 (New Style 1609) were punctuated by a miscellany of encounters with the Indians, only one more of which need concern us. The theft of a pistol was attributed to an absent Indian, two of whose friends were brothers and frequent visitors to the fort. To get the pistol back, Smith seized both brothers, sent one off to retrieve the gun, and promised to hang the other if he was not successful. The captive was imprisoned in what was twice described as a dungeon, a place so cold that his captors took pity on him and gave him charcoal for a fire. When his brother returned with the pistol and the guards went to release their prisoner, they found him apparently dead of smoke inhalation. Smith managed later to revive the man and was given credit among the Indians for being able to raise the dead. Although that must have pleased Smith no end, the incident's importance lies in its reference to the dungeon, for the word was most often used to refer to a subterranean place of imprisonment. The fact that the charcoal's smoke asphyxiated the prisoner implies that the cell's walls were not aboveground, where they would have been of wood boards between which air could circulate.

The affair of the stolen pistol occurs in the *Generall Historie* after that of the capture of the king of the Paspaheghs, who was housed in chains within the fort but who, to Smith's fury, managed to escape. It's fair to speculate that in the aftermath of that embarrassment Smith ordered the dungeon to be dug. Because several timber-lined storage cellars have been found on Virginia sites dating from the first half of the seventeenth century, we can legitimately conclude that the dungeon was five or six feet deep and lined with studs and boards. There remains the question of how deep such a hole could have been dug on Jamestown Island before water seeped up from below. Although most of the wells archaeologically excavated on the island date no earlier than the mid-seventeenth century, the majority terminate at a depth of between nine and eleven feet. The shaft closest to the alleged James Fort site was partially excavated in 1955 and drew water at seven feet. However, the report added that "It may be assumed that the original ground surface was 1 to 3 feet higher."[33] Assuming that the fort lay nearer to the river, one must suppose that Smith's dungeon was not only cold but at the very least unpleasantly damp.

The dungeon was not the only deep hole to be dug early in 1609, for during that time Smith ordered the digging of James Fort's first well, which, so he said, yielded "excellent, sweet water, which till then was wanting."[34] A year later a less enthusiastic chronicler claimed that "by drinking of the brackish water of James Fort [its inhabitants were] weakened and indangered."[35] Perhaps by the standard of the settlers' previous water supply, the well's bounty did indeed taste sweet, for as George Percy has told us, they had drunk out of the river, which was salty when the tide was high, and "full of slime and filth" when it was low.[36]

Enumerating his achievements in the first months of 1609, Smith claimed to have built twenty houses, to have re-covered the church (again?), as well as produced samples of tar, pitch, and soap ashes; also a "tryall of Glasse."[37] You may recall that he previously had told us that a similar range of samples had been produced in the fall of 1608 and been shipped home with Newport. The possibility exists, therefore, that these claims are a reiteration of the previous year's achievements. After all, if the remaining Dutchmen were last year's glassmakers, they should by now be in production, not claiming another "triall" as progress. Included in this listing is the settlement's most important advance since the fort palisades were erected in 1607. At Smith's insistence the colonists constructed a blockhouse "in the neck of our Isle, kept by a Garrison to entertaine the Salvages trade, and none to passe nor repasse Salvage nor Christian without the presidents order."[38]

The new minifort was at the island end of the tidal causeway leading to the mainland and effectively prevented any further illicit communication or transference of stolen goods to dissident Dutchmen at the glasshouse. Although the blockhouse could not prevent Indians from invading the island by crossing the Back River in canoes, it did exercise control over those who came to trade. Nothing is known about the construction of the blockhouse, and its site about a quarter of a mile from the glasshouse was long ago washed away and now lies beneath the modern causeway. Consequently, details for blockhouse building included in the instructions to M. Bonnavolia for his 1630 Anglo-French settlement venture in modern South Carolina are a real help. So, too, is the fact that the manuscript provides the kind of marginal sketch that must have graced many a contemporary document and journal, but that were omitted when Purchas printed them.

Trees were to be cut in twenty-foot lengths, each split or pit-sawn into four, and the pieces laid on the ground in squares, "and so put the squares one upon another; and that itt be laid 2 stories high and every story 8 foote deep: and that the Garrett be 4 foote & ½ deepe; Under the house you must make sufficient seller and therein put or keep all your provisions. . . ."[39] This, then, was akin to the kind of log construction that continued to be standard military building procedure through the nineteenth century and as far away as Fort Walla Walla, Washington.[40]

A second Virginia blockhouse was built across the river on Hog Island to protect the colony's stock of pigs, which had grown from three starter sows to more than sixty. However, the garrison was not there solely to pig-watch; it was also to look out for enemy or friendly shipping approaching upriver. As Hog Island can be seen only from Jamestown Island's extreme east end, one wonders how warnings were communicated to the fort. To make sure that the Hog Island garrison had something to do besides sitting and watching, Smith put it to work splitting and sawing clapboard and wainscot boards, while back at the fort the still healthy were kept busy clearing and planting fields, which by now reportedly extended over thirty to forty acres.

The satisfaction of these accomplishments was short-lived. Working across the river, building a fort in what is now Surry County, Smith received word that another disaster had befallen the James Fort storehouse. Rats from the ships had come ashore and bred in such numbers (their population was put in the thousands) that they had eaten half the remaining corn supply. The rest was found to have rotted in its casks. So once again the colony's food supply was down to crisis level, and once again we find ourselves asking, "Who was minding the store?" That the rats should have remained unnoticed until they had finished eating is

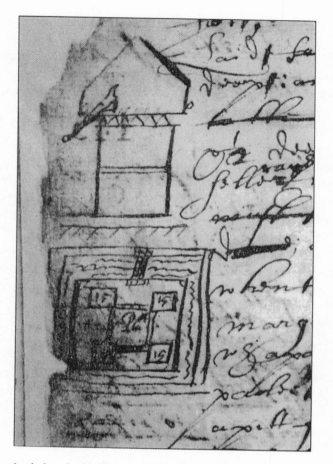

A marginal sketch showing a blockhouse to be erected by an Anglo-French expedition to settle in modern South Carolina in 1630. Below it a plan shows how four such buildings were to be connected.

hard to believe—particularly when rats made as good meat as squirrels and were a lot easier to catch. No easier is it to believe that no one would have checked the precious casks to be sure that they remained dry and their contents fresh.

Just how far Smith had progressed with his Surry fort when the bad news made him leave it one cannot be sure. Two editions of his *Generall Historie* differ on this point, one saying that work halted "ere it was finished"[41] and the other that it stopped "ere it was halfe finished."[42] Although nothing is later said about its completion, this can be dismissed as just one of the innumerable facts that have slipped between the historical cracks. Later versions of the map John Smith published in 1612 mark "The new fort" alongside what evidently is Gray's Creek. At least as early as 1637 "Smith's fort" had become a sufficiently well recognized landmark to serve as a property boundary marker.[43] Smith himself, however, tells us only that it was "neere a convenient River upon a high commanding hill, very hard to be assalted and easie to be defended," and that it was to serve as a "retreat,"[44] but *for* whom and *from* whom are left unspecified. Following National Park Service historian Charles E. Hatch, Virginia's Division of Historic Landmarks defined the new fort's purpose as "a refuge for the Jamestown settlers should the island be attacked."[45] But that makes very little sense, particularly if the fort was located where it is traditionally thought to be and where state archaeologists made "positive identification" of it through test digging in 1968 and 1981.

The site, now owned by the Association for the Preservation of Virginia Antiquities, lies some distance up Gray's Creek on high ground that well fits Smith's description, but it would not have been of much help to the people on Jamestown Island. Had a Spanish fleet lain off James Fort and pounded it from the river, the colonists would have been more than usually foolhardy to evacuate into the muzzles of Spanish guns. If, on the other hand, James Fort had been overrun by the Indians, the best escape would have been downriver rather than toward other Powhatan confederates waiting, with arrows nocked, on the Surry side. It makes much better sense to see Smith's "retreat" as a refuge for trading and punitive parties exploring beyond the territory of the area's then-friendly Quiyoughcohanock Indians.

Archaeological work at the supposed "Smith's Fort" site has been limited to slicing through the filling of a ditch and its much-eroded rampart. In the absence of any tightly datable artifacts one cannot be sure that it was Smith's 1609 work, but if (as seems likely) this is the right site, then the mode of construction harks back to the kinds of earthwork reconstructed on Roanoke Island, not to the palisaded defenses pioneered across the James River. We have to ask ourselves to what extent, if any, earthworks were a part of the James Fort configuration, for up to this point in the chronicle there is no documentary evidence that banks and ditches had a part to play.

The food crisis that erupted so unexpectedly in the spring of 1609 once again taxed President Smith to his limit, but it was the kind of challenge on which he thrived. He quickly ordered about a third of the population out of the fort and sent them downriver to live off the oysters which were so prolific in the lower reaches that their beds protruded from the water at low tide. It was not a diet to gladden the hearts of nutritionists, but it was noticeably better than nothing. Perhaps recognizing the need for dietary variety, Smith dispatched George Percy to Point Comfort with another twenty men and instructions to try their luck at fishing. This being a period in which, thanks to editor Purchas, Percy's journal is lost, we have only Smith's word on what went wrong: "but in six weekes they would not agree once to cast out the net, he [Percy?] being sicke and burnt sore with Gunpouder."[46]

Gunpowder accidents were by no means rare, often as a result of overloaded firearms whose barrels burst (which is probably what happened to ex-President Ratcliffe), as well as through careless handling of the uncompressed powder. Because the combination of potassium nitrate, sulfur, and charcoal readily absorbed atmospheric damp, keeping it dry enough to ignite was always a problem. One popular remedy was to spread the gunpowder out on the conveniently dished iron backplate from a cuirass and to warm it gently over the embers of a fire. An Indian at Werowocomoco learned this trick but failed to grasp its finer points. Several apparently shortsighted friends who had gathered around to watch the demonstration were peering closely at the roasting gunpowder on the armor plate when the inevitable happened. Those who survived the flash reportedly "had little pleasure to meddle any more with powder."[47]

If Smith was amused by the ignorance of the Indians, he found little to laugh at among his fellows at the fort. He called them "distracted Gluttonous Loyterers" and claimed that "had they not beene forced *nolens, volens*" ("whether they liked it or not") to gather and process such as food as could be found, "they would all have starved or have eaten one another."[48] Many were ready to give the Indians anything they wanted in exchange for corn, were it the kettles the settlers needed to cook in or the guns that protected their lives. Others clamored to take the next boat home.

It arrived early in July. The *Mary and John* was probably the same vessel of that name used by the Popham expedition to Maine in 1607. This time she was not serving as another supply ship but rather as the first vessel commissioned by the London Council for Virginia to make use of James Towne in the way it was intended—namely, as a going concern, a port for English ships crossing the Atlantic on independent commercial enterprises. This one proved to be a fishing trip for sturgeon and sent "the ready way, without tracing through the Torrid Zoan,"[49] meaning that she had sailed across by the Azores route, not by the longer southerly Caribbean course. Although it may have been the *Mary and John* which a Spanish reconnaissance ship spotted lingering at anchor in the Chesapeake Bay on July 24 (by the Spanish calendar, but the fourteenth by the

English),[50] when she reached James Towne, her news from London was still relatively fresh. Her captain, Samuel Argall, was no simple fisherman; he was a cousin by marriage of Sir Thomas Smythe, the Virginia Company's new treasurer, and related to the wife of Lord De La Warr, and it was news of him that Argall brought to James Towne. A member of the king's Privy Council, De La Warr had been on the council of the Virginia Company from the beginning and was now appointed governor-general for life. As such he was the moving force behind "a great supply,"[51] which, even as Argall sailed, was boarding a fleet of seven ships lying in the Thames at Woolwich. Less reassuring, however, was Argall's news of a new Company charter, the appointment of an on-site lieutenant governor in the person of Sir Thomas Gates, and the revocation of the Virginia colony's existing form of government. In short, London was sending in a new and untested management team—and six hundred novice settlers.

CHAPTER IX

"Lewd and naughtie practices"

SAMUEL Argall's information was correct as far as it went. The largest and best-outfitted English supply fleet to sail to the New World was on its way to the relief of the James Towne settlers. What Argall may not have known was that even then plans were going forward for yet another major reinforcement under the command of Thomas West, Baron De La Warr. Although Sir Thomas Gates had been made governor, Lord De La Warr would be officially named governor-general on May 23, when the king signed and sealed the Company's second charter eight days after the fleet left the Thames. If the appointment had been a secret at all, it had not been well kept. Ambassador Zúñiga had known about it for the best part of three months, and thanks to his diligence, Philip III of Spain was aware of it on March 27—along with a good deal of other disturbing (if not necessarily accurate) information.

According to Zúñiga, his king's perceived lack of concern about the growing British presence in Virginia was emboldening its backers to send much larger implantations of men and materials. Sir Thomas Gates, "who is a very remarkable soldier who has served the [Dutch] Rebels,"[1] would leave in about six weeks—it was then March 15—with four hundred to five hundred men and a hundred women. Once word reached London that they arrived safely, so Zúñiga's spies told him, Lord De La Warr would be departing with as many as eight hundred more. And that wasn't to be the end of it. When Gates got back, he would immediately turn around to take over yet another load. The ambassador's information was essentially correct, though he probably got his De La Warr and eight hundred linkage from the fact that in February the plan had been for De La Warr to lead the first fleet, which was to sail in March with just such a number aboard. Lest Philip might be wondering where all the volunteer colonists were to come from, Zúñiga reported that after the Dutch States General had signed a truce with Spain, soldiers previously fighting for the Protestant Dutch would be available for boarding. Historian Philip Barbour has seen these as Dutch rather than as English troops,[2] but from what we know of those who actually went, that interpretation seems doubtful. So, too, does Zúñiga's claim that they (presumably meaning the Company) had asked James I "that all the pirates who are out of this kingdom will be pardoned . . . if they resort there." Virginia, he pointed out—as he had several times before—is a place "so perfect (as they say) for piratical excursions that Your Majesty will not be able to bring silver from the Indies without finding a very great obstacle there."[3] Fearing that Philip might prefer to dismiss this letter (as he had others) as the overreaction of an excitable man, Zúñiga added that "I confess to Your Majesty that I am writing this in anger, because I see the people excited and insolent over this business."[4]

With plans going forward for the shipment of eight or even six hundred people, and prodded by Company propagandists, London could hardly fail to be agog with excitement. From the merchants in the Exchange to the sailors on the wharves, Virginia had become a name to conjure with; Captain Seagull's time had arrived! And as Zúñiga evidently had discovered, English Protestants saw the venture as another opportunity to spit in the eye of Spain.

Ever since the discovery of the Gunpowder Plot, a fear of covert Catholics had kept Protestants on their sacerdotal toes, and with good reason. Many of the country's premier families coupled loyalty to the Crown with secret adherence to the old religion—with varying degrees of success. Zúñiga reported that Thomas, Baron Arundell (who had sponsored George Waymouth's 1605 expedition to plant a Catholic colony) had applied again for a patent to take out "a crowd of people" but had been turned down "because he is suspected of being a Catholic."[5] Perhaps out of spite and jealousy toward the Protestant adventurers, Arundell allegedly passed the word that if properly rewarded, he would assist Spain to dislodge the James Towne settlement. Philip, however, later warned Zúñiga to be careful lest Arundell turn out to be a double agent. The latter's scheme involved a proclaimed voyage of discovery that would pick up a Spanish agent at the Canaries or Puerto Rico and show him "the entrance of the River and the sites occupied by the English, and the fortifications they have, and that he will then tell Your Majesty how those people can be removed without recourse to arms."[6] It wasn't a scheme likely to excite enthusiasm, for the Spaniards already knew their way to the James River, but it does provide graphic evidence of the treachery thought to lurk in the hearts of prominent English Catholics.

Although the Virginia Company's management was well aware that if Spain really put its mind to it, the James Towne settlement could be wiped out long before anyone in England could draw a sword to prevent it, that was not the kind of message it wanted to leave in the minds of potential investors. Instead, perhaps early in April, the company distributed a pamphlet written by one Robert Johnson giving his reasons for wanting to contribute to the new adventure, a copy of which, needless to say, Zúñiga obtained and promptly sent to Spain. Titled *Nova Britannia,* the pamphlet called Virginia an "earthly Paradice"[7] and claimed that it had belonged to England since the reign of Henry VII. The Indians were "generally very loving and gentle,"[8] food of every kind was there for the hunting and harvesting, and the opportunities for industry and profit were scarcely imaginable. Not only that, said Johnson, warming to his theme, but here was a heaven-sent opportunity to be rid of "swarmes of idle persons, which having no meanes of labour to releeve their misery, doe likewise swarme in lewd and naughtie practices." If employment was not found for them abroad, Johnson went on, "we must provide shortly more prisons and corrections for their bad conditions."[9] As the French so often observe, "The more things change, the more they remain the same."

Numerous undesirables boarded the waiting fleet, but there is no evidence that they were rounded up at the end of a pitchfork. Most of them, like their predecessors, were people who signed on of their own volition and at their own charge, if for all the wrong reasons. No record survives to tell us when and where the majority of the passengers and most of the cargo went aboard. Individual ships may have loaded at different points below London Bridge, some people boarding there, while others waited until closer to sailing time and were carried down the eight miles of river on wherries to Woolwich, there to join the great Virginia fleet.

The lead ship, named the *Sea Venture* (or *Sea Adventure*), became the "admiral" because the fleet commander, Sir George Somers, was aboard. The second-largest ship, the *Diamond,* was called the vice admiral, and the third, the *Falcon,* the rear admiral. The others in the fleet were the *Blessing,* the *Unity,* the *Lion,* the *Swallow,* and two smaller vessels, an unnamed ketch (a small two-masted vessel) and a pinnace named the *Virginia,* both of which joined the seven larger ships at Plymouth. The *Virginia* was the one built on the Sagadahoc by the Popham colonists (the first English ship constructed in America) and was now captained and mastered by Robert and James Davies, from that expedition.

Like Davies, the majority of the senior officers were men with prior New World experience—but men whose names would not be music to the ears of John Smith at James Towne: Christopher Newport would be returning as captain of the *Sea Venture;* John Ratcliffe (that "sillie president") would be vice admiral aboard the *Diamond;* the ever-sickly John Martin was rear admiral on the *Falcon,* with Francis Nelson (late of the *Phoenix*) as his master, and on the *Blessing,* Gabriel Archer. In short, the three men who had given Smith the most trouble would be back mantled in the Company's favor. The only hope for Smith was that they all were answerable to Sir Thomas Gates and, while he remained, to Sir George Somers, both of them the Company's senior officers under the original charter, who with luck could be relied on to put the public good ahead of personal vendettas.

When the *Sea Venture* left Woolwich carrying Governor Gates and under Newport's command, fleet Admiral Somers was not aboard. He was to join the ship at Plymouth, thus putting all the top management together in one boat or basket—a risk few modern companies care to take.

The fleet dropped anchor in Plymouth Sound on May 20 and remained until June 2, somewhat lethargically taking on supplies, including six terrified horses and two mares that had to be hoisted aboard and lowered into the *Blessing.* When at last the convoy put to sea, it ran into strong winds blowing out of the southwest, forcing it to shelter in the port of Falmouth on the Cornish coast, where it remained until June. The delay eventually brought the ships bow to billow into the teeth of a hurricane tearing out of the Caribbean and across the Bahamas. The ships were scattered, sails ripped to shreds, and masts and spars sent crashing to the decks as holds filled with water and deck cargoes disappeared into the boiling ocean.

The fleet met the leading edge of the storm on Monday, July 24, having no idea of its impending severity. But with "the clouds gathering thick upon [them] and the winds singing and whistling most unusually,"[10] every captain knew he was in deep trouble. Aboard the *Sea Venture* from noon on Tuesday, night and day until the following Friday, the crew manned the pumps as the ship was hurled like a tiny cork, blown northeast toward the foaming reefs of the dreaded Bermudas. But rather than striking broadside and breaking up, as many another ship had and would through the centuries, the *Sea Venture* drove bow ahead into a V between two coral outcrops and there stuck. Although a total loss, she remained above water for all 150 passengers, crew, and dog to get safely ashore and, when the weather cleared, for much of her superstructure to be dismantled and transported the three-quarters of a mile to the westerly island. Saved also were those of the stores not ruined by the salt water in the ship's holds and so, too, were the carpenters' and boatswain's tools and supplies.

Once safely ashore, the crew set about building two new vessels out of the remains of the wreck and from cedars growing on the islands. In popular folklore, building the seventy-ton pinnace they called the *Deliverance* and the thirty-ton *Patience* has been hailed as a remarkable achievement, and so it was. But with ship's carpenters to hand, it was by no means unique, as the Popham people's building the *Virginia* had demonstrated. Nor, indeed, was it the first time that mariners shipwrecked in the Bermudas had escaped in that way. The crew of a wrecked Portuguese slaver did it in 1543, as did men from a lost Spanish prize ship thirteen years later, and so did several crews thereafter.[11] What turned the story of the *Sea Venture* and its company's deliverance into one of the great epics in the history of seafaring was the presence aboard of William Strachey.

At thirty-seven, Strachey was a man still looking for a niche and hoping to find it in Virginia. He was well educated, had minor experience as an aide to the English ambassador to the Sublime Porte at Constantinople, and was on more than nodding acquaintance with most of London's literary and theatrical luminaries. Not surprisingly, therefore, Strachey was a man of creative and literary talent, who saw in the drama of the foundering *Sea Venture* an irresistible opportunity to exercise his descriptive powers.

Historian David Quinn has described William Strachey's *True reportory of the Wreck and Redemption of Sir Thomas Gates, Knight . . . &* as "one of the finest pieces—clear, specific, descriptive, critical—in the literature of the whole period of early-seventeenth-century American enterprise."[12] It's also one of the most exciting.

> . . . there might be seen master, master's mate, boatswain, quarter master, coopers, carpenters, and who not, with candles in their hands, creeping along the ribs viewing the sides, searching every corner, and listening in every place if they could hear the water run. Many a weeping leak was this way found and hastily stopped, and at length one in the gunner room made up with I know not how many pieces of beef. But all was to no purpose, the leak (if it were but one) which drunk in our greatest seas and took in our destruction fastest could not then be found, nor ever was. . . .[13]

Top, left: A pewter candlestick, still with the stub of a candle
in its socket, found in the wreck of the *Sea Venture*. Height 9¾ inches.
Top, right: Allan J. Wingood recovering a Rhenish stoneware bottle
from the wreck of the *Sea Venture*. *Bottom:* The *Sea Venture* in
course of excavation.

Strachey's claim that the crew tried to plug the leaks with lumps of beef is somewhat surprising, but less so than the likelihood that in the midst of a hurricane the crew would be searching for them with candles in their hands. But skepticism ebbed when divers excavating the wreck came up with a pewter candlestick—the stub of the candle still in its socket!

The wreck was discovered in 1958 by the Bermudian diver Edmund Downing, who retrieved, among other artifacts, a late-Elizabethan-period Rhenish stoneware jug and an iron cannon. The remains of the ship snuggled, bow in, between two walls of the coral reef, paralleling the description written by Silvester Jourdain, another *Sea Venture* survivor, who told how she "fell in between two rocks, where she was fast lodged and locked for [from] further budging."[14] Convincing though this evidence was, an ordnance expert at the Tower of London identified the cannon as dating from the eighteenth rather than the early seventeenth century, thus casting doubt on the wreck's identity. Although no one seems to have recognized the rebutting evidence of the jug, Downing remained convinced that he had found the *Sea Venture,* and to be on the safe side the Bermudian government designated the wreck as a protected historic site to discourage its further exploration. In retrospect, this was extraordinarily fortunate, for in the late 1950s underwater archaeology was in its infancy, and any extensive digging on the site would have ruined it. By 1978 the Tower had changed its mind about the date of the cannon, and a new investigation of the site was begun under the auspices of the Bermuda Maritime Museum, the project directed by a Bermudian professional diver, Allan J. Wingood, who, though a keen amateur archaeologist, recognized his need for professional help. So, in 1982, he turned over the direction of the excavation to one of the world's best, Jon Adams, who had been deputy director of the famed *Mary Rose* (1545) project in England. Adams and Wingood created the ideal team, and by 1992 the *Sea Venture* remains had been fully documented, and virtually every surviving artifact, from pins to the pewter candlestick, retrieved.

Strachey's *True Reportory* was eventually published by Samuel Purchas—and his manuscript lost—and so it remains known only in its printed form. Late in the eighteenth century, the Shakespeare scholar Edmond Malone was the first to suspect that the playwright had seen a copy of Strachey's manuscript and used it as the genesis for *The Tempest.* It was clear, too, that when in 1610 the Company needed to put out another reassuring pamphlet, it made use of descriptions of the *Sea Venture* miracle written both by Jourdain and by Strachey. The scholarly world assumed that Strachey had written only *one* account of the wreck and the survivors' year on the Bermudas—until the summer of 1988, when an old trunk of family papers yielded another.

The handful of historical sources for Virginia's and Bermuda's early history has been studied and restudied ever since the mid-nineteenth century, with nothing of consequence being added since George Percy's second manuscript, his "Trewe Relacyon," was first published in 1922. Decades of scouring libraries public and private have fostered the conclusion that what we've seen is all we'll get. Then a friend wrote saying that he had found some papers relating to the *Sea Venture* that might be of use to me in writing this book and that looked as though they could be "of the right period." They turned out not to be. What they are, however, is a twenty-page copy, probably made in the early to mid-nineteenth century, of another version of Strachey's narrative, one whose wording strongly suggests that this was the one used by Shakespeare and by the Company's 1610 propagandist, not the extended and more polished *True Reportory* printed in 1625 by Purchas. The transcriber evidently was unacquainted with *Purchas, His Pilgrimes* and had no idea that Strachey might be the author of the letter he so laboriously copied under the title "Sir George Somers' Shipwreck."

"The following account of a shipwreck," wrote the copyist, "less interesting from comcomitant calamaties than from the turbulance of the crew and its ultimate consequences, is contained in a letter from one of those whose safety was endangered. Though we are not acquainted with his peculiar capacity on occasion of the voyage, both his experience and intelligence are sufficiently conspicuous."[15] With that rather ponderously said, the yet-to-be-identified transcriber proceeded to preserve for us one of the most remarkable treasures of early American literature, prose in some respects even tauter and better than that rightly praised by Professor Quinn. One cannot help asking albeit churlishly, and too late: "But what did you do with Strachey's original?"

Like the Purchas version, the "Strachey" manuscript details the year of turbulence that beset Gates, Somers, and the rest as they worked to survive and to build the pinnaces that would get them off the islands. But for the time being, that's where we must leave them—along with two salvaged black boxes containing Gates's instructions on how he was to reorganize the Virginia colony.

The rest of the Virginia fleet, though badly battered, had survived the hurricane, and six days after the skies cleared, the *Lion* caught up with the *Blessing*, followed shortly afterward by the *Falcon* and the *Unity*, the last in sorry shape. Of her seventy settlers, only ten remained fit, and of her crew, only the master, his servant boy, and one sailor were well enough to sail the ship. Together these four vessels arrived in the James River on August 11. Three more came in later: first the *Diamond* (the vice admiral) and a few days later the *Swallow*, both with their mainmasts gone and many of their passengers and crew sick unto death. According to Gabriel Archer, "The Viceadmirall was said to have the plague in her."[16] The third ship, presumably the *Virginia* pinnace, is not mentioned, but the figure of eventual arrivals is put at seven and eight, though most reports mention the loss of a pinnace or ketch, perhaps the one towed behind the *Sea Venture* and cast adrift when the hurricane struck.

With 32 of their dead thrown overboard from the *Diamond* and *Swallow* and 150 marooned on the Bermudas, the total number of James Towne's new arrivals still numbered close to 400 souls of varying physical and dispositional quality. In the section of Smith's *Proceedings* attributed to Richard Potts and William Phettiplace, they are described as "this lewd company, wherein were many unruly gallants packed thether by their friends to escape il destinies. . . . Happy had we bin had they never arrived."[17] On seeing Archer, Martin, and Ratcliffe come ashore, Smith was ready to throw in his hand and return to England, but on discovering that they came without any specific authority (the orders being with Gates in his black boxes), he changed his mind. His commission as president was not to expire until September 10, and no one could take it from him save by force. Nevertheless, at one point Smith volunteered to surrender the job in favor of John Martin, believing him to be the least of the three evils. Martin accepted, kept it for three hours, and then thought better of it. Earlier, in an effort to offset the attempts made by Archer & Co. to blacken his name among their shipboard fellows, Smith did what he could to make himself agreeable to the crews. George Percy, who by this time was no friend of Smith's, complained that he "so Jugled w^{t}h them [the seamen and "thatt factyon"] by the way of feasteinges Expense of mutche powder and other unnecessary Tryumphes That mutche was Spente to noe other purpose butt to Insinewate w^{t}h his Reconcyled enemyes and for his owne vayne glory for the w^{c}h we all suffred."[18]

Just what these feastings and powder expenditures amounted to is unclear, but evidently Smith did everything possible to keep the uncommitted happy and the opposition muzzled while he decided what best to do with all these new people. We have to remember that the number of deaths on Jamestown Island through the recent months had greatly diminished. Settlers who survived from the First and Second supplies were fully or at least partway seasoned and, thanks to Smith's firm discipline, were even beginning to get the hang of scratching a life out of Virginia's soil. Thus, when the fleet arrived, there were still close to two hundred people either in James Towne or lodged by Smith in the villages of neighboring and at least temporarily amicable Indians. In spite of expanding the palisades into their "five-square forme,"[19] the enclosure was not large enough to hold all of them. What could one do with four hundred more? As long as the ships stayed, some might remain aboard, but eight vessels (Argall's *John and Mary* was still there) could not long afford to lie idle.

It makes no sense to assume that Archer, Martin, and Ratcliffe were totally ignorant of the contents of Sir Thomas Gates's orders. They must have been composed as the result of extended debate among the London council's members and advisers. Consequently, we can fairly suppose, for example, that the trio were aware that James Towne had been rejected as the permanent capital settlement in favor of a location "removed some good distance from any navigable river, except with small boats, by which no enemy shall dare to seeke your habitation." James Towne, considered in London a place "unwholsome and but in the marish [marsh] of Virginia," was to be used only as a port. It was not to be the storehouse for arms, victuals, or goods "because it is so accessable with shippinge that an enemy may be easily uppon you."[20] If one of the new arrivals told Smith that, he would have been justified in sending expeditions out to set up new towns, and that is what he did.

One large party said by Percy to number 140 men (and by Smith 20 less), under the command of Lord De La Warr's brother Captain Francis West, was dispatched upriver to the falls on the border between Powhatan's confederacy and the lands of the Monacans. Given six months' supplies, they were a larger contingent than the entire 1607 Virginia enterprise and clearly intended to settle no less permanently or securely. Preceding this departure went another led by John Martin and George Percy, this one going downstream into the Nansemonds' territory.

Part of Martin's sixty-man force marched overland commanded by his lieutenant, Michael Sicklemore (apparently unrelated to President Ratcliffe alias Sicklemore); the rest went by boat. Precisely where they were to rendezvous is not known, but later evidence suggests that it was on the west bank of the Nansemond River, perhaps on high ground opposite modern Trotman Wharf and in sight of the large, now largely marsh-surrounded rise called Dumpling Island, where a preliminary archaeological survey has revealed extensive evidence of Indian occupation. Although the Indians had a very different view of land title from the

English, Martin nevertheless sent messengers to the Nansemonds' king offering to buy the island on which he lived in exchange for copper and hatchets. The messengers, however, did not return; instead, according to Percy, certain Indians were persuaded to reveal that the envoys had been executed and that "their Braynes weare cutt and skraped outt of their heades w^{t}h mussell shelles."[21] Percy is silent on just how that information was extracted.

As previously explained, the official policy regarding the Indians required that every effort be made to get along with them. In Johnson's *Nova Britannia*, which had been published just before Martin boarded the *Falcon*, the Company professed that "wee require nothing at their hands, but a quiet residence to us and ours" and that "they shall be most friendly welcome to conjoyne their labours with ours, and shall enjoy equall priviledges with us, in whatsoever good successe, time or meanes may bring to passe."[22] Not everyone was so sure that this was a good idea. In 1609 a less positive English view of the Indians and their culture was voiced in London by Robert Gray, rector of the oddly named Church of St. Bennet Sherehog. Located in Sise Lane close to the City's mercantile heart, it almost certainly included in its congregation many people prominently involved in the new Virginia adventure. Those who missed hearing the Reverend Gray's sermon had an early opportunity to read it, for it was published on April 28, seventeen days before the fleet left the Thames.

"The report goeth, that in Virginia the people are savage and incredibly rude," Gray declared, "they worship the divell, offer their young children in sacrifice unto him, wander up and downe like beasts, and in manners and conditions, differ very little from beasts, having no Art, nor science, nor trade, to imploy themselves. . . ." On the other hand, Gray continued, they "are by nature loving and gentle, and desirous to imbrace a better condition." Consequently, in dealing with them, all men should "use their wits in the first place, and weapons should alwayes be the last meanes in all our projects."[23]

For Messrs. Martin and Percy, the distance from first means to last was scarcely longer than a sword's blade. Not waiting to be sure that their messengers were dead, they "Beate the Salvages outt of the Island burned their howses Ransaked their Temples Tooke downe the Corpses of their deade kings from their Toambes And caryed away their pearles Copper and bracelettes, wherew^{t}h they doe decore their kings funeralles."[24]

Martin's combination of vengeance and Christian zeal knocked yet another nail into the coffin of the *Nova Britannia*'s vision of productive coexistence. To make matters worse (if that were possible), Martin captured the king's son on the mainland and took him and another Indian prisoner to the island, where an English boy shot one or the other of them in the chest. The wounded prisoner escaped, swam to the mainland, and spread the news of their treatment. At this point Percy returned to James Towne after advising Martin to raid the mainland, where a large store of corn could be seized. Martin, however, preferred not to risk it.

Meanwhile, Francis West's expedition to build a fort at the falls also managed to get itself into trouble. Having built the fort (alas, we know nothing of its character), whenever West's men ventured out, they tended either to disappear or to come back damaged. When Smith went up to try to learn why the previously good relations with weroance Parahunt and his Powhatan Indians at the falls had broken down, he found the settlement in total disarray, discipline tossed to the wind, gold fever raging, and looting the neighboring Indians' gardens and homes the easiest means of augmenting the rations. Several Indians were being held hostage in the fort—to the chagrin of their relatives, who complained to Smith that these people he had claimed were coming to protect them from the Monacans were worse than their traditional enemies. West being temporarily absent, Smith could do little to solve the problem without bringing up reinforcements of loyal men from James Towne. To that end, therefore, he set sail. But the ship went only a short distance before it lodged in a sandbank. Meanwhile, at the falls a handful of Indians attacked stragglers outside the fort, drove the rest back into it, and retrieved their hostages. Word was sent to Smith, who left the stranded ship and returned to the fort in its boat to try to patch up a truce.

George Percy would later portray the incident entirely differently, claiming that Smith, driven by fury that his instructions and authority had been flouted, had incited the Indians to attack, telling them that the fort's defenders "had noe more powder lefte them then wolde serve for one volley of shott."[25] There's no doubt, of course, that this was a canard eagerly seized upon by Percy. Nevertheless, the fact that the fort was successfully assaulted by barely a dozen Indians suggests that the powder supplies were as low as the inhabitants' morale.

Although testimonies are conflicting, it seems that West returned after the attack and became involved in a heated dispute with Smith over the latter's charge that he had chosen a ridiculous location to build the fort, one on such low ground that it would be inundated whenever the river flooded. Smith opened negotiations with Parahunt to buy a better placed and already fortified Indian village, to be paid for with copper and an English boy named Henry Spelman. The boy, who admitted leaving England "beinge in displeaseur of my frendes,"[26] claimed that he had no idea what he was in for until "unknowne to me he sould me to him for a towne called Powhatan and leavinge me with him ye litle Powhatann."[27] The deal struck, Smith ordered a reluctant Francis West to move his people to the purchased village. With its two to three hundred acres of plantable ground, protected by poles and the bark of trees, in Smith's view no place was "so strong, so pleasant and delightfull in Virginia,"[28] and so he called it Nonsuch—there being none such as could compare with it. West called it something quite different, and as soon as Smith departed, he took himself and his men back to his own fort.

While returning by boat to James Towne, John Smith suffered the famous accident that brought his Virginia career to an abrupt and painful end. Historians invariably have taken him at his word when Smith claimed that he "was neare blowne to death with Gun-powder."[29] But he was renowned for bluster and for making any bang bigger than it was. Following his lead, and Purchas's marginal note "Captaine Smith blowne up with powder,"[30] modern accounts of what happened usually read like this: "While Smith was returning in a boat from the falls of the James, he was severely burned by an explosion of gunpowder,"[31] or "a bag of gun-powder he was carrying exploded, burning him severely."[32] Perhaps because the mixing of gunpowder is not part of a historian's required education, none seems to have asked whether the story (at least as it has come down to us) really makes pyrotechnical sense.

Even if Smith's bag had contained only a quarter of a pound of powder, its explosion would have blown Smith, leg and thigh, all around the boat. Uncompressed, as the powder would have been when loose in a bag, it would only burn, albeit creating a brief flash, a cloud of smoke, and tremendous heat. There's no disputing the severity of Smith's injury, which he says in his *Generall Historie* "tore the flesh from his body and thighes, nine or ten inches square in a most pittifull manner."[33] That it did happen, we know, but how it *could* happen is something else again. Was it really an accident?

Both Smith's *Proceedings* and his *Generall Historie* are careful to say that "Sleeping in his Boate . . . accidentallie, one fired his powder bag, which tore the flesh. . . ."[34] Percy (who wasn't there) coupled his account of the accident with Smith's alleged leak to the Indians of the powder shortage at West's fort: "And so Capte: SMITHE Retouringe to JAMES TOWNE ageine fownd to have too mutche powder aboutt him The wch beinge in his pockett where the sparke of A Matche Lighted very shrewdly [severely]

A musketeer with his match burning. Unlike Smith, who is said to
have carried a large bag of powder at his waist, this marksman carries
his charges in individual cylinders, his priming powder in a small flask,
and his bullets in a leather bag. Engraving by Jacob de Ghyn, 1612.

burned him."[35] In the seventeenth century (and in the eighteenth, for that
matter) the word "pocket" meant a bag or purse hung from a belt, not a
container sewn into one's clothing. The reference to a match is to flax or
hemp cord soaked in a solution of potassium nitrate that, when dry, was
used as a slow-burning ignition for matchlock muskets.

Although fuses could be a yard long and were often kept burning at
both ends, they needed only to glow until blown on. The likelihood of a
spark's accidentally falling onto Smith's bag of gunpowder was remote,
and even if it had, the chances of its burning through a leather bag before
going out were equally slight. But if the end of a lit match were deliberately laid against the bag, ignition (but not explosion) could very easily
result. But who might have done that, and why?

Smith had left the Indian-built fort at Nonsuch at odds with West
and with any others among the men who resented his disciplinarian
approach to their problems. They were also (or so it seemed) desperately
short of powder. If Smith's bag contained enough to load and fire even

one more volley, his failure to donate it before departing could have caused fierce resentment, even among the crew of his own boat. Furthermore, the crew knew that Smith's continuing presidency was a thorn in the shank of James Towne's triumvirate of Archer, Ratcliffe, and Martin. Looking to the future, therefore, who could win more brownie points than the bearers of news that their out-of-step commander had met with an unfortunate and fatal accident? All in all, then, a case can be made for adding attempted murder to the colonists' tally of lewd and naughtie practices.

Unfortunately for the conspirators (if such they were), Smith was not sufficiently injured that he could not throw himself overboard to quench his burning clothes, whereupon his crew deplored the accident and helped him back into the boat. Skeptics may counter that if the crew had gone so far as to stage the accident, they would have seen it through to the end by hitting Smith over the head with an oar as he struggled in the water. But a manufactured accident known to perhaps only two or even one, was very different from the cold-blooded assassination of their president witnessed by everyone aboard.

The likelihood that this scenario is correct, and that the attempt's failure prompted others to see merit in preventing Smith from returning to England to tell his side of the James Towne story, is bolstered by a reported second escape as he lay ill in the fort. Smith's *Proceedings* describe how Martin, Ratcliffe and Archer, "their guiltie consciences fearing a just reward for their deserts, seeing the President unable to stand, and neare bereft of his senses by reason of his torment, they had plotted to have him murdered in his bed. But his hart did faile him that should have given fire to that mercilesse pistol."[36] Whether this is Smithian hyperbole or an assassin with pistol in hand actually stood over his sickbed, one cannot say, but recognizing that he was in no condition to defend himself, and assuming that there was neither a physician nor a surgeon in James Fort (what, we may wonder, had become of Dr. Russell and surgeon Bagnall?), Smith made arrangements with one of the fleet's captains to go aboard and return with him to England.

So ended the first phase in the development of James Fort, for after the formidable Smith's departure the quarreling leadership preferred to sit on its hands through the six months or so that it would take to get word to England that Governor Gates and his black boxes were lost and for new instructions to be shipped over.

Smith's departure prompted Richard Potts, the council's clerk and his supporter, to inventory the colony's assets. Potts was the author of much of Smith's *Proceedings,* and it is there that his listing appears: After the first four ships sailed, three remained, as did seven boats. The harvest was in, and there were provisions in the store to last ten weeks. As for live-stock, the colony possessed six mares and a horse, between five and six hundred pigs, as many hens and chickens, as well as an unspecified num-ber of goats and sheep. This looked pretty good on the ledger, but the inventory also listed 490 "odde persons" as consumers.[37] How many of those were women, alas, has gone unrecorded. Cannon of various sizes numbered twenty-four, and the small arms ran to three hundred "mus-kets, snaphaunces and firelocks." This last description leaves us with some problems, however, for Randle Holme in his firearm terminology says that "A Snaphaunch Lock is the generall name for all fire Locks." Elsewhere in the same essay Holme distinguishes between the "parts of a Fire lock and a match lock, and wheele lock,"[38] this last being an ignition system operated by a serrated wheel grinding sparks from a lump of iron pyrites. However, writing in 1590, Sir John Smythe identified only the wheel lock as a "firelock,"[39] and there is every reason to conclude that Potts was using the term in that way. Mechanically simpler and more effi-cient than the wheel lock, the snaphaunce used a cock-gripped flint to strike a steel plate and produce the same result.

In addition to the cannon and small arms, and in spite of continuing attrition by the Indians, Potts's inventory showed that the colony could boast more helmets, body armor, swords, and pikes than it could muster men to wear and bear them. When Smith partially rewrote the contents of the *Proceedings* for inclusion in his *Generall Historie,* he added impor-tant fort-related information that had been previously omitted from Potts's manuscript but that presumably had been part of it. In using it, however, we have to recognize that it was written retrospectively and that there is no knowing how much time had elapsed or how flawed the writer's memory might have become. With that caveat borne in mind, here is what the *Historie* says:

> Besides James towne that was strongly Pallizadoed, containing some fiftie or sixtie houses, he [Smith] left five or sixe other sever-all Forts and Plantations: though they were not so sumptuous as our successors expected. . . . All this time we had but one Carpen-ter in the Countrey, and three others that could doe little, but desired to be learners.[40]

The summary goes on to list two blacksmiths and a couple of sailors and to note that those who had been categorized as "Labourers" among the earlier arrivals were really "foot men," meaning servants to the gentlemen and therefore not bred to hard labor. This was almost certainly true, for as long as the worker emigrants were drawn largely from London and their fares paid by a private master, few, if any, would have been brought as farm-trained field hands.

The statement that by the time Smith left, dwellings numbered in the fifties is the surprising first claim that the total exceeded twenty. But although there is no later corroboration, the dramatically increased number makes sense. Even assuming a maximum James Towne population of two hundred, averaging six to the house, that would still call for thirty-three, not twenty, dwellings. Reduce the body density only slightly to meet the social needs of council members and other senior gentlemen, and fifty-five houses becomes a by no means unreasonable number. The trick (as we shall see when more evidence becomes available once the *Sea Venture* survivors arrive) is how to fit that many houses inside the James Fort laid out by Wingfield and the first council and only slightly modified after the 1608 fire. It may be significant, therefore, that Smith refers no longer to James Fort but to a strongly palisaded James Towne.

Counting heads and houses is, in reality, a far more risky game than I have indicated. The total colonist population of 490 and the James Towne house total of "fiftie or Sixty" cited by Potts must be weighed against others' testimony that the Third Supply (minus the *Sea Venture*) added "neere five hundred persons" to a James Towne that possessed "howses few or none to entertain them." So bad was the situation that "being quartered in the open feilde they fell upon that small quantitye of corne, not being above seaven acres, which we with great penury and sufferance had formerly planted, and in three days, at the most, wholly devoured it."[41] The new arrivals therefore were divided into three groups, one remaining with Smith at James Towne, the second going upriver with Francis West to the falls (Percy put the number at 140), and the third down with John Martin to the island base in the Nansemond River. No one mentioned any burst of building at James Towne between August 11, when the six (Percy called it eight) ships arrived, and September 10, when Smith was replaced as president. Indeed, as we have seen, through much of that time Smith had been absent from James Towne, grappling with West and growing Indian problems below the falls, and was in no position to supervise a major structural expansion that would have called for both domestic and defensive planning.

With Smith's regime ended, his place both as president and as chronicler was to be taken by George Percy. Eighth son of Henry Percy, eighth earl of Northumberland, thus brother to the ninth earl, George was the scion of an ancient and noble family, but like many a seventh or eighth son, he found his ego and his assets often at odds. Nevertheless, his social status had set him several cuts above that of his longtime council superior, the yeoman's son John Smith, a distinction that helps explain Percy's growing dislike for his president, whom he later condemned as an "Ambityous unworthy and vayneglorious fellowe."[42] Smith might have countered that it took one to know one, for this was the same George Percy who in 1611 helped explain his deficit spending to his brother Henry by his need as governor at James Towne "to keep a continual and daily table for gentlemen of fashion."[43]

Charles R. Beazley, who contributed the essay on Percy to the *Dictionary of National Biography*, stated that his *A Trewe Relacyon of the Precedeinges and Occurrentes of Momente wch have hapned in Virginia . . . &c.* was written in rebuttal after John Smith's *Generall Historie* was published in 1624. Subsequent authors have accepted this conclusion and are at pains to point out that because thirteen years thus elapsed after Percy's own return to England, his spite is likely to have driven his quill more forcefully than did his memory. On the other hand, much of his narrative is so detailed that it must surely be drawn from his own notes or journal written while he was in Virginia. That such sources existed we know from Purchas's published extracts, but that Percy evidently made no immediate effort to publish his recollections suggests that he lacked any literary ambition. If he had, Smith's publication of the *Proceedings* in 1612, the same year that Percy returned to England, must have discouraged him. But when, in 1624, the *Generall Historie* expanded the *Proceedings* to comment on events in Virginia after Smith left, Percy may have felt compelled to justify himself to his brother—hence the longhand and undated manuscript of the *Trewe Relacyon* which was destined to remain library-locked for almost three centuries.[44]

Be all that as it may, George Percy becomes our principal, if sometimes vindictive, guide through the next seven months, and it is primarily through his retrospective eyes that we watch James Towne's condition slip from better to infinitely and horrifyingly worse.

CHAPTER X

A Ship in Time

❧

FOR THE unruly settlers at James Towne, John Smith's departure was akin to seeing their drill sergeant drive out of camp. The men would be free to amuse themselves, creating their own hierarchy, whereby the strong and belligerent influenced and intimidated those who were neither. This, however, was a situation that quickly could lead to mutiny, as Virginia's new but still-instructionless leadership well recognized.

With George Percy the senior member of the council established under the old charter, it made sense to elect him interim president. Besides, by doing so, Ratcliffe, Martin, and Archer could avoid responsibility for any mistakes that might be made during what was likely to be a very difficult winter. Knowing that even if the *Sea Venture* had gone down with all hands, Lord De La Warr and another supply fleet would eventually be on its way, these men needed to be sure that they continued to have the winds of favor at their backs. Should Smith fail to die of his injuries on the way home, there was always the danger that he might influence enough Company members to undo the damage that Ratcliffe & Co. had previously and carefully done him. No doubt they felt reasonably certain that Smith's abrasive soldier's personality would find little favor among the Company's courtiers and merchants; but just to be on the safe side, Ratcliffe made sure that along with Smith and the departing ships went a letter to Secretary of State Salisbury, informing him that "This man [John Smith] is sent home to answere some misdeamenors whereof I perswade me he can scarcly clear him selfe from great imputation of blame." This, of course, differed markedly from Smith's claim to having left of his own volition to seek medical treatment in England. The letter's implication, therefore, is that together, and perhaps with the vengeful Percy's help, the new council "of the best and worthyest that inhabitie at James towne"[1] wrote up an indictment and, unbeknownst to Smith, shipped it to London. Although Ratcliffe referred only to misdemeanors, young Henry Spelman's account claimed that Smith had conspired with the Powhatan Indians at the falls to kill Francis West. West being Lord De La Warr's brother, such a charge would certainly get London's attention. As Spelman told it, "Capt Smith was Aprehended, and sent abord for England,"[2] thus reinforcing Ratcliffe's statement to Lord Salisbury.

Continuing the policy established by John Smith of creating satellite settlements at the falls under West, and on the Nansemonds' island under Martin, Percy sent John Ratcliffe to the mouth of the James at Point Comfort to build another fort, this one to be named Algernon— in the hope of scoring points with Percy's noble and wealthy brother, whose eldest son bore that name. The name aside, Fort Algernon was a good idea; it had a commanding view of approaching shipping, it was a good place for fishing, and with Martin on the south side of the river and Ratcliffe on the north, the entrance to the James was well covered. At least that's the way it looks on paper. In reality, with Martin's Dumpling Island base some nine miles up the Nansemond River, the distance between the two settlements was such that there could be no speedy communication between them.

From its beginning, John Martin's island settlement had been more defensive than an intimidating demonstration of English firepower. Indeed, in the mind of one George Forrest the intimidation and firepower were better handled by the Nansemonds, who shot seventeen arrows into him, one of them passing right through. Forrest died a week later "for want of Chirurgery."[3] To Percy's evident disgust, Martin left his people in Lieutenant Sicklemore's charge and returned to James Towne, "pretendinge some occasions of busyness, but indede," Percy added, "his owne saffety moved him thereunto feareinge to be surprysed by the Indyans."[4] Although in Smith's opinion, Michael Sicklemore was "a very valiant, honest, and a painefull Souldier,"[5] Martin's men were evidently more than he could handle. Seventeen mutinied, seized a boat, and set out across the James to the Indian town of Kecoughtan to trade for food. Several days later, Sicklemore and several still-loyal men went after them. All were later found dead "wth their mowthes stopped full of Breade."[6] To Percy the message was loud and clear, and he saw in it a parallel to the fate of a Spanish general in Chile whom the Indians forced to drink molten gold.

Théodore de Bry's engraving of South American Indians pouring
molten gold into the mouth of a European prisoner, a practice
described by Girolamo Benzoni in 1565 and remembered by
George Percy at James Towne.

With Sicklemore dead and Martin fled, Percy pulled out the last of
the Nansemond garrison, leaving Fort Algernon as the colony's sole
downriver presence. That setback was quickly followed by another. After
losing eleven more men and a boat, Francis West withdrew from his post
at the falls and returned with his people to James Towne, further overcrowding the fort and reducing its supplies, now estimated at "halfe a
Cann of meale for A man A Day"[7] for three months. Percy did not record
the date when that estimate was made, but it was probably in late November. If so, that meant empty mugs by the end of February, by which time
the Indians, too, would be short of grain. Indeed, they had already made
it clear that supplies were low, the shortage blamable in part on the
colonists' endless "trading" and in part on the instability that the English
presence had injected into the orderly process of Indian life. Percy concluded that the wisest course would be to send another awe-inspiring
deputation to King James's good friend and fellow monarch, the emperor
Powhatan.

After Smith's last trading trip had created chaos up and down Prince
Henry's (York) River, Powhatan had abandoned Werowocomoco and
moved his capital to an earlier ceremonial center at Orapakes, which lay
farther west between the Chickahominy and Pamunkey rivers and was far
less easily reached by the English. It was to Orapakes, therefore, that

Percy now sent John Ratcliffe as emissary and trader. Details of the trip are sketchy and somewhat contradictory; but it seems that with fifty men (another account put the figure at only twenty-four) Ratcliffe sailed in the *Discovery* or *Virginia* pinnace up Prince Henry's River and when partway up the Pamunkey, transferred sixteen of them to a barge. At some point Ratcliffe invited "Powhatans sonne and dowghter [Pocahontas?] Aboard his pinesse"; but instead of holding them hostage he let them go again—a courtesy seen in hindsight by Percy as a seriously missed opportunity. Failure to keep a proper watch on his arms, and allowing his men to "straggle into the Salvages howses"[8] were among other charges Percy leveled. Ratcliffe, however, would not be around to hear them, for he was to pay a terrible price for his incompetence.

At the outset, the negotiations with Powhatan were encouraging. Yes, he did have some corn, and yes, of course, bygones should be bygones. Bread and venison were exchanged for copper and beads, and out of respect for King James's friends, Powhatan offered accommodation close by his own lodge—half a mile from the barge. The next day Ratcliffe and his men were taken to the main grain store, where the heavy trading was to begin. When they got there, all seemed well until they discovered that the Indians were using their hands to push up the bottoms of the soft woven baskets used to measure out the grain, thus reducing the size of the units. Words were exchanged, and Powhatan walked out, taking with him his wives, one of his Dutchmen, and Henry Spelman, the boy whom Smith had traded to Powhatan's son Parahunt at the falls, and to whom we are indebted for the only eyewitness account of what happened.

With the trading angrily terminated, Ratcliffe and his men gathered up the corn they had already bought and set out on the half-mile walk to the boat. They never made it. Indians in ambush in the woods and fields beside the trail picked them off one by one. Two escaped into the forest and eventually got home overland; but Ratcliffe was seized and tied naked to a tree, and a fire was lit at his feet. Then out came the razor-sharp mussel shells, this time in the hands of women, who scraped the flesh from his bones and, while he lived, tossed the pieces into the fire. "And so," as Percy later put it, Virginia's second president "for want of circumspection miserably perished."[9]

Not content with their accomplishment, Powhatan's warriors tried to capture the waiting pinnace, but were driven off by Captain William Phettiplace, though at the cost of further English losses. He eventually returned to James Towne with only sixteen of the fifty would-be traders. President Percy could be forgiven for feeling that an alien world was closing in on him.

At some time in the autumn of 1609 Captain James Davies and sixteen men had arrived at James Towne aboard the *Virginia* pinnace. Davies, who had played a leading role in the 1607 Popham enterprise on the Kennebec, was a man of some experience. Percy therefore appointed him to the vacant command at Fort Algernon and sent Francis West and thirty-six men up the Chesapeake Bay to try to trade for corn with the Patawomeke Indians. In the dead of winter this was not an overnight trip. The Patawomekes had their principal village in what is now Stafford County on Potomac Creek above Fredericksburg. Although still part of Powhatan's Confederacy, the tribe had seen less of the English than had those closer at hand and with luck might be more friendly. And so it proved.

Though West was able to load his pinnace with grain, the success involved "some harshe and Crewell dealinge by cutteinge of towe of the Salvages heads and other extremetyes."[10] The pinnace and her lifesaving cargo returned to Point Comfort, where Captain Davies came out from the fort to tell West of the increasingly dire straits in which he and the rest at James Towne were finding themselves. No one doubted that this new supply of grain would help, but it would not be enough to last the winter. On the other hand, decided the pinnace's crew, it was plenty to get them fatly home to England. So it was that Francis West "by the perswasion or rather by the inforcement his company hoysed upp Sayles"[11] and headed out into the Atlantic, leaving the colonists to the Indians and to God.

As the food supplies at James Towne dwindled, a sick and starving Hugh Pryse concluded that there was no God and shocked his fellows by running into the marketplace crying out that "if there were A god he wolde nott suffer his creatures whom he had made and framed to indure those miseries." The same day the emaciated Pryse in the company of a contrastingly and surprisingly corpulent butcher took to the woods, where they were soon shot by Indian snipers and left where they fell. Animals tore Pryse's bony corpse to shreds while less than twenty feet away the butcher's fat and inviting body was found untouched. Although today this is the kind of phenomenon that enjoys endless speculation on the part of writers for tabloid newspapers, at James Towne in the winter of 1609 the explanation was simple: Hugh Pryse had received the justice of "gods Indignacyon."[12] To those of us forever scratching for clues to the settlement's character and content, Pryse's outburst revealed that the palisades enclosed an area that George Percy could define as a "markett place."

Once Smith had gone, Powhatan had begun to turn the screws on the English wherever they were to be found. Except as a means of trapping the settlers (as he had Ratcliffe at Orapakes), he proscribed any trading in food; his warriors were to attack anyone who ventured into the woods and shoot at every fisherman who took to the water. As a result, the settlers remained caged behind their wooden walls and, like animals at bay, fought one another for the foulest of bones. With their pigs on Hog Island slaughtered by the Indians, they gnawed their way through their chickens, their sheep, their goats, and even the hides of their horses. They killed their dogs and their cats and chased the rats and mice themselves, until finally, as the "gastely and pale" face of famine bared its teeth, they stared hungrily at one another.

An anonymous eyewitness quoted in John Smith's *Generall Historie* confessed that a slain and buried Indian was dug up by "the poorer sort" and eaten.[13] Percy corroborated the admission but drew no distinction between Indian and English dead, saying only that the hungry were moved to "digge up dead corpses outt of graves and to eate them," adding that "some have Licked upp the Bloode w^{c}h hathe fallen from their weake fellowes."[14] Through the centuries, however, one harrowing tale has stood out above all others as the desperate embodiment of the months that have gone down in Virginia history as the Starving Time. Some tellers claimed to have been witnesses, others attributed the story to this person or to that, but within a year and in one form or another it was being told and embroidered upon in every London tavern: An Englishman had eaten his wife.

John Smith's informant told how the man had salted and eaten part of her before he was discovered and, with a touch of gallows humor that transcends all centuries, added, "Now whether shee was better roasted, boyled or carbonado'd [grilled], I know not, but of such a dish as powdered [salted] wife I never heard of."[15] The jokes no doubt took the edge off the story's true horror, but for the Virginia Company's promoters it was publicity that they could well do without. To keep investors steadfast, a new promotional pamphlet was hastened into print, explaining (amid much else) that although a James Towne settler had killed his wife, he had done so not out of hunger but out of "mortal hatred." While it was true that he had dismembered her, explained the writer, the man did so to hide the evidence of his crime. When discovered, he claimed that his wife had died and that only hunger had driven him to cannibalism. According to the London version, the man's house was searched and found to contain a "good quantitie of meale, oatmeale, beanes and pease,"[16] thus refuting his starvation defense. He was promptly arraigned, judged, sentenced—and burned alive. The sentence was unusual in that burning was generally a death reserved for those guilty of treason and for women, a statute which, despite its brutality, would not be repealed in England until 1794.

Neither of the surviving eyewitness accounts mentions the burning, nor do they support the published motive. The testimony of George Percy, who heard the evidence and passed the sentence, cannot be dismissed. His version is even more ghastly than Smith's, recalling that the man "murdered his wyfe Ripped the childe outt of her woambe and threw itt into the River and after chopped the Mother in pieces and salted her for his foode [,] The same not beinge discovered before he had eaten parte thereof. . . ."[17] A much later reporter claimed that before being caught, the husband had chewed his way through a good deal more than a "parte thereof." He had "clean devoured all partes saveinge her head."[18] When the suspect was slow to confess, Percy had him hauled up by the thumbs and left him hanging with weights on his feet. Fifteen minutes proved sufficient, and Percy, as counsel, jury, and judge, passed sentence of death—by means he avoided defining.

The calendar of James Towne's suffering is unclear, but the popular perception that the Starving Time was limited to the deep winter months cannot be true. Percy goes on to relate that having recovered from his own sickness, but with James Towne's misery still at its height, he went downriver to Fort Algernon to find out how its garrison was faring. External evidence suggests that it was now mid-May. To Percy's surprise, he found Captain Davies and his men so well fed that they were feeding crabs to their hogs. This is a significant statement, for in modern times, at least, the crabbing season does not begin until April. In somewhat elliptical language Percy accused Captain Davies of deliberately concealing his supplies from the sufferers at James Towne and even with plotting to keep his men healthy enough that they could commandeer the pinnaces and sail home to England. Davies's response is lost, but he might well have asked why as the colony's leader Percy had waited until the spring to visit his people at Fort Algernon. Finding them obscenely healthy, however, Percy declared his intent to bring down some of his James Towne survivors to reap the benefits of Davies's prudence.

While the president and his fort commander were debating the merits of the plan, two pinnaces were spotted on the horizon and heading toward the bay—this on the evening of Sunday, May 20, 1610. Fearing that the ships were Spanish, the fort's forty defenders stood to their arms throughout the night. When dawn found the pinnaces lying offshore, Davies fired a warning cannon, and all waited nervously as a boat put out from one of the vessels and headed toward the fort. Only then did they discover that the pinnaces were the Bermuda-built *Deliverance* and *Patience*, bringing Gates, Somers, and all but two of the wrecked *Sea Venture*'s passengers and crew safely to the end of their journey, albeit a year late.

The record of Sir Thomas Gates's arrival provides us with yet another example of the dangers inherent in accepting the word even of eyewitnesses. Although Percy tells us that the ships were sighted before dark and came to land the next morning, the generally invaluable William Strachey aboard the *Deliverance* describes how, at about midnight on the twentieth, they encountered a "marvellous sweet smell from the shoare" but did not sight the coast until an hour after daybreak the next morning when from the foretop "one of the saylers descryed Land."[19] We are left wondering, therefore, how a sentry at the fort could identify two tiny dots on the horizon when the *Deliverance*'s lookout failed to spot something as large as Virginia. Nevertheless, regardless of who saw what first, the miracle of Governor Gates's survival was received with unbridled joy—until it became apparent that the pinnaces brought about 148 mouths and no food. Conversely, the relief of the *Sea Venture*'s survivors was quickly tempered by the sight of their welcomers at James Towne, some of whom came stumbling from their beds "so Leane thatt they Looked lyke Anatomies [medical students' skeletons] Cryeinge owtt we are starved."[20]

Thanks to the arrival of William Strachey, we at last have a stranger's first impression of James Towne's appearance. I wish I could reveal that this comes, hitherto unseen, from the pages of the newly discovered Strachey manuscript, but unfortunately that crams the Virginia story into a single paragraph and offers only one piece of information not in the long version published by Samuel Purchas. "In a short time," it says, "scarcely sixty of 600 survived," differing from Percy, who noted that of "fyve hundrethe men we had onely lefte Aboutt sixty,"[21] closely paralleling the "490 and odde persons" cited by Richard Potts in Smith's 1612 *Proceedings*.

The *Deliverance* and *Patience* took two days in a dead calm to ride the tides to James Towne, thus arriving on May 23. The fortifications, which we have to assume were in good condition when Smith left, were by now in a deplorable state. Reporting to the Company in London on Gates's arrival, a spokesman for the council in Virginia—who almost certainly was William Strachey—wrote that "entering the towne, it appeared raither as the ruins of some auntient [for]tification, then that any people living might now in habit it."[22] The description continues in words almost exactly paralleling those used by Strachey in his *True Reportory* to capture the same scene: "We found the Pallisadoes torne downe, the Ports open, the Gates from off the hinges, and emptie houses (which Owners' death had taken from them) rent up and burnt, rather then the dwellers would step into the Woods a stones cast off from them, to fetch other firewood."[23] It's a description that raises several puzzling questions: How could starvation have led to the tearing down of an apparently substantially built palisade? And what of the gates? What possible circumstances would cause heavy timber gates to be raised up and freed from their hinge pintles? It's understandable that the settlers might destroy abandoned houses for firewood, but even if they had the strength, they would not breach the walls and gates which provided their only refuge from the Indians' arrows. However, what starving men could not accomplish, violent weather might. But although Strachey reported a major storm on the day the two pinnaces reached Point Comfort, it would take a hurricane to wreck a fort's gates, and the hurricane season was long over.

Strachey's brief description of the fort's condition contains two more elements, referring as it does to the open ports and to the nearby woods. The word "port" (or "portal") comes from the Latin *porta* and generally means either "a door" or "a gate," but in this instance it occurs in tandem with gates, so means something else: either secondary and smaller door openings in the palisades or, more probably, musket slits between the pales. A spying Spaniard, Don Diego de Molina, who in 1611 was taken first to Fort Algernon and afterward to James Towne, later commented disparagingly on the quality of the English fortifications, saying that "the forts which they have are of boards and so weak that a kick would break them down, and once arrived at the ramparts those without would have the advantage over those within because its beams and loopholes are common to both parts,"[24] meaning that Spanish attackers could shoot the defenders through their own gunports. Using that interpretation, therefore, we can read Strachey as saying that the slots were not covered as they should have been to prevent their use by attackers be they Spanish or Indian. That the Indians might be capable of winging arrows through slits nine inches high and only three wide would have surprised no one. "I suppose the world hath no better marke-men with their bow and arrowes then they be," admitted the Reverend Alexander Whitaker in 1613; "they will kill birds flying, fishes swimming, and beasts running: they shoote also with mervailous strength," Whitaker added, "they shot one of our men being unarmed quite through the bodie, and nailed both his armes to his bodie with one arrow."[25] Clearly, therefore, leaving one's musket ports uncovered would have been dangerously dumb. That brings us to Strachey's last point—namely, the proximity of the Indian-concealing woods.

A James Towne–style palisade of posts, rails, and planks pierced by
musket ports, as reconstructed on the John Boyse site at
Wolstenholme Towne.

Describing the forest as "a stone's cast off" belies the previously cited
evidence of extensive tree-felling and the clearing of up to forty farmed
acres adjacent to the fort. If the woods were a only a stone's-throw distance even in one direction from the triangular walls, it meant that the
trees were still standing within an arrow's flight of the defenses. This
question of cleared cover (or the lack of it) resurrects another question—
to wit, where did the colonists bury their dead? The question was pertinent enough in 1607, when the numbers were in the tens, but when they
rose into the hundreds (maybe four or even five hundred) in the winter of
1609–10, the spatial problem became immense. Clearly the settlers could
not have gone into the woods to do it. We may recall, too, that some of
the graves were sufficiently to hand that the hunger-driven settlers could
dig them up. The anonymous survivor's account published much later by
Smith identifies one such disinterment as the grave of "a Salvage we slew,
and buried," adding that "the poorer sort tooke him up againe and eat
him" and then somewhat cryptically, "and so did divers [a word or words
missing?] one another boyled and stewed with roots and herbs."[26]

The burial of an Indian by the colonists is in itself a clue. Since we
know both that the attackers were careful to carry away their dead and
that the colonists would never have taken the trouble to bury Indians
killed outside the James Towne palisades, logic dictates that the eaten
Indian was killed outside—and probably buried inside. If true, it's possi-

ble that at least some of the colonists were interred within the walls, where the burial detail would be protected from Indian marksmen. Although today the notion of burying one's friends and relations within yards of one's house would be morally improper—not to mention illegal—we have archaeological evidence from Wolstenholme Towne that at least a dozen were interred beside one dwelling, the closest only three feet from its end wall. Although it is true that the house was destroyed in the Indian attack of 1622 and that the dead may have been its victims, it is fair to assume that survivors expected to rebuild on the same site.

That the Indians were continuing to apply pressure on James Towne when Gates and his fresh people arrived is revealed by Strachey, who followed his comment on the survivors' understandable reluctance to gather kindling from the woods by saying: "and it is true, the Indian killed as fast without, if our men stirred but beyond the bounds of their Blockhouse, as Famine and Pestilence did within."[27] His reference to "their Blockhouse" may be misleading. Taken at face value, it may seem to relate to the interior of the log structure built at the neck connecting the island to the mainland at Glass House Point, yet the rest of the sentence almost certainly refers to the inhabitants of the island east of the neck and the blockhouse's protection.

Were Strachey not the source, one might be tempted to suggest that in some way the writer perceived James Fort as a single large unit comprising three palisade-linked blockhouses. That is not as farfetched as it may appear, for in the aftermath of the massacre that was to come in 1622, notes on Virginia's defenses submitted to Commissioner Lord Chichester stated that "The fortifications antientlie used were by Trench and Pallizado and diverse blockhouses made of great Tymber built uppon passages and for scouring the Pallizadoes: all w^{c}h are now gone to ruyne."[28] In addition, there are several other supportive references to blockhouses and bulwarks as associated elements in a fortification. The previously cited instructions to M. Bonnavolia (1630) on how to erect a log-laid blockhouse went on to tell him to build three more "80 Foote Distant one tower fro[m] another, with a pa[ssage] or Alley to goe from one to another in quarters."[29] Both the quoted sources mention the blockhouses' being linked by passages, thus reinforcing the likelihood of their similarity. Such passages can be interpreted as palisaded trenches or as wooden versions of the elevated walkways behind the stone battlements connecting the towers of medieval fortresses. If such raised walkways existed at James Fort as early as 1607, they would have provided the firetraps needed to ignite the otherwise hard-to-burn palisades.

By 1610 it was rare for anyone to refer to the island settlement as James Fort; now it was invariably identified as James Towne. We have to ask, therefore, whether the change resulted from structural alterations that had turned a wooden castle into a demonstrably walled town or whether having become the postal address for several hundred people, it assumed its urban status by presumption. In the absence of any recorded shape or spatial changes since the 1608 fire, the latter explanation is the more reasonable. Certainly, in the London Company's vision, the sight of departing fleets crammed with settlers (leaving behind city desks piled with invoices and bills) promoted the idea of a burgeoning New World colony with a capital to rival the Spaniards' St. Augustine or Santo Domingo.

The pathetic reality, however, was all too evident to Governor Gates. With his own food supplies almost exhausted, this being the planting and not the reaping time, and with no certainty as to when, if ever, Lord De La Warr might arrive with a new supply, there seemed no alternative but to abandon the colony and head north to the Newfoundland fishing banks, where English ships could be found to help carry the survivors home. Strachey makes it clear that with his Bermuda survivors back aboard the *Deliverance* and *Patience,* everyone else would have to crowd onto the two remaining pinnaces, the *Discovery* and *Virginia.* The voyage would not be pleasant (few voyages ever were), but the alternative was nobody's preference.

Once the decision had been reached, Gates set about orchestrating an orderly evacuation. Lists were drawn up showing who should board which ship, and an inventory was made of all arms and of any materials worth loading into the holds to be sold when they reached England—a puny gesture to offset the enormous lost investment. Some of the survivors wanted to leave nothing for the Indians but ashes. Gates, however, refused to fire the settlement, arguing that in time "as honneste men as our selves may come and inhabitt here."[30] The point is pertinent, for in spite of Strachey's description of decay and collapse, Gates must have found some merit in what he saw. To make sure that no arsonist had his way, Gates and his guards were the last to leave.

Largest of the colony's assets were its cannon, but they also were the heaviest. Gates consequently ordered their burial "before the Fort gate, which looked into the River."[31] That must have been a lot more easily said than done. When, in 1624, the mechanics of dissolving the Virginia Company were under review, John Smith wrote a summarizing essay opposing the move. In it he stated that within the fort (ca. 1608) were twenty-four pieces of ordnance defined as culverins, demiculverins, sakers, and falcons, whose respective weights (using Smith's own table) were fifty-five hundred pounds, forty-five hundred pounds, thirty-five hundred pounds, and eleven hundred pounds. Support for Smith's large number of cannon comes from another document in the Spanish archives, this one dated July 1, 1610. Describing James Fort, it reads: "And in this fort they put twenty pieces of artillery and afterwards they sent there from England much more artillery."[32] However, as we shall see, three years later the spy Diego de Molina was providing quite different intelligence.

Regardless of the numbers, we know that artillery was removed and buried and that even if the cannon were mounted on large-wheeled field carriages, getting them down from the bulwarks could have been no easy task, while dismantling and burying them would have daunted even the most hale and hearty. One might assume, therefore, that the guns were dumped into an open ditch and covered with dirt shoveled from its banks. But if that is what happened, it is the first indirect evidence we have for James Towne's palisades' being enclosed within or fronted by a ditch. Nothing was said in 1607 about digging ditches, and no English description of the fort directly mentions such a feature, though there are hints. The 1624 memo to Lord Chichester mentioned the ancient use of "Trench and Pallizado," but James Towne is not specified, and the description could as well apply to ditch, rampart, and palisade forts at the mouth of the James akin to Ralph Lane's proposed sconces in modern North Carolina. The 1610 Spanish report, on the other hand, refers specifically to "This fort which the English call James Fort" when it tells how "the English built a well intrenched fort."[33] Before rushing to take "intrenched" literally, you have to remember that this is a translation and that the 1610 correspondent may have meant only that armed with twenty and more cannon, James Fort would be hard to dislodge. Countering that argument, however, we have the eyewitness Molina citing ramparts as an element of English palisades, and you cannot build ramparts without digging a ditch to obtain the dirt.

There is, however, another possibility—namely, that between the fort and the river the settlers had dug a deep infantry trench of World War I character, in which musketeers could stand as a first line of defense against a boatborne invasion. At face value, this sounds farfetched, but it would provide a much better repository for abandoned artillery than would the soft-contoured and partially silted concavity of a ditch. More important, the ever-helpful London instructions to M. Bonnavolia told him precisely how to shape what they described as a pit: "Then make a pitt fro[m] the Tower six foot distant square round about 20 foot broade and eight foote Deep the earth you must Carrey without the paile, and make itt like a shelf so as your men may stand in the pitt, and discharge their shot with security."[34] The words "broade" and "Deep" are puzzling until one realizes that they mean "broad across the front of the defenses" (i.e., long) and "deep outward from the palisade" (i.e., wide). The actual depth into the ground is not given; instead the diggers are told to create a firing step within the pit, which would put it about four feet six inches below grade. That there should be a shelf for the men to stand on rather than leaving them to stand on the floor of a pit of shallower depth would have had two advantages: first, that the musketeers could step down from the shelf for greater protection while reloading and second, that if water collected at the bottom, they wouldn't have to stand in it.

The 20-foot-long pit proposed for M. Bonnavolia protected a fortification about 80 feet wide, so it might be argued that to defend properly a wall, say, 420 feet long (and the significance of this figure will soon be apparent), one might need four or five such musketry pits. Why, then, you may ask, not make them into one long trench? There are two answers to that: A continuous man-deep slot would hamper access to the river if the fort had to be evacuated in the face of an attack from its landward sides, and in the absence of turns and zigzags, the longer the trench, the more vulnerable are its defenders to enfilade fire.

One must not lose sight of the fact that this musketry trench thesis is based on no direct evidence. We are told only that Gates ordered the burial of the artillery outside the fort's entrance on the river side. The big guns, those of culverin and demiculverin bore, were not only heavy but large, their barrels ten or eleven feet long, and when mounted on carriages, they occupied fifteen or sixteen feet and stood about four feet six inches high. Considering the huge weight of the tubes, it would have been a lot easier to have built a ramp at one end of a long pit and to have run the guns down into them while still on their wheeled carriages—easier, but space-hungry. Even if the majority of the twenty-four were of only falcon caliber, the smallest would still have been six feet long. Thus the preexisting musket pit proposition gains credence.

Although Strachey recorded the artillery's burial, he said nothing about its being dug up. However, he had a friend in London who said it was. Writing in 1613 and claiming that he got his information directly from Gates, the Reverend William Crashawe stated that not only did the departing settlers bury their guns, but they also interred their armor. This makes very little sense. Left in the ground for a few months (as John White recalled after Indians had dug up and looted his chests on

Roanoke Island), armor and particularly its leather would decay to the point of being useless. The departing colonists may as well have thrown it into the river. But we have also been told that Gates ordered the inventorying of the arms and the salvaging of anything that could be considered a salable asset—and armor certainly was that. Consequently, when the Reverend Crashawe tells us that Gates's people soon turned around and "with as much joy returned, as with sorrow they had come away, and making as it were a new entrie and possession, took up their Ordnance and their Armour,"[35] a quizzically raised eyebrown may not be out of place—particularly when Crashawe claims that it was all done in the space of twenty-four hours.

If as many as twenty guns had been at James Towne the day before the evacuation, nothing like that number was ever again reported. Two years later Don Diego de Molina (the spy who sent his secret reports to Spain's ambassador in London hidden in coils of rope and sewn between the sole and inner sole of a shoe) wrote that there were four iron guns at Fort Algernon and only *six* at James Towne. Much more reliable, though years later in date, the official Virginia census of 1624 listed only four pieces of ordnance of unspecified size as belonging to James City. Was Molina hopelessly wrong, or was it that in believing the official view that the place could not defend itself, Gates and his successors allowed some of the cannon to stay where they lay? Assuming the latter, it is possible that if (as is generally believed) the site of James Fort slowly eroded into the river, one of the first elements to go would have been the dirt-filled musketry pits, in which case the big guns may yet rest deep in the silt of the modern James River, serving as relatively accurate markers for the location of the fort's south wall.

With the artillery and perhaps the armor buried, and everything portable and of value loaded, a beating drum summoned the settlers to file out of the fort and down to their appointed ships. By noon all were aboard. After firing a rather pointless volley of small shot as a departing salute, and doubtless watched by scores of hidden Indian eyes, they cast off shore lines, hauled anchors, and set sails, and away they went—for all of five miles. By nightfall the fleet had reached Hog Island, presumably having set out when the tide was against it. By that time abandoned James Towne must have been crowded with curious and even incredulous Indians, and word was on its way to Powhatan that he had won.

The next morning, June 8, Gates's melancholy flotilla ran with the ebb tide down to Mulberry Island at the mouth of what later became the Warwick River and now is home to the United States Army's base at Fort

Thomas West, third Baron De La Warr, appointed governor for life of
Virginia in 1610. Engraving ca. 1883, from a portrait attributed to
Nicholas Hilliard.

Eustis. To the surprise of a lookout (probably aboard the anchored *Deliv-erance,* that being the tallest pinnace) he spotted a longboat coming
upriver on the flood. Lord De La Warr and the new supply fleet had
arrived in Hampton Roads. With him came provisions to last four hundred men a full year—good news doubtless received by many with glum
disappointment. They weren't going home after all; instead they could
look forward to more Indian arrows and the hard labor of making James
Towne habitable. They could also look forward, though none can have
been instantly aware of it, to a level of discipline even more strict than
John Smith had tried to impose.

Appointed for life, the Right Honorable Thomas West, the Lord De
La Warr, lord governor and captain general of the colony planted in Virginia, was not a man to be trifled with. He also suffered from gout. On
stepping ashore, he knelt and "before us all made a long and silent Prayer
to himselfe" and then "marched up into the Towne,"[36] where, after prayers
were said and commissions read, his lordship delivered his maiden speech
to the assembled company. Rather than praise the survivors for their for-

titude he set about "laying many blames upon them for many vanities and their Idlenesse, earnestly wishing, that he might no more find it so, least he should be compelled to draw the sword of Justice, to cut off such delinquents."[37] He was quite right, but it wasn't what the halt and the hungry expected to hear.

William Strachey, who had boarded the *Sea Venture* without a job, now had one. De La Warr appointed him secretary and recorder for the colony, public tasks for which he was well equipped, as his privately penned *True Reportory* attests. Before setting down the history of Lord De La Warr's administration, Strachey digressed to provide the most detailed surviving account of Jamestown's appearance and fortifications, along with some none-too-flattering observations about its location. It stood, he said, on "an extended plaine & spot of earth, which thrust out into the depth & middest of the channell,"[38] and was attached to the mainland by a neck as narrow as the distance a man could spin a potsherd. The ground was low and marshy and lacked any freshwater, and the air, in Strachey's opinion, was unwholesome and sickly.

In the preamble to his description of the habitation which he defined uncertainly as "this our fort, or James Towne,"[39] Strachey made it clear that he was describing the place as it "is now at this present" after "growing since [its first building] to more perfection."[40] It is for this reason, and because one cannot be sure when and to what extent the growing to perfection had been achieved, that I have hitherto refrained from presenting Strachey's testimony—even though much of it might previously have been admissible in evidence.

He begins by telling us that the fort occupied "A low levell of ground about halfe an Acre," a statement that has generated centuries' worth of trouble, for half an acre is about the area of today's fair-size single-family-home lot. In Strachey's terms, how "about" was about half an acre? He was a man who liked to display his classical education, particularly when trying to impress his betters back home, so he followed his half acre with the following parenthetical amplification: "or (so much as Queene Dido might buy of King Hyarbas, which she compassed about with the thongs cut out of one Bull hide, and therein built her Castle of Byrza)."[41] In an attempt to squeeze something useful out of the allusion, we have to digress long enough to take a look at the Dido legend.

The queen in question was Elissa, daughter of Mutton, king of Tyre, who fled from her wicked brother Pygmalion and with her followers landed on the North African coast in 850 B.C. There, in what is now Tunisia, she made a deal with a local chieftain named Iarbas whereby she purchased as much land for her settlement as could be contained by the skin of an ox. Iarbas named his price, expecting to be selling at best a few square yards. But with the deal struck, Elissa proceeded to cut the hide into shoelace-thin strips and with them encircled the entire hill on which the city of Carthage was to rise. The hill came to be known as Byrsa from the Greek *bursa*, meaning "hide," and covered a great deal more than half an acre. Geographically, though not necessarily in hide-thong area, it was nearly three miles long and half that wide. But give or take a mile, the acreage seems to have had no James Fort relevance. Furthermore, the Jamestown Island site was not purchased from the Indians either legitimately or by Didoesque cheating—at least not directly. Just as the emigrant queen took much more from Iarbas than he had expected, so it is true that the English in planting their colony took much more than the Indians had anticipated. However, it is unlikely that when beginning to define the dimensions and appearance of palisaded James Towne, this otherwise well-ordered chronicler would have digressed into an obtuse and not particularly apt parable touching on the impact of English colonization on the Powhatan Confederacy. So what, then, was the Carthaginian connection?

Although the last attribute that could be claimed for James Fort was that it was built on a hill, Strachey may have seen it as relatively high ground flanked around by marshes which dictated the palisades' triangular shape, for in the next breath he goes on to say that they were "cast almost in the form of a triangle." Essentially, therefore, the shape remained pretty much as it had been when first laid out in May 1607—the postfire "five-square" modification notwithstanding—perhaps because the terrain permitted no expansion of the triangle. If so, it presaged a physical separation from the fort and the eventual expansion of James Towne upriver or down.

Because so little hard information survives, every straw tends to be clung to with grim-faced tenacity. It is entirely possible, however, that Strachey's Dido and Iarbas allusion is one of the weakest. He may have meant only that like Dido and her followers, the James Towne settlers were isolated in a foreign and hostile land, their territory defined by the thin, thonglike line of the palisades. If so, Strachey would have better served posterity by simply saying what he meant.

We must not be too unkind to Strachey, however, for his is the only detailed surviving description of the fort and its palisades, which, he says, were built of "Plankes and strong Posts, foure foote deepe in the ground, of yong Oakes, Walnuts, &c.,"[42] therefore not from vertically abutting tree trunks, as John White had found when he returned to Roanoke Island in 1590, or as would be reconstructed at the Jamestown Festival Park in 1956. But before dismissing the latter as a mistake, we must remember that prior to Strachey's arrival the fort had burned and been subjected to at least one shape change. It is conceivable, therefore, that it was first built from "great trees" and later improved by substituting planks.

Describing Fort Algernon, the spying Molina called it "a weak structure of boards ten hands high."[43] Although his statement may have lost something in translation (ten hands being only three feet four inches), the fact that the fort walls were of boards and not pointy-headed poles is important. The latter method, however, was used at two small forts built at Kecoughtan which were much later reported to have been "encompassed with small young trees."[44] That technique was the one employed by the Indians to encircle their villages against the ill intentions of other Indians and probably was chosen by the English for the same reason. Fort Algernon, in contrast, was supposed to provide shelter from Spanish artillery, and there the short boards made sense—as a breastwork set atop an earthwork combination of rampart and ditch.

Construction similar to that described by Strachey at James Towne would be called for when the palisades at Plymouth, Massachusetts, were rebuilt in 1633 and 1634. There the posts were to be "10 inches square, & not to stand above 10 foote assunder [apart], to be done with 3 rails between every post, of fitt scantling," all to be sawed. The plank pales were to be "9 foote high, & then to be cut sharp at ye tope, & either listed or shote with a plaine."[45] Supporting archaeological evidence for the spacing of palisade posts has come from Colonial Williamsburg's excavations at Wolstenholme Towne, where the fort's walls were set on nine-foot centers.

Although Strachey tells us how far the support posts went into the ground at James Towne (and one wonders how he knew that), he says nothing about their height. For that we have to rely on the memory of John Smith, who recalled that the "palizado" stood fourteen or fifteen feet high, "and each as much as three or foure men could carrie."[46] That, coupled with his reference to "our extreame toile in bearing and planting Pallisadoes,"[47] may have misled the 1956 reconstruction's designers into building utility pole–style palisades, perhaps unaware that in the sixteenth century the word "palizado" could mean anything from an entire wall to a single stake. Had the reconstruction been erected to follow Strachey's very clear description, the walls would have needed at least 113 massive support posts some eighteen feet long. Carrying each of them in from the forest would have taxed the strength of four men and constituted extreme toil, thus fitting Smith's descriptions.

If, in fact, the pales really stood fifteen feet high, the support posts may have been set even deeper than Strachey said. The most detailed description of a post, rail, and pale palisade dates from 1641 and comes from Ulster, where the duke of Ormond planned to impale the bounds of the villages of Kilbride, Kilgerny, and Kilkely. The carpenters were to "fell, cut, lop, cleave [split] and make up" pales seven feet in height and secure them by rails to posts nine feet long, three of them set in the ground. The ratio, therefore of seven to nine suggests that to support a wall fifteen feet high (and strong enough to withstand hurricane-force winds), the posts should have gone five to six feet into the ground. The Irish document adds another useful detail: that the rails and pales were to be secured with treenails (tapering wooden dowels, not iron nails) "made of dry timber and strongly fastened in setting."[48]

The need for the treenails to be dry must have posed a problem for the hasty builders of James Fort, for none of their wood had time to cure and shrink, and pegs that shrink after they are driven eventually come loose. However, when we built the first Wolstenholme fort reconstructions, we deliberately used green wood to see what would happen after a season in Virginia's scorching sun. Pegs shrank less than did the pales, which contracted to such a degree that two-inch gaps developed—enough for an arrow to zip between them.

After stating that the James Towne palisades enclosed an area of about half an acre, Strachey gave specific measurements, and these we need to read with infinite care: "The South side next the River (howbeit extended in a line, or Curtaine six score foote more in length, then the other two, by reason the advantage of the ground doth so require) contains one hundred and forty yards: the West and East sides a hundred onely." He went on to add that "At every Angle or corner, where the lines meete, a Bulwarke or Watchtower is raised."[49] When National Park Service historians advised the Virginia's Festival Park designers on the fort's dimensions, they failed to ponder as carefully as they should have what you have just read. Instead they followed in the misplaced footsteps of historian Lyon G. Tyler, who, in *The Cradle of the Republic*, assumed that Strachey's measurements represented the total lengths of each side of the triangle. The result was a palisade 420 feet broad on the river side, with the two landward sides 300 feet in length. It was an interpretation that ignored one crucial word: "Curtaine." In the military parlance of that time, a cur-

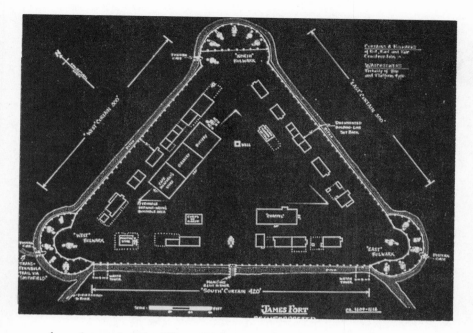

A conjectural plan of James Fort, using Strachey's measurements as the lengths of the settlement's three curtain walls. In their number and distribution, the buildings shown are based on the sketchy information and hints provided by the documents. The size of the flankers is based only on the reported maximum number of artillery pieces.

tain was a wall connecting (not including) two towers, bulwarks, or flankers. Thus, for example, Laurence Sterne in his novel *Tristram Shandy* (1759) paints a portrait of the narrator's uncle, an old soldier obsessed with military structures, who explains that "The curtain, Sir, is the word we use in fortifications for that part of the wall . . . which lies between the two bastions."[50] Nothing could be less equivocal. Nevertheless, the Festival Park's consultants included the bastions in Strachey's measurements and drew a fort significantly too small.

The size of the increased livable space within the palisades depends on one's knowing the size of the bulwarks. The wider they are, the larger the triangle becomes. Alas, we have no such measurements and must base estimates only on the often contradictory numbers and sizes of the guns mounted in or on them. On that evidence it is conceivable that the gun platforms could have been as much as eighty feet wide between the abutting curtain walls, thus expanding the settlement's interior space almost 70 percent above that of the still-standing 1956 reconstruction.

Such a reassessment helps address, though does not entirely solve, the spatial problem posed by Smith's claim that after the fire (he doesn't say how *long* after) the fort contained "fortie or fiftie severall houses to keepe us warme and dry."[51] Unfortunately, by expanding the interior square footage, we run foul of Strachey's half acre—unless that defined only the area of the marketplace within the flanking rows of houses. In truth, his 21,780 square feet far more closely matches the 19,400 square feet occupied by the reconstruction than it does the expanded plan, which takes in 63,854 square feet. On the other hand, there is no way that 19,400 can accommodate forty or fifty houses—plus the church, *corps de garde* (guardhouse), marketplace, public store, kitchen, dungeoned prison, and the 30-foot building-line setback from the palisades.

Because most of the settlers' coming and going was to and from the river, it made sense that the "principall Gate from the Towne, through the Pallizado"[52] opened in that direction. But whether Strachey's use of the singular "gate" meant exactly what it said or meant one gateway with two gates, no one can be sure, though in paintings, on models, and at the reconstruction, the latter is the chosen interpretation. It also makes the best architectural sense. Although two gates are more easily forced than one, the Indians were not in the battering ram business, so that level of strength was not a factor. More important was the need to have the gateway wide enough to permit the passage of carts. But the weight of a single gate to close an opening eight feet wide would either be too much for the hinges or cause the gate to scrape and bind on the ground. So, for those reasons, if for no other, double gates would have best met the needs. Strachey goes on to state that there were secondary gates at each of the three bulwarks, "and at every Gate a Demi-Culverin, and so in the Market Place."[53]

Strachey's statement gives us three subsidiary or postern gates and four cannon of the second-largest caliber in John Smith's listed arsenal. If we assume, for the sake of argument, that when Strachey put a "peece of Ordnance or two" on each bulwark platform, he meant not one but two, these, coupled with another at each gate and yet another in the marketplace, bring the total to ten—still fourteen short of Smith's two dozen. That heavy guns would be placed at the side (Indian-facing) gates as well as in the marketplace, where only antipersonnel weapons were of any use, suggests one of two things: Either there were more demiculverins than sakers or falcons (as is unlikely) or the officers were reluctant to waste energy hauling an unnecessary number of big guns up onto the platforms—always supposing, of course, that the platforms were elevated and not mere pads laid on the ground within the bulwarks. Although Smith put the artillery "upon convenient plat-formes"—which would have been convenient even if the platforms were at ground level—we have also to remember that Percy's 1607 description put the artillery *in* rather than on the bulwarks. If, indeed, this is the correct interpretation, it renders James Towne's cannon far more maneuverable for flexible deployment and, for that matter, for hasty burial.

As noted in an earlier chapter, the best paralleling information we have about the placement and sizes of guns used in defending an English American settlement comes from the Popham Plantation's Fort St. George on the Kennebec. The plan shows its largest piece, a demiculverin, on a bulwark facing out to sea, and because it had a point-blank range of about 830 yards and a maximum of about 5,000 yards, that made good sense. Although Fort St. George had no cannon in its marketplace, it did have one (a saker) at the entrance to the inner defense enclosing the president's house and pointing toward the fort's interior. As a rule, and as the 1624 muster in Virginia showed, most of the few settlements that boasted any kind of ordnance relied on small swivel guns of the sort left behind by the Roanoke Island colonists, which were listed as murderers or falconets. We have no evidence, however, that James Fort or James Towne possessed that kind of breech-loading and quick-firing weapon.

Having said all he was going to about James Towne's defenses (and we could wish for much more), Strachey turns to the church, which to the prayerful Lord De La Warr evidently was a pious priority. Finding it "ruined and unfrequented" served to confirm his worst doubts about the quality of the people he had come to govern. Repairing their place of worship, therefore, was but the first step toward rebuilding their hearts and minds. The result was a "pretty chapel," perhaps coincidentally the same term used by the Fort St. George mapmaker to describe what had previously in Virginia been called the "church." The Popham plat shows its chapel as four bays long and, if we assume that no structural bay (the spread between any two main vertical framing posts) is likely to be wider than ten feet, suggests a nave about forty feet long, plus belfry at the altar end perhaps fifteen or twenty feet square, and thus a building maybe sixty feet long. Again, perhaps coincidentally, James Towne's chapel was "in length threescore foote" (sixty feet)[54] and twenty-four wide.

Churches of comparable character to the one shown for Fort St. George are to be seen in drawings made in 1620 of English settlements in Ulster, and although those appear to be of stone and so lack measurable bays, they may have been of similar size. Evidently smaller are two early English chapels drawn (or perhaps redrawn) in the mid-nineteenth century (p. 279), both of which have externally hung bells suggestive of a

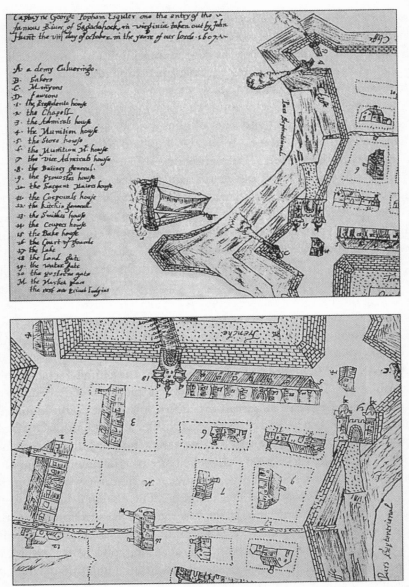

Top: Detail of the 1607 Fort St. George on the Kennebec, showing the placement of cannon and listing by letter of the types represented. *Bottom:* Detail of the 1607 Fort St. George on the Kennebec, showing the church (2) and the store (5).

Two small post-medieval chapels in England, as shown in nineteenth-century engravings; *top*, at Bishopton in Yorkshire, and *bottom*, at Seathwaite in Lincolnshire.

mounting that may have been common to village chapels lacking the grandeur of towers or steeples and are still to be seen on old village school buildings in the British Isles. One of these chapels, that at Seathwaite in Lincolnshire, is closely paralleled in John Smith's drawing of the church in Bermuda (p. 281).

In the seventeenth century, prior to the rise of the nonconformist movement, the term "chapel" most often defined small places of worship frequented by Catholics or by those in rural communities too small to warrant a large building and clergy of the established church. However, both at Fort St. George and at James Towne the inference may have been that the buildings served both ecclesiastical and secular gatherings.

The urgency of the James Towne chapel's need for refurbishment is evident from Strachey's reference in a single sentence both to Lord De La Warr's order and to the fact that "at this instant, many hands are about it."[55] Later in the same paragraph, however, the immediacy is gone, and Strachey is talking about sermons twice a day on Sundays and another on Thursdays. He goes on to note that daily at ten and four o'clock the sexton rang the bell, sending every man to his prayers. The new piety by decree may not have sat too well with the old-style settlers, but it provides us with a useful piece of information: that the chapel bell was used as a means of communicating with the population. Earlier, in describing the arrival of Sir Thomas Gates, Strachey recalled how he had "caused the Bell to be rung, at which (all such as were able to come forth of their houses) repayred to Church."[56] One might be tempted to use that as evidence that warnings and other public communications with out-of-earshot settlers was always provided by the church bell—until we remember that on leaving, Gates used a drum to summon his evacuating settlers. Then, too, the arriving Lord De La Warr used his shipboard trumpeter to bring his fleet to anchor off James Towne.

De La Warr was a stickler for discipline and the pomp of power—and with good reason, considering the ragtag and belligerently lazy company he was trying to whip into shape. On the other hand, the Sunday church parade seems at least mildly ridiculous in a settlement allegedly restricted to a cramped half acre.

> Every Sunday, when the lord governor and captain generall goeth to church, he is accompanied with all the councilors, captains, other officers, and all the gentlemen, and with a guard of halberdiers in his Lordship's livery, fair red cloaks, to the number of fifty, both on each side and behind him; and being in the church, his Lordship hath his seat in the choir, in a green velvet chair, with a cloth, with a velvet cushion spread on a table before him on which he kneeleth; and on each side sit the council, captains, and officers, each in their place; and when he returneth home again he is waited on to his house in the same manner.[57]

Top: John Smith's illustration of the church at St. George Towne, Bermuda. Whether it bears any resemblance to the actual building, only future archaeology may tell. An illustration from Smith's *Generall Historie*, 1624. *Bottom:* The church in the reconstructed James Fort.

If the whole palisaded enclosure was as small as Strachey claimed, the marketplace can hardly have been large enough to get the procession lined up, let alone to process, yet here we have the governor marching between his house and the church. To this we can add the question of how large a house did he have and how many people could he receive in it. With that in mind, it helps to take a look at the new hierarchy which seemed to adopt the questionable late-twentieth-century management theory that more is better and that a lot more is better still.

Sir Thomas Gates, who had succeeded George Percy as interim governor, now became lieutenant general; Sir George Somers remained as admiral; Percy became captain of the fort's fifty-man garrison; Sir Ferdinando Wainman (who had come over with De La Warr) was master of the ordnance; Christopher Newport stayed as vice admiral; and as previously noted, Strachey became secretary. These, then, were the members of the new council. A severely demoted John Martin was put in charge of ironworking, Captain George Webb became sergeant major of the fort; Edward Bruster (or Brewster) took charge of De La Warr's ceremonial halberdiers; George Yeardley (later to be governor) captained Gates's company, while Samuel Argall, Thomas Holecroft, and Thomas Lawson were given captaincies of other fifty-man militia companies. Ralph Hamor (another who later rose to prominence) was appointed one of two clerks to the council, and Daniel Tucker and Robert Wilde got the tricky jobs of clerks to the stores. Although Strachey mentioned but did not name the appointment of "divers other officers," notably absent is John Smith's old antagonist Gabriel Archer, who is believed to have been among the many who failed to survive the Starving Time.

Strachey tells us nothing about the governor's house beyond the fact that Lord De La Warr processed to and from it. But when we remember that President Ratcliffe had been building himself a "palace" in the woods, it is fair to conclude that any president's or governor's home inside James Towne's palisades was relatively modest and could accommodate no more than the council. How early a dwelling was set aside specifically to house the governor is unclear. We know only that in 1625 a report to the Privy Council by unnamed "Ancient Planters nowe remaining alive in Virginia" noted that since the governorship of Sir Thomas Gates there had been one house "wherein the Govr allways dwelt" and that it had been enlarged in 1618.[58] In Lord De La Warr's time, therefore, full-blown staff meetings would have taken place in one or another of the public buildings, most probably in either the church or the storehouse.

In addition to his cargo of supplies, Lord De La Warr had brought "many gentlemen of quallety And thre hundredthe men"[59] to add to the 150 saved by Gates from Bermuda. Thus, with the 60 surviving from the earlier arrivals, by the time De La Warr took charge on June 10, 1610, the English expecting to live in America numbered about 500, most, if not all, of them to be housed at least temporarily at James Towne. How many or few of these were women, a factor of enormous significance in assessing the settlers' quality of life, has gone unrecorded. Even if we set aside the fact that in the Popham Colony people like the blacksmith and the cooper aspired to their own homes and workshops, the incomplete listing of James Towne's senior management identifies eighteen men with the right to expect superior housing, which, if forthcoming, would have left little room for anyone else. Clearly, therefore, there was a pressing need for what the Germans in another century called Lebensraum, living space to be secured by reestablishing lost satellite settlements and by devising a satisfactory solution to the Powhatan problem.

CHAPTER XI

Strong Pales and Shivered Arrows

L ORD DE LA WARR announced his staff appointments on June 12, and the next day at his first council meeting Sir George Somers volunteered to return to Bermuda to bring back supplies of fish and hogs. His offer was seen as brave and generous. No one was churlish enough to suggest that the winds of self-interest might be speeding his return to the place of his salvation previously known as the Isle of Devils and shortly to be renamed the Sommer Islands. Bermuda had been remarkably good to the castaways; they had planted gardens whose produce grew, the climate was mild, the fishing was fabulous, turtles were there for the hauling, birds lined up to be shot, and the wild pig progeny of those stranded there in the sixteenth century from Spanish and Portuguese shipwrecks had so multiplied, we are told, that the *Sea Venture*'s dog killed them by the hundred. Furthermore, unlike Virginia, the islands lacked "snakes or any creeping beast"; and best of all, there were no Indians.

Somers's proposition was enthusiastically endorsed at James Towne. He was to make the eleven-day trip aboard the smaller of his two Bermuda-built pinnaces, the thirty-ton *Patience*, and he hoped "to bee back againe before the Indians doe gather their harvest."[1] As the Indians reaped while their corn was still green, Somers should have returned by mid-August at the latest. With him went Samuel Argall as captain of the veteran *Discovery*, and together they received their commissions in sealed boxes on June 15. Adverse winds delayed them for a month, and on July 16 Somers decided to change the plan and sail north toward Cape Cod and the New England fishing grounds. Caught in dense fog on the evening of the twenty-sixth, Argall received a message from his admiral that they

Sir George Somers, appointed admiral of Virginia in 1609, was shipwrecked in Bermuda that year, and died there in 1610.

should "stand in for the River of Sagadahoc [the Kennebec]," but when he got there, the *Patience* was nowhere to be seen.

After six days of searching, Argall instructed the *Discovery*'s master to "open the boxe wherein my commission was, to see what directions I had, and for what place I was bound to shape my course."[2] Argall's log-based record does not reveal what his commission said, and it is hard to understand why he would be sailing under sealed orders when he knew he was supposed to be on course to Bermuda. Instead, loaded with a good haul of cod, he was back off the Virginia capes on the evening of August 31—still with no sign of the *Patience*.

Where Somers had been and what he had been doing between the time his last message reached Argall on July 26 and his arrival in Bermuda at the beginning of November is one of early American history's enduring mysteries. He would die there on November 9, allegedly from eating a surfeit of pork. To cement his association with the islands, Somers asked that his heart and entrails be extracted and buried there. And so they were. Soon afterward the *Patience,* under the command of Sir George's nephew Mathew, ignoring the dying admiral's instruction to return to Virginia, sailed on to England, carrying his embalmed body (to be buried at Whitchurch in Dorset) and, more advantageously, a quantity of marketable ambergris.

In a letter written on the day he had sailed from Virginia, Sir George Somers noted that the Indians had long since ceased trading with the James Towne settlers, adding that "The Trothe is they had nothing to trade withal but mulberries."[3] Nevertheless, their harvesttime was approaching, and once again the Indians' diligence could be used to the advantage of the slothful English. Lord De La Warr therefore decided that another diplomatic approach to Powhatan could do no harm. As Strachey put it, the new governor-general thought "it possible by a more tractable course to win them to a better condition." When publishing this passage, the Reverend Samuel Purchas asked in a marginal note: "Were not Caesar's Britons as brutish as Virginians?," then added in a tone not entirely Christian, that "The Roman swords were best teachers of civility. . . ."[4] Nevertheless, regardless of this clerical opinion, De La Warr was following stated Company policy, regardless of his own views on its validity. His lordship was not a subtle man, and diplomacy not his strong suit. Consequently, his idea of a more tractable course was more an ultimatum than an offer of renewed friendship. He began with a listing of Indian crimes against the English and only then allowed that he "did not suppose that these mischiefes were contrived by him [Powhatan], or with his knowledge, but conceived them rather to be the acts of his worst and unruly people."[5] Nevertheless, it was up to Powhatan to tell them to desist, or otherwise it would be the worse for him. Furthermore, since he had benefited from these unauthorized activities to the tune of unspecified quantities of armor and muskets, as well as at least "two hundred Swords, besides Axes, and Pollaxes, Chissels, Howes [hoes], to paire and clense their grounds, with an infinite treasure of Copper,"[6] he should at least return the weapons and any prisoners he happened to be holding. If he did not, soldiers would be sent to get them.

The message ended by reminding Powhatan of his allegiance to King James and how, on his knees, he had received the crown and regalia as the symbols of "Civill State and Christian Soveraigntie." Although some of the symbolism may have escaped him, Powhatan did like his crown and wore it at harvest ceremonies. He also liked beads, which he tossed to his eager subjects on these and other occasions. But he liked neither enough to comply with Lord De La Warr's demands. He preferred to send a message as irritating as the one he had received: The English could either remain at James Towne or get out of his country. He wanted no more explorations up his rivers, and if the English disobeyed, he would instruct his people to shoot at will. He wanted no more unscheduled messengers "unlesse they brought him a Coach and three Horses, for hee had understood by the Indians which were in England, how such was the state of great Werowances and Lords in England, to ride and visit other great men."[7] End of message.

If there was humor in Powhatan's request, De La Warr failed to recognize it. He saw only "prowde and disdaynefull Answers."[8] The savages had had their chance to bury the hatchet and return the swords. Now it was time to make them wish they had. Following a July 6 incident in which a man from Fort Algernon was seized and sacrificed by Nansemonds on the south of the river, Gates received permission to launch an attack on Kecoughtan on the north shore. Although Strachey cited that none-too-clear rationale for the assault, few can have forgotten the slaughter near Kecoughtan of Lieutenant Sicklemore and his men in the autumn of 1609, when George Percy was president. The latter, however, cited no reason beyond Gates's "beinge desyreous for to be Revendged."[9] He got it but earned no medals for sportsmanship.

The size of the force is not recorded, but it was probably large, considering that someone as senior as William Strachey went along for the show. On July 9 they landed from a flotilla of boats, advanced on the Indian settlement, and, while still some distance from it, set up an ambushing trap using one of Gates's own men as bait. Named Dowse, the man was described as a taborer, a tabor being a small single-sided drum. However, taborers also doubled as fifers and as dancers. This taborer was called upon "to play and dawnse thereby to Allure the Indyans to come unto him."[10] And they did. Five were killed, but others, some seriously wounded, managed to escape and to warn the Kecoughtan villagers.

Strachey carefully avoided any reference to the dancing entertainer but did admit that the spoils of the victory were nothing to write home about (though he did): "a few Baskets of old Wheate, and some other of Pease and Beanes, a little Tobacco," and his own loot, a collection of women's silk grass girdles, which he described as "not without art, and much neatnesse."[11] Neat or not, they ranked fairly low in the annals of British battle trophies.

With Kecoughtan and its valuable planted acres in English hands, Gates returned to James Towne and on July 20 sailed for England aboard

Richard Tarlton, a famed comic actor, shown in the role of a taborer playing a drum and blowing on a pipe. Tarlton died in 1588, and the ca. 1638 woodcut is derived from a drawing illustrating an elegy written at the time of his death. His clothing and instruments may well have resembled those of taborer Thomas Dowse when he lured the Indians of Kecoughtan with his music.

the *Blessing* to report to the Company. With him went a cargo of lumber, samples of iron ore, and an Indian prisoner: Kainta son of Sasenticum, king of the Warraskoyacks, who lived in modern Isle of Wight County near the mouth of the Pagan River. Kainta's arrival in England would provide another opportunity for Londoners to inspect "these naked slaves of the divell."[12] More useful, however, were the packets of dispatches from the colony, among them one of more versions of Strachey's *True Reportory*—regrettably bringing his on-the-spot chronicle to its end. Thereafter George Percy continues as our primary and certainly most colorful witness.

As leader of the troops at James Towne, Percy was given the command of the next adventure against the Indians. This time it was to be the Paspaheghs and the Chickahominies, who were responsible for most of the attacks on settlers in the vicinity of the fort and the island's neck-defending blockhouse. On the night of August 9, 1610, Percy set out with two bargeloads of troops and landed at the mouth of the Chickahominy River within three miles of modern Sandy Point and the village of Wowinchopunck, king of the Paspaheghs. Led there by a handcuffed Indian whose services as a guide were improved by intimidation, Percy invaded the settlement with colors flying and in something resembling European battle order. This time there was no comic taborer. Fifteen or sixteen Indians were killed, and one was taken prisoner, as was the queen of the Paspaheghs and her children. Percy ordered the male prisoner decapitated, but the queen and her family he took aboard the boats, intending to carry them back to James Towne. Before departing, the soldiers burned the village and cut down all the growing corn. What happened next is best left to Percy to explain:

> And after we marched wth the quene And her Children to our Boates ageine, where beinge noe sooner well shipped my sowldiers did begin to murmur becawse the quene and her Children weare spared. So upon the same A Cowncell being called itt was Agreed upon to putt the Children to deathe the wch was effected by Throweinge them overboard and shoteinge owtt their Braynes in the water[,] yett for all this Crewellty the Sowldiers weare nott well pleased And I had mutche to doe To save the quenes lyfe for thatt Tyme.[13]

Although Percy expressed a degree of horror at what had been done and blamed his men for murdering the children, the responsibility was his. Indeed, if he considered himself in some way absolved, we are left with the impression of an officer incapable of controlling his own men—men no less savage than their victims.

On their way back, and about two miles downriver, incited by threatening Indians on the bank, Percy sent half his force ashore under Captain James Davies, formerly his commander at Fort Algernon. When the Indians fled, Davies marched fourteen miles inland, attacking and burning every structure he could find, among them "A Spacyous Temple cleane and neattly keptt A thinge strange and seldome sene amongste the Indyans in those Partes."[14] The buildings and crops destroyed, Davies returned to the waiting boats and continued downriver to James Towne.

Since the first days of his arrival Governor-General Lord De La Warr had run the gamut of every available illness, and so, perhaps on the orders of his personal physician, Dr. Lawrence Bohun, he was now living aboard one of the ships away from the island's unhealthy air. Percy and Davies therefore reported to their commander aboard his ship—or did they? Percy tells us that "we" rowed to the ship, but although he had led the expedition, it was Davies, the second-in-command, to whom De La Warr appears to have talked in private about the fate of the captive queen. Here again Percy had best speak for himself:

> My Lord Generall . . . Seamed to be discontente becawse the quene was spared as Captayne Davis towlde me and thatt itt was my Lords pleasure thatt we sholde see her dispatched The way he thowghte beste to Burne her. To the first I replyed thatt haveinge seene so mutche Bloodshedd thatt day now in my Cowldbloode I desyred to see noe more and for to Burne her I did not howlde itt fitteinge butt either by shott or Sworde to geve her A quicker dispatche.[15]

Davies then took the queen ashore and into the woods, where we can but hope he there did no more than he was ordered. Percy, whom Lord De La Warr later described as a "gentleman of honour and resolution,"[16] did his best to distance both his leader and himself from responsibility by adding that "Capte: Davis towlde me itt was my Lords direction [,] yet I am perswaded to the contrary."[17] Here was a crime reminiscent of Macbeth's murder of Lady Macduff and all her pretty ones and in modern eyes one of the most barbarous acts recorded in early Anglo-American history, yet Percy, by his own admission, first allowed himself to be overruled by his men and subsequently failed to check with his commander to be sure that Davies had heard the order correctly. It was an extraordinary end to an infamous day.

At about this time Captain Argall returned from his failed attempt to reach Bermuda, but carrying his compensatory cargo of fish. He was the next to lead an assault on the Indians, his target the Warraskoyacks, who perhaps could be blamed for having killed the settlers' pigs on Hog Island during the Starving Time. Although led by an aged king, with his son a hostage in England, the Warraskoyacks were not sitting ducks. By the time Argall had crossed the James, disembarked his troops, and marched inland, every Indian in the region had long since vanished, leaving the English to wreak their vengeance on defenseless crops and empty homes.

Unintimidated by Powhatan's warning that he would not tolerate any more exploratory expeditions into his territory, Lord De La Warr next sent a boatload of men up the James to the falls to reestablish the foothold previously abandoned by his brother Francis West and to search for the still-elusive minerals. With them went Dowse, the taborer, perhaps with a view to repeating his success as a dancing Judas goat. When they passed the village of Appomattoc, the home of Queen Oppossunoquonuske, her subjects came down to the river's edge and graciously invited the travelers ashore to rest, eat, and drink, "butt our men forgetteinge their Subtellties lyke greedy fooles," wrote Percy, "accepted thereof more esteameinge of A Little foode then their own lyves."[18] It turned out to be a bad mistake and resulted in "the unfortunate losse of all our chieffe men skilfull in findeinge out mines."[19] Only the tabor player escaped to the boat, whose rudder he successfully used as a shield against a hail of arrows.

Hunting for the minerals to make the James Towne enterprise a financial success was going to be expensive. Nevertheless, the hints of riches beyond the falls remained the driving force, and sick as he was, Lord De La Warr intended to succeed. A second boat loaded with what passed for soldiers went upriver under Captain Edward Brewster, who doubtless was instructed to ignore the Lorelei calls from hospitable Indians. Although Brewster had several encounters with them, he reached the falls relatively unscathed and there camped to await the arrival of his governor-general. Shortly afterward, De La Warr joined him, and together they set to work to build a fort which His Lordship named after himself. No description of it survives. Meanwhile, Percy was again in charge at James Towne and remained so throughout the winter of 1610–11.

In the absence of any dated chronology, there is no knowing how long Wowinchopunck waited before seeking revenge for the murder of his wife and family. As had happened many times before, the blockhouse was approached by an advance party of Paspaheghs, led by the intimidating figure of the king himself, his body painted black and, as Percy put it, with horns on his head like a devil. The idea was to draw the defenders out in pursuit. The ploy had worked before, and it did so again. Percy sent a troop forward led by his standard-bearer, Captain Powell, who ran into a shower of arrows and was forced to retreat, but not before he had twice thrust his sword through Wowinchopunck, who was so seriously wounded that he had to be carried away on a litter. Percy said he lived, but Strachey reported that both the king and another stabbed Indian soon died.

We know nothing of the day-to-day activities at James Towne during this time, but with the early wrangling between the original council members behind the settlers and with the sense that with Lord De La

Warr on hand (albeit upriver), a degree of order had been brought to the settlement. No longer were Indians freely coming and going to trade and steal, and consequently, there were few opportunities for dishonest settlers to loot the stores of hardware to trade for food. Before the governor-general went up to the falls, several Indians had been sent by Powhatan "as spyes to our foarte"[20] and were apprehended. The event is pertinent in that it shows Percy (the writer of the report) still on occasion referring to James Towne as "our fort." The inference has to be that as far as building space was concerned, the settlement remained locked and cramped within the triangular "half" acre. Perhaps that was what the Indian spies wanted to find out. If so, they got the information the hard way. On Lord De La Warr's orders, one of them was sent back with his hand cut off as a warning to others.

Apart from occasional small-scale probing by the Indians, those of the settlers still at James Towne were able to go about their business relatively safe from interruption. Thus they had ample time to improve the defenses and to build better houses, but whether they so used it remains unanswered. Such construction as we know of took place downriver near the burned Indian village at Kecoughtan, where two new outposts were built: Forts Charles and Henry. Each manned by a maximum of fifteen men and sometimes by none at all, the former was at Strawberry Bank, four miles from Point Comfort and Fort Algernon, and Fort Henry was reportedly only a musket's shot away to the west. The spying Spaniard Diego de Molina saw the forts, built solely as defenses against the Indians, as posing no problem to an invading army.

As the supply of corn daily dwindled in the storehouse at James Towne, and with next year's harvest too distant even to be looked forward to, something bold needed to be done. The destruction of the neighboring Indians' crops may at the time have given the colonists heady satisfaction, but the knowledge that in consequence, the enemy was also on short rations did nothing to placate rumbling English stomachs. Although there are many of us, even in our affluent Western world, who through poverty or misadventure have known the debilitating effect of hunger, most of us have no idea how vast is the separation between survival food and the satisfaction of a good meal. Previously in England, Virginia's gentlemen and craftsmen (and perhaps even many of the laborers) had been able to take daily culinary pleasures for granted, and even those who could not afford them never had to face the prospect of there simply being no food to beg or steal. In short, therefore, at James Towne even *better* times were pretty bad, and although in the winter of 1610-11, thanks to Lord De La Warr's supply fleet, there was no repetition of the previous year's Starving Time, summer was still a long way off. Looking to the future, therefore, and believing that the Pata- womeke Indians might again be willing to ignore Powhatan's embargo and trade corn to the English, De La Warr sent Samuel Argall up the bay to see what he could get.

The king of Patawomeke, though ostensibly a member of Powhatan's Confederacy, carefully exercised a visible degree of independence, a fact attested to by his welcoming a fugitive with a familiar name. It was Henry Spelman, the boy who claimed that John Smith had sold him to Powhatan's son in part exchange for the ready-built Indian fort near the James River falls. Spelman soon escaped and returned to James Towne. Later used as a messenger to Powhatan, the lad decided that eating was the better part of valor, and sought permission to stay with him. As a result of becoming part of the emperor's household, the boy (as we have seen) had been present at the killing of John Ratcliffe. Perhaps recogniz- ing that his new master's policy toward the English was becoming more openly belligerent, Spelman began to wonder whether he had backed the wrong horse and was in danger of being trampled by it. Consequently, when the king of Patawomeke paid a visit and was kind to him, the boy decided to escape and join the returning king's party. And so he did, though not before Powhatan had sent men to catch him or kill him. When Argall reached the Patawomekes' territory, he heard about an English boy named Harry who turned out to be Henry Spelman and thus he became the interpreter and go-between in subsequent trading, which included an unspecified quantity of copper in exchange for himself. In his *Generall Historie* John Smith mentioned the boy but credited Pocahontas with saving him to live "many yeeres after, by her meanes, amongst the Patawomekes."[21] Young Harry, however, remembered the duration only as "a year and more"[22] and recalled nothing about any help from Poca- hontas. For his part, Smith forgot to remember that he had sold the boy in the first place.

Young Harry Spelman returned to James Towne with Argall, having played an important role in securing a cargo of corn from the Patawom- eke Indians. He would go back to England about eighteen months later, would return to Virginia as the colony's principal interpreter, rise to the level of captain, and thirteen years later, in another starving time, would lead a further corn-seeking expedition to the Patawomekes—who would kill him.

By spending the winter in his fort at the James River falls, Lord De La Warr was following John Smith's lead toward shifting the colony's administration inland to modern Richmond, a step not finally to be achieved for a further 169 years. For De La Warr, however, his stay had not been an unqualified success; constantly on the defensive against the Indians, he had lost several men, including his nephew Captain William West, while others were taken prisoner or had narrow escapes. It would not, however, be the Indians who defeated him, but the illnesses that had beset him at James Towne and had followed him to the falls. Dr. Bohun advised his patient that another month would see him dead and prescribed a rest cure in the Caribbean, specifically at the hot spring baths on the island of Nevis. De La Warr left on March 28, 1611, presumably intending to return as soon as his health improved. As it turned out, though governor-general for life, Lord De La Warr was gone for seven years and died on his way back.

Among the many hard-to-explain decisions made by Virginia's leaders in the colony's teething years was the fact that De La Warr took more than fifty men with him on what sounds, for them, like a Caribbean vacation. But if that was what they expected, they were disappointed. Adverse winds persisted so long that in the interests of his lordship's health, the ship steered east for the Azores, where she arrived with forty of her passengers "neare sicke to death, of the Scurvie, Callenture, and other diseases."[23] Eight days of fruit-eating restored them all to health, and on June 11 they reached England, where De La Warr's unexpected return sent shock waves among the already nervous Virginia Company investors.

Shortly before De La Warr docked, the Company's council had sent out three ships loaded with men, cattle, and materials, under the command of Sir Thomas Dale, who, with the titles of marshal and temporary lieutenant governor, was substituting for Sir Thomas Gates, then back in England lobbying for more support. It had not been an easy task. When Gates arrived home with little to give the subscribers but more promises and the realization that new supplies would have to be paid for not from the Company's profits but from additional investment, even the council debated long and earnestly over "whether it were fit to enter into a new Contribution, or in time to send for them home, and give over the action."[24] Consequently, Lord De La Warr quickly had to issue a statement reassuring fainthearted contributors seeking any excuse to cut their losses.

"There is no want of any thing," he claimed, "if the action can be upheld with constancy and resolution."[25] Along with a tabulation of the available resources (from which gold was conspicuously absent) De La Warr reported that he had left upward of two hundred colonists "the most in health, and provided for of at least tenne moneths victuals, in their store-house."[26] Others assessed the food supplies as enough to last only three months, and then only in small helpings, while those of his lordship's readers who coupled good memories with an ability to count may have asked, "What happened to the rest of the people?" Although the number De La Warr shipped to the colony has been put as low as 150 or as high as Percy's "thre hundrethe," a conservative estimate of those who died in the ten months of the De La Warr administration stands at about 150 and ran a social gamut from humble soldiers to the council member and master of the ordnance Sir Ferdinando Wainman.

With Lord De La Warr gone to take the cure, George Percy once again found himself the senior man and official temporary deputy governor. It was a good opportunity for the Paspahegh Indians to be avenged for the slaughter of their royal family, and they seized it before De La Warr's ship was scarcely clear of Point Comfort. "After my Lords depture," Percy explained, "the Indyans did fall to their wonted practyses ageine."[27] As dusk settled, shadow-cloaked Indians moved into woods close to the blockhouse and began calling to the guard to come out. Percy claimed that on learning of the Indians' presence (he doesn't say how), he sent word to the guard commander, Lieutenant Puttock, that under no circumstances were he or any of his men to be lured out. Later Percy sent more men to double the guard and repeated his instruction. Stay where you are, Percy insisted, and in the morning he would send a detachment to find out how many Indians were involved. But Puttock chose otherwise. When, in the early-morning light, the Indians made a noisy production of departing, he "w^{t}h the small number of men he had[,] Sheowinge more vallour then will [,] more fury then Judgementt," sallied out after them.

> . . . he followed them w^{t}houtt apprehensyon of that w^{c}h ensewed for the Salvages still Retyreinge he followed them untill they browghte him into their ambuskado where beinge five or six hundrethe of Salvages lett flye their Arrowes as thicke As hayle amongste our handfull of men And defeated and Cutt them all of in A moment[;] The Arrowes w^{c}h they had shott beinge so many in Number thatt the grownd there aboutts was allmoste Covered w^{t}h them.

Shouting, "Paspahegh! Paspahegh!" the Indians fell back when Percy sent out a force of fifty men led by Lieutenant Jeffrey Abbott, who soon found himself with little to do but to recover "the deade bodyes of our men whome he browghte to our foarte where they weare Buryed."

The slaughter of the blockhouse guard provides us with several not altogether cohesive bits of information. According to Percy, it was the Indians' victory shouts, "The wch filleinge our eares in the Foarte presently wth all Spede," that prompted him to send out the troops. He went on to say, however, that he did not know "derecttly whatt had befallen" the guard.[28] From this it is safe to assume that James Towne and its blockhouse were not in sight of each other but that they were in earshot or trumpeting distance. How, one cannot help asking, did Percy transmit his order to Puttock to keep his door shut when the blockhouse was evidently surrounded in the darkness by taunting Indians? From Percy's own evidence, it would have been unwise to send a force out at night to disperse them. But if so, what chance had the "stay inside" messenger? In view of Percy's previous handling of the murder of the queen of Paspahegh and her children, we may be forgiven for concluding that no such order was sent, and that years later (1624) Percy fabricated it to put the blame on the conveniently dead Lieutenant Puttock.

Regardless of what the incident may tell us about the character of George Percy, Lieutenant Abbott's burial detail contributes another clue to where the settlers interred their dead. The bodies were "browghte to our foarte where they weare Buryed," said Percy, making it fairly evident that they were not interred in an established burying ground at some hygienic and psychologically divorced distance from the living. While that much is clear enough, we have to be careful not to jump to alternative conclusions. Bringing the dead to the fort for burial is not necessarily the same as bringing them *into* the fort. Furthermore, we cannot be sure whether this was another isolated instance wherein Indian pressure forced a deviation from normal procedure or whether this *was* the normal practice, as the Starving Time cannibalism had suggested. From an archaeological perspective, if we knew that Jeffrey Abbott's men were digging graves alongside those found in 1955 under the later statehouse foundations, then we should be within an Indian's taunt of the grail— James Fort itself (see p. 210).

There can have been little cause for optimism in the first days of Percy's command, and much reason to wonder what lay in store. More lives had been lost at the falls to no purpose. The governor-general had gone off with a ship and fifty lucky men. When, if ever, would he and they be back? The lieutenant governor, Sir Thomas Gates, had gone to England. Did he make it? And what of the admiral, Sir George Somers?

He had gone on a short trip to Bermuda, and nine months had slipped away without a word. No gold or silver mines had been opened at the falls, and nothing of any real value had been shipped home to England. How long would the Company keep pouring money into fresh supplies? Suppose it had already decided to cut and run? Perhaps there would be no more ships. And what about the Spaniards? What were they up to? While some colonists lived on hope and others in fear, both fed on endless and futile speculation. And now the Indians were back in business.

In such an atmosphere, the debacle at the blockhouse must have done significant damage to the colonists' morale, and with Percy more interested in setting a good table for gentlemen of fashion than in giving orders that subordinates respected and obeyed, esprit de corps at James Towne must have been on the skids when three ships dropped anchor in the river. It was May 10, 1611.

Their arrival was not unexpected. Two months earlier the *Blessing* (commanded by Captain Adams, who had brought her through the 1609 hurricane and had returned from delivering Sir Thomas Gates to London) had moored off James Towne, bringing an unrecorded inventory of men and supplies and the news that Sir Thomas Dale was on his way. Dale had seen military service in the Low Countries and was a close friend to Lord De La Warr, whom he was expecting to join as marshal. As the title suggests, together they planned to shift from a civil to a military government with all the "no-nonsense" discipline that implied. Gates, too, had risen through the military ranks as the result of campaigning in the Low Countries. Consequently, both he and Dale were cast in the same mold and were well equipped to carry on where Lord De La Warr had left off. Thus, for the first time, when Gates returned, Virginia would have two hard-nosed professionals at the helm. And with the marshal came martial law.

English common law honed on the stone of long experience had reached America with the 1607 colonists, who from the outset had been guaranteed the rights, liberties, and immunities of all true-born Englishmen—as loosely interpreted by those in charge. With the arrival of Sir Thomas Gates and Lord De La Warr in 1610, the first written code was penned by William Strachey. These *Lawes Divine, Morall and Martiall* were sharpened and expanded by Dale. Now every man knew where he stood and, more important, where not to stand. Death was to be the price of a wide range of crimes, from speaking impiously of the Holy Trinity (Article 2) to willfully plucking a flower from a neighbor's garden (Article 31). Should this kind of rule be thought too tough and, like young

Harry Spelman, one contemplated a more democratic life with the Indians, Article 29 could be discouraging: "No man or woman, (upon paine of death) shall runne away from the Colonie, to Powhathan, or any savage Weroance else whatsoever."[29]

Sir Thomas Dale had gained his first impression of conditions in Virginia when he landed at Fort Algernon and assessed the somewhat half-hearted defenses at the neighboring Forts Henry and Charles. His inspection of the evidently inadequate progress in planting corn in the abandoned Indian fields left him no better satisfied. Before heading upriver in the hope of finding greater efficiency demonstrated at James Towne, Dale set his own men to planting from the seed he had brought with him. "About the end of May, we had there an indifferent Crop of good corn."[30] That statement introduces us to a new witness, Ralph Hamor, whose undramatic, if sometimes rose-tinted, narrative overlaps with that of the more often sensationalist and self-serving Percy and has the added advantage of being written soon after Hamor returned to England in June 1614, while his memory was fresh. Through the three years following Sir Thomas Dale's arrival, Hamor was to become the measured eye of history, and it was he who described what met Dale's critical gaze on reaching Percy's James Towne.

> This businesse [the corn planting at the downriver forts] taken order for, and the care and trust of it committed to his under officers, to James Towne he hastened, where the most company were, and their daily and usuall workes, bowling in the streetes, these he imployed about necessary workes, as felling of Timber, repairing their houses ready to fall upon their heads, and providing pales, posts and railes to impaile his purposed new Towne. . . .[31]

Dale had arrived at James Towne on May 19; a week later he was writing to the Company in London that work had begun on a wide range of construction projects, including "reparation of the falling Church and so of the Store-house, a stable for our horses, a munition house, a Powder house, a new well for the amending of the most unholsome water which the old afforded." Among others were the construction of a building for the curing of sturgeon and a cattle shed, a blacksmith's forge "to be perfected," and launching a brickmaking operation. In addition, another blockhouse was to be built, this time "on the North side of our back river to prevent the Indians from killing our cattle."[32] This last clearly means the landward side of the Back River (across from Jamestown Island) where a long-established cattle farm still exists. More significant in terms of James Fort, however, is Dale's reference to the "falling Church," for this is the same "pretty chapel" on which Lord De La Warr's men had labored so hard barely a year before. The storehouse, too, had received his lordship's attention, and it likewise was already in need of repairs. As for the stable, the munition house, powder magazine, and the rest, Dale's wording can be read to say that they all were in existence but needed fixing up or that they were new construction. The latter seems the more likely, for none of these buildings were mentioned in previous reports.

The parlous state of the fort, the indolence of its inhabitants, and Dale's intent to focus on his "new Towne," as described by Hamor, provide three important pieces of information: The work of rebuilding houses that had allegedly gone forward during Governor-General De La Warr's stay had been either incomplete or ineffective. The new town which Dale planned to build at the falls was to be defended by palisades constructed similarly to those described by Strachey at James Towne—namely, posts, rails, and pales. Thirdly, the contemptuous reference to the layabout settlers bowling in the streets says that there had to be streets of some kind in which to play.

Although the original London Company's 1606 instructions had told the on-site planners to set out the houses "even and by a line, that your streets may have a good breadth, and be carried square about your market place, and every street's end opening into it,"[33] the Company had not counted on a triangular configuration. Consequently, on the basis of available evidence, it appears that no streets opened onto the marketplace and that the only passages that can be called streets are those avenues created by the thirty-foot building-line setback from the palisades. It seems likely that it was here that the sportsmen set up their bowling alleys.

Dale's voyage from England had taken only eight weeks and had been uneventful. Consequently, he and his men, some three hundred of them, arrived fit and ready to work. Dale being a military man with a military mission, these men were enforcers first and husbandmen a distant second, and as the *Lawes Divine, Morall and Martiall* made abundantly clear, they were "souldiers emprest in this sacred cause," answerable to "the King of kings, the commaunder of commaunders, and Lord of Hostes."[34] In short, they had come to do God's work and were eager to get on with it. Not content, however, to let truth be their shield against the arrow that flyeth by day, they came generously supplied with arms, munitions, and armor.

An outer "street" at the reconstructed James Fort.

From Percy's continuing recollections, it appears that in previous years armor had more often than not been limited to helmets and quilted jack coats in which arrows could lodge and sometimes lethally penetrate. Now, with the coming of Gates and Dale, heavier plate armor and shirts of mail were being issued. "And nott beinge acquainted nor acustomed to encownter wth men in Armour mutche wondered thereatt especyally thatt they did nott see any of our men fall as they had done in other conflictts,"[35] the Indians may have had a reaction akin to that of the Germans when, on September 15, 1916, the British sent their first tanks lumbering into their trenches. Indian marksmen whose arrows hitherto had landed with a satisfying thud and remained in their targets (even if they did no real damage) were now finding their shafts shivered or ricocheting harmlessly off into the woods.

Dale's orders were short and clear: Search and destroy. He himself led a force of "a hundrethe men in Armour" against the Nansemonds and only narrowly escaped ending his Virginia career before it had begun. Percy tells us that "An arrow light, juste upon the edge or Brimme of his headepiece The wch if itt had fallen A thowght Lower mightt have Shott him in the Braynes and indangered his Lyfe."[36] Dale evidently was wearing not one of the fully face-covering helmets of the type found at Wolstenholme Towne (1622) but either a simple morion or a cheek-protecting burgonet. Two of his captains were wounded: Francis West in the thigh (West must have returned from England with Dale, if not before) and

John Martin, shot in the arm. From both men's injuries we can deduce that in those instances their armor was limited to torso protection and were not full half suits. That certainly made good sense, considering the time of the year and the weight of all-encasing armor. Nevertheless, it is evident from Percy's wording that Dale's troops were wearing more protection than the Indians were used to encountering. Much else, however, was becoming all too commonplace: files of steel-helmeted infantry, ammunition slung across their chests, guns gripped in tense hands, warily advancing through the woods; lightly clothed villagers fleeing with whatever they can carry, looking back only long enough to see the black smoke billowing up above the treetops. Others less fortunate are rounded up for interrogation; mothers plead for the lives of their children in a language most of the invading troops do not understand; old people stand dazed, watching with uncomprehending eyes as flames roar up through wall mats and reed roofs, quickly leaving nothing but a few scorched earthen pots standing amid creaking and gently smoking sticks, all that remains of their homes.

Confronted with dramatically changing odds and by men whose chests were impervious to arrows, the Indians (like every race and tribe throughout history) turned to their gods for help, "Throweinge fyer upp into the skyes[,] Runneinge up and downe wth Rattles and makeinge many dyabolicall gestures," calling for rain to put out the soldiers' burning musket match and to "wett and spoyle their powder." Unfortunately for the Indians, as Percy put it, "nether the deivall whome they adore nor all their Sorcerres did anytheinge Avayle them[,] for our men Cutt downe their Corne Burned their howses and besydes those wch they had slayne browghtt some of them prisoners to our foarte."[37]

Although Percy spoke with evident scorn of the Indians' religious rituals, he was not ready to deny that their "Sorceries and Charmes" contained some powerful magic. Case in point: While leading his troops on one of his punitive expeditions, Sir Thomas Dale and his officers paused to rest in an Indian house where something very strange happened.

A fantasy possessed them thatt they imagined the Salvages were sett upon them[,] eache man Takeinge one another for an Indyan And so did fall pell mell one upon An other beateinge one another downe and breakeinge one of Anothers heades, thatt Mutche mischiefe mighte have bene donn butt thatt itt pleased god the fantasy was taken away whereby they had bene deluded and every man understood his errour.[38]

Was it magic, or did the house offer both shelter and a tempting brew containing an hallucinatory drug perhaps derived from mushrooms or jimsonweed? If that interpretation is correct, here was white America's first recorded case of group substance abuse, albeit unintentional. More worthy of attention, however, is the question of whether the drugged food was a booby trap or whether Dale merely stumbled onto a narcotic prepared for Indians who reacted to it in an entirely different and benign way from Europeans.

Because Percy mentioned no village but only that Dale and "Some of the better sorte [were] sitteinge in an Indyans howse," it may have been an isolated structure, perhaps that of a quoikosough, or priest. Dale's own priest, the Reverend Alexander Whitaker, was sure he knew a devil when he saw one and declared the Indian priesthood "no other but such as our English Witches are"[39] and "a generation of vipers even of Sathans owne brood. The manner of their life," he explained, "is much like to the popish Hermits of our age; for they live alone in the woods, in houses sequestered from the common course of men." No one entered the house unless the priest invited them, yet as with the clergy of many another culture, his people turned to him when they needed rain or even when they had lost something. "If they be sicke, he is their Physitian, if they bee wounded he sucketh them. At his command they make warre and peace, neither doe any thing of moment without him." Unfortunately the Reverend Whitaker had not yet learned the tricks of the quoikosough's trade and could only assure his readers that "when I have more perfectly entered into their secrets, you shall know all."[40] Alas, if he ever discovered these secrets, the minister kept them to himself.

Had Dale's hallucinatory experience been unique, it could the more easily be filed away as an inexplicable aberration, but it was not, as both Dale and Whitaker had reason to know. A second occurred when Dale and a company of his men were on a scouting expedition to the James River falls. As was normal precautionary military practice, the troops had dug themselves a trench and rampart wall around their camp and were at their evening prayers when they heard a strange noise coming from the adjacent Indian cornfields. Whitaker described it as a "hup hup" and an "oho oho." That may not sound particularly frightening or intimidating, but coming out of the darkness beyond the flickering light of the camp-fire, it evidently got the nervous troops' attention:

> . . . some say they sawe one like an Indian leape over the fier and
> runne into the corne with the same noyse. Att the which all our men

were confusedly amazed. They could speak nothing but "Oho Oho," and all generally taking the wrong end of their armes. . . . But thanks be to God, this Alarum lasted not above a quarter of an hower, and no harme was done excepting 2. or 3. that were knockt downe without any further harme For suddenly as men awaked out of a dream they began to search for their supposed enemies, but findeing none remained ever after very quiett.[41]

The Reverend Whitaker offered no explanation, being content to stick with his previous conclusion that "there be greate witches amongst them and they very familiar with the divill."[42] However, in his preamble to the story Whitaker gives us a clue. He recalled that Parahunt, Powhatan's son who ruled in the falls area, had "threatened to destroy us after strange manner. First he said he would make us drunke and then kill us."[43]

In both hallucinatory instances those involved seem to have become almost simultaneously disoriented; they saw Indians in their midst either in the persons of their companions or as intruders, and in each case the result was the same: Believing themselves attacked by Indians, the men fought among themselves. That they did no lasting harm to one another may be explained by the second instance, when they seem to have lost the ability to handle their weapons correctly. The final similarity is provided by the speed at which their belligerence evaporated, leaving the men shamefaced and emotionally drained.

Although professionals in the field of drug abuse have agreed that plants such as *Datura stramonium* (popularly known as jimsonweed, having been first identified while growing wild at James Towne) can, in combinations, produce violence-generating hallucinations, they have been unable to cite any modern instances in which groups of imbibers have been uniformly affected or the symptoms pass so quickly. The key question, of course, is how could such a drug have been administered. In the falls instance, Whitaker linked the event to Parahunt's intent to make the English drunk, but he also said that the men were at prayer when the noises were first heard in the fields—noises which may have been in their heads rather than in the corn. It is unlikely, nevertheless, that the victims were drinking at Episcopalian prayers.

That the Algonquian Indians had a sophisticated understanding of mind-distorting herbal-based drugs is proved by Robert Beverley's 1705 account of their methods of achieving mental purification. Young men chosen for leadership roles in the tribe had first to endure the rigors of "Huskanawing," wherein they were sequestered in cages in the woods for several months and there given "no other sustenance, but the Infusion, or Decoction of some Poisonous Intoxicating Roots; by virtue of which Physick, and by the severity of the discipline, which they undergo, they become stark staring Mad."[44] As a result, they "lose the remembrance of all former things, even of their Parents, their Treasure, and their Language." Thus, with their minds cleansed of the memories and emotions of boyhood, the young men were slowly withdrawn from the drug called wysoccan and restored to empty-headed sanity. They were then ready to be taught the secrets and disciplines of government, unquestioning and unadulterated by childhood prejudices—in short, they were victims of brainwashing at its most elemental.

I am not suggesting that wysoccan was the drug used to cause Dale's men to hallucinate and attack one another but cite it only as an example of the Indians' knowledge of botanically derived drugs capable of creating mental disorders which, if continued, could lead to total and permanent memory loss, and were it to be repeated, "the usage is so severe, that seldom any one escapes with Life."[45] Although jimsonweed may have been involved, it would not have been the sole ingredient, for as Beverley described the symptoms of some soldiers who used it in a boiled salad, their hallucinations were more comical than lethal:

. . . they turn'd natural Fools upon it for several Days: One would blow up a Feather in the Air; another wou'd dart Straws at it with much Fury; and another stark naked was sitting up in a Corner, like a Monkey, grinning and making Mows at them; a Fourth would fondly kiss and paw his Companions, and snear in their Faces, with a countenance more antick, than any in a *Dutch* Droll.

Beverley added that the men had to be confined for fear that they might "in their Folly destroy themselves; though it was observed that all their Actions were full of Innocence and good Nature."[46] The ubiquitous jimsonweed (which in the eighteenth century was brewed as a tea) was by no means the only suspect; equally readily, if seasonally, gatherable was (and is) the *Amanita muscaria* mushroom, whose parallel in northern Europe is known as the Berzerka mushroom, a name shared by a breed of ancient Scandinavian warriors who reputedly ate it before going into battle and in consequence fought in a berserk frenzy. The American Medical Association's handbook on toxic plants describes the mushroom's effects as increased motor activity, illusions or delirium, sometimes coupled with manic excitement, during which phase patients may need protection against injury. The symptoms pretty well fit the Dale parties' experiences—with one major exception: The effects can take up to two hours to be felt, and alternating bouts of drowsiness and excitement can persist for several more after the trip is essentially over. In both the Nansemond and the falls incidents the hallucinations reportedly started suddenly and ended as abruptly, though the victims would have had an imprecise awareness of elapsed time.

A skeptical consultant has noted that Percy's account of the Nansemond experience made no mention of eating or drinking, any more than did the Reverend Whitaker, who said only that Parahunt had threatened to kill the English after first making them drunk. Consequently, there is no proof that the men ingested any toxic substance. If, however, we reject that theory, we are left with what is to us in the enlightened twentieth century an even less digestible explanation—namely, telepathic witchcraft.

Before Lord De La Warr and then Sir Thomas Dale arrived with their reinforcements, the ratio of Indians to English was in the former's favor. Rarely had Smith or Gates fielded more than 50 or 60 musketeers, whereas the principal militant Indian tribes (if we assume that about a third of their populations were fighting men) could each mobilize at least as many, and some considerably more: the Chickahominy about 300, the Pamunkey 360, the Nansemond 200 to 250, the Weanoc 125, the Appomattoc 80, the Warraskoyack 60, and the Paspahegh, substituting belligerence for numbers, between 40 and 55. In all, by Strachey's reckoning, the Powhatan Confederacy could field about 3,220 warriors. Though based on contemporary sources[47] these estimates must be somewhat adrift if Percy's figure of "five or sixe hundrethe" who lay in ambush for Lieutenant Puttock and his blockhouse guard is anywhere near correct. But, then, how could it be? Puttock was dead, and by the time the relief column went out, the Indians had made their point and were retreating and hard to count. No one, however, could have been counting heads with more care than Powhatan. For him there were not plenty more where those came from, but for the English there would be, as was soon to be demonstrated.

On August 2, 1611, Sir Thomas Gates returned with nine ships by Percy's count (six by Hamor's), all heavily laden. It was the largest supply yet committed to Virginia, an achievement that owed much to Gates's success in renewing the confidence of the wavering London Company's council and investors. No doubt his decision to bring with him both his wife and his two daughters had had a dramatically reassuring effect; but if he made it solely as a public relations ploy on the colony's behalf, he

Caravel-rigged ships decorating Théodore de Bry's map of
Spanish Florida.

paid a tragic price. Lady Gates died on the voyage, forcing him to send
his girls back with the returning fleet.

Regardless of whether the lookout at Point Comfort saw six or nine
ships, one detail is undisputed: Three of them were Mediterranean-style
caravels. Not waiting for further identification, the messenger boat set
out for James Towne with the long-expected news that the Spaniards
were coming. That fear had been heightened soon after Dale's arrival,
when a lone Spanish caravel anchored off Point Comfort. For ship spot-
ters, caravels offered a very distinctive silhouette, having a high poop and
three masts supporting a predominance of triangular (lateen) sails
extended by long spars, rather than the square rig of most English vessels.
While Fort Algernon's commander, Captain Davies, waited in ambush, a
senior Spaniard and two companions went ashore and were promptly
detained. Their spokesman was said by Percy to be "A comawnder of
some foarte" in the West Indies, his name: Don Diego de Molina. Those
with him were an ensign named Antonio Pereos (or Peres), and the ship's
pilot "who wentt under the name and habitt of A Spanyard."[48] Whether
or not Molina was captain of the ship is unclear; nevertheless, it was he
who explained that the vessel was carrying supplies and had inadvertently
strayed off course. Could he please borrow an English pilot who knew the
James River to bring the ship to a safe anchorage?

Davies thought that a fair request, particularly when Molina was prepared to remain with his own pilot while his English counterpart guided the ship into safe water. But no sooner was the English pilot aboard than the Spaniard hoisted sail and departed—leaving Molina, Pereos, and their pilot behind. An embarrassed and doubtless enraged Captain Davies had much explaining to do. It really didn't help that the abandoned Spanish pilot, Francisco Lembri, was soon suspected of being "a hispanyolated Inglishe man." The subsequent detention of Molina would create an unwelcome international incident. Meanwhile, according to Percy, the three men were "broughtt to James Towne and sentt as prissoners A board severall shippes,"[49] where he and others went to interrogate them. Sir Thomas Dale's decision to keep the cleverly devious Molina in Virginia would prove to be a tactical mistake, for it provided an opportunity for intelligence leaks that would have been best plugged with a bullet. At the outset, however, the three prisoners must have been of less concern than the whereabouts of their caravel and the fate of the purloined pilot. How far had the Spaniards taken him? All the way to the West Indies to instruct Spanish chart makers? Or would he soon be back, a pistol at his head, piloting a fleet of galleons to put an end to England in America? All were questions guaranteed to promote apprehension. And now galleons and caravels had been sighted heading in toward the river.

Once the news reached James Towne, trumpets and drums (or perhaps the church bell) brought soldiers stumbling into their equipment and hurrying to their colors. At an emergency council meeting, during which Dale invited comments on whether it was better to meet the invaders at the fort or afloat, Percy can have endeared himself to no one by advising "Thatt is [it] was dowttfull whether our men wolde stande unto itt A shoare and Abyde the Brunte, butt A shippboard of necessety they muste for there was noe runneinge Away."[50] Convinced that was the right answer, if tactlessly put, Dale hastily loaded provisions aboard the three ships then lying off Jamestown Island, the *Star,* the *Prosperous,* and the old *Discovery* workhorse. Aboard these Dale proposed to fight the enemy, telling his assembled people that "if by these meanes God had ordained to set a period to their lives, they could never be sacrificed in a more acceptable service, himselfe promising, rather to fire the Spanish Shippes with his owne, then either basely to yeelde, or to be taken."[51] This was good strong stuff but not tremendously encouraging to those likely to go down with their burning boats. Fortunately for all, they soon discovered what you already know: The nine ships weren't Spaniards;

they came from England with massive new supplies of arms, tools, food, and several hundred more settlers.

For the Indians the return of Lieutenant Governor Gates and his additional troops marked the beginning of an end still several decades away, but for colonial Virginia it was the start of a new era whose impact was immediate. In London the Virginia Company had reiterated its demand that the colony's administration should be seated somewhere safer from Spanish assault than was James Towne, and the only way to do that was to go inland yet to remain sufficiently close to the river for it to serve as the kind of highway that the Thames gave to London. Although Dale had explored the Nansemond River, it remained clear that a site up the James below the falls would be far safer. Besides, it was on the way to the mines and to the South Sea.

Because most Americans can draw a relatively accurate map of the continent virtually with their eyes shut, it is difficult for us to imagine what it was like to live in Virginia not knowing whether there might be another ocean just beyond the next unexplored hill. The notion that the China Sea might indeed be close at hand persisted as late as the mid-seventeenth century, when a published map of Virginia based on a draft by its onetime deputy treasurer, John Farrar, showed "The Sea of China and the Indies" beyond a mere hiccup of a mountain range. The accompanying explanation stated that the "happy shores" could be reached "in ten dayes march with 50 foote and 30 horsmen from the heade of Jeames River, over those hills and through the rich adjacent vallyes beautyfied with as proffitable rivers, which necessarily must run into ^{y}t peacefull Indian sea," which discovery would be "to the exceeding benefit of Great Brittain, and joys of all true English."[52]

With Lieutenant Governor Gates's approval, Dale was to establish a town below the falls to serve both as the replacement for James Towne and as the jumping-off point for the adjacent valleys and profitable rivers. This time there would be no reliance on Indian acquiescence, no fraternization, and no retreat. The force sent to do the job would be large enough to suffer casualties and keep right on building. And what they intended to build, and indeed did build, is critically important to an understanding of both the colonists' aspirations and capabilities not only at the new town site but at James Towne as well.

The new town was to be called Henrico (or Henricus) in honor of Henry, prince of Wales. Its builders and defenders set out at the beginning of September, 350 of them according to Hamor and "aboutt towe hundrethe" in Percy's recollection. Dale and a few senior men went the

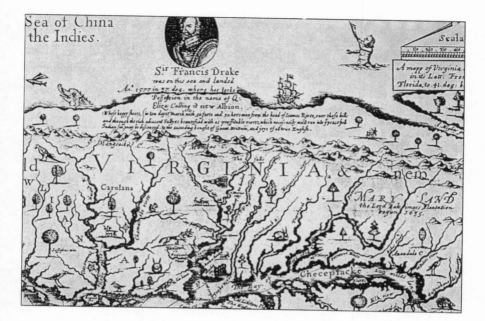

Part of John Farrar's map of Virginia showing how the China Sea could be reached in only ten days' march beyond the source of the James River. Though not published until 1651, the map made use of much earlier and outdated information.

easy way by boat, but the majority marched overland, beating off several Indian attacks along the way, one of them led by a weroance whose name Percy said was Munetute (Smith called him Nemattanow) and whom the English soldiery knew as Jack of the Feather, "By Reason thatt he used to come into the felde all covered over wth feathers and Swans wings fastened unto his showlders as thowghe he meante to flye."[53] One of Powhatan's, and later Opechancanough's principal lieutenants, Jack was a fierce and enterprising leader who encouraged his followers to believe him immune to English guns. Years later a boy's bullet proved otherwise. Now, however, he was doing his best to make good Powhatan's threat to thwart any further expeditions through his land and up his river.

It took the English marchers a day and a half to cover the fifty-nine-mile distance to the chosen site at what today is called Farrar Island, then a promontory described by Hamor as standing on a high neck of land embraced in three sides by the river. In the space of ten days Dale's men had "very strongly impaled seven English Acres of ground for a towne,"[54] a space thirteen times larger than the palisaded James Towne—if Strachey's half acre is to be believed. At the corners Dale erected "very strong and high commanders or watchtowers." Later in the same description

Hamor refers to "five faire Block houses, or commaunders, wherein live the honester sort of people, as in Farmes in England,"[55] and it seems likely that the blockhouses and watchtowers are one and the same. Lest Hamor's reference to the "honester sort of people" drag a red herring across the path of my reasoning, one should understand that he was not distinguishing between the honest and dishonest (though Dale had plenty of the latter) but used the adjective in the *Oxford English Dictionary*'s sense of "a vague epithet of appreciation or praise, esp. as used in a patronizing way to an inferior."

As Dale's blockhouses served the dual purpose of dwelling and watch-tower and were placed at the corners of the town, the thinking is reminis-cent of Strachey's description of the James Towne palisades, where "At every Angle or corner, where the lines meete, a Bulwarke or Watchtower is raised, and in each Bulwarke a peece of Ordnance or two well mounted."[56] This statement has always been a problem, for bulwarks on (or in) which cannon can be mounted do not look in the least like watch-towers. However, a tall blockhouse of the kind shown in the Bonnavolia sketch (p. 233) could easily be described as a watchtower or "commander," the latter meaning a place having a commanding view. Although every modern reconstruction of James Fort, on paper, as a model, or on the ground, has shown a large, cannon-mounting bulwark facing inland across the island to the Back River, a strong argument can be made that by 1610 the landward corner was protected by a blockhouse-style watch-tower of the kind being erected by Dale at Henrico.

It made very little sense to mount heavy guns which, even if the forest were completely cleared to the Back River, could only have fired at out-of-range canoes. By 1614 there were two blockhouses on Jamestown Island (one probably the original defense at the neck), both serving "to observe and watch least the Indians at any time should swim over the backriver, and come into the island."[57] There is here no reference to their use of canoes, and such early evidence as we have indicates that the Indi-ans were content to invade the island from the neck. Although the Back River narrows and is easily swimmable toward the west end of Jamestown Island, on the other side lies a treacherous marsh a quarter of a mile wide at its narrowest point and thus a natural deterrent to any invader. If, how-ever, we assume that the colonists cleared and planted behind the fort, it makes sense that they should raise a tall blockhouse to watch over their crops, but none that they should defend them with artillery.

The basis for the James Towne fort's landward bulwark reconstruc-tions is derived in part from Strachey's equivocal description and in part

Aerial view of Jamestown Island and the Back River. The wide marsh
can be seen in the left background, and beyond it the modern
causeway, Glass House Point, and the frozen-edged James River.

from the tiny sketch on Smith's map (the one Pedro de Zúñiga sent to
Spain) which does show an oval rather than a squared projection facing
north. Several explanations are possible: The map may have been drawn
before the 1608 fire and does not reflect the configuration after the
rebuilding. Then again, other changes may have been made to the bulwarks after the postfire repairs and before Strachey shipped his *True
Reportory* back to England. A third possibility might be that the copy of
the map sent to Spain was hurriedly drawn by someone who saw the original rendering of the fort as a symbol rather than an actual plan and so
took minor liberties in the redrafting. Crude and small though the sketch
is, the sloppy-copy theory is easily dismissed. If a symbolic location was
all that was intended, the draftsman could have settled for an unadorned
triangle or even a circle. Instead he showed all three flankers and even
stuck what appears to be a flag on one of them. More than that, he
showed two boxlike projections facing the river, which have been interpreted as secondary gates.

Because the boxes add a level of difficulty to drawing the triangle, we
have to allow that the structures really did exist, though there may be less
agreement about their on-site character. Military engineers liked gate-
ways that made visitors turn a corner or pass through a second gate before
entering a fortress. The device was much used in medieval castle archi-

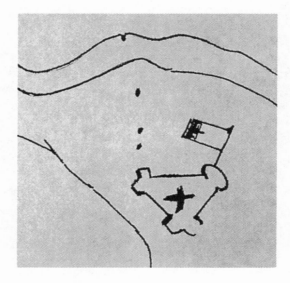

A redrawn detail from the Smith-Zúñiga Map, the only surviving
rendering of James Fort's configuration in 1608. Although these are
among the most thoroughly studied details of any American map,
there is still no knowing whether the enclosure's projecting flankers are
anything more than a draftsman's stylization. The flaglike projection
above the fort is interpreted by some as a fenced garden similar to that
on the plan of Fort St. George (see p. 100).

tecture where the gatehouse leading to the inner ward had a passage
between its outer and inner gates, the flanking walls pierced by archery
slots and the ceiling by holes through which boiling water or oil could be
poured onto the heads of unwelcome visitors.

The same general idea was manifest in palisaded and earth-built forts
where a right-angled wall protected the inner gate, thus limiting the
number of men who could attempt to break in and making them boxed
targets for the defenders. At James Towne, however, the existence of a
main river-fronting gate made a pair of adjacent defensible secondary
gates a pointless embellishment. A more likely explanation is that the two
drawn projections were small watchtowers (like medieval castle turrets),
enabling musketeers to enfilade the otherwise poorly protected main
gate. At first glance one might think that the corner flankers projected far
enough to do the same job and so made the towers unnecessary. Not so.
With the gate in the center of a wall 420 feet long, marksmen firing from
the flankers would be shooting a distance of about 200 feet—with mus-

kets whose accurate point-blank range was said in 1590 to be between 72 and 90 feet.

Hamor's description of James Towne's defenses (which can represent conditions as they were as late as the spring of 1614) offers the surprising information that "a faire platforme for Ordenance in the west Bulwarke [is] raised," suggesting—because he mentions no other—that the west bulwark was the only one with a platform and cannon. However, the passage can equally well be read in the context of *new* construction, and it may be safer to suppose that only the west bulwark required such attention. Hamor's use of the word "raised" may also be significant, perhaps telling us that previous references to artillery platforms were to mere lumber pads laid not on the ground but elevated above it. On the other hand, in seventeenth-century usage "raised" had several meanings, not the least of them being "to restore or reconstruct." But even in that context we have a sense of elevating, of lifting, a term unlikely to have been applied to fixing something that lay flat on the dirt. An alternative interpretation of Hamor's entire bulwark statement and one that helps support the conventional wisdom regarding James Fort's location, may be that by 1614 the old triangular structure had been redesigned to permit the town to expand in an easterly direction and in the process did away with the east, river-fronting bulwark. Here is what Hamor tells us:

> The Towne it selfe by the care and providence of Sir Thomas Gates, who for the most part had his chiefest residence there, is reduced into a hansome forme, and hath in it two faire rowes of howses, all of framed Timber, two stories, and an upper Garret, or Corne loft high, besides three large, and substantiall Store-howses, joyned togeather in length some hundred and twenty foot, and in breadth forty, and this town hath been lately newly, and strongly impaled. . . .[58]

Then follows the bit about the bulwark. Hamor's passage is full of valuable information—or it would be, if only we knew what he meant. Here, once again, is that confusing word "reduced," as previously used by John Smith when he described changes made in the wake of the 1608 fire: "the Fort reduced to a five-square forme."[59] Both then and here the sense demands that the meaning be either "improved" or "expanded." Supportive of the latter interpretation is Hamor's news that the town had been recently and newly impaled. On the one hand, we can read that the old palisades had simply been replaced by new work on the same lines; on the other, we can claim it as evidence of a major expansion. Governor Gates and his marshal were thinking big when they decided to impale seven acres for their new upriver town, so doesn't it follow that they would see James Towne's future in comparably expansive terms? Answer: not necessarily.

Later recollections of Gates's structural contributions to James Towne were both less informative and less enthusiastic than Hamor's, saying only that "Sir Thomas Gates likewise in his time erected some buildinges in and about James Towne, which by continuall cost in repaireinge of them doe yet for the most part in some sort remaine."[60] In assessing Gates's work, we have to remember that James Towne was being written off as the colony's seat of government in favor of Henrico. Henceforth it should serve only as a port of entry for the temporary housing of stores. The need, therefore, was to make it strong—but not big. Perhaps significantly, Hamor tells us that by 1614 James Towne had "two faire rowes of howses." But it had had *three* before, as described by Strachey, who saw that "To every side, a proportioned distance from the Pallisado, is a setled streete of houses, that runs along, so as each line of the Angle hath his streets."[61] How, we may wonder, did 1610's three streets get changed (one hesitates to use "reduced") to only two? Here again a possible interpretation might be that Hamor was describing new work ordered on Gates's watch. Strachey had talked about *streets* of houses, and a street implies that it has two confining sides, interpreted inside the fort by a row of houses on one side and the palisade on the other. But Hamor cites only two *rows* of houses, suggesting, perhaps, that they were built outside the fort, either to east or west, and flanked an open space like a village green.

Hamor's houses themselves offer clues: They obviously were better built than those Dale found in May 1611, which reportedly were ready to collapse about their occupants' ears. Unlike the simplest post-supported (known as earthfast) cottages, they were all of framed timber, as they would have to be, for these houses were remarkably high, standing two stories and a loft from the ground, thus about seventeen feet to the ridge. Were buildings of that height to stand close to the palisades inside the fort, the pales would need to be of at least equal height to protect the roofs from direct shots by bowmen using fire arrows. It would have made no sense for the houses to be taller than the walls behind which they hid.

Other factors, too, are hard to rationalize. The houses Hamor said were falling down in May 1611 had been in relatively good shape when Strachey saw them nine months earlier, at which time he described them thusly:

Very few post-in-the-ground or earthfast dwellings survive in
England. This nineteenth-century engraving of the cottage birthplace
of Samuel Butler at Pershore in Worcestershire is comparable to many
of Virginia's early dwellings.

The houses have wide and large country chimneys, in which it is to
be supposed (in such plenty of wood) what fires are maintained;
and they have found the way to cover their houses now (as the
Indians) with bark of trees, as durable and as good proof against
storms and winter weather as the best tile, defending likewise the
piercing sunbeams of summer and keeping the inner lodgings cool
enough, which before in sultry weather would be like stoves, whilst
they were, as at first, pargeted and plastered with bitumen or tough
clay. And thus armed for the injury of changing times and seasons
of the year we hold ourselves well apaid [satisfied]. . . .[62]

These sound like simple but adequate dwellings, and if the colony's secretary pronounced them so, his testimony is not easily challenged. It is
unlikely that even the most voracious of termites would chew through the
houses in a single season, and while a hurricane could wreck them in
moments, we have no reports of storm damage between July 1610 and
May 1611. So what is the explanation? Although Hamor is generally considered an honest witness, he was a staunch advocate of the new order,
and one cannot dismiss the possibility that he was unduly critical of the
old buildings, thus to make more of the new.

Top: A "country chimney" in the reconstructed James Fort, probably of the kind described by Ralph Hamor in 1611. *Bottom:* Typical story-and-a-half wattle-walled dwellings in the reconstructed James Fort.

If, as has been suggested, the dwellings Hamor described were not the ones in the fort, they may well have been the product both of new architectural skill and of a new philosophy based on the belief that thanks to hard-line policies pursued by De La Warr, Gates, and Dale, Jamestown Island was now safe from Indians—or at least sufficiently safe to adopt the kind of bawn village planning concurrently being employed in the Anglicized provinces of Northern Ireland: Keep the fort close by to provide refuge if the worst should happen, but otherwise build on an open and undefended plan. Hamor's continuing description is wholly supportive of that concept, "there are also without this towne in the Island," he tells us, "some very pleasant, and beutifull howses,"[63] the first evidence of off-base housing since the abandoning of John Ratcliffe's unfinished palace. Though the message was buried in a few lines of ill-spelled text, Ralph Hamor was telling us that the history of James Towne's confinement inside James Fort was virtually over. That being so—or appearing to be so—what thenceforth was to remain within its palisades?

If the Irish bawn village analogy is valid, the house of the governor becomes the centerpiece of an essentially military compound, and it may be that Hamor is obliquely supporting that assumption when he says that Acting Governor Sir Thomas Gates "for the most part had his chiefest residence" at James Towne. When we remember that Lord De La Warr had resided inside the fort and paraded back and forth across the market square between church and home, it seems highly likely that Gates would have continued to reside within the walls like the lord of any castle. More on this later. It makes equal sense to assume that the colony's storehouse would have remained within the palisades' protection.

With the church measuring sixty feet by forty, the company store had become, by Hamor's day, the largest building at James Towne: "three large, and substantiall Store-howses, joyned togeather in length some hundred and twenty foot, and in breadth forty,"[64] thus twice as long as the church. This proportional relationship had its parallel at Popham's Fort St. George, where the chapel measured about forty feet in length and the storehouse about eighty feet (see p. 278). Hamor's statement that the James Towne store complex comprised three buildings can be read simply as two additions to the old postfire building, growing as more supplies demanded more space, or it can be interpreted as three separate but abutting buildings to house different materials. A clue to how those could have been divided comes from the London Company's instructions to Gates, telling him that James Towne should not continue to be his "principall Storehowse or magazin either of armes, victualls or goods."[65] The three elements could therefore be a weapons magazine, a food store, and a repository for tools, rope, canvas, Indian trade goods, clothing, and so forth, all under the control of the cape merchant.

There is evidence that the storehouse remained within the fort at least until 1624—but also that it didn't. First the clue that it did: At a court hearing on June 24, 1624, one George Ungwine, testifying about a break-in at cape merchant Abraham Piercey's store, said that "haveinge beene one of the watch last night [he] did not see any persone that night about the forte."[66] From this we can deduce that if the store had not been within the fort, Ungwine would have been quickly told to get to the point. The contrary evidence stems from an incident which occurred in December 1622 and was reported in testimony taken from "divers sufficient and understanding sea men" in London the following year. It related to the arrival and off-loading of supplies from the ship *Abigail*.

It is reported by the same persons that they have seene goods so landed from the Abigall this Voyage right Against the companies store howses, and the governors howse, Armours, swords, musquets, truncks and such like goods, lye a fortnight together uncared for, everie tide beeing overflowed with water and the trunks readie to bee swallowed.[67]

What matters here is not the arms and armor but the indication that both the company storehouses and the governor's residence were then within a tide's lap of the river—quite impossible if they had remained behind the fort's river-facing palisade. No one is likely to buy the proposition that the rate of the river-driven erosion was such that the wall had already been washed away to expose both store and house. A more reasonable alternative, therefore, is that at some time during the ten years after Hamor wrote his report a new store and a new governor's residence had been erected away from the aging fort, but that the old store building was turned over to the cape merchant for his personal use—hence the fact that at the hearing the robbery was repeatedly said to have occurred in Mr. Piercey's rather than the Company's store.

Sir Thomas Dale's intent had been to follow London's instructions to the letter and to move the permanent storehouses to Henrico—along with anything else that mattered. "There is in this town" wrote Hamor, "3 streets of well framed howses, a hansom Church, and the foundation of a more stately one laid of Brick, in length, an hundred foote, and fifty foot wide, beside Store houses, watch houses, and such like."[68] Note that here

A 1950s interpretation of James Towne ca. 1620, as it may have looked after expanding beyond the confines of the palisaded triangle. A three-part storehouse, replacing the one originally located inside the fort, is shown at the river's edge. A blockhouse is to be seen commanding the curve of the Back River and the marshes beyond it.

Hamor speaks of three *streets*, not the *rows* of houses he described at James Towne.

In spite of attempted Indian discouragement, the work at Henrico went forward at a phenomenal pace, the town's public buildings and dwellings being completed in only four months. But here again, they may not have been as well constructed as Hamor would have us believe. Some fourteen years later a company employee who had lived there remembered the architecture very differently:

... those buildings that weare erected, coulde not in any man's judgement, neither did stande above five yeares and that not without continuall reparations; true it is that there was a Bricke Church intended to be built, but not soe much as the foundation thereof ever finished, but we contentinge our selves with a church of wood answereable to those houses.

The anonymous settler added that Dale undertook "Many other workes of like nature" in and around Henrico, but that they were all done "so slightly as before his departure hence, he himself saw the ruine and desolation of most of them."[69]

North of the town site the slender neck of Farrar Island provided a natural and readily defensible entry. It made better sense, therefore, to look to the south side of the narrow James River for future expansion. Dale consequently set his men to impaling twelve miles of ground (an enormously labor-intensive undertaking), called it Coxendale, and protected it with five forts, one of them, named Mount Malado, doubling as an isolation hospital for the sick. That proto-anthropologist the Reverend Whitaker (he sent the council an "Image of their god . . . painted upon one side of a toade-stoole"[70]) was given four hundred acres as glebe land, where a "faire framed parsonage" was built for him and named Rocke Hall.

Gates and Dale had much to be pleased about, but not all their workers were as thrilled. Rather than continue a life of cleaving, sawing, and digging, several who were "Idile and not willeinge to take paynes" preferred to ignore the *Lawes Divine* and decamped to the Indians. They were later made to realize that this was not a good idea. Caught by Dale in the course of his several sweeps through Indian country, they became grisly warnings to any comrades who harbored similar inclinations. Those who were hanged got off lightly. Some Dale ordered burned alive, "Some to be broken upon wheles, others to be staked and some to be shott to deathe[;] all theis extreme and crewell tortures he used and inflicted upon them To terrefy the reste for Attempteinge the Lyke and some wch Robbed the store he cawsed them to be bownd faste unto Trees and so sterved them to deathe."[71]

That description's creative spelling should have identified George Percy as its author. Although today in America capital punishment in even its least painful form is widely considered cruel and unusual, Percy's opinion of Dale's cruelty is surprising for an age wherein one could be crushed under rocks for declining to plead to a charge and could be pulled apart on the rack for failing to give the right answer to a political quiz. In the context of his time Dale may have been cruel, but he was not unusual. As I noted earlier, the barbarity of punishment continued in England through the eighteenth century, and in Spain Catholic Inquisitors did

A suspect "put to the question" in Tudor England.
The methods employed by Sir Thomas Dale were no
less barbarous and equally effective.

God's work with fiendish ingenuity. At the dawn of the seventeenth century there were some two hundred crimes on the English books for which death was the penalty, the conventional wisdom being that even if execution was not the deterrent that people like Dale thought it to be, it made sure that the transgressors wouldn't be around to do it again. It was a philosophy linked to the brevity of human life in earlier centuries and perhaps to a more universal belief in the merciful hands of angels and the searing damnation of hell. But no matter how one interprets the thinking, in judging how harshly the English treated the Indians, we must always remember how they behaved to one another.

As each new mile of wooden walling went up, the Indians saw their way of life changing. Although the tribes recognized and usually respected one another's hunting grounds, the idea of erecting barriers denying their neighbors free passage from place to place was entirely foreign to them. Furthermore, the English were making it very clear that they offered only two choices: Accept or die.

Shortly before Christmas in 1612, having ensured the security of Henrico, Dale and his troops turned their attention to the Indian lands five miles east (or fourteen miles downriver) at the mouth of the Appomattox River. Here was the second principal village of the Appomattoc Indians, where lived Queen Opposunoquonuske, who, like her brother King Coquonasum, was a thorn in Dale's hide. No doubt because he remembered that it was here that Lord De La Warr's advance party had been fed, watered, and wiped out, the queen's village and all its crops were destroyed. The following year (1613) Dale occupied the area, impaled it, and began to build another major community, which he named Bermuda Citty and the lands around it "the new Bermudas."[72] Although relatively little is known about Bermuda Citty, its site is vaguely recalled today by a headland on the edge of the town of Hopewell and marked on maps and charts as "City Point." A distant and inadequate state historical marker on Route 36 tells anyone who pauses to read it that "City Point is five miles northeast. There Governor Sir Thomas Dale made a settlement in 1613."

At the same time that Marshal Dale was founding his second city, he was expanding on both sides of the James River, dividing the land up into semiautonomous minicounties, which he called hundreds, thus: Rochdale and Bermuda Nether Hundreds on the south bank, and Bermuda Upper Hundred, Digges Hundred, and West and Shirley Hundred all on the north. Part of these annexed lands were impaled to contain the growing hog population, and the rest to claim the Indians' cornfields.

By the spring of 1614, thanks to Sir Thomas Dale's efforts, a little England was growing up around the confluence of the James and Appomattox rivers. Theoretically, therefore, James Towne henceforth could expect its growth to be limited to wharves and transit warehouses—watched over by the guns of James Fort. But as so often is the case, a gulf yawned between theory and practice, this one created by the forty-three nautical miles' sailing and rowing distance between James Towne and Henrico. Hiding out of reach of the Spaniards was all very well, but being unable to adequately support one's coastal defenders could result in blockade and starvation. Whereas James Towne was strategically placed at the pivot of the river, Henrico, for all its palisades and watchtowers, teetered precariously on the edge of the unknown, as the Indians and history would demonstrate.

CHAPTER XII

No Fayre Lady

"THERE IS a ship come from Virginia with newes of theyre well dooing." So wrote John Chamberlain from a friend's home in England to his perennial correspondent, Sir Dudley Carleton, on August 1, 1613. The "well dooing" turned out to be another dirty trick played on the increasingly embattled emperor Powhatan.

> They have taken a daughter of a king that was theyre greatest ennemie, as she was going a feasting upon a river to visit certain friends: for whose ransome the father offers whatsoever is in his power, and to become theyre frend, and to bring them where they shall meet with gold mines: they propound unto him three conditions, to deliver all the English fugitives, to render all manner of armes or weapons of theyrs that are come to his handes and to give them 300 quarters of corne. . . . But this ship brought no commodities from thence but only these fayre tales and hopes.[1]

As a shareholder in the Company, Chamberlain was among the many who, regardless of Sir Thomas Gates's blandishments, was becoming increasingly disenchanted with the "good newes" from Virginia. As for his account of the capture of Pocahontas and her father's willingness to give away the store to get her back, only the abduction was true.

The notion of capturing or purchasing Indian children who could be Christianized and Anglicized and then sent back like rotten apples into Powhatan's barrel was by no means new. The Virginia Company's instructions to Lord De La Warr written in 1609 had told him "to procure from them some of theire children to be brought up in our language and manners"[2] and at the same time to seize Indian priests, some of whom might be shipped to England to be converted. By April 1613 Pocahontas was no longer a child, but if there was to be an ideal candidate for indoctrination, she certainly was it. Indeed, capturing her mind might not be necessary, for if she was, as Hamor said, "Powhatans delight and darling,"[3] the very fact of seizing her might bring the old man to the bargaining table. To what extent, if any, this idea had been discussed by Gates, Dale, and the council at James Towne is unrecorded, but it's unlikely that the capture would have been executed without at least tacit approval at the highest level.

Planned or not, Samuel Argall, described by historian Edward Neill as "the bold and unscrupulous Captain,"[4] found the opportunity—and took it. He had returned from England in June 1612 and throughout the year had been of service to Lieutenant Governor Gates in various enterprises to or against the Indians. In December he had made another trip to the previously helpful Patawomeke Indians, and in an effort to cement good relations with their king, he had left a junior officer named Swift as a combination ambassador, spy, and hostage. When Argall returned four months later (April 1613), he learned that Pocahontas had been living with the Patawomekes for the past three months as a corn agent for her father. Here, then, was an opportunity not to be missed. By promising the king that the English would protect him from Powhatan's wrath if he would not stand in the way of Pocahontas's abduction (just how this support could be provided is not and probably was not clear), Argall had only to devise the trap and spring it.

Among the Patawomekes was a weroance named Iapazaws, who had been befriended first by John Smith and since by Argall. It followed that thus being partial to the English at large, he was also a confidant of the still pro-English Pocahontas—though she had not visited James Towne since Smith's departure. Argall persuaded Iapazaws that his help in trapping Pocahontas would be the best and safest means of creating an enduring peace between the Indians and the English. That reasoning became the more persuasive when Argall threw in "a small Copper kettle and som other les valuable toies so highly by him esteemed, that doubtlesse he would have betraied his owne father for them."[5]

The plan involved both Iapazaws and his wife. Together with Pocahontas they would walk down to the creek, where Argall's frigate *Treasurer* lay at anchor. The wife would want to visit the ship, Iapazaws would refuse, tears would be shed, and eventually he would relent—provided Pocahontas went, too. It was not the first time that she had been aboard an English ship, and she did not suspect a trap. Besides, Iapazaws was her friend, and so, too, she believed were Argall and all the English. As Smith put it in his *Generall Historie*, "thus they betraied the poore innocent Pocahontas aboord."[6] After a tour of the ship and then a convivial supper, Argall persuaded all three to remain overnight. However, by morning Pocahontas had become suspicious and urged Iapazaws to be up and away, at which point she was detained. Shortly thereafter Judas and his wife (Smith called him "the old Jew") took their money, or rather their kettle and toys, and departed. In a classic understatement Hamor reported that Pocahontas's response was to become "exceeding pensive, and discontented."[7]

Although she was well treated by Argall, one doubts whether Pocahontas was any less pensive by the time she was brought prisoner to James Towne. Before leaving the Patawomekes, however, Argall had sent an Indian runner to Powhatan to tell him that his daughter was a prisoner who could be ransomed in exchange for all English prisoners and runaways currently in his hands, as well as for all the captured or stolen weapons and tools, plus, of course, large quantities of corn. The messenger soon returned with Powhatan's assurance that if Argall would bring his ship up Prince Henry's River to him at his current residence on the Pamunkey, he would pay the ransom. With that encouraging news in hand, on April 13, 1613, Argall returned instead to James Towne and there handed his prize over to Sir Thomas Gates.

Although Powhatan's immediate response to the news of his daughter's abduction was to agree to pay up, he probably hoped to outwit Argall and seize his ship. Certainly thereafter Powhatan did not think that trading arms for hostages was a particularly stellar idea, for he let three months elapse before replying to a further demand from Gates. He then sent back seven prisoners, a broadax, a whipsaw, and seven unserviceable muskets—claiming that all the rest had been lost or stolen—and one canoeful of corn. He would supply a further five hundred bushels of corn and his lasting friendship *after* his daughter was released. Gates rejected both the offer and the notion that the vast quantities of arms known to be in Indian hands had inadvertently been mislaid.

No further exchanges on the hostage issue occurred for maybe nine months. In the meantime, according to author Grace Steel Woodward,[8] Pocahontas was taken to Henrico and placed in the charge of Parson Whitaker at his Rocke Hall, with instructions to transport her from the devil's darkness into the sunlight of Christian goodness. Curiously, however, it was Dale who took the credit and piously declared that "were it but the gayning of this one soule, I will thinke my time, toile, and present stay well spent."[9]

While Dale and Whitaker paid sustained attention to Pocahontas's soul, Powhatan, who had at least twelve sons and nine more daughters, seemed content to forget her. His silence became increasingly irritating to Gates, Dale, and Argall, for there is nothing more irksome than holding a trump card in a game nobody wants to play. So, shortly after Gates had returned to England in March 1614, leaving Dale as deputy governor, the latter decided to force Powhatan's hand. Using Argall's *Treasurer* and several boats to transport 150 heavily armed men, Dale sailed up Prince Henry's River with Pocahontas aboard, intending either to trade her or to use her to provoke Powhatan's warriors into a pitched battle.

En route Dale had several verbal exchanges with various groups of Indians, to whom he made it clear that he came in peace or war and that the choice was Powhatan's. When the fleet entered the mouth of the Pamunkey at what is now West Point, Dale got his answer in a shower of arrows that left one of his men with a head wound. Thus provoked, his troops went ashore and "burned in that verie place some forty houses," wrote Hamor, "and of the things we found therein, made freeboote and pillage."[10] Farther up the narrowing river Dale came to Powhatan's current seat at the Indian town of Matchcot (historian Philip Barbour puts it about fifteen miles northeast of modern Richmond) and there found four hundred bowmen ranged along the shore and daring the English to land. When they went right ahead, the Indians were unsure how to respond and so did nothing. Powhatan, fearing that he might be captured and killed, had retreated to a safe distance, leaving no clear directions on how to deal with the invaders. Consequently, a truce was called while messengers, both Indian and English, were sent to find him. But first two of his sons went aboard the *Treasurer* to talk to Pocahontas and to see how she was being treated. Satisfied on that score, they assured Dale that their father could be talked into paying the ransom.

The two Englishmen chosen to go as emissaries to Powhatan were a Master Sparkes, about whom we know nothing, and Master John Rolfe, who was about to make his indelible (if slightly smudged) mark on the pages of Virginia history. Both men were refused an interview with the aged Powhatan but did talk to his brother, identified by Hamor as Apachamo and by Smith as Opechancanough, who said he would do what he could to work out an agreement. Somebody pointed out that this might take awhile and that since it was already April and corn-planting time, both sides would be better employed doing that than waiting around for Powhatan to make up his mind. Dale surprisingly agreed to the delay, though warning that next time he would destroy everything the Indians possessed and had planted if he did not get his weapons, his tools, and the five hundred bushels of corn.

At this point the sequence of events becomes more than usually unclear. Immediately after reporting that threat, Hamor went on to relate the following:

> Long before this time a gentleman of approved behaviour and honest cariage, maister John *Rolfe* had bin in love with *Pocahuntas* and she with him, which thing at the instant that we were in par-lee with them, my selfe made known to Sir Thomas *Dale* by a let-ter from him, whereby he intreated his advise and furtherance in his love, if so it seemed fit to him for the good of the Plantation, and *Pocahuntas* her selfe, acquainted her brethren therewith: which resolution Sir Thomas *Dale* wel approving, was the onely cause: he was so milde amongst them, who otherwise would not have departed their river without other conditions.[11]

No matter how you slice it, this was an extraordinary turn of events. Here we have John Rolfe, an officer in Dale's enterprise against the Indians, apparently secretly in love with Parson Whitaker's version of Eliza Doolittle, who, if all went well, was about to be given back to her heathen relatives. In the midst of the negotiations, presumably while Rolfe was off trying to arrange for Pocahontas's repatriation, Hamor handed to Dale Rolfe's letter revealing his love and offering to marry the girl "for the good of this plantation for the honour of our countrie, for the glory of God, for my owne salvation, and for the converting to the true knowledge of God and Jesus Christ, an unbeleeving creature, namely Pokahuntas."[12]

If the letter is the same one later published as an appendix to Hamor's treatise, it was no hurriedly scribbled note passed to Hamor as Rolfe left on his mission. The document runs to 217 printed lines, expends 46 of them saying absolutely nothing, and then adds, "But to avoid tedious preambles. . . ." It was the kind of letter that gets put away to be read when one is less busy. That Dale did read what Rolfe left him cannot be disputed, but why Rolfe gave it to Hamor to deliver and why he did not simply discuss his proposal face-to-face with his commanding officer are questions unlikely to be answered. The style and length of the missive, however, were questioned as long ago as 1869, when Edward Neill pub-lished his *History of the Virginia Company of London* and in a footnote called the letter "a labored treatise, giving reasons when a Christian should marry a heathen, and has the musty smell of the dusty study of a London divine, rather than the fragrance of a letter written by a man in love."[13] No less to the point is the fact that if the letter was not expanded later to help justify what in England could be viewed as rather dodgy behavior, then Rolfe emerges as a pretty dull fellow—at least for the "well featured but wanton young girle" who used to turn cartwheels naked in the fort for the amusement of the boys and who, by 1612, had been married for two years to an Indian named Kocoum. Although, in 1953, historian Louis B. Wright tried to gloss over the prior marriage by casting doubt on whether "Pocohunta" the entertainer was the same daughter of Powhatan who was to marry Rolfe, a careful reading of the sources leaves no doubt that they were one and the same.[14]

Hamor's narrative says only that the intended marriage "came soone to Powhatans knowledge,"[15] and that it proved acceptable to him. Just how Powhatan got the information and whether his permission was formally requested, we do not know, nor for that matter, do we know what was to become of Dale's trading ace once his hostage was married to Rolfe. In short, the details of this important event are strangely lacking, while those provided by Hamor are chronologically adrift. You will recall that the hostage negotiations had been suspended to allow for corn planting "the time of the yeere being then April."[16] Hamor next tells us that ten days after receiving news of the marriage, Powhatan sent an old uncle of Pocahontas's to represent him at the celebration. At the very earliest, therefore, the wedding would have taken place in mid-April. But Hamor goes on to say that the marriage was solemnized "about the fift of Aprill."[17] This can be read either as the fifth or, as Smith chose to do in his *Generall Historie,* the first—if we assume Hamor's second *f* to be a mistaken archaic long *s*. Either way, the first or fifth must be wrong. The only logical explanation seems to be that Hamor or his printer omitted a "twentie" before misspelling the second digit, be it "first" or "fift of Aprill." We know that the marriage took place in "the Church," but not knowing who officiated, we cannot be sure which church was meant. The logical choice to read the vows would have been Pocahontas's teacher, Alexander Whitaker, but he was the parson at Henrico, whereas the Reverend Richard Buck, who had come over on the *Sea Venture,* was the senior cleric and the incumbent at James Towne. The likelihood, therefore, is that the ceremony took place in James Fort and that both clergymen were involved.

As John Rolfe and Sir Thomas Dale had hoped, the marriage proved to be the magic ingredient needed to bring Powhatan's war with the

English to a peaceful end. Although Hamor's narrative stopped only two months later, he had the confidence to report that "ever since we have had friendly commerce and trade, not onely with Powhatan himselfe, but also with his subjects round about us; so as now I see no reason why the Collonie should not thrive a pace."[18] In this same period the Chickahominy Indians, who, along with the Paspaheghs, had been James Towne's principal threat, made peace overtures which led to the first Indian treaty.

The Chickahominies were then ruled not by a single weroance but by an eight-man council, which volunteered to accept James as their king and Dale as his deputy, provided that they were allowed to live by their existing laws, which the eight would continue to administer. They also proposed to renounce their tribal name and asked that they should henceforth be recognized as Englishmen or, as the treaty put it, *new* Englishmen. For those empty and anthropologically rather pathetic blessings, the Chickahominies agreed not to kill or otherwise interfere with old Englishmen's persons and property, not to enter any English town without first declaring their new English status, to pay annual tribute of two bushels of corn per fighting man, and to be always willing to provide "three or foure hundred bowmen to aide us *against the Spaniards*, whose name is odious amongst them, for *Powhatans* father was driven by them from the *west-Indies* into those parts, or against any other *Indians* which should, contrary to the established peace offer us any injurie."[19]

The treaty's passing reference to Powhatan's father's having fallen foul of the Spaniards in the West Indies has long intrigued historians, but there seems to be no more than that on which to build a rather unlikely Spanish connection. More to the point, however, is the wording's reminder that Spanish ogres continued to lurk in British imaginations.

In exchange for keeping the peace and doing all that the treaty required of them, each of the Chickahominies' eight elders would annually be given a red coat in the king's name, as well as a "picture of his Majesty, ingraven in Copper, with a chaine of Copper to hang it about his necke, wherby they shall be knowne to be King James his noble Men."[20] The other side of the medal, however, was that if anyone breached the treaty, the eight noblemen would be the ones to pay the price. The agreement ceremony took place not at James Towne but at the Chickahominies' principal village seven miles upriver, to which Dale, Argall, and a fifty-man escort went by boat. For reasons about which we can only speculate, Dale "concealed himself, and kept aboarde his barge,"[21] leaving the smiling to Argall, perhaps because Dale as stand-in governor thought that the submission of one tribe ought not to get the attention that should be reserved for Powhatan.

With the old emperor now his declared adopted brother, Dale (who seems not to have reopened the purloined-weapons issue) was constrained to make another, extraordinary request, for which Ralph Hamor was to be his spokesman. Probably in May 1614, Hamor set out overland from the Bermuda settlement accompanied by the now-grown boy Thomas Savage, who had been left with Powhatan by Captain Newport, had spent three years living with the Indians, and thus could serve as interpreter. Powhatan was still living where we last left him, at Matchcot near modern Richmond and a prudent distance from the English.

Powhatan received Hamor and Savage graciously enough and began the meeting by offering "a pipe of Tobacco, which they call Pissimore,"[22] which Powhatan first puffed from, then handed to Hamor, who drew on it and returned it. Amid the pissimore smoke, the two men exchanged pleasantries, which inevitably gravitated to Pocahontas, who Hamor said was "so well content that she would not change her life to returne and live with him."[23] Though this was a slightly risky observation, Powhatan took it well, laughed, and said he was glad to hear it. Thus encouraged, Hamor got to the point, saying in effect: You have another daughter, your youngest, whose beauty is renowned throughout the land and whose exquisite perfection has even come to the attention of your brother Sir Thomas Dale.

Hamor does not tell us what Powhatan said to that, though he does allow that "many times he would have interrupted my speech." Here, however, a fatherly smile would have sufficed. Hamor plunged on, saying that he had come on behalf of Sir Thomas "to intreate you by that brotherly friendship you make profession of, to permit her (with me) to return unto him, partly for the desire which himselfe hath, and partly for the desire her sister hath to see her of whom, if fame hath not bin prodigall, as like enough it hath not, your brother (by your favour) would gladly make his neerest companion, wife and bedfellow." It would, said Hamor, serve to make the Indians and English one people "in the band of love,"

Opposite: De Bry's interpretations of various incidents in Indian-English relations: *top,* Powhatan's sons checking on the condition of Pocahontas when she was held captive by Sir Thomas Dale in 1613; *center,* Samuel Argall receiving the submission of the Chickahominy elders; *bottom,* Ralph Hamor visiting Powhatan as Sir Thomas Dale's proxy in securing the hand in marriage of another of the king's daughters.

principally because Sir Thomas "hath taken resolution to dwel in your country so long as he liveth."[24] In his *Generall Historie* John Smith put the proposition more succinctly: Dale "intended to marry" the twelve-year-old Indian girl.[25] For the record, Sir Thomas Dale already had a wife in England to whom he would return in less than two years.[26]

Not until Hamor was through did Powhatan finally get a chance to say what he had been trying to interject throughout the long and florid pitch. Giving up one daughter to his English brothers, he said, was sacrifice enough; and while he appreciated this added assurance of English friendship, he believed that he could manage with what he had. Furthermore, although he had many children, "he loved his daughter as his life" and "delighted in none so much as she." Besides, he had already sold her to a great weroance for two bushels of beads.

We can do better than that, Hamor assured him. Why not call the deal off and give the chief back his beads? Brother Dale would give three times their number, as well as hatchets and all sorts of other eye-catching goodies. But Powhatan was losing patience and told Hamor to "urge that suite no further."[27]

The idea that Dale, the already married English governor of Virginia, would formally take an Indian child for his wife is hard to countenance, for had Powhatan agreed, he could and should have expected the union to have been solemnized with even greater ceremony than had been afforded Pocahontas at her wedding to the commoner John Rolfe. Would Parson Buck or Whitaker have conducted the service knowing the union to be bigamous? And who in London on the Virginia Company's council would have been assigned to break the news to Lady Dale? All in all, it was just as well that Hamor arrived too late.

Nothing is known about John Rolfe's life with Pocahontas through the next eighteen months. We do know, however, that as early as 1612 he had been at work experimenting with the cultivation of tobacco, introducing varieties from Spanish South America and the Caribbean to substitute for the less popular strain grown by the Virginia Indians—research that was to elevate production from its secondary status in Indian agriculture to the Virginia gold that the London investors were so anxious to receive. Under Dale's governorship, however, there was no tobacco boom. He saw agriculture primarily as sustenance, assigning each free man three acres, two of which were to be planted in corn. Not until 1616, after Dale had been succeeded as lieutenant governor by Captain George Yeardley, were those restrictions lifted, allowing tobacco to become not only the colony's money crop but also its money.

Samuel Argall and the *Treasurer* (of which he was part owner) returned to England late in June 1614, taking Ralph Hamor with him, thus ending the latter's narrative. His news of the end of Powhatan's War and of the treaty with the Chickahominies was music to the Company's ears, though as usual, crass shareholders would have preferred a cargo more glittery than sassafras and lumber to fill the ship's hold. Some of the merchants and gentry who had made pledges to the Company still had not paid up, and others who had made their first installments were being sued for payments that failed to follow. Consequently, beginning in 1612, fund-raising took a new turn. The Virginia Company secured a new royal charter extending its dominion between the forty-first and thirtieth degrees of latitude three hundred leagues offshore (thus annexing the Bermudas) and authorizing the council to set up lotteries to be held in London and other towns. However, they were not wildly successful and were criticized for being illegal, immoral, and a public nuisance. Four years later, in 1616—dividend time for shareholders under the first Virginia charter—creative new thinking was urgently needed. The outcome would be the issuance of land patents to individuals and groups of contributors, a hundred acres for each £12.10s. share purchased. Although this new policy did not get off the ground until a year or more later, it was to change the way in which land was managed, create as many as forty new settlements, and close the door even tighter on the Indians.

But that, as I say, was later. In the winter of 1616 Sir Thomas Dale (regardless of his having advised Powhatan that he intended to live out his life in Virginia) was thinking about returning to England. Although not everyone loved him for it, he had been fairly successful in instilling discipline into the ragtag lot of colonists. Enough land had been cleared and planted to feed the Company's employees, whose number had by now been somewhat reduced because survivors of the early supplies had worked out their indentures, were on their own, and no longer needed to be fed from the "common kettle." On the other hand, an insufficient number of new settlers had been sent over to offset those who had died by accidents or at the hands of the Indians or had failed to make it through the first acclimatizing months. Consequently, plans for expanding inland beyond the falls had stalled, and Dale's favorite project, the new city of Henrico, was languishing for want of inhabitants.

John Rolfe, who was to accompany Dale aboard the ship *Treasurer* in April 1616, wrote a detailed assessment of the colony at their time of their departure. At Henrico he counted only thirty-eight men and boys, twenty-two of them described as farmers, and the rest "officers and oth-

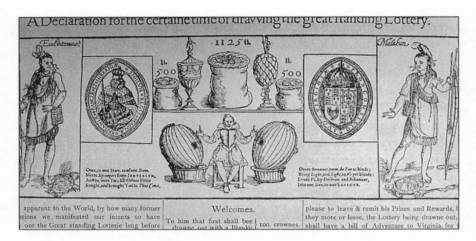

The ornamental header for a broadsheet announcing the Virginia
lottery of February 1615.

ers."[28] Rolfe listed three categories of male settler: officers, who served
the Company and the colony but provided for themselves and their servants through their own industry; farmers, who were free men yet were
required to provide corn annually to the Company's store and to serve
militarily as the need arose; and laborers, who fell into two classes—
namely, those who worked solely for the Company and those who were
tradesmen (blacksmiths, coopers, tanners, etc.) working both for the
colony and for themselves.

The Reverend Whitaker would have been considered one of the Henrico officers had he still been there. His place had been taken by one
William Wickham, who had not taken holy orders, while Whitaker
moved to Bermuda Nether Hundred (later part of Charles City), a much
larger parish with 119 male inhabitants, all initially serving the colony
through a separate charter. The Reverend Richard Buck remained at
James Towne, whose population was down to 50, 31 of them farmers. At
West and Shirley Hundred were 25 men employed only in raising tobacco
for the Company, while downriver at Kecoughtan were 20, 11 of whom
were farmers. A sixth and dangerously isolated settlement had been
established across the Chesapeake Bay at Cape Charles and named
Dales-Gift. There 18 Company laborers were employed in fishing and
panning salt to cure the catch. The colony's total complement tallied to
205 Company officers and laborers, 81 farmers, and 65 women and children, a total of 351 people thinly scattered and still vulnerable to whatever
ill wind might blow. Nevertheless, they were at peace with those that
Hamor called the "naturalls," and they were relatively well supplied. Livestock of the bovine variety totaled 144 (with 20 cows expecting); they had

6 horses, 216 goats, and more pigs and poultry than anyone could count.[29] All this was enough for Dale to congratulate himself and give thanks to God for having "with pour means left the Collonye in great prosperytye & pease contrarye to manye mens exspectatyon."[30]

Captain Samuel Argall and his *Treasurer* left Hampton Roads in April 1616, carrying an extraordinarily mixed bag of passengers. Sharing the "great" and other stern cabins with him were Sir Thomas Dale and the 1607 veteran John Martin and perhaps also James Towne's most familiar foreigner, Don Diego de Molina, who was at last ending his five years of at least quasi-imprisonment. Going with him, too, was his companion, Francisco Lembri, the "hispanyolated Inglishe man" (by now unmasked as Francis Limbrecke, a pilot for Spain in the 1588 Armada), who was led to believe that he was going home but got no closer than the sight of the Devon coast before dangling and dying at Argall's yardarm. No such surprises awaited the ship's now most famous passengers; John Rolfe, his Indian princess wife, and their infant son, Thomas, were coming on what amounted to a promotional visit sponsored by the Virginia Company, in part to gain support for a proposed soul-winning school for Indians to be set up near Henrico. To make sure that Pocahontas was recognized as real royalty, she came with a retinue of about a dozen Indians headed by Tomocomo, her brother-in-law (at least in English law), along with his wife and her half sister Matachanna, three female servants, and four Powhatan men. Some in this group of "divers men and women of thatt countrye"[31] would stay to be educated in England.

On or about June 3 the *Treasurer* docked at Plymouth, where the distinguished passengers were greeted by Devonshire's vice admiral, Sir Lewis Stukley, who may have have been surprised by the behavior of Pocahontas's guidance counselor. Tomocomo had been instructed by Powhatan to remember everything and everybody he saw, specifically to count the people, as he dutifully began to do by cutting notches on a long stick. However, probably even before he left the Plymouth quay, in John Smith's words, "he was quickly wearie of that taske."[32] With the civic reception over and the national census stick tossed aside, the Rolfes and their retinue set out on the 173-mile journey to London, riding in the kind of coach that Powhatan had wanted for himself. As such vehicles had no springs and the roads no surface, by the time Pocahontas saw the tower of St. Paul's, she doubtless concluded that coach travel was less fun than her father had been led to believe.

It may have been someone's idea of a joke to book the Rolfes into the Belle Sauvage Inn on Ludgate Hill. But lest it be supposed that the name was changed to capitalize on the inn's American guests, records show that

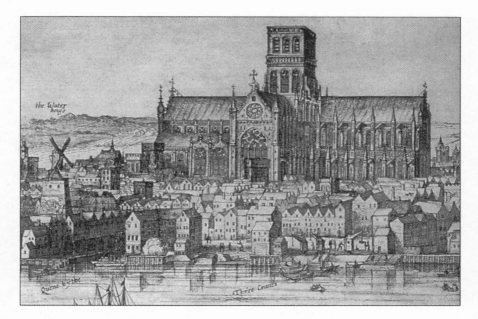

St. Paul's Cathedral dominated the London skyline when in 1616 Claes Visscher drew his panorama. In the same year Pocahontas and her retinue lodged at the Belle Sauvage Inn, which stood amid the tenements to the left of the cathedral.

both the building and the name dated back to at least 1453. A hundred and sixty-three years later the inn was no four-star hotel, and indeed had slipped down the hostelry ladder to the level of a tavern, as Ben Jonson recalled in his 1625 play *The Staple of News*. In it lawyer Picklock is talking to Pennyboy, a beggar, who says: "Let your meat rather follow you to a tavern."

> *Penny.* A tavern's as unfit too for a princess.
> *Pick.* No, I have known a princess, and a great one, come forth of a tavern.
> *Penny.* Not go in, sir, though.
> *Pick.* She must go in, if she came forth: the blessed Pocahontas, as the historian calls her, and great king's daughter of Virginia, hath been in womb of tavern."[33]

The historian was John Smith, who in 1624 had referred to "the blessed Pocahontas" in the dedicatory introduction to his *Generall Historie*, but the play's "princess" was a young woman from Cornwall, where, like many Indians, the people were commonly swarthy-skinned and black-haired.

Once in London, the Rolfes quickly became the city's latest curiosity. Just as they would be today, opinions were sharply divided on the wisdom of such a marriage, not so much on racial grounds as on religious. The Virginia Company's own enthusiasm for the idea of bringing over this example of a fair princess plucked from the devil's talons had wilted more than somewhat when the king made it clear that he considered John Rolfe's behavior little short of treason, prompting the council to debate the possibility that it might indeed be so. Whether these deliberations occurred before or after the couple's arrival is not clear, but James's opinion evidently softened to the point where he allowed Lord and Lady De La Warr to escort Pocahontas and Tomocomo (no mention of Rolfe) to Twelfth Night revels which both he and his queen, Anne of Denmark, attended to watch a masque written by Ben Jonson. There may, however, have been a degree of irony in the invitation, for Twelfth Night was traditionally the time to do honor to the swarthy biblical wise men of Bethlehem, "who are supposed to have been of royal dignity."[34] Mock kings and queens, each chosen by finding a bean or a pea in a slice of cake, ruled the revels. Consequently, Jonson's *Masque of Christmas,* which he wrote for that occasion, included an usher "bearing a great cake with a bean and a pease."[35] In the midst of such turnabout hilarity an Indian princess dressed like an English lady attended by Tomocomo in Indian attire would have provided London's smart set with added amusement.

Some authorities doubt that Pocahontas and Tomocomo were ever formally received by the king and queen, yet from John Smith's *Generall Historie* it seems clear enough that shortly after the Rolfes' arrival, and before Smith left for Plymouth to plan a New England voyage, Smith met Tomocomo in London, where the following conversation resulted:

> . . . hee told me Powhatan did bid him to finde me [Smith] out, to shew him our God, the King, Queene, and Prince, I so much had told them of: Concerning God, I told him the best I could, the King I heard he had seene, and the rest hee should see when he would; he denied ever to have seene the King, till by circumstances he was satisfied he had: Then he replyed very sadly, You gave Powhatan a white Dog, which Powhatan fed as himselfe, but your King gave me nothing, and I am better than your white Dog.[36]

The logic of his argument may be weak, but it is evident that Tomocomo did see the king, possibly at a levee along with so many other splendidly dressed people that he did not know who among them was the English Powhatan.

Whether or not Pocahontas was received by the king or queen would be of little pertinence to the James Towne story were it not that it relates to an object which allegedly survives as the sole relic of that meeting. I saw it first in 1968 in a singularly unlikely place—namely, in an office at the Sloane Street branch of Barclays Bank in London. I had been asked to go there on behalf of the Smithsonian Institution to examine a silver-mounted stoneware mug allegedly given by Queen Anne to Pocahontas, whose owner had a mind to sell it to the nation. The jug was genuine enough. Made at Siegburg in the Rhineland in about 1580, it boasted a very ordinary silver mount on which were crudely engraved the initials T M R. Assuming that the middle letter stood for Pocahontas's Indian name Matoaka, the combination was supposed to represent the initials of Mr. and Mrs. Rolfe, a reasonable supposition, provided one forgot that John does not begin with a *T.*

The jug's thin mount lacked any London silversmith's marks and therefore was probably Continental, while the mug itself was the kind of drinking vessel the Rolfes would have found in the better bar at the Belle Sauvage—hardly, therefore, a princely or queenly gift to bestow on for-eign royalty. Because the 1968 asking price of two hundred thousand dollars owed much to that premise, the Smithsonian declined to buy it. Eighteen years later the mug was again offered for sale, and this time it was purchased by the state of Virginia and placed on exhibition, legend intact, at its Jamestown Settlement park.

To help promote Pocahontas's acceptance in London's cruel society, John Smith had written to Queen Anne recalling all that Powhatan's daughter, "this tender Virgin," had done to help the colonists at large and himself in particular. Now that she had arrived from Virginia "the first Christian ever of that Nation, the first Virginian ever spake English, or had a childe in marriage by an Englishman,"[37] Smith begged that she be well received. Seeking financial generosity (for which James was not renowned), Smith noted, too, that John Rolfe's financial status was such that he could not afford to dress his wife appropriately to be received at court, as was true. Although the Virginia Company did give the family four pounds a week, as historian Philip Barbour points out, the Levant Company hosting a single minor diplomatic visitor to London allowed him that much per diem solely for food, plus twenty pounds a month for lodging.[38] In short, the Virginia Company was being extraordinarily stingy, reflecting its persisting ambivalence toward its colorful guests.

When Smith wrote his appeal to the queen, he claimed that he was "preparing to set saile for New-England" and so could not be of as much

Top: A silver-mounted Siegburg mug of about 1590, which according
to family tradition was given to Pocahontas and her husband,
John Rolfe, by Queen Anne. Neither mug nor mount is of the
quality one would expect of a royal gift. Height 8 inches.
Bottom: Detail of the Pocahontas jug's silver mount showing
its crudely engraved T M R initials.

service to Pocahontas as he would have wished. That was true, as far as it went, but since Smith's grand design to reunite the Plymouth adventurers with the London Company in a new James Towne–like venture in Maine came to naught, it is surprising that he recorded details of only one meeting with Pocahontas in the seven months of her visit. It took place at the village of Brentford, possibly at Syon House, one of the homes of George Percy's illustrious brother Henry, earl of Northumberland. He, however, would not have been there to receive the guests. At first an enthusiastic supporter of Scotland's James VI when he came south to accept the English crown, Northumberland soon had difficulty concealing his conclusion that a very few Scotsmen were more than enough. When the king learned that the earl's kinsman Thomas Percy, a ringleader in the Gunpowder Plot, had dined at Syon House the day before the scheduled explosion, Northumberland's loyalty came to be doubted, a suspicion that led to his prolonged imprisonment in the Tower of London—where Pocahontas reportedly was taken to visit him. That she should have been received at Syon House by his wife, Dorothy, is entirely possible, for like her husband, the countess of Northumberland was an outspoken supporter of another longtime but recently released Tower prisoner, Sir Walter Ralegh.

Tradition has it that it was Ralegh who escorted Pocahontas to the Tower to meet his friend Northumberland, whose scientific interests had earned him the sobriquet of the Wizard Earl. He was also an all-purpose tinkerer, and during the meeting with Pocahontas he noticed that one of her earrings was in need of attention. A pair of silver-mounted mussel shell earrings displayed in the National Park Service's visitor center at Jamestown reputedly exhibits the Wizard Earl's handiwork.

However much John Smith may have professed affection for Pocahontas, his description of their Brentford meeting, though intensely human and likely to be true, does not stamp it as a social success. Perhaps overwhelmed by the glittering company, or perhaps by the emotion of seeing him for the first time since her childhood, Pocahontas failed to project a particularly sparkling or engaging personality. Smith recalled that "After a modest salutation, without any word, she turned about, obscured her face, as not seeming well contented; and in that humour her husband, with diverse others, we all left her two or three houres, repenting my selfe to have writ she could speake English."[39] She later demonstrated that she could; but she evidently, and not surprisingly, felt herself a tropical fish in an empty tank.

Although through the months that she was in England, Pocahontas was well treated and entertained by many distinguished people having

A pair of mussel-shell earrings set in silver and steel, traditionally believed to be those that the earl of Northumberland repaired for Pocahontas in his cell at the Tower of London.

Virginia interests, behind her back she was considered an oddity, and was referred to by the gossipy letter writer John Chamberlain not as Mrs. Rolfe or Pocahontas, or even as Matoaka, but repeatedly as "The Virginian woman."[40] On February 22, 1617, just a month before she was due to return to Virginia, Chamberlain wrote to his friend Dudley Carleton:

> Here is a fine picture of no fayre Lady and yet with her tricking up and high stile and titles you might thincke her and her worshipfull husband to be sombody, yf you do not know that the poore companie of Virginia out of theyre povertie are faine to allow her fowre pound a weeke for her maintenance.[41]

In a classic demonstration of the historian's problems in interpreting such evidence, Samuel Purchas reported on precisely the same action, but saw the Company's "provision for her selfe and her sonne" as evidence of its generosity and its respect for the Virginian princess.[42] With two such different views of the Company's largess, it remains to us to pick the more likely, but had fate ordained that either be tossed into the trash can, we would have had a fifty-fifty chance of being left with the wrong impression—and the documentation to "prove" it. In this instance we have the previously cited evidence from historian Philip Barbour to tip the balance. It is, therefore, merely an example of the kinds of trap that historical attrition lays in the path of the time walker.

Two engraved portraits of Pocahontas, both frequently published as
contemporary, but one looking more European than the other.
Left: engraved in 1616 by Simon van de Passe; *right:* the portrait
reengraved and published in 1793.

We might expect to be much better served by illustrations of the
period, but alas, that holds true only of unfaked photos. In the seventeenth century every picture, from the studio of the finest portraitist to
the blade of the humblest woodcut chiseler, was compromised by the
artist's limitations and by the wishes and wealth of his sitters and customers. Chamberlain evidently had sent his friend an engraving by the
Flemish artist Simon van de Passe, one apparently commissioned by the
compiler and publisher Henry Holland and sold by his supposed brother
Compton at his shop near the Royal Exchange, where merchants associated with the Virginia Company were likely to see it. The engraving
shows a fierce-eyed, high-cheekboned, dark-countenanced woman with a
strikingly regal yet witchlike look. A surrounding oval identifies her as
Matoaka alias Rebecca (the name given her at her baptism), daughter of
Powhatan, emperor of Virginia. As was common among engravings of
this period, a lengthy inscription below the portrait repeats the information and adds that "Matoaks" was wife to the Worshipful Mr. John Rolfe.
Were it not for van de Passe's additional statement that his subject was
aged twenty-one, we might be forgiven for guessing at forty.

The engraving is striking but by no means flattering, and one Pocahontas biographer has dismissed it as "mere caricature," a cheap copy of a

Ætatis suæ 21. Aº.1616.

Matoaks als Rebecka daughter to the mighty Prince
Powhatan Emperour of Attanoughkomouck als Virginia
converted and baptized in the Christian faith, and
Wife to the worⁿᵗᵗ Mʳ Tho: Rolff.

The Booton Hall portrait of Pocahontas, its inscription identifying
her as the wife of Thomas rather than John Rolfe.

portrait painted at the time of Pocahontas's presentation at court.[43] There
is no doubting, however, that the engraving came first and the portrait a
possibly belated second. The painting is stated in the *Dictionary of
National Biography* to be the work of an Italian artist and to have come
down in the Rolfe-related family of the Reverend Whitwell Elwin of
Booton Rectory, Norfolk. In 1882 or 1883 the painting's then owner, Hast-
ings Elwin, wrote that his grandfather had been given it by a Mrs. Zuccelli and that he thought that Mr. Zuccelli might have been the artist.
Perhaps because Elwin admitted to being unsure of the spelling, artist
Zuccelli (if, indeed, he was an artist) has not been traced. All that can be
said, therefore, is that the painting has no known history prior to the
mid-eighteenth century.

Now in the National Portrait Gallery in Washington, D.C., the
famous picture shows that the artist tried to Anglicize and soften the features, eliminating the chin cleft, weakening the cheekbones and the shadows under the eyes, and giving the flesh a warming injection of pink. In

The Spanish ambassador, Diego Conde de Gondomar, engraved after
the painting by Daniel Mytens. The ambassador's feathered hat is
similar to that worn by Pocahontas in the van de Passe engraving.

the engraving Pocahontas wears a tall hat with a broad band and a handsome side feather, but in the painting the feather is gone, and the plain
hat begins to merge into the muddy background. The painter's changes to
the hat, which seem to include a slight shortening of the crown as well as
to omit the feather, might be construed as part of the gentling process in
the belief that van de Passe's hat was too theatrical. In fact it wasn't
(though it may well have been made for a man), for it is closely paralleled
in Daniel Mytens's portrait of Spain's then ambassador to England, the
Conde de Gondomar. The treatment of other clothing details in the
"Zuccelli" portrait suggest that the artist did not fully understand how
early-seventeenth-century garments were put together, thus supporting
the likelihood that the engraving was copied some while after Pocahontas's death. But then again we cannot be sure that the "Zuccelli" portrait
is not itself an imprecise copy of a now-lost original.

That the portrait was not painted from life is amply demonstrated by the fact that the long inscription under the engraving has been more or less slavishly transferred to the painting, something rarely, if ever, incorporated in that way into family portraits. The inscription reads like this:

Matoaks als [alias] Rebecka daughter to the mighty Prince Powhatan Emperour of Attanoughkomouck als virginia converted and baptized in the Christian faith, and Wife to the wor^ll Mr Tho: Rolff.

Thomas Rolfe? Like the stoneware mug which came down through the same family, John Rolfe has been given the name and initial of his son. The "mistake" has to be deliberate, but why? There is no evidence that John changed his name, for after returning to Virginia, he continued to sign himself in that way. On the other hand, as we shall shortly see, the John-Thomas confusion is not the result of retrospective memorializing or fakery, for it began in March 21, 1617. One thing is certain: The painting was not commissioned by John Rolfe. But if not, then by whom?

The London historian William Kent has recorded that the landlord of the Belle Sauvage so profited from the fame or notoriety of his exotic lodgers that he put up a new sign bearing a portrait of Pocahontas. According to Kent, the association lasted at least until 1672, when the inn issued the second of two monetary tokens depicting "an Indian woman holding a bow and arrow."[44] Is it possible, therefore, that the crude sign-like quality of the "Zuccelli" portrait is no accident and that it was the work of the Belle Sauvage sign painter, either as a gift to the Rolfes or perhaps to hang in the taproom in the way that today's publicans hang signed portraits of celebrity visitors in their bars?

If that theory is to hold water, one needs to be able to produce the two tokens, the first of which (according to Kent) was issued in 1648. However, the standard catalog of English seventeenth-century tokens[45] lists none for the Belle Sauvage, and the British Museum's Department of Coins and Medals states that it has no examples in its collection, nor has it heard of their existence. With the tokens sidelined, one has to wonder whether Kent's inn sign story is any more reliable.

Out of all this uncertainty, only the Simon van de Passe engraving survives as an undeniably contemporary portrayal of the Virginian princess. Although the engraving seems to have been later bound with a book of English royal portraits printed by Henry Holland and published in 1618,[46] it appears to have been first rushed out as a single sheet to exploit a short-

lived market—the haste suggested by the absence of the corner embellishment common to these cartouche-style portraits. This, then, is the rationale for claiming that it was the Simon van de Passe portrait that John
Chamberlain sent to his friend. It remains an open question whether the
van de Passe rendering was taken from life or was copied from another,
now-lost painting or drawing. That period still being the era of the portrait miniaturist, it is entirely possible that there was the source and even
that the proof may still lie unrecognized and forgotten at the back of a
drawer in some country house attic. But this is all speculation.

The van de Passe engraving is described by Thomas Seccombe in his
notes on John Rolfe in the *Dictionary of National Biography* as portraying
features both agreeable and modest. Modesty, of course, is in the eye of
the beholder, but with nothing but one hand and her head visible, only a
wanton's wink could have made her appear immodest. Whether or not
the engraving is agreeable is another question.

In 1966 the Huntington Library's 1624 copy of John Smith's *Generall
Historie* was reprinted in what was claimed to be a facsimile edition, and
in it, on facing pages, were not one but two portraits of Pocahontas, the
van de Passe version on the left and another, healthier and more European version on the right. Assuming that "facsimile" meant an exact copy,
I developed a thesis that Smith, believing that the van de Passe engraving
failed to do justice to Pocahontas's memory, had the gentler version
drawn for inclusion in his history's first edition. Although there are several ways to distinguish between the two versions when they are not seen
side by side (p. 342), the easiest is to note that the hat's feather breaks the
oval in the first version but not in the second. The latter is by far the better known, for it was used to illustrate Edward Arber's edition of Smith's
Travels and Works (1910), which remained the standard text for more than
seventy years. What Arber did not reveal, any more than did the 1966 facsimile edition, was the fact that a crucial line had been omitted from the
bottom of the engraving. It reads "Pub^d. Augt 10. 1793. by W. Richardson
Castle S^t. Leicester Square." Thus John Smith had nothing to do with
the short-feather engraving, and my thesis promptly collapsed. Only the
van de Passe engraving had given Londoners their lasting impression of
their exotic visitor, thin-visaged, regal, yet still rather frighteningly "savage" beneath her European attire, and, as Chamberlain had slyly put it,
no fayre lady.

One cannot help feeling sorry for John Rolfe. He came from a
respectable Norfolk family of rural gentry who for generations had lived
at Heacham Hall near King's Lynn. The area was a seedbed of Puri-

tanism, and that clearly had influenced the young man. It is clear, too, that he was a loner, more interested in growing tobacco than in involving himself in Virginia politics. As his letter to Sir Thomas Dale revealed, Rolfe was concerned lest God and his peers take a dim view of his marrying "an unbelieving creature," and he knew that once in London, he was even more likely to encounter "the vulgar sort, who square all mens actions by the base rule of their own filthinesse" and who he feared would tax and taunt him for what he saw as his godly labor.[47] Lodged in an inn later renowned for its bedbugs and then frequented by fencers and theater people, where plays were performed in the yard, the quiet John Rolfe as the sole white gentleman in the midst of an Indian circus must have prayed for the day when he could return to Virginia and to isolated respectability. In dramatic contrast with the retiring and increasingly ill Pocahontas, Tomocomo enthusiastically assumed the role of spokesman both for the Native American culture and for the great Powhatan, and it was he, therefore, who gave the gawking visitors what they wanted. Samuel Purchas recalled Tomocomo as "a blasphemer of what he knew not" who preferred his own god; nevertheless, this latter-day Hakluyt seized any opportunity to watch the Indian "dance his diabolical measures"[48] and to listen to him talk through an interpreter about his country.

Had the Rolfes gone to England without Tomocomo and the rest of Pocahontas's entourage, Rolfe might have kept his hand on the tiller of events; instead he slipped into the background to become simply a minor curiosity as the Englishman who had married into a family of savages that, in his own words, was a "generation accursed."[49]

Although Pocahontas was no better able to grapple with the climate and common sicknesses to which the English were hardened than were they to those of Virginia, she seems to have enjoyed her seven months in England. On January 18, 1617, Chamberlain, after describing the royal masque and Pocahontas's presence, wrote that "She is on her return (though sore against her will) yf the wind wold come about to send them away."[50] This suggests that the Rolfes were by then aboard ship waiting for a favorable wind. Although winter was a vile time of year to sail out into the English Channel, it seems unlikely that the departure would have been delayed by all of nine weeks. Nevertheless, we know from both Smith and Chamberlain that Samuel Argall, as admiral of a three-ship fleet, was not ready to sail until about March 20—the day that Pocahontas died.

The ship *George* was then anchored at the mouth of the Thames off Gravesend. A small town of less distinction, it was nevertheless a major arrival and departure point for foreign visitors. Because it was closer to London than Dover and within rowing distance of the city, Queen Elizabeth had ordered that its lord mayor, aldermen, and officials of the civic companies were to go to Gravesend to receive all "eminent strangers and ambassadors . . . and attend them to London in their barges."[51] It is likely, therefore, that the Rolfes went down the Thames to Gravesend by open barge. Anyone who has taken a tour boat from Westminster (if only as far as Greenwich) on a gray and windy March day can attest to the fact that you disembark with skin as blue as a blue-footed booby's feet. The probability that the already sickly Pocahontas caught a chill en route to Gravesend has more credence than the often favored view that her death was caused by exposure to the sea air while she waited aboard the *George* or while she lodged in a Gravesend cottage.[52]

There is, however, another possibility, and it takes us back to the Simon van de Passe engraving and forward to 1620, when one of the Indian women left behind to be educated reportedly became "very weake of a concumpcon."[53] Pulmonary diseases, which were common in seventeenth-century London, were exacerbated in the winter, when the city lay under a pall of yellow, choking fog and the houses reeked of smoke from countless aging and often poorly built chimneys. As later bills of mortality show, hundreds died of tuberculosis and the other lung diseases collectively described as consumption. John Chamberlain's letter of January 18 had indicated that Pocahontas was leaving and waited only for a fair wind. It is conceivable, therefore, that the Company wanted her out of town before her deteriorating health generated critical gossip and that she did, in fact, go down to Gravesend several weeks before Argall's ships were to sail. That her drawn features were the product of a wasting disease and did not mirror her previous healthy appearance cannot be proved, yet it is hard to believe that any artist would have drawn the twenty-one-year-old "poor innocent Pocahontas," as Smith described her, in so unflattering a portrait had there been no reason to do so. However, Wendy Ricks Reaves, curator of prints at the National Portrait Gallery, has warned against a close interpretation of the portrait, contending that in van der Passe's day "such perfection was not sought or expected," and that one should resist a "close psychological or physical reading of the likeness."[54]

The funeral of Pocahontas took place in the parish Church of St. George at Gravesend on March 21, 1617, the entry in the register reading "Rebecca Wrothe[,] wyff of Thomas Wroth gent. a Virginia lady borne, here was buried in ye Chauncell"[55] The church burned down in 1727, and if a carved stone was laid in the floor (as seems likely, she being placed in so prominent a place in the church), it has long since disappeared. The parish registers survived, however, keeping alive the mystery of why, as on the mug and on the painted portrait, John Rolfe was there cited as T or Thomas.

As she lay close to death, Pocahontas had told her husband that though all must die, it was enough that her child should live.[56] But would he? The infant Thomas Rolfe had also been sick and remained frail and ill prepared for the rigors of an Atlantic voyage. The Indian women who had been Pocahontas's servants and were now the child's nurses were also sick and themselves in need of nursing. Consequently, when the *George* reached Plymouth, John Rolfe sadly and reluctantly turned the boy over to Sir Lewis Stukley, the vice admiral who had greeted Pocahontas and all the others at quayside only ten months earlier. Rolfe never saw his son again.

CHAPTER XIII

Questionable Answers

LIKE MOST seamen cast in the Elizabethan mold, Captain Samuel Argall liked to get things done, preferably without help from committees. He was the kind of fellow to have on your side in a fight, but who would be more helpful out of town when diplomacy was needed. Nevertheless, he had been an effective lieutenant to hard-liners Gates and Dale, as his opportunistic seizure of Pocahontas had demonstrated. More than that, when late in 1613 news reached Virginia of French settlements being planted on the St. Croix River and on the coast of Nova Scotia, Argall aboard his fourteen-gun *Treasurer* went up and surgically excised them, returning to James Towne with their ships, fifty prisoners, and the products of their Indian trade, an exploit which, in Hamor's words, "will ever speake loud his honour, and approved valour."[1] Now, four years later, as Argall assumed the mantle of governorship, his attributes of valor and boldness were to be less in demand than an ability to govern. Thus the delay at Gravesend caused by the death of Pocahontas may have been the first test of Samuel Argall's patience.

Because the Company had appointed John Rolfe to succeed Ralph Hamor as secretary to the council and thus made him Virginia's chief conduit to the London management, Rolfe was no longer just another colonist. Although he may not have impressed sophisticated society writers like John Chamberlain, Rolfe had used his months in England to establish valuable contacts. He had written and dedicated *A True Relation of the State of Virginia* to the enthusiastic tobacco smoker and immensely wealthy William Herbert, earl of Pembroke. He sent a copy to Sir Robert Rich, soon to become the second earl of Warwick, a powerhouse in one arm of a Virginia Company increasingly divided between supporters of its longtime treasurer, Sir Thomas Smythe, and the disenchanted stockholders, led by the earl of Southampton and Sir Edwin Sandys, who became treasurer in 1619. Rolfe, rather than cling to the friendship of his Virginia superiors, De La Warr, Gates, and Dale, wisely looked to the future rather than to the past and courted Sandys—so successfully that by the time he returned to James Towne he could write to him as one who had become "a father to me, my wife and childe."[2] As admiral of the Virginia fleet Samuel Argall must have been very conscious of the pious John Rolfe's rising star and was perhaps glumly aware that his opinions could make or break his governorship in the eyes of Sandys and his Company supporters. Had this not been so, when Pocahontas's illness threatened to delay the ships' departure, Argall might very well have put Rolfe ashore at Gravesend to deal with his family problems and sailed without him. Instead he sent Ralph Hamor as his vice admiral aboard the *Treasurer* on ahead to Plymouth, presumably (as was common) to take on the last food and water before heading out into the Atlantic. Meanwhile, Argall remained at Gravesend to attend Pocahontas's funeral.

It was April before the *George* joined the *Treasurer* at Plymouth and the tenth before they landed Rolfe's sick son and set sail for Virginia, accompanied by a pinnace captained by the durable John Martin.[3] Left behind in London were two and possibly three Indian "maydes" who were to be brought up in English households to be educated and Christianized. It would take awhile, and in May 1620, the girl assigned as a servant to a Cheapside mercer was the one who grew "verie weake of a Consumpcon,"[4] causing the never overly generous Company to contribute a pound a week for two months to help her recover. By June of the following year the Company evidently had tired of supporting the students, and at the quarterly meeting of its court it resolved that the "two Indian maydes haveinge byne a longe time verie chargeable to ye Company itt is now ordered that they shalbe furnished and sent to the summer Ilands [Bermuda] whether they were willinge to goe wth one servante apeec towards their preferm^t in marriage wth such as shall accept of them."[5] The intent was then to send them and their resulting children (and presumably their husbands) on to Virginia to civilize their kindred. In October 1621 they reached Bermuda, where one soon found a husband described by John Smith as fit for her. In London, however, the educational experiment had not been deemed a great success, and when six months later someone suggested trying again with some likely Indian lads, the Company's late treasurer, Sir Edwin Sandys, observed that "to have them educated here, he found upon experience of those brought by Sir Tho. Dale, might be far from the Christian work intended."[6]

Above: Sir Robert Rich, second earl of
Warwick; engraved in 1827 after a painting
by Sir Anthony Vandyck. *Above, right:*
Simon van de Passe's 1616 engraved portrait
of longtime Virginia Company treasurer Sir
Thomas Smythe.

When Dale sailed for England in the spring of 1616, leaving the
colony in the hands of his appointed deputy governor, George Yeardley,
all had been allegedly in good order, or so both Dale and John Rolfe
claimed when they reported to the Company in London. However, by the
time Argall returned to relieve Yeardley, and in the space of less than a
year, the place had gone to hell in the proverbial hand basket. Yeardley
had encouraged the colonists to plant tobacco in preference to corn (of
which, thanks to Dale's prudence, they had plenty), with the result that

they became so obsessed with the get-rich-quick potential of their money crop that virtually everything else was neglected, including their spiritual guidance. James Towne's Reverend Buck seems to have been on leave, and Henrico's worthy Alexander Whitaker had drowned, consequently "here being no other parson."[7] To make matters worse, the treaty with the Chickahominy Indians had broken down. When Yeardley demanded the annual corn tribute required under the agreement, the Indians dared him to try to get it. With a force of a hundred men he did so, killing a dozen Indians and taking as many prisoner, two of them from among the eight elders held responsible under the treaty. But as had happened before, the river was on the Indians' side, and while returning from the attack, one of the boats overturned, losing its cargo of looted grain and drowning all eleven occupants.

Powhatan, who was by now leaving most of the administration of his empire to his younger half brothers, Opitchapam and Opechancanough, expressed dismay at the behavior of the Chickahominies and assured Yeardley of his continuing friendship. Indeed, the friendship with at least some of the Indians went so far that Yeardley trained two of them to be skilled in musketry and kept them as bird hunters. Another (or perhaps one of the two) led the right-hand file of halberdiers on parade to receive the new deputy governor when he landed at James Towne. It was the 16th of May, 1617, and Argall was appalled by what he saw:

> In James towne he found but five or six houses, the Church downe, the Palizado's broken, the Bridge in pieces, the Well of fresh water spoiled; the Store-house they used for the Church, the market-place, and streets, and all other spare places planted with Tobacco, the Salvages as frequent in their houses as themselves, whereby they were become expert in our armes, and had a great many in their custodie and possession, the Colonie dispersed all about, planting Tobacco.[8]

How neglect resulting from a season of tobacco planting could have brought James Towne again to ruin is hard, if not impossible, to explain. Because the foregoing description comes from Smith's *Generall Historie*, one is tempted to dismiss at least part of it as an attempt to show that since he, Smith, left, nothing had gone right. However, he cited as his sources letters from both Argall and Rolfe, and although the former's do not survive, the latter's do. Rolfe tells us that they found the "buildings, fortyficacons and . . . boats, much ruyned and greate want."[9]

Although the structures, whether boats or buildings, seemed to be at the point of collapse, the people and livestock appear to have been doing surprisingly well—with the possible exception of the goat population. When he left, Rolfe had listed 351 men, women, and children; when he got back, there were "about 400. but not past 200. fit for husbandry and tillage."[10] They had tended 144 cattle before, and now they were down by only 16; but the 216 goats had shrunk to a mere 88. Curious though that is, and though we allow for some eccentric counting, the number pales beside the diminution of James Towne's buildings. After the fire of 1608 "we had about fortie or fiftie severall houses to keepe us warme and dry," wrote Smith.[11] Hamor talked about "two faire rowes of howses" in 1614, all two and a half stories high and frame-constructed.[12] Rolfe had reported 50 people living at James Towne in the spring of 1616. Now, a year later, Argall "found but five or six houses!"

And what of the church? What kind of structure was it that could go up and down like a yo-yo? Strachey recalls how in 1610 one of Lord De La Warr's first steps had been to rebuild it and to provide "a Chancell in it of Cedar, and a Communion Table of the Blake Walnut, and all the Pewes of Cedar, with faire broad windowes to shut and open, as the weather shall occasion, of the same wood, a Pulpit of the same, with a Font hewen hollow, like a Canoa, with two Bels at the West end."[13] De La Warr's successors, Gates and Dale, had been equally fervent in their insistence on religious discipline, and it makes no sense to suggest that during their administrations the church had been allowed to run down; but then again it makes no more to argue that such a building could within a year become so dilapidated that its services had to be held in the company store. If, as seems likely, the store was divided into three parts for arms, food, and general materials, one wonders which part or parts accommodated the worshipers.

The reference to "the Well of fresh water spoiled" seems to link all the other complained-about features to the area of the old fort. The first shaft had been dug in 1608 by Newport's men and been replaced by Sir Thomas Dale in 1611 because of "the unholsome water which the old afforded."[14] That no other wells should have been sunk at James Towne in the succeeding seven years is astonishing; nevertheless, Argall's quoted summary of decay refers to "the," and not to "a" well. Smith's mentioning the bridge's being in pieces has long caused historians trouble. "What bridge?" they ask. Biographer Philip Barbour suggests that it may have spanned "the thin neck of muddy sand that tied Jamestown to the mainland" and might already have been partly awash at high tide.[15] However, the word "bridge" was almost certainly being used in a sense foreign to the modern ear. The *Oxford English Dictionary* has the following as its third definition: "A gangway or movable landing-stage for boats. A fixed or floating landing-stage, jetty, or pier." In May 1611 Sir Thomas Dale reported that one of his first acts upon taking over from Lord De La Warr was to use Captain Newport's mariners to build "a bridge to land our goods safe and dry upon."[16]

As the dictionary definition makes clear, the term "bridge" did not necessarily mean a permanent structure; it could also describe a portable gangway between ship and shore that could be run out as needed. Some support for that interpretation may be drawn from a 1620 report from James Towne to Sir Edwin Sandys: "It is not long agone, since ye Governo^r made those that watched here at James Citty to contribute some labo^r to a bridge, and to certaine platformes to mounte greate ordinance upon, being both for ye use and defense of ye same Citty. . . ."[17] The platforms here mentioned may have been no more than planked pallets or mats placed under the wheels of the guns to prevent their sinking into the ground. In 1617 a Spanish fleet being assembled at Gibraltar was reported to be loading "1,500 three-ynche planke to land ordnance or to make platformes on the water,"[18] meaning rafts on which to float the guns ashore. Longer and narrower versions of such platforms would make good movable gangways or bridges. That both bridge and platforms are mentioned consecutively and were to be constructed by the same people having the same skills could point to a relationship in both mind and practice. Were the bridge to be a permanent jetty, it would have involved driving piles into the riverbed, a much more laborious and skilled operation than cutting and pegging boards and rails. Rebutting evidence exists, however, in the shape of an undated description of Virginia, written no earlier than the end of April 1619, which referred to the Dale bridge thusly: "A framed Bridge was alsoe then erected which utterly decayed before the end of Sir Thomas Smith's government, that being the only bridge (any way soe to be called) that was ever in the country."[19] If, therefore, the anonymous author knew whereof he wrote, a post-supported jetty was indeed built but had come apart by the time Governor Argall arrived in 1617. That this could happen continues to be demonstrated along the James River, where combinations of floods and high winds lift boat ramps, jetties, and breakwaters and send their planks drifting to the sea.

In spite of the fact that in 1620 Governor Yeardley ordered James Towne's watchers and warders to contribute their labor to a bridge, we know that by 1623 either the fruits of it had come and gone or the work was never done, for in December 1622 the supply ship *Abigail*'s cargo of arms, "trunckes and such like goods"[20] were left where the tides flowed over them, as would not have happened had there been a permanent jetty onto which to off-load them.

Unhappily (or perhaps happily for historians for whom disputable speculation is the staff of life), James Towne's remaining written legacy can be interpreted to support whatever thesis one happens to be pushing this week. For example, the foregoing bridge evidence can be interpreted quite differently. Because Smith's statement follows immediately after the words "the Palizado's broken," one can argue that the bridge and the palisades were physically related, thus supporting the proposition that a draw or tongue of marsh lying outside the palisades' west gate needed to be spanned by a bridge—to which others can counter that even the laziest of tobacco-growers would have fixed the bridge if that was the only way out of town.

The bridge puzzle is but one small example of the problems that beset everything we think we know about early James Towne. In many, if not most, instances the sum of it is no more than what the Virginia Company of London *wanted* the world to know. Unfavorable reports were destroyed or severely edited, while those that were supportive were transcribed into the Company records and even published. Thus, for example, Alexander Whitaker, in writing to his cousin in London, defended Sir Thomas Dale, who he said had been "much debased, by the letters which some wicked men have written from hence, and especially by one C.L."[21] Needless to say, none of those letters has survived, nor, for that matter, has the identity of the critical C.L.

When bad news did get into the record, it was often because it was sugar coated. "All men cheerefully labor about their grounds," wrote John Rolfe, "their harts and hands not ceasing from worke"—now comes the downer—"though many have scarce ragges to cov^r their naked bodyes."[22] That was unfortunate, but it meant only that these cheerful, hardworking men needed the Company's reluctant subscribers to fulfill their pledges. Positive mileage could be culled from the shirt shortage, whereas there was nothing very useful to be extracted from a report that James Towne's palisades had collapsed or that its houses had vanished. It may, therefore, be no accident that the full text of John Rolfe's generally optimistic letter of June 8 has come down intact but that another written on the following day by the outspoken "Admiral, & for ye time present, principal Govr of Virg^a," Samuel Argall, has not. Instead we have only a clerk's summary, which includes absolutely nothing about the dilapidated state of James

Towne or the colonists' obsession with tobacco.[23] All that information comes from Smith, who attributes it to Argall and to Rolfe. As Rolfe was not specific, it follows that Argall was and that Smith managed to obtain a full copy of his letter.

For that we have to be eternally grateful—while recognizing that Smith, too, was selective, using bits that supported his postures and omitting those that didn't. Although Smith was restrained in his sorrow at the death of Pocahontas, his account omits anything that might be construed as critical of her surviving relatives. Not so with Argall, whose summarized letter recalls how the news of the princess's death was reported to the Indians, saying, "That he sent Tomakin [Tomocomo] to tell Oppachancano of his arrival & he came to James Town recd a present wth great joy. Tomakin rails ag[t] Engl[d] English people and particularly his best friend Tho: Dale [;] all his reports are disproved before opachank[o] & his Great Men whereupon (to the great satisfaccion of y[e] Great men) Tomakin is disgraced."[24]

We had a hint of Tomocomo's resentment in his "white dog" comment to Smith, but now he had come home to tell his brothers what he really thought of the English and their crass, commercialized, and arrogant society. So Tomocomo was disgraced. There is no denying that Argall and the Company would draw comfort from thinking so, and as long as Powhatan and Opechancanough wanted to keep the peace, it made sense for them to disavow publicly the views of their disgruntled envoy. But privately it was almost certainly a different story. They needed to hear everything that he had seen, heard, and thought, and in the long run they were far more likely to believe him than they were the outraged rebuttals voiced by the blustering English. Indeed, Tomocomo's experiences may ultimately have influenced Opechancanough to conclude that "Eastern Civilization" was something that America would be better off without.

For the time being, however, the Indians were content to watch and wait. Besides, 1617 brought them other problems more pressing than the replacement of Yeardley by the less manipulable Argall. A major smallpox epidemic broke out in the summer and coincided with a virus that played havoc with the deer population. Although smallpox also hit the English in the same year, the knowledge that the Indians were hurting without assistance from English gunpowder was in itself cause for complacent satisfaction. Powhatan was now an old man, probably in his late eighties; in Argall's absence, no longer able to dictate the rules of the game, he had left his village on the Pamunkey River and gone to live with the Patawomekes. However, in March 1618, a month before his death, Argall reported that Powhatan "goes from place to place visiting his Country taking pleasure in good friendship wth us."[25] In spite of all this encouragement, many colonists needed no reminding that whites were whites and Indians weren't. Thus in 1618 Argall was to issue a directive banning any trade with "ye perfidious Savages."[26] Even so, the omens were not such as would justify forcing the farmers of James Towne to expend time and effort on rebuilding their fort. Indeed, from this point forward its existence is rarely mentioned.

Samuel Argall's governorship had not been a success. So persistent were complaints about his dictatorial and self-serving decisions that the London Company voted to recall him and substitute the previously ineffective George Yeardley, who, to give him more clout, received a knighthood from the king. John Chamberlain called him "a meane fellow" whose elevation "hath set him up so high that he flaunts yt up and downe the streets in extraordinarie braverie, with fowrteen or fifteen fayre liveries after him."[27] The prospect of another inept governor was tempered by the Company's decision to make the term of appointment three years (Lord De La Warr, the first and last governor for life, being dead) and, more important, to establish America's first attempt at democracy by creating a General Assembly akin to the English parliamentary system.

Earlier in 1618 the ship *Treasurer,* having previously returned to England, was refitted in London allegedly for a fishing trip, but instead of being supplied with "salte hookes lynes, fishermen, or men skilled in fishing," she was secretly armed as a man of war.[28] When the *Treasurer* (commanded by Captain Daniel Elfrid, Elfrey, or Elfrith) reached Virginia, Argall sent her out, allegedly to obtain salt and goats from the Azores. Instead she sailed south into the Caribbean, taking with her "an olde commission of hostility from the Duke of Savoy against the Spanyards"[29] provided by Argall's mentor the piratically inclined Sir Robert Rich (soon to be earl of Warwick) in what amounted to an Elizabethan-style privateering expedition. To man the ship, Argall reportedly conscripted some of the colony's best men and sent them "rovinge in ye Spanish Dominions in the West Indies."[30] In short, and in the view of the Warwick faction's opponents, Rich and Argall had deliberately, and for personal gain, dispatched the *Treasurer* to poke a stick into the Spanish hornets' nest.

In April 1619, before the *Treasurer* returned, Argall heard that he was being replaced, and so departed to face the music on his own terms, leaving the governorship temporarily in the hands of another 1607 survivor, Nathaniel Powell, whom he had previously appointed captain of the guard, lieutenant governor, and commander of James Towne and its blockhouses and people—in that order.

At the end of August a 160-ton Dutch warship with an English pilot arrived at Point Comfort, its captain reporting that he had met up with the *Treasurer* in the Caribbean and that they had agreed to sail together but had lost sight of each other. Short of victuals for the transatlantic voyage, the Dutchman offered Yeardley and cape merchant Piersey the only commodity he had to exchange—namely, "20. and odd Negroes."[31] Although some confusion persists, it appears that the Dutch ship was carrying additional slaves belonging to Argall and the *Treasurer* and that those were later left in the Bermudas.[32] If true, the dubious credit for the intent to introduce blacks to Virginia in the seventeenth century belongs to Argall. Yeardley, on the other hand, was simply agreeing to help out a visitor in distress and probably saw the landing only as a not particularly advantageous deal. Africans had been traded in the Americas for more than a century, but they had not hitherto been imported by the post-1607 English into Virginia for three simple reasons: The London-controlled settlement system was not geared to lifelong slave labor; the laboring and servant needs of the colony were better drawn from those whom England would be glad to see gone; and thirdly, the early supply ships being fully fitted out and paid for in England, they were expected to make the fastest possible crossing to ensure that everything and everybody arrived intact. As we have seen in the previous century, English slave trade experience had taught that visits to African slave ports or buying already enslaved blacks in the Caribbean courted both sickness and the ire of the Spaniards, either of which could sever the supply lifeline to Virginia.

Four days after the Dutchman's departure the *Treasurer* came into Hampton Roads, but when Captain Elfrid learned that Argall was gone and that Yeardley had received orders from London that "the shipp be seased upon ymediatly upon her returne,"[33] he upped anchor and headed for the treacherous yet more friendly shores of the Bermudas, where his ship was to end its life "starke rotten and unserviceable."[34] Before quitting Virginia, Elfrid voiced a warning: Unless Yeardley quickly installed cannon at Point Comfort, the colony would be lost. He had heard from Spaniards in the West Indies that come the spring, they would be on James Towne's doorstep. In view of the fact that the *Treasurer* had been down in the Caribbean stirring them up, the likelihood of an invasion must have seemed very real, and according to John Rolfe, the prospect did "much to disharten the people ingenerall." In a letter to Sir Edwin

Sandys, Rolfe outlined just how unready Virginia was to repel a Spanish invasion:

> wee have no place of strength to retreate unto, no shipping of certeynty (wch would be to us as the wodden walles of England) no sound and experienced souldyers to undertake, no Engineers and arthmen [i.e., earthmen: sappers] to erect works, few Ordenance, not a serviceable carriadge to mount them on; not Amunycon of powlder, shott and leade, to fight 2. wholl days, no not one gunner belonging to the Plantacon.[35]

Rolfe did not address his letter from James Towne, but when he wrote that nowhere was there a strong place to which to flee, he hardly could have overlooked the worth of James Fort. As for the cannon, without carriages to support them or a trained gunner to load and fire them, James Towne in 1620 was more vulnerable than ever before.

Nothing specific is known about the Spanish threat, but Captain Elfrid may have heard that the Spaniard who knew Virginia best, Diego de Molina, had returned to Spain, "where he was made Generall of six tall shippes . . . and as we weare after certenely informed sett outt of purpose to Supplantt us."[36] To secure royal support, Molina had shown his king a piece of silver he had obtained while in Virginia and convinced Philip that there was a silver mine there worth the taking, or so it had been reported in London in June 1618.[37] The enterprise was planned and manned in Spain rather than in the Caribbean, for George Percy, who is the source of most of what little we do know, went on to tell how, after being a month at sea, Molina's crew mutinied and stabbed him to death, "Whereupon their Course was alltered and their former determinacyon ceased."[38] Had Diego de Molina or any other Spanish general sailed up the James River with malice in mind, no one can doubt that James Towne would quickly have collapsed in a pile of splinters. With the heart destroyed, resistance at the isolated, undermanned, and powder-poor plantations would have been brief, while those homesteads overlooked by the Spaniards would soon have fallen to the Indians.

Since the death of Powhatan, his Tidewater empire had been ruled by his half-brother Opitchapam, about whom very little is known other than that he confusingly changed his name to Itopatin and very soon disappeared to be replaced by the redoubtable Opechancanough, who continued to smile and accede to the wishes of the colonists. The latter's generic attitude toward coexistence with the Indians was well put by another clerical gentleman, Jonas Stockham (or Stockton), who explained that he saw "no probability by faire meanes alone to draw the Savages to goodnesse . . . and till their Priests and Ancients [Elders] have their throats cut, there is no hope to bring them to conversion."[39]

Powhatan's long life had made him an institution in the minds of both the Indians and the English, but in his waning years he had become easy-going and indecisive, leaving it to younger men to look to the future with practical and increasingly concerned eyes. It is significant, however, that when Opechancanough finally grasped the reins, he reportedly tied his most fateful decision to the ritual burial of his great predecessor.

Just as the English had Westminster Abbey in which to bury their kings and keep their sacred relics, so the Powhatan Indians had their royal shrine at Uttamussack beside the Pamunkey River. But instead of a single structure, they had three, each sixty feet long and "filled with images of their Kinges and devills, and tombes of their predicessors."[40] Although details provided by Strachey and his Roanoke forerunner Thomas Hariot are not entirely clear, it is evident that the dead king was not immediately placed in the tomb. First the corpse was disemboweled, and then the skin was stripped from the flesh with razor-sharp shells and dried. Next, most of the remaining flesh was cut away, leaving what must have been a some-what messy skeleton, which was then placed on a bier and allowed to dry in the sun. Once the decay had advanced to the point where the last of the flesh was gone but the bones were still held together by sinews, the artic-ulated skeleton was taken down, encased in leather, and its body cavity stuffed "with perle, Copper, beades, and such Trash sowed in a skynne."[41] That done, the king's own skin was then replaced and sewn over the leather base to re-create his original appearance. Neither Hariot nor Stra-chey commented on the quality of the likeness, probably because neither had an opportunity to view a weroance both immediately before and after his cosmetic surgery.

Hariot's account, as well as De Bry's accompanying illustration, makes it clear that the royal entombing described to him ended with the mummified king's being laid naked on a raised platform within the tomb house alongside his predecessors. Strachey's description, on the other hand, ends with the rebuilt cadaver rolled in a mat. Either way, it is clear that the transference of the remains (at which stage is not clear) to the tomb house paralleled any European royal funeral.

In 1621 word reached James Towne that Opechancanough intended to use the ceremony of "the takinge upp of Powhatans bones" as an empire-wide cue to destroy simultaneously every English plantation.[42] Opechan-

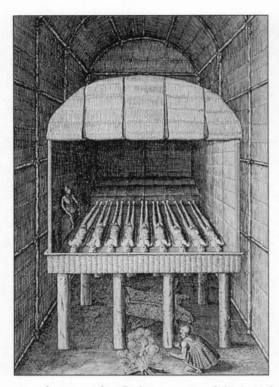

Left: De Bry's 1590 engraving of the tomb of Virginian "Cheiff Lordes," illustrating Hariot's report and adapted from John White's rendering of 1585. Hariot explained that the priest-custodian lived under the platform supporting the mummies. Although he is shown here, he is absent from White's original drawing. *Above:* Tubular copper "beads" wrapped around the forearm of an Indian as part of the burial procedure. From an ossuary of ca. 1550–1610 discovered on a Paspahegh village site five miles above James Fort.

canough denied it, but Governor Yeardley was taking no chances. He visited each English settlement, took a general census of all their men and weapons (a record which, alas, does not survive), and called on them to keep constant guard. But nothing happened, and in time everyone relaxed. So it was that on the "fatal Friday" of March 22, 1622, only James Towne was prepared for the slaughter and destruction that followed.

Although, according to John Smith (who wasn't there), the massacre was triggered by the death of Nemattanow, alias Jack of the Feather, the gun of retribution had long been loaded and aimed. In the previous five years the English presence had expanded dramatically. Between 1619 and 1621 forty-two ships had been sent out, carrying 3,570 male and female settlers. Although attrition brought about primarily by disease had been incredibly heavy, an estimated English population of about 350 in 1618, when Powhatan died, had grown to somewhere between 1,200 and 1,400 by March 1622. Whereas the earlier colonists had been fairly well controlled by the Company's leaders, the newcomers were an increasingly inconsiderate and scrofulous lot, as the quality of volunteers culled from the taverns and alleys of London, Plymouth, or Bristol declined. Not only their attitude but their physical diseases were having their impact on the order and health of Indian life. Then, too, the creation of the many subsidiary English companies, some such as Martin's Hundred claiming exclusive ownership of twenty thousand acres and more, generated territorial disputes with the Indians on a scale unknown in Powhatan's lifetime. Thus, for Opechancanough the squeeze was on, and his regret must have been that he had not done what needed to be done when Powhatan died and the odds were in his favor.

The Jack of the Feather spark, if such it was, resulted from his visit to the house of a man named Morgan and an invitation for the latter to go trading with the Pamunkeys. Morgan accepted and was not seen again. Three days later Jack returned to the house and told two of Morgan's youthful servants that their master was dead. The story here becomes increasingly improbable, for Jack came wearing Morgan's cap, causing the boys to conclude that the Indian had murdered him. They then shot and severely wounded Jack. Uncertain what to do next, they bundled him into a boat and set out on an eight-mile trip downriver to deliver their bleeding prisoner to then Governor Sir Francis Wyatt. Jack, who had for years had boasted that no bullet could harm him, pleaded with his captors that they keep the truth a secret; then he died.

According to Smith, Opechancanough first sent Wyatt threats of revenge, but when he got back "such terrible answers," he substituted "the greatest signes he could of love and peace." Two weeks later he struck—to the inexplicable surprise of the English.

It's true that we do not know the specifics of Opechancanough's "great threats of revenge,"[43] but the fact that he got an answer from the English makes it clear that his reaction to Jack's death was not merely for effect. Coupling these threats with those made at Powhatan's funeral, the colonists had good reason to look to their defenses, yet they seem to have done nothing until a small boat grounded before dawn on the shore at James Towne. Out of it clambered a breathless Richard Pace. He had rowed three miles in the dark from his plantation in Quiyoughcohanock territory, carrying a warning from a friendly Indian named Chanco who, though "belonging to one Perry," was living in Pace's house. Waking Pace, who the subsequent report stated "used him as a Sonne," Chanco revealed that he had received instructions to kill him and that in the morning others would come "from divers places to finish the Execution."[44] Chanco had received his orders from his brother (another of William Perry's Indi-

ans) who was spending the night with him, and we may deduce that
Chanco got out of bed ostensibly to do the murder and instead gave his
warning.

There is no evidence that Chanco intended anything more teacherous
to his own people than saving the life of a man who had been like a father
to him, and as he turned up again a year later as an envoy for Opechancanough, it is possible that none of his people knew that his was the weak
link in the chain of Indian vengeance. Indeed, a letter written by retired
Virginia Company treasurer Sir Edwin Sandys after all the post-massacre
reports had been analyzed in London indicated that warnings had come
from more than one Indian. However, that documentation being lost, we
are left only with the story of Richard Pace's famous rowing exploit carrying Chanco's warning to James Towne.

No details survive to tell us what happened there after Governor
Wyatt received Pace's report and the settlers braced themselves for the
impending onslaught. The only detailed account was later published in
London, using information derived from several eyewitness reports, and
like most Company-approved releases, it no doubt edited out bits that
failed to fit the scenario. Virtually nothing is said about any attack on
James Towne beyond the statement that as the result of Pace's warning, an
attack "was prevented there, and at such other Plantations as was possible
for a timely intelligence to be given." Without specifying whether it meant
James Towne or the other warned plantations, the report added only that
"where they saw us standing upon our Guard, at the sight of a Peece [mus-
ket] they all ranne away."[45] So there went our best hope of learning anything specific about James Fort's ability to withstand assault—the closing
of its gates, the method of manning its palisades, or the firing of its guns.
Indeed, there is no certainty that it was even attacked.

Years later, in the last volume of the De Bry family's *Historia Americae*,
a highly fanciful engraving shows men, women, and children being
slaughtered while eating their breakfast, trimming timbers, and generally
going about their normal business, and in the background a riverside town
defended by belching cannon and about to be invaded by four Indian-
filled canoes. Over the years this detail has been separately redrawn and
hailed as the only contemporary illustration of James Towne. By the time
it was published by Virginia historian Lyon G. Tyler in 1900, the town had
taken on the appearance of a Victorian military cantonment.

That no deaths were reported from Jamestown Island or from plantations on either side of the river in its immediate vicinity indicates that the
report was correct in saying that Wyatt had time to warn a few of his

Detail from de Bry's engraving of Indians attacking unsuspecting
colonists in 1622. In the background a typically European fortified
community represents James Towne, its defenders firing cannon
at boatloads of approaching Indians. Not published until 1632,
the engraving may have derived from a broadsheet woodcut
printed in London as company propaganda in the immediate
aftermath of the massacre.

neighbors. But seven miles downstream, and at points above the Chickahominy all the way to the falls, the settlers were taken completely by surprise. This is how a survivor described what happened:

> . . . as in other dayes before, they came unarmed into our houses,
> without Bowes or arrowes, or other weapons, with Deere, Turkies,
> Fish, Furres, and other provisions, to sell, and trucke with us, for
> glasse, beades, and other trifles: yea in some places, sate downe at
> Breakfast with our people at their tables, whom immediately with
> their owne tooles and weapons, eyther laid downe, or standing in
> their houses, they basely and barbarously murthered, not sparing
> eyther age or sexe, man, woman or childe; so sodaine in their cru-
> ell execution, that few or none discerned the weapon or blow that
> brought them to destruction.[46]

The reported death toll was put at 347, but we know it to be inaccurate.
Some 20 people, 15 of them women, who were listed as dead were instead

The fort at Wolstenholme Towne, ca. 1621.

taken hostage. Then again, at the other end of the scale, several of the dead may have been in remote sectors and failed to make the list. At Martin's Hundred, one of the few major plantations of the pre-massacre period to have been extensively studied both archaeologically and historically, about half its population survived, protected, we must suppose, by the walls of its palisaded fort. How many more plantations possessed such substantial retreats only archaeology will tell. As for James Fort, if it provided a refuge for the island's beyond-the-pale inhabitants, no record has survived to tell us so. Indeed, were it not that we have passing references to it in 1624, one might be tempted to conclude that it had ceased to exist before Opechancanough played his ace.

Like modern newspaper stories which invariably report the anomalous but rarely the commonplace, so it has been throughout recorded history. Consequently, much of what we know about life in early Virginia we owe to its lawbreakers, to the people who wound up in court. Richard Barnes was one of them. Sentenced on May 10, 1624, for having uttered derogatory remarks about the governor, he would live to regret it—though not in the fort.

The Counsell have therefore ordered that Rich: Barnes (for his opprobrious & base speeches of the Governour) shall be disarmed, & have his armes broken & his tongue bored through wth a awl.

shall pass through a guard of 40 men & shalbe butted by every one of them, & att the head of the troope kicked downe & footed out of the fort: that he shall be banished out of James Cittye & the Island.[47]

Such was the price of unduly free speech. It was not, however, as bad as it reads, for the broken arms were not his limbs but his weapons. At the same time, being turned out into the forest with a hole in one's tongue and without any means of defense was nobody's idea of fun.

The second case involving the fort went to trial five months later, when John Proctor was accused of killing his servant Elizabeth Abbott. She evidently was not the best of maids; but that seemed hardly to warrant a beating of five hundred lashes. Nor was it her first such punishment. A witness who had seen her bruised and bleeding testified that she said she had been whipped with fishhooks. True or not, the last beating was one too many. Another witness reported finding her body "aboute two stones cast of the houses within the forte."[48] We know, therefore, that as late as October 10, 1624, houses were still standing inside its palisades.

A third case, this one heard on August 10, proves that Argall's 1618 complaint about tobacco-growing within the fort had been ignored. The charges involved the alleged theft of privately grown tobacco and the claim by one witness that "some Parte of the tobacco wch grew in the forte was caryed and mixt wth the Companies Tobacco."[49] The grower, Mr. Utie, claimed that he had raised a sufficient number of plants within the palisado to generate about 100 pounds of tobacco. In 1619 John Rolfe stated that a single man could successfully tend 4 acres of corn and 1,000 plants of tobacco, and Professor of Agriculture Lyman Carrier has estimated that that number would generate about 112 pounds of tobacco.[50] Another witness in the Utie case testified to having packed a "chest full of Tobacco wch was growne wth in the Forte and to his Judgment there could be no less then 150^{li} waight." Yet another witness told the court that give or take 40 or 50, one could grow 3,000 tobacco plants to the acre.[51] Colonial Williamsburg's landscape architect Kent Brinkley independently arrived at fairly similar figures: 2,723 plants to the acre, each plant occupying 16 square feet, thus a total of 43,560 square feet.

The seventeenth-century witnesses were providing posterity with the only substantive clue to the size of James Fort since 1610, when Strachey had put it at half an acre. Now they were saying that one 150-pound barrel of tobacco grown inside the fort would take about 1,500 plants occupying approximately half an acre—thus in Strachey's terms, palisade-to-palisade planting, with no space left over for buildings, for booting sore-tongued lawbreakers, or anything else.

The record of yet another court appearance may or may not relate directly to the fort. Captain Richard Quaile had been found guilty of delivering intemperate speeches and on March 11, 1624, was sentenced to be "igominiously degraded from his degree of Capt[,] his sword broken and he sent out o[f] the port of James Citty with an ax on his shoulder afterwards to be broughte in agai[n] by the name of Richard Quaile, Carpenter And that he sha[ll] sett uppon the pillory wth his eares nayled thereto & they either to be cutt of or redeemed by payinge the fine of 100^{li} sterl[ing]."[52] The point here is that ex-Captain Quaile was sent out through the "port" of James City. Although this could be a misreading of "fort," it almost certainly means the city gate. If it is the latter, the reference may still be to the entrance described by Strachey in 1610 as "the principall Gate from the Towne, through the Pallizado, [which] opens to the River."[53]

Putting all these clues together, we are left with the reasonable certainty that the old palisaded James Fort was still standing in 1624, that there were several houses and the old storehouse still inside it, but that much of the interior had been given over to growing tobacco, which, in August, stood sufficiently high for Elizabeth Abbott's battered body to lie unnoticed in it for several days. Witness Thomas Gates had found her "about two stones cast" from the fort's houses. Had she been outside the fort, Gates would not have mentioned the houses but only the palisades. But how long was a stone's cast? In James Fort's heyday, its houses ranged in rows parallel to the three palisade walls, leaving a marketplace toward the center, but Gates seems to be saying that those houses still in the fort were grouped together and that the planted area extended away from them to a distance considerably more than two stone's throws, for had that distance put Miss Abbott's body close to the palisaded perimeter, the witness would almost certainly have used the shorter measurement.

If Thomas Gates's 1624 testimony seems to separate the houses from the tobacco, how does it equate with the 1617 description attributed to Governor Argall which says that "the market-place, and streets, and all other spare places [were then] planted with Tobacco"?[54] The inference here is that James Towne remained pretty much as it had when Strachey described it in 1610. If not, then the marketplace and tobacco-sprouting streets must have been moved out of the fort. There is, however, no documentation to say so. An alternative could be that between the years 1617 and 1624 major changes *did* occur within the fort and that the interior had looked very different to the newly arrived Governor Argall from the way it did to the dying Elizabeth Abbott. However, the previously quoted "Briefe Declaration" says otherwise. In its description the condition of James Cittie at the time of Governor Yeardley's arrival (eleven years after the fire) there "were only those houses that Sir Thom. Gates built in the time of his government, with one wherein the Govr allways dwelt, an addition being made therto in the time of Captaine Saml Argoll."[55] This crucial statement persuasively argues against any expansion since Gates's departure in 1614.

Into this pot one has to stir another passage from the "Briefe Declaration," which, in discussing both Henrico and James Towne, says this: "Fortifications against a foreign enemy there was none, only two or three peeces of ordinance mounted, & against a domestic [enemy] noe other but a pale inclosinge the Towne, to the quantitye of four acres within which those buildings that weare erected, could not in any man's judgement, neither did stand above five yeares & that not without continuall reparations."[56] While recognizing some ambiguity as to whether the description related to Henrico or to James Towne, the engineer and archaeologist Colonel Samuel Yonge plumped for the latter, accepting the four-acre enclosure reference as important James Towne documentation. In reality, however, there can be very little doubt that the description related to Henrico. Several passages scattered throughout the "Briefe Declaration" show that the anonymous author had lived there and that when he wrote that "we built such houses as before and in them lived with continual repairs, and building new where the old failed, untill the massacre,"[57] he could only be meaning Henrico, which was attacked and abandoned, and not James Towne, which was spared.

If the space within the James Towne fort remained more or less constant from 1607 to 1624, by the latter date the nomenclature had become increasingly grandiose. James Fort had become James Towne, and that in turn expanded into James Cittie. The census or muster tabulated on January 24, 1625, listed James Cittie as having twenty-four households comprising 58 family members and 67 servants, 9 of whom were black. These 125 people were distributed through twenty-one houses; collectively, therefore, a community not much larger than that of 1607. Lest it be argued that "James Cittie" included the whole of Jamestown Island, I should add that the muster provided a separate listing for "James Iland" where 50 more people were distributed through eleven houses.

The James Cittie muster also listed three storehouses, two of them belonging to Abraham Piersey, the cape merchant. The third was owned

Houses built beyond the protection of the James Fort palisades.

by the governor, Sir Francis Wyatt, under whose name is listed the property "Belonging to James Citty: Church 1; A Large Court of Guard, 1; Peeces of Ordnannce Mounted, 4; Quilted Coats, 16; Coates of Male, 77; The rest dispersed in the Cunttrie."[58] Ex-Governor Sir George Yeardley had the largest number of servants, twenty-four of them (eight black), seven of whom made up the crew of his forty-ton three-masted barque. He also owned a shallop and a skiff. Four other people had among them five boats of unspecified type, all moored or beached at James Cittie.

As the muster gives a total of twenty-one houses in James Cittie and as we know that much of the interior of the fort had been given over to tobacco-growing, it follows that many of the dwellings were outside the palisades, thus supporting the thesis of a bawn village, with its rows of unprotected houses and its fort wherein lived the leader. As previously noted, an official governor's residence had been built during the Gates administration (1611–14) "at the charges and by the Servants of the Company and since enlarged by others by the very same means"[59] and certainly as late as 1619 remained where it had begun. Logic dictates (Ratcliffe's palace notwithstanding) that this location was within the protective walls of James Fort and was still there in 1624. We also know from testimony in the Elizabeth Abbott case that there were still plural "houses within the forte." One may reasonably suggest, therefore, that Sir George Yeardley's three dwellings were also within the palisades.

An added puzzlement is provided by the fact that while the muster lists several forts at neighboring plantations, it lists none on Jamestown Island. The only sensible conclusion has to be that James Cittie's cited "Large Court of Guard" was then how the fort was officially described. But sensible though it may be, the interpretation is not well supported by the term's accepted usage. Chambers's *Cyclopædia* (1738) describes a *corps de garde* thusly: "a post in an army, sometimes covert, sometimes in the open air, to receive a body of soldiery, who are relieved from time to time, and are to watch in their turns, for the security of a quarter, a camp, station, &c."[60] About half a century earlier Randle Holme called it "the place where the cheife gard is kept, from whence rounds and grand rounds are continually sent to keepe other gards watchfull."[61]

Because, in 1625, Governor Wyatt is shown as having only four male servants at James Towne (one of them aged thirteen), the guarding obviously did not come from his immediate household. However, the muster also lists a dozen of "The Governors Men" on the mainland beyond the glasshouse on the three-thousand-acre tract laid out by Argall in 1617 and initially called Pasbehaighs—ironic recognition of the fact that it had been a Paspahegh village and hunting territory. The governor's dozen men are shown to have been somewhat haphazardly armed and armored. Among them they sported eight or ten guns and ten swords, but only two helmets, eight assorted types of body armor, and no reported housing. However, a thirteenth man, John Swarbeck, may have been their sergeant, and he is listed as having his own gun, sword, and armor as well as one house. The inference, therefore, is that by 1624 the military situation had so changed that the governor felt confident enough to put his troops to farming off the island and more than a mile from James Fort. Just who did duty at the *corps de garde* or performed the nocturnal watching and warding remains (like so much else) open to speculation.

Collectively, the evidence points to the fort's having become a civic center where the governor lived, where the court sat, and where, in 1619, in the church, the first General Assembly was held—always supposing that the church was still within the old palisades.

You may recall that when Argall returned with John Rolfe et al. to take over the governorship in May 1617, he found the church not merely crumbling but "downe." He therefore had to erect an entirely new structure. It was slightly smaller than the original one, measuring only fifty by twenty feet; nevertheless, it was in this that the first General Assembly convened. Because excavations within the later brick church in 1901 revealed the foundations of an underlying structure of uncertain length but twenty-foot width, the conventional wisdom has been that these were the remains of Argall's church—therefore, *outside* the fort. That one church should rise on the site of another makes perfect sense. At the same time, however, one cannot ignore the fact that a structural width of twenty feet was not unique to churches. Nor, as I shall suggest in the next chapter, is it wise to dismiss out of hand the possibility that the brick church was inside the fort.

Since we know that it was in Argall's new church that the 1619 General Assembly met, logic dictates that the courts also convened in the church. As the available evidence points to justice being meted out within the fort, it is probable, too, that the jail stayed there and that the pillory still stood in the old marketplace. That the banished Richard Barnes and the humiliated Captain Quaile both were evicted through the fort and city gate is persuasive evidence that at least as late as 1624 the fort remained the ceremonial and administrative heart of James Towne and of the colony. Whether it had any military value is another question.

The January 1625 census had been the product of a royal commission set up to study the state of the colony in the aftermath of the 1622 massacre and to review its by then much-criticized management system. Feuding between the Virginia Company and the semi-independent Sommer Islands Company (for Bermuda) had become an open scandal and led to the Privy Council's putting Virginia Company treasurer Sir Edwin Sandys under house arrest for abusing the earl of Warwick. That led to another Virginia Company council member, Lord Cavendish, challenging Warwick to a duel, which would have taken place in the Netherlands had not the English government intervened. This, and much else, made the king decide to be "graciously pleased to take into his royall care the State of the Plantation of Virginia and of the government thereof."[62] That was not a step to take without first very carefully testing the waters, to which end the Privy Council issued an order that three lords, Gradison, Carew, and Chichester, should put together a report based on a set of ten proposals, the first of which was that forts were "to be erected in places healthfull and best for safety and defence."[63]

A month or so later a set of responses was forthcoming, though unfortunately there is no documentation to prove whose views they represent. Here is the first of them:

> The places antientlie best fortified were the Cities of Henrico and Charles [originally Bermuda City] wch are now utterlie demolished by th'Indians: And the fortifications about James Citie &

Elizabeth Citie [Kecoughtan] have ben suffered by the Colonye of late to grow to such decay that they are become of no strength or use[,] so that as to the first point the truth is That at this tyme there are no places fortified for defence & safetie for the Access of Shipping from the Sea and Boates uppon the Rivers.[64]

That crushing dismissal of James Towne's fortifications is not reflected in the previously cited court references to the fort. However, the reported destruction of Henrico in the 1622 massacre was true enough. With the exception of Martin's Hundred and Edward Bennett's plantation on the south side of the James at Warraskoyack, Henrico and its environs had been hardest hit. Five miles above it, on Falling Creek, the ironworks operated by Captain John Berkeley lost 27 people, including Berkeley himself; three miles downstream at Thomas Sheffield's settlement, Sheffield, his wife, and 11 others were killed; at Henrico Island only 5 died (suggesting that the much-vaunted city was scarcely inhabited), but across the river at the site of the new college "for the training up of the Children of those Infidels"[65] 17 men were lost. And so on down the river, to a reported total of 347 dead out of a total population of about 1,400.

The answers to Lord Chichester had more to say about the destruction wrought by the Indians, yet at the same time they provided generic information about the quality of housing: "But the plantacons are farr asunder & their houses stand scattered one from another, and onlie made of wood, few or none of them beeing framed houses but punches sett into the Ground And covered w^t Board so as a firebrand is sufficient to consume them all."[66] Although, as I have noted, there is no proving who provided this information or whether its supplier had actually seen what he reported, the finger of suspicion points, at least in part, to the ex-governor of the Sommers Islands, Captain Nathaniel Butler, who in October 1622 decided to pay a call on Virginia before returning to England. There is good reason to believe that he, the earl of Warwick's man, was sent to gather ammunition for Warwick to fire at Sir Edwin Sandys. If so, Butler did his job well. On his way back to England he wrote a vitriolic treatise titled *The Unmasked face of o^r Colony in Virginia as it was in the Winter of ye yeare 1622*. Circulated while the London investors were still reeling from the impact of the Indian massacre, Butler's broadside came close to sinking the Company. It also precipitated the clash between Warwick and Sandys.

Butler's testimony has to be heard with caution, for if, as some believe, he was angling for the governorship of Virginia, it was to his advantage to paint as grim a picture as he could of the current administration's short-comings. On the other hand, he was the first known Englishman to visit the colony solely to observe and report. We cannot doubt, therefore, that he actually inspected the palisades of James Fort and crossed the thresholds of its houses. To do so, therefore, he must also have landed at the site chosen in 1607 because the "shippes doe lie so neere the shoare that they are moored to the Trees in six fathom water."[67] Butler recalled: "I found the shores and sides . . . every wher soe shallow as no Boate can approach the Shores Soe that besides the difficulty daunger and spoyle of goods in ye Landinge of them, the poore people are forced to a continuall wadinge and wettinge of themselvs."[68] Although Butler was speaking in general terms of riverside conditions along the James, had those at James Towne been any different, someone surely would have said so. Instead his criticism endorses the sailors' account of how, while Butler was still in the colony, the *Abigail's* relief supplies rotted at the water's edge. As for the fort, he had this to say:

> I found not the least peec of Fortificacon: Three peeces of Ordinance onely mounted att James Citty and one att Flowerdue hundred [Yeardley's plantation] butt never a one of them serviceable; Soe y^t itt is most certaine that a Small Barke of 100 Tunn may take itts time to pass upp the River in spite of them; & cominge to an Anchor before ye Towne may beat all their houses downe aboute their ears and soe forceinge them to retreat into the woods may Land under ye favour of their Ordinance and rifle the Towne att pleasure.[69]

The author of the ca. 1625 "Briefe Declaration" said much the same thing, but was a little more specific. He recalled that "For fortification against a forreign ennemie there was none at all; two demi culverin only were mounted uppon rotten carriages and placed within James Citty, fitter to shoot downe our houses then to offend an ennemie."[70] Although these witnesses are telling us that when Yeardley returned as governor in 1618, and certainly by late 1622, no fort survived at James City, one remembers that the court records reveal that it was still serving a civic, if not a military, function in 1624.

Butler did not comment specifically about the quality of the James Cittie houses, but he did have some characteristically pithy observations about dwellings in general. They were, he said, "the worste that ever I sawe[,] the meanest Cottages in England beinge every way equall (if not superior) wth the moste of the best." He also inspected what was left of Henrico and Charles City and found both "wholly quitted and lefte to ye spoyle of the Indians who . . . burned the houses said to be once ye best of all others."[71]

When, in London on April 23, 1623, the court of the Virginia Company heard to its dismay that a copy of Butler's report had been submitted to the king, it hastily launched a campaign of counterpropaganda, rounding up witnesses who would testify that his charges were false and scandalous. A week later at a meeting (attended also by Butler and his supporters), Sandys was ready to present "The Answers of divers Planters" who claimed (along with much else) that arriving boats drawing three to four feet of water could safely land and that nobody had to wade to bring goods ashore. While allowing that all the colony's defenses were of palisade construction, they reported that "allmoste everie Plantacon hath one" and that some also had trench protection.[72] As for the guns, all were in good working order, four of them at James City, six at Flowerdew Hundred, seven at Henrico, two at Charles City, three at Kecoughtan (Elizabeth City), and three more at Newport News.

Sandys's supporters had more trouble finding good things to say about the houses, admitting that most were "built for use and not for ornament," then hastily adding that since they were the homes of laboring men, "wch wee cheifly professe our selvs to be," their English parallels were "in no wise generally for goodnes to be compared unto them."[73] That, of course, can be read in any way you care to choose. Less equivocation was required when it came to the houses of "men of better Ranke and quallety." Those, claimed the Company's promoters, were so much better than their English counterparts that "noe man of quallety wthout blushinge can make excepcon against them."[74] As we have seen, the later questions and answers stemming from Lord Chichester's inquiry took those claims with several grains of salt, concluding that few, if any, of the dwellings were anything better than puncheon structures (meaning posts set directly into the ground and not into sills atop brick or stone foundations) all ready to burn at the spilling of a candle. Three and a half centuries later, archaeologists produced the evidence to support that conclusion.

Excavations on sites beside the James River in the 1970s and 1980s have uncovered the remains of several dwellings dating from the 1620s and 1630s, and although ranging from cottages to relatively large houses, virtually all have been of the puncheon type, their quality progression limited to the increasingly regulated spacing of postholes' dark stains into pairs back and front, indicative of the formalized framing units called

Patterns of post-constructed buildings at Wolstenholme Towne
erected around 1620 and typical of construction practices in the first
years of colonization.

bays. Unlike the tells of Mesopotamia, the towering obelisks of Egypt, or
the pillars of Greece and Rome, the first ruins of America are often so
ephemeral that once they are exposed, a sudden shower of rain or an
overzealous student shoveler can wipe them out. Can we be surprised,
therefore, if conservative historians suspect that our archaeological conclusions are enhanced by generous ingestions of jimsonweed?

CHAPTER XIV

Stinking Beer and Other Calamities

W HEN ONE stands on the Park Service's manicured lawns at Jamestown today, it is hard to imagine how much hope, regret, fear, hatred, hunger, pain, and dying were experienced at this place or at least *near* this place in the seventeen years between the first landing and the dissolution of the Virginia Company in 1624. Mortality throughout the colony in that period has conservatively been put at about six thousand, and in the first years the majority of those who succumbed to sickness, disease, and starvation ended their lives at James Towne. Other estimates put the overall mortality much higher, and we know that of some five thousand settlers sent over between 1620 and 1623, the number had been reduced to about fourteen hundred by the time of the 1622 massacre. On more than one occasion, however, there was a significant but, alas, undefined difference between the number who were recorded as sailing and those who actually arrived. A single letter from James Towne speaks more eloquently to that point than can any statistics:

Deare Sister eare this yo^u should have heard from me, had not th'extremitie of sicknes till now hindered me. For o^r Shipp was so pestered wth people & goods that we were so full of infection that after a while we saw little but throwing folkes over boord: It pleased god to send me my helth till I came to shoare and 3 dayes after I fell sick but I thank god I am well recovered[.] *Few els are left alive that came in that Shipp:* for here have dyed the Husband, wife, children & servants: They tould me they sent the Shipp less pestered for me, but there never came Shipp so full to Virginia as ours.[1]

The writer was Lady Margaret Wyatt, wife of the governor, and the ship the *Abigail,* the one whose cargo of arms lay rusting in their crates on the James Towne beach.

On May 18, 1622, before news of the massacre reached London, the Virginia Company had signed an agreement with Captain Samuel Each, the *Abigail*'s master, to transport Lady Wyatt and numerous new settlers. But when the first reports of the tragedy arrived and were magnified by every retelling, many an intended settler changed his and her mind. Indeed, the initial response of Company members was to blame the survivors as an ungodly lot who had earned His retribution and so should be left to their fate.

Had that view prevailed, the history of American colonization might have taken a very different turn. With the English dislodged from their still-precarious foothold in Virginia, Spain would almost certainly have moved in, planting a culture perhaps never to be superseded. But the view did not prevail; a heavy propaganda campaign by the Company convinced waverers that with a little more perseverance all would be incredibly well. Consequently in October the *Abigail* and her companion ship, the *Seaflower,* rode at anchor off the Kentish coast in the sheltered waters behind the Goodwin Sands, waiting for Lady Wyatt and her retinue to board.

The colonists had asked for a regiment of trained soldiers to drive out the Indians once and for all, but troops were not forthcoming. Instead, as a gift from the king, a large quantity of arms and armor, described as "unfit for modern service," was loaded aboard the *Abigail*—with the exception of a supply of England's traditional weapon, the longbow. Because, in the minds of unnamed bureaucrats, sending the bows directly to Virginia might help the Indians learn to make more powerful bows of their own, the longbows were to be carried aboard the *Seaflower,* which would stop at Bermuda on the way and leave them there until needed.

Captain Each was a seaman long on experience and short on patience, and the slowness with which the relief supplies of corn were arriving for loading, coupled with his desire to get clear of the English Channel before the worst of the winter turned even the safe anchorage into a hazard, made him decide to sail alone, leaving the *Seaflower* and the corn and other supplies to follow as soon as they were stowed. Lady Wyatt's letter to her sister is the only surviving account of the *Abigail*'s nightmare voyage, and it fails to tell us how soon after she sailed the contagion broke out among the passengers and crew. It is evident, however, that by the time the ship reached James Towne on December 20, 1622, the overcrowding of which the governor's lady complained had been no little alleviated—resulting, it was claimed, from the drinking of contaminated beer.

"I would you Could hang that villaine Dupper who with his stinking beere hath poisoned most of the Passengers, and spred the Infection all over the Collonie wch before the Arrivall of the Abigall were recovered."[2] So wrote the colony's secretary, George Sandys, three months later. The charge against the brewer Jeffrey Dupper may or may not have been just, though the records show that it was not the first time he had been accused of selling a poisonous product; but regardless of the cause, the effect was indisputable.

Most of the *Abigail*'s passengers were replacements sent out by the subsidiary companies, like the Society of Martin's Hundred, to substitute for their people killed in the March massacre. When the ship reached James Towne, it clearly was the responsibility of the colony's physician, Dr. John Pott, to quarantine the ship and everyone on it. His decision not to do so (always supposing that he was allowed to make the determining judgment) was almost certainly colored by the presence aboard of the not-yet-ill Lady Wyatt. To have bottled her up with the dying would have been awkward at best, but to have allowed her ashore while leaving other seemingly well passengers on the ship would probably have started a riot. Consequently, the new arrivals were permitted to travel to their assigned plantations, where, it would seem, no efforts were made to sequester them until they proved themselves to be healthy. That this should have been allowed to happen is extraordinary. We know, for example, that an isolation hospital or pesthouse had been erected at Henrico. Nevertheless, like firing a poisoned shotgun into the colony, the carriers went where their papers instructed. Thus the 1,400 population, which had been reduced to about 1,050 by the massacre, was now whittled down to scarcely 500 by the bounty of the *Abigail*.

Demoralized by the massacre and intimidated by the still-militant Indians (who in a subsequent mini-massacre reportedly killed another 30), the survivors had done little through the summer of 1622 to replenish their food supplies. Instead they were content to rely on the expected relief ships from England. One can well imagine, therefore, the reaction at James Towne when the *Abigail* arrived with crates of arms and armor and very little food. Fear not, Captain Each doubtless told them, the corn would be close astern aboard the *Seaflower*.

For more than three months all eyes were on the river for the first sight of a sail. But none came. From Martin's Hundred, Richard Frethorne, one of the *Abigail*'s passengers who had come as a servant to that plantation's governor, wrote this on April 3, 1623:

> Wee are as like to perish first as anie Plantacion, for wee have but two Hogsheads of meale left to serve us this two Monethes, if the Seaflower doe stay so long before shee come in, and that meale is but 3 Weeks bread for us, at a loafe for 4 about the bignes of a pennie loaf in England, that is but a halfepenny loafe a day for a man. . . . What will it bee when wee shall goe a moneth or two and never see a bit of bread. as my M^r [master] doth say Wee must doe, and he said hee is not able to keepe us all, and then wee shalbe turned up to the land and eate barks of trees, or moulds of the Ground. . . .[3]

But the *Seaflower* never did come in—and Richard Frethorne died.

Though much delayed, the ship had made a relatively uneventful passage to Bermuda, where she dropped anchor in St. George's Harbor on or about March 18, 1623. Although a few men and boys were reported dead (as was only to be expected and was taken in stride), her captain celebrated the safe arrival by throwing a party in the great cabin for numerous distinguished Bermudian friends. Meanwhile, below in the gun room his eldest son, the gunner, entertained at a more modest level where "drinckeinge [smoking] Tobaco by neclygense of ther fyer Blue uppe the Shyppe."[4] With her stern blown apart, the *Seaflower* quickly sank into the harbor, where she remains today.

News of the *Seaflower*'s fate was slow to reach Virginia, and as we have seen, Richard Frethorne was still in hopes two weeks after the last splinter splashed down into the blue Bermudian water. Luck, good or bad, is said to run in threes; it was to do so for Virginia's sick and starving colonists. And all of it was bad.

In the aftermath of the massacre Governor Wyatt had launched several counterattacks against the Indians, the details of which are both sparse and confused. Sorties against the Appomattoc, Chickahominy, Quiyoughcohanock, and other tribes along the upper James River resulted in many villages burned, fishing weirs destroyed, and corn seized, but few Indians killed. "The Salvages are so light and swift," John Smith explained, "though wee see them (being so loaded with armour) they have much advantage of us though they be cowards."[5]

According to Virginia Company records, no fewer than ten ships sailed for Virginia in April and May 1622, their passengers and crew unaware of the bad news awaiting them on the other side. The smallest of the ships, the 50-ton *Bonaventure,* carried only 10 passengers, while the two largest, the *White Lion* and *Furtherance,* each of 180 tons, boarded 100 men and 40 cattle between them. In all, in the space of two spring months the Company shipped out 580 unsuspecting settlers and 120 cattle. Few, it seems, ever arrived, and the historian Alexander Brown, who could find only that the *Bonaventure* and the 130-ton *Gift of God* reached James Towne, observed that the others' "fate is unknown to me; but it probably lies concealed, with other tragedies of American colonization, within the bosom of the Atlantic."[6] John Smith, Monday-morning-quarterbacking in London, identified none of the ships by name but dismissed those that did arrive as "some pety Magazines."[7]

Augmenting supplies brought aboard the English ships, Governor Wyatt sent the *Discovery* and other vessels as far north as New England in search of food. Most reliance, however, was placed on the Patawomeke Indians and their weroance, a longtime friend to the English who, in spite of the polarization generated by the massacre, was no friend to Opechancanough. Consequently, several expeditions sailed up the bay to the Patawomekes in a continuing quest for food. The polarization was two-sided, and with Wyatt's blessing and commissions, his expedition leaders were free to treat any Indian as a foe and to take what they wanted "by force and any other meanes they can devise."[8] Through planted rumors, crossed signals, or possibly an inept interpreter, Captain Isaac Madison, the leader of one such expedition, concluded that the king of the Patawomekes had entered into a secret agreement with Opechancanough and intended to murder the English traders. The king denied it, claiming that he was the victim of a plot "to kill mee for being your friend."[9] Madison nevertheless seized the king, his son, and two others, promising to hold them hostage only until his own men were safely back on their ship. Instead Madison took the prisoners aboard, hoisted sail, and carried them back to James Towne. Several days later Ralph Hamor, who was setting out on a voyage to Newfoundland, paused long enough en route to return the four prisoners to their tribe, but not before demanding an unspecified quantity of corn as ransom.

Such treatment of their premier Indian friend was not only dishonorable but incredibly stupid, as John Smith was at pains to point out. "Ever since the beginning of these Plantations," he wrote, "it hath beene supposed the King of Spaine would invade them, or our English Papists indevour to dissolve them. But neither all the Councels of Spaine, nor Papists in the world could have devised a better course to bring them all to ruine, then thus to abuse their friends. . . ."[10] That happened in November, before the arrival of the contagion-ridden *Abigail*. Although the various ploys to obtain corn had been marginally profitable, the colonists' success in burning Indian fields not only denied the Indians their sustenance but also meant that they had less to be looted. Furthermore, the massacre and the month or more of indecision that followed had meant that the colonists' own planting was late and the crop poor, much of it either harvested too soon or, in tit-for-tat retaliation, destroyed by the Indians. Thus it was that the English went into the winter with their food supplies dangerously low and emerged from it facing the prospect of being turned out into the forest to grub for roots and to eat bark off the trees.

When weeks slipped by without sight of the supply-carrying *Seaflower*, Governor Wyatt ordered another trading expedition up the Chesapeake to the Patawomekes, this time sending as leader the man most able to paper over the autumn's disgraceful betrayal. We met him first as a twelve-year-old boy, when John Smith sold him without his knowledge to Parahunt, weroance of the Powhatans. Harry Spelman had spent his youth in and out of Indian service, and as you may recall, having tired of living with Powhatan at Werowocomoco (and having witnessed the slow and gruesome execution of President Ratcliffe), he had secretly joined the retinue of the visiting king of the Patawomekes and had returned with him and remained with the tribe until Samuel Argall found him there in 1610. Although Spelman subsequently went home to England, he was soon back in Virginia, spending in all about fourteen years there and becoming, in Smith's opinion, "one of the best Interpreters in the Land."[11] He had, however, a reputation for speaking out of turn, and in 1619 had paid the price for undermining the authority of the then governor, Sir George Yeardley, by telling Opechancanough that "within a yeare there would come a Governor greatter then Him that nowe is in place."[12] Charged with treason, Spelman could have lost his life; instead he lost only his captaincy and was made to serve the colony for seven years as an interpreter.

It may have been Yeardley's successor, Sir Francis Wyatt, who recognized that good men were too thin on the ground for Harry Spelman to serve out his years in the doghouse, and even before the massacre he had been reinstated. Now, given command of the ship *Tiger* and with an unidentified pinnace (also described as a shallop) in support, Spelman set out with a complement of about thirty-one of the colony's best available men, at least four of whom were sailors aboard the *Tiger*. Arriving in

Patawomeke territory, Spelman learned from a passing Indian the scarcely unexpected news that his old friend and mentor the king was no longer any Englishman's brother.

Thus warned, Spelman and his men approached the town in full armor and with swords drawn and muskets primed. When asked by the king why they came in so belligerent a fashion, "Spillman tauld him of his distrust and shewed him the man that gave him Warninge, Wheere upon ye kinge in his presence caused the fellowes head to bee cut of & cast into the fire beefore the sayd Capten his face."[13]

One would have thought that, being the best interpreter in the land, Spelman would have gotten the message; but the next morning he and twenty-five men returned to open trading negotiations. With only the four sailors and perhaps one or two others left on the *Tiger,* Spelman and the rest went ashore in the pinnace, leaving aboard it all their armor and most of their weapons. That was a mistake.

There are four very different accounts of what happened next. In one the sailors on the *Tiger* were approached by several canoes filled with Indians who were not recognized as unfriendly until they actually invaded the ship. Vastly outnumbered, one of the sailors had the presence of mind to fire a cannon, whereupon the shocked attackers leaped overboard and swam ashore, abandoning their canoes. In this, Smith's version, the crew later heard a great shouting among the Indians onshore and saw a man's head (presumably Spelman's) thrown down the bank. There being no point in lingering longer, the sailors weighed anchor and headed home.

In another telling, the *Tiger's* crew knew that something was amiss when they saw a group of Indians smashing up the beached pinnace. When sixty canoes of Indians headed in the ship's direction, the sailors "whiffed up sayles & went faster then theyr canowes & so left her."[14] In the third version the Indians captured not only the pinnace but also "a Shallopp, and a small Boate wth 26 men all in Compleat Armour the 27th of March 1623."[15] However, in the fourth narrative, having seized the pinnace, the Indians mounted Captain Spelman's head atop a pole at its stern "and so rowed home." Later they attempted an assault on the *Tiger,* not with sixty canoes, but with two hundred, manned by a thousand warriors![16] That was the way Richard Frethorne of Martin's Hundred heard it: twenty-six valuable men slain and the pinnace and its contents captured. For the always excitable Frethorne, the disaster at the Patawomeke had nightmarish possibilities. The Indians "have gotten peeces [muskets], Armour, swords, all thinges fitt for Warre," he wrote, "so that they may now steale upon us and wee Cannot know them from English till it is too late. . . ."[17]

That the Indians would have been foolish enough to strap on the heavy English armor is hardly likely; but Frethorne was undoubtedly right when he added that they "can use peeces, some of them, as well or better then an Englishman."[18] However, the most circumspect post-mortem came from the quill of settler Peter Arundel:

> Wee our selves have taught them how to bee trecherous by our false dealinge with the poor kinge of Patomeche that had alwayes been faythfull to the English, whose people was killed[,] hee and his sonne taken prisoners brought to Jeames towne, brought home agayne, ransomed, as if he had beene the greatest enemy they had: Spilmans death is a just revenge. . . .[19]

For most survivors of the 1622 massacre no needles of guilt pricked their consciences. They had seen and buried the scalped and skin-stripped corpses of their relatives and friends, and no treachery was too base if it led to the death of a savage.

When Governor Wyatt heard that some of the men taken by the Pata-womekes at the time of Captain Spelman's death were still alive, he dispatched Captain Daniel Tucker and ten men to obtain their release and "withall in culler [appearance] to conclude a pease with the great Kinge Apochanzion."[20] Special preparations for the project were handled by one of the more odious characters to stain the pages of Virginia history. Dr. John Pott, who had been introduced to the Virginia Company in 1621 as "well practised in Chirurgerie and Phisique, and expert allso in Distill-inge of waters and that hee had many other ingenious devices,"[21] demonstrated his skills by preparing the special drink wherewith the peace would be toasted. And so it was:

> After a manye fayned speches the pease was to be concluded in a helthe or tooe in sacke which was sente of porpose in the butte with Capten Tucker to poysen them. Soe Capten Tucker begane and our interpreter tasted before the kinge woulde tacke yt, but not of the same. So thene the kinge with the kinge of Cheskacke, [their] sonnes and all the great men weare drun[k] howe manye we canot wryte of but yt is thought some tooe hundred weare poysned[,] and thaye comying backe killed som 50 more and brought hom part of ther heades.

The seal granted to the Virginia Company of London in April 1606.

It was perhaps a fitting conclusion to so heinous a crime that the perpetrators should sink to the level of those they considered savages and bring home the scalps of their victims. Colonist Robert Bennett, who wrote the account, ended it by declaring, "God sende us vyctrie, as we macke noe question god asistinge."[22] In England, however, men of conscience reacted with horror, and when in July the king expanded his investigative commission to include on-site members in Virginia, at the insistence of the earl of Warwick, Dr. John Pott's name was stricken from the list because "he was the pysoner of the salvages thear."[23]

Collectively these events contributed to the demise of the Virginia Company and to changing attitudes and policies that were to shape the colony's future while hastening the death also of Powhatan's empire. The troika disasters of the *Abigail*, the *Seaflower*, and Harry Spelman's expedition had been nails driven hard into the coffins of the old order.

In London the Company, already torn by factional animosities, received little joy from the returning *Abigail*. Captain Each had died, more than half his passengers who had reached shore were already dead, and more were expected to follow, and there was still no news of the *Seaflower*. What the ship did take back, however, were letters from survivors in Virginia amounting to a litany of misery, from Frethorne complaining about his clothes being in rags and a colleague's having stolen his cloak (and then dying without telling him what he had done with it) to a man who considered himself relatively well off but whose "wife doth nothing but talke of gooing home."[24] Another spoke for the less fortunate who had no wives, could not afford to buy one, and had to pay exorbitant prices to get their washing done.

Women are necessary members for the Colonye [wrote settler Thomas Niccolls to Sir John Wolstenholme], but the poore men are never the nearer for them they are so well sould, for I myselfe have ever since my coming payd 3^{li} ster p An [pounds sterling per annum] for my washing & find sope. A hard case not having had for all the service I have done the Company not one pipe of Tobacco consideracon. I am sure for all these women yor poore Tenants that have nothing dye miserablie through nastines & many depte the World in their owne dung for want of help in their sicknes[;] Wherefore for prevention I could wish women might be sent over to serve the Company for that purpose for certayne yeares whether they marry or no. For all that I can find that the multitude of women doe is nothing but to devoure the food of the land without dooing any dayes deed whereby any benefitt may arise either to ye Company or Countrey.[25]

Doubtless Niccolls was writing in both frustration and jealousy, but his reference to "the multitude of women" is a useful reminder that by the time of the massacre the number of women in the colony had greatly increased. Indeed, fifteen were among twenty hostages taken by the Indians, one of whom enjoyed the dubious privilege of being ransomed by Dr. Pott for two pounds of beads. Once freed, Jane Dickenson found herself bound in servitude to Pott to compensate him for their value and later petitioned the governor to be released on the ground that "shee hath already served teen months, tow much for two pound of beads," and that her treatment by Dr. Pott "much differeth not from her slavery wth the Indians."[26]

In 1619 the Company had sent out eight ships, between them carrying 650 people "sent for Publicke and other pious uses," among them 90 "Young maids to make wives for so many of the former Tenants."[27] In June 1620, 100 more (plus a like number of servant boys) were being assembled. The quality of possibly earlier shipments would be questioned later, when the conduct of Sir Thomas Smythe's administration of the Company came under fire, charging (among many another accusation) that "He sent but few women thither & those corrupt." Defender Sir Nathaniel Rich answered that on the contrary, "He sent a great many & those of the best hee could gett & some such whose Husband since hath ben knighted & made Governo^r of Virg."[28]—this a telling riposte, using Sir George Yeardley and his wife in evidence.

Regardless of Rich's defense, complaints that previous shipments had been of uneven quality had almost certainly filtered back to London by

1621, prompting the Company in its next supply to insist that aboard the *Marmaduke* "Wee send youe in this Shipp on[e] Widdow and eleven Maids for Wives for the people in Virginia," each carefully screened and all accepted "uppon good Commendacons." They were not to be wasted on servants, said the Company, but were to be offered "only to such freemen or Tenn[an]ts as have meanes to manteine them."[29] In September fifty more quality "maids & yong woemen" were dispatched aboard the *Tiger*—probably the same ship later used by Captain Spelman. With the cost of shipping taken into account, the women were to be priced to prospective husbands at not less than "one hundredth and fiftie [pounds] of the best leafe tobacco," and proportionately more if any should die on the way over. They came, said the Company, with a packet of testimonies to "theire honest life and cariadge, wch together wth theire names we send here inclosed for the sattisfaccon of such as shall Marry them."[30] Although the council in Virginia made no complaint about the quality of the shipments, it wrote back complaining that the maids had not been provided with food, and asking that the next lot "bringe some smale pvisione wth them to help them . . . untill they may bee convenientlie disposed of."[31]

Regardless of the exported women's true moral character—and one cannot help wondering who of moral character and sound mind would have volunteered to go to the edge of the earth to be sold like breeding stock to men they didn't know—the popular English presumption was less than flattering. Thus a Londoner introduced to a woman who had come back from the colony turned to the by then aging but still-contentious John Martin and asked, "is this one of you^r Virginia whoores?"[32]

The Company's rationale for shipping the women was sound enough, and it could hardly be blamed for the moral turpitude of a few. Indeed, a cynic might argue that, as in frontier towns of the American West, they served a useful function. Much more important was the Company's recognition that if the colony was to be controlled and to prosper, its male inhabitants had to put down roots, and "wifes, children and familie might make them lesse moveable and settle them, together with their Posteritie in that Soile."[33] It was true, and there can be no doubting that Virginia's "maids," though looked upon as chattels, and often most cruelly treated (as was the pregnant seamstress who made a shirt too short and whose court-ordered whipping caused her child to miscarry), played a role no less important in cementing the colony than did the men. Tragic it is, therefore, that so few of their names survive.

As is so often true of major enterprises in their early phases, much more careful recording was maintained when the numbers were small, manageable, and pioneering. Thus we know the names of most of the people who went as Ralegh's settlers to Roanoke Island as well as those who landed on Jamestown Island in 1607 and those who followed in the 1608 supply. But once exporting working people became old hat, numbers were of more lasting concern than names: so many on this ship and so many more on that. It's true that we have lists of the dead in the 1622 massacre, a tabulation of those who survived in 1624 and those who didn't, and the magnum muster of 1625; but between 1608 and 1622 we have only the occasional name—most often those lucky enough to survive to be listed in the muster, which usually noted the year of arrival and the name of the ship that brought them.

Even when the lesser names survive, learning whence they came and what they contributed is rarely possible. Across four centuries, when many people had the same names and when any one of them would be spelled in whatever way the scribe cared to write it, being sure that you had the right John Smith (unless, of course, he was *the* John Smith) is defiantly difficult. On the other hand, like the cast of any memorable drama, the biographies of the stars are a matter of record, but nobody remembers who played the maid—unless, like Elizabeth Abbott, she happened to be whipped almost to death with fishhooks.

The star of the great Virginia adventure, though offstage throughout the later acts, unquestionably was Sir Walter Ralegh. Imprisoned in the Tower of London in 1606, he remained there for ten years, though under sufficiently liberal arrest to be able to provide the Company with the benefit of his experience. In 1610, or thereabouts, Ralegh had appealed to the king through a letter to Queen Anne reminding her that "I long since presumed to offer your Majestie my service in Virginia, with a short repetitio of the commoditie, honor, and safetye which the King's Majestie might reape by that plantation, if it were followed to effect."[34] But the king was taking no chances. Six years later, when Ralegh finally was paroled, he was able to raise enough money from old friends to mount one more expedition, not to Virginia but to the Orinoco in search of the fabled El Dorado, the Indian king who, clad in gold, bathed in a lake whose bed was strewn with golden tribute.

James somewhat hesitantly approved the project, but warned that if harm was done to Spanish property, it would cost Ralegh his life. Even with that assurance, Philip's ambassador, Don Diego Sarmiento de Acuña [Count Gondomar], raised merry hell, claiming that Ralegh was also planning to attack Spain's annual treasure fleet—which was true. When Ralegh admitted as much to Francis Bacon and the latter warned that it

Detail from de Bry's engraving showing Sir Walter Ralegh conferring with aboriginal leaders in Guiana in 1595, their revelations providing the rationale for the last disastrous expedition to the Orinoco in 1617 that led to his execution in the following year.

would be sheer piracy, Ralegh retorted, "Did you ever hear of men being pirates for millions?"[35] But the Orinoco expedition failed, and in the resulting clash with the Spaniards a town was burned—and Sarmiento hit the roof. Ralegh's companions, fearing James's wrath, rejected his argument that if the prize was big enough the king would forget his threat, and refused to join in attacking the Spanish *flota*. They elected instead to scatter. Four ships went north, Ralegh's among them, intending to catch fish off Newfoundland. So it was that in 1618 Sir Walter Ralegh finally reached what once had been *his* Virginia, sailing up the Carolinian Outer Banks, past Hampton Roads and the Chesapeake Bay, and on beyond Cape Cod and the abandoned Fort St. George on the Kennebec, but visiting none of them as he sailed brokenly homeward to face arrest, trial, and execution—to satisfy the king of Spain. On October 29, when Ralegh mounted the scaffold in Old Palace Yard and placed his head on the block looking west toward the New World, someone advised him to turn it eastward to Calvary. "What matter how the head lie," he replied, "so the heart be right?"[36] Then the ax fell.

Ralegh's widow kept his head in a red leather bag until she died in 1647 at the age of eighty-two. The bag then passed to Carew, their second son, and thereafter into his grave—which probably was just as well.

Although even unto his last moment Ralegh had continued to look westward, other key players turned east to end their careers. Sir Thomas Dale had taken part in an Anglo-Dutch expedition to open trade with the Chinese and died at Masulipatam on the Malabar Coast in 1619; two years later Sir Thomas Gates followed him to the East Indies and reportedly died there. Samuel Argall was cleared of his piracy charges, knighted, and put forward for a second term as governor of Virginia in 1624 but lost out to Sir Francis Wyatt. Characteristically, Argall quickly overcame that setback and in the following years went on to command the Anglo-Dutch fleet that seized seven Spanish ships worth a hundred thousand pounds and then, following in the wake of Drake, launched a successful attack on Cádiz. He died on the way home, perhaps from a stroke following a row with his ship's master.

There would be no such dramatic exit for John Smith, who made repeated efforts to get back into the American swim. Shifting his interest from the southern colony northward to New England, he made three attempts to launch new settlements, two in 1615 and the last in 1617. All failed, and he spent the remaining frustrated years of his life being helpful about Virginia to anyone who would listen. In the aftermath of the 1622 massacre he called on the Company to provide him with a ship, thirty sailors, and a hundred soldiers, and with them he would "inforce the Salvages to leave their Country, or bring them in that feare and subjection that every man should follow their business securely."[37] Smith and his men would remain as a standing army ready to defend the colony against all comers. It was a prospect that did not excite a company whose aging leaders had long memories and who concluded that the last thing they needed was a loose cannon to add to their American troubles. It was a nice idea, they told him, and good of him to offer, but right now they couldn't afford it. John Smith died at the age of fifty-one in London in 1631, leaving as his legacy his books, his maps, and his controversial personality, which together will keep his memory flamboyantly alive as long as there is a Virginia.

George Percy never came again to Virginia. Instead in 1625 he returned to military service in the Low Countries and in 1627 had a finger shot off—an inconvenience which had nothing to do with his death in 1631. His fellow chronicler William Strachey, after returning to England in the expectation of advancement within the Company, and through it the prospect of making advantageous friendships, was disappointed, and like John Smith, he was destined to remain an outsider; but unlike Smith, he did not suffer the pain of obscurity for long. Strachey died in 1621.

Title page from John Smith's legacy to America, *The Generall Historie of Virginia . . . &c.*, first published in 1624.

After returning to Virginia as secretary in 1617, John Rolfe married again and more conventionally, choosing Joane, daughter of William Pierce, who had come over aboard the *Blessing* in 1609. Rolfe made his will in 1622 and admitted to being "sick and weak in body," foretelling his death in the same year.[38] The often heard conclusion that he was killed in the 1622 massacre is not supported by the documents, which failed to list him among the dead. His son, Thomas Rolfe, whom we last saw left behind in Plymouth, grew up to become a respected Virginia planter holding two thousand acres across the river from James Towne. When news of Pocahontas's death reached Opechancanough, the latter is said to have proposed proclaiming the infant Rolfe to be the Indians' king, thus to do a leadership end run around James Towne's administration. But nothing came of it.

Ralph Hamor aspired to the title of captain not because he had been Governor Argall's vice admiral aboard the *Treasurer* but because, like many another leading settler, he took command of a company of fifteen men in defense of the colony under the system originally set up by Sir Thomas Gates. The title, however, carried no salary, and in 1623 the then secretary George Sandys wrote that "Capt. Hamor is miserablie poore,"[39] a comment seemingly at variance with the evidence of the 1625 muster, which listed him as having three servants at James Citty and seven more on Hog Island, where he owned an unspecified number of houses but only armor for four of his men. Although I have been unable to find documentation for the use of the word "poor" in the sense of "poorly" before 1758, the fact that Sandys's comment was written at a time when the colony was racked with the contagion brought aboard the *Abigail* almost certainly points to Hamor's having been poor in health but not in pocket. If so, he proved luckier than most who took sick in the winter of 1623, for he lived until 1626, having married twice and sired two children. Unfortunately the will that would have resolved the question of Hamor's wealth or lack of it is lost.

Sir George Yeardley also died in the colony, but certainly not in penury. Until he sold them in 1624, he had owned twenty-two hundred acres at Weyanoke and across the James River from it the thousand acres of Flowerdew Hundred, where sixty-three people were then living, eleven of them blacks. In the next year's muster Yeardley and his family were resident at James Citty with three houses and twenty-four servants. He died in 1627, leaving his widow and three children, among them his only son, named Argall as evidence of the warm relationship that had existed between two very different governors.

Of the old guard's spiritual leadership, the Reverend Whitaker had drowned in 1617, but James Towne's minister and *Sea Venture* survivor the Reverend Richard Buck fared better. He enjoyed the distinction of delivering the opening prayer at Virginia's first General Assembly, and when he died in 1624, he left some 750 acres planted in the Corporation of James City, as well as two dwellings, numerous cattle, and at least four sons, one of whom, Benoni (meaning "son of my sorrow"), had the distinction of being "the first idiot born in that plantation."[40]

And then there was Gates's decoy, Dowse, the dancing drummer— James Towne's "Everyman," put upon, always good for comic relief, but smart, courageous, and lucky. Thomas Dowse rose to represent the decaying Henrico at the 1619 General Assembly, survived the massacre there, and by 1624 he and Mrs. Dowse had moved to Elizabeth City (Kecoughtan), where they employed at least two men. He also retained four hundred acres at Charles City, which he was still planting in 1626. In short, Dowse, the taborer, was one of the first to scale the great American ladder of capitalistic opportunity.

Not so lucky, yet luckier, Opechancanough outlived them all, surviving long enough to witness the death of freedom as the Indians knew it, and the destruction of a civilization and of the environment that had nurtured it for the best part of a thousand years. His was not a European-style culture of the kind that the Spanish destroyed in Peru and Mexico. Its architecture aspired to no towering temples of stone, nor its art to dizzying heights of the goldsmith's or potter's fancy, yet it lived in harmony with the seasons, respecting the environment, worshipping the universal God, and finding fulfillment in ways that only European poets cared to recall.

That assessment rests upon the presumption that Opechancanough was the younger half brother of the great Powhatan, and that his own roots were buried deep in the Algonquian culture. As long ago as 1703, when Robert Beverley was writing *The History and Present State of Virginia,* he reported hearing from the Indians that Opechancanough was not related to Powhatan, but was "a Prince of a Foreign Nation, and came to them a great Way from the South-West: And by their Accounts, we suppose him to have come from the Spanish Indians."[41] Were that so, however, it is almost certain that in the aftermath of the 1622 massacre, Company apologists would have found in it some hint of a Spanish connection.

For twenty-two more years Opechancanough ruled the old Powahatan Confederacy, keeping his distance yet coexisting with the English as best he could, until in 1644 he saw a second, and almost certainly his last, opportunity to be rid of them. By then he was about ninety years old, so frail that he had to be carried on a litter and so weak that aides had to hold his eyelids open. His mind, however, needed no assistance. Hearing that England was embroiled in a debilitating civil war and likely to be too preoccupied to pay attention to the fate of its Virginia colony, Opechancanough once again called in his markers and on April 18 attacked the plantations in a second massacre. Although it was more successful than the first in that it resulted in more than five hundred English dead, its impact, proportionately to the by then much greater population, was far less serious.

Retribution was swift and relentless. Opechancanough was captured, taken to James Towne, and there imprisoned with a view to shipping him to England as a gift to the beleaguered Charles I. Mercifully, in that the Indian patriarch was spared the voyage and the subsequent humiliation, the James Towne English proved so ill-disciplined that they could not protect their prisoner from themselves. Unable to see or to recognize his danger, the defenseless old man died at the hands of a soldier who boldly shot him in the back.

With Opechancanough's murder, the last link with the pioneering years of John Smith and James Fort came to an end. With him, too, went the memory of the fort's evolution from its first brushwood bulwark, through the fire, the five-square form, and the renewed triangle. What, if anything, remained of the old palisades in 1644 is hard to say, for so much depends on precisely where the fort stood in relation to the growing town.

In an enthusiastic attempt to resolve that question, but only vaguely aware of what to look for, in the summer of 1934 the United States Department of the Interior assembled the prescribed numbers of picks and shovels, marshaled its Civilian Conservation Corps troops on Jamestown Island—and began to dig.

CHAPTER XV

Day of the Diggers

T HE HISTORY of historical archaeology as a definable research
discipline in America began at Jamestown in the 1930s, albeit
lacking any prefatory adjective until it came to be known to the
National Park Service as "historic sites archeology." That is not to say that
digging for American history was unknown before the 1930s. Far from it.
As we have seen at Roanoke Island, exploratory trenches had been dug
there by Talcott Williams as early as 1895. Two years later, at Jamestown,
Mary Jeffery Galt took credit for digging with her own hands "quite deep
inside of the south wall of the church."[1] She is, however, better remembered as the originating spirit behind one of America's oldest and most
prestigious preservationist organizations, the Association for the Preservation of Virginia Antiquities, generally known as the APVA.

The association had been preceded in Williamsburg in 1884 by the
founding of the Katherine Memorial Society by Cynthia B. T. Coleman
in memory of her daughter and dedicated to preserving and restoring the
old colonial capital's Bruton Parish Church. But Mrs. Coleman and her
largely distaff associates soon recognized the need for a statewide organization to "preserve just such records of the past as are attracting the interest and attention elsewhere." Their stated aim was not only to repair
church monuments and tombs but to preserve "buildings in which stirring deeds have been enacted, and where they have been destroyed to
mark the spot on which they stood."[2] This, then, became the APVA's
conceptual mandate, and four years after its creation it accepted twenty-
two and a half acres of Jamestown Island from their owners, Mr. and Mrs.
Edward E. Barney, patriotic benefactors who themselves undertook
quasi-archaeological digging on their remaining property in 1901. This

was the same year that the APVA with the help of engineer John Tyler, Jr., excavated the interior of the brick-towered church, a site previously described as "a picture of desolation."[3]

From the first days of its Jamestown stewardship, the APVA looked upon its island acres with an almost mystic reverence, and beginning in May 1895, it conducted a pilgrimage to eulogize the memory of the first heroic, even saintly settlers, an annual event which still occupies an important place in the Virginia calendar. To old families struggling to recapture their historic identity in the aftermath of the Civil War and the embarrassment of Reconstruction, Jamestown ensured Virginians their right to a place at the high table of American history. As a 1907 guidebook explained it, the Far East had its Mecca, Palestine its Jerusalem, and the French their Lourdes, "but America's only shrines are her altars of patriotism—the first and most potent being Jamestown; Jamestown, the sire of Virginia, and Virginia the mother of this great Republic."[4]

James Towne had ceased to be of political importance when its fourth statehouse burned on October 21, 1698, prompting in the following year the long-discussed moving of the colony's administration to an embryonic Williamsburg, where it remained through the rest of the colonial era. Jamestown Island was never completely abandoned, however. Much of it became the eighteenth-century plantations of the Travis and Ambler families, though the Travis "mansion house . . . by the water side,"[5] which had been the focal point for a bicentennial pilgrimage for some two thousand visitors in 1807, had gone by 1837, leaving little but the brick Ambler House and its dependencies to keep Jamestown alive. By that date the last of the Amblers had departed, leaving the property to pass through several ownerships before the house burned for the third and last time in 1898.

A surviving photograph of the plantation house, though admittedly taken in winter, showed it to be a bleak and grim pile devoid of any environmental embellishment save for a dirt path flanked by rows of paper mulberries, trees renowned for their gnarled and forbidding appearance. Hyphen-linked wings that had given the building its magestic, river-fronting spread reputedly had been torn down by Union troops camped on the island during the Civil War. Thus it came to pass that by the close of the nineteenth century the sole monuments to Jamestown's three hundred years' history were the new Ambler ruin and the old church tower.

Other remains were said to have existed at the beginning of the century and were recalled by former President John Tyler when he addressed celebrants of the founders' 250th anniversary and spoke of ruined houses running in "a connected street" east and west from the Ambler House as

Top: Early stages of excavation within the brick church at Jamestown, ca. 1901. There can be little doubt that valuable information was lost as a result of such haphazard digging. *Bottom:* Ruins of the eighteenth-century Ambler House on Jamestown Island.

far as the church.[6] Historian Lyon G. Tyler interpreted these as the remains of seventeenth-century James Towne's "Back Street," though no archaeological excavation has yet revealed any trace of such a line flanking the Ambler ruin.

Nineteenth-century paintings and engravings of the crumbling church tower show it surrounded by a picturesque jungle of trees and vines, its brickwork in the firm grip of the ubiquitous Virginia creeper: in short, a New World manifestation of Britain's Gothic Revival taste for romantic ruins. The truth, at least in the mid-century, was otherwise. When it came time to celebrate the 1857 anniversary, William Allen, then the landowner, had planted crops in the immediate vicinity of the church, forcing the pilgrims to pay their respects elsewhere. Two years later Massachusetts Senator Edward Everett and a group of friends visited the tower to plant ivy around its base as a substitute for creeper that had died off, the donors blissfully unaware that nothing is more damaging to mortared brickwork than is ivy.

As early as 1816, in addition to the ferry plying between Surry County on the south side of the James and Jamestown on the north, the steamship *Powhatan* provided service between Richmond and Norfolk, stopping at Jamestown to transfer passengers to a horse-drawn bus which shook them back and forth over the rutted road to Williamsburg. Consequently, there was continuing activity at Jamestown's wharf and wooden reception buildings over the years. Because, after 1865, the landing jetty ran out into the river close by the old church tower and its adjacent gravestones, travelers from either boat or bus must often have had time to contemplate the past while awaiting their vehicular futures. Those passengers aside, there was too little of interest to draw visitors to the historic site save on commemorative occasions, but with the advent of the APVA and the approach of the 1907 tercentennial of the first landing, a new vitality was expected. In 1894 the federal government appropriated ten thousand dollars to enable the Corps of Engineers to build a concrete breakwater to arrest erosion along the river frontage, and following the APVA's excavations within the church, the Society of the Colonial Dames of America built the still-standing memorial church overlying the remains of the excavated seventeenth-century foundations. Bronze statues of John Smith and Pocahontas were commissioned, but, like much else planned for the 1907 exposition, they weren't installed in time. The Smith bronze was unveiled in May 1909, and the now-famous demurely buckskinned figure of Pocahontas did not reach Jamestown until 1922.

The Jamestown ferry landing and the churchyard as visitors saw them in the waning years of the nineteenth century.

Bronze statue of Pocahontas by William Ordway Partridge, commissioned for the Jamestown Exposition of 1907 but not installed at Jamestown until 1922.

In line with the enigmas surrounding Pocahontas's life and death in England and the evolution of her engraved and painted portrait, the history of her bronze statue is curiously incomplete. In the spring of 1905 the APVA's Jamestown committee received a letter from "Mr. Davis of Oklahoma" seeking permission to erect a memorial to Pocahontas at Jamestown.[7] After approving the plan, the committee got word that a society to be called the Pocahontas Memorial Association had been formed in Washington for the same purpose. Not wishing to reverse itself, the APVA prudently put the Washington group in contact with Mr. Davis and was gratified to learn that with his help the Memorial Association had "succeeded in raising funds" to erect the monument.[8]

In October 1906 the Jamestown Committee heard that another letter had been received, this from "Mr. A. M. Davies," who may or may not have been the Mr. Davis of Oklahoma, with a somewhat unnerving archaeological request. He wanted to dig up the bones of Pocahontas from her Gravesend grave and bring them to Jamestown "and place a monument over them."[9] This, of course, raised all sorts of ethical and practical problems, not the least of them being how to separate the right bones from the many other interments in the nave of St. George's Church, which, to compound the problem, had burned down in 1727 and been rebuilt four years later. The committee wisely ducked the issue and referred it to the Pocahontas Memorial Association, which in turn did nothing.

In December 1906 the chosen sculptor, William Ordway Partridge, visited the island with Colonel Samuel Yonge of the Army Corps of Engineers and others and selected a site for his creation. But four years later work was still in progress on the pedestal, and no one was saying anything about the statue. Although intended for Jamestown, it had been set up in 1907 outside the administration building on the Norfolk exposition grounds and thereafter disappeared. Eight years later the APVA minutes recorded that "Mrs. Lightfoot hopes that the monument to Pocahontas will be finished and in place by another year."[10] But it wasn't. In March and April 1917 the minutes reported "much discussion" and ended with the confession that "the money has not all been raised."[11] Five years later still, Mrs. Lightfoot reported that the Pocahontas statue "was almost complete" and would be unveiled on May 13, 1922, a ceremony that actually took place in June.[12] Where the statue had been since 1907 and why Mr. Davis of Oklahoma and the Washington-based association had disappeared from the record remain another of Jamestown's mysteries. The most plausible explanation may be that their fund-raising carried the project no farther than the original sculpture and a painted plaster cast used at Norfolk, and that the price of pouring the bronze took sixteen years to collect.

The 1907 exposition had sired two building projects on Jamestown Island. One built by the APVA itself was a museum called the Relic House (later the Dale House) to hold artifacts from the 1901 church excavations and such treasures as Pocahontas's bead and bark basket and the pair of earrings allegedly repaired for her by the Wizard Earl. The other structure was funded by the nation's premier distaff patriotic organization, the Daughters of the American Revolution, and provided the APVA with a residence for its on-site superintendent. At first rather surprisingly named the Sir Walter Raleigh House, today it is more appropriately known as the Yeardley House. These buildings, coupled with the 103-foot commemorative obelisk contributed by the United States government, represented the legacy of the great Jamestown Exposition, and as invariably is the case, when the show was over and Pocahontasmania faded and the last portrait souvenir was consigned to the attic, public interest in Jamestown waned and lay dormant for a quarter of a century.

The APVA's 1901 excavations, coupled with additional digging by Colonel Yonge in 1903, had prompted compilers of the official report on the tercentennial exposition to announce that "The recent excavations conducted at Jamestown under the direction of the United States government have brought to light the foundations of block houses, a fort, the first capitol and many of the houses of the early settlers as well as the foundations of the church."[13] Readers unaware that forts were built on the island many years after the first disappeared could be forgiven for concluding that the original James Fort had been found and uncovered. But that, as we have seen, was not so.

At least two later fortifications were erected in the vicinity of James Towne in the seventeenth century: One was of dirt (described as turf), which may have been built in 1663 to defend against a feared insurrection and which survived in a ruined state as late as 1689; the other of brick is believed to have been completed around 1676. The latter's construction had been ordered by an act of the General Assembly in 1667 which called for its walls to be ten feet high and ten feet thick when facing the river. Consequently, having found "what appear to be masses of masonry submerged from one and one and one-half to two and one-half feet below low water" about three hundred feet from the 1903 shoreline,[14] Colonel Yonge concluded that it came from that last brick fort. No doubt his published assumption to this effect gave rise to the claim that government excavations had revealed what the writer wisely defined as "a" rather than "the" fort.

As I have previously noted, the official view, and by that I mean National Park Service opinion, has been that the original James Fort

Top: Aerial view of Jamestown today. The Yeardley House and, in front of it, the outline of the Ludwell and fourth/fifth statehouse foundations are in the extreme left foreground. The church stands in the trees to the right of the 1901 obelisk. The open area of later James Towne ("New Towne") lies behind it, and behind the tree line is the controversial Elay-Swann tract. *Bottom:* Detail from Colonel Yonge's 1901 interpretive map of Jamestown Island's historical features. No. 22 identifies the church, 6 the fourth/fifth statehouse site, 21 the existing Confederate fort, 8 the site of the brick-walled fort of 1670–76, and 25 Yonge's conjectural location for the 1607 James Fort.

stood on a now-eroded promontory adjacent to the brick church which extended outward into the river along a broad front approximately five hundred feet wide. That was Yonge's carefully arrived-at conclusion, and it was shared by Jamestown's pioneering historian, Dr. Lyon G. Tyler, whose 1906 map closely paralleled that of the engineer colonel. Although neither map showed any appreciable erosion eastward from the church, subsequent excavations have demonstrated that the easterly frontage suffered significant land loss over the years, thus raising doubts about the promontory thesis. That may owe its genesis to testimony attributed to Francis Magnel, the Irish sailor who told the Spaniards that twenty leagues up the James from its mouth "the English built a well intrenched fort, standing on a point which goes out from the land into the river," adding that "the English determined to cut this point so that the water should surround them on all sides."[15] Because the point to be cut was not a point at all but the neck linking Jamestown Island to the mainland, it follows that Magnel's reference to the "point" is to the island in its entirety (really a peninsula reached across an isthmus), not to any projection from it.

National Park Service archaeologist John. L. Cotter, in his masterly analysis of all the Jamestown Island excavations up to 1956, followed Yonge in contending that the main area of erosion occurred to the west of the church, adding that in 1607 it represented the northwest arm of a crescent-shaped shoreline creating an "embayment . . . protected from the prevailing wind and down-river ebb tide acceleration as long as the arm on which the First Fort stood remained intact." With a disarming degree of finality Cotter went on to say that "as the First Fort site disappeared into the river in the 18th century, this protective arresting of wind and wave grew less and less." He later explained that prior to completion of the westerly seawall in 1906, there had been "at least 200 years of steadily increasing erosion of the south shore between Church Point and Orchard Run"—Church Point being the bend in the frontage adjacent to the ruin.[16] There can be no denying, however, that until the close of the nineteenth century the land immediately upstream from the Confederate fort did project significantly farther, for in 1896 the ground was deliberately cut back by seventy feet "to bring it to a fair line to receive protective work" prior to building the concrete sea wall.[17] That protective work may well have destroyed crucial information relating to the fort's environs, if not to the structure itself.

As one who lives beside the James in sight of the island and has fought the river's encroachment for some thirty years, I would argue that regardless of the Church Point projection, the erosive force has been spread

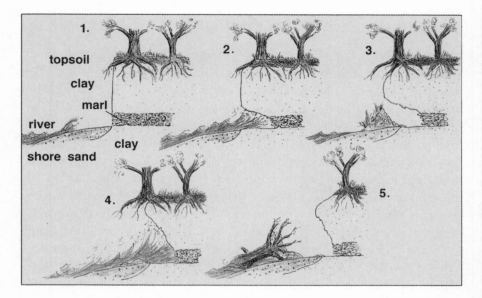

Sketch showing a typical erosion sequence at a clay bluff on the James River near Jamestown Island: (1) clay bank is capped by shallow-rooted trees with weak bed of marl at tidal level; (2) high tides wash out marl to begin undercutting; (3) clay falls and deposits temporary barrier onshore, bonded by fast-growing summer grasses; (4) spring storms and tides wash out barrier, erosion continues, rain washes clay from around tree roots; (5) tree falls, taking top of bluff with it, but lies on the shore providing longtime protection for the marl and clay immediately behind it.

fairly evenly along the island's shore all the way from the isthmus to the marshes southeast of Orchard Run. Furthermore, such baying by wind and tide could not have disproportionately focused east of the church unless some major obstruction prevented the clay scarp to the west from washing out first. In reality, the firm ground of the island is of essentially uniform clay composition and can be expected to give way at much the same rate.

When a tree-capped clay escarpment erodes along the north bank of the James River, the sequence goes like this: First the windblown water (usually in March and April) undercuts the clay at the spring tidal level, moving slowly where the clay is stiff, but fast where it is sandy or rests on a stratum of fossil shell (marl). The overlying clay bed is undercut, often to a distance of two or three feet. Meanwhile, spring and summer rains wash clay from around the roots of trees at the cliff edge, and this, coupled with alternate drying and shrinking of the clay, causes it to spall and pile up on the shore in front of the developing cave. Because the resulting pile lies above the normal high-water mark, it settles down, dries hard, and is bonded by the roots of weeds that grow on it through the summer. Consequently, it is not until prolonged high tides wash that protective wall away that the cycle of undercutting begins again. In time the cave or inward-sloping cliff reaches such a point that the trunks of the overlying trees have become part of the ledge and are held up only by their landward extending roots. Eventually high winds coupled with rain-soaked ground cause the weight of the trees to topple them from the cliff onto the shore below and, in falling, take as much as ten or fifteen feet of the bank with them. Once down, and with their root systems standing up along the waterfront like protective hands, the fallen trees create minibreakwaters that can slow the erosion process immediately in their lee.

Erosion in marshland areas behaves very differently. In sectors where nothing but grasses holds the mud together, a hurricane can strip away huge areas, lowering the land surface sufficiently to effect drastic changes in its environment; but when (as is common along the James River frontage) the marshes are bonded with the protruding roots of cypress trees, the land loss can be imperceptibly slow.

In sum, therefore, and as the map on page 402 shows, the fastest and most dramatic destruction along the Jamestown Island frontage has occurred where the clay escarpment is most vulnerable. Thus the nine teeth of high ground extending northward into the marshes at the east end of the island, which are held together by a strip resembling the back of a comb, are all that remains of much more solid ground that once reached outward into the river—and into the prevailing wind. Compare this modern environmental relationship with the outline of the island shown on the Smith-Zúñiga Map of 1608 (p. 407), and the similarities are immediately apparent.

There is no denying that the 1608 map is far from accurate; nevertheless, it is reasonable to argue that the closer Smith (if, indeed, he was the cartographer) got to James Fort, the more precise he would have been. Had the fort stood on a westerly projecting landmass with a bay to its east, Smith surely would have shown it so. Instead the fort is drawn in the curve with the projection to its east, a very similar site-to-land relationship that appears on William Hack's 1684 map of Carolina (p. 407). Robert Tindall's 1608 chart of the James River, on the other hand (p. 205), shows neither bay nor projection but moves the triangular mass of James Fort somewhat farther to the west.

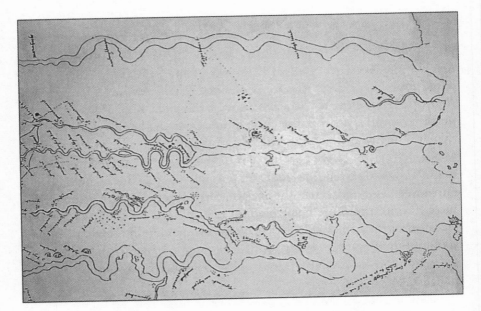

Part of the Smith-Zúñiga Map showing a dotted trail extending
from James Fort's west flanker beyond the Back River to
Indian settlements on the York River.

Slender though the evidence is, the burden of it rests on the Smith-
Zúñiga Map, which provides the only extant rendering of the fort in sufficient detail to define its defensive features. Questionable though even
those remain, it provides another clue of undeniable importance. Extending away from the upstream (west) bulwark is a row of dots crossing the
peninsula to the York River immediately opposite Powhatan's seat at
Werowocomoco. Other comparable rows of dots crisscross the map to
link several Indian settlements, leaving no doubt that they represent
existing trails. That one row ends (or begins) at the fort's west bulwark is
no accident, for it would have been much neater to have shown it arriving
in the midsection of one of the curtain walls, the most appropriate perhaps being the one facing the river, which Strachey told us was the "principall Gate from the Towne." However, Strachey also noted that "at each
Bulwarke there is a Gate likewise to goe forth."[18]
    Although the Smith-Zúñiga Map is very rough, its salient features
remain recognizable, and for that reason the course of the line of dots crossing Jamestown Island and continuing on the other side of the Back River
can be used to support the thesis that James Fort stood somewhat farther
east than is usually believed. Were the fort to be sited west of the church
ruin, the line of dots would plunge into an extensive swamp on the land-

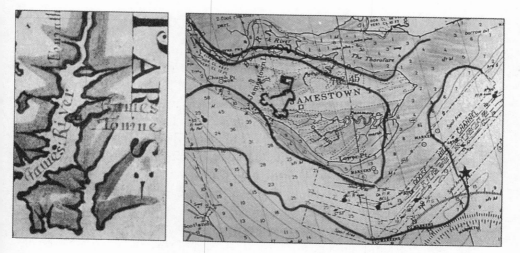

Left: A detail from William Hack's 1684 map of North Carolina showing his location for James Towne. *Right:* Jamestown Island from the Smith-Zúñiga map superimposed on a modern chart of the same area.

ward side, but when it is moved downstream perhaps as far as Orchard Run, the dots cross the Back River onto solid, traversable ground—a factor to bear in mind (along with the map's uncertain reliability) when we come to look more closely at the Orchard Run alternative.

Returning to the fort and the importance of its western bulwark gate, we now add what John Smith has to say after providing his enigmatic description of the fort's being "reduced to a five-square forme." He tells us that "the whole Company every Saturday exercised, in the plaine by the west Bulwarke, prepared for that purpose, we called Smithfield: where sometimes more then an hundred Salvages would stand in an amazement to behold, how a fyle would batter a tree, where he would make them a marke to shoot at."[19]

Next we have the testimony of the anonymous author of the "Breife Declaration" (ca. 1625), who, though recalling conditions as many as seventeen years earlier, had lived in the fort and so wrote with some authority. He remembered that after the arrival of the First Supply in 1608 "there were some few poore howses built, & entrance made in cleeringe of grounde to the quantitye of foure acres for the wholl Collony." The same witness told how when the 1609 fleet limped in with the Third Supply, so many new settlers went ashore that there being no vacant houses to lodge them in, they were "quartered in the open feilde."[20] Together these statements may be telling us that the Smithfield plain beyond the west bulwark was created as a result of the four-acre clearance. Both Colonel Yonge and Lyon G. Tyler concluded that it was into those same four acres that James Towne spread beyond James Fort, though they saw the expansion eastward, rather than westward from the west bulwark.

Unquestionably there was an open space or parade ground beyond the bulwark, one sufficiently large not only for the settlers' militia to drill and for its fifteen-man files to practice their marksmanship but for a sizable audience of Indians to watch them and at times to participate by demonstrating their own archery skills. Some historians have concluded that the ground was named Smithfield in honor of the Company's treasurer Sir Thomas Smythe, but it is equally likely—even *more* likely—that it took the name from its London counterpart, an area of three acres outside the walled city's northwest gate which as early as the twelfth century was known as "Smethefelde" and described as follows: "In the suburb outside one of the gates there is a smooth field both in fact and in name . . . where there is a much frequented show of fine horses for sale."[21] It later became the site for the annual Bartholomew Fair, for jousting contests, for public hangings, burnings, and boilings, and for the cattle market which still bears its name. As permanent buildings went up to serve Smithfield's customers, a suburb of London developed outside its walls and around the open acres. That an activity area flanked by rows of houses might remind an Englishman of London's Smithfield was demonstrated two years after the James Fort space was created, when George Sandys (Sir Edwin's youngest brother) visited Constantinople and reported seeing a large open square which looked to him for all the world like Smithfield.[22] From Turkey he went on to Egypt, where he made detailed drawings of the interior of the Great Pyramid of Cheops and earned himself an honored place as a pioneer among British Egyptologists, and thus, by being appointed the Virginia Company's treasurer at James Towne in 1621 and remaining there until about 1628, he can claim to be America's first archaeologist.

The point, however, is not the strength of such a claim but that the Smithfield so identified by John Smith paralleled the London space in relation to both its location and public usage. If that association extended to the growth of dwellings around the cleared area, then James Towne first grew westward, not eastward, from the fort. Assuming major erosion along the island frontage west from the brick church, one can argue that there would have been room for a three- or four-acre cleared area in that direction, yet one too small to accommodate the expected growth of the post-fort James Cittie, in which case Smithfield might have been aban-

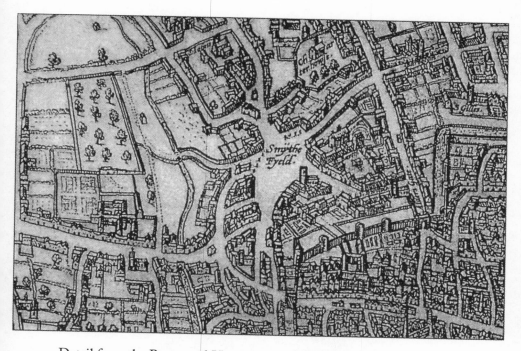

Detail from the Braun and Hogenberg map of London (1574) showing
the open market area of Smithfield north of the ancient city wall and
its northwest gate, a relationship perhaps paralleled by that of
Virginia's Smithfield and the James Fort's palisades.

doned—perhaps to be converted into a burial ground as the town
extended eastward away from both it and the fort.

Militarily it makes more sense for the settlement's defenses to be
downstream of it so that attacking Spanish ships would have to pass its
artillery before bombarding the town. On that basis, an argument can be
made for locating James Fort downriver at the opposite end of the later
seventeenth-century "New Towne" site, beyond Orchard Run and on the
ground now known as the Elay-Swann tract. If James Fort had been
the Elay-Swann tract, and Smithfield had been cleared upstream from
the fort's west bulwark, one could presume that the houses that first grew
up around the fort became the nucleus of the "New Towne" lots. Such a
scenario would push the alleged cobblestone-foundationed church discovered beneath the brick church away from the protection of the fort,
always supposing that the earlier foundation had carried a church. Even
so, there is contemporary Irish bawn village precedent for the fort to be at
one end of the settlement and the church at the other.[23]

To give credence to this east-to-west growth, one would need to find
the majority of the 1607–15–period artifacts in the vicinity of Orchard

George Sandys, treasurer of the council in Virginia and arguably
America's first archaeological antiquary. An 1823 engraving
from an earlier drawing.

Run, their numbers rapidly decreasing in favor of later material as one
heads toward the church. The sad truth, however, is that we archaeologists are unable to date the majority of our seventeenth-century artifacts
with the necessary degree of precision. English and most European pottery of 1610 is generally indistinguishable from that of 1620, yet in that
time bracket the changes at James Towne may have been many and far-
reaching. Difficulties in dating the artifacts tie one hand behind our
backs; the way in which the early digging was conducted fetters the other.

Let me explain.

Archaeological reasoning is founded on two childishly simple rules:
The ground is made up from a series of layers, some deposited by people
and others by nature, but the last is always the most recent. Dig a hole
through it, and the filling of the hole takes its place as the last disturbance,
relegating the previous *last* to the one before the last—and so on as each
successive change to the layering occurs. That, then, is rule number one.
Number two states that we date each layer by the most recent artifact

we find in it. Thus the presence of a 1960 penny in the one-before-the-last layer means that this stratum cannot have been deposited before 1960 and that any backfilled hole dug through it must be later still. To preserve these relationships and to keep the artifacts from each layer together (thus to provide the dating) require that the excavator be scrupulously careful in peeling away the layers in the right order. That necessitates having not only a keen eye for the nuances of soil changes but also the ability to recognize what the artifacts are saying while still in their contexts.

Artifacts, whether potsherds, fragments of weapons, broken bottles, or whatever, are to the archaeologist as words are to the conventional historian. Set out on the page as the author intended, words communicate; but cut them from it and reassemble them alphabetically, and yesterday's sonnet becomes today's dictionary. Jamestown archaeologists of the early 1930s did not fully grasp these rules and distinctions, and because most of the actual artifact recovery was done by Job Corps–style laborers, the subtleties of stratigraphy and artifact relationships went unrecognized. Although the supervisors knew enough to record the locations of artifacts by both horizontal and vertical measurements, the layer relationships were limited to arbitrary depths, thus taking the ground down five or six inches at a time, regardless of the fact that each such increment might embrace two or three layers or, alternatively, might be part of only one layer.

There is no denying that these limitations have seriously impaired the interpretive value of the vast collections of artifacts recovered from Jamestown excavations which are now preserved at the site's visitor center. Nevertheless, because the horizontal placement of the artifacts was recorded, their distribution could still be mapped. But knowing geometrically where they were does not necessarily tell us how or when they got there. An early-seventeenth-century pitcher could have been in use for fifty years before it was dropped and thrown away. If it is found and kept together with associated artifacts of the 1670s its longevity is proved, but if it is found in isolation, we can say only that an early pitcher was used at some time or other at such and such a location. Because objects having potentially long lives may be inadmissible as evidence, we needed to find readily datable things that were discarded soon after their first use. Clay tobacco pipes were easily broken and almost as expendable as cigarettes, and thanks to the pioneering work of British archaeologist Adrian Oswald and Jamestown's own J. C. Harrington, their bowl shape evolution has been exhaustively studied. I dared hope, therefore, that if we

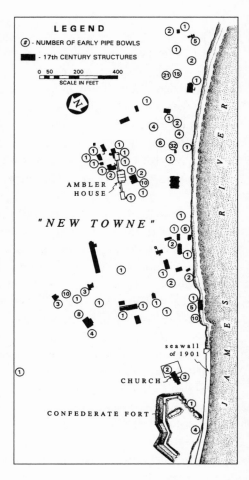

Left: Diagram illustrating the basic premise of archaeological stratification and time sequencing: If Feature A cuts through layers B, C, and D and contains a bottle resting on layer E, that bottle cannot be as old as the knife in layer B, the bone in C, or the cup in D. Consequently, Feature A must be removed in its entirety before disturbing layer B.

Right: Sketch plan of James Towne's excavated areas showing the distribution of tobacco pipe bowls of shapes dating prior to ca. 1625. The circled numbers identify the number of bowls from each location.

mapped the distribution of the earliest bowls, a growth pattern might emerge. And it did.

Of the 201 pipe bowls tentatively identified as dating from before 1620, 95 (48 percent) came from locations to the extreme eastern end of the excavated "New Towne" area, while only 10 were found west of the brick church—and 4 of those came from dubious locations and were found during the erection of the 1901–06 seawall. On the other hand, 4 of the earliest bowls came from the immediate vicinity of the church, while a group of 15 from about 1620 came from a partially eroded foundation on the waterfront only a short distance to its east. With those reservations aside, the pipe bowl distribution analysis did point to intensive early occupation at the Orchard Run extremity of the excavated site.

The Smithfield and westward expansion possibility had emerged by accident, growing out of my study of the reconstructed fort on behalf of the then Jamestown Festival Park. Not until that work was completed did I learn that I was not the first to look eastward to the Elay-Swann tract for traces of James Fort. I was fifty-one years late. Using reasoning based on recorded property lot relationships, Richmond banker and antiquary George C. Gregory voiced the same possibility in a report distributed in 1934.[24] It had landed with a thud on the desk of Lyon G. Tyler, who, as doyen of Jamestown historians, told Gregory in no uncertain terms that he was "upsetting the views of the investigators" who had preceded him.[25] Two weeks earlier Tyler had written saying, "I have given very attentive consideration to your location of Jamestown, and frankly speaking cannot give it my approval."[26] Tyler went on to counter Gregory's conclusions item by item, but because no new evidence was forthcoming, there, for the time being, the matter rested.

Early in 1934 the United States National Park Service had acquired all of the island save for the APVA's twenty-two and a half acres. The 1934 acquisition thus took in the whole of the "New Towne" sector and everything beyond, including, of course, the Elay-Swann tract (Fig. XV-8A). Key personnel from the archaeological team who had first assembled at Williamsburg in 1928–29 to excavate foundations as part of John D. Rockefeller's restoration project, and were let go late in 1933, had gravitated to the Park Service at Yorktown, where Civilian Conservation Corps (CCC) troops were excavating and restoring the 1781 battlefield. Consequently, when the nation took over Jamestown Island, the Williamsburg-Yorktown–trained archaeologists shouldered their shovels and their assorted talents, ready and eager to address the site of the oldest English-speaking capital in the Western Hemisphere.

On Wednesday, July 11, 1934, the advance guard "with fitting ceremonies began the actual work of exploratory excavations on the island,"[27] under the direction of ex-Williamsburger John Zaharov. Twelve days later a hundred men from CCC Company 247, commanded by foremen reportedly experienced in archaeological work, began to dig. Even when the supervisors *are* fully trained, the prospect of launching fifty untrained diggers onto a fragile and complex archaeological site is enough to chill the blood. In this instance the supervisors were not and could not have been trained to do justice to the remains of a hitherto unstudied archaeological

National Park Service personnel excavating at Jamestown in 1934.

period. Zaharov, naturally enough, thought otherwise and defended his technique of digging small holes all over the site, insisting that "it was the only method which would work on this type of job."[28] In hindsight, of course, it was a totally inappropriate means of locating the dirty marks of postholes and not even a reliable method for finding brick foundations.

As the search for James Towne progressed, the more dramatic became its parallels to the weaning years of the colony itself: the National Park Service headquarters in Washington, on the one hand, representing the Virginia Company, but divided within itself among bureaucrats, anthropologists, and architects, and, on the other hand, their equally faction-ridden "colonist" minions digging on Jamestown Island. Representing the Company was National Park Service Director Arno B. Cammerer, and under him the distinguished restoration architect Charles E. Peterson. Within weeks of the work's commencement, Henry Chandlee Forman, assistant architect in the Branch of Plans and Design, became Peterson's man on the site, and it was to him that Zaharov answered. Representing traditional archaeology was W. J. Winter, whose fieldwork spurs had been won in Arizona and Illinois and whose none-too-reassuring Park Service job title was Junior Park Naturalist (Archeology). In April 1935 he was to assume field responsibility for the Jamestown excavations, but not before fierce territorial battles had been fought with Forman and Zaharov. To reinforce Winter, the Park Service sent two more anthropologists, Alonzo Pond and H. Summerfield Day, who served as "technical foremen" and who, like everyone else on the project, could claim no prior experience of excavating a seventeenth-century British colonial site.

By January 1935 squabbling between the architects and anthropologists prompted Director Cammerer to let it be known that he did "not want to have Jamestown stand out as the one place where problem after problem accumulates for [his] personal attention."[29] It was the kind of comment that Company treasurer Sir Thomas Smythe might have voiced more than three centuries before. Indeed, the archaeological staff at Jamestown in the 1930s might as well have been puppets manipulated by the ghosts of Ratcliffe, Archer, Martin, and the other protagonists whose wrangling so nearly wrecked the Virginia adventure before it could take root. Cammerer's wish was not fulfilled, and in April we find Winter in Washington sending a telegram to Alonzo Pond instructing him to SUSPEND HOSTILITIES UNTIL I ARRIVE TONIGHT OR TOMORROW.[30]

In an attempt to define responsibilities, the Washington office had agreed to divide the excavating between the anthropologists and the architects, though Winter later admitted (with considerable justification) that staffing an archaeological project "with three archeologists and five architects appears rather disproportionate."[31] Nevertheless, Forman's proposal that his people should "excavate to the width of approximately three feet from parts of the basement walls"[32] and that the anthropologists should encroach no farther was accepted. On a site where structures were umbilically linked to the land use around them, such a division made little theoretical sense, and in practical terms it made none at all. Winter, in his role as senior archaeologist, correctly claimed the right to control the techniques employed by everyone digging on the site and so stepped in when he found one of the architects beginning to "use the worst excavating method that any of us have seen in some time"—this after a telegram from the architects complaining that Winter "was digging in our foundation" reached Peterson in Washington.[33]

For months memos and telegrams flew back and forth as the CCC crews dug on, only half aware of the professional turmoil swirling around them. Eventually, in the summer of 1936, so legend has it, the dispute extended to the troops in the trenches. Across one of Forman's arbitrary three-foot frontiers, pickaxes and shovels were wielded in malice as invaders and defenders faced off. Shortly thereafter Washington decided that enough was enough, and the Jamestown project was temporarily closed down, leaving only the laboratory supervisor (later curator) Worth Bailey to look after the artifacts and the records.

The methodological war at Jamestown has taken its place in the folklore of American archaeology and has encouraged those who have not studied the records to conclude that neither the architects nor the anthropologists understood what the site was all about or how to tackle it. That is grossly unfair. On the contrary, in the context of archaeological knowledge at the time, the anthropologists were remarkably enlightened, and thoughts expressed by Winter in April 1935 still make excellent sense today:

> I have reached the conclusion that the combination of archeologi-
> cal and architectural activities at the same time will never work in
> a satisfactory manner. . . . After all[,] the most important things
> on Jamestown Island are not the brick foundations. We are
> attempting to make a study of a culture, to gain *all* of the informa-
> tion that the ground has to yield. The only way to do this is to
> make use of the skill of trained archeologists. The evidence of the
> Indian occupation should not be ignored. The very first English
> habitations had no brick foundations, yet a trained archeologist
> can read in the ground any evidence of wooden structures and
> secure data that would escape the best of architects. . . . We have
> need of architects as consultants, it is true, just as we have need of
> geologists, conchologists, numismatists and other specialists.
> Their work, however, comes *after* that of the archeologist.[34]

Perhaps because the archaeology of historical sites was so new, and because the pioneers in Williamsburg had been architects, surveyors, and architectural draftsmen (with nary an anthropologist in sight), Park Service Director Cammerer was reluctant to take sides. His dilemma was made the more difficult by the strength of his own architectural office and by the knowledge that the architectural "archeologists" then at Jamestown were the same ones who reputedly had accomplished so much in Williamsburg. But whatever the reason, Winter's argument was ignored.

Three months later anthropologist Summerfield Day put his very similar point of view to the project superintendent, B. Floyd Flickinger:

> Jamestown does represent the beginning of English architecture in
> America. But it represents much more than that. It was the begin-
> ning of English *culture* in America. By culture I mean every phase
> of life, social, political, religious, and material, in other words, cul-
> ture in the anthropological sense. Architecture is only one phase of
> material culture. We cannot neglect all the other beginnings that

are to be found at Jamestown. Architecture may be the most important to the architect, but America is not populated solely by architects. . . . We must study everything, find the correct interpretation for every object, we must omit no detail that will help build up the complete story of life on Jamestown Island whether it be how the colonist dressed, how he ate, what tools he used, what his amusements were, or what kind of house he lived in—in short we must find out all that is to be found out from the soil that will tell us the answer to any question that anyone might ask.[35]

He was absolutely right. Those were the correct goals then, and they remain so today. But no matter how laudable the intent, the harsh reality was that neither Day nor Pond nor Winter had the knowledge to do what needed to be done—if it *could* be done, and there is no certainty that it could.

Seventeenth-century James Towne was not a sealed Pompeii-like time capsule waiting only for the ashes of time to be swept aside to reveal all as once it was. As we have seen from groping our way through the history of the first seventeen years from 1607 to 1624, constant changes were occurring in terms of personnel and cultural personality. The James Fort of John Smith was very different from the James Cittie of Governor Wyatt. But to achieve what Summerfield Day envisaged, the archaeologist would have to separate and identify not only those extremities but every evolutionary phase in between. It couldn't be done in 1935, and it can't be done now.

To complicate the task further, James Towne remained Virginia's seat of government until 1699, and as we have seen, even after the legislature had moved inland to Williamsburg, Jamestown survived as a ferry landing and as the worked soil of the eighteenth-century Ambler family's plantation. Armies camped and crossed the river there in the Revolutionary War, and Confederate troops were stationed there eighty years later during the Civil War. It was they who built the earthworks adjacent to the brick church ruin that may have obliterated traces of James Fort. Consequently, to reach back to the seventeenth-century colonists, as Day hoped to do, he had first to peel away, and understand fully, whatever survived of the succeeding 250 years.

Even those of us for whom the past is our present and constant concern have difficulty keeping it in perspective. The hours from lunchtime to dinner are vivid enough, but the distance from July back to January is recalled only by means of remembered highlights along the way. Without those dividers there is nothing to keep summer and winter apart. And so it is with years, decades, centuries; without milestones culled from our own memories and experience, they rub together, compacting into mere words: Victorian, Georgian, Stuart, Elizabethan, medieval, Dark Age, and so on into the forests of prehistory. But just as life in America at the close of the twentieth century is far removed from the way it was in the 1950s and light-years from 1900, so life in seventeenth-century James Towne was not all of a piece. The thinking and the possessions of the 1607 settlers were essentially Elizabethan and in some respects even medieval.

Forty years later England was to suffer through the traumas of its own civil war, and with the restoration of the monarchy in 1660 the country was to change its hats yet again, throwing aside its insularity and becoming much more a part of Europe. Consequently, allowing for the inevitable transatlantic delays and the reluctance of old planters to embrace new ideas, Virginia moved away from the world of Dr. Dee, Shakespeare, and Sir Walter Ralegh and followed the mother country into the Age of Enlightenment, of Newton, Dryden, and of foreigners on the throne. The seventeenth century's changes in everything from architecture to haberdashery and from religious expression to weaponry were enormous, and yet we are prone to think of it as somehow different from the eighteenth century, but otherwise as a single neat package. It was, believe it or not, a hundred years long, and if Jamestown's early archaeologists were unable to dissect it accurately, some would say that they would have done better to leave it alone. Indeed, J. C. Harrington, from his perspective as elder statesman of American historical archaeology, said as much while being honored at a Jamestown meeting in the fall of 1988.

Arriving there to pick up the administrative pieces late in 1936, Harrington was the right man at the right time—or at least as right as was then possible. He enjoyed the possibly unique distinction of having been registered as an architect before earning a degree in anthropology and thus straddled Forman's old battle line. Nevertheless, when he first took the job, Harrington did not even know where Jamestown was, and he has never shrunk from admitting that "when it came to digging a colonial site and carrying out related research, we were all babes in the woods."[36] With the help of the held-over Worth Bailey and the goodwill of the remaining CCC workers, there began what is now known as the Harrington Era in the history of Jamestown, one marked by first-rate field drawings (the product of his architectural training) and by improved digging and recording techniques designed to address the kinds of concerns expressed in 1935 by the beleaguered and frustrated anthropologists.

Henry Forman had left to bring his architectural skills and research philosophy to bear on another seventeenth-century colonial site—

namely, St. Mary's City in Maryland, which was founded in 1634 and whose remains could therefore be compared with those of mid-century James Towne. His efforts quickly resulted in a memorable and still much-sought-after book flamboyantly titled *Jamestown and St. Mary's, Buried Cities of Romance* (1938). In it Forman made clear his views on who should excavate the sites of colonial buildings:

> When, in an excavation, the foundation of a colonial building commences to meet the light of day, there is only one person who can rightly step forward to take charge—the specialist in colonial construction. A person who has spent years in studying antique buildings understands the ruins as no one else can. The secrets of the foundations are revealed to him, where others would pass them by.[37]

This, of course, was what he had been saying all along, and it had prompted the eloquent responses of Messrs. Winter and Day, neither of whom denied that architectural scholars could best interpret foundations or even that their advice could be helpful as the anthropologically directed digging progressed. Much more disturbing to traditional Jamestown theoreticians was the book's categorical statement that "George C. Gregory, Esq., of Richmond, Virginia, is the discoverer of the true site of original Jamestown." Equally firm was Forman's flat assertion that ". . . the Old Town must have been on the *east side of the New Town*."[38] His reasoning was the same as Gregory's, based on the interpretation of property boundaries and on the disposition of key arms of swampland referred to in the records, which Gregory believed he had correctly identified on the modern terrain. It was all very complicated and open to alternate interpretations. Nevertheless, the public (or at least the Virginia public) had been taught that Jamestown was the birthplace of the nation and that the birthing took place not among the brick foundations uncovered by the Park Service's excavations but in the palisaded James Fort, which it had failed to find—and whose traditional location was currently under attack. Something needed to be done to restore confidence—even if it only meant exploring the Elay-Swann site and, with luck, finding nothing.

In the summer of 1937 junior archaeologist Carl F. Miller was put in charge of cutting four ten-foot-wide trenches extending back from the river on the Elay-Swann site in the sector where Gregory and Forman thought the fort might have stood. They revealed the remains of a brick house which Miller dated to about 1750 and in whose foundation he

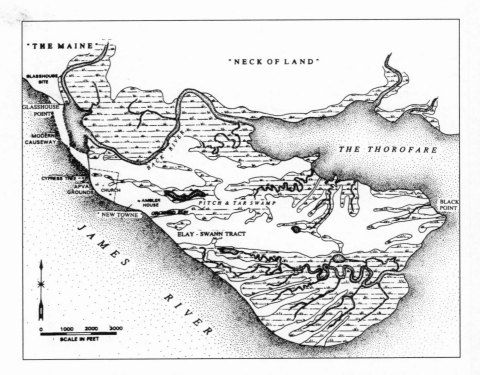

Map of Jamestown Island and its environs showing the marshes
and the Elay-Swann and APVA areas, along with other
existing historical landmarks.

encountered many decorative bricks reused from an earlier structure. He
reported finding "hundreds of post holes and other features," including
the remains of several ditches. "At the present time," wrote Miller, "it
appears to be unquestionable that these ditches were early, as some of our
earliest artifacts, both European and aboriginal, came from them."[39] On
the strength of these encouraging discoveries, Miller advised Harrington
that the site "should be carefully and meticulously approached and by a
trained man and not just someone who has had just a season or two in the
field." He urged that the individual be put in sole charge "and then be let
alone to do it as he sees fit, taking his time, for in the long run," Miller
added, "this is one of the key-stones in building up the complete historical story of Jamestown and one which should not be be treated lightly."
He concluded with a short list of specific proposals, prefixing them with
the comment "Of course, these are only suggestions, and I don't believe
they will be given any consideration by those now in charge."[40]

    More than three years later Harrington wrote the formal report on
Miller's work, dismissing his dating of the building to the mid-eighteenth

century but allowing that part might have been erected at its end. As for the artifacts, Harrington reported that "we found not over a dozen fragments which could possibly have dated from the seventeenth century" and concluded that the archaeological evidence indicated that the excavated area "was not occupied during any of the seventeenth century, and probably not until at least as late as the end of the eighteenth."[41] A careful reader could be forgiven for asking how, if the site was unoccupied until the close of the eighteenth century, there could be even a dozen seventeenth-century artifacts in its ditches? Then, too, what did Miller mean by "some of our earliest artifacts"? How early was early?

As Miller had suspected, and in spite of his insistence that more thorough excavations led by men more experienced than he were warranted, no further attention was focused on the Elay-Swann tract during Harrington's tenure at Jamestown. As Harrington's report summed it up, "The evidence seems to be fairly conclusive that the first fort and early settlement were not located in the area suggested by Gregory and Forman."[42] So that was that—until 1955. Then in a belated countdown to celebrating the 350th anniversary of the 1607 landing, more Park Service money was allocated to Jamestown, and a new team of archaeologists recruited, this time under the direction of the experienced prehistorian John L. Cotter. Once again the scarred earth of James Towne was trenched in search of whatever it cared to yield. The 1930s work had demonstrated that much remained to be learned about the later township, so that was where most of the effort focused, regardless of the fact that the discovery the nation needed had been enclosed within the pales of James Fort. It was imperative, however, that that goal should not be ignored, so Director Cotter assigned assistant archaeologist Joel Shiner to the task.

Renewed excavation on the Elay-Swann tract, which Miller had thought "should consume the greater part of three field seasons,"[43] took Shiner only five April days, two narrow trenches, and seven small test pits to conclude that "It can now be stated with finality that James Fort could not have been located at the Elay-Swann Tract."[44] In reviewing Miller's 1937 discoveries, Shiner reported that "Seventeenth and even eighteenth century artifacts were completely absent," explaining that "with the more complete understanding of 17th century materials that is available in 1955, it is even more certain that no colonists were living at the Elay-Swann tract during the 1600's."[45] Cotter, in his published study of the archaeology of Jamestown, made certain that the bottle of controversy remained firmly corked, using the alleged "absence of 17th-century traces of any kind"[46] east

Tobacco pipe bowls from 1937 excavations on the Elay-Swann tract, indicating English activity there by, and perhaps before, 1625.

of Orchard Run to reinstate the Tyler-Yonge conclusion that the 1607 fort site lay out in the river in the vicinity of the Confederate fort.

A reexamination of Miller's notes, photographs, and artifacts leaves no doubt that somebody was living east of Orchard Run as early as the second quarter of the seventeenth century. Rather than be a surprise, such occupation is only to be expected in the light of the expansion on the island documented by the 1625 census. On the other hand, in terms of James Towne's evolution, the period 1625–50 was several life-spans removed from the fort builders of 1607, and there is as yet no archaeological evidence for any occupation at so early a date. Nevertheless, the fear that the recovery of *any* seventeenth-century artifacts might be so construed may have encouraged Park Service authorities to say as little about them as possible.

Reviewing the fort site controversy in about 1936, the temporary acting archaeologist in charge, Charles S. Marshall, advocated resuming the Elay-Swann investigation, adding that if the fort was not found there, "its location will be proven only negatively as the Association for the Preservation of Virginia Antiquities, who now own the other possible location are strongly opposed to any archeological work being carried on in their area."[47]

Staunchly conservative and rightly proud of its preservationist accomplishments, the APVA considered Jamestown the jewel in its tiara. It could hardly, therefore, be expected to assist Johnny-come-latelies from Washington in proving that their statues of John Smith and Pocahontas belonged somewhere else. For its part, the Park Service was anxious to operate in harmony with its ultrasensitive neighbor and had no wish to rock the political boat. Consequently, it would be much better for all concerned if the Gregory-Forman theory could be disproved and James Fort could be left where the association was content for it to be: out in the river but off its own property.

Aerial view of National Park Service trenching across "New Towne" in 1956. The Ambler House ruin lies to the right rear, and the agency's laboratory and museum are at the extreme left.

By 1955, with both Tyler and Yonge deceased and with the Elay-Swann threat dormant, the APVA was ready to let the Park Service excavate in and around the Confederate fort in the hope that recognizable traces of James Fort might be found. Consequently, with Elay-Swann out of the way, Joel Shiner shifted his attention to this more promising site, explaining in his report that because descriptions of the fort indicated that it was built "entirely of logs, timber and earth" and had a ditch on the outside with a palisaded behind, it was "imperative that excavation techniques be designed to detect ditches and post holes."[48] That was absolutely right—except that the chosen technique of digging narrow trenches and sinking random test holes was no better a means of detecting posthole patterns around the Confederate fort than it had been on the Gregory-Forman site. As the 1950s models, paintings, and reconstructions have repeatedly demonstrated, the prevailing wisdom was that James Fort's palisades were built from side-by-side vertical logs, not from the posts, rails, and planks described by Strachey. Furthermore, Strachey said nothing about any exterior ditch. As we have seen, it wasn't until 1977, when the Wolstenholme Towne fort was found in Martin's Hundred, that anyone realized that rather than look for continuous lines of

cheek-by-jowl postholes, the excavators should be designing their digging to locate holes that could be nine, ten, or even twelve feet apart.
Because it is an old archaeological truism that any two holes make a
straight line, one has to find three or four before any construction pattern
emerges. To do so requires opening an area at least thirty-five feet long,
and since only luck will put that line in a three-foot-wide trench, it follows that one should be studying an area as broad as it is long.

Not surprisingly, Shiner's trenches and pits failed to locate any palisade, though they did find several ditches of uncertain date. One of the
cuts revealed a shallow pit containing iron slag, eight sword guards, parts
of matchlock musket mechanisms, bar iron, and other evidences of military blacksmithing of the kind attributable to the first half of the seventeenth century. This pit was identified as the site of the blacksmith's
forge, although forges do not require pits and no evidence of burning was
noted. Nevertheless, Shiner's report included a conjectural reconstruction
of an overlying shed, thus establishing the forge notion. Because he
attributed it to about 1620, Shiner's forge has since entered the folklore as
evidence for the proximity of James Fort. And it might be—just as the
predominance of early clay pipes (there was one from the "forge") can be
used to push the fort eastward into the Gregory-Forman ball park, relegating the forge to evidence for the westward growth of New Towne in
the second quarter of the century. Furthermore, it was common practice
in English towns for combustible manufacturing processes to be kept
outside the walls and away from dwellings, as was the glass factory across
the isthmus from James Towne. However, losing one's glass to the Indians was one thing; losing one's weapons and the tools for repairing them
quite another. It seems highly likely, therefore, that as long as the settlers
huddled behind their palisades, any military blacksmithing would have
been similarly protected.

With the Shiner "forge" temporarily on hold, we now need to turn
back the clock to 1901, when the APVA began digging in and around the
brick church prior to its reconstruction in time for James Fort's tercente-
nary. Mary W. Garrett, the association's Jamestown Committee's chairman, reported that "When the committee began their excavations at
Jamestown there was no one present except Miss Galt, myself, and one
laborer."[49] She later conscripted the custodian and, more important, amateur antiquary John Tyler, Jr., who was a member of the engineering team
building the seawall under Colonel Yonge's direction. If we ignore a relic-
hunting trench dug behind the tower in 1854, and the hole dug in 1897 by
Mary Jeffery Galt that first revealed the cobblestone foundation, we can

call this the first historical archaeological team to dig at Jamestown. Thus it fell to John Tyler to expose fully the cobblestone footings of what was thought to be an earlier church under the buttressed foundations of the brick building. This last is assumed to have been the church completed around 1647 (the tower added later), which usually is identified as the fourth church. Not surprisingly, the cobblestone foundation beneath it is thought to represent the third church, a frame structure which Henry Forman equated with a "new" one built in 1636, thus disagreeing with the more popular theory that the stone footings belonged to another third-church candidate—namely, the one built by Samuel Argall in 1617, wherein the General Assembly convened in 1619. Forman's argument against that interpretation rests on the knowledge that the interior width of Argall's building was twenty feet whereas the cobblestones define a structure twenty-one feet six inches wide. But as Lyon G. Tyler gave the same span as twenty-two feet, and as the measurements in "A Breife Declaration" might have been given in round numbers—nobody in England giving a hoot about the precise dimensions—the discrepancies may not be significant.

If we accept the 1617 church as the third, its predecessors are usually defined as the one built to replace the tent in 1607 but destroyed in the January 1608 fire and the second, its successor, erected in the aftermath by Captain Newport's sailors. The chronology thus leaves Lord De La Warr's church of 1610 as no more than repairs to the second church, yet (if Strachey is to be believed) the renovations were so extensive that the result was the first really churchlike church built at James Towne. No one doubts that until Samuel Argall returned in 1617, James Towne's churches stood within the fort, but the consensus has been that Argall's new (third) church did not. However, there is no proof of that, for our only information comes from "A Breife Declaration" stating that the building was of timber, twenty feet wide and fifty long, and that the "inhabitants of that cittie" had had the privilege of paying for it.[50] If, as I have suggested, the fort continued to serve as a civic center for some years after the town had spread away from it, a case might be made for the third church's remaining within the walls—always supposing that some tangible clue can be found on which to hang it.

With that in mind, we turn again to the APVA's researches, which were to resume in June 1902, this time with custodian "Mr. William Leal to carry on the work of excavating,"[51] watched over by Mary Garrett and other interested ladies. Focusing as it would on the interior of the church, it was about to disturb (and thus destroy) what was perhaps the site's most

The interior of Jamestown's brick church after the excavation in 1901.

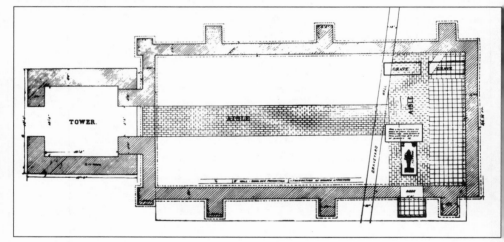

Plan of the excavated James Towne church foundation drawn by John Tyler, Jr., in 1901. The paralleling trench within the south wall marks the location of part of the earlier cobblestoned foundation.

critical archaeological feature—namely, the sequence of floors and graves associated with the fourth and third churches. Well-meaning though the excavators were, and remarkably intelligent as their conclusions proved to be, one weeps even at the thought of what was done.

Subsequent accounts of their discoveries written by the APVA ladies give tantalizing hints of the datable artifacts found in the many graves

The church at Jamestown seen from the southwest, the nave and chancel reconstructed over, and preserving, the earlier seventeenth-century foundations.

opened in the course of their researches. Alas, in 1958, John Cotter concluded that "No artifacts found by the A.P.V.A. in church or churchyard excavations were preserved with their provenience."[52] However, while visiting the Park Service's collections at Jamestown in 1989 in pursuit of Joel Shiner's "forge," I came upon two small boxes containing labels which read "Found in Grave in S.E. corner of chancel, July, 1902" and "Found in grave of Governor Sir George Yeardley at the south-east corner of chancel, 1617 church." I have found no documentation to confirm this identification; but with the knowledge that Yeardley died in November 1627, this would be the strongest possible evidence that the cobblestone foundation really had supported Argall's church.

As intriguing as the faded 1902 labels are the contents of their boxes. They include a scrap of waste copper, a cock screw from a snaphaunce or flintlock gun mechanism, the pan from another, and a lead cap from a musketeer's bandolier—the kinds of odds and ends commonly found on military and armament servicing sites. In short, these were the same kinds of artifacts that could have come from the blacksmithing operation encountered by Shiner about a hundred yards to the west. The presumption has to be that these military artifacts were scattered on the land surface, perhaps near the *corps de garde, before* the cobblestone-foundationed church was built and stayed there to get shoveled into the grave.

Having denounced the temptation to push unsupportive artifacts under the rug, I have to admit that the "Yeardley" box also contained a copper-alloy button which by no feat of imagination could date before the mid-eighteenth century. Nevertheless, because the military items are consistently of the first half of the previous century, it seems safe to dismiss the button as the intrusive product either of poor excavating or of lax collections' management.

The same search that turned up the "Yeardley" grave artifacts yielded another equally surprising. Its label reads as follows:

Fragment of a tiny fire-clay glass pot. Found near the Pocahontas monument in July, 1938. The excavation of the site which yielded this crucible disclosed the presence of field stones used in the construction of the glass furnace.

A second, related label suggested that the crucible might have been used in the manufacture of beads. It is, however, the same kind of crucible used for all sorts of small metallurgical work and is almost indistinguishable from the fragments attributed to Joachim Gans on Roanoke Island. The James Towne artifact, however, represents not one crucible but two, fused together mouth to mouth, one having served as a cover to the other in the melting process. They were found south of the church close to the southeast corner of the APVA property, before the Pocahontas statue was moved to its present location north of the church. The reference to a 1938 excavation is harder to pin down, for I could find no record of any archaeological digging in that area. However, the "excavation" may relate to utility work behind the post office at what was then the entrance to the APVA's property.

The crucible's association with stones from the glass furnace at first sounds highly improbable, for as far as one knows, both the glasshouse of 1608, where the devious Dutchmen plotted with the Indians, and a second glassmaking attempt, staffed by less devious but no more productive Italians in 1621, were located beyond the island's causeway at what is today known as Glass House Point, where Harrington skillfully excavated one of them in 1946. Unlikely though the notion of hauling rocks from Glass House Point onto the island might seem, John Cotter's 1955 excavations proved that this was done. While uncovering a series of foundations and pits to the back of "New Towne," he found a broken rock which actually fitted a break on another recovered by Harrington on the glasshouse site. Thus the stones found near the church in 1938 are likely to have been salvaged from a glassmaking operation and reused in building a metal-working furnace on the island. The key question, of course, is *which* glassmaking operation did the stones come from, that of 1608–09 or the later on-and-off enterprise of 1621–24. The stones, unfortunately, were not retained, so one cannot be sure that just because vitreous material clung to them, they actually came from a glassmaking furnace. Similar glazing effects can result from pottery manufacture and even from brickmaking. If we assume the 1938 label to be essentially correct, all one can say of it is that some kind of industrial work seems to have gone on in the vicinity of the APVA's post office and that only new and careful excavations can tell us what it was and, more important, how it related to the cobblestone or later church.

Putting all these scraps of evidence together, one is left with the impression that at some time in the relatively early seventeenth century considerable lay activity went on in the immediate vicinity of the church and that the "Yeardley" grave material came from a source surrounded by and predating the laying of the cobblestone foundation. Once James Towne had spread beyond the confines of the fort, the likelihood of industrial activities' clustering around the church becomes increasingly remote. So what is the alternative?

Although the discarding dates for the crucible and the gun parts can only be guessed at, there are the four very early tobacco pipes from the church itself and another pipe not quite so early from Joel Shiner's forge waste pit. Admittedly the slenderest of evidence, but together the pipes and the military artifacts may be saying that they and all four churches stood *within* James Fort in one or another of its phases. However, to explain the gun parts in the "Yeardley" grave, one would have to argue that the cobblestone church was not erected on the same site as churches one and two, for otherwise the artifacts could not have been found beneath it.

With that said, another possible though improbable scenario can be written: In it, Cotter was right in saying that none of the APVA's artifacts retained their provenances. The 1902 Yeardley grave labels have been mistakenly or capriciously inserted into the boxes with the military artifacts. Thus, with that evidence of prior lay activity eliminated, there is no proof that the first and second post-built churches did not precede the cobblestone and brick buildings on the same site, for no one trained to do so has yet looked for postholes under and sealed by the rock-laid footings.

With the exception of Shiner's Confederate fort dig in 1955 and the APVA-sponsored excavations prior to the 1907 celebration, no archaeological exploration has been carried out immediately around the church and its graveyard or southward from it to the seawall—an area large enough to conceal much of James Fort. (In the summer of 1994, however, the APVA began a new dig in this area, and one can only look forward with anticipation to its results.)

In 1969, tempered by nary a "perhaps" or "maybe," historian Philip Barbour declared that the fort "is a site now under water some 175 yards west of the Old Church Tower and 300 yards south of a partly submerged cypress tree," and lest he be charged with lack of precision, he added the spot's exact bearings: 37° 12′ 30″N., 76° 47′ 0″W.[53]

If one accepts the church vicinity thesis—regardless of whether the site lies partially on land or entirely submerged—it must follow that it was there, too, that in 1607 the three ships lay "so neere the shoare that they are moored to Trees in six fathom water."[54] With six feet to the fathom we would looking at an inshore depth of approximately thirty-six feet, an extremely unlikely figure. Modern charts show about two feet of water along the Jamestown frontage at mean low tide with a quick drop-off to about fifty-eight feet as the result of dredging.

Crude attempts in 1955 to grab up artifacts from the riverbed as a means of locating the fort proved singularly uninformative. That any trace of its palisading might lie offshore is highly unlikely. William Strachey stated that the posts were set four feet into the ground, and if we accept that the seventeenth-century ground encountered by Dr. Shiner was close to the present land surface, that would place the bottoms of the posts at least eight feet *above* the riverbed. Save for the possibility that some of the fort's buried and never retrieved artillery might have settled into the river mud, it is equally improbable that the recovery of random artifacts can provide sufficiently convincing proof of its location. If answers are to be found, and there is every reason to believe that they can, they will be obtained by renewed investigation on land.

Knowing this to be true and recognizing that in archaeological research terms the nation's 400th birthday in 2007 is just around the corner, in 1992 the National Park Service invited bids to begin a long-term interdisciplinary study of the island and its environs. The successful application submitted jointly by the College of William and Mary and the Colonial Williamsburg Foundation cited their need to know much more about the growth and decline of James Towne in the late seventeenth century as they prepare to commemorate the 300th anniversary of the founding of its successor at Williamsburg in 1999. Although the Park Service plan involves archaeologists, emphasis has been placed on the need for the archaeology to be "noninvasive"—which, in common parlance, means *no* digging.

Recalling J. C. Harrington's admission that in retrospect there would have been merit in deferring the 1930s excavations until the archaeologists had been better trained, and recognizing that full-scale excavation can be almost prohibitively expensive, the Park Service stressed the importance of preserving the site for future and wiser generations to excavate. That, of course, can be said of any historic site. The fact remains that if the project's purpose is to learn more about either the James Fort era or the later years of "New Towne," geophysical surveying and computer-generated theory and supposition must be tested by extensive digging—the cost of which calls for a larger budget and a program far more invasive than was first proposed.

The APVA, while ready and anxious to cooperate with its Park Service neighbor, took a more pragmatic view of its responsibility to its acres and to preparing to commemorate not the unrelated founding of Williamsburg but the 1607 landing on Jamestown Island. In 1993, therefore, the association appointed Dr. William Kelso to be its archaeological director and began raising the funds needed to finance several years of carefully programmed, albeit traditional, excavation, drawing on the talents of experienced archaeologists who learned their craft at such sites as Martin's Hundred and Roanoke Island. Although this is a fundamentally different approach from that of the National Park Service, the prospect of both techniques' being employed simultaneously offers hope that proving the validity of one or the other may have a lasting impact on the future course of historical archaeology in America. And if, as I believe likely, the new APVA excavations succeed in uncovering a landward corner of James Fort, and the National Park Service gains a better understanding of seventeenth-century life on the rest of the island, few will doubt that the nation's quatercentennial will have been eminently well served.

* * *

In 1994 the APVA's archaeological director, Dr. William Kelso, asked me where I thought he should start digging. I pointed to a low spot between the seawall and the churchyard. "If I were you, I'd start there," I told him. Two years later he was able to announce that a corner of the fort had been found.

NOTES

ॐ

PROLOGUE

1. Whitaker, *Good Newes from Virginia*, p. 11.

CHAPTER I: WHOSOEVER COMMANDS THE SEA

1. Chetwood, *Memoirs of the Life and Writings of Ben Jonson Esq.*, pp. 97–98; also Brown, *The Genesis of The United States*, vol. I, pp. 30–31; *Eastward Hoe*, Act III, Scene 2.

2. Cited by Lacey Baldwin Smith in Sears, *The Horizon History of the British Empire*, p. 15.

3. Quinn, *New American World*, vol. I, p. 161: Patent granted by Henry VIII providing protection to John Rastell and others, March 5, 1517.

4. Ibid., p. 170; John Rastell's *A New Interlude and a Merry of the Nature of the Four Elements* (c. 1519), spoken by the character Experiens.

5. Rastell's *A New Interlude*. . . .

6. Ibid., p. 171.

7. Ibid., pp. 190–91; Richard Grafton, *A Chronicle at large . . . of the affayres of England* (London: 1568), p. 1149.

8. Hakluyt, *The Principal Navigations*. . . ., vol. V, p. 136: Christopher Hall's account of Frobisher's first voyage, 1576.

9. Ibid., p. 197: George Best's account of Frobisher's 1576 voyage.

10. Ibid., p. 198. The sample has been identified as horneblende; cf. Vilhjalmur Stefansson, *The Three Voyages of Martin Frobisher* (London: Argonaut Press, 1938), p. 249.

11. Hakluyt, op. cit., p. 198.

12. Ibid., p. 199: an account of Frobisher's second voyage, 1577.

13. Known as Mistake Bay through the eighteenth century, it was later renamed Frobisher Bay.

14. William Harrison, *Description of England*, 1587; cited by David Gaimster et al., "The Continental stove-tile fragments from St. Mary Graces, London, in their British and European Context," *Post-Medieval Archaeology*, vol. 24 (1990), p. 16.

15. *Calendar of State Papers, Domestic, 1581–1590*, p. 357.

16. *Dictionary of National Biography*, vol. I, p. 919.

17. Hakluyt, op. cit., vol. VII, p. 20: John Sparke's account of Hawkyns's voyage to Guinea and the Indies, 1564.

18. Ibid., p. 31.

19. Ibid., p. 52.

20. Ibid., p. 60: Hawkyns's own account of his third voyage to Guinea and the West Indies in 1567 and 1568.

CHAPTER II: THE NEW FORT IN VIRGINIA

1. Hakluyt, *The Principal Navigations . . .*, vol. V, p. 350: Sir Humphrey Gilbert's Letters Patent, June 11, 1578.

2. Ibid., vol. VI, p. 14: Edward Haye's account of Sir Humphrey Gilbert's 1583 voyage.

3. Ibid.

4. Ibid., p. 16.

5. Ibid., p. 18.

6. Ibid., p. 35.

7. Ibid., p. 122: Arthur Barlowe's report of his 1584 voyage.

8. Wright, *Further English Voyages to Spanish America 1583–1594*, p. 175: Marqués de Villalobos to the Crown, from Jamaica, June 27, 1586.

9. Ibid.

10. Hakluyt, op. cit., vol. VI, p. 125: Arthur Barlowe's report of his 1584 voyage.

11. Ibid., p. 128.

12. Ibid., p. 130.

13. Ibid., p. 124.

14. Ibid., p. 117: Letters Patent to Sir Walter Ralegh, March 25, 1584.

15. Aubrey, *Brief Lives*, p. 261.

16. Quinn, *Set Fair for Roanoke*, p. 50: Richard Hakluyt the Elder, "Inducements to the Liking of the Voyage intended towards Virginia in 40. and 42. degrees," 1584(?).

17. Hakluyt, op. cit., p. 133: An anonymously authored report of "The voiage made by Sir Richard Grenvile, for Sir Walter Ralegh, to Virginia, in the yeere, 1585."

18. Ibid., p. 134.

19. Ibid.

20. Ibid., p. 138.

21. Ibid.

22. Ibid., p. 140: Ralph Lane to "M. Richard Hakluyt Esquire, and another Gentleman of the middle Temple, from Virginia."

23. Ibid.

24. Ibid., p. 156: Ralph Lane's "account of the particularities of the imployments of the English men left in Virginia by Sir Richard Greenevill under the charge of master Ralph Lane generall of the same, from the 17. of August 1585. until the 18. of June 1586," submitted to Sir Walter Ralegh.

25. Ibid., pp. 155–56.

26. Harrington, *Search for the Cittie of Ralegh*, p. 3; also Stick, *Roanoke Island: The Beginnings of English America*, p. 226.

27. Lawson, *Lawson's History of North Carolina*, p. 61.

28. Harrington, op. cit., quoting Edward C. Bruce, "Lounging in the Footsteps of the Pioneers," *Harper's New Monthly Magazine*, vol. 20, no. 120 (1860), pp. 733–35.

29. Ibid.

30. Hakluyt, op. cit., vol. VII, p. 87; "A summarie and true discourse of sir Francis Drakes West Indian voyage, begun in the yeere 1585."

31. Ibid., p. 105.

32. Ibid., p. 113: Baptista Antonio's "A relation of the ports, harbors, forts and cities in the west Indies, which have been surveied, edified, finished, made and mended . . . &c., Anno 1587."

33. Quinn, "Turks, Moors, Blacks, and Others in Drake's West Indian Voyage," *Terrae Incognitae*, vol. 14 (1982), p. 94: Letter of Nicholas Clever to Nicholas Turner, May 26, 1586.

34. Wright, *Further English Voyages to Spanish America 1583–1594*, p. 204: Diego Fernández de Quiñones to the Crown, Havana, September 1586.

35. Hakluyt, op. cit., vol. VI, p. 160: Ralph Lane's account, see note 24.

36. Hakluyt, op. cit., p. 162.

37. Hariot, *A briefe and true report of the new found land of Virginia* (1588), p. 11.

38. Quinn, op. cit., p. 100: Dispatch from Ambassador Edward Stafford to Francis Walsingham from Paris, August 20, 1586.

39. Hakluyt, op. cit., vol. VII, p. 107: See note 30.

40. Ibid., vol. VI, p. 162: See note 24.

CHAPTER III: THE CITTIE THAT NEVER WAS

1. Hakluyt, *The Principal Navigations . . . &c.*, vol. VI, p. 163: A summary of "The third voyage made by a ship sent in the yeere 1586, to the reliefe of the Colony planted in Virginia, at the sole charge of Sir Walter Ralegh."

2. Quinn, *The Roanoke Voyages*, vol. II, p. 790: "Relation of Pedro Díaz," March 21, 1589.

3. Hakluyt, op. cit., p. 165: Thomas Hariot's *A briefe and true report*, first published in 1588. Also in Hariot (see Chapter II, note 37), p. 5, facsimile with different spelling.

4. Hakluyt, op. cit., p. 166: Also Hariot, p. 6.

5. Hakluyt, op. cit., p. 196: John White's "The fourth voyage made to Virginia with three ships, in the yere 1587. Wherein was transported the second Colonie."

6. *Oxford English Dictionary*, citing François Froger's "Relation of a voyage made in 1695–97 on the coasts of Africa . . . &c.," translated and published in 1698.

7. Hakluyt, op. cit., p. 197.

8. Ibid., p. 195. Also Hariot, p. 32.

9. Hakluyt, op. cit., p. 201.

10. Ibid.

11. Quinn, *The Roanoke Voyages*, vol. II, p. 790; See note 2.

12. Ibid., vol. I, p. 262: "Ralph Lane's Discourse." Also Hakluyt, op. cit., vol. VI, p. 144.

13. Harrington, *Search for the Cittie of Ralegh*, p. 46.

14. Ibid., p. 4.

15. Hakluyt, op. cit., vol. VI, p. 201: See note 5.

16. Ibid., pp. 201–02.

17. Ibid., pp. 204–05.

18. Ibid., p. 206.

19. Aubrey, *Brief Lives*, p. 264.

20. Quinn and Quinn, *Virginia Voyages from Hakluyt*, p. 114: John White's "Narrative of the Abortive Virginia Voyage, 1588." Not included in the 1600 edition of Hakluyt's *Principal Navigations . . . &c.*

21. Hakluyt, op. cit., p. 212: John White in a letter to Richard Hakluyt from Kilmore in Ireland, February 4, 1593.

22. Ibid.

23. Ibid.

24. Barbour, *The Complete Works of Captain John Smith*, vol. III, p. 71: "The Sea Grammar."

25. Hakluyt, op. cit., vol. VI, p. 221: John White's account of "The fift voyage of M. John White into the West Indies and parts of America called Virginia, in the yeere 1590."

26. Ibid., p. 222.

27. Ibid.

28. Ibid., p. 203.

29. Harrington, *An Outwork at Fort Raleigh*, p. 33.

30. Quinn, *The Roanoke Voyages*, vol. II, p. 835: Deposition from Gonzálo Méndez de Canzo to Philip III, February 8, 1600.

31. Quinn, *New American World*, vol. IV, p. 35: Edward Hayes's narrative of Sir Humphrey Gilbert's voyage, 1583.

32. Hariot, op. cit., p. 10.

33. Harrington, *Search for the Cittie of Ralegh*, p. 21.

34. Ibid., p. 22.

35. Hariot, op. cit., p. 10.

36. Hakluyt, op. cit., vol. VI, p. 222: "The fift voyage of M. John White into the West Indies and parts of America called Virginia in the yeere 1590."

37. Lawson, *Lawson's History of North Carolina*, p. 61.

38. Hakluyt, op. cit., vol. VI, p. 222: See note 25.

39. Quinn, *The Roanoke Voyages*, vol. II, p. 835: Depositions sent by Gonzálo Méndez de Canzo to Philip III, February 8, 1600.

40. Hakluyt, op. cit., p. 222.

41. Ibid., pp. 222–23.

42. Barbour, *The Complete Works of Captain John Smith*, vol. I, p. 244: "The Proceedings."

43. Ibid., pp. 265–66: See footnote.

44. Kingsbury, *Records of the Virginia Company*, vol. III, p. 17, May 1609.

45. Lawson, *Lawson's History of North Carolina*, p. 62.

CHAPTER IV: WEST FROM THE AZORES

1. Hakluyt, *The Principal Navigations . . . &c.*, vol. VII, p. 149: John Twitt's "A True report of a voyage for the West Indies by M. Christopher Newport Generall of a fleete of three shippes and a pinnesse . . . &c.," ca. September 1592.

2. Ibid., p. 152.

3. Ibid., p. 153.

4. Hakluyt, op. cit., vol. VI, p. 61: Sir George Peckham's "A True Report of the late discoveries, and possession taken in the right of the crowne of England of the Newfound Lands, By that valiant and worthy Gentleman, Sir Humphrey Gilbert Knight."

5. Ibid., p. 62.

6. Kingsbury, *Records of the Virginia Company,* vol. III, p. 259: Sir Edwin Sandys to Sir Robert Naunton, January 28, 1620.

7. Aubrey, *Brief Lives,* p. 253.

8. *Dictionary of National Biography,* vol. II, p. 1620: Entry for Sir George Peckham.

9. Strachey, *Historie of Travaile into Virginia Britannia,* p. 155.

10. Ibid., p. 157.

11. Quinn, *New American World,* vol. III, p. 360: Chronicle of Martin Pring's voyage in 1603.

12. Ibid., vol. III, p. 390, n. 21: James Rosier, "A Virginian Voyage made Anno 1605 . . . &c."

13. Hariot, *A briefe and true report of the new found land of Virginia* (1590), Dover reprint, p. 75.

14. Daniel, *A Short History of British Archaeology,* p. 36.

15. Quinn, *New American World,* vol. III, p. 392: Agreement between George Waymouth and Sir John Zouche, October 30, 1605.

16. Bemiss, *The Three Charters of the Virginia Company of London,* p. 2.

17. Ibid., p. 1.

18. Ibid., p. 3.

19. Strachey, op. cit., pp. 162–63.

20. Quinn, op. cit., vol. III, p. 404: John Stoneman, "The Voyage of Master Henry Challons intended for the North Plantation of Virginia, 1606."

21. Ibid, p. 406, n. 1.

22. Brand, *Popular Antiquities,* vol. II, p. 364: James I's "Counterblaste to Tobacco," written 1604, published 1616.

23. Quinn, op. cit., vol. III, p. 417: "Opinion relative to the term 'Indies' at the Treaty with Spain & whether Virginia bee considered in them," 1606.

24. Ibid., p. 416: Sir Charles Cornwallis to the earl of Salisbury, from Madrid, May 24, 1607.

25. Brand, op. cit., vol. I, p. 397.

26. James I, "Counterblaste to Tobacco," 1604: See note 22 above.

27. Quinn, op. cit., vol. III, p. 434: A now anonymously written "Relation of a Voyage, unto New England." Begun June 1, 1607.

28. Ibid.

29. Strachey, op. cit., p. 178.

30. Ibid., p. 179.

31. Wahll, "Fort St. George Reconsidered," p. 9.

32. Quinn, op. cit., vol. III, p. 438: Sir Ferdinando Gorges to the earl of Salisbury, December 3, 1607.

33. Ibid., p. 437.

34. Ibid., p. 439: George Popham to James I, December 13, 1607.

35. Ibid, p. 440.

36. Maverick, *A Briefe Description of New England,* n.p.

CHAPTER V: MOST WELCOME AND FERTILE PLACE

1. Quinn, *New American World,* vol. V, p. 267: George Percy's "Discourse of the Plantation of the Southerne Colonie in Virginia by the English, 1606."

2. Barbour, *The Complete Works of Captain John Smith,* vol. I, pp. 207–09: "Proceedings"; and vol. II, pp. 140–42: "Generall Historie."

3. Jonson, *Every Man Out of His Humor,* 1600.

4. Irwin and Herbert, *Sweete Thames,* pp. 65–66.

5. Quinn, op. cit., p. 173: Examination of Henry Ravens in the case of the *Susan Constant,* December 13, 1606.

6. Ibid., p. 180: Examination of John Harvey in the case of the *Susan Constant,* December 13, 1606.

7. Barbour, op. cit., vol. I, p. xliv.

8. Quinn, op. cit., p. 197: Instructions for the Council of Virginia, December 10, 1606.

9. Barbour, op. cit., vol. III, pp. 188–89: "True Travels."

10. Hatch, *The First Seventeen Years, Virginia, 1607–1624,* p. 3; and Barbour, op. cit., p. lxvii.

11. Quinn, op. cit., p. 198: Instructions for the Council of Virginia, December 10, 1606.

12. *Dictionary of National Biography,* vol. II, p. 1945: Entry for John Smith. Also ibid., p. 2300: Entry for Edward Maria Winfield.

13. Jones, *The Literature of Virginia in the Seventeenth Century,* p. 19.

14. Quinn, op. cit., vol. V, p. 275: "The Discription of the now discovered River and Country of Virginia; with the Liklyhood of ensuing ritches, by Englands ayd and industry." This account, though anonymous, is generally attributed to Gabriel Archer, as is another in the same vein.

15. Arber, *Travels and Works of Captain John Smith,* vol. I, p. xxxiv: "Instructions by Way of advice, for the intended Voyage to Virginia," 1606.

16. Carrier, *Agriculture in Virginia, 1607–1699,* p. 7.

17. Barbour, *Complete Works of Captain John Smith,* vol. I, p. 29: "True Relation."

18. Quinn, op. cit., p. 270: Percy's "Discourse."

19. Carrier, op. cit., p. 8.

20. Ibid.

21. Cotter, *Archeological Excavations at Jamestown,* p. 6.

22. Quinn, op. cit., p. 276: Archer's "Description."

23. Ibid., p. 268: Percy's "Discourse."

24. Ibid., pp. 268–69.

25. Ibid., p. 269.

26. Ibid., pp. 269–70.

27. Wright, Strachey's *Historie of Travell into Virginia Britania,* pp. 57–58.

28. Quinn, op. cit., p. 270.

29. Ibid.

30. Ibid.

31. Barbour, op. cit., vol. I, pp. 205–06: "Proceedings."

CHAPTER VI: ARROWS OF OUTRAGEOUS FORTUNE

1. Arber, *Travels and Works of Captain John Smith*, vol. I, p. xl.

2. Ibid., p. xxxv: "Instructions by Way of advice, for the intended Voyage to Virginia," 1606.

3. Quinn, *New American World*, vol. V, p. 272: Percy's "Discourse."

4. Arber, op. cit., p. xlvi: Archer's "Discovery of our River," May 24, 1607.

5. Ibid., p. xliii: May 23, 1607.

6. Ibid., p. xlvii: May 25, 1607.

7. Ibid., p. liii: May 27, 1607.

8. Barbour, *Complete Works of Captain John Smith*, vol. I, p. 206: "The Proceedings," and vol. II: "Generall Historie," p. 138.

9. Ibid.

10. Arber, op. cit., p. liii: May 27–28, 1607.

11. Barbour, op. cit., vol. I, p. 206, and vol. II, p. 139.

12. Arber, op. cit., vol. I, pp. liii–liv (several entries omitted).

13. Ibid., p. lv: June 14, 1607.

14. Quinn, op. cit., vol. V, p. 271: Percy's "Discourse."

15. Hunter, *Plantations in Ulster*, Facs. 163.

16. Arber, op. cit., vol. I, p. xxxvii.

17. Barbour, op. cit., vol. II, p. 138: "Generall Historie."

18. Arber, op. cit.

19. Quinn, op. cit., p. 272: Percy's "Discourse."

20. Arber, op. cit., p. xxxviii: Robert Tindall to Prince Henry.

21. Ibid., p. liv: Archer's "Relatyon."

22. Barbour, op. cit., vol. III, p. 295: "Advertisements."

23. Ibid., vol. I, p. 35: "True Relation."

24. Ibid., vol. II, p. 144: "Generall Historie."

25. Barbour, *The Jamestown Voyages*, vol. I, p. 219: Wingfield's "Discourse," May 1608.

26. Ibid., p. 214.

27. Quinn, op. cit., vol. V, p. 272: Percy's "Discourse."

28. Barbour, *The Jamestown Voyages*, vol. I, p. 215: Wingfield's "Discourse," May 1608.

29. Quinn, op. cit., p. 273.

30. Ibid.

31. Ibid.

32. Barbour, *The Complete Works of Captain John Smith*, vol. I, p. 33: "True Relation."

33. Ibid., vol. II, p. 104: "Generall Historie."

34. Ibid., vol. I, p. 33: "True Relation."

35. *Encyclopaedia Britannica*, 1953 edition, vol. 23, p. 425: "Water Purification."

36. Barbour, *The Complete Works of John Smith*.

37. Barbour, *The Jamestown Voyages*, vol. I, p. 156: "Francis Magnel's Relation of the First Voyage and the Beginnings of the Jamestown Colony," Madrid, July 1, 1610.

38. Barbour, *The Complete Works of Captain John Smith*, vol. I, p. 212: "Proceedings."

39. Ibid., p. 41: "True Relation."

40. Barbour, *The Jamestown Voyages*, vol. I, p. 244: Smith to Council of Virginia, fall 1608.

41. Ibid., p. 176: Newport to Lord Salisbury, July 29, 1607.

42. Ibid., pp. 79–80: Council in Virginia to Council in England, June 22, 1607.

43. Ibid., p. 108: Sir Walter Cope to Lord Salisbury, August 12, 1607. Cope's spelling and punctuation being so bad, the text is here presented after copy-editing.

44. Ibid., p. 111: Sir Walter Cope to Lord Salisbury, August 13, 1607.

45. Ibid.

46. Ibid., p. 79: Council in Virginia to Council in England, June 22, 1607.

47. Ibid., p. 112: Sir Thomas Smythe to Lord Salisbury, August 13, 1607.

48. Ibid., p. 112: Sir Thomas Smythe to Lord Salisbury, August 17, 1607.

49. Ibid.: East India Company, court minutes, September 4, 1607.

50. Ibid., p. 115: Pedro de Zúñiga to Philip III, London, September 22, 1607. N.B.: Here and elsewhere Spanish texts, being translations, read with the clarity of the translator's modern spelling. Some words have been chosen to approximate their most appropriate modern equivalents.

51. Ibid.

52. Ibid., p. 113: Dudley Carleton to John Chamberlain, August 18, 1607.

53. Ibid., p. 118: Pedro de Zúñiga to Philip III, London, October 8, 1607.

54. Ibid.

55. Ibid., p. 121: Pedro de Zúñiga to Philip III, London, October 16, 1607.

56. Ibid., p. 122, n.1: Minutes endorsement, November 10, 1607.

57. Barbour, *The Complete Works of Captain John Smith*, vol. I, p. 45: "True Relation."

58. Ibid., vol. II, p. 146: "Generall Historie."

59. Barbour, *The Jamestown Voyages*, vol. I, p. 150: William White's account, written prior to 1614.

60. Barbour, *The Complete Works of Captain John Smith*, vol. II, illustration, pp. 98–99.

61. Ibid., vol. I, p. 47: "True Relation."

62. Ibid., vol. II, p. 147: "Generall Historie."

63. Ibid., p. 151.

64. Ibid., p. 148.

65. Ibid.

66. Ibid., p. 151.

67. Ibid.

68. Ibid., vol. I, p. 274: "Proceedings."

69. Ibid., vol. II, p. 151: "Generall Historie."

70. Ibid., p. 152.

71. Ibid., vol. I, p. 61: "True Relation."

72. Barbour, *The Jamestown Voyages*, vol. I, p. 226: Wingfield's "Discourse," May 1608.

CHAPTER VII: ALARUMS AND EXCURSIONS

1. Barbour, *Jamestown Voyages,* vol. I, pp. 227–28: Wingfield's "Discourse," May 1608.

2. Barbour, *The Complete Works of Captain John Smith,* vol. I, p. 211: "The Proceedings."

3. Ibid., vol. III, p. 295: the "Advertisements."

4. Ibid.

5. Ibid., vol. II, p. 157: "Generall Historie."

6. Ibid., vol. I, p. 217: "The Proceedings."

7. Barbour, *Jamestown Voyages,* vol. I, pp. 158–59: Francis Perkins to a friend in England, March 28, 1608. Translated into modern English from a Spanish copy in the Archivo General de Simancas.

8. Ibid., p. 160.

9. Ibid., vol. I, p. 228: Wingfield's "Discourse," May 1608.

10. Barbour, *The Complete Works of Captain John Smith,* vol. I, p. 61: "True Relation."

11. Ibid., pp. 217–18: "The Proceedings." Note that the 1607 date follows the Old Style calendar.

12. Barbour, *Jamestown Voyages,* vol. I, pp. 161–62: Perkins to a friend in England, March 28, 1608.

13. "Mons. Bonnavolia his directiones for a Voyage and settling a Plantation under the deg. of 35 Nor:lat[?] the coast of Florida in the west Indies." March ?, 1630. British Public Record Office, CO1/5. 2627; unpublished.

14. Barbour, *The Complete Works of Captain John Smith,* vol. I, p. 219: "The Proceedings."

15. Quinn, *New American World,* vol. V, p. 273: Percy's "Discourse," September 5, 1607.

16. Wright, Strachey's *Historie of Travell into Virginia Britania,* p. 34.

17. Barbour, *The Complete Works of Captain John Smith,* vol. I, p. 65: "True Relation."

18. Ibid., vol. II, p. 151, n. 1.

19. Ibid., vol. I, p. 65: "True Relation."

20. Ibid., vol. II, p. 156: "Generall Historie."

21. Ibid.

22. Ibid.

23. Ibid.

24. Ibid., p. 154.

25. Chetwood, *Memoirs of the Life and Writings of Ben Jonson Esq.,* p. 97.

26. Barbour, *The Jamestown Voyages,* vol. I, p. 161: Perkins to a friend in England, March 28, 1608.

27. Ibid., p. 112: Sir Thomas Smythe to Lord Salisbury, August 17, 1607.

28. Barbour, *The Complete Works of Captain John Smith,* vol. I, p. 218: "The Proceedings."

29. Ibid.

30. Ibid.

31. Ibid., vol. II, p. 159: "Generall Historie."

32. Ibid., vol. I, p. 93: "True Relation."

33. Ibid.

34. Ibid., p. 95.

35. Ibid., vol. II, p. 158: "Generall Historie."

36. *Dictionary of National Biography*, vol. II, p. 1720.

37. Quinn, *New American World*, vol. V, p. 274, n. 10.

38. Barbour, *The Complete Works of Captain John Smith*, vol. I., p. 83: "True Relation."

39. Ibid., p. 85.

40. Ibid.

41. Arber, *Travels and Works of Captain John Smith*, vol. I, p. lv: Archer, Sunday, June 14, 1607.

42. Barbour, *The Complete Works of Captain John Smith*, vol. II, p. 169: "Generall Historie."

43. Ibid., vol. I, p. 233: "The Proceedings."

44. Ibid., vol. II, p. 160: "Generall Historie."

45. Ibid., vol. I, p. 97: "True Relation."

46. Ibid., p. 24.

47. McClure, *Letters of John Chamberlain*, vol. I, p. 259: Chamberlain to Dudley Carleton, July 7, 1608.

48. Barbour, *The Complete Works of Captain John Smith*, vol. I, p. 228: "The Proceedings."

49. Ibid.

50. Ibid., p. 229.

51. Ibid., vol. II, p. 171: "Generall Historie."

52. Ibid., p. 179.

53. Ibid.

54. Cotter, *Archeological Excavations at Jamestown*, p. 23.

55. Barbour, *The Complete Works of Captain John Smith*, vol. I, p. 233: "The Proceedings."

56. Ibid.

57. Ibid., vol. II, pp. 180–81: "Generall Historie."

58. Ibid., vol. I, p. 242: "The Proceedings."

59. Ibid., vol. II, p. 182: "Generall Historie."

60. Ibid.

61. Ibid., vol. I, p. 127.

62. Directions to M. Bonnavolia, March ?, 1630: See note 13.

CHAPTER VIII: CROWNING AND OTHER ACHIEVEMENTS

1. Barbour, *The Complete Works of Captain John Smith*, vol. II, pp. 189–90: "Generall Historie."

2. Morton, *Colonial Virginia*, vol. I, p. 16.

3. Barbour, op. cit., p. 188.

4. Barbour, *Jamestown Voyages*, vol. II, p. 269: Pedro de Zúñiga to Philip III, Highgate, July 5, 1609.

5. Barbour, *The Complete Works of Captain John Smith*, vol. I, p. 259: "The Proceedings."

6. Nugent, *Cavaliers and Pioneers*, p. 240: Entry for Major Francis Morrison.

7. Wright, Strachey's *The Historie of Travell into Virginia Britania*, p. 78.

8. Barbour, *The Complete Works of Captain John Smith*, vol. II, p. 189: "Generall Historie."

9. Ibid., vol. I, p. 238: "The Proceedings." Much of this work was contributed by others, in this case by one of three: Richard Wiffin, William Phettiplace, or Anas Todkill.

10. Ibid., vol. II, p. 189: "Generall Historie."

11. Ibid., p. 181.

12. Ibid., p. 182.

13. Ibid., p. 183.

14. Ibid., p. 184.

15. Ibid.

16. Allen, *The Tradescants*, pp. 114–15.

17. Barbour, *The Complete Works of Captain John Smith*, vol. II, p. 186: "Generall Historie."

18. Ibid.

19. Ibid., vol. I, p. 238: "The Proceedings."

20. Ibid., vol. II, p. 185: "Generall Historie;" also in a slightly different version in vol. I, p. 238: "The Proceedings."

21. Ibid., pp. 186–87.

22. Ibid., vol. I, p. 244: "The Proceedings."

23. Ibid., vol. II, p. 198: "Generall Historie."

24. Ibid., vol. III, p. 77: "A Sea Grammar."

25. Ibid, vol. II, p. 203: "Generall Historie."

26. Ibid., vol. I, p. 254: "The Proceedings."

27. Ibid., vol. II, p. 201: "Generall Historie."

28. Ibid., vol. II, p. 202: "Generall Historie"; and vol. I, p. 252: "The Proceedings."

29. Ibid., vol. II, p. 206: "Generall Historie."

30. Ibid., p. 208.

31. Ibid., p. 209.

32. Mann, *European Arms and Armour*, vol. II, p. 365, pl. 130.

33. Cotter, *Archeological Excavations at Jamestown*, p. 159: Well no. 24.

34. Barbour, *The Complete Works of Captain John Smith*, vol. II, p. 212: "Generall Historie."

35. Quinn, op. cit., vol. V, p. 300: Strachey's "True Reportory," 1610.

36. Ibid., p. 273: Percy's "Discourse," 1607.

37. Barbour, *The Complete Works of Captain John Smith*, vol. II, p. 212: "Generall Historie."

38. Ibid.

39. Public Record Office, CO1/5. 2627; see Chapter VII, p. 161, and n. 13.

40. Haas, *Citadels, Ramparts & Stockades*, p. 146.

41. Barbour, *The Complete Works of Captain John Smith*, vol. II, p. 212: "General Historie."

42. Arber, *Travels and Works of Captain John Smith*, vol. I, p. 154. The word "halfe" present in this version is not found in the first (1624) edition of the *Generall Historie*.

43. Nugent, *Cavaliers and Pioneers,* p. 61: Entry for William Mills, who patented 350 acres in James City County on July 19, 1637, "On S. side of James Riv., bounding N. upon Smith fort. . . ."

44. Barbour, *The Complete Works of Captain John Smith,* vol. II, p. 212: "Generall Historie."

45. Loth, *The Virginia Landmarks Register,* p. 457. Also Hatch, *The First Seventeen Years, Virginia, 1607–1624,* p. 79.

46. Barbour, *The Complete Works of Captain John Smith,* vol. II, p. 213: "Generall Historie."

47. Ibid., p. 211.

48. Ibid., p. 213.

49. Barbour, *Jamestown Voyages,* vol. II, p. 281: Gabriel Archer, August 31, 1609.

50. Ibid., vol. II, pp. 307–08: Report of Francisco Fernández de Ecija, after September 24, 1609, when the ship returned to St. Augustine.

51. Barbour, *The Complete Works of Captain John Smith,* vol. II, p. 217: "Generall Historie."

CHAPTER IX: "LEWD AND NAUGHTIE PRACTICES"

1. Barbour, *Jamestown Voyages,* vol. II, p. 255: Pedro de Zúñiga to Philip III, Highgate, March 15, 1609.

2. Ibid., pp. 258–59 and fn. 1: Pedro de Zúñiga to Philip III, Highgate, April 1, 1609.

3. Ibid., p. 255: See note 1.

4. Ibid., p. 257.

5. Ibid., p. 255: See note 1.

6. Ibid.

7. Quinn, *New American World,* vol. V, p. 237: Robert Johnson's *Nova Britannia,* April–May 1609.

8. Ibid., p. 239.

9. Ibid., p. 243.

10. Wright, Strachey's *True Reportory,* p. 4. Note that here and throughout, in the interests of consistency, the Wright transcription is used rather than the more accurate but incomplete version published by Dr. Quinn in his *New American World.* Both are drawn from the 1906 edition of *Purchas, His Pilgrimes . . . ,* vol. XIX, pp. 5–72.

11. David Beers Quinn, "Bermuda in the Age of Exploration and Early Settlement," unpublished paper read at an Institute of Early American History and Culture colloquium, November 15, 1988.

12. Quinn, op. cit., vol. V., p. 288.

13. Wright, op. cit., p. 9.

14. Wright, *A Voyage to Virginia in 1608,* with Silvester Jourdain's *Discovery of the Bermudas,* p. 107.

15. The manuscript is the property of Mr. and Mrs. Edward B. Tucker of Bermuda and is at present in the hands of the author pending its editing and publication.

16. Quinn, op. cit., p. 286: Gabriel Archer's account of the Third Supply, written at James Towne, August 31, 1609.

17. Barbour, *The Complete Works of Captain John Smith*, vol. I, p. 269: "The Proceedings."

18. Percy, "A Trewe Relacyon," p. 262.

19. Barbour, *The Complete Works of Captain John Smith*, vol. II, p. 181: "Generall Historie."

20. Bemis, *The Three Charters of the Virginia Company*, p. 59: "Instruccions Orders and Constitucions . . . To Sir Thomas Gates Knight Governor of Virginia," May 1609.

21. Percy, op. cit., p. 263.

22. Quinn, op. cit., vol. V, p. 240: Robert Johnson's *Nova Britannia*, April–May 1609.

23. Gray, *A Good Speed to Virginia*, April 26, 1609, pp. 12–13 (no printed pagination).

24. Percy, op. cit., p. 263.

25. Ibid., p. 264.

26. Arber, *Travels and Works of Captain John Smith*, vol. I, p. ci: Henry Spelman's *Relation of Virginea*, written ca. 1613.

27. Ibid., p. cii.

28. Barbour, *The Complete Works of Captain John Smith*, vol. I, p. 271: "The Proceedings."

29. Ibid, vol. II, p. 325: "Generall Historie."

30. Ibid., p. 272.

31. Morton, *Colonial Virginia*, vol. I, p. 23.

32. Woodward, *Pocahontas*, p. 113.

33. Barbour, *The Complete Works of Captain John Smith*, vol. II, p. 223: "Generall Historie."

34. Ibid., vol. I, p. 272: "The Proceedings."

35. Percy, op. cit., p. 264.

36. Barbour, *The Complete Works of Captain John Smith*, vol. I, p. 272: "The Proceedings."

37. Ibid., p. 273. The section of the *Proceedings* is actually attributed by Smith to Richard Potts and to W.P., who is assumed to be William Phettiplace. Similar collaborations occur throughout Smith's works, attributions which are authoritatively analyzed by his editor Philip Barbour. Here and elsewhere in the interests of readability I have elected to cite only one contributor.

38. Holme, *An Academie of Armory*, p. 135. Much of Holme's manuscript was assembled in the 1640s, but his first volume was not published until 1688.

39. Smythe, *Certain Discourses Military* (1590), p. 115.

40. Barbour, *The Complete Works of Captain John Smith*, vol. II, p. 225: "Generall Historie."

41. "A Breife Declaration . . . &c.," p. 70.

42. Percy, op. cit., p. 264.

43. *Dictionary of National Biography*, vol. II, p. 1627: Entry for George Percy (1580–1632).

44. Percy, op. cit., p. 259.

CHAPTER X: A SHIP IN TIME

1. Quinn, *New American World*, vol. V, p. 287: John Ratcliffe to Lord Salisbury, October 4, 1609.

2. Arber, *Travels and Works of Captain John Smith*, vol. I, p. cii: Henry Spelman's *Relations of Virginea*, ca. 1613.

3. Barbour, *The Complete Works of Captain John Smith*, vol. II, p. 221: "Generall Historie."

4. Percy, "A trewe relacyon," p. 264.

5. Barbour, op. cit., p. 193.

6. Percy, op. cit., p. 265.

7. Ibid.

8. Ibid., p. 266.

9. Ibid.

10. Ibid.

11. Ibid.

12. Ibid., p. 269.

13. Barbour, *The Complete Works of Captain John Smith*, vol. II, p. 232: "Generall Historie."

14. Percy, op. cit., p. 267.

15. Barbour, *The Complete Works of Captain John Smith*, vol. II, pp. 232–33: "Generall Historie."

16. Quinn, op. cit., vol. V, p. 256: *A True Declaration of the state of Virginia*, 1610.

17. Percy, op. cit., p. 267.

18. *Colonial Records of Virginia*, "A Breife Declaration of the Plantation of Virginia . . . &c.," ca. 1625.

19. Quinn, op. cit., p. 289: Strachey's *True Reportory*.

20. Percy, op. cit., p. 269.

21. Ibid.

22. Brown, *The Genesis of the United States*, vol. I, p. 405: Governor and Council of Virginia to the Virginia Company of London, July 7, 1610.

23. Quinn, op. cit., p. 289.

24. Tyler, *Narratives of Early Virginia*, p. 221: Pedro de Molina, probably to Don Alonzo de Velasco, who in 1610 succeeded Pedro de Zúñiga as Spanish ambassador in London, 1613.

25. Whitaker, *Good Newes from Virginia*, p. 25.

26. Barbour, *The Complete Works of Captain John Smith*, vol. II, p. 232: "Generall Historie."

27. Quinn, op. cit., vol. V, pp. 289–90: Strachey's *True Reportory*.

28. Kingsbury, *The Records of the Virginia Company*, vol. IV, p. 259: Notes for an Answer to the Propositions made by Lord Chichester, August or September 1623.

29. Public Record Office, London, CO1/5. 2627. See Chapter VII, p. 161, and n. 13.

30. Percy, op. cit., pp. 269–70.

31. Quinn, op. cit., p. 293.

32. Brown, op. cit., vol. I, p. 394: Report on Virginia to the Spanish Council of State, July 1, 1610.

33. Ibid.,

34. See note 27 above.

35. Whitaker, op. cit.: "The Epistle Dedicatorie" by Rev. William Crashawe, p. 9.

36. Quinn, op. cit., vol. V, p. 295: Strachey's *True Reportory.*

37. Ibid., p. 296.

38. Ibid., p. 294.

39. Ibid., p. 295.

40. Ibid., p. 294.

41. Ibid.

42. Ibid., p. 295.

43. Tyler, op. cit., p. 223: See note 24 above.

44. *Colonial Records of Virginia*, p. 72: "A Breife Declaration of the Plantation of Virginia . . . &c., c. 1625.

45. *Plymouth Colony Records, Court Orders*, vol. I, pp. 33–34, March 13, 1635.

46. Barbour, *The Complete Works of Captain John Smith*, vol. II, p. 325: "Generall Historie."

47. Ibid., p. 143.

48. Bodleian Library, Oxford. Ms. Carte 176 ff, 170–71v: Article of Agreement between James, Earl of Ormond, and Edmond O'Magher and Mortegh O'Conner, August 26, 1641.

49. Quinn, op. cit., vol. V, p. 294: Strachey's *True Reportory.*

50. Laurence Sterne, *The Life and Opinions of Tristram Shandy* (York: 1759), vol. II, p. xii.

51. Barbour, *The Complete Works of Captain John Smith*, vol. II, p. 324.

52. Quinn, op. cit., p. 295.

53. Ibid.

54. Ibid., p. 294.

55. Ibid.

56. Ibid., p. 289.

57. Wright, *A Voyage to Virginia in 1609*, pp. 80–81, being the modernized spelling and punctuation of William Strachey's *True Reportory*. For the Purchas spelling, see Quinn, op. cit., vol. V, p. 294.

58. *Colonial Records of Virginia*, p. 80: "A Breife Declaration of the Plantation of Virginia . . . &c.," c. 1625.

59. Percy, op. cit., p. 270.

CHAPTER XI: STRONG PALES AND SHIVERED ARROWS

1. Lefroy, *Memorials of . . . the Bermudas*, p. 11.

2. Brown, *The Genesis of the United States*, vol. I, p. 435: "The Voyage of Captaine Samuel Argal, from James Towne in Virginia, to seeke the Ile of Bermuda, and missing the same, his putting over toward Sagadahoc and Cape Cod, and so backe againe to James Towne, begun the nineteenth of June, 1610."

3. Lefroy, op. cit.

4. Wright, Strachey's *True Reportory*, p. 89 and n. 116.

5. Quinn, *New American World*, vol. V, p. 297: Strachey's *True Reportory*.

6. Ibid.

7. Ibid., p. 298.

8. Percy, "A trewe relacyon," p. 271.

9. Ibid., p. 270.

10. Ibid.

11. Quinn, op. cit., p. 297.

12. Whitaker, *Good Newes from Virginia*, pp. 23–24.

13. Percy, op. cit., p. 272.

14. Ibid.

15. Ibid.

16. Tyler, *Narratives of Early Virginia*, p. 212: "The Relation of the Right Honourable the Lord De-La-Warre, Lord Governour and Captaine Generall of the Colonie planted in Virginea," 1611.

17. Percy, op. cit., p. 272.

18. Ibid., p. 273.

19. *Colonial Records of Virginia*, p. 73: "A Breife Declaration of the Plantation of Virginia . . . &c.," ca. 1625.

20. Percy, op. cit., p. 273.

21. Barbour, *The Complete Works of Captain John Smith*, vol. II, p. 232: "Generall Historie."

22. Arber, *Travels and Works of Captain John Smith*, vol. I, p. civ: Henry Spelman's *Relation of Virginea*, ca. 1613.

23. Barbour, op. cit., p. 237.

24. Ibid.

25. Tyler, op. cit., p. 214.

26. Ibid., p. 212.

27. Percy, op. cit., p. 275.

28. Ibid., p. 276.

29. Strachey, *Lawes Divine, Morall and Martiall . . . &c*, June 22, 1611, p. 20.

30. Hamor, *A True Discourse of the Present Estate of Virginia . . . till the 18 of June, 1614*, p. 26.

31. Ibid.

32. Brown, op. cit., vol. I, p. 492: "Sir Thomas Dale to the President and Counsell of the Companie of Adventurers and Planters in Virginia," James Towne, May 25, 1611.

33. Arber, op. cit., vol. I, p. xxxvii: *Instructions by Way of advice, for the intended Voyage to Virginia*, 1606.

34. Strachey, op. cit., p. 10.

35. Percy, op. cit., p. 277.

36. Ibid.

37. Ibid.

38. Ibid., pp. 277–78.

39. Whitaker, op. cit., p. 24.

40. Ibid., p. 26.

41. Brown, op. cit., vol. I, p. 498: Alexander Whitaker to Mr. Crashawe, James Towne, August 9, 1611.

42. Ibid., p. 499.

43. Ibid., p. 498.

44. Beverley, *The History and Present State of Virginia* (1705), p. 207.

45. Ibid., p. 208.

46. Ibid., p. 139.

47. McCary, *Indians in Seventeenth-Century Virginia*, pp. 3–10; Wright, Strachey's *The Historie of Travell into Virginia Britania*, pp. 63–69.

48. Percy, op. cit., p. 278.

49. Ibid., pp. 278–79.

50. Ibid., p. 279.

51. Hamor, op. cit., p. 28: See note 30.

52. Cumming et al., *The Discovery of North America*, p. 269: A map of Virginia by John Farrar (Ferrar), published 1651.

53. Percy, op. cit., p. 280.

54. Hamor, op. cit., p. 29.

55. Ibid., p. 30.

56. Quinn, *New American World*, vol. V, p. 294: Strachey's *New Reportory*.

57. Hamor, op. cit., p. 33.

58. Ibid.

59. Barbour, op. cit., vol. II, pp. 180–81: "Generall Historie."

60. *Records of Colonial Virginia*, p. 75: "A Breife Declaration of the Plantation of Virginia . . . &c.," ca. 1625.

61. Quinn, *Now American World*, vol. V, p. 294.

62. Wright, *A Voyage to Virginia*, pp. 81–82; the modernized text of Strachey's *True Reportory* is used here for easier reading. For the Purchas version, see Quinn, *New American World*, vol. V, p. 295.

63. Hamor, op. cit., p. 33.

64. Ibid.

65. Bemis, *The Three Charters of the Virginia Company of London*, p. 59: "Instruccions orders and constitucions . . . to Sir Thomas Gates, Knight . . . &c.," May 1609.

66. McIlwaine, *Minutes of the Council and General Court of Colonial Virginia*, p. 15: June 24, 1624.

67. Kingsbury, *Records of the Virginia Company*, vol. IV, p. 93: "Statements of Seamen as to Conditions in Virginia Between April and June, 1623."

68. Hamor, op. cit., p. 30.

69. *Records of Colonial Virginia*, p. 75. See note 60 above.

70. Whitaker, op. cit., p. 24.

71. Percy, op. cit., p. 280.

72. Hamor, op. cit., p. 31.

CHAPTER XII: NO FAYRE LADY

1. McClure, *The Letters of John Chamberlain*, vol. 1, pp. 470–71: Chamberlain to Sir Dudley Carleton, Ware Park, August 1, 1613.

2. Bemis, *The Three Charters of the Virginia Company of London*, p. 73.

3. Hamor, *A True Discourse*, p. 4.

4. Neill, *History of the Virginia Company of London*, p. 85.

5. Hamor, op. cit., p. 5.

6. Barbour, *The Complete Works of Captain John Smith*, vol. 2, p. 243: "Generall Historie."

7. Hamor, op. cit., p. 6.

8. Woodward, *Pocahontas*, p. 158, n. 20.

9. Hamor, op. cit., p. 56: Sir Thomas Dale to D.M., James Towne, June 18, 1614.

10. Hamor, ibid., p. 8.

11. Ibid., pp. 10–11.

12. Ibid., p. 63: John Rolfe to Sir Thomas Dale, undated.

13. Neill, op. cit., p. 91, fn. 1.

14. Wright, Strachey's *The Historie of Travell into Virginia Britania*, pp. 62 and 72, n. 1.

15. Hamor, op. cit., p. 11.

16. Ibid., p. 10.

17. Ibid., p. 11.

18. Ibid.

19. Ibid., p. 13.

20. Ibid., p. 14.

21. Ibid., p. 12.

22. Ibid., p. 39.

23. Ibid., p. 40.

24. Ibid., p. 41.

25. Barbour, op. cit., vol. 2, p. 249: "Generall Historie."

26. Neill, op. cit., p. 93, n. 1.

27. Hamor, op. cit., p. 42.

28. Neill, op. cit., p. 109: John Rolfe's "Relation of the State of Virginia," 1617.

29. Ibid., pp. 107–12.

30. Morton, *Colonial Virginia*, vol. 1, p. 44: Quoting Sir Thomas Dale to Sir R. Wynwood, Plymouth, May 1616.

31. Neill, op. cit., p. 96.

32. Barbour, op. cit., vol. II, p. 261: "Generall Historie."

33. Jonson, *The Complete Plays of Ben Jonson*, vol. 2, p. 380: *The Staple of News*, Act II, Scene 1.

34. Brand, *Popular Antiquities*, vol. 1, p. 21.

35. Ibid., p. 24.

36. Barbour, op. cit., vol. II, p. 261: "Generall Historie."

37. Ibid., pp. 259–60.

38. Ibid., p. 260, n. 1.

39. Ibid., p. 261.

40. McClure, op. cit., vol. II, pp. 50 and 66: Chamberlain to Sir Dudley Carleton, London, January 4, 1617, and London, March 29, 1617.

41. Ibid., pp. 56–57: Chamberlain to Sir Dudley Carleton, London, February 22, 1617.

42. Purchas, *Purchas, His Pilgrimes*, vol. IV, p. 1774.

43. Woodward, *Pocahontas*, p. 177 and fn. 8.

44. Kent, *An Encyclopaedia of London*, p. 395.

45. Boyne, *Trade Tokens Issued in the Seventeenth Century*, vol. I, pp. 688–89.

46. Hind, "The Bazili Logia 1618, and Expanded Bazili Logias," *Engravings in England in the Sixteenth & Seventeenth Centuries*, Part II, pp. 115–20.

47. Hamor, op. cit., p. 67.

48. Purchas, op. cit., p. 1774.

49. Hamor, op. cit., p. 64.

50. McClure, op. cit., p. 50.

51. *The Universal British Directory of Trade, Commerce, and Manufacture*, 1793, vol. III, p. 202.

52. Woodward, *Pocahontas*, p. 184, n. 1.

53. Kingsbury, *The Records of the Virginia Company of London*, vol. I, p. 338: Minutes of the court, London, May 21, 1620.

54. Wendy Rick Reaves, personal communication to the author, January 24, 1989.

55. Neill, op. cit., p. 98, n. 2, where the date is given as May, not March, 21, along with the Old Style year 1616.

56. Kingsbury, op. cit., vol. III, p. 71: John Rolfe to Sir Edwin Sandys, James Towne, June 8, 1617.

CHAPTER XIII: QUESTIONABLE ANSWERS

1. Hamor, *A True Discourse*, p. 36.

2. Kingsbury, *The Records of the Virginia Company of London*, vol. III, p. 72: John Rolfe to Sir Edwin Sandys, James Towne, June 8, 1617.

3. Ibid., p. 70. The pinnace has been incorrectly identified as the *Lizard* on the basis of this quotation which reads "and the next daie lost sight of the Lyzard" but which actually refers to a Cornish promontory, the last land visible on leaving the English Channel.

4. Ibid., vol. I, p. 338: Minutes of the court of the Virginia Company, London, May 21, 1620.

5. Ibid., p. 496: Minutes of the court of the Virginia Company, London, June 13, 1621.

6. Neill, *History of the Virginia Company of London*, p. 105.

7. Kingsbury, op. cit., vol. III, p. 74: Summary of letter from Samuel Argall to the Virginia Company (?), James Town, June 9, 1617.

8. Barbour, *The Complete Works of Captain John Smith*, vol. II, p. 262: "Generall Historie," drawn from letters from Samuel Argall and John Rolfe.

9. Kingsbury, op. cit., p. 71: John Rolfe to Sir Edwin Sandys, James Towne, June 8, 1617.

10. Barbour, op. cit., vol. II, p. 262.

11. Ibid., p. 324: "General Historie," Smith to the commissioners for the reformation of Virginia, 1624.

12. Hamor, op. cit., p. 33.

13. Quinn, *New American World*, vol. V, p. 294: Strachey's *True Reportory*.

14. Brown, *The Genesis of the United States*, vol. I, p. 492: Sir Thomas Dale to the Virginia Company, James Towne, May 25, 1611.

15. Barbour, op. cit., p. 262, fn. 3.

16. Brown, op. cit.

17. Kingsbury, *London*, vol. III, p. 302: John Pory to Sir Edwin Sandys, James Citty, June 12, 1620.

18. Maclean, *Letters from Lord George Carew*, p. 92: Carew to Sir Thomas Roe, 1617.

19. *Colonial Records of Virginia*, p. 75: "A Breife Declaration of the Plantation of Virginia . . . &c.," ca. 1625.

20. Kingsbury, op. cit., vol. IV, p. 93: Attestation of divers seamen, possibly in the hand of Nathaniel Butler or John Harvey, London, between April and June 1623.

21. Hamor, op. cit., p. 60: Alexander Whitaker to Reverend M. Gough, Virginia, June 18, 1614.

22. Kingsbury, op. cit., vol. III, p. 71: John Rolfe to Sir Edwin Sandys, James Towne, June 8, 1617.

23. Ibid., p. 73: Summary of letter from Samuel Argall to the Virginia Company (?), James Towne, June 9, 1617.

24. Ibid.

25. Ibid., p. 92: Samuel Argall to the Virginia Company, March 10, 1618.

26. Kingsbury, op. cit., vol. III, p. 93: Governor Argall's proclamation of May 18, 1618.

27. McClure, *The Letters of John Chamberlain*, vol. II, p. 188: Chamberlain to Sir Dudley Carleton, London, November 28, 1618.

28. Kingsbury, op. cit., vol. III, p. 419: Admiralty Court, London, earl of Warwick versus Edward Bruster concerning the ship *Treasurer*, 1621.

29. Neill, op. cit., p. 120.

30. Ibid.

31. Kingsbury, op. cit., p. 243: John Rolfe to Sir Edwin Sandys, Virginia, January 1620.

32. Neill, op. cit.

33. Kingsbury, op. cit., p. 147: Treasurer and Council of the Virginia Company to Sir George Yeardley, June 21, 1619.

34. Barbour, op. cit., vol. II, p. 376: "The Generall Historie of the Bermudas."

35. Kingsbury, op. cit., p. 244: John Rolfe to Sir Edwin Sandys, Virginia, January 1620.

36. Percy, "A trewe relacyon," pp. 278–79.

37. Brown, *The First Republic,* p. 269.

38. Percy, op. cit., p. 279.

39. Purchas, *Purchas His Pilgrimes,* vol. IV, p. 1779: Reverend Jonas Stockham to the Reverend Alexander Whitaker, May 28, 1619.

40. Wright, Strachey's *The Historie of Travell into Virginia Britania,* p. 95.

41. Ibid., p. 94.

42. Kingsbury, op. cit., vol. IV, p. 10: Council of Virginia to Virginia Company of London, James Cytty, January 20, 1623.

43. Barbour. op. cit., p. 293.

44. Kingsbury, op. cit., vol. III, p. 555: Edward Waterhouse's "A Declaration of the State of the Colony and Affaires in Virginia . . . &c.," compiled from letters and other sources, London, 1622.

45. Ibid.

46. Ibid., p. 551.

47. McIlwaine, *Minutes of the Council and General Court of Colonial Virginia,* p. 14: James Towne, May 10, 1624.

48. Ibid., p. 22: James Towne, October 10, 1624.

49. Ibid., p. 19; James Towne, August 16, 1624.

50. Carrier, *Agriculture in Virginia,* p. 21.

51. McIlwaine, op. cit.

52. Ibid., p. 12: James Towne, March 11, 1624.

53. Quinn, op. cit., vol. V, p. 295: Percy, *True Reportory.*

54. Barbour, op. cit., vol. II, p. 262: "Generall Historie," drawn from letter of Samuel Argall and John Rolfe.

55. *Colonial Records of Virginia,* p. 80: "A Breife Declaration of the Plantation of Virginia . . . &c.," ca. 1625.

56. Ibid., p. 75.

57. Ibid.

58. Meyer, *Adventurers of Purse and Person,* pp. 28–34: "Muster of the Inhabitants in Virginia 1624/1625."

59. Kingsbury, op. cit., vol. III, pp. 101–02: Virginia Company's instructions to Sir George Yeardley, London, November 18, 1618.

60. Chambers, *Cyclopædia,* vol. I, n.p.

61. Holme, *An Academie . . . of Armory,* p. 100.

62. Brown, *The First Republic,* p. 543.

63. Ibid.

64. Kingsbury, op. cit., vol. IV, p. 259: "Answers to the propositions made by Lord Chichester," London, August or September, 1623.

65. Ibid., vol. III, p. 102: See note 59 above.

66. Ibid., vol. IV, p. 259: See note 64 above.

67. Quinn, *New American World,* vol. V, p. 270: Percy's *True Reportory.*

68. Kingsbury, op. cit., vol. II, p. 374: Nathaniel Butler's *The Unmasked face of o^r Colony . . . &c.,* presented at the Virginia Company's court, London, April 23, 1623.

69. Ibid., p. 375.

70. *Colonial Records of Virginia,* p. 80: See n. 55 above.

71. Kingsbury, op. cit., pp. 375–76.

72. Ibid., p. 383: "The Answers of divers Planters" to Butler's *The Unmasked face . . . &c.,* presented at the Virginia Company's court, London, April 30, 1623.

73. Ibid.

74. Ibid.

CHAPTER XIV: STINKING BEER AND OTHER CALAMITIES

1. Kingsbury, *Records of the Virginia Company of London,* vol. IV, p. 232: "The Lady Wyatt to her Sister Sandys," James Towne, April 4, 1623.

2. Ibid., p. 65: George Sandys to Samuel Wrote, James Cittie, March 28, 1623.

3. Ibid., p. 62: Richard Frethorne to his parents, Martin's Hundred, April 3, 1623.

4. Ibid, p. 120: Captain Miles Kendall to Sir Edwin Sandys, Somers Islands, April 15, 1623.

5. Barbour, *The Complete Works of Captain John Smith,* vol. II, pp. 310–11: "Generall Historie."

6. Brown, *The First Republic in America,* p. 474. See also Kingsbury, op. cit., vol. IV, p. 639: "A note of the shipping, men, and provisions sent and provided for Virginia, . . . in the Yeere 1621," May 1622.

7. Barbour, op. cit., p. 311: "Generall Historie."

8. Kingsbury, op. cit., vol. III, p. 700: Governor Wyatt's commission to Captain Isack Maddison and Robert Bennet, James Towne, November 12, 1622.

9. Barbour, op. cit., p. 314: "Generall Historie."

10. Ibid.

11. Ibid., p. 320.

12. Kingsbury, op. cit., p. 175: "A Reporte of the manner of proceeding in the General assembly convented at James citty in Virginia, July 30, 1619," entry for August 4, 1619.

13. Ibid., vol. IV, p. 89: Peter Arundel to William Caninge, April (?), 1623.

14. Ibid.

15. Ibid., p. 234: Edward Hill to John Hill, April 14, 1623.

16. Ibid., p. 61: Richard Frethorne to his parents, Martin's Hundred, April 3, 1623.

17. Ibid.: April 2, 1623.

18. Ibid.: April 3, 1623.

19. Ibid.: See note 13 above.

20. Ibid., p. 221: Robert Bennett to Edward Bennett, Bennetes Wellcome, June 9, 1623.

21. Ibid., vol. I, p. 516: Court of the Virginia Company held July 16, 1621.

22. Ibid., vol. IV, pp. 220–21: See note 20 above.

23. Brown, op. cit., p. 639.

24. Kingsbury, op. cit., vol. IV, p. 235: William Rowlsley to his brother, James City, April 2, 1623.

25. Ibid., pp. 231–32: Thomas Niccolls to Sir John Wolstenholme, April 2, 1623.

26. Ibid., p. 473: Jane Dickenson, Widdowe, to the Governor and Counsell of Estate in Virginia, March 30, 1624.

27. Ibid., vol. III, p. 115: See note 6 above.

28. Ibid., p. 82: Charges against Sir Thomas Smythe by Captain John Bargrave, with answers by Sir Nathaniel Rich, London, April (?), 1623.

29. Ibid., pp. 493–94: Virginia Company to the Governor and Counsell of State in Virginia, London, August 12, 1621.

30. Ibid., p. 505: Virginia Company to the Governor and Counsell of Virginia, London, September 11, 1621.

31. Ibid., p. 583: Council in Virginia to the Virginia Company of London, James Towne, January, 1621/22.

32. McIlwaine, *Minutes of the Council and General Court of Colonial Virginia*, p. 61: Court held at James Towne, testimony of Mrs. Elizabeth Hamor, May 23, 1625.

33. Kingsbury, op. cit., vol. I, p. 269: Virginia Company's Great and Generall Court Session Houlden for Virginia, Wednesday, November 17, 1619.

34. Brown, op. cit., vol. I, pp. 443–44: Ralegh to Queen Anne, n.d. (ca. 1610).

35. *Dictionary of National Biography*, vol. II, p. 1732: Sir Walter Ralegh.

36. Ibid.

37. Barbour, op. cit., vol. II, p. 306: "Generall Historie."

38. Meyer, *Adventurers of Purse and Person*, p. 508: will of John Rolfe, March 10, 1622.

39. Kingsbury, op. cit., vol. IV, p. 110: George Sandys to John Ferrar, April 11, 1623.

40. Brown, op. cit., vol. II, p. 835; also Neill, *History of the Virginia Company of London*, p. 111, n. 1.

41. Beverley, *The History and Present State of Virginia*, p. 61.

CHAPTER XV: DAY OF THE DIGGERS

1. Cotter, *Archeological Excavations at Jamestown*, p. 222: untitled report by Mary Jeffery Galt to the APVA, n.d. (1901?).

2. Kelly, *The First Restoration in Williamsburg*, p. 11.

3. Cotter, op. cit., p. 222.

4. Packer, *White Gloves & Red Bricks*, p. 11.

5. Tyler, *The Cradle of the Republic*, p. 91.

6. Ibid., p. 95.

7. APVA, Jamestown Committee Minutes, December 5, 1905.

8. Ibid., May 2, 1906.

9. Ibid., October 2, 1906.

10. Ibid., February 2, 1915.

11. Ibid., April 3, 1917.

12. Ibid, February 1922.

13. Jamestown Exposition *Blue Book*, p. 22.

14. Yonge, *The Site of Old "James Towne,"* p. 76.

15. Brown, *The Genesis of the United States*, vol. II, p. 394: testimony of Francis Magnel (Francisco Miguel) taken and signed in Madrid, July 1, 1610.

16. Cotter, op. cit., p. 6. The wall was begun in 1901.

17. Yonge, op. cit., p. 76.

18. Quinn, *New American World,* vol. V, p. 295: Strachey's *True Reportory.*

19. Barbour, *The Complete Works of Captain John Smith,* vol. II, p. 181: "Generall Historie."

20. *Colonial Records of Virginia,* "A Breife Declaration of the plantation of Virginia . . . &c.," ca. 1625, p. 70.

21. Kent, *An Encyclopaedia of London,* p. 581.

22. George Sandys, *A Relation of a Journey begun An Dom: 1610* (London: 1615).

23. Noël Hume, *Martin's Hundred,* p. 238.

24. Gregory, "Jamestown Site of First Fort," Ms., n.d. (September 1934?)

25. Tyler, letter to Gregory, November 8, 1934, p. 1; copy in NPS files, Jamestown.

26. Tyler, letter to Gregory, October 25, 1934, p. 1; copy in NPS files, Jamestown.

27. Malcolm Gardner (historical technician), memo to Verne E. Chatelain (chief of Historical Division), weekly progress report for July 9–14, dated July 16, 1934; copy in NPS files, Jamestown.

28. H. Summerfield Day, memo to W. J. Winter, December 20, 1934; copy in NPS files, Jamestown.

29. Cammerer, memo to Zaharov, Washington, D.C., January 16, 1935; copy in NPS files, Jamestown.

30. Winter, telegram to Pond, Washington, D.C., April 18, 1935; copy in NPS files, Jamestown.

31. Winter, memo to Cammerer, Jamestown, June 11, 1935; copy in NPS files, Jamestown.

32. Forman, letter to Winter, March 4, 1935; copy in NPS files, Jamestown.

33. Winter, memo to Chatelain, May 18, 1935; copy in NPS files, Jamestown.

34. Winter, memo to Walter Damaray (associate director, NPS), April 25, 1935; copy in NPS files, Jamestown.

35. Day, memo to Flickinger, July 16, 1935; copy in NPS files, Jamestown.

36. Harrington, "Jamestown Archaeology in Retrospect," *The Scope of Historical Archaeology,* p. 36.

37. Forman, *Jamestown and St. Mary's,* p. 82.

38. Ibid., p. 331 and fn. 1.

39. Carl F. Miller, report in form of memo to Harrington; Jamestown, December 18, 1937, pp. 5–6; copy in NPS files, Jamestown.

40. Ibid., p. 6.

41. Harrington, "The Elay-Swann Tract," p. 45.

42. Ibid., p. 53.

43. Miller, op. cit., p. 7.

44. Shiner, "Final Report . . . Confederate Fort Area," p. 2.

45. Ibid., p. 3.

46. Cotter, op. cit., p. 163.

47. Marshall, "The First Settlement at Jamestown, Virginia," n.d., p. 17.

48. Shiner, op. cit., p. 3, quoted by Cotter, op. cit., p. 11.

49. Cotter, op. cit., p. 220: Preamble by Mary W. Garrett and Annie Galt to their report to the APVA, 1902.

50. *Colonial Records of Virginia,* "A Breife Declaration . . . &c.," p. 80: See note 20.

51. Cotter, op. cit., p. 220: Mary W. Garrett's report to the APVA, on the 1901–02 Jamestown excavations, December 15, 1905.

52. Ibid., p. 225, fn.

53. Barbour, *Jamestown Voyages,* vol. II, p. 465.

54. Quinn, *New American World,* vol. V, p. 270: Percy's "Discourse."

BIBLIOGRAPHY

❧

WORKS CITED AND CONSULTED

Anonymous: "A Breife Declaration of the plantation of Virginia, duringe the first Twelve Yeares, when Sir Thomas Smith was Governor of the Companie, & downe to this present tyme. By the Ancient Planters nowe remaining alive in Virginia." n.d. (c. 1625), *Colonial Records of Virginia* (originally published as *Senate Document—Extra.* Richmond, Va., 1874); Baltimore, Md.: Genealogical Publishing Co., Inc., 1964, pp. 69–83.

The Dictionary of National Biography, compact ed. London: Oxford University Press, 1975. 2 vols.

Middlesex County Records (Old Series), vol. II, 1603–1625, ed. John Cordy Jeaffreson. London: Greater London Council, 1974.

The Official Blue Book of the Jamestown Ter-centennial Exposition, 1907. Norfolk: The Colonial Publishing Company, Inc., 1909.

Report of the Virginia 350th Anniversary Commission. Richmond: Commonwealth of Virginia, 1958.

The 350th Anniversary of Jamestown 1607–1957. Final Report to the President and Congress. Washington, D.C.: Jamestown-Williamsburg-Yorktown Celebration Commission, 1958.

The Times Atlas of World History. London: Times Books Limited, 1978.

The Universal British Directory of Trade, Commerce, and Manufacture. London: Peter Barfoot & John Wilkes, 1793. 6 vols.

Allen, Mea. *The Tradescants, Their Plants, Gardens and Museum.* London: Michael Joseph, 1964.

Arber, Edward, ed. *Travels and Works of Captain John Smith.* Edinburgh: John Grant, 1910. 2 vols.

Athens, William P. "Soil Resistivity Investigations at Fort Raleigh National Historic Site." Final internal report. National Park Service, Southeastern Archeological Center, Tallahassee, Florida, 1984.

Aubrey, John. *Brief Lives,* ed. Richard Barber. Woodbridge, U.K.: Boydell Press, 1982.

Axtell, James. *After Columbus: Essay in the Ethnohistory of Colonial North America.* New York: Oxford University Press, 1988.

Baker, William A. *Colonial Vessels: Some Seventeenth Century Ship Designs.* Barre, Mass.: Barre Publishing Company, 1962.

Barbour, Philip L., ed. *The Complete Works of Captain John Smith (1580–1631).* Chapel Hill: University of North Carolina Press, 1986. 3 vols.

———. *The Jamestown Voyages Under the First Charter, 1606–1609.* Cambridge: Hakluyt Society Cambridge University Press, 1969. 2 vols.

———. *The Three Worlds of Captain John Smith*. Boston: Houghton Mifflin Company, 1964.

Barret, Robert. *The Theorick and Practike of Moderne Warres*. London: 1598. Facsimile ed., New York: Da Capo Press, 1969.

Bemiss, Samuel M., ed. *The Three Charters of the Virginia Company of London*. Richmond: Virginia 350th Anniversary Celebration Corporation, 1957.

Beverley, Robert. *The History and Present State of Virginia* (1705), ed. Louis B. Wright, Charlottesville: University Press of Virginia Dominion Books, 1968.

Boyne, William. *Trade Tokens Issued in the Seventeenth Century in England, Wales, and Ireland, by Corporations, Merchants, Tradesmen, Etc.*, ed. George C. Williamson. New York: Burt Franklin, 1970. 2 vols. Reprint of the 1889–91 edition.

Brand, John. *Observations on the Popular Antiquities of Great Britain: Chiefly Illustrating the Origin of Our Vulgar and Provincial Customs, Ceremonies, and Superstitions*. London: Henry G. Bohn, 1849. 3 vols.

Bridenbaugh, Carl. *Jamestown 1544–1699*. New York: Oxford University Press, 1980.

Brown, Alexander. *English Politics in Early Virginia History*. New York: Russell & Russell, 1968. First published 1901.

———. *The First Republic in America*. New York: Russell & Russell, 1969. First published 1898.

———. *The Genesis of the United States*. Boston: Houghton, Mifflin and Company, 1890. 2 vols.

Carrier, Lyman. *Agriculture in Virginia, 1607–1699*. Jamestown: Virginia 350th Anniversary Celebration Corporation, 1957.

Chambers, Ephraim. *Cyclopædia: Or An Universal Dictionary of Arts and Sciences . . . &c.* London: D. Midwinter et al., 1738, 2 vols.

Chetwood, William Rufus. *Memoirs of the Life and Writings of Ben Jonson Esq.* New York: Garland Publishing, Inc., 1970. Facsimile printing of the Dublin edition of 1756.

Cocke, John Esten. *My Lady Pokahontas, A True Relation of Virginia, Writ by Anas Totdkill, Puritan and Pilgrim*. Boston: Houghton, Mifflin and Company, 1907.

Cole, Anna Cunningham. *The Jamestown Princess*. Norfolk, Va.: privately printed, 1907.

Cotter, John L. *Archeological Excavations at Jamestown . . . Virginia*. Archeological Research Series Number Four. Washington, D.C.: U.S. Department of the Interior, 1958.

Craven, Wesley Frank. *The Virginia Company of London, 1606–1624*. Jamestown: Virginia 350th Anniversary Celebration Corporation, 1957.

———. *White, Red, and Black, the Seventeenth-Century Virginian*. Charlottesville: University Press of Virginia, 1971.

Culliford, S. G. *William Strachey, 1572–1621*. Charlottesville: University Press of Virginia, 1965.

Cumming, W. P., R. A. Skelton, and D. B. Quinn. *The Discovery of North America*. London: Paul Elek Productions, Ltd., 1971.

Daniel, Glyn. *A Short History of Archaeology*. London: Thames and Hudson, 1981.

Davis, John. *The First Settlers of Virginia*, 2d ed. New York: I. Riley & Co., 1806.

Davis, Richard, ed. *Hakluyt's Voyages*. London: Chatto & Windus, 1981.

Davis, Richard Beale. *George Sandys, Poet-Adventurer, A Study in Anglo-American Culture in the 17th Century*. New York: Columbia University Press, 1955.

Eburne, Richard. *A Plan Pathway to Plantation*, ed. Louis B. Wright. Ithaca, N.Y.: Cornell University Press, 1962. First published 1624.

Ehrenhard, John E., et al. "Remote Sensing Investigations at Fort Raleigh National Historic Site, North Carolina." Internal report. National Park Service, Southeast Archeological Center, Tallahassee, Florida, 1983.

————, and Gregory L. Komara. "Archeological Investigations at Fort Raleigh National Historic Site, Season 2, 1983." Final internal report. National Park Service, Southeastern Archeological Center, Tallahassee, Florida, 1984.

Fausz, J. Frederick. "The Invasion of Virginia: Indians, Colonization and the Conquest of Cant." *Virginia Magazine of History and Biography*, vol. 95, no. 2 (April 1987), pp. 153–56.

————. "Middlemen in Peace and War, Virginia's Earliest Indian Interpreters, 1608–1632." *Virginia Magazine of History and Biography*, vol. 95, no. 1 (January 1987), pp. 41–64.

Fitzhugh, William, and Jacqueline S. Olin, eds. *The Archeology Of The Frobisher Voyages*. Washington, D.C.: Smithsonian Institution Press, 1993.

Forman, Henry Chandlee. "The Bygone 'Subberbs of James Cittie.'" *William and Mary College Quarterly Historical Magazine*, vol. 20, no. 4 (October 1940), pp. 475–86.

————. *Jamestown and St. Mary's, Buried Cities of Romance*. Baltimore: Johns Hopkins University Press, 1938.

Foss, Michael. *Undreamed Shores, England's Wasted Empire in America*. London: George G. Harrap & Co., Ltd., 1974.

Gibson, Susan, ed. *Burr's Hill, A 17th Century Wampanoag Burial Ground in Warren, Rhode Island*. Providence, R.I.: Haffenreffer Museum of Anthropology, Brown University, 1980.

Gradie, Charlotte M. "Spanish Jesuits in Virginia: The Mission That Failed." *Virginia Magazine of History and Biography*, vol. 96, no. 2 (April 1988), pp. 131–56.

Grassl, Gary C. "Joachim Gans of Prague: America's First Jewish Visitor." *Review of the Society for the History of Czechoslovak Jews* (1987), pp. 53–90.

Gray, Robert. *A Good Speed to Virginia*, ed. Wesley F. Craven. New York: Scholars' Facsimiles & Reprints, 1937. First published 1609.

Gregory, George C. "Jamestown Site of First Fort." Ms. report; copy in National Park Service files, Jamestown, n.d.

Haag, William G. *The Archeology of Coastal North Carolina*. Technical Report No. 8, Part B. Baton Rouge, La.: Coastal Studies Institute, Louisiana State University, December 15, 1956.

Haas, Irvin. *Citadels, Ramparts & Stockades, America's Historic Forts*. New York: Everest House, 1979.

Hakluyt, Richard. *The Principal Navigations Voyages Traffiques & Discoveries Made by Sea or Overland to the Remote & Farthest Distant Quarters of the Earth at any time within the compasse of these 1600 Yeares*. London: J. M. Dent & Sons Ltd., 1927. 8

vols. Published along with Hakluyt's two additional volumes, *The Voyages, Traffiques and Discoveries of Foreign Voyagers . . . &c.*

Hamor, Ralph. *A True Discourse of the Present Estate of Virginia, and the successe of the affaires there till the 18 of June, 1615.* Reprinted from the London edition of 1615. Richmond: Virginia State Library, 1957.

Hariot, Thomas. *A briefe and true report of the new found land of Virginia . . . &c.* New York: History Book Club, 1951. Facsimile edition of 1588 publication.

Harrington, Jean C. *An Outwork at Fort Raleigh.* Philadelphia: Eastern National Park and Monument Association, 1966.

——. *Archaeology and the Enigma of Fort Raleigh.* Raleigh, N.C.: North Carolina Department of Cultural Resources, 1984.

——. "Archeology as an Auxiliary Science to American History." *American Anthropologist,* vol. 56, no. 6 (December 1955), pp. 1121–30.

——. "The Elay-Swann Tract, Jamestown Island, Virginia. Preliminary Historical Study and Archeological Report on the 1937 Exploratory Excavations," May 15, 1941, Ms. on file in National Park Service library, Jamestown.

——. "From Architraves to Artifacts: A Metamorphosis," 1977. Privately circulated autobiographical manuscript.

——. *Glassmaking at Jamestown.* Richmond: Deitz Press, 1952.

——. "Jamestown Archaeology in Retrospect." *The Scope of Historical Archaeology,* ed. David G. Orr and Daniel G. Crozier. Philadelphia: Department of Anthropology, Temple University, 1984, pp. 29–51.

——. *Search for the Cittie of Ralegh, Archaeological Excavations at Fort Raleigh National Historic Site, North Carolina.* Washington, D.C.: Department of the Interior, 1962.

Harrington, Virginia S. "Theory and Evidence for the Location of James Fort." *Virginia Magazine of History and Biography,* vol. 93, no. 1 (January 1985), pp. 36–53.

Hatch, Charles E. *The First Seventeen Years, Virginia, 1607–1624.* Charlottesville: University Press of Virginia, 1957.

Hind, Arthur M. *Engraving in England in the Sixteenth & Seventeenth Centuries,* Part II, *The Reign of James I.* Cambridge: Cambridge University Press, 1955.

Holme, Randle. *An Academie or Store House of Armory & Blazon.* Vol. II. London: Roxburghe Club, 1905. First printed 1688.

Hubell, Jay B. *South and Southwest, Literary Essays and Reminiscences.* Durham, N.C.: Duke University Press, 1965.

Hulton, Paul. *America 1585: The Complete Drawings of John White.* Chapel Hill: University of North Carolina Press, 1984.

Hunter, R. J., comp. *Plantations in Ulster.* Educational Facsimiles 161–180. Belfast: Public Record Office of Northern Ireland, 1975.

Irwin, John, and Jocelyn Herbert, eds. *Sweete Thames.* London: Max Parrish, 1951.

Ives, Vernon A., ed. *The Rich Papers, Letters from Bermuda 1615–1646.* Toronto: Bermuda National Trust, 1984.

Jones, H. G. "The Genesis of the Quadricentennial," *Carolina Comments,* vol. 33, no. 8 (September 1985), pp. 142–50.

Jones, Howard Mumford. *The Literature of Virginia in the Seventeenth Century,* 2d ed. Charlottesville: University Press of Virginia, 1968.

Jonson, Ben. *The Complete Plays of Ben Jonson.* London: J. M. Dent & Sons Ltd., Everyman's Library, 1946 ed. 2 vols.

Kelly, Jeannette S. *The First Restoration in Williamsburg.* Richmond: Association for the Preservation of Virginia Antiquities, 1933.

Kent, Barry C. *Susquehanna's Indians.* Harrisburg: Pennsylvania Historical and Museum Commission, 1984.

Kent, William, ed. *An Encyclopaedia of London.* London: J. M. Dent & Sons Ltd., 1937.

Kingsbury, Susan Myra, ed. *The Records of the Virginia Company of London 1607–1626.* Washington, D.C.: U.S. Government Printing Office, 1906–35. 4 vols.

Lampe, Kenneth F., and Mary Ann McCann. *AMA Handbook of Poisonous and Injurious Plants.* Chicago: American Medical Association, 1985.

Lavery, Brian. *The Colonial Merchantman Susan Constant 1605.* Annapolis: Naval Institute Press, 1988.

Lawson, John. *Lawson's History of North Carolina,* ed. Francis Latham Harris. Richmond: Garrett and Massie, 1952. First published 1714.

Lefroy, Sir John Henry. *Memorials of the Discovery and Early Settlement of the Bermudas or Somers Islands 1515–1685.* Bermuda: Bermuda Historical Society, 1981. 2 vols. First published 1887–89.

Lewis, Clifford M., and Albert J. Loomie. *The Spanish Jesuit Mission in Virginia, 1570–1572.* Chapel Hill: University of North Carolina Press, 1953.

Loth, Calder, ed. *The Virginia Landmarks Register.* Charlottesville: University Press of Virginia, third edition, 1986.

Luccketti, Nicholas, and Martha W. McCartney. "An Archaeological Survey of Smith's Fort, Surry County, Virginia." Ms. report for Virginia Historic Landmarks Commission, 1982.

Lyster, Mrs. Henry F. Le Hunte. *Jamestown. Its Foundation and Ter-centennial.* A paper read before the National Society of Colonial Dames in Michigan, January 6, 1906. Detroit: private printing, 1906.

M.T. *A Discourse of Trade, From England unto the East-Indies: Answering to diverse Objections which are usually made against the same.* London: John Pyper, 1621. Reprinted New York: Facsimile Text Society, 1930.

Maclean, John, ed. *Letters from George Lord Carew to Sir Thomas Roe, Ambassador to the Court of the Great Mogul, 1615–1617.* London: Camden Society, 1860.

Mann, Sir James. *European Arms and Armour.* Catalogs of the Wallace Collection. London: William Clowes and Sons Ltd., 1962. 2 vols.

Manucy, Albert. *Artillery Through the Ages.* Washington, D.C.: U.S. Government Printing Office, 1955.

Marshall, Charles S. "The First Settlement at Jamestown, Virginia," n.d. (ca. 1936). Ms. report in National Park Service library, Jamestown.

Maverick, Samuel. *A Briefe Description of New England and the Severall Townes Therein Together with the Present Government Thereof.* Ms. in the British Museum, published 1885.

McCary, Ben C. *Indians in Seventeenth-Century Virginia.* Williamsburg: Virginia 350th Anniversary Corporation, 1957.

McClure, Norman Egbert, ed. *The Letters of John Chamberlain.* Westport, Conn.: Greenwood Press, 1979, 2 vols. Reprint of the 1939 edition.

McIlwaine, Harold Read, ed. *Minutes of the Council and General Court of Colonial Virginia,* 2d ed. Richmond: Virginia State Library, 1979.

Meyer, Virginia M., and John Frederick Dorman, eds. *Adventurers of Purse and Person VIRGINIA 1607–1624/5.* Richmond, Va.: Published by Order of the First Families of Virginia, Dietz Press, 3rd edition, 1987.

Morton, Richard L. *Colonial Virginia.* Chapel Hill: University of North Carolina Press, 1960. 2 vols.

Neill, Edward D. *History of the Virginia Company of London.* New York: Burt Franklin, 1968. Reprint of 1869 edition.

Noël Hume, Ivor. *Here Lies Virginia.* New York: Alfred A. Knopf, 1963.

———. *Martin's Hundred.* New York: Alfred A. Knopf, 1979.

———. "The Reconstructed Jamestown Fort: A Re-examination of the Documentary and Interpretive Evidence." Ms. report for the Jamestown-Yorktown Foundation, May 29, 1983.

Nugent, Nell Marion. *Cavaliers and Pioneers, Abstracts of Virginia Land Patents and Grants, 1623–1666.* Baltimore: Genealogical Publishing Co., Inc., 1983. First published 1934.

Padfield, Peter. *Armada.* London: Victor Gollancz Ltd., 1988.

Packer, Nancy Elizabeth. *White Gloves & Red Bricks: APVA 1889–1989.* Richmond: Association for the Preservation of Virginia Antiquities, 1989.

Percy, George. *A Discourse of the Plantation of the Southern Colony in Virginia by the English, 1606,* ed. David B. Quinn. Charlottesville: University Press of Virginia, 1967.

———. "A Trewe Relacyon of the Precedeinges and Occurrentes of Momente w^{c}h have hapned in Virginia from the Tyme Sr Thomas GATES was shippwrackte uppon the BERMUDES an^o 1609 untill my depture outt of the Country w^{c}h was in an^o Dñi 1612–." *Tyler's Quarterly Magazine,* vol. III (1922), pp. 259–82.

Peterson, Harold L. *Arms and Armor in Colonial America 1526–1783.* New York: Bramhall House, 1956.

Phillips, E. *The New World of Words, or a General English Dictionary.* London: Nathaniel Brook, 1671.

Powell, William S. *Paradise Preserved.* Chapel Hill: University of North Carolina Press, 1965.

Purchas, Samuel. *Purchas, His Pilgrimage, or Relations of the World . . . &c.* London: Henry Fetherstone, 1617.

———. *Purchas, His Pilgrimes . . . &c.* London: Henry Fetherstone, 1625. 4 vols.

Quinn, David B. *New American World, a Documentary History of North America to 1612.* New York: Arno Press and Hector Bye, Inc., 1979. 5 vols.

———. *North America from Earliest Discovery to First Settlements, the Norse Voyages to 1612.* New York: Harper & Row/Harper Colophon Books, 1977.

————. *Set Fair for Roanoke, Voyages and Colonies, 1584–1606.* Chapel Hill: University of North Carolina Press, 1985.

————. *The Roanoke Voyages 1584–1590.* London: Hakluyt Society, 1955. 2 vols.

————. "Turks, Moors, Blacks, and Others in Drake's West Indian Voyage." *Terrae Incognitae,* vol. 14 (1982), Wayne State University Press, pp. 93–100.

Quinn, David B., and Alison M. Quinn, eds. *Virginia Voyages from Hakluyt.* London: Oxford University Press, 1973.

Rich, Robert. *Newes from Virginia. The lost Flocke Triumphant.* Bound with Robert Gray's *A Good Speed to Virginia.* New York: Scholars' Facsimiles & Reprints, 1937. First printed in 1610 and 1609, respectively.

Rodríguez-Salgado, M. J., et al. *Armada 1588–1988.* London: Penguin Books and the National Maritime Museum, 1988.

Rosier, James. *A True Relation of the most prosperous voyage made this present yeere 1605, by Captaine George Waymouth, in the Discovery of the land of Virginia.* Readex Microprint facsimile edition, 1966.

Rountree, Helen C. *Pocahontas's People, the Powhatan Indians of Virginia Through Four Centuries.* Norman: University of Oklahoma Press, 1990.

————. *The Powhatan Indians of Virginia, Their Traditional Culture.* Norman: University of Oklahoma Press, 1989.

Rowse, A. L. *Ralegh and the Throckmortons.* London: Macmillan & Co., 1962.

Sears, Stephen W., ed. *The Horizon History of the British Empire.* New York: American Heritage Publishing Co., Inc., 1973.

Sheehan, Bernard. *Savagism & Civility, Indians and Englishmen in Colonial Virginia.* Cambridge: Cambridge University Press, 1980.

Shiner, Joel L. "Final Report Archeological Explorations in the Confederate Fort Area in the APVA Grounds (Jamestown National Historic Site) at Jamestown. Park Research Project No. 100," June 24, 1955. Ms. in National Park Service Library, Jamestown.

————. "Report on Archeological Excavations in the Area of the Statehouse Group in the Association for the Preservation of Virginia Antiquities Grounds (Jamestown National Historic Site) at Jamestown. Research Project No. 105," June 16, 1955. Ms. in National Park Service Library, Jamestown.

————. "Report on 1955 Excavations in the Elay-Swann Tract on Jamestown Island, First Fort (Gregory-Forman Site) Project #235," June 23, 1955. Ms. in National Park Service Library, Jamestown.

Simmons, William Scranton. *Cautantowwit's House, an Indian Burial Ground on the Island of Conanicut in Narragansett Bay.* Providence: Brown University Press, 1970.

Sinclair, Andrew. *Sir Walter Raleigh and the Age of Discovery.* Harmondsworth (U.K.): Penguin Books, 1984.

Smith, John. *The Generall Historie of Virginia, New England, & The Summer Isles . . . &c..* Glasgow: James MacLehose and Sons, 1907. 2 vols. See also under Arber, Edward, and Barbour, Philip L.

Smythe, Sir John. *Certain Discourses Military,* ed. J. R. Hale. Ithaca, N.Y.: Cornell University Press for Folger Shakespeare Library, 1964. First published 1590.

Stick, David. *Roanoke Island: The Beginnings of English America.* Chapel Hill: University of North Carolina Press, 1983.

Stith, William. *The History of the First Discovery and Settlement of Virginia.* New York: Johnson Reprint Corporation, 1969. Facsimile of the 1747 edition.

Strachey, William. *For the Colony in Virginea Britannia. Lawes Divine, Morall and Martial, etc.,* ed David H. Flaherty. Richmond: Association for the Preservation of Virginia Antiquities, 1969. First established June 12, 1610, enlarged June 22, 1611.

————. *The Historie of Travaile into Virginia Britanna . . . &c.* London: Hakluyt Society, 1849. See also under Wright, Louis B.

————. *A True Reportory of the Wreck and Redemption of Sir Thomas Gates, Knight, upon and from the Islands of the Bermudas: His coming to Virginia and the Estate of that Colony Then and After, under the Government of the Lord La Warr, July 15, 1610.* See Wright, Louis B., *A Voyage to Virginia in 1609.*

Trevelyan, G. M. *History of England,* 3d ed. London: Longmans Green and Co., 1945.

Tuck, James A. "Unearthing Red Bay's Whaling History." *National Geographic,* vol. 168, no. 1 (July 1985), pp. 50–57.

Tuck, James A., and Robert Grenier. *Red Bay, Labrador: World Whaling Capital A.D. 1550–1600.* St. John's, Newfoundland: Atlantic Archaeology Ltd., 1989.

Tyler, Lyon Gardiner. *The Cradle of the Republic,* 2d ed. Richmond: Hermitage Press, Inc., 1906.

————. *Narratives of Early Virginia, 1606–1625.* New York: Charles Scribner's Sons, 1907.

Vaughan, Alden T. *American Genesis, Captain John Smith and the Founding of Virginia.* Boston: Little, Brown and Company, 1975.

Wahll, Andrew J. "Fort St. George Reconsidered." Unpublished ms., 1986.

Wallis, Helen. *Raleigh & Roanoke, the First English Colony in America, 1584–1590.* British Library exhibition Catalogue. Raleigh: North Carolina Museum of History, 1985.

Whitaker, Rev. Alexander. *Good Newes from Virginia.* New York: Scholars' Facsimiles & Reprints, n.d. First printed 1613.

Wilkinson, Frederick. *The World's Great Guns.* London: Hamlyn Publishing Group, 1977.

Willan, T. S. *The Early History of the Russia Company, 1553–1603,* 2d ed. Manchester (U.K.): Manchester University Press, 1968.

Williamson, James A. *The Ocean in English History.* Oxford: Clarendon Press, 1941.

Wingood, Allan J., et al. *Sea Venture, the Tempest Wreck.* Hamilton, Bermuda: Sea Venture Trust, 1986.

Woodward, Grace Steel. *Pocahontas.* Norman: University of Oklahoma Press, 1969.

Wright, Irene A., ed. *Further English Voyages to Spanish America, 1583–1594.* Second Series, No. XCIX. London: Hakluyt Society, 1949.

Wright, Louis B., ed. William Strachey's *The Historie of Travell into Virginia Britania.* 2d ed. Series II, vol. CIII. London: Hakluyt Society, 1849. First published 1612. See also under Strachey, William.

————. Robert Beverley's *The History and Present State of Virginia.* Charlottesville: University of Virginia Press/Dominion Books, 1968. First printed 1705.

————. *A Voyage to Virginia in 1609.* Charlottesville, Va.: University Press of Virginia, 1964. Comprises the texts of William Strachey's *True Reportory of the Wreck and Redemption of Sir Thomas Gates, Knight,* and Silvester Jourdain's *A discovery of the Bermudas, Otherwise Called the Isle of Devils.* Both first published 1610. See also under Strachey, William.

Yonge, Samuel H. *The Site of Old "James Towne" 1607–1698.* Richmond: Association for the Preservation of Virginia Antiquities, 1904.

INDEX

๑๏

Page numbers in boldface indicate illustrations.

A NOTE ABOUT THE AUTHOR

IVOR NOËL HUME is chairman of the Association for the Preservation of Virginia Antiquities' Jamestown Rediscovery Advisory Board. He was born in London, studied at both Framlingham College and St. Lawrence College in England, and served during World War II in the Indian Army. In 1949 he joined the staff of the Guildhall Museum in London as an archaeologist. He moved to Colonial Williamsburg as chief archaeologist in 1957 and eight years later became director of the Department of Archaeology. Since 1959 Mr. Noël Hume has been an honorary research associate of the Smithsonian Institution; he is also a fellow of the Society of Antiquaries of London and a past vice-president of the British Society of Post-Medieval Archaeology. He was made an Officer of the British Empire (O.B.E.) in 1992 for services to British cultural interests in Williamsburg. Mr. Noël Hume is the author of *Archaeology in Britain* (1953), *Treasure in the Thames* (1956), *Great Moments in Archaeology* (1958), *Here Lies Virginia* (1963), *1775: Another Part of the Field* (1966), *A Guide to Artifacts of Colonial America* (1970), *All the Best Rubbish* (1974), and *Martin's Hundred* (1982), as well as two pseudonymous novels in 1971 and 1972.

A NOTE ON THE TYPE

THIS BOOK WAS SET in a modern adaptation of a type designed by William Caslon (1692–1766). The first of a famous English family of type designers and founders, he was originally an apprentice to an engraver of gunlocks and gun barrels in London. In 1716 he opened his own shop, for silver chasing and making bookbinders' stamps. The printers John Watts and William Bowyer, admirers of his skill in cutting ornaments and letters, advanced him money to equip himself for type founding, which he began in 1720.

In style Caslon was a reversion to earlier type styles. Its characteristics are remarkable regularity and symmetry, and beauty in the shape and proportion of the letters; its general effect is clear and open but not weak or delicate. For uniformity, clearness, and readability it has perhaps never been surpassed. After Caslon's death his eldest son, also named William (1720–1778), carried on the business successfully. Then followed a period of neglect of nearly fifty years. In 1843 Caslon type was revived by the firm of Caslon for William Pickering and has since been one of the most widely used of all type designs in English and American printing.

Designed by Virginia Tan